Angels and Ministers
of Grace Defend Us!

Ann Savage bewitchingly rides an anti-aircraft gun instead of a broomstick in this World War II cheesecake pin-up.

Angels and Ministers of Grace Defend Us!

More Dark Alleys of Classic Horror Cinema

GREGORY WILLIAM MANK

McFarland & Company, Inc., Publishers

Jefferson, North Carolina

ALSO OF INTEREST AND BY GREGORY WILLIAM MANK AND FROM McFARLAND: *Laird Cregar: A Hollywood Tragedy* (2018; paperback 2019); *Bela Lugosi and Boris Karloff: The Expanded Story of a Haunting Collaboration, with a Complete Filmography of Their Films Together* (2009; paperback 2017); *The Very Witching Time of Night: Dark Alleys of Classic Horror Cinema* (2014); *Women in Horror Films, 1930s* (1999; paperback 2005); *Women in Horror Films, 1940s* (1999; paperback 2005); *Hollywood Cauldron: Thirteen Horror Films from the Genre's Golden Age* (1994; paperback 2001); *Karloff and Lugosi: The Story of a Haunting Collaboration, with a Complete Filmography of Their Films Together* (1990)

LIBRARY OF CONGRESS CATALOGUING-IN-PUBLICATION DATA

Names: Mank, Gregory W., author.
Title: Angels and ministers of grace defend us! : more dark alleys of classic horror cinema / Gregory William Mank.
Description: Jefferson, North Carolina : McFarland & Company, Inc., Publishers, 2022 | Includes bibliographical references and index.
Identifiers: LCCN 2022013809 | ISBN 9781476665535 (paperback : acid free paper) ∞
ISBN 9781476644035 (ebook)
Subjects: LCSH: Horror films—United States—History and criticism. | Motion pictures—United States—History—20th century. | BISAC: PERFORMING ARTS / Film / Genres / Horror | LCGFT: Film criticism.
Classification: LCC PN1995.9.H6 M314 2022 | DDC 791.43/61640973—dc23/eng/20220405
LC record available at https://lccn.loc.gov/2022013809

BRITISH LIBRARY CATALOGUING DATA ARE AVAILABLE

ISBN (print) 978-1-4766-6553-5
ISBN (ebook) 978-1-4766-4403-5

Front cover: Bela Lugosi as Dr. Mirakle in the 1932 film *Murders in the Rue Morgue* (author's collection)

Printed in the United States of America

McFarland & Company, Inc., Publishers
Box 611, Jefferson, North Carolina 28640
www.mcfarlandpub.com

To my beautiful Barbara,
who did so much to make this book happen.
My Sun, Moon, Stars … and Beyond!

"Angels and ministers of grace defend us!"
—*Hamlet*, Act I, scene IV

Table of Contents

Acknowledgments   ix

Introduction   1

1. Bela, Bestiality and the *Amours* of Erik the Ape: *Murders in the Rue Morgue*   3

2. "Why Won't You *Die*?": *Rasputin and the Empress*   39

3. The Vanity of the Panther Woman: *Island of Lost Souls*   73

4. "A Sin Against the Holy Ghost!": Early Drafts, Studio Politics and Censorship Sagas of *Bride of Frankenstein*   109

5. "It's the Devil ... Creeping Out of Hell": *WereWolf of London*   138

6. Procuring *Mad Love*   177

7. Unholy Royalty: Universal's *Tower of London*   209

8. "A Madman's Dream": *Dr. Jekyll and Mr. Hyde* (1941)   238

9. Monogram's Nazi Horror Peep Show: *Women in Bondage*   272

10. The Odyssey of Mildred Davenport—to Acquanetta—to Paula the Ape Woman   296

11. How to Make a Monster Rally: The Production of *House of Frankenstein*   331

12. His 20-Year-Long Last Bow: The Final Act of Basil Rathbone   360

13. Horror Box Office   394

Chapter Notes   417

Bibliography   434

Index   437

Acknowledgments

This book had many friends who helped make it happen. Coming together ultimately at a time of a worldwide pandemic, "peaceful" protests and all the ensuing perils, it needed all the friends it could get.

Several people deserve special thanks. In alphabetical order:

John Antosiewicz generously provided many of the stills in the book, as noted in the captions. He also made available fascinating information from his files, including the pages on *Murders in the Rue Morgue* from Bela Lugosi's scrapbook, formerly in John's possession. This book, in its published form, could never have happened without him.

Frank Dello Stritto, prolific horror writer-historian, proofed every chapter, making many helpful suggestions, and alerting me to various material that made the book more colorful and comprehensive. He also dynamically contributed to Chapter 13 in its present form. Frank and I for some years have annually given presentations at the Monster Bash convention in Mars, Pennsylvania, and I hope we will continue this tradition for many years to come.

Scott Gallinghouse is a remarkable researcher whose recent biography of Rondo Hatton won him a well-deserved Rondo Award. His generosity in sharing the jaw-dropping discoveries is almost saintly, and his dynamic contributions, notably in the Acquanetta chapter, were vital to this book. He himself is horror history's top "discovery" of recent years.

Kristine Krueger of the Margaret Herrick Library of the Academy of Motion Picture Arts and Sciences has been her unfailingly helpful self, especially in providing copies of the censorship papers from the Library's MPPDA file. As the reader will see, these are a very crucial part of several of the chapters in this book.

Constantine Nasr has produced a staggering number of special Blu-ray releases over the past several years. During that time, he did me the honor of engaging me to write and narrate audio commentaries for *The Black Cat*, *Murders in the Zoo*, *Murders in the Rue Morgue* and *Jungle Woman*, and to appear in several special features. He's a generous friend and colleague.

Tom Weaver has been assisting me on my labors in these vineyards for almost 40 years, and I'm sure the readers of this book are well aware of Tom's prestige in this business. He claims that, when we first became associates, he was still a little boy, and I used to bounce him on my knee, but don't believe him.

Thanks also to:

Ron Adams (and the folks at Monster Bash), Lionel Anthony Atwill, Lawrence Bennie, the late Richard Bojarski, Michael Brunas, David Colton (and the Classic Horror Film Board), Clive Dawson, Michael Druxman, Donnie Dunagan, John Eccles, Jack

Gourlay, Julie Graham, Martin Grams Jr., G.D. Hamann, Charles Heard, Roger Hurlburt, Cortlandt Hull, Dr. Robert J. Kiss, David Knight, Mark Martucci, Julie and Dick May, Bill Nelson, Neil Pettigrew, the late Philip J. Riley, Gary Don Rhodes, Gary and Sue Svehla, Dr. Karl Thiede, Mark A. Vieira, Laura Wagner and Scott Wilson.

I must mention those who provided interviews and who are now gone: Acquanetta, DeWitt Bodeen, Carroll Borland, Mae Clarke, Lillian Lugosi Donlevy, Frances Drake, Susanna Foster, Verna Hillie, Valerie Hobson, Zita Johann, Elsa Lanchester, Reginald LeBorg, Hope Lugosi, Evelyn Moriarty, Alan Napier, Gil Perkins, Curt Siodmak, Gloria Stuart, Elena Verdugo and Robert Wise. It was an honor to have talked with all of them.

Finally, very special thanks to…

For over three decades, Ned Comstock, USC's legendary Film and TV History archivist, has been the patron saint of film researchers. He's helped me on all my projects with such expertise and generosity that I honestly can't imagine any of my work ever having come into the light without his amazing assistance. Having Ned in your corner was like having a gung ho, uncredited, indefatigable co-author. His retirement date was June 30, 2020, and the world of film history will never be the same without Ned Comstock.

Barbara Klein Mank, my wife, has always been the inspiration for my books and everything else in my life. She's done a great deal to make all my published work happen over the past 49 years, but never as much as on this book. Barbara proved a devoted, diligent editor, proofreader, advisor on photo selections, photo restorationist and much more. She also convinced me this project was worthwhile, even when I came perilously close to losing faith.

So, if you enjoy this book, tell her. If not, tell me.

Introduction

I had imagined this book would be, emotionally, a vacation.

My two previous books were biographies of Colin Clive and Laird Cregar. Living vicariously the tragic lives of those two men, each with his own demons, was at times a torturous task. Both projects still give me the occasional nightmare.

In this book, ten of the 13 chapters are about specific horror movies or, to split hairs, "melodramas." This would be a far less tempestuous adventure, I'd figured … researching and writing about specific movies, not tormented people.

There are such things, however, as tormented movies.

A film, in a sense, takes on its *own* personal identity and personality. Like a human being, it's the result of conflicting experiences, frequently emerging *not* as what it ideally was set on *becoming*, but what it ultimately *became*. It always starts off with its goals, ambitions and dreams; it very often ends up scarred, broken and compromised.

A movie proceeds with its allies and enemies. Some films even develop their own personal demons, be it the egos of the creative forces who fashion them, or the ruthlessness of the studio heads who produce them. Some are over-appreciated at the time of their release; some, unfairly scorned.

People often claim they "love" certain movies. Film researchers, aware of what happened behind the scenes, often "love" them for different reasons. Virtually every film covered in this book faced major obstacles in coming into being; each of them alternately inspired admiration and loathing; and each of them still do today, even though the most recent one in the book was released 77 years ago.

People "get" other people or they don't. People "get" certain movies or they don't. And sometimes, certain movies get *us*. We don't choose to admire them, like them, or own them on DVD, Blu-ray or both. *They* choose *us,* casting a lasting, inexplicable spell that we're powerless to resist.

In this book, I relied as much as possible on primary source material, which included everything from Bela Lugosi's scrapbook pages on *Murders in the Rue Morgue,* to producer Victor Saville's personal production file on 1941's *Dr. Jekyll and Mr. Hyde.* This discovery of new information prompted the re-examination of several films I've covered previously in books and magazine articles. It seemed to me, for instance, that I'd wrung every drop of blood out of *Bride of Frankenstein* over the years, but the fresh facts learned about Universal's in-house civil war at the time, the hang-ups of the scenarists, and the many censorship travails persuaded me to revisit the film from a new and sharply different angle.

Of course, personalities figure dynamically in the backgrounds of these films. How can one delve fairly into *Rasputin and the Empress,* for example, without due attention to the brilliance and torments of the three Barrymores? Still, the spotlight is on production, release, impact and legacy.

The acknowledgments, chapter notes (which contain some colorful information) and bibliography cite the many people who made this book possible, and I hope entertaining.

Also, "a word of friendly warning": This book scorns contemporary conventional wisdom and "progressive" re-evaluations which lurk everywhere, including film history. The concerns they raise in 2022 are often more absurd and outrageously judgmental than anything the much-maligned Joseph Breen and his widely despised Production Code offered over 85 years ago. Indeed, in a world where some people actually take such films as *The Mask of Fu Manchu* seriously, it's likely that the current Big Brother "enlightenment" will continue trying, as Fu would say, to "conquer and breed."

As such, this book defies all present and future sledgehammer attacks on *Dr. Jekyll and Mr. Hyde* for its abuse of women, *Island of Lost Souls* for its abuse of animals, *Murders in the Rue Morgue* for demonizing an oversexed gorilla, *Rasputin and the Empress* for siding with royalty, *Bride of Frankenstein* for its Christian iconography (even though it's irreverently used), *WereWolf of London* for killing the WereWolf rather than sending him to a sanctuary in Yellowstone National Park, *Tower of London* for its prejudice against a hunchback, *Mad Love* for pejoratively presenting a short, bald-headed man, *Women in Bondage* for being titled *Women in Bondage*, etc. We won't even get into the probable hysterical burning-in-the-streets of Acquanetta's *Captive Wild Woman* and *Jungle Woman*—not because they're bad movies (which they are), but because … well, you'll see.

So, if this book moves you to watch (or re-watch) any of the films it covers, or to buy them on DVD or Blu-ray, you might want to do so before it's too late.

Keep the faith!

1

Bela, Bestiality and the *Amours* of Erik the Ape

Murders in the Rue Morgue

I am in the prime of my strength ... and I am lonely!
—Erik the Ape, as translated by Bela Lugosi's Dr. Mirakle,
in *Murders in the Rue Morgue*

[I]t is a pity that [Edgar Allan Poe's] name is associated with it. There is something bestial and offensive in those portions of the picture which insinuate that Erik, the gorilla, nourishes a hopeless passion for young girls, in which fancy he is encouraged by his insane master....
—Donald Kirkley, *The Baltimore Sun,*
reviewing *Murders in the Rue Morgue,* 1932

How long are such pictures as Frankenstein, Freaks *and* Murders in the Rue Morgue *to be permitted? How long are such films to be sent to mark and mar our children, horrify morons, stimulate all that is vilest in the human heart and disgust decent people with the whole motion picture business?*
—Adela Rogers St. Johns, *The San Francisco Examiner,* 1932

Yuletide, 1931.

The residence at 2643 Creston Drive sits very high in the Hollywood Hills, accessible by steep, twisty roads. Renting quarters in this house over 90 years ago was the star who had recently triumphed in the title role of the film version of *Dracula*: Bela Lugosi.

The moon, which would turn full Christmas night, shone on nearby Lake Hollywood. Lugosi dwelt in this hideaway with his mistress, Lulu Schubert. The apartment was sparsely furnished, at least for the abode of a movie star. A piano. A painting of naked "It Girl" Clara Bow, with whom Lugosi allegedly had a sex fling.[1] A full-length painting of Lugosi in Prince Albert attire by the same artist, his friend Geza Kende. Several suits. Furniture. Tapestries.

A scrapbook.

With an actor's pride and a boy's enthusiasm, Lugosi maintained this scrapbook devoted to his stardom. Most recently, he had been filling pages with clippings about his latest movie, *Murders in the Rue Morgue*, set to premiere in the New Year of 1932. Among them was this October 17, 1931, notice from *Hollywood Filmograph*:

Carl Laemmle Jr. has put Murders in the Rue Morgue *into production at Universal Studios.... Bela Lugosi, featured in the sensational* Dracula *on stage and screen, will have the outstanding role in this production of Edgar Allan Poe's dramatic mystery story....*[2]

3

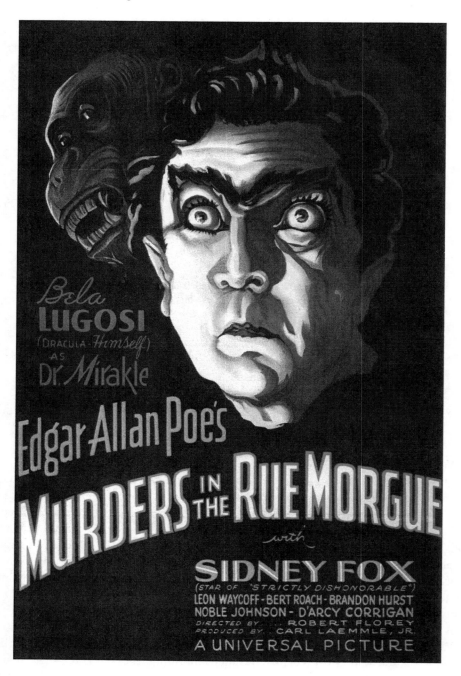

This dramatic *Murders in the Rue Morgue* poster gives top-billing to Bela Lugosi, although leading lady Sidney Fox enjoyed star billing in the film itself.

It was Lugosi's long-awaited follow-up to *Dracula*—Poe, "sexed-up," as they said in Hollywood. As a ragingly insane doctor, amok in 19th-century Paris, Lugosi had virtually crucified a "Woman of the Streets" whom he had hoped to mate with a gorilla, and dumped her carcass into the Seine.

"Will my search never end?" his mad Dr. Mirakle mournfully laments in the movie.

Lugosi hoped *Murders in the Rue Morgue*, for all its excesses, would be a great success. It *had* to be. *Frankenstein*, the film he had scorned last summer, was now in theaters—and a sensation. Universal had signed the Karloff fellow, who had played the Monster, to a star contract. They were hailing James Whale, the director, who hadn't even wanted Bela in *Frankenstein*, as a genius.

Bela had missed out on the biggest film hit in the country.

Murders in the Rue Morgue must make up for it. It had given Lugosi a fine showcase. So spellbinding a role! Such bravura dialogue! Yet this sensitive, passionate man privately had nagging doubts. Junior Laemmle, the producer, had awarded top billing to the leading lady, Sidney Fox, Junior's lover. Robert Florey, the director, had been far more interested in painting shadows on the walls for atmosphere than in unleashing great acting. Universal had put the film back into production two weeks ago, to make it a match for *Frankenstein*, but devoted most of those scenes to the gorilla.

Christmas was coming … Lugosi's first as a known-worldwide movie star. So much to enjoy. Cigars. Wine. Fan mail. Lulu. For now, Bela, isolated in the Hills, played the waiting game. He was aware of Universal's publicity, which extolled him:

> *Bela Lugosi is the screen's strangest, most mysterious personality. No one has approached him in the depiction of fascinating horror … [I]n* Murders in the Rue Morgue, *Lugosi delivers a characterization which makes Dracula look pale in comparison.*[3]

However, it was *Frankenstein*, Lugosi realized, that must pale in comparison. Lugosi approached Christmas of 1931 with pride, anticipation … and perhaps visions of Karloff's Monster, dancing nightmarishly in his head.

Yes, *Murders in the Rue Morgue* had to be a success. It *had* to be….

Part One: Pre-Production

> [A] search was made in the chimney, and (horrible to relate!) the corpse of the daughter, head downward, was dragged herefrom; it having been thus forced up the narrow aperture for a considerable distance….
>
> —From Edgar Allan Poe's tale
> "The Murders in the Rue Morgue" (1841)

Hollywood's "Ape Man"

Fall, 1931. As *Frankenstein* was shooting at Universal City, an alleged murderer-pervert haunted Hollywood, infamously known as the Ape Man.

He first struck Friday night, September 25, 1931, with what the *Los Angeles Times* called the "brutal slaying" of Mrs. Wilma McFarland, "comely 22-year-old clerk in a Hollywood candy shop." The newspaper quoted Inspector of Detectives Davidson:

> *By some threat the murderer compelled Mrs. McFarland to go with him to the rear room in the shop. There, when she resisted his attempts to force his attentions upon her, he strangled her into unconsciousness with a towel. Then he shot her in the head as she regained consciousness.*

The *Times* went on in gruesome detail:

> That Mrs. McFarland made a desperate struggle against her brutal assailant even after a pistol bullet had torn through her cheek and neck was evident in the splattering of blood over the walls and ceiling of the little room....[4]

The perpetrator quickly earned his soubriquet "the Ape Man," as later sightings had him lunging out of alleys at night, terrifying women, running away.

Wednesday, September 30: Wilma McFarland's funeral took place at Forest Lawn, Glendale. The women who worked with her were honorary pallbearers. *The Los Angeles Times* reported the next day:

> On the theory that a morbid urge might have sent the slayer to the scene, a score of detectives mingled in the crowd that surged about the Little Church of the Flowers.... They scrutinized all faces carefully for a hint of possible guilt, but observed nothing.[5]

Thursday, October 1: The Ape Man was allegedly amok again this night. A 22-year-old woman reported that, after she went out her back door, a "giant loomed out of the darkness, grabbed her by the throat with one hand, and with the other attempted to tear her dress off." She screamed and fought and the attacker ran away. A few minutes later, police got a report that a second woman had seen "a giant man rise from behind some bushes and run toward her." She took refuge in a pharmacy. Shortly after that, police learned from a boy that "a giant stepped from behind a tree waving a club." The boy outran the "giant."[6]

Saturday, October 3: *Frankenstein* wrapped up at Universal.

Sunday night, October 4: The Ape Man made the news again, as reported in the October 6 *Los Angeles Times*:

> A 14-year-old girl was terrified by an "ape man" who crawled into her bedroom.... Screams arousing her parents possibly saved Bernice Arnsbiter from a vicious attack from the "ape man" in her bedroom at 203 North Bixel Street. The prowler had cut a screen and crawled in through a window. The girl awoke to find the fiend bending over her. Terror-stricken, she screamed for help. Her mother and father rushed into her bedroom just as the intruder dived head-first out the window....[7]

Ironically, as the Ape Man continued terrorizing Hollywood, Universal Studios prepared to unleash a filmic "Ape Man" in its new horror show, Edgar Allan Poe's *Murders in the Rue Morgue*, starring Bela Lugosi.

The Shadow of Frankenstein

Monday, October 5: The morning after the Ape Man crawled into the 14-year-old's bedroom, Universal City seemed a ghost town.

For almost six weeks, Universal-at-large had been on the lookout for Boris Karloff's Frankenstein Monster. Now the actor had checked out, waiting to see if Universal would pick up the option on his *Frankenstein* contract. Fearing his performance would sink his career, he had grave doubts. Colin Clive, portrayer of the title role, was off to Lake Arrowhead and Palm Springs, playing golf and tennis, keeping his alcoholism at bay. Mae Clarke, *Frankenstein*'s leading lady, had immediately gone into *Three Wise Girls* at Columbia, co-starring with Jean Harlow. *Frankenstein* director James Whale was carefully screening the footage, to see if any retakes or revisions were necessary.

Amidst this uneasy atmosphere reigned Carl Laemmle Jr., Universal's 23-year-old "Crown Prince." Presented the job of studio general manager by his father, Universal founder Carl Laemmle Sr., before "Junior" had turned 21, he was still craving the respect of Hollywood. A Best Picture Academy Award for 1930's *All Quiet on the Western Front* had helped only marginally, as had the smash hit *Dracula*. Fretful over *Frankenstein*— was it *too* horrifying?—"Junior" had nevertheless greenlighted a new horror show that was preparing to shoot.

The problem: *Murders in the Rue Morgue* wasn't really a horror saga. It was, in fact, the first modern detective story. The tale, published in 1841, focused on Poe's master of deduction, C. Auguste Dupin, who predated Sir Arthur Conan Doyle's Sherlock Holmes by 46 years.[8] In Poe's story, the orangutan was the escaped pet of a sailor: It had run off with the sailor's shaving razor and, in a panic, had killed the L'Espanaye ladies, mother and daughter. The horror is primarily in the orangutan having stuffed the daughter feet-first up a chimney—and the demise of the mother:

> *After a thorough investigation of every portion of the house, without farther discovery, the party made its way into a small paved yard in the rear of the building, where lay the corpse of the old lady, with her throat so entirely cut that, upon attempt to raise her, the head fell off and rolled to some distance....*

Junior Laemmle, his notorious hypochondria raging in the wake of *Frankenstein*, was painfully aware that *Murders in the Rue Morgue* had to compete with *Dracula*, boasting its 500-year-old vampire from Hell, and *Frankenstein*, with its Monster from the charnel house. Always a gambler, he rolled the dice that a man who had worked as a teenager with the famed Grand Guignol Theatre in Paris could make lightning strike at Universal for a third time.

Adaptor and Director Robert Florey

Thirty-one-year-old Robert Florey, who stood more than a foot taller than Junior Laemmle, loved the movies.

In Hollywood, he had directed 1928's *Johann the Coffin Maker*, a Poe-esque three-reeler he reportedly shot in a weekend for under $200. He had co-directed (with Joseph Santley) the Marx Brothers in 1929's *The Cocoanuts*.[9] And he had adapted *Frankenstein*, as well as shooting the legendary long-lost screen test with Lugosi. As Brian Taves wrote in his superbly researched book *Robert Florey: The French Expressionist*, Florey excelled at "bizarre set design, shadowy lighting, [and] *avant-garde* compositions and camera angles."[10]

In the gospel of *Frankenstein*, according to Florey, he was a bloody but unbowed martyr, sacrificed by Universal Studios.

As Florey remembered the *Frankenstein* test, Bela Lugosi did *not* appear *à la Der Golem*, as test reel player Edward Van Sloan claimed, nor (again in Van Sloan's words) like "something out of *Babes in Toyland*."[11] Nor did the test cause Junior Laemmle, as later reported, "to laugh like a hyena."[12] These were fables, claimed Florey, made up by the studio to "create a mythos for *Frankenstein*" and glorify James Whale, Boris Karloff and makeup artist Jack P. Pierce. If Florey told the truth (and it's increasingly difficult to tell as the years go by)—that Lugosi wore a Monster makeup "identical" to what Karloff later wore, and that the test (as photographed by cameraman Paul Ivano) was so impressive

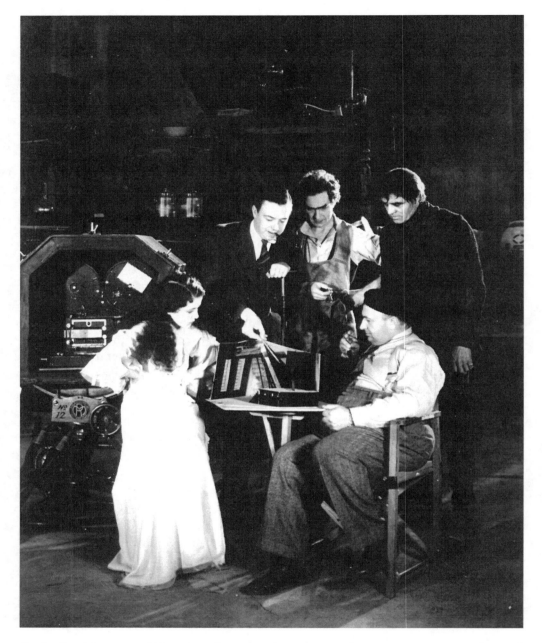

On the *Rue Morgue* set: Sidney Fox, director Robert Florey, Bela Lugosi, cinematographer Karl Freund (seated) and Noble Johnson.

that every director on the lot wanted to make the movie—he indeed got one of the great raw deals in motion picture history.[13]

Nevertheless … if Florey's truly the martyr of the story, there's one problem having too much sympathy for the hero. Florey's *Frankenstein* adaptation presented most of the film's horror highlights, but fell flat on characterization. Frankenstein is simply a power-hungry mad doctor who bullies his Monster; the Monster is merely a monstrosity.

James Whale would see the poetry in Henry Frankenstein, whom Colin Clive played with such Byronic glamour; and Whale would also see the beauty in the Monster, for whom Karloff provided a soul.

Whale saw *Frankenstein* as "insane passion."[14] Florey saw it as camera angles.

Florey went his own way on *Murders in the Rue Morgue*. For example, he named the villain after the 1857 one-act operetta *Le docteur Miracle*, by Georges Bizet. His major interest: the film's *look*. He wanted to evoke *The Cabinet of Dr. Caligari* and *Nosferatu*, and he won a huge break with his vision as Universal provided Karl Freund as cinematographer. Freund, Tod Browning's cameraman on *Dracula*, was already a legend in cinema, with such celebrated European credits as *Der Golem* (1920), *Variety* (1925) and *Metropolis* (1927).

Florey's stylistic approach was exciting, but again, it all came together at the cost of the *dramatis personae*. In his late years, Florey told interviewers that he saw Dupin as the script's major character (which made sense), and resented the very presence of Dr. Mirakle (which made no sense). "[T]he story would have been much better without the Mirakle character," said Florey.[15]

Indeed, a strange "vibe" was in the air at Universal at this time: Lugosi's "rejection" of *Frankenstein*'s Monster role (in fact, James Whale hadn't wanted him) was already creating a real-life legend and melodrama, unfairly casting the Hungarian star as a loser. Possibly this fed Florey's opinion. Decades later, author James Curtis, in his book *Featured Player*, asked Mae Clarke, who was "Queen of Universal" the summer of 1931, what her impression had been of Bela Lugosi during that highly eventful season. "I didn't know anything about Bela Lugosi," she replied. Nevertheless, Clarke would go on to say:

"Well, he seemed like a ham actor who didn't know how to live a life and messed up everything as he went."[16]

The Censors

If Bela Lugosi wasn't receiving the respect he deserved, neither was Robert Florey. For that matter, neither was George Melford, who directed Universal's Spanish version of *Dracula*, and was set to direct *Murders in the Rue Morgue* until Junior Laemmle gave it to Florey.

Then a bombshell exploded. After months of work on the project, Universal decided to slash the budget: *Murders in the Rue Morgue*—Edgar Allan Poe be damned—would become a contemporary thriller! Dr. Mirakle, perhaps on the loose in 1931 Hollywood … with the real-life Ape Man?

Aghast, Robert Florey walked out of the studio. However:

Tuesday, October 6: Variety ran this notice, titled "Poe Victory":

Universal has changed story of Murders in the Rue Morgue *back to the time in which Edgar Allan Poe placed it. Studio had attempted to give it a modern treatment but couldn't get a satisfactory script. John Huston and Dale Van Every are preparing the latest treatment.*

Florey returned but had to guarantee to keep down the costs in its 19th-century setting. Among Florey's assurances: He was aware that all the beautiful costumes created for MGM's *La Boheme* (1926), directed by King Vidor and starring Lillian Gish and John Gilbert, were hanging at Western Costume. Florey, a production assistant on *La Boheme*, knew they could be had for an economy rental.

The final script gave credit to Tom Reed, Dale Van Every and 25-year-old novice John Huston, who worked on the dialogue.[17] Destined for big things, Huston came to Universal after his father, Walter Huston (the star of Universal's recent *A House Divided* with Helen Chandler), implored Junior Laemmle to give his ne'er-do-well son a chance as a writer. "He starts tomorrow,"[18] Junior promised, and he kept his word. John worked primarily on the romantic dialogue. Alas, Florey would rewrite most of it on the set.

The Hollywood-ized *Murders in the Rue Morgue*: A mad doctor in 19th-century Paris, with a pre–Darwin theory of Evolution, keeps a gorilla by the name of Erik … whom he wishes to mate with a Parisienne coquette.

The Poe story had become a sex saga of bestiality.

Tuesday, October 13: The Motion Picture Producers and Distributors Association of America (MPPDA) was the lily-livered enforcer of the Production Code, and headed by Col. Jason Joy, formerly a colonel in the U.S. Army General Staff and executive secretary of the American Red Cross. Fred W. Beetson of the MPPDA seemed relatively oblivious to the gorilla-mates-with-woman story as he wrote to Junior Laemmle:

> *We have read with interest your script of* Murders in the Rue Morgue *and believe it is satisfactory under the Code and reasonably safe from censorship difficulties, provided the picture is not regarded as too gruesome and too full of horrors. It seems to us the two major situations which offer concern are: first, the scenes in which the unknown woman is murdered in the opening episode, especially shadows of her apparently strapped to a cross; and second, the scene when the body of Camille's mother is discovered in the chimney.*
>
> *The only other suggestion we have regards the Nautch dancer…. If this is developed in an exaggerated manner so as to be offensive, it probably will be censorable. But we feel sure you, in your usual splendid manner, will make certain this is not the case.*

To amplify Beetson's suggestions:

- The "unknown woman" was a prostitute, who Mirakle wanted to mate with his gorilla, and she was indeed strapped to a cross. Also, note that the scene with the prostitute was the *opening* episode in the script.
- As for the body in the chimney, the scenarists made the *mother* the victim, not the daughter, as Poe had written. The film planned a Happy Ending for the daughter (the movie's ingénue).
- And as for the "Nautch" dancer … a "Nautch" is defined as "a sinuous Oriental dance resembling the cooch." Performing this dance was the character of "Lady Fatima," who would appear in the Carnival night episode, bumping and grinding with her sideshow "Arab Angels."

Apparently "off the record," the Production Code eventually warned Universal that the concept of gorilla-mating-with-woman was potentially trouble. Florey and company came up with camouflage: Mirakle claimed he wanted to mix the blood of Erik and a human.

Nobody was fooled, but it got the script past the Code.

Junior, frazzled by the pressures of his job and his epic fights with his father (who hated horror movies), became ill. He would be at Lake Arrowhead, at Cedars of Lebanon Hospital, and at a "desert retreat" for the next five weeks, and wouldn't reply to Beetson until November 14, the day after shooting of *Murders in the Rue Morgue* originally wrapped.[19]

It all came together—at least on paper. Florey, in a February 17, 1979, letter to Richard Bojarski (author of *The Films of Boris Karloff* and *The Films of Bela Lugosi*), related:

> In Rue Morgue, *I used the same device I had employed in* Frankenstein. *Bela Lugosi became Doctor Mirakle—a mad scientist desirous to create a human being—not with body parts stolen in a graveyard and a brain in a lab, but by the mating of an ape with a woman.*[20]

Florey had previously claimed he had outwitted Universal by ripping off his own conception of *Frankenstein*. Actually, Florey might have perpetrated a *different* joke on Universal—or maybe his writers had played one on *him*.

Ingagi

Ingagi was a 1930 movie about a gorilla who has a bevy of human female sex slaves. They bear him children, who in turn grow up to be ape women.

The notorious film was from Congo Pictures, which came into being specifically to produce this atrocity. It tried to pass itself off as a documentary, actually shot in the Congo, on an expedition led by "Sir Hubert Winstead," who also narrated. It boasted that it featured real apes and genuine native ladies. The publicity proclaimed:

AN AUTHENTIC INCONTESTABLE CELLULOID DOCUMENT SHOWING
THE SACRIFICE OF A LIVING WOMAN TO GORILLA HORDES!

Ingagi, upon release, was a smash hit, but … rumors circulated that the show was an unabashed "hoax":

- There was no evidence there really was a "Sir Hubert Winstead."
- In his narration, the British explorer had a distinct American accent.
- The photography was terrible. (Sir Hubert claimed in the film that this was due to the African heat.)
- Sir Hubert appeared to have a beard in some shots, and no beard in others.
- The pygmies didn't resemble pygmies at all, but looked like black children.

The climax, as reported by the press at the time, saw Ingagi, in all his glory, leading a promenade of native women. The ape was lugging a baby. A native bride was led into the jungle, and as the crowd cheered the amorous Ingagi, the gorilla acknowledged their fandom—then carried off the virgin. Sir Hubert followed, fatally blasting him with his elephant gun. Ingagi died—and the film showed several native women *weeping*, as if mourning a dead lover. The bestial inference was horrifically clear.

One critic wrote, "In all the latter scenes of *Ingagi* … the camera work is so good that it might have been made in a well-lighted movie studio in Hollywood."[21]

Well, sure enough…. *Ingagi* was a fraud. Among the discoveries that came to light:

- There was no such person as Sir Hubert Winstead.
- The head of Congo Pictures had actually provided the "Winstead" narration.
- The location footage was ripped off from a 1915 documentary titled *Heart of Africa*, by Lady Grace MacKenzie, known as the first white woman to lead an expedition in Africa. Her son sued Congo Pictures.
- The "location" footage new in the film had actually been shot at Los Angeles' Selig Zoo.
- Some (if not all) the native women in the film were white women in blackface.

The MPPDA, due to *Ingagi's* "nature faking,"[22] ordered theaters to stop exhibiting it. Congo Pictures sued the MPPDA for $3,365,000. The MPPDA hired a Better Business Bureau detective to investigate, which brings us to our punchline:

The detective learned that "Ingagi" had been a man in an ape suit: Charles Gemora. In 1930, Gemora had also played an ape in MGM's *The Unholy Three* (Lon Chaney's last film) and the title role in First National's *The Gorilla.* The detective convinced Gemora to sign an affidavit admitting the masquerade.[23] More on Gemora later.

Clearly *Ingagi* influenced *Murders in the Rue Morgue* ... and *King Kong.* Just how *much* it influenced them, fans can now determine for themselves, as the long-unavailable film has made its bow in a new millennium, as a January 2021 Kino Classics Blu-ray release.

Thus, in the wake of *Ingagi,* Florey and his writers provided *Murders in the Rue Morgue* its true horror element. After all, it sounded promising: Before the MPPDA shot down *Ingagi,* the film, according to several sources, had taken in $4,000,000.[24]

Murders in the Rue Morgue's next problem: no assigned leading lady. On October 14, only five days before shooting started, Llewellyn Miller of the *Los Angeles Record* reported:

> *Sidney Fox, Universal's little dark-eyed beauty, has been given the feminine lead in* Murders in the Rue Morgue, *in which Bela (Dracula) Lugosi is starred. Horror stories invariably have such sweet little ingenues for leading women. It makes just that much more excitement, I suppose. Helen Chandler had to battle old man Dracula, you remember.*

The Hollywood press enjoyed describing Sidney Fox as "angelic." In fact, she eventually fell in flames as Universal's Dark Star of the early 1930s.

Sidney Fox

December 2, 1930: Elizabeth Yeaman reported in the *Hollywood Daily Citizen:*

> *A new star arrived in Hollywood yesterday under contract to Universal Pictures. She is Sidney Fox.... A diminutive little creature with the charm and poise of a veteran, she made her first visit to Universal yesterday and left everyone on the lot gasping at her beauty.... She has great luminous dark brown eyes that spark fire and personality.... Junior Laemmle has planned great things for her, and she is exceedingly anxious to start work.*

Junior had seen Sidney in the play *Lost Sheep,* which had opened

A signed portrait of Sidney Fox from May 1931 (from the Roger Hurlburt Collection).

May 5, 1930, at Broadway's Selwyn Theatre. The risqué comedy concerned a reverend who moved his family into a house recently vacated by a madame and six prostitutes. Hilarity ensued. Of Sidney, who played the reverend's youngest daughter, the *New York Times* wrote, "[L]ittle Sidney Fox won the hearts of the audience at once…. Nothing could be more tenderly disarming than the freshness of her acting."[25]

She certainly disarmed Junior. He signed Sidney to a Universal contract, and she and the "Crown Prince" allegedly became lovers.[26]

In at least one way, they were a good match: Junior was barely over five feet tall, so Sidney, at 4'11", could wear high heels without looming over him, the way many other starlets did. Nevertheless, the affair was a mixed blessing for Sidney. Although Junior had won the Best Picture Oscar for *All Quiet on the Western Front*, many figured Junior himself was no prize: a hypochondriacal playboy who had a gift for selecting talent, but had none himself. As Junior was regarded in Hollywood as rather a joke, Sidney, his rumored lover, quickly and unfortunately became something of a joke too.

It was a pity. The lady was no fool and told a reporter:

> *My greatest cross is that my face and body don't match my mind and soul. People expect me to be an ingenue, a baby doll, and they're terribly disappointed when they find I'm not…. Men, in Hollywood especially, don't like intelligent women.*[27]

Publicized as 19 years old (she was 23), Sidney made her Universal debut in the title role in 1931's *Bad Sister*, in which she first appears languishing in bed surrounded by photos of herself. Bette Davis, who played the "good sister" in *Bad Sister,* complained for decades that Sidney got the title role because of her relationship with Junior.

Throughout the summer of 1931, Sidney made the news:

Wednesday, July 29: The Hollywood Daily Citizen reported that Sidney had attended a Universal City luncheon honoring Mrs. Knute Rockne, visiting during the filming of the studio's *The Spirit of Notre Dame*. (Rockne had died in a plane crash March 31 while flying to California regarding the film.) Among those also in attendance: James Whale and Bela Lugosi.

Wednesday, August 12: The Los Angeles Examiner announced that Sidney was one of the 13 "WAMPAS Baby Stars" of 1931. The others included freelancer Frances Dade (Lucy in *Dracula*), Warner Bros.' Marian Marsh (leading lady to John Barrymore in *Svengali*) and MGM's Karen Morley (the heroine in Karloff's *The Mask of Fu Manchu* in 1932).

Thursday, September 10: The Los Angeles Record reported that Harry Rosenthal's orchestra had opened at the Embassy Club. Jimmy Durante was emcee, and amidst the "tremendous crowd" were Jean Harlow, Evelyn Brent and Sidney, who was dressed "all in white."

Most significantly, Sidney has landed the plum female role in Universal's *Strictly Dishonorable,* based on the Preston Sturges play, as a dainty Southern damsel seduced by an opera star (Paul Lukas). Plenty of actresses had desired that part, and tongues had been viciously wagging about Sidney sleeping with the boss.

"Angelic" Sidney Fox was walking a high wire. Caught in the prattle, Sidney flashed a Jekyll-Hyde personality with the press. She purred to the *Los Angeles Times,* "Love? Oh, I would have to be very seriously in love even to get engaged…. I know if I ever do marry, I shall want two houses—intimacy is so romance-destroying."[28]

In a more hostile mood, she scratched and clawed to the *Los Angeles Examiner*: "I can't help it if I didn't go about tossing myself into people's laps when I arrived here.

Or if I didn't maul and paw everyone to whom I was introduced. I can't gush over everybody...!"[29]

Sidney hoped *Strictly Dishonorable*, set to premiere in November, would establish her as a top star and extinguish the jokes mocking her as the paramour of "the Baby Mogul." She was now starring in Universal's *Nice Women*, which would wrap the same day *Murders in the Rue Morgue* began shooting. As such, she would have no break between films.

There was a consolation. Junior awarded Sidney top billing in *Murders in the Rue Morgue*, although it was blueprinted as Bela Lugosi's vehicle after *Dracula*.

There's no record of Lugosi's response when he learned the news.

* * *

Everything was in place. The budget was $164,220. The shooting schedule was 18 days. This was almost $100,000 less than the budget for *Frankenstein*, and the schedule 12 days shorter.[30]

Finally, there was one more piece of pivotal casting. Playing the role of Erik the gorilla: Ingagi himself ... Charles Gemora!

Monday, October 19: *Murders in the Rue Morgue* began shooting.

Part Two: The Shoot

I bring news, from Erik! He speaks only of you. He can't forget you!
　　　—Bela Lugosi as Dr. Mirakle, to Sidney Fox as
　　　Camille L'Espanaye, in *Murders in the Rue Morgue*

The Carnival

As released, *Murders in the Rue Morgue* opened with Carnival Night in Paris, 1845.

Atmospherics abound. Couples ride on large swings. Sideshow acts play with a touch of midnight burlesque. Sidney Fox's Camille, lovely in her *La Boheme* hand-me-downs, is wide-eyed at the wonder of it all.

Just how different was Sidney from the cooing, baby-talking, kewpie doll heroine she played? Well, shortly after *Murders in the Rue Morgue* was released, Sidney backed her Cadillac coupe out of her garage at 6774 Wedgewood Place, Whitley Heights, Hollywood, felt her brakes fail, and was trapped inside the car as it tumbled 40 feet backwards down an embankment. The car somersaulted to the street, finally landing upside down. Sidney emerged with "a few cuts and bruises about the head and shoulders."

"I seemed to just bounce around inside the car when it landed," she said nonchalantly, and with *chutzpah*.[31]

Accompanying Camille at the carnival was her beau, Pierre Dupin, our lovesick version of Poe's C. Auguste Dupin. John Boles, who had played Victor Moritz in

The Carnival Night set, as seen in this candid shot from a soundstage catwalk. Note the "Arab Angels" in all their tempting glory, to the left of the shot. Was "Lady Fatima and Her Arab Angels" an intended sacrilegious reference on director Robert Florey's part?

Frankenstein, had been announced for the role. However, it went to 29-year-old stage actor Leon Waycoff, aka Leon Ames, later the father in MGM's beloved 1944 Technicolor musical *Meet Me in St. Louis*.[32]

Joining our ingénues at the carnival: Dupin's chubby roommate Paul (Bert Roach, an original Keystone Cop) and his lady friend Mignette (Edna Marion, formerly in Laurel and Hardy comedies). The foursome takes in all the sights and sounds.

Most memorably, they behold Lady Fatima and her Arab Angels.

The unbilled, half-naked Lady Fatima performs her "cooch" dance with a ditzy expression and strip-joint abandon. A pair of aged lechers ogle:

> LECHER 1: *Do they bite?*
> LECHER 2: *Oh, yes—but you have to pay extra for that!*

Just as the Production Code had warned, Lady Fatima and her undulating "Angels" were headed for trouble. The Virginia state censor attacked with the scissors:

> *Reel 1—Eliminate all C.U. scenes of dancing girls wiggling their bodies in unseemly fashion to show their navels.*

Pennsylvania's censor demanded, "Eliminate all views whatsoever of girls dancing," and cut out the two geezers and their "Do they bite?" dialogue. Ontario would scissor scenes of Lady Fatima and the dancers "wriggling," Kansas would snip the dance scene "except shots of hands and arms and comments of crowd," Australia and Alberta would cut the close-ups of the dancers, and Massachusetts would eliminate the scene for "Sunday showings."

Murders in the Rue Morgue, only two minutes and twenty seconds into the film, was already in censorship trouble.

As for "Lady Fatima and her Arab Angels," the Roman Catholic Church was deeply

Edna Marion, Bert Roach, Sidney Fox and Leon Ames observe the "cooch dance" of Lady Fatima and Her Arab Angels (from the John Antosiewicz Collection).

devoted in 1931 to Our Lady of Fatima. The Blessed Virgin Mary had reportedly appeared to three shepherd children in Fatima, Portugal, in 1917. Millions of 21st-century pilgrims still visit the site of Our Lady of Fatima's apparitions.

Was it coincidence that, in *Murders in the Rue Morgue*, Florey presented "Lady (of) Fatima," who did a "cooch" dance? And that her back-up dancers were called "Angels"? How coincidental does this seem after one sees in the same film a crucifixion of a prostitute and a bevy of iconic religious images?

Had Florey put one over on Universal, the Production Code and the Catholic Church?

Meanwhile, Camille sticks out her tongue at Lady Fatima, and Florey and Freund delight in shadows and camera angles. The film is a treat for the eyes. Looming at the carnival is a giant towering cut-out of a gorilla. Playing the Barker: Michael Visaroff, the innkeeper from *Dracula*.

"Erik … the Ape Man…. The beast with a human soul!" spiels the barker.

The crowd enters the tent under the "loins" of the gorilla figure and into the "womb" of the tent—a nice visual touch, suggesting both the evolution speech we're about to hear, and the bestiality the film so gleefully presents. Inside, we see Lugosi as Dr. Mirakle—the actor's favored left side toward the camera as he speaks to Camille: "Take a seat up front where you can see everything!" Then he goes up on stage, his giant shadow looming behind him.

"What a funny-looking man!" Camille says girlishly to Dupin of Mirakle. "He's a show in himself!"

Indeed, Jack P. Pierce clearly tried hard to make Lugosi "funny-looking" as Mirakle. The two men had clashed on *Dracula* and the *Frankenstein* test, and Pierce's work here seems vindictive: a curly wig and a long, caterpillar eyebrow. Additionally, Freund lit and shot Lugosi's close-ups here to suggest an evil Man in the Moon.

It didn't matter. Lugosi's Mirakle has dash and demonic glamor. Claiming he had rejected *Frankenstein* because the Monster had no dialogue, Lugosi has a juicy soliloquy here. With his rich accent and epic pauses, Lugosi virtually sings:

> *I'm Dr. Mirakle, monsieurs and medames, and I'm not a sideshow charlatan. So if you expect to witness the usual carnival hocus-pocus, just go to the box office and get your money back. I am not exhibiting a freak … a monstrosity of nature … but a milestone in the development of life!*

À la Dwight Frye's Fritz in *Frankenstein*, Mirakle has a warped assistant: Janos, the Black One, played by black actor Noble Johnson. Johnson's fascinating career dated back to 1916, when he founded the all-black Lincoln Motion Picture Company, which produced "race" films. Johnson's horror credits will include the Nubian in *The Mummy* and the native chief in *King Kong* and *The Son of Kong*.

Things start to get wonky as Mirakle introduces Erik.

Charles Gemora, born in the Philippines, was 28 years old at the time of *Murders in the Rue Morgue*. His 1931 state-of-the-art gorilla mask was very expressive. As shooting began, he leered early and often as Erik. Gemora had no idea (nor perhaps did Florey at this time) what would happen two months later: Florey would visit the Selig Zoo, shoot close-ups of a monkey, cut Gemora's close-ups, and splice in close-ups of the wildly mugging chimp.

Florey never told Gemora what he had done. Bob Burns, himself a noted gorilla actor, met Gemora in 1957 and they discussed *Murders in the Rue Morgue*. Gemora remembered going to see the film during its original release.

His response to the monkey close-ups? He was, as he told Burns, "in shock."[33]

There follows a remarkable moment. Lugosi's Mirakle announces that Erik will relate his history to the crowd, and Mirakle will translate. Lugosi smiles at Erik, speaking to him in what's supposed to be ape language. The bit would sink almost any other actor, but Lugosi plays it so sincerely, so compassionately, that he absolutely transcends the hoke. Erik chatters, and Mirakle soulfully translates:

> My home is in the African jungle, where I lived with my father and my mother ... and my brothers and sisters. But I was captured by a band of hairless white apes, and carried away to a strange land. I'm in the prime of my strength ... and I am lonely!

Again, Lugosi almost sings the dialogue, especially the words "and I'm lonely," with sadness and tenderness.

Lugosi struts his stuff, acting with the fervor of a star who knows the producer is in love with the leading lady, and the director is in love with shadows and camera angles. He rips into his Darwinian speech, pointing his gnarly twisted cane at a large, evolutionary chart with its drawings of fish and reptiles: "Here—is the story of Man. ... Crawling reptiles grew legs...."

Darwin's *On the Origin of Species* was published in 1859, so Mirakle's theories are 14 years ahead of that date. It's also worth noting this film was produced only six years after the Scopes Monkey Trial.

"Behold! The first man!" proclaims Mirakle, pointing his cane at Erik.

The crowd responds. A man cries "*Heresy!*" prompting another bevy of great

"You liked her—didn't you, Erik?": Lugosi as Mirakle and Charles Gemora as the "lonely" Erik (from the John Antosiewicz Collection).

Lugosi lines: "*Heresy*? Do they still burn men for heresy? Then burn me, monsieur. Light the fire!"

The film now takes its first plunge into the *Ingagi* veldt: Mirakle invites the crowd to step up to the cage and "make the acquaintance of Erik." This offer scares away the majority of the audience, although Camille, Dupin, Paul and Mignette remain in the tent. The film almost becomes a comedy as Fox's Camille approaches the cage with fascination, and Lugosi's Mirakle plays matchmaker: "Erik is only human, mademoiselle!" smiles Lugosi. "He has an eye for beauty.... You have made a conquest, mademoiselle!"

Erik, overly ardent, grabs Camille's bonnet. Dupin tries to retrieve it and Erik gets him by the neck. "You fool!" shouts Mirakle, intervening. Then he asks for Camille's address so he can replace the bonnet, "with Erik's compliments." Dupin declines to provide it. Mirakle dispatches Janos to find where Camille lives.

Our First Act nears its curtain. We've met our 4'11" heroine, our clunky hero, our supercharged villain, and our ape, who has a fetish for Camille's bonnet. We've seen the stylistics the director and cinematographer are impressively creating, and have caught wind of the racy and possibly profane way the writers have thoroughly bastardized Edgar Allan Poe's story. The look in Lugosi's eyes gives away what's up here: Camille has indeed made a conquest, with Dr. Mirakle, as well as with Erik. And Lugosi's last line sets up what's to come:

"You liked *her* ... didn't you, Erik?"

"Lonely" Erik, fondling Camille's bonnet, chatters appreciatively.

*   *   *

Two notes:

On October 20, 1931, Bela Lugosi turned 49 years old. He wasn't on call at Universal on his birthday.

Also: As if to celebrate *Murders in the Rue Morgue*'s first week's shooting, on Friday, September 23, police captured the Ape Man—or so they thought. As the *Los Angeles Times* reported the next day:

> Hollywood's bogey man, "the Ape Man," who terrorized the film capital almost nightly for a fortnight with attacks on defenseless women following the brutal candy-store murder of Wilma McFarland ... was believed captured early yesterday with the arrest of Fred Peterson, 45 years of age, of 413 Coll Street, Ventura, police stated....

Peterson was described as 6'2", over 200 pounds, with a four-day growth of beard. A police officer arrested him "standing in a shaded nook near a clump of hedges" at Lillian Way and Romaine Street in Hollywood. Peterson tried to make a break for freedom from the Hollywood Police Station twice, unsuccessfully. Among the charges facing him: stealing four dollars from the milk fund cash box of the Vine Street School.[34]

But Peterson proved not to be "Hollywood's bogey man." Police never captured the Ape Man, and the murder of Wilma McFarland was never solved.

The Passion of the Woman of the Streets

Frankenstein haunted the shoot of *Murders in the Rue Morgue*.

The week of October 26 saw Colin Clive start his trip home to England; hating the sight and sound of himself onscreen, he was gone by the time James Whale previewed

Frankenstein on Thursday night, October 29, in Santa Barbara. Junior Laemmle, although still battling a nervous breakdown, was there for the preview.

Nobody invited Boris Karloff.

Frankenstein's big horror episode had been the "Flower Game," filmed at Lake Malibou in the Santa Monica mountains, where Karloff's Monster drowned Marilyn Harris' Little Maria. (The scene, of course, had been in Florey's adaptation.) Whale had directed the tragic episode brilliantly, and Karloff and seven-year-old Marilyn Harris played it hauntingly.

Could Florey top this scene for sheer horror in *Murders in the Rue Morgue*? He was certainly hellbent on trying.

It was a shocking episode for its day ... and frankly, still is in 2022. The victim: a Woman of the Streets, as the credits billed her. Her fate: hung on a cockeyed cross in Mirakle's laboratory as the madman viciously takes a blood sample. His dream: to mate her with Erik. Her fate: dying on the cross, her body dropped through a trap door into the Seine.

Incredibly, it all plays even more savagely and sacrilegiously than it sounds ... and it was originally the opening episode of *Murders in the Rue Morgue*.[35]

Night. Fog. Two men are battling on a bridge for the prostitute. Playing the Woman of the Streets is Arlene Francis, who had just turned 24 on October 20 (sharing a birthday with Bela) and who would later be the smiling, *tres*-sophisticate panelist of TV's *What's My Line?* A Universal executive had spotted Arlene dining in a restaurant in Los Angeles, promptly offered her the role of the Woman of the Streets and said she would "have to swim."[36] This suggested two things:

- She would be in water in the film.
- None of Universal's starlets were willing to play the part.

The two men on the bridge kill each other as the prostitute screams. Mirakle's carriage, driven by a leering Janos, glides to a stop. Lugosi, in cloak and a tall hat worthy of a satanic pilgrim, alights and moves through the mist, superbly captured by Karl Freund, in an episode that was scripted and shot as Lugosi's entrance.

"A lady ... in distress?" asks Mirakle.

The Woman of the Streets laughs in hysteria, Mirakle leers with abandon, and he gets her into the carriage. As it pulls away, the Woman of the Streets becomes even more hysterical: As edited in the final print, she's sharing the carriage with Mirakle *and* Erik.

The laboratory ... a revamp of the *Frankenstein* tower and dungeon set. The Woman of the Streets screams wildly, stripped to her 1845 lingerie and boots, bound to an X-shaped crucifix. Mirakle lances her for a blood sample. It reveals under his microscope that she has venereal disease.

"*Rotten blood!*" he howls.

The prostitute dies from her tortures, and Mirakle orders Janos to drop the doxy through a trap door and into the Seine.

Before examining this remarkable scene in detail, let it be known that censors in New York, Pennsylvania and Kansas cut this scene almost entirely, as did the Chicago city censor, Ontario and Alberta. Virginia trimmed the footage of Arlene Francis on the cross, as did Massachusetts ("for Sunday showings"). Perhaps the best way to describe this baroque episode is to quote from the Pennsylvania censor, who was extremely detailed:

Eliminate all views whatsoever, in silhouette or otherwise, of girl tied to crossed timbers, of her writhing, twisting and moaning in agony, of Dr. Mirakle coming to her, talking to her, stabbing her in arm with lance, of her screaming, twisting and straining away from him, of Dr. Mirakle getting angry and holding her arm while he tortures her....

The same censor was also specific about cutting this dialogue:

DR. MIRAKLE: *Be patient. Are you in pain, Mademoiselle? It will only last a little longer.*
GIRL: *Oh! Oh!*
DR. MIRAKLE: *Ahhh, you are so stubborn! Hush! It will only last one more minute and we
    shall see. We shall know if you are to be the Bride of Science!*

The "Bride of Science" line, as roared by Lugosi, is significant. For all the action and dialogue about mixing blood, Mirakle is clearly hoping for a wedding night for Erik and the caterwauling Woman of the Streets.

The Pennsylvania censor continued its eliminations

...of camera panning and bringing his laboratory apparatus into view, of him leaving girl and going to work table, of girl crying and moaning and of him turning to her and raving at her, of him arranging microscope and looking through it, showing displeasure as he looks, of him knocking his microscope and other things off table in his fury, raving at girl,....

DR. MIRAKLE: *Oh, hush! Hush! Now, Mademoiselle, now. The clots—the black spots—Rotten
    blood! You!*

This same censor noted that he was allowing only a shred of the scene to survive, as described:

This allows scenes from where Dr. Mirakle is standing in front of girl and says, "Your blood is rotten! Black as your sins! You cheated me—your beauty was a lie!"—until Janos starts to cut ropes.

The Pennsylvania censor was being liberal. Other censors cut this particular action as well.

Of course, the crazy sexuality is wacky, but what about the sacrilegious concept—a "Woman of the Streets" as a tortured Christ symbol? Later horror films flirted with the Crucifixion concept. Karloff, as Anti-Christ, appears to be crucified on a rack in *The Black Cat*, as Lugosi skins him alive. Karloff's Monster hangs crucified by the villagers in *Bride of Frankenstein*.

Yet Florey and Freund created a unique blasphemy, as it were. After the death of the Woman of the Streets, there's a darkly lit close-up of her, with her flowing hair and peaceful expression.

Murders in the Rue Morgue's Passion Play evokes the Virgin Mary Crucified ... a truly startling image.

The follow-up action reinforces this interpretation. "You're dead," pitifully laments Lugosi, who falls to his knees before the corpse, hands clasped in prayer, as if beholding a beatific Vision, and pleading to the Virgin for forgiveness. Again, a sacrilegious flourish: a man praying at the foot of a cross, where there hangs the body not of Jesus, but a slaughtered doxy.

"Get rid of it," Mirakle commands Janos. The vision has passed; the dead woman is now "it." Janos cuts the ropes with an axe, springs a trap door, and we hear a splash. Whether Arlene Francis actually fell into water under the scaffolding, or whether the splash was dubbed, isn't known.

"Will my search never end?" sings Lugosi.

The Woman of the Streets (Arlene Francis) bound to an X-shaped cross, Mirakle (Bela Lugosi) kneeling in holy reverence, in one of the most perversely blasphemous episodes in Universal Horror (from the John Antosiewicz Collection).

Fade out.

Incidentally, on October 28, 29 and 30—the eve, actual date, and day after *Frankenstein's* Santa Barbara preview—Florey shot this outlandishly profane, sadistic, macabre episode. Learning of the sensation *Frankenstein* had created, he was likely glad he had dared film so savage a scene. Had he matched, or topped, *Frankenstein's* flower game?

Would his search never end?

A Morgue Keeper, Camille Sings, and Swinging with Sidney

Naturally, *Murders in the Rue Morgue* had scenes in a morgue complete with a large cross on its wall. Religious touches continued to adorn the film.

Nicely ghoulish comic relief creeps into the film at this point via D'Arcy Corrigan, from County Cork, Ireland, as the Morgue Keeper. In his first close-up, he blows his nose, then looks at what's in his handkerchief. Appearing to have crawled out of a dusty Dickens first edition, Corrigan's morbid Morgue Keeper delivers one of the best lines in the movie: "Since that whole body disappeared last week, the inspector is very strict about medical students."

Speaking of Dickens, Corrigan later played the Ghost of Christmas Future in MGM's 1938 *A Christmas Carol*. It was ironic casting. A certain future Christmas wasn't festive for Corrigan: He died on Christmas in 1945.[37]

"D'Arcy Corrigan gives a representation of a morgue-keeper that simply knocks you for a ghoul," the *San Francisco News* critic saluted, while *The Hollywood Herald* reported, "Next to Lugosi for acting honors comes D'Arcy Corrigan, who lives and breathes the part of the Morgue Keeper...."

If Corrigan was "next to Lugosi," how was Sidney Fox doing?

Camille receives a gift from Dr. Mirakle, which she opens in front of her mother, Mme. L'Espanaye (Betsy Ross Clarke, an attractive and rather youthful-looking choice for the role). It's the bonnet Mirakle promised Camille, with a letter:

> *Mademoiselle—*
> *You are lovely. Who knows what the future holds for you? Great things are written on the stars. Erik and I will read them for you. Tonight—the Carnival—come.*
> *Admiringly,*
> *Doctor Mirakle*

Here, the film offers one of its hard-not-to-laugh-out-loud moments. In the stationery's return address right corner, there's a cartoon of a wild-eyed, mugging Erik.

The leading lady next gets a showcase in an episode in Universal's historic European village. Sidney's Camille stands on a top floor balcony, Dupin and frolickers on horseback, calling up to her and singing. She sports her new bonnet here, warbles a few lines of the song "A Funny Little Man," and throws a kiss.

Fox's shining moment in *Murders in the Rue Morgue*, however, is surely the picnic scene. Camille sits on a swing by a lake, Dupin pushes her, and she shows off the bonnet sent with Erik's compliments. Karl Freund's camera swings along with her, forward and back, the star leaning into the camera for smiling, giggling closeups. Freund had used the same "Swing" gimmick in Germany's *Variety* (1925), directed by E.A. Dupont.

Yes, Lugosi was taking the show. There was little Sidney could do about it. Strangely, several horror heroines of this halcyon era would face grim tragedy. Helen Chandler, of *Dracula*, was an alcoholic who never conquered her curse. Mae Clarke, of *Frankenstein*, battled anxiety that caused a breakdown and, early in 1932, placed her in a sanitarium.[38]

Sidney Fox, probably unaware of the bleak secrets these ladies kept, was nevertheless savvy and knew the dangers of Hollywood and stardom. She was determined to override them.

Would she?

Rue Morgue **director Robert Florey (right) prepares the swing scene, in which Karl Freund's camera swings along with Sidney Fox. Leon Ames stands behind her (from the John Antosiewicz Collection).**

Halloween

The second week's shooting of *Murders in the Rue Morgue* ended Saturday, October 31 … Halloween.

Work took place at the exterior of Mirakle's house and the street. It was a chilly All Hallows Eve, and the scenes of Lugosi and Erik, chattering together as they entered the towering old house—"I'll swear they were talking to each other!" marvels Leon Ames' Dupin—certainly fulfilled the spirit of the evening.

There was an odd atmosphere on the set. Florey and the company found Bela very aloof. Arlene Francis, who had attempted to make friends during the stretch where Bela had her bound to a cross, had received the same distant response.

Florey remembered:

Bela Lugosi was habitually silent and not given to conversation. Between scenes he retired in his dressing room.

I was very busy directing a number of players and spoke to Lugosi only to discuss scenes we were about to shoot and how I would want him to interpret them. It was at times difficult to control his tendency to chew the scenery.

I am sorry to say that I had more relationship with actors I directed in 65 films and 300 TV shows than with this taciturn artist.[39]

A candid shot survives from *Murders in the Rue Morgue*, perhaps taken Halloween night: Florey and Freund heavily bundled-up for the evening's chilly shoot. Leon Ames sits in a star's chair in his top hat and overcoat and smiles ear to ear. Lugosi stands to the side, in his cloak and hat, looking slightly away from the camera, remote even in this group shot. A group of brilliant émigrés … all gathered under the mountains at Universal City, creating horror on All Hallow's Eve.

Perhaps Lugosi was nursing resentment about Sidney Fox's first-billing. Maybe he had picked up that Florey felt the film would be better if Bela weren't in it. Or perhaps he was having apprehensions about the release of *Frankenstein*.

Always the pro, Lugosi proved garrulous for Universal's *Murders in the Rue Morgue* pressbook. Indeed, he put on quite a show:

> *Strange creatures—women. They love horror.*
> *There is something in the makeup of a woman which glories in association with horror. She gloats over repulsive things which cause the average man to turn away....*
> *When I was on stage in* Dracula, *my audiences were composed mostly of women. They came again and again, thrilling to the shocking story. True, many men were in the audience, but most of them had been brought by women, who craved the subtle sex intimacy brought about when both sat watching the terrifying incidents of the play.... The blood-sucking monster of the story excited strange thoughts and strange feelings.*
> *Women are the ones who constantly visit cemeteries, ostensibly to grieve for departed ones, but subconsciously to gloat over death.... Women are in the majority as spectators at murder trials, and the more gruesome the killing, the more breathless will be their attention....*
> *Women put forth every possible effort in their frantic desire to get to the front-line trenches during the World War. Granted that their great wish was to give aid and comfort to the wounded. But subconsciously they sought the savage thrill that came from being in the midst of suffering and horrible mutilation....*
> *It is women who flock to spiritualistic seances. They feel that, in a sense, they are coming in contact with Death, and thus is fed the morbid longing of the sex.* Dracula *fed this longing and* Murders in the Rue Morgue *is* Dracula and Frankenstein *combined.*[40]

Whatever his private musings, Lugosi spent Halloween of 1931 playing Dr. Mirakle, his most savagely passionately crazed mad doctor.

The Climax

Strictly Dishonorable, starring Sidney Fox, had its gala Hollywood premiere at the Carthay Circle Theatre on Friday night, November 6, 1931—the 17th day of *Rue Morgue* shooting. Sidney won mostly nice notices, although the bitchery remained. Jimmy Starr of the *Los Angeles Evening Express* felt it necessary to write that "one tiny glimpse" revealed the star as "somewhat overweight."

"Don't eat starchy foods, Sidney," sniped Starr.[41]

Murders in the Rue Morgue was originally scheduled to wrap Saturday, November 7. But the picture had fallen behind and the pressure was on to finish.

Mirakle and Erik take a carriage ride with Janos to the street outside Camille's rooming house. Mirakle goes up to pay a midnight call.

"I have a message for you, from Erik!" Mirakle insists as Camille, prepared for bed and holding a candle, opens the door a crack. "He speaks only of you. He can't forget you! There is something … you must know…!"

Lugosi takes a strange spin here, thespically. As played, it's clear that Mirakle is as lovesick over Camille as he claims Erik is. In fact, when Camille asks, "Are you insane, monsieur?" and closes the door in his face, Lugosi's Mirakle appears heartbroken, and close to tears. He recovers, grimly returns to the streets, and hisses to the gorilla, with vengeful glee: "There, Erik! She's up there!"

Next comes *Murders in the Rue Morgue*'s "other" Big Horror Episode—this one actually related to Poe. Erik climbs the wall of the house. Inside the L'Espanaye apartment, we see Camille praying. A crucifix glows celestially on the wall, prophetic of the crucifix in the Hermit's cottage in *Bride of Frankenstein*. Madame L'Espanaye is in her bed. Camille snuggles in her bed as well.

Enter Erik.

Here, Florey's eccentric style makes its masterpiece. We see on the wall the shadow of Charles Gemora in his gorilla suit, arms raised above his head. Sidney Fox's Camille awakens, looks up and sees in close-up…

The Selig Zoo monkey!

Camille screams and faints. The still photographer took a "hotcha" picture of Sidney, passed out in her bed, her nightgown raised, displaying her legs and thighs as Gemora loomed over her. The film itself offers no such view. Nevertheless, the shot of Sidney prone and showing her legs became part of the major imagery Universal used to sell *Murders in the Rue Morgue*.

Betsy Ross Clarke's Mme. L'Espanaye runs to her daughter's rescue, only to have the gorilla attack her. In Poe's story, the ape stuffs the daughter up the chimney (and tosses the mother out the window after slicing her throat). Some audiences, familiar with the Poe story, are likely surprised that Camille escapes the chimney.

Based on Sidney Fox's super-saccharine performance, they might be disappointed.

Erik, although we can't tell in the mayhem what he's doing, works on shoving Madame L'Espanaye up the chimney. Florey again splices in close-ups of the zoo ape, bobbing his head furiously, clearly hot and bothered. The dramatic effect, with all the screaming: Erik is furiously raping Mme. L'Espanaye.

The Mirakle coach speeds off into the night, Camille's scream sounding from inside it.

The film delays the discovery of the up-the-chimney body, interjecting more comic relief—and one of the few elements from Poe's story that's actually used in the film! A German (Herman Bing, from Frankfurt, Germany), an Italian (Agostino Borgato, from Venice, Italy) and a Dane (Torben Meyer, from Arhus, Denmark) all debate the language the killer spoke, having heard, of course, the ape's growls and roars.[42]

Playing the prefect at the makeshift inquest: Brandon Hurst, already a veteran of such horror films as John Barrymore's 1920 *Dr. Jekyll and Mr. Hyde* and Lon Chaney's 1923 *The Hunchback of Notre Dame*. Shortly after this movie, he appeared as the butler in Lugosi's *White Zombie*.[43]

As this scene reaches its apex of hilarity, the three men bellowing at each other, a gendarme opens the chimney. Quick close-ups of the gaping-in-horror German, Italian, Dane … and of Madame L'Espanaye's head dangling down into the firebox. The Chicago censor cut the latter shot. So did Australia. Alberta demanded, "Eliminate screams of woman when mother's body is discovered in chimney."

The laboratory. Bela's Mirakle prepares for the great consummation. Sidney Fox lies sprawled on a lounge, unconscious in her nightgown.

"Her blood is perfect!" rejoices Mirakle.

The line plays as a euphemism: The mad doctor is likely delighted that Camille is a virgin. How nice for Erik … although, with Lugosi's Mirakle gaga over Camille, it's clear

A dash of pure Poe: Leon Ames' Dupin and Brandon Hurst's police inspector find the corpse of Camille's mother shoved feet first up the chimney (from the John Antosiewicz Collection).

why he's so jubilant. The Chicago censor presumably took this interpretation and cut the line.

Led to Mirakle's by Dupin, gendarmes try to break in. Erik's simian hormones are completely topsy-turvy by now, so much so that the Alberta censor will cut "Ape making impatient and whining noises" and Kansas will scissor "close-ups of ape panting."

Mirakle lets Erik out of his cage with a "Let the games begin!" expression. Erik, however, perhaps having caught scent of a romantic rival, stalks Mirakle. "Erik ... back into your cage!" Mirakle commands. The gorilla attacks Mirakle, strangling his maniacal matchmaker. Lugosi's death agonies are captured in shadow on the laboratory wall.

The gendarmes shoot Janos the Black One. Erik takes to the rooftops with Camille. A crowd watches from the street. Dupin climbs to the roof and shoots Erik, who tumbles over the edge and plummets into the Seine. Dupin rescues Camille. The crowd cheers.

The final scene: D'Arcy Corrigan's Morgue Keeper presides as a gendarme presents Mirakle's off-camera corpse.

"Death caused by?" asks the Morgue Keeper.

"Ha ha ha!" laughs the gendarme. "An *ape*!"

As Robert Florey would have said it, FINIS.
Or so he thought.

Retakes and Revisions

Friday, November 13: *Murders in the Rue Morgue* originally wrapped after 23 days of shooting. Filmed on the last day was the episode by the Seine, where a hag (Tempe Pigott), flanked by dregs, cackles as gendarmes fish the Woman of the Streets out of the river and carry away her corpse. The figure probably isn't Arlene Francis, but it's nice that her tragic character got an acknowledgment on this final day of shooting.

This movie had come in five days *over* schedule, but the cost was $161,781.11 ... $2,432.89 *under* budget.

The completion date was significant. On this Friday the 13th, *Motion Picture Daily* ran its review of *Frankenstein*: "Karloff has truly created a Frankenstein Monster.... Women come out trembling, men exhausted."

Friday, November 20: *Frankenstein* opened to smash hit box office at various East Coast theaters. Universal picked up Karloff's contract on December 2. On December 4, *Frankenstein* opened at New York's RKO-Mayfair Theatre. It was a show business phenomenon.

In Junior Laemmle's eyes, *Murders in the Rue Morgue* paled in comparison. Frightened that the film might kill off the studio's horror golden goose, Junior decreed emergency action.

Thursday, December 10: As Sidney Fox celebrated her 24th birthday, "Retakes and Added Scenes" began for *Murders in the Rue Morgue*. The estimated cost was $21,870. On the first day of retakes, Florey made new shots in Mirakle's laboratory, and reshot the duel of the two men for the Woman of the Streets. The second day saw retakes in Dupin's room and Camille's room.

Saturday, December 12: Four nights' work began on the exterior rooftops, to boost the climax. Joe Bonomo, the famed strongman, donned a gorilla suit and doubled Charles Gemora in the new chase footage. The story goes that he wore Gemora's gorilla suit, but as Bonomo was just shy of six feet and Gemora just 5'5", one wonders if that is even possible.

The company worked hard. On Monday, December 14, they started at 12:30 p.m. and carried on until 3:10 a.m. Shooting continued the next two nights on the rooftops of Universal's German Street. Bonomo dangerously cavorted over the rooftops, high above the back lot street, performing a fireman's carry of a bewigged dummy of Sidney Fox, the acrobatics worthy of the Big Top as a mob of extras watched from below.

Tuesday and Wednesday, December 22 and 23: Florey visited the Selig Zoo and filmed what the production sheet called "close-ups of monkey." As noted, these infamous shots would appear throughout *Rue Morgue*, including a mugging chimpanzee with wide-open mouth during Erik's last stand on the rooftops. Meanwhile, Gemora's own close-ups fell on the cutting room floor.

It was a disastrous directorial decision.

There had been nine additional days (or nights) of shooting on *Murders in the Rue Morgue*. The final estimate cost, including the retakes, came to $186,090; the total final cost would be $190,099.45.

It was all over in time for Christmas.

Part Three: The Release and the Impact

Beauty and the Beast—and the Mad Dr. Mirakle!
—Universal Publicity for *Murders in the Rue Morgue*

Friday, January 1, 1932: After its giant success in the East, *Frankenstein* opened in Los Angeles at the Orpheum Theatre. It set a house record.

Wednesday, January 6: *The Hollywood Reporter* reviewed a preview of *Murders in the Rue Morgue*, writing that it "gave Santa Ana a perfectly delightful scare and a sleepless night." The review had nice things to say about Junior Laemmle, Robert Florey, Karl Freund, Sidney Fox and especially Bela Lugosi:

> *Lugosi is type, if any actor ever was. He has the physical necessities and is so legitimately trained than even though his performance does smack of the old legit, he is perfection in a role of this sort. Lugosi chews scenery, but he makes an audience like it.*

Also, on January 6: *The Los Angeles Evening Herald Express* ran an interview with James Whale, aglow in the triumph of *Frankenstein*. Whale, one suspects, had seen *Rue Morgue* rushes, or maybe had attended the preview. Without mentioning the name Robert Florey, he said:

> *As the director, you should be completely out of sight; no queer camera angles ... no exhibitionist tricks to jockey yourself into fame at the expense of the picture. Such tricks are the worst kind of self-aggrandization. It is imitation of self—the worst kind. It is like a pig eating his own hams. Cannibalistic art!*

Friday, January 8: The MPPDA's Col. Jason S. Joy wrote to Junior Laemmle that *Murders in the Rue Morgue* was

> *satisfactory from the standpoint of the Code with the exception of the Nautch dancing in front of the side show at the carnival. The last shot of the dancers, a close-up of the lower parts of their bodies, ought to be eliminated in order to save the whole scene from serious criticism as a violation of the Code....*
>
> *Our feeling is that the screaming of the Woman of the Street in the scene in which she is being subjected to a test by Dr. Mirakle is over-stressed, not only from the standpoint of possible audience reaction but also censorship objection.... We therefore suggest that you ought to consider making a new sound track for this scene, reducing the constant loud shrieking to lower moans and an occasional modified shriek.*

It's quite remarkable that Col. Joy didn't suggest that the tortures of the Woman of the Streets be reduced, but rather, her screaming*!*

Sunday, January 10: *The Pittsburgh Press* reported that Universal would produce *The Invisible Man*, starring Boris Karloff. The blurb noted that Florey and Garrett Fort had adapted the H.G. Wells novel, and that Florey was set to direct.

Monday, January 11: Although Col. Joy was basically upbeat with Universal about *Murders in the Rue Morgue*, he expressed his actual concerns in a letter to Will H. Hays, who headed the Production Code headquarters in New York City. Joy wrote that, as far as horror films went, "resentment is surely being built up":

How could it be otherwise if children go to these pictures and have the jitters, followed by nightmares? I, for one, would hate to have my children see Frankenstein, Jekyll *or the others.... Not only is there a future economic consideration, but maybe there is a real moral responsibility involved to which I wonder if we as individuals ought to lend our support. It occurs to me that you might want to call the attention of the company heads to the situation and see how they feel about it. The latest picture of the type is* Murders in the Rue Morgue. *It lacks the punch of* Frankenstein, *but the idea of the ape pursuing the girl is sufficiently disturbing.*[44]

Also January 11: By this time, Universal had re-edited *Murders in the Rue Morgue* to its release form. As originally synopsized by the studio after shooting, the film began with the Woman of the Streets episode. It now opened with the Carnival sequence. Other scenes were juggled as well, causing continuity problems.[45]

Thursday, January 14: Junior wrote to Col. Joy, claiming the studio had "complied" with his suggestions. As for Lady Fatima and her Arab Angels, Junior replied the studio had "substituted a longer shot of a different part of the dance which is innocuous in comparison with the shot we eliminated." He also claimed that the studio had "toned down" the Woman of the Streets' screaming during the duel and her laboratory agonies.

Whatever the trims, the accent was on sex and horror as Universal prepared the ad copy for *Murders in the Rue Morgue*:

> DEMON EYES GLEAMING RED GREAT BEAST OF THE JUNGLE
> MUST THIS DAINTY CHILD ON HER WEDDING NIGHT SUFFER A HORRIBLE FATE?

The words appeared below a lurid picture of "dainty" Sidney Fox, raised thighs revealed, a cartoon of Erik lecherously leering over her. Of course, Camille has no wedding night in the actual film. Was the publicity hinting that her "wedding night" was to be shared with "the great beast of the jungle" ... as Mirakle intended?

Also, Universal realized that, to sell the film most effectively, Lugosi should receive first billing on most of the posters. Sidney Fox retained first billing on the film's onscreen credits.

Wednesday, February 3: Universal planned to open *Murders in the Rue Morgue* at Chicago's State-Lake Theatre. The city's censor promptly banned it. The previously detailed cuts were made, as well as trims in the scene of the two men fighting for the Woman of the Streets. As an "Adults Only" attraction, the show went on.

Wednesday, February 10: Murders in the Rue Morgue, with "Swan Lake" playing during its credits, opened this night at 9:00 p.m. at New York's RKO-Mayfair Theatre, where *Frankenstein* had shattered records. As previously noted, the New York censor had eviscerated the episode of the Woman of the Streets, her crucifixion, and her "rotten blood." *Variety* critiqued:

> *Edgar Allan Poe wouldn't recognize his story. They dropped everything but the gorilla killer and the title, completely changed the characters, motives and developments and sexed up the whole affair to the limit.... At the Mayfair a cynical audience hooted the finale hokum, but away from Broadway the chase and its finish shouldn't meet such hard-boiled resistance....*[46]

The *New York Times* review also noted "irreverent squeals" from the audience during the climax. *Harrison's Reports*, a trade journal, reported that the Broadway audiences "did not seem to accept it in the same spirit they accepted *Frankenstein* and *Dracula*, for many of them 'kidded' it, laughing in serious parts, and treating it as if it were a travesty on thrilling pictures...." If the New York engagement had kept the crucifixion episode intact, the film surely would have cowed the audiences into a more respectful reception.

Murders in the Rue Morgue **publicity material (from the John Antosiewicz Collection).**

By the way, although the New York Censor had cut Arlene Francis' role severely, the RKO-Mayfair exhibited a giant cut-out of her from the film, showing her tied to the cross with Lugosi kneeling at her feet. Arlene's father Aram Kazanjian, a prominent Manhattan portrait photographer, passed the Mayfair, saw the picture of his daughter crucified in her underwear with "Dracula" bowing before her, and telegrammed her in Hollywood:

"I have seen you half-naked on Broadway Stop Our friends have seen you too Stop Come home at once."[47]

Saturday, February 13: Everhardt Armstrong championed *Murders in the Rue Morgue* in his *Seattle Intelligencer* review:

> *Hats off to Bela Lugosi!*
>   *Here is a great actor who can coin new thrills … always dominating the big scenes is the weird figure of Dr. Mirakle. Lugosi makes him as fascinating as he is fantastic.…*
>   *Murders in the Rue Morgue is one of those pictures that "get you." Never have I seen an audience follow a film more intently that did yesterday's matinee crowd. Seeing it is an adventure.*

Tuesday, February 16: Famed writer-reporter-"sob sister" Adela Rogers St. Johns let loose at horror films in the *San Francisco Examiner*, citing *Frankenstein*, *Freaks* and *Murders in the Rue Morgue*. She warned Will Hays that unless these films were "cleaned up from within," the Women of America would rise:

> *Mothers are beginning to realize the dreadful consequences of such pictures.… They are becoming conscious of the fact that ten years from now a sight such as* Frankenstein *may bear bitter fruit, in nervous disorders, sleepless nights and morbid tastes.…*
>   *The motion picture has more influence today than anything in the world. To employ it to bring to life the ugliest and most ghastly and most abnormal sights ever conceived by the human brain is a desecration of its art and purpose.*

Tuesday, February 23: *Variety* announced that Universal was preparing star campaigns for three players: Boris Karloff, German *émigré* Tala Birell and Sidney Fox.

February 28: "Reaction Against Morbid Type Of 'Movie' Foreseen," headlined the *Seattle Times*. "Like paths of glory that lead but to the grave," warned Seattle critic Richard E. Hays, "the horror cycle in today's 'movies' is becoming more and more an invitation to censorship." Hays knew his film history: "The present cycle of morbidity did not begin, as some believe, with *Dracula*.… It had an earlier inspiration in *Ingagi*, a fake picture that made a ton of money … it ran long enough and fast enough to indicate a demand for 'sensation' and 'shock.'"

Hays mentioned not only *Dracula* but also *Frankenstein*, and *Dr. Jekyll and Mr. Hyde*, writing that these films represented skill in acting, direction and photography. He then added, "But along came *Murders in the Rue Morgue*.… It is a revolting picture.…"

April 3: *The New York Times* ran an interview with Junior Laemmle, who was visiting the Big Apple. Junior crowed about *Frankenstein*, chatted enthusiastically about Boris Karloff and Tala Birell, and said:

> *We had a lot of trouble making* Murders in the Rue Morgue. *After all, there wasn't anything in Poe's original story that made good cinema and we naturally had to adapt it very liberally. I wouldn't think of comparing it with* Frankenstein. *I'm really proud of the men who made that. James Whale is a fine director.*

Junior made no mention of Bela Lugosi or Robert Florey.

April 4: In Baltimore, where Edgar Allan Poe lies buried in Westminster Hall and Burying Ground, *Baltimore Sun* critic Donald Kirkley was aghast at *Murders in the Rue Morgue*:

> *It is as far from the Poe story as it would be possible to get.… A great portion of the scenes*

depicting tortures, gruesome things and places, shrieks, groans, killings and kidnappings serve no dramatic purpose.... It's dime-novel stuff.

May 1932's *Photoplay* magazine review: "Here's another shocker for you with plenty of thrills and chills. Bela Lugosi and the ape deserve a big hand."

July 29: The MPPDA took heed of the following communiqué from Bela Lugosi's native Hungary, which had rejected *Rue Morgue* and explained why:

> *The film deals with certain perverse tests on the part of a mysterious individual who wants to cultivate a gorilla by means of human blood and for the purpose of attaining his goal he commits crimes. The problem in question is disgusting, the direction of the film is causing a feeling of horror and the effect of same against all civilization. Neither morals nor good taste should permit the showing of such subjects in the moving picture houses. On the grounds of the aforesaid the picture was banned unanimously.*

Despite reports to the contrary, *Rue Morgue* did fairly well at the box office, earning a respectable profit of $63,000.[48] It was, however, a very distant third in the triad with *Dracula* and *Frankenstein*. Robert Florey followed up *Rue Morgue* by working on adapting *The Invisible Man* (which he was supposed to direct), a werewolf film and a *Frankenstein* sequel. Junior passed on all of them for the time being, and Florey left Universal. The next film he directed was *The Man Called Back* (1932) for K.B.S. productions.

As for Bela Lugosi: In early 1932, Universal invited him to visit the lot to pose with Boris Karloff, then starring in the film *Night World*, in a series of publicity pictures. Both men wore tuxes and, for most of the shots, large smiles. Karloff went into 1932's *The Old Dark House* and *The Mummy*.

Lugosi wouldn't return to Universal for two years, when he and Karloff co-starred—magnificently—in *The Black Cat*.

Part Four: Aftermath and Legacy

> *...Film benefits from expressionistic photography by Karl Freund and Lugosi's sinister portrayal.... Most interesting aspect of the film is the perverse sexuality that is implicit in Mirakle's work, and the ape's attraction to Fox.*
> —*Guide for the Film Fanatic* by Danny Peary[49]

> *One can't but feel that if* Murders in the Rue Morgue *was shot five years earlier, [the] seeming defects would be forgiven and the film would be ranked as one of the great Silent horror masterpieces.*
> —*Universal Horrors*, by Tom Weaver, Michael Brunas and John Brunas[50]

October 2, 1936: Joseph Breen wrote to Harry Zehner of Universal regarding the Production Code Administration's approval of a re-release of *Murders in the Rue Morgue*. The PCA, which Breen had powerfully strengthened in 1934, agreed, but the cuts were extensive: Lady Fatima, her Arab Angels, and the "Do they bite?" dialogue; a cut of the knife plunging in the duel; and almost the entire Crucifixion episode.

Today, *Murders in the Rue Morgue*, reassembled, rages away as a controversy among Golden Age horror disciples. Perhaps this is most obvious in the film's coverage in the aforementioned *Universal Horrors*. The original 1990 edition panned the film unmercifully. The revised 2007 edition, however, praised it as "very likely the most underrated of the Universal Horrors."

The wildly negative response to *Murders in the Rue Morgue* likely influenced how Universal designed its later 1932 horror films: *The Old Dark House*, directed by James Whale, was primarily a dark comedy (until its harrowing climax), and *The Mummy*, the directorial debut of Karl Freund, was a macabre romance about reincarnation. The next horror film to rattle the censors—utterly—came from Paramount: *Island of Lost Souls*, released at Yuletide of 1932, and again dealing with the mating of an animal with a human. (See Chapter 3.)

Over 90 years after its release, *Murders in the Rue Morgue* has its blessings, as well as its multitude of sins.

As far as its sins go, *Rue Morgue*, with its infectious injection of *Ingagi* blood, falls far short of the lasting impact of *Dracula* and *Frankenstein*. The story can't compete with the lore of a 500-year-old vampire and a pitiful man-made Monster. A 2022 audience member can still fall in love with Lugosi's charismatically undead Dracula, who believes it's "glorious" to be "really dead," and Karloff's beautiful-eyed Monster, who reaches to the light for a soul. No such profound attractions exist in *Murders in the Rue Morgue*.

As for its blessings: The film scores today for its daring (and most tasteless) episodes—the outrageous gorilla-mates-with-human twist, and its blasphemous Woman-of-the-Streets-as-Crucified-Christ (or Virgin Mary) show-stopper. Cinematically, the film is still a dazzler; Florey and Freund splendidly make Paris so *Caligari*-esque that one almost expects Conrad Veidt's Cesare to step out of the myriad of shadows and join Erik during the rooftop chase. While the film is set in Paris, it has the scent—perhaps more than any other 1932 Hollywood movie—of depraved and decadent Weimar Berlin. One can imagine that only a soundstage away, Marlene Dietrich's Lola-Lola of *The Blue Angel*, sporting her top hat and garter belt, is warbling "Falling in Love Again" and debasing Emil Jannings.

Bela Lugosi, however, is the show. In my opinion, Lugosi as Dr. Mirakle is more diabolically convincing than he is in *White Zombie* or *The Raven*, and radiates more star quality than he displayed even in *Dracula*. The depth isn't there—that's the script's fault—but the passion certainly is. It's Lugosi's dashing savagery, unleashed against the backdrop of *Caligari* stylistics, a kewpie doll heroine, a screaming crucified Woman of the Streets, and a sex-crazed ape, that makes *Murders in the Rue Morgue* one of Universal's most perversely striking Horror Classics.

*   *   *

A few last words about the talents of this film:

Robert Florey, after *Murders in the Rue Morgue*, eventually did nicely. He directed Warner Bros' *The Florentine Dagger*, a 1935 murder mystery, and Warner Bros.' 1946 horror film *The Beast with Five Fingers,* starring Peter Lorre and a dismembered hand. The latter was scary stuff, and Jack L. Warner, after a screening, said to Florey, "The maker of *Frankenstein* would be jealous of this film!"[51]—unfortunately reminding Florey of James Whale, who had managed to take *Frankenstein* away from him.

At any rate, Florey had a far longer and more prolific film career than Whale, whose last Hollywood work was in the early 1940s. In fact, in 1957, the year Whale drowned himself in his pool in Pacific Palisades, Florey directed episodes of TV's *General Electric Theatre*, *Schlitz Playhouse*, *M Squad*, *Zane Grey Theatre* and two episodes of *Wagon Train*, one of which earned him an Emmy nomination. He later directed episodes of *Alfred Hitchcock Presents*, *The Twilight Zone*, and one of *Thriller*'s most frightening episodes, "The Incredible Dr. Markesan," hosted by and starring Boris Karloff. His last credit, in 1964: the "Moonstone" episode of *The Outer Limits*.

In the aforementioned 1979 letter to Richard Bojarski, Florey, who had become a Knight of the French Legion of Honor, briefly revisited the *Frankenstein* controversy, recalled Lugosi's aloof nature on *Rue Morgue*, sadly listed the film's stars and featured players who had died, and concluded:

> *Year after year I receive letters similar to yours and really do not know what to say about a small film made so many years ago.*

Not quite three months later, on May 16, 1979, Robert Florey died. He was 78 years old. He passed away four months before Carl Laemmle Jr., who never produced another picture after new management took control of Universal in 1936.

As for "Erik": Charles Gemora went on to a prolific career as a Hollywood gorilla. Two notable performances: "Ethel" in Laurel and Hardy's three-reeler *The Chimp* (1932) and the sad-eyed ape (with a transplanted human brain) in Paramount's *The Monster and the Girl* (1941). In 1954, when Warner Bros. released a 3-D and color *Phantom of the Rue Morgue*, starring Karl Malden and Patricia Medina, Gemora again played the ape ... and was doubled in some stunt scenes, as he had been 22 years before in *Murders in the Rue Morgue*. Gemora died in 1961.

Finally, what became of *Murders in the Rue Morgue*'s Camille L'Espanaye, Sidney Fox?

She was one of the attractions Universal showed off in 1932's *The Cohens and Kellys in Hollywood*, in a cameo at the Cocoanut Grove with Boris Karloff, Tom Mix, Lew Ayres, Genevieve Tobin and Gloria Stuart ... but the gossip about her affair with Junior Laemmle only festered. She landed a desirable role in Universal's 1932 *Once in a Lifetime* as a daffy starlet who incongruously auditions by reciting the Kipling poem "Boots." Universal loaned Sidney out for productions in Europe, including *Don Quixote* in which she acted the niece with the legendary Feodor Chaliapin, directed by the famed G.W. Pabst; and *The Adventures of King Pausole* in which she appeared with Emil Jannings.

While she was away, Universal dropped her contract. Her affair with Junior Laemmle, obviously, was over.

In December 1932, Sidney married Charles Beahan, Universal's New York–based story editor. Beahan had written the play which was the basis for the 1931 Paramount horror film *Murder by the Clock* (in which Blanche Friderici installs a siren in her crypt in case she's buried alive—a very grim movie). Beahan weighed 250 pounds, and the press made much of the difference in size between portly Beahan and petite Sidney.

It was a wildly dysfunctional marriage. They constantly broke up and reconciled. At one point, during a ride along Malibu Beach, Beahan proceeded, in Sidney's words, to "choke and curse" her.[52] She declared her intention to divorce him in April 1934.

"I was afraid to go near him, most of the time," said Sidney. "He would insult me and call me horrible names."[53]

She and Beahan reconciled. Beahan declared bankruptcy. Her career nosedived. Sidney starred in 1934's *School for Girls*, a Poverty Row reform school melodrama. (Also in the cast: *Island of Lost Souls*' Panther Woman, Kathleen Burke.) She nearly landed a major comeback role in the MGM epic *The Good Earth* (1937) as Lotus, second wife of

A photograph of Sidney Fox and her writer spouse Charles Beahan, shortly after their December 1932 marriage. It was a tragically abusive union. Fox committed suicide in 1942.

Wang (Paul Muni), but lost the plum part to Tilly Losch. It was that film, incidentally, for which *Rue Morgue* cinematographer Karl Freund won his Oscar.

Sidney and her abusive tubby hubby continued to wage their marital war, to the point where the *Los Angeles Examiner* ran an open letter to Sidney from "The Courthouse Reporters," reading:

It is our sincere wish that you refrain from further divorce suits against Mr. Beahan. It is our understanding that almost everyone in the film colony shares the latter wish with us. Thank you, Miss Fox.[54]

Sidney did some theater work. In 1940, almost forgotten, she announced again that she would divorce Beahan; "This time the decree will become final,"[55] said Sidney. But it wasn't. The aberrant marriage continued, and word spread that she was ill.

Saturday night, November 14, 1942: Sidney and Beahan had company at their home, 516 North Crescent Drive in Beverly Hills. Sidney suggested late that night they all go dancing, but then decided, according to Beahan, to go to bed and attend church in the morning. The next morning, November 15, Beahan found Sidney dead in bed, an empty prescription bottle nearby. Death was ruled "Barbiturate Poisoning,"[56] without determination if death was accidental or a suicide.

Sidney Fox was 34 years old. She's buried in Mt. Lebanon Cemetery in Queens, New York. Her large monument reads, "Our Beloved Daughter."[57]

As for Charles Beahan, he died following surgery at Valley Doctors Hospital in North Hollywood on August 18, 1968. He was 65 years old. The funeral took place in Beahan's hometown of Clearfield, Pennsylvania. He had remarried after Sidney's death, and his widow survived him.[58]

* * *

December 1942.

Only a month after Sidney Fox's death, Bela Lugosi was at Monogram Studios, starring in *The Ape Man*, directed by William "One Take" Beaudine. Bela played a mad doctor, who once again kept a caged gorilla (played by Emil Van Horn). This time, Lugosi himself was part-ape, due to his experimentation. Times had changed since *Murders in the Rue Morgue*; World War II was raging, and Hollywood censors would never have allowed a film in which a madman dreams of mating the leading lady with a gorilla.

The feminine lead, blonde Louise Currie, got her own licks in here, lashing Bela with a whip in the climax ... far feistier than Sidney Fox's ever-dainty Camille. *À la* the late lamented Erik, the ape mauled Bela to death. Beaudine's direction had none of Robert Florey's stylistics. And as for the star, he had recently turned 60 years old, was married, had a four-year-old son, and had toned down his act quite a bit since the prodigal pre–Code days of *Murders in the Rue Morgue*.

Nevertheless, Bela Lugosi was still chewing the scenery ... and still making the audience like it.

Murders in the Rue Morgue

Universal, 1932. Producer, Carl Laemmle Jr. Associate Producer, E.M. Asher. Director, Robert Florey. Screenplay, Tom Reed, Dale Van Every, from an adaptation by Robert Florey of Edgar Allan Poe's 1841 short story *Murders in the Rue Morgue*. Added Dialogue, John Huston; Uncredited Writer, Ethel M. Kelly. Cinematographer, Karl Freund. Scenario Editor, Richard Schayer. Art Director, Charles D. Hall. Recording Supervisor, C. Roy Hunter. Editor, Milton Carruth. Supervising Editor, Maurice Pivar. Special Effects, John P. Fulton. Set Designer, Herman Rosse. Makeup Artist, Jack P. Pierce. Music, Heinz

Roemheld. Special Process Photographer, Frank D. Williams. Technical Advisor, Howard Salemson. Running time, 61 minutes.

New York opening, RKO-Mayfair Theatre, February 10, 1932.

The Cast: Sidney Fox (Mlle. Camille L'Espanaye), Bela Lugosi (Dr. Mirakle), Leon Waycoff [aka Leon Ames] (Pierre Dupin), Bert Roach (Paul), Betsy Ross Clarke (Mme. L'Espanaye), Brandon Hurst (Prefect of Police), D'Arcy Corrigan (Morgue Keeper), Noble Johnson (Janos, the Black One), Arlene Francis (Woman of the Streets), Charles Gemora (Erik the Ape), Agostino Borgato (Alberto Montani), Herman Bing (Franz Odenheimer), Torben Meyer (The Dane), Harry Holman (Victor Albert Adolph Jules Hugo Louis Dupont, the Landlord), Edna Marion (Mignette), Michael Visaroff (Mirakle's Sideshow Barker), Tempe Pigott (Crone at River), Christian J. Frank (Gendarme Using Snuff), Charles Millsfield (Bearded Man at Sideshow), Iron Eyes Cody (Indian at Sideshow), Joe Bonomo (Double for Charles Gemora as Erik).

"Why Won't You *Die*?"

Rasputin and the Empress

Get back in Hell! … Anti-Christ!
—John Barrymore to Lionel Barrymore
in *Rasputin and the Empress*

A "mad monk" with a resplendent black beard, resurrecting from a bloody corpse, brains oozing from his shattered scalp, demonically chanting, "The great day of wrath is come!"

His wild-eyed assassin, screaming hysterically, tearing his hair, making the Sign of the Cross, spitting out a glob of phlegm and madly shrieking, "Why won't you *die*?"

Add hypnosis, poison, an orgy, a rape (originally dramatized, later cut), mind-blown singing female sex slaves, the seduction of an underage princess, and a blistering fade-out finale showing the massacre of the tsar, tsarina and their children

Lurid MGM publicity for *Rasputin and the Empress*, 1932.

before your eyes, and you have MGM's *Rasputin and the Empress* ... the great unsung horror classic of 1932.

Few film historians see it that way. *Rasputin and the Empress* generally rates its distinction as a filmic High Mass in praise of the Barrymore Trinity: John as the assassin, Ethel as the tsarina, Lionel as Rasputin. It was the celebrated siblings' only film together. Others regard it as the movie that spawned a sensational libel suit—won by Grigori Rasputin's self-proclaimed assassin Prince Felix Youssoupoff and his royalist wife Irina. It was so disastrously costly that Hollywood forever-after used the "Any similarity between persons living and dead..." disclaimer.

Be that as it may, *Rasputin and the Empress* packs more sex-driven, startlingly violent horror flourishes into its prodigal 121 minutes than most of the venerable 1932 horror classics ... combined! Film history all-hails MGM for its glamour, but in this movie, Leo the Lion showed off his bloodthirsty appetite for red-meat melodrama.

As Pre-Code.com salutes *Rasputin and the Empress*, "It's more *Murders in the Rue Morgue* than *Dinner at Eight* for damned sure."

Part One: Background

The Historical Facts(?)

The real-life assassination of Rasputin in 1916 Russia co-starred two fascinating and possibly intimate adversaries.

Rasputin, born Grigori Yefimovich Rasputin in Siberia in 1869, was a wildly sexed peasant whose ability to effect seemingly miraculous cures won him glory as a "Living Christ." In 1905 or 1906 (historians differ), he cured the tsarevich, son of Nicholas and Alexandra, of a hemophilia attack at the Royal Palace in St. Petersburg. In 1912, Rasputin again saved the boy after a severe attack, via a long-distance "miracle" sent from Siberia. "God has seen your tears and heard your prayers," Rasputin wrote to the tsarina. "Do not grieve. The little one will not die. Do not allow the doctors to bother him too much." The 6'4" "Living Christ" won a place within the tsar and tsarina's innermost circle, enjoying enormous and glutinous power during Russia's war with Germany.

Prince Felix Felixovich Youssoupoff, born in the Moika Palace in St. Petersburg in 1887, was of a family richer than the Romanoffs. He was the son of Princess Zenaide, who had so wanted a daughter that she had dressed little Felix as a girl. A beautiful man (rather than a handsome one), he later became a female impersonator singer in a nightclub and met Rasputin in 1909. "He walked up to me, said 'Good evening, my boy,' and attempted to kiss me," claimed Youssoupoff. "I drew back instinctively." Perhaps he did with Rasputin, but rumors of Youssoupoff's homosexual promiscuity were rampant—so much so that, as Sir David Napley wrote in his 1990 book *Rasputin in Hollywood,* a colloquialism used at the time by Russian royals for anal intercourse was, "do a Youssoupoff."[1]

The story spread that Youssoupoff visited Rasputin in hopes of a cure for his "disease" of homosexuality. Other accounts claim the prince and the ecumenically sexual

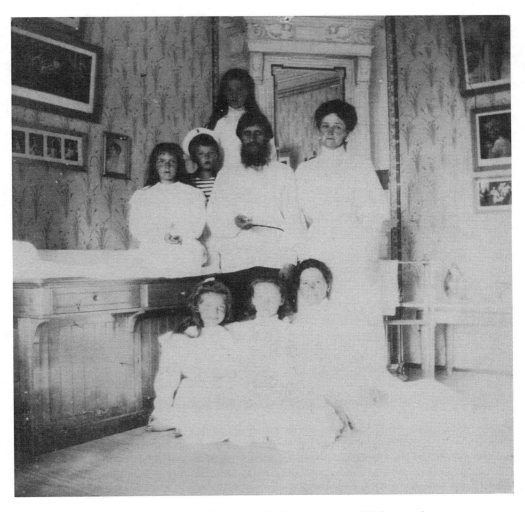

The real Tsarina Alexandra Feodorovna with Rasputin, her children and a governess.

Rasputin were lovers. At length, Prince Felix wed the tsar's darkly beautiful niece, Irina, in 1914. A daughter was born the following year.

After midnight, Sunday, December 17, 1916: Prince Felix assassinated Rasputin (or did he?) at the Moika Palace. Historians reluctantly concede that nobody will ever know with certainty the actual details of Rasputin's assassination. Nevertheless, various reputable writers have taken gory stabs at it.

Joseph T. Fuhrmann wrote in his 2013 book *Rasputin: The Untold Story* that Rasputin came to party at the Moika palace basement after midnight. The fireplace was lit and "Yankee Doodle" played over and over on a gramophone. "Play something cheerful, I like your singing," said Rasputin to Youssoupoff, who had spearheaded the assassination plan. Youssoupoff serenaded him on his guitar as Rasputin gobbled cakes and swilled wine poisoned by Dr. Stanislaw Lazovert, one of the other conspirators who were hiding upstairs. Rasputin seemed invulnerable to the poison, and Youssoupoff approached hysteria. As Rasputin admired a rock crystal crucifix, the prince made his move.

The real Romanovs. Seated in front is the Tsarevich Alexei (portrayed in the movie by Tad Alexander). Seated middle row from left to right are the Grand Duchess Maria (played in the movie by Jean Parker), the Tsarina Alexandra (portrayed in the movie by Ethel Barrymore), Tsar Nicholas II (played in the movie by Ralph Morgan) and the Grand Duchess Anastasia (played in the movie by Anne Shirley). Standing are the two oldest children, the Grand Duchesses Olga and Tatiana; the actresses are unidentified.

"Grigori Yefimovich," warned Youssoupoff, "you had best look at that crucifix and say a prayer before it!"[2]

Youssoupoff fired. Rasputin, shot in the chest, gave "a wild scream," falling onto a white bearskin rug. The other conspirators (some sources claim there were several women among them) ran down the stairs, and saw what they presumed to be the corpse. Two of them proceeded with a plan to fake driving Rasputin home, posing in the car as Rasputin and Youssoupoff. After they returned, the highly strung Youssoupoff claimed he needed to see the body, still locked in the basement. There, according to Greg King's 1995 book *The Man Who Killed Rasputin*, Youssoupoff "abused the body sexually in some way." Imagine the prince's surprise as Rasputin's eyes suddenly opened, "greenish and snake-like," and he rose from the floor, foaming at the mouth, catching his attacker by the shoulders, ripping off one of his tunic's epaulets.

"Felix!" roared Rasputin menacingly, over and over. "*Felix!*"[3]

"I realized now who Rasputin really was," wrote Youssoupoff in his 1953 memoir, *Lost Splendour*. "It was the reincarnation of Satan himself who held me in his clutches and would never let me go until my dying day."

Youssoupoff screamed, freed himself, and ran. Rasputin escaped into the snowy courtyard. A conspirator named Purishkevich pursued him, shooting him in the back. When Rasputin fell into the snow, Purishkevich shot him in the forehead from a distance of about eight inches. Rasputin, at last, was dead.

Maybe.

Youssoupoff's co-conspirators dragged Rasputin back inside into the entrance hall. A comedy of errors proceeded after police heard a shot and investigated; ultimately, no one was arrested. The conspirators planned to toss the body off the Great Petrovsky Bridge into the Malaya Neva River. Before they could leave, Youssoupoff, who'd been sick in the bathroom, saw the body and again went into hysterics. He grabbed a two-pound rubber-coated dumbbell, smashing at Rasputin's head again and again. Blood sprayed the walls.

"In my frenzy, I hit anywhere," Youssoupoff admitted. "All laws of God and man were set at naught."

His hysteria was possibly contagious. As Rasputin's daughter Maria wrote in her book *Rasputin: The Man Behind the Myth* (published in 1977, the year Maria died), blood-lust exploded as Rasputin helplessly mumbled. "What do they want of me?"

> *… There was much kicking and gouging at the inert body…. One of the men drew a dagger and, pushing aside the man who was still straddled across the lower extremities of my father, rapidly tore away at the remains of his trousers. Some say it was Felix who wielded the knife; other say differently…. With the skill of a surgeon, these elegant young members of the nobility castrated Grigori Rasputin and flung the severed penis across the room.*[4]

Youssoupoff fainted and was carried to his bedroom. The other assassins took Rasputin's corpse (or was he still alive?), drove it to the bridge (the sentry was asleep), and tossed it into the frozen Malaya Neva, through a hole in the ice. Some accounts claim Rasputin still lived; he sank, but shot, beaten, castrated, mad as hell—and after all, being Rasputin—he swam to the surface, failing to break through the ice, drowning as he made the Sign of the Cross.

The autopsy report, cited by Fuhrmann (acknowledged as the world's authority on Rasputin), refutes these more colorful accounts and claims Rasputin died from a shot to the head. Then again, there's the argument that he *might* have drowned, and that the police and autopsy reports eliminated the more sensational findings. King, whose book is also thoroughly researched, addresses Youssoupoff's alleged sexual abuse of Rasputin's supposed corpse: "By this time, Felix was indeed probably capable of such action, and certainly his dealings with the peasant were dominated by sexual fascination." He also gives credence to the castration story:

> *The removal of Rasputin's penis would have been a symbolic act in light of the scandalous rumors surrounding his sexual adventures. In addition, if some form of homosexual relationship existed between Felix and Rasputin, castration might have been a further way for the prince to free himself from the sexual hold the peasant had on him.*

King specifies, however, "[T]here is no authoritative evidence that Rasputin was castrated."

As noted, details vary—wildly—but the evidence is that Prince Felix Youssoupoff, while heading the assassination plot and surely a hysterical witness, was not Rasputin's actual assassin. His castrator, maybe, but not his assassin. Also, a story in many accounts casts light on Youssoupoff's personality: To create an alibi for the sound of the shot and the blood at the scene, he told police that someone had shot his dog. To back it up, Youssoupoff killed his own dog, firing a gun into its mouth.[5]

The Rasputin assassination was, of course, sensational movie material. In October 1917, less than ten months after Rasputin's death, World Film released *Rasputin, the Black Monk*, shot in Fort Lee, New Jersey. Montagu Love had the title role, and while Irving Cummings played Prince Felix, the actual killer was a revolutionary named Raff (played by Arthur Ashley). Portraying Kerensky, who champions the Duma and argues for the tsar's exile: future *WereWolf of London* Henry Hull.

Youssoupoff and Irina had fled Russia before the Revolution, holding onto a residue of their tremendous fortune and property. After Nicholas abdicated, Youssoupoff returned to Moika Palace to retrieve two paintings by Rembrandt, as well as the blue Sultan of Morocco diamond, the Polar Star diamond, and diamond earrings that had belonged to Marie Antoinette. The prince lived in France, becoming an international celebrity, recognized as Rasputin's assassin, always using it to his advantage.

In 1927, Youssoupoff published his book *Rasputin—His Malignant Influence and Assassination*. When Rasputin's daughter Maria wrote a memoir in 1929 and sued Youssoupoff for killing her father, the prince claimed he'd simply been in the room as part of the plot, but hadn't actually killed Rasputin.

The French court tossed out Maria's suit.

*   *   *

By 1932, Felix Youssoupoff and Irina were living in Paris. It was a strange, morbid existence: traveling the luxury locales of the world, taking credit (when it suited him) for a murder he probably never personally committed, dogged by sordid rumors about his sexuality, largely surviving on a notoriety that scavenged the corpse of Rasputin. Meanwhile, the prince became almost absurdly litigious.

However, MGM, in Hollywood, feared nothing and no one.

Leo the Lascivious Lion

> *"All Out for Sex in 1932"*
> —MGM's corporate motto[6]

Metro-Goldwyn-Mayer, for all its glory, was the ugliest studio in Los Angeles. The joke was that even the lot's water tower was ugly.

Nevertheless, for MGM, 1932 was its Circus Maximus year. By early summer, the studio had produced such fare as *Tarzan the Ape Man*, in which Johnny Weissmuller's Tarzan fights a gorilla monster with crocodile teeth who wants to rape Maureen O'Sullivan's Jane; *Red-Headed Woman*, in which Jean Harlow, in red wig, shows off her fishnet stockings and takes a shot at her lover's wife. And of course, there was *Freaks*, in which a posse of actual circus sideshow attractions wend their vengeful way after blonde Olga Baclanova in a rainy night storm … and mutilate her into the Chicken Woman.

Freaks proved an epic disaster, but the other films were smash hits. So, of course, was *Grand Hotel*, all-starring Greta Garbo, John Barrymore, Joan Crawford, Wallace Beery, Lionel Barrymore and Lewis Stone. The film premiered in Hollywood on April 29, went on to reap $2.5 million in worldwide rentals, and won the 1932 Best Picture Academy

Award. The studio was proudly charging toward a 1932 fiscal profit of $8 million as rival Hollywood studios fought bankruptcy.[7]

The formidable team of corporate chief Louis B. Mayer, and "Boy Wonder" producer Irving Thalberg appeared unbeatable. An exiled Russian prince of dubious sexuality whose tale of killing Rasputin morphed to suit his circumstances seemed hardly a formidable threat.

Nevertheless, MGM, discussing a Rasputin film early in 1932, should have taken some heed of Youssoupoff's litigious reputation. Conrad Veidt starred in that year's German-produced *Rasputin, Demon with Women*, playing the role (despite the title) with a certain amount of sympathy. Portraying "Furst Jussupoff" in the film was Karl Ludwig Diehl. The real-life Youssoupoff sued. The London *Daily Telegraph* reported in March:

> *The film is largely based on Prince Youssoupoff's own account of how he fired the first shot at Rasputin. It deviates, however, from the prince's story in some particulars. Prince Youssoupoff at first demanded either that the film should be suspended or that he should be paid 50,000 marks compensation for the liberty taken with historical facts in which he was concerned. As both alternatives were refused, he instructed his lawyer to sue for an injunction. According to the Berlin newspapers, the question at issue is whether or not the producers of the film were under the obligation to represent the murder strictly in accordance with the account given by the participants in it, or whether they were at liberty to make it a subject of an artistic interpretation.[8]*

Metro was at its apex. In early 1932, MGM had cast John and Lionel Barrymore in *Arsene Lupin*, John as the dapper thief, Lionel as the detective who hounds him. After casting them again in *Grand Hotel*, the studio decided *Rasputin* would be a spectacle starring all *three* Barrymores ... including sister Ethel. The Russian Revolution would be merely their backdrop.

And if Prince Felix dared sue Leo the Lion regarding this epic production, Mayer and Thalberg would very likely tell him to "do a Youssoupoff."

The Royal Dysfunctional Family of the Theater

> *When Irving Thalberg, the producer, decided a few months ago that he wanted to make a story based upon the life of Rasputin, he conceived the idea of bringing the three Barrymores together. Hollywood had just been imbued with the all-star idea.... The three Barrymores, the producers thought, would have some box office value—something, perhaps, like a circus with three white whales.*
>
> —John Barrymore[9]

> *What poor son of a bitch is going to direct this picture?*
> —Lionel Barrymore[10]

> *Hollywood is a factory. My brothers have become institutionalized factory hands.*
>
> —Ethel Barrymore[11]

In 19th-century Baltimore, audiences had two major options for weekend entertainment: Attend the fights and watch two boxers beat the living hell out of each other, or attend a performance of a Shakespearean villain by Junius Brutus Booth, the acclaimed tragedian who lived at Tudor Hall, north of the city in rural Bel Air.

The thrill of bloody boxers in the ring and Booth on stage were equally visceral … with Booth enjoying the edge.

The Philadelphia Barrymores were of this rarified breed of spellbinder, strutting and fretting in 20th-century theater. Their audiences saw them as super-actors, preternaturally gifted, with all the electricity and glamour that major rock stars enjoy nowadays. By

John Barrymore, the hero in *Rasputin and the Empress*, preferred demonic roles. Here he appears as Ahab in *The Sea Beast* (Warner Bros., 1925) (from the Bill Nelson Collection).

the time of *Rasputin,* each was over 50, yet the showcasing of the trio in a single movie was dazzling showmanship.

The three titans, from youngest to eldest:

John Barrymore, 50, had made film history in 1920's *Dr. Jekyll and Mr. Hyde*—terrifying in his largely-without-makeup transformation. The same year, he conquered Broadway as *Richard III,* and in 1922, became the century's most celebrated stage Hamlet—audacious with his Oedipus complex interpretation. In 1931, "The Great Profile" created what many consider his greatest screen performance in *Svengali,* for Warner Brothers.

Ethel Barrymore, who turned 53 during the shoot of *Rasputin and the Empress,* was the First Lady of the American Theatre, with such New York successes as *The Constant Wife* (1926). She hadn't appeared in a film since 1919's *The Divorcee.* "Ethel scorned the cinema," said Lionel, "as a Metropolitan diva might scorn hog-calling."[12] At this point, she wasn't faring well theatrically; a 1930 production, *Scarlet Sister Mary,* saw Ethel playing a "vagrant Negro wench" in blackface to withering reviews—especially from the *Afro-American* newspaper.

As for Lionel, 54, he'd enjoyed such New York stage successes as *Laugh, Clown, Laugh!* (in the role played by Lon Chaney in MGM's 1928 film version), and was, in 1932, the outstanding character actor of the movies.[13] He won a Best Actor Academy Award for MGM's *A Free Soul* (1931), as a lawyer who, defending his daughter (Norma Shearer) for killing her lover (Clark Gable), gives a dazzling speech—then drops dead. He also directed features for Metro, including *Madame X* (1929).

All three Barrymores had demons … livid ones. John had been an alcoholic since he was 14 and feared he would end his life in an asylum, as had his father, Maurice. Ethel was also having alcohol bouts that threatened to capsize her stage career; she accepted *Rasputin* because she desperately needed money. As for Lionel, the rumor was that he was addicted to morphine and cocaine, provided by L.B. Mayer (who, a great admirer of the actor, joked that the "L.B." stood for "Lionel Barrymore").[14]

Nevertheless, in 1932, the adoring public knew virtually nothing of these problems, although John had a reputation for his drinking that, during these Prohibition days and nights, played colorfully rather than tragically.

The *Rasputin* project approached production.

Wednesday, April 27, 1932: John Colton—who co-authored the play *Rain,* authored the play *The Shanghai Gesture,* and later wrote the screenplay of *WereWolf of London* (1935—see Chapter 5)—submitted a 121-page "Temporary Complete Screenplay."

Saturday, May 21: Ethel Barrymore appeared in two performances of *The School for Scandal* at Baltimore's Maryland Theatre. *The Baltimore Sun* critic Donald Kirkley wrote that she appeared "more than a little worn and tired after many weeks of trouping in this play. She seemed to lack much of her usual spirit…."[15] The rumor was that she was intoxicated.

Friday, May 27: Ethel arrived by train in Pasadena, California, with her three children: 19-year-old John Drew Colt, 20-year-old Ethel Colt, and 23-year-old Samuel Colt. John met them at the station. A reporter asked Ethel if she was nervous about acting with her brothers, both notorious scene-stealers. "You need not worry about Mrs. Colt getting nervous," said John. "She'll be standing right before the camera—in front of us."[16]

Saturday, June 4: "I swore that if God would give me a son, I'd never drink again,"

John Barrymore would say, and on this date, his wife and former leading lady Dolores Costello gave birth to a healthy baby boy. John promptly went on a bender. "What happens to a man, who makes a sacred oath," Barrymore will later ask with sincerity, "—then breaks it?"[17]

Friday, June 17: Lenore Coffee and C. Gardner Sullivan provided a 93-page "treatment" for *Rasputin*. Reportedly, the Motion Picture Producers and Distributors Association of America (the MPPDA) would reject it, just as they had rejected John Colton's draft and four others in between, because they made the Romanoffs look "stupid and unsympathetic." Thalberg was unhappy about this interpretation as well, even though he was Jewish—and the tsar was a notorious persecutor of Jews.

"The tsarina was the granddaughter of Queen Victoria," said Thalberg. "Fifty percent of our foreign receipts come from England. I am not going to risk harming our foreign market because I'm a Jew. It wouldn't be fair to the stockholders."[18]

Tuesday, June 28: "BRABIN GETS BARRYMORES," headlined *Variety*, writing, "Charles Brabin replaces Raoul Walsh on direction of three Barrymores in *Rasputin* at Metro. Walsh gets another assignment." The Liverpool-born Brabin had just directed Jean Harlow's first film as an MGM contract star, *The Beast of the City*. He had a hangdog distinction at Metro: He'd started filming the 1926 *Ben-Hur* in Italy, only to be sacked from the epic and replaced by Fred Niblo. Happily wed since 1921 to silent film vamp Theda Bara, Brabin hoped *Rasputin* would restore him to full prestige at MGM.

Tuesday, July 5: *Variety* reported:

> Script of *Rasputin* *is being tailored to fit five Barrymores instead of three. John Drew Colt and Samuel Blythe Colt have been added to cast and parts must be written in to suit. More writers have been placed on the story so that the script may be ready for production next Monday (11). Lenore Coffee and C. Gardner Sullivan are working on one script. John Meehan has another in hand. Best one will be used or the two combined.*

As things evolved, neither John nor Samuel had any interest in being in *Rasputin*, nor did their sister Ethel, who was also considered for the film. The siblings preferred to play, not work, in Hollywood. Ethel rented British humorist P.G. Wodehouse's estate in Benedict Canyon, with a swimming pool and tennis courts, and began prodigally spending her Metro salary.

Thursday, July 7: Elizabeth Yeaman reported in the *Hollywood Citizen News* that RKO had started rehearsals for the shooting of *A Bill of Divorcement*, in which John Barrymore would star as an insane man, terrified that his mania would pass to his grown daughter (Katharine Hepburn, in her film debut). He made the film concurrent with *Rasputin*. The role was uncomfortably close to Barrymore's greatest fear: that his father's insanity would pass on to him. He was also fearful, of course, that his own mental illness would pass on to his infant son. It appeared a precarious role choice.

Saturday, July 9: MGM released *The Washington Masquerade*, starring Lionel Barrymore as an idealistic D.C. Senator betrayed by a blonde charmer (Karen Morley). The director: Charles Brabin.

Monday, July 11: The start date for *Rasputin* arrived. How much shooting took place this day is questionable; the studio was still casting the picture, and there was still no script. Among those who had taken or *would* take stabs at a scenario: Ben Hecht, John Lee Mahin, Robert E. Sherwood, Laurence Stallings, Carey Wilson, Bernie Hyman (the film's producer) and Mercedes de Acosta, the alleged lesbian paramour of MGM super-star Greta Garbo.

Pressure was on for the film to begin. Ethel Barrymore had a new play vehicle titled *Encore*, to be produced by Arthur Hopkins, scheduled for a Broadway opening late in 1932. She insisted on being back east in time for rehearsals.

Wednesday, July 13: "ETHEL BARRYMORE SUED FOR $509 GROCERY BILL," headlined page one of the *Baltimore Sun*. A county judge in Mamaroneck, New York, where Ethel usually resided, had given permission for a process server, who'd tried 17 times to present the bill only to find Miss Barrymore away from her house, to leave the bill with her servants while she was in Hollywood, or tack it to her front door.

Thursday, July 14: Lionel and his actress wife Irene Fenwick celebrated their ninth wedding anniversary. There was some sensitivity between the brothers about Lionel's wife, as John had a fling with Fenwick before she and Lionel wed. He even claimed to have bedded her. "She's nothing but a whore," John had advised Lionel.[19]

Tuesday, July 19: *Variety* reported that MGM had cast British actress Diana Wynyard in *Rasputin*, her first film under her new Metro contract. Wynyard, 26 years old, was to play Princess Natasha, the true love of Rasputin's assassin (renamed Prince Paul Chegodieff in the film). Tall, stately and doe-eyed, Wynyard had made her Broadway bow on January 4, 1932, in *The Devil Passes*, co-starring with Basil Rathbone and Ernest Thesiger.[20] Her role in *Rasputin* would prove profoundly significant.

Also on July 19: Howard Strickling, MGM's young publicity chief, formally announced the studio's new motto, "All Out for Sex in 1932." This spice would apply, generously, to *Rasputin*.

* * *

By late July, *Rasputin* was shooting. The Barrymores saw little of each other away from the studio. At one point, John had the brood at his home, Bella Vista, at No. 6 Tower Road, high in Beverly Hills. Overlooking the estate was a 29'-tall totem pole John had stolen from the village of Tuxecan on Prince of Wales Island in Alaska during a 1931 cruise on his yacht. Lionel, believing it to be a funerary totem pole that contained the ashes of indigenous people and carrying a curse, would blame the totem for John's imminent downfall.[21]

Normally, Lionel wasn't a superstitious man.

Part Two: The Shoot

Act I—Rising Action

> CREST OF IMPERIAL RUSSIA ... *painted on the side of a carriage which is rolling through the streets of Moscow.... The* CAMERA *moves along with the carriage, then recedes far enough to show the Grand Duke Sergie and his daughter Natasha....*
>
> WOMAN WITH BABY CARRIAGE...*There's something striking about her look as Natasha's carriage rolls toward the camera ... the woman gives the*

baby buggy a quick push. It rolls into the street toward the carriage. ... The
baby carriage explodes with a terrific roar....
SHOT OF GRAND DUKE'S DRESS HELMET *As it rolls slowly into the gutter.*
—Original opening of *Rasputin*, as scripted
by Charles MacArthur, dated November 8, 1932[22]

Note the above scene carries the credit of Charles MacArthur, co-author (with Ben Hecht) of such plays and films as *The Front Page*. Ethel had visited MacArthur at his home, demanding he take over the floundering script. When he demurred, Ethel allegedly called him, to his face and in front of his wife Helen Hayes, a "lazy, cowardly, impertinent, loafing, good-for-nothing ass!" She also knocked a pile of books and magazines onto the floor.

"Do you want me to tear down this house?" threatened Ethel.[23]

MacArthur agreed to the job. On August 30, *Variety* reported, "Metro has assigned Charles MacArthur to rewrite several sequences of *Rasputin*. Author is working against time, with company photographing the stuff as he bats it out."

At any rate, the original assassination scene opening of *Rasputin and the Empress* (as it was eventually retitled) does *not* appear in the film. It was to have proceeded with John Barrymore's Prince Paul Chegodieff, officer of the Chevalier guards, finding Diana Wynyard's Natasha, the victim's daughter, amidst the debris and carrying her to safety.

"Her clothes are torn in Adrian's most voluptuous style," in-joked MacArthur in the script—Adrian, of course, being MGM's legendary costume designer, creating the fashions for this film.

Instead, the opening scene of *Rasputin and the Empress* is a solemn religious ceremony inside a cathedral. It's 1913, and the opulent celebration of the Romanoffs' 300th anniversary sets a tone of epic pageantry. Brabin shot the episode on a 400'-long cathedral set that filled two stages and featured the Los Angeles Greek Orthodox Church Choir.

Among the guests who watched the shoot of the ceremony: Tallulah Bankhead, Evalyn Walsh McLean (a personal friend of Ethel's who happened to own the Hope Diamond) and Walt Disney, who discovered that all three Barrymores were huge fans. Disney, delighted, caricatured the trio in their *Rasputin and the Empress* roles in his 1933 cartoon *Mickey's Gala Premiere*, which also featured such luminaries as Lugosi's Dracula, Karloff's Frankenstein Monster, and Fredric March's Mr. Hyde.

The spectacular opening also takes sides. With its soaring hymns and a white-bearded bishop intoning a religious chant, *Rasputin and the Empress* unabashedly glorifies the Romanoffs.

First "white whale" sighted: Ethel. She looks rigidly, reverently beautiful, at first seen only in medium and long shots, as if cinematographer William Daniels is reluctant to move in too close and too fast. Daniels, Garbo's cinematographer, filmed Ethel as if she were a piece of religious statuary; John had suggested Ethel demand Daniels, promising, "He'll make you look like Mona Lisa on her wedding day."[24]

Ethel repeatedly repelled any attempt by Brabin to direct her—"I knew Her Majesty personally," she told him.[25] Also introduced in this opening: bearded Ralph Morgan, whose quietly played performance as Tsar Nicholas virtually screams "martyr," Nebraska-born Tad Alexander, who turned ten on August 7, as the tsarevich (called Aloysha by his intimates); and the teenage Grand Duchesses: Anastasia (14-year-old

Anne Shirley), Maria (17-year-old Jean Parker) and Tatiana and Olga (played by actresses whose names were never listed by MGM).

"White whale" number two breaches: John, as Prince Paul Chegodieff. Sporting an immaculate white uniform, along with knee-high black boots, John's Prince Paul is clearly the heroic archangel in this giant battle between Good and Evil, Heaven and Hell.

A candid on-the-set shot: John Barrymore out of costume, Diana Wynyard and Ethel Barrymore.

He brings news to his sweetheart Natasha (Wynyard), the tsarina's lady-in-waiting, that her (Natasha's) father, a grand duke, has been assassinated—an economical option to the previously described opening scene.

John still had his classical handsomeness, although a few shots reveal cosmetics daubing "The Great Profile." Also, under his uniform he had to wear a corset that was so tight that he couldn't sit down.[26]

During the prolonged shooting of the opening sequence, John disappeared on another bender, this one lasting two days. Then, one morning, he was suddenly back on the *Rasputin* set in his white uniform, "beautiful in my eyes," said Anne Shirley, who played the Grand Duchess Anastasia.[27] Aware of the company's tension regarding his off-the-wagon episode and the stony silence on the set, John walked up to Ms. Shirley, who was in costume.

"Don't you ever do that again!" he playfully scolded the 14 year old, as if she were the drunk who'd caused the delays. The company roared with laughter.

One has to wait a while for "white whale" number three to surface.

As *Rasputin and the Empress* continues, MGM, the aristocracy of Hollywood studios, stays clearly on the side of the tsar. In one episode, we see John Barrymore's prince mercifully halt the firing squad execution of a singing, screaming coven of Bolsheviks, including a raving female revolutionary, played by a wild-eyed Helen Freeman. (The script notes that she's the same character who'd rolled the baby buggy bomb into the original opening assassination scene.) The woman repays the prince's clemency by spitting in his face. As soldiers restrain her, John elegantly removes his handkerchief (presumably silk), suavely wipes his face—and then coyly throws the spoiled handkerchief into the woman's fierce face. The bit was detailed in the script, not a Barrymore flourish; Mayer and Thalberg, Republicans both, must have loved it.

Three months later, the tsarevich falls while playing. The doctors can't stop the bleeding....

Finally, 27 minutes into the film, Rasputin appears—Lionel Barrymore's introductory shot masterfully captured in diabolic shadow by William Daniels. We've met the angels, and now we meet the Devil himself. Natasha, a zealous believer in the man's powers, has brought him to the royal family. Lionel's presence is instantly immense, and he hypnotizes the boy, spinning a watch on a chain as he purrs a fanciful, almost psychedelic tale:

> We'll go riding in that golden house, Aloysha—on your elephant—through the black, dark forest ... yellow tigers are going to be hiding in the trees—and we're going over beautiful blue rivers in the snow, filled with silver fish—we'll ride on that elephant of yours, Aloysha, all the way to the moon, Aloysha—all the way to the moon....

In his 2019 book *Forbidden Hollywood*, Mark A. Vieira notes that Lionel's Rasputin was "the most licentious character ever written for an MGM film, a crude, lip-smacking lecher." Not surprisingly, considering Rasputin's notoriety and MGM's political stance, *Rasputin,* after Lionel's entrance, rapidly becomes ominously dark. His hold over the boy—and the royal family—chillingly increases. We learn that a boy he'd previously "cured" went stark mad. And Aloysha, very well-played by Tad Alexander, seems to be going insane ... almost as if he's possessed.

A vivid episode has Rasputin forcing the frightened crown prince to look at a fly and an ant that Rasputin places under a microscope, the scene festooned with gruesome close-ups of the ant killing and gnawing the fly:

Boo! Lionel Barrymore, getting the full-blown MGM showmanship treatment as Rasputin.

RASPUTIN: *Now, suppose those two should start in fighting, who do you think will win? You'd
say the fly. Big "General Fly." But that little ant has power—and he knows how to use it.
Power's the only thing in the world—but you must know how to use it.... Look, look, look!
Poor "General," first crippled, and then destroyed.... He's tearing him apart! He's eating him
up! ... That's the kind of power we can have, you and I, if you do as I tell you.... We can have
Russia! ... You're the fly [laughs] and I'm the ant—but I'll always be your friend....*

Prince Chegodieff appears, shocked to see the boy so woefully under Rasputin's control. In a scene added to the preceding action by Charles MacArthur, Paul takes Aloysha's
hand: Aloysha, under Rasputin's power, bites Paul's hand like an animal.

John Barrymore, Ralph Morgan, Edward Arnold (as Dr. Remezov), Ethel, Gustav von Seyffer-titz (as Dr. Franz Wolfe), Tad Alexander, Lionel (from the Bill Nelson Collection).

PAUL: (in horror) *Aloysha!* (Rasputin chuckles. Paul wheels on him.) *What damnable thing is this? … You filthy swine! Meddling in politics is one thing—but if you've tampered with this boy's soul…!*

Paul grabs Rasputin. The tsarina enters and intervenes.

In a later episode, filmed before Ethel left for New York, Rasputin turns a lecherous eye on the Grand Duchess Maria. The scene was the creation of a writer other than Charles MacArthur—it isn't clear whom it was—and Ethel exploded when she learned about the seduction scene.

"With one of the tsar's daughters! Do you realize that the king of England is this girl's cousin? How could you ever show the picture in England?"[28]

The approved scene went before William Daniels' camera. The refreshingly lovely Jean Parker, who played Maria, had turned 17 on August 11 and in some shots appears even younger. *Rasputin* was her second film.

The scene instantly repels. "Lionel gives Rasp a little of the old Svengali-Frankenstein treatment," *Variety* would report of his performance. "Lionel is a debaucher of women, a scarer of children, and a cabalistic ghoul who gives out the Frankie-Dracula stuff when ogling an adolescent princess."[29] *Variety*'s tone was almost one of amusement, but the scene with the "adolescent princess," as she stands before the seated Rasputin, is hardly humorous:

RASPUTIN: (in silky tones) *I heard you went to the hospital the other day.*
MARIA: *Yes, Father.*

RASPUTIN: *What did you see there?*

MARIA: *Oh…. Mother and I talked to a boy. The first day he was at the front he lost both his hands. And he was so brave—and beautiful.*

RASPUTIN: *Do you like beautiful boys?*

MARIA: *I don't know what you mean.*

RASPUTIN: *Oh, that's all right. It's perfectly natural for girls to think about boys. You must never be ashamed of life, my dear….*

HE TAKES A LITTLE LOCKET FROM HIS POCKET:

RASPUTIN: (standing) *I've got something for you. A little locket, a holy image, to wear around your neck.*

MARIA: (pulling at her hand) *Father, I don't know if I should….*

RASPUTIN: (smiling) *See, you're afraid of me…. You mustn't be. Your mother wouldn't like to hear that. Would she? Well, then, you'll have to be a lot nicer.* (Slipping the locket around her neck, dropping the locket inside her dress) *Now we'll put this on around your neck— and every day you wear it, you'll be blessed. Wear it next to your warm little heart. It's beating so fast! Like a little bird I once held in my hand. It was so afraid I would hurt it. But I didn't.*

Consequently, Rasputin doesn't molest Maria, but not for lack of trying … he creeps into her bedroom that night; sensing his presence, she wakes up screaming.

Natasha, hysterical, attacks Rasputin. Rasputin smacks her in the face, knocking her to the floor. The tsarina witnesses his brutality. Ethel's face magnificently registers horror and guilt as she realizes she's trusted her family to a madman.

As things evolved, the attempted seduction scene got by in England. It would be a different sex episode, shot later in the production, that gave *Rasputin and the Empress* its epic notoriety.

Intermission

> *Ethel has been marvelous. Lionel, who loves his sarcasm, has never been in better humor. I have, ladies and gentlemen, conducted myself magnificently. Never, at any time, have we betrayed less of that "Barrymore temperament," whatever that may be!*
>
> —John Barrymore, regarding the shooting
> of *Rasputin and the Empress*[30]

At MGM, they nicknamed the film, despite what John Barrymore claimed, *Disputin'*.

During the summer of '32, MGM was a hothouse of scripted and real-life melodrama. On August 6, Metro started shooting *The Mask of Fu Manchu*, in which Karloff cavorted with snakes, lizards and Myrna Loy as his nymphomaniacal daughter Fah. Thirty nights later, September 5, Metro producer Paul Bern, 65 days after wedding the studio's Platinum Blonde Jean Harlow, stripped naked and shot himself in the head in his Bavarian-style hideaway in Benedict Canyon, leaving a suicide note inferring sexual inadequacy.

All the while, the Barrymores, *Rasputin's* "three white whales," spewed talent and temperament.

There were reports of Olympian upstaging contests, primarily between the two brothers. Of course, John had recently triumphed as Svengali—also a hypnotist who seduces the heroine (played in *Svengali* by 17-year-old Marian Marsh)—and followed at

The Barrymore brothers, Lionel and John … spellbinders both.

Warners in the title role of *The Mad Genius*. Both characters wore whiskers. One imagines John craved the role of Rasputin for himself. Aware of these rumors, he denied them:

> [N]obody had ever met a crazy old duck like Svengali, nor encountered, even in his nightmares, a Mad Genius. No matter what I did, no critic could say I wasn't true to type. So, all I had to do was to ad lib to hellangone—make faces, clutch the air, gargle and gasp and groan, and fall on the floor and writhe. That was acting!
>
> I was writhing my bewhiskered way right into oblivion and didn't know it.[31]

He was right, partially: Both *Svengali* and *The Mad Genius* had lost money, while MGM's *Grand Hotel*, in which he'd played Garbo's lover, was making a mint. Yet John was clearly bridling to break loose in certain episodes of *Rasputin*. He and Lionel sparred and sparked in their tandem scenes, and reportedly, Lionel one day, fed up with John's upstaging trickery, left the set and sequestered himself in his dressing room, moodily playing the piano.[32]

In fact, the script encouraged such rivalry. In the episode where Rasputin attends

A candid shot of Lionel as Rasputin, in shades and with cigarette.

a dinner at the prince's palace and Rasputin roars, "I will *be* Russia!" Lionel belches on borscht and spits out the butt of a cigar. It's in the script. John poses and plays with a rapier as Lionel rants—the swordplay is in the script too. It appears the boys are indulging in a can-you-top-this? contest, but in fact, they're fulfilling what the scenario wanted.

There was, however, one rather bizarre bit as the brothers sparred in this episode. John began to place a cigarette in his mouth, nearly inserted the wrong end, mugged in surprise, then righted and lit the cigarette!

It was Ethel, actually, who proved the most formidable sibling. She refused early calls to the set. She even fought about how to pronounce Rasputin. She said "Ras-poo-tin." A Russian technical advisor corrected her, saying, "Ras-pew-tin." Brabin reluctantly backed up the Russian.

"Good God!" shouted Ethel, looking at the studio-at-large. "What kind of place *is* this?"[33]

Eager to get back East for her play, Ethel became increasingly exasperated with the myriad delays. She vented her wrath on the hapless director. "See here, Mayer," she ultimately demanded on an on-set phone so all the cast and crew could hear her, "let's get rid of this Brahbin or Braybin or what's his name."[34]

She got her way. Metro fired Charles Brabin—or actually, switched him to direct *The Mask of Fu Manchu*, sacking Charles Vidor, that film's original director. Brabin found himself directing another production with no script—a trouble-plagued horror show that Karloff, in later years, laughingly called "a shambles."

Rasputin and the Empress' new director: Richard Boleslavsky (sometimes spelled Boleslawski). He had fought for the tsar in the Russian Revolution and had later been a Polish lancer. Formerly of the Moscow Art Theatre, Boleslavsky and Maria Ouspenskaya had taught Method acting in New York City. He had little reputation as a movie director in 1932; his previous film, *The Gay Diplomat*, had been a disaster that proved to be RKO's lowest-grossing film of 1930. Yet he was quite a brilliant talent, destined to direct such films as MGM's *Men in White* (1934) and 20th Century's *Les Misérables* (1935), temperamentally (and politically) suited to *Rasputin*.

Eventually, the off-screen antics grew dark ... and in at least one case, mirrored the melodrama in the film.

It was John who discovered Jean Parker for the role of Maria, seeing her on the Metro lot and asking, "Are those your own eyelashes?" She replied affirmatively. "Ungodly beautiful ones!" admired John, phoning Mayer's office and saying, "I think we've cast Maria."

Lionel played the scene where Rasputin tried to seduce Maria; John actually did—or attempted to—seduce Jean Parker. He was 50. She was 17. She adored John Barrymore, and was so naïve that, as she remembered decades later, "I'd have kissed anybody who asked me." He entered her dressing room, and looked at her up and down.

"Love those little brown ankles," he flirted.

However, before the heavily made-up, tightly corseted "Great Profile" could make his move on the trembling teenager, a wardrobe lady entered.

"A premeditary error," said John, and fled the scene.[35] A potentially sordid situation had been cut off at the pass.

As if the Barrymore trio weren't enough of a circus ... on September 27, *Variety* headlined on page one, "Rasputin's Daughter as Metro Sideshow":

Maria Raspoutine [sic] *who claims to be the daughter of Rasputin, "the mad monk," may appear over here. It is proposed to use her in a presentation with Metro's forthcoming* Rasputin *film with the Barrymores. Mlle. Rasputin is known to the Paris stages. Her routine includes Russian folk songs and dances. Several years ago, she published a biography in which she set forth her parentage.*

Ultimately, Maria Rasputin, surely sensing the way Metro was presenting the father she adored, had nothing to do with the movie.

The troubles went on … and on. MGM was in the aftershock of Paul Bern's death as Jean Harlow resumed work in *Red Dust* with Clark Gable. "*Rasputin* Delayed" headlined *Variety* on September 20:

Rasputin *was held in production for three days last week with the studio trying to get an ending. Story is being written as it went along and on account of the Paul Bern death, writers were handicapped in getting ending approved through Thalberg being absorbed in straightening out the Bern matter.*

Then there was the misery caused by former Russian army officers, working in Hollywood as extras. "Loyal Russians Refuse *Rasputin* Parts: Seek Pic Ban," headlined the October 11 *Variety*, explaining that the ex-officers believed the film might reflect badly on the Imperial family:

These royalists, drifting here after the revolution, are organized as the Russian Army Officers' Club, which is ostensibly social and practical, inasmuch as it is active in endeavoring to get film work for its members. There are about 40 of them ranging from generals up.

Taking themselves seriously, the royalist extras reported to their fellow expatriate organization in Paris on their peeve, and it is understood that they demanded that influence be brought to bear through the British royal court to get Metro to lay off the picture. Nothing came of the plan.

Meanwhile, the army officers refused to work in the picture with other nationalities filling the Muscovite berths. Theodore Lodijensky, former officer in the Russian army, is working as technical advisor on the film. He has been an American citizen for six years, and is not a member of the officers' club.

There was also the Diana Wynyard problem. Fox Studios had cast Wynyard as the star of its epic *Cavalcade,* destined to win the Academy's Best Picture Award of 1933. Her leading role was a work-out, in which her character aged 34 years. Fox needed its star, but MGM still had her on call as the *Rasputin* company batted around ideas for new episodes.

October 18: "Ethel Barrymore's Eyes Prolong Metro's *Rasputin*," headlined *Variety*:

Due to eye trouble, Ethel Barrymore was only able to work six hours last week on Rasputin *(Metro), with the result that she has not left for New York. She will remain here another week, Arthur Hopkins having agreed to postpone rehearsals for her play.*

Finishing date for Rasputin *is now November 15. Original schedule called for completion September 1.*

On October 21, RKO premiered *A Bill of Divorcement*—the film John Barrymore had started about the same time as *Rasputin*—at the RKO Hillstreet Theatre. As *A Bill of Divorcement* opened, *Rasputin* continued with no end in sight. Incidentally, although Katharine Hepburn was the rage of *A Bill of Divorcement*, John won laudatory reviews for his haunting portrayal. Reportedly Ethel also saw *A Bill of Divorcement* and gave John her assessment.

"You're very good," said Ethel. "In this one, you're not an ass."[36]

Before Ethel's departure, John and Dolores had their baby boy baptized at Saint

Andrew's Church in Pasadena. Ethel headed home. In Chicago, reporters got into her train compartment, where the Great Lady voiced her feelings on her movie colony adventure:

> *The whole place is a glitzy, glaring nightmarish set, built up in the desert. It looks, it feels, as though it was invented by a Sixth Avenue peep-show man. Come to think of it, it probably was.*[37]

Ethel was adamant that she simply wasn't able to sell out to the Movies as her brothers had. She also hadn't been able to handle her finances. MGM had paid her $57,500 for *Rasputin and the Empress*, and she'd tallied Hollywood expenses of $65,482.[38]

As for Ethel's play: *Encore* would have a disastrous opening night in New Haven on November 28. The word was that Ethel had a severe cold. The play never reached Broadway.

Act II—Falling Action

> *For jealousy is as cruel as the grave … and we're going to punish Paul—you and I….*
>
>   —Lionel Barrymore's line as Rasputin, as he's about
>   to rape Diana Wynyard as Natasha

After Ethel vacated MGM, *Rasputin* focused on John and Lionel. It truly became a horror movie … and in more ways than one.

The script delved deeper and deeper into sex and horror. On November 12—four months and one day after shooting started—Charles MacArthur submitted this episode, set in Rasputin's dining room. Natasha, still believing Rasputin to be a holy man, comes to warn him of Paul's assassination plan. The script read:

> *Rasputin sits at the head of a groaning table, eating with his hands. Miss Barondess is beside him, in an enormous attitude—but not enormous enough to startle Natasha; a little hand-holding, possibly….*

"Miss Barondess," by the way, was MGM starlet Barbara Barondess, who was having an affair with *Rasputin*'s producer, Bernie Hyman.[39] Perhaps MacArthur specifically added "Miss Barondess" here to heed Hyman's request to provide a role for his protégée; or maybe MacArthur, at this late date in the hapless shoot, decided to be bold and reveal that he knew about the married producer's mistress.

At any rate, the script continues its focus on Rasputin's women, who appear to be in the throes of sexual and religious mania, singing, delirious:

> **WOMAN** (to Rasputin): *Father, let me touch your holy hands!*
> Natasha arrives among the disciples. The women eye her.
> **RASPUTIN:** *My daughter! … This way, my daughter….* (He leads her toward a door.)
> **ANOTHER WOMAN** (to Natasha, holding a picture of Rasputin, hysterical): *Blessed among women! It's the way of holiness!!*
> **RASPUTIN** (as Natasha nervously regards the women): *Children—happy in their faith!*

The script had the women creepily reaching to touch Natasha, which Boleslavsky tones down in the film. However, "Barondess," as the script refers to Barbara Barondess, comes through with her big line:

BARONDESS: *Father—There's something that's troubling me … that I must know—Why do you always bless the young and pretty ones?*
RASPUTIN (angry, sotto voice): *Keep this up and I'll break your thick skull!*

The sight and sounds of the nearly orgasmic disciples, the not-surprising revelation that Rasputin always "blesses" the "young and pretty ones" … it all led to the episode that would spell disaster.

Sure enough, Prince Paul arrives and attempts to assassinate Rasputin, who leaves Natasha locked in a private room as he goes to confront Paul. Having been warned by Natasha, Rasputin wears a shield under his clothing. The bullets aimed at the heart do no harm, and Paul suspects the trickery … and says that next time, "I'll aim at your head."

Paul departs. Rasputin returns to Natasha. In this scene, dated November 15, 1932—only two days before the first public preview(!)—Lionel Barrymore and Diana Wynyard play this doomed-for-infamy episode as Rasputin's women sing insanely in the other room. It's a scene that nobody has seen for the past 87 years:

Natasha has been praying hysterically before the icon. She leaps up as Rasputin enters.

NATASHA: (wildly) *He did shoot….* (tearfully) *Forgive him, Father—*
RASPUTIN: (piously) *Of course, my child. I only pray that his eyes may be opened—It was the Evil One within him—not Paul—*

Natasha wants to go to Paul, but Rasputin won't let her leave the room—and starts drawing her toward a couch. "Look into my eyes," he purrs, hypnotizing her.

Rasputin: *Yes. Angels are hovering over us. Hear their wings. Keep looking, Natasha. They're singing a new song—a song of love—*
He reaches behind him and locks the door.
NATASHA: (thickly) *Let me go—*
RASPUTIN: (sweetly—amused) *But you can't walk any more….*
Close shot Natasha's face as it reflects her terror and helplessness.
RASPUTIN: *Let go, my love—my undefiled, while I kiss you with the kisses of my mouth. Thy lips drop as the honeycomb. Milk and honey are under thy tongue. Come, my beloved.*
NATASHA (hardly audible) *Open the door—*
RASPUTIN: *Not till the daybreak and the shadows flee away. Come.*
(He picks her up. Her hand, reaching out hits the gazing ball. It begins to spin.)
For jealousy is as cruel as the grave … and we're going to punish Paul—you and I—
We see and hear Natasha scream….
FADE OUT.

* * *

As will be explained, MGM was forced later to cut this scene, recreated here from the original script pages. Dialogue in the current version only vaguely infers that Rasputin has ravaged Natasha, and as such, Wynyard's haunted performance of Natasha for the remainder of the film as almost a zombie, devastated by her rape, can't be fully appreciated.

For Diana Wynyard—who later became "Lady Diana Wynyard" in her native England—her brief Hollywood sojourn ended with another offscreen cinema rape. In Universal's *One More River* (1934), directed by James Whale, Colin Clive, playing Wynyard's perverted spouse, attacked her with his riding whip.

* * *

MGM quickly edited the rape episode into the film, already heady with sex and melodrama. Boleslavsky had shot the climax of the film—Chegodieff's assassination of Rasputin—only a short time before, the episode dashed off by MacArthur starting Halloween and ending November 5.

As shot, Prince Paul has hated Rasputin all through the film. He despises him now

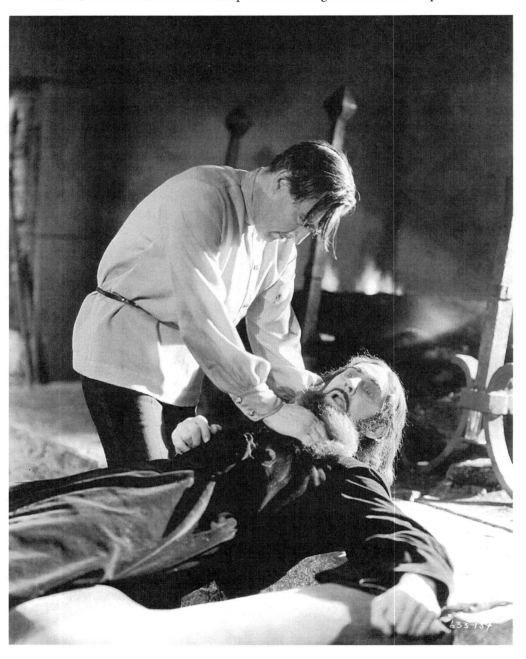

The must-be-seen-to-be-believed assassination scene. One critic described John Barrymore's bloodthirsty performance as "abhorrent savagery." Pictured: John and Lionel Barrymore.

because of what he's done to the Royal Family, and because Natasha has inferred to Paul that Rasputin has raped her—and therefore she feels she can never marry Paul.

The assassination episode, power-packed with motivations, and the performances of Lionel and John, must be seen to be fully appreciated ... and believed.

An orgy. Music. Laughter. A female reveler pours wine over a man's bald head, then falls on the floor, sprawled in her backless evening gown. The women chant for Rasputin as he downs a goblet of wine, which drenches his mouth and beard. Meanwhile—unbeknownst to Rasputin, of course—he's gobbling cyanide-laden cakes with enough poison in each one to kill five men.

At length, Rasputin recognizes Paul's servant (played by unbilled Mischa Auer), roars in fear and anger, and apprehends Paul. He leads the would-be-assassin at gunpoint to the cellar, where Paul stands defiantly before the burning fireplace. In the room above, the party goes on, a Gypsy singing "Nights of Love." Rasputin takes his first shot at Paul—"Just a nip," he says—wounding him in the upper left arm. Paul winces but stands proudly.

All the while, Lionel's Rasputin, his eyes monstrously large, eats another poisoned cake.

The song goes on upstairs. Rasputin enjoys it greatly. "Life, and death, and love," he says, still devouring a poisoned cake. Then he begins coughing. The poison has finally taken effect, and John's Prince Paul explodes into what the script calls a "maniacal laugh."

> RASPUTIN: *What are you laughing at?*
> PAUL: *You! You're full of poison, you fool! Don't you believe me? Look at your eyes! They're like red jelly! Didn't you eat too many cakes, Holy Father?*
> RASPUTIN: (throwing away the cake) *Aggh!*
> PAUL: *They were loaded with poison—and how you stuffed them down, you swine! It's the same music—Life and love ... and death! Are you getting cold, Holy Father? It's the first sign!*

Rasputin fires again. Paul springs over a table and knocks Rasputin to the floor. They roll and fight before the fireplace, and Rasputin sticks his fingers down his throat to try to vomit up the cakes.

"You're a little late for that!" laughs Paul, who crawls atop Rasputin.

The magic of the episode is that John, as the assassin, is as wildly crazed as Lionel, as Rasputin. In fact, John almost appears ready to perform his famed Jekyll-into-Hyde transformation as he sits on Lionel's chest, shrieks, choking and beating him as the "mad monk" calls for an ally upstairs to rescue him:

> PAUL: *Don't disturb him! He's with his girl! That's where you'll be, Holy Father! You'll be with yours—and the little children who believed in you.... You'll see them all now—those dead little faces that you killed!*

Rasputin breaks away, shatters a cellar window, calls out into the street for help. Paul drags him back into the room and they struggle for a poker at the hearth. The prince gets the poker and strikes Rasputin across the head.

> RASPUTIN (scalp bleeding): *You can't kill me! You can't! If I die, Russia dies—do you hear that? ... You'll be dragged down, down to the bottomless pit.... I tell you that!*
> PAUL: (eyes glaring) *The poison's working. You're turning* blue, *Father....*

In an unscripted bit, John spits out a large glob of phlegm, which surely must have gotten a rise out of the audiences. Then he screams, hysterically, "Why won't you *die*?"

John's "Hyde" transformation peaks: Smiling in bloodthirsty savagery, he brings down the poker time and again, over and over, smashing Rasputin's (offscreen) skull. The prince hears the revelers trying to break into the locked cellar, and opens the door to remove the corpse as he hears the "corpse's" voice:

Babylon has fallen … fallen….

Paul makes the Sign of the Cross and sees the bloody corpse rising from the floor. Rasputin's droning voice sounds as if it's coming from underwater. Blood and brains drip through the hair, Lionel's makeup so horrible that MGM forbade still photographers to take pictures.

RASPUTIN: (raising two fingers, as if prophesying, approaching Paul) *The great day of wrath is come!*
Paul tears his hair and screams.
RASPUTIN: *The tsar, Aloysha, all of them gone…. I see their bodies, lying in the snow….*
PAUL: GET BACK IN HELL!

Paul attacks again. This time he drags the risen corpse out into the night, the snow, and the howling wind, to the ice-covered river. There's a hole in the ice and Paul dunks Rasputin into it. The head, its eyes open, sinks last.

"Anti-Christ!" says Paul. "Drown in the lake of Hell—Anti-Christ!"

*   *   *

As scripted, the scene was even wilder. Rasputin has these lines to Paul:

No man can kill me … but they'll kill you! … I'll make up a death for you—and I'll make Natasha watch it! … I'll drag her there—and while you're screaming, I'll have her in my arms…. Natasha!—in my arms—and it won't be the first time!

Paul, meanwhile, had these zingers for Rasputin[40]:

- *You unclean horror!*
- *You belching swill!*
- *You wallowing hog!*
- *You sick cat!*
- *You obscene corpse!*

The scene, as originally shot, had a surprise finish for those watching on the set. Samuel Marx, then story editor at MGM, remembered decades later in his book *Mayer and Thalberg* that John got so crazed in playing the murder scene that, on the soundstage river ice, he lost his balance, and he himself fell into the water.[41]

At any rate, the episode is a show-stopper, wildly horrific even without the missing dialogue, and both actors are magnificent. The John vs. Lionel battle in *Rasputin and the Empress* is among the greatest blood-and-thunder episodes of pre–Code Hollywood.

*   *   *

The film has only a short way to go; what followed was shot while Ethel was still in Hollywood. Aloysha recovers his sanity after Rasputin's death. The Royal Family, publicly condemning Paul, privately thank him. They ask him to take the shattered Natasha with him as he joins the British army. The assassin bids farewell to his friends; in one of John's best-played moments, he fights tears as he says goodbye to Aloysha, his hand tightening on the boy's shoulder.

Newsreel footage presents the Russian Revolution. Nicholas abdicates. The Royal Family departs on a train, with only the tsarina sensing the execution to come. The sinister-looking Bolsheviks lead the family into a dark room. The parents and children huddle together in the cold and darkness, Nicholas holding Aloysha. Then suddenly, the Bolshevik thugs reveal their guns. The family members bless themselves and are shot down in cold blood.

An angelic chorus. THE END.[42]

Meanwhile, Bernard Hyman, the film's supervising producer, added a foreword, reading:

This concerns the destruction of an empire, brought about by the mad ambition of one man. A few of the characters are still alive. The rest met death by violence.

One of the few "still alive" characters, of course, was Prince Felix Youssoupoff.

Part Three: The Release and the Lawsuit

"Beautiful Girls Who Came to Pray—Caught in the Web of Debauched Rasputin!"
—From the *Rasputin and the Empress* trailer

The Release

Thursday, November 17: MGM took *Rasputin* to seaside San Luis Obispo, about 160 miles up the coast from Los Angeles, for a preview. The film was on 17 reels, which means it ran approximately three hours. The MGM hierarchy decided the movie needed revisions.

Tuesday, November 22: "*Rasputin* a Headache," headlined *Variety*:

Odd-shot schedule is being held up because Metro cannot get Diana Wynyard from Fox, where she is loaned for Cavalcade. *Several times during early production on the Fox picture, work was held up because the studio couldn't get Miss Wynyard from Metro where she was working on the Russian opera.*

Tuesday, December 6: "Retakes for *Rasputin* After 17-Reel Preview," reported *Variety*:

Rasputin *has been called back for ten more days of retakes at Metro. Picture has already been in production 22 weeks and has cost $1,000,000.*

Time was now of the essence. The film was set to world-premiere as the Christmas 1932 attraction at the Astor Theatre in New York City.

Meanwhile, MGM settled on a new title: *Rasputin and the Empress*. This was possibly to appease Ethel, who had demanded first billing. John had protested, and the three stars agreed to allow Irving Thalberg to make the final decision. John received first billing, Ethel second and Lionel third.

Friday, December 23: *Rasputin and the Empress* premiered this night at New York's Astor Theatre, the first of the film's roadshow attraction engagements. It was an offbeat

December 23, 1932: *Rasputin and the Empress* **premieres at New York City's Astor Theatre.**

Yuletide attraction, although not as strange as the one on this same date in Chicago—where Paramount's *Island of Lost Souls* opened. (See Chapter 3.)

None of the Barrymores was in attendance. Nevertheless, the opening night so fascinated the public that riot police had to keep the crowds in line. The Christmas Eve review in the *New York Times* praised the three stars, called the film "an engrossing and exciting pictorial melodrama," and noted the power of the assassination sequence: "When Lionel Barrymore … lifted his bloody head and face, a shudder went through the audience."

Rasputin and the Empress was an immediate smash hit. In its first week at the Astor—a small, posh theater with only 1141 seats—the film played at $2 a ticket and took in $22,522,[43] just short of the $24,216 record high set the previous year by MGM's *Hell Divers*. The reviews were almost reverential, such as this one in *Motion Picture Herald* on New Year's Eve:

> *The Barrymore family will, in a hundred years, be a legend, or a historical fact both glamorous and romantic. They are the Medici Family of the stage.... Rasputin and the Empress will, I believe, be shown eventually in every picture house in the country. It is a major event, both from an artistic and a box office point of view.*

But *Harrison's Reports*, a trade journal that never pulled punches, let it rip in its New Year's Eve critique:

> *During the first two or three reels one gets the feeling that* Rasputin *will be the best drama produced to this day, and that the other producers will go a long way before they will duplicate it; but after that one discovers that the Hollywood mind could not have kept that dramatic pace. It would have been unbelievable for such minds not to resort to their cheap, tawdry and disgusting lustful scenes.... Lionel Barrymore takes the part of Rasputin with realism, but such part is unpleasant and in many places to people with decent feelings. For instance, the sight of his entering the room of one of the princesses, a mere child, not older perhaps than seventeen, with the intention of seducing her, coming immediately after his seduction of another princess, cannot help but create a feeling of revulsion to persons with some tenderness in their heart....*
>
> *In addition to being revolting on that score,* Rasputin *is also horrible, at least in one situation. This is where the Prince is shown striking Rasputin on the head with a poker, then dragging him out and throwing him into the river, and drowning him. The sight of Rasputin with his head covered with blood, almost unrecognizable, will sicken the heart of many a person. At the opening night I heard expressions of horror by women around me.*

Still, *Harrison's Reports* admitted the film "holds the interest; at times it grips it."

The battle between John and Lionel, of course, captured the most awestruck attention. *The Wall Street Journal* noted that John "kills Rasputin with abhorrently savage glee."[44] Donald Kirkley of *The Baltimore Sun* cited the "grand finale" fight between the brothers as "the roughest, goriest, longest-drawn-out, most brutal murder this witness has ever seen in pictures." Kirkley wrote that, by the end of the fight, "the monk looks like the by-product of a slaughterhouse, and the audience is thoroughly horrified." It was, in Kirkley's words, "realism run amuck."[45]

March 30, 1933: Rasputin and the Empress had its Los Angeles opening at Loew's State Theatre. Although the historic epic had morphed into a horror spectacle, the critics and crowds were impressed properly. "A feast of personal art rarely exceeded in the picture realm," praised *Photoplay.*[46] *Rasputin and the Empress* came in tenth in the *Film Daily* Ten Best 1933 Poll. (It was the only MGM film in the top ten; Fox's *Cavalcade* was #1.) *Rasputin and the Empress* received one Academy nomination, for Charles MacArthur's screenplay.

Exhibitors wrote to *Motion Picture Herald*. J.J. Medford of the Orpheum Theatre in Oxford, North Carolina, enthused, "A wonderful picture, expertly produced, directed, and the acting is marvelous.... [I]t is the year's best picture." But in the same September 15, 1933, issue, Walter Odom Sr. of the Dixie Theatre in Durant, Mississippi, carped, "When the last showing was over, I sure had one big job waking them up and getting them out."

The Lawsuit

In England, where *Rasputin and the Empress* opened at the Empire Theatre in Leicester Square, the film whipped up its supreme notoriety.

Felix Youssoupoff, naturally, threatened MGM with a lawsuit, citing the same cause used with the German *Rasputin, Demon with Women*: namely, that the film distorted the manner in which he had killed Rasputin. It was remotely possible Youssoupoff resented John Barrymore's savagery in the assassination scene (although considering pre–Code Hollywood, he should have been relieved the film didn't show the prince castrating Rasputin). More likely, the ex-prince was just engaging in his customary litigation.

MGM, believing he had no case, ignored his threats.

Enter Fanny Holtzmann, a 32-year-old superstar lawyer with worldwide connections. She sniffed the big publicity potential of such a lawsuit, met with Irina Youssoupoff in the Riviera, and explained a new attack: The Youssoupoffs would sue MGM for dramatizing that Rasputin had raped the character of Natasha—who represented (they'd claim) the ex-princess. Such a sordid fictionalization, Holtzmann suggested, was harmful to Irina's international reputation.

There was an irony in the alliance: Holtzmann was a Jew and Prince Youssoupoff was violently anti–Semitic.

Of course, the assassin in the movie was named Prince Paul Chegodieff; Natasha wasn't his wife, but fiancée. No matter. Fanny Holtzmann visited MGM's London office and expressed the royal couple's complaint. Her original presentation: It was "only a question of money." Holtzmann allegedly claimed she was doing MGM a favor: The studio would get an avalanche of publicity, and the Youssoupoffs would get a payoff. The sum she requested, by at least one account, was a fairly modest $5000.

MGM, feeling it needed no such favor, refused.

Holtzmann, rejected, went for blood. Preferring to stay in the background, she ignited the lawsuit but did not personally represent the royal couple in British court. The trial would be an Olympian match between two renowned lawyers: Sir Patrick Hastings, K.C., representing Youssoupoff, and Sir William Jowett, K.C., representing MGM. The judge was the celebrated Horace Edmund Avory. The trial proceeded on the crux of whether or not people who saw *Rasputin and the Empress* believed that Chegodieff represented Felix Youssoupoff, and that Natasha represented Irina Youssoupoff.

Tuesday, February 27, 1934: The trial began. Youssoupoff took the stand. So did Irina. Some of the testimony was absurd. Jowett argued that several of the film's *dramatis personae* were composites, and that Natasha, who tended to the tsarina in the movie, might as well have been suggestive of Madame Vyroubova, who actually tended to the tsarina. Meriel Knowling, daughter of the British Ambassador at St. Petersburg, testified for the defense on this score. The plaintiff's Sir Hastings cut in and the questioning eventually centered on Diana Wynyard's figure:

> **Hastings:** *How many times did you see Madame Vyroubova?*
> **Knowling:** *I saw her several times at court ceremonies.*
> **Hastings:** *Was she a middle-aged, fat woman?*
> **Knowling:** *She was not very fat.*
> **Hastings:** *I do not know what "very fat" means. Was she fatter than Miss Diana Wynyard?*
> **Knowling:** *I do not think so, when I first saw her.*
> **Hastings:** *You do not call Miss Diana Wynyard fat, do you?*

KNOWLING: *No.*

HASTINGS: *Then what do you mean by saying this other woman was not very fat?*

KNOWLING: *She was not any fatter than Miss Wynyard when I first saw her.*

Meanwhile, MGM took emergency action: The studio cut the foreword and, of course, the scene where Rasputin raped Natasha. Other dialogue cuts were made as well, as the 133-minute film became the 121-minute version seen today. Nevertheless, a snippet of the rape sequence—Rasputin saying "We must punish Paul," and Natasha screaming as Rasputin's women sing in a nearby room—remained in the trailer. It still does today.

March 5: The Youssoupoffs won. The amount originally announced was $125,000. There was ominous talk, however, that the Youssoupoffs could magnify their windfall by suing any theater in the world that had shown *Rasputin and the Empress.* MGM made a deal, ultimately paying so allegedly staggering an amount that the studio was loath to disclose it. The unofficial assessment: Fanny Holtzmann got $200,000 and the Youssoupoffs got $700,000.[47]

The available financial figures on *Rasputin and the Empress* are:

Cost: $1,019,404.39.
Worldwide rentals: $1,379,000.
Loss: $182,404.[48]

Note that "rental" is not "gross." Rental is the money that comes directly to MGM after its split with the theaters. Also, these numbers surely don't reflect the lawsuit. The nearly one million dollars reportedly came from a contingency fund that MGM kept for such corporate disasters. At any rate, the studio nicely weathered the storm: MGM's 1932 profit was $8 million; its 1933 profit, $4.3 million; and its 1934 profit (the year of the trial), $8.6 million.[49]

Still, there seemed to be no escaping the curse of *Rasputin and the Empress.* In the fall of 1937, a Russian exile whose name actually was Chegodieff—Prince Alexis Pavlovich Chegodieff—emerged in London and sued MGM, claiming *Rasputin and the Empress* had subjected his wife, Princess Elena Chegodieff, to "the gravest libel." On November 15, 1937, they won the suit. The amount MGM paid was not publicized.[50]

Part Four: The Legacy

I thought I was pretty good, but what those two boys were up to, I'll never know.

—Ethel Barrymore, after seeing *Rasputin and the Empress*
on *The Late Show* in Los Angeles in the late 1950s[51]

The fortunes and follies of the Barrymores are well-covered in their full-length biographies, especially Margot Peters' *The Barrymores.* Briefly, John and Lionel acted together again in MGM's *Dinner at Eight* and *Night Flight,* both in 1933. John's last great performance was *20th Century* (Columbia, 1934); his alcoholism and fragile emotional state nearly overwhelmed him, and his cruel self-satirizations earned him the money that kept him from ending up—as he had always feared—in an asylum. He died in 1942. Lionel,

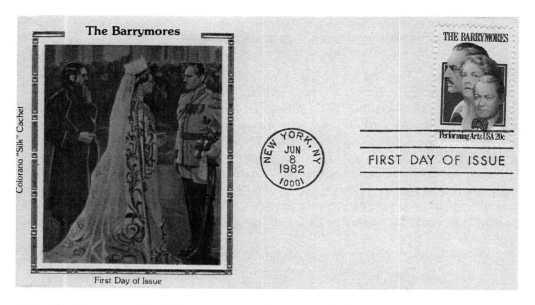

The Barrymores

Colorano "Silk" Cachet

THE BARRYMORES

NEW YORK, N.Y.
JUN
8
1982
10001

Performing Arts USA 20c

FIRST DAY OF ISSUE

First Day of Issue

A 1982 first-day issue of the U.S. postage stamp honoring all three Barrymores, on a card with a *Rasputin and the Empress* image.

wheelchair-bound by the late 1930s, grumbled on, under contract to Metro, a beloved old trouper in control of his addictions; he died in 1954. Ethel floundered for a while, then enjoyed a major stage comeback in 1940 in *The Corn Is Green*. Back in Hollywood, she won a Best Supporting Actress Oscar for *None but the Lonely Heart* (1944), and worked steadily, her demons seemingly at bay. She died in 1959.

Lionel and Ethel are both interred in the mausoleum at Calvary Cemetery in East Los Angeles. John was too, until December 1980, when his son John Drew Barrymore, whose acting career had gone up in a blaze of mania and addictions, forged papers to claim the body, removed the coffin from the mausoleum, insisted on looking at the 38-years-dead corpse before it was cremated, and took the ashes to the family plot at Mount Vernon Cemetery in Philadelphia (where Maurice Barrymore is buried, and where John Drew Barrymore claimed his father wanted to be buried). John Drew Barrymore buried the ashes himself, by hand. A small marker, placed in 1998, reads: *Alas Poor Yorick*.

John Drew Barrymore died in 2004, having fulfilled the most agonizing fears of his father.

*   *   *

There have been many dramatic versions of the Rasputin saga. On March 17, 1953, Boris Karloff played the role on the *Suspense* TV series in an episode titled "The Black Prophet."

In October 1962, *The Night They Killed Rasputin*, a 1960 Italian-French film, was released in the U.S. Edmund Purdom played Rasputin and—an irony—John Drew Barrymore played the assassin, referred to in the film as Prince Felix Youssoupoff.

Then, in January 1963, CBS presented a TV drama, "If I Should Die," based on the Rasputin assassination.

Fanny Holtzmann, after her *Rasputin and the Empress* payday, had assisted far more worthy causes, such as getting Jewish European refugees into the U.S. in the 1930s and 1940s. After the 1963 TV show, perhaps for *auld lang syne*, she persuaded Felix Youssoupoff to sue CBS. Seventy-six years old, frail, bald as an egg and wearing dark glasses, the former prince went to court in the fall of 1965, suing for $1.5 million. He was no longer game for the spotlight and at one point during the 18-day trial, he collapsed in the witness box. If it was a play for sympathy, it failed; CBS won the case.[52] To add insult to injury, *Izvestia*, the Soviet Union's newspaper of record, accused Youssoupoff of "living off the murder of Rasputin" and called him "a revolutionary reject" who "has been thrown onto the garbage heap of history."[53]

Hammer's 1966 *Rasputin the Mad Monk* starred Christopher Lee (who'd claimed that, as a boy, he'd met Felix Youssoupoff). The film played it safe with a disclaimer: "This is an entertainment, not a documentary. No attempt has been made at historical accuracy. All the characters and incidents may be regarded as fictitious."

Felix Youssoupoff wasn't finished yet. On May 3, 1967, *J'ai tu'e Raspoutine* was released in France. Gert (*Goldfinger*) Frobe played Rasputin, Peter McEnery played Youssoupoff, Ira von Fursternburg played Princess Irina, Robert Hossein directed the film in Eastmancolor ... and the movie gave Youssoupoff onscreen credit for his book. The real surprise: Youssoupoff *and* Irina appeared before the credits in an interview!

It was the prince's last hurrah. Felix Youssoupoff died on September 27, 1967, in Paris. He was 78. Irina died on February 26, 1970. Some sources report that she died from lingering grief after Felix's death; another claims she caught pneumonia after crawling onto her roof on a cold winter's night to fetch her cat. She was 74.

Fanny Holtzmann died in 1980. She was 78.[54]

*   *   *

Strangely enough, only two days before Felix Youssoupoff's death, the *Los Angeles Times* ran a story, "Rasputin's Daughter Maintains Father Was Wise and Generous." Maria Rasputin was living in a small apartment at 3431 Larissa Drive, near the Hollywood Freeway. "His power came from belief in God," vowed Maria of her father. "He healed by power of prayer."[55]

She had two pet dogs, which she'd named—pejoratively, no doubt—Youssou and Poff. Maria Rasputin died on September 27, 1977, the tenth anniversary of Felix Youssoupoff's death. She was 79.

*   *   *

Despite the outrageous legal attack, and for all the derision that it's a travesty of history, *Rasputin and the Empress* survives defiantly, almost gloriously. It's a tribute to MGM's Golden Age of pomp and arrogance, but its major distinction, always, is the Barrymore trio, together for the one and only time. The film's a time machine trip back to the age of theatrical spellbinders, and showcases the legendary siblings, with just enough of their demons peeking through the Metro façade to add to the film's fascination.

The Barrymore triumvirate had proceeded to upstage history, Rasputin's real-life legend and lore, and the Russian Revolution itself.

Finally, as for the real-life Rasputin: The story goes (and one may choose to believe it or not) that a woman present at the assassination had found Rasputin's severed penis, allegedly cut off and tossed on that fateful December night in 1916 by the Youssoupoff gang. The organ passed down as a holy relic, eventually arriving in Paris, worshipped by a coven of women who all-hailed it as a fertility charm. Maria Rasputin, learning of its existence, allegedly demanded it as rightful heiress. After Maria's death, the organ was supposedly found, preserved by her, pickled in a jar.

Tests revealed it to be a sea cucumber.[56]

All three Barrymores would have roared with laughter.

Rasputin and the Empress

MGM, 1932. Executive Producer, Irving Thalberg. Supervising Producer, Bernard H. Hyman. Director, Richard Boleslavsky and (uncredited) Charles Brabin. Screenplay, Charles MacArthur and (uncredited) Lenore J. Coffee, John Colton, Ben Hecht, Bernard H. Hyman, John Lee Mahin, John Meehan, Milton Raison, Robert E. Sherwood, Laurence Stallings, C. Gardner Sullivan, Carey Wilson, Mercedes de Acosta. Cinematographer, William Daniels. Editor, Tom Held. Music, Herbert Stothart. Composer, William Axt. Art Directors, Alexander Toluboff, Cedric Gibbons. Costume Designer, Adrian. Makeup Artist, Cecil Holland. Sound, Douglas Shearer, G.A. Burns. Assistant Director, Cullen Tate. Cavalry Trainers, General Lodijensky, John Peters. Still Photographers, Milton Brown, Clarence Sinclair Bull. Running time, 121 minutes.

New York Premiere, Astor Theatre, December 23, 1932. Los Angeles Premiere, Loew's State Theatre, March 30, 1933.

The Cast: John Barrymore (Prince Paul Chegodieff), Ethel Barrymore (The Tsarina Alexandra), Lionel Barrymore (Rasputin), Ralph Morgan (Tsar Nicholas), Diana Wynyard (Natasha), Tad Alexander (The Tsarevich Alexei), C. Henry Gordon (Grand Duke Igor), Edward Arnold (Dr. Remezov), Jean Parker (Grand Duchess Maria), Anne Shirley (Grand Duchess Anastasia), Henry Kolker (Chief of Secret Police), Gustav von Seyffertitz (Dr. Franz Wolfe), Frank Reicher (German Language Teacher), Mischa Auer (Butler at Chegodieff's Party), Sarah Padden (Duna, the Landlady), Barbara Barondess (Rasputin Disciple), Helen Freeman (Hysterical Woman Facing Execution), Louise Closser Hale (Lazy Spoiled Woman), Mary Alden (Natasha's Lady-in-Waiting), Henry Armetta (Photographer), Luis Alberni (Photographer's Assistant), Richard Cramer (Revolutionary Given Birdcage), Nigel De Brulier (Priest), Murray Kinnell (Prof. Kropotkin), Lucien Littlefield (Reveler at Party), Eily Malyon (Rasputin Disciple Crying "Blessed Among Women!"), Evelyn Selbie (Tsarevich's Head Nurse), Michael Mark (Revolutionary Soldier).

3

The Vanity of the Panther Woman

Island of Lost Souls

Charles has never really enjoyed a visit to the Zoo since.
—Elsa Lanchester, regarding her husband,
Charles Laughton, after he starred
in *Island of Lost Souls*[1]

A large gong, echoing in the jungle night.

"What is the Law?"

Island of Lost Souls, 1932 … based on H.G. Wells' novel *The Island of Dr. Moreau*, 1896. The tropical island jungle was actually the Paramount Ranch in the Santa Monica Mountains, about ten miles from the Pacific Ocean. It was Halloween time, and the night was cold.

Behold: Charles Laughton's Moreau, vivisectionist-as-God, sporting a goatee, a white suit, sounding the gong, cracking his bullwhip, and lording it over a horrific tribe of Beast Men, gathered below by a bonfire.

"Not to spill blood. That is the law. Are we not … men?"

A hirsute Bela Lugosi led the litany. The werewolf-like hair disguised his handsome features, but the dynamic voice, almost singing this hymn to the all-hallowed Moreau, was unmistakable. The chanting Beast Men lugubriously backed him up, a creep-out chorus in various degrees of Wally Westmore makeup. Some of the cosmetics were hideously extreme. The creatures were described by one critic as "something out of Boris Karloff's wilder dreams."[2]

Richard Arlen, our hero, observed the macabre ritual. Close beside him was Kathleen Burke, a 19 year old from Chicago, the winner of Paramount's Panther Woman Contest. Playing a character not in Wells' novel, she wore a wildly teased dark wig, eye-ringed makeup that suggested she was actually the Raccoon Woman, and a skimpy costume that evoked a 1932 South Seas stripper. She was a sexpot Hollywood curio—a foxy starlet, playing a woman surgically created from a beautiful but vicious carnivore. The Panther Woman, who only months before had been living with her mother in Chicago, slinked this night on the cold, remote location, appearing in her first film, surrounded by moaning Beast Men.

The Sayer of the Law passionately delivered the prayers, as only Lugosi could:

His *is the Hand that makes!*
His *is the hands that heals!*
His *is the House of Pain!*

73

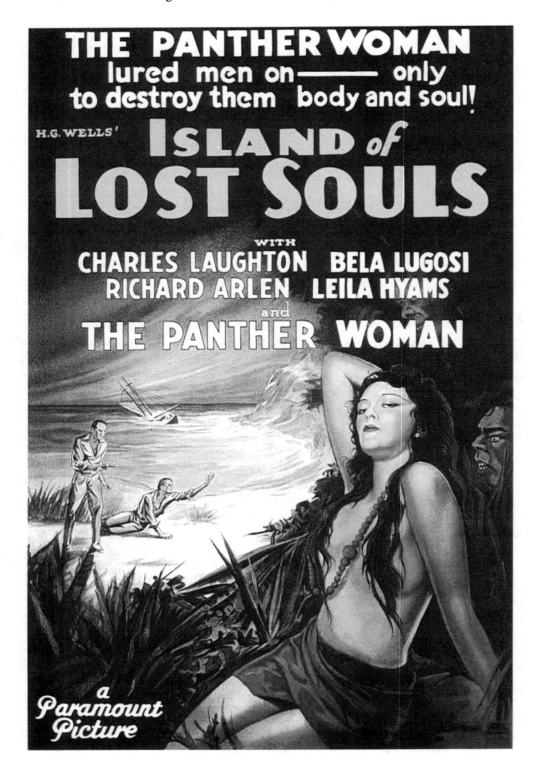

Poster for *Island of Lost Souls*, Paramount, 1932.

The Beast Men dispersed ... and *Island of Lost Souls,* a tropical mix of *Frankenstein* and *Freaks*, went on its mad, blasphemous way, destined to be banned in 12 countries, fated to amaze and appall H.G. Wells privately and professionally, and proceeding to inspire rock stars not yet born at the time of its filming. Charles Laughton's Moreau, hell-bent on mating Kathleen Burke's Panther Woman with a human, would spawn, as Danny Peary writes in *Guide for the Film Fanatic,* "one of the most repellent" sagas in film history.

Time hasn't diluted its exotic, erotic, pre–Code power.

Part One: Pre-Production

Each preserved the quality of its particular species: the human mask distorted but did not hide the leopard, the ox or the sow....
—From H.G. Wells' novel *The Island of Dr. Moreau*

H.G. Wells' Nightmare and the Vivisection Controversy

H.G. Wells claimed that, at age 12, he suffered a nightmare in which he saw God slowly roasting a sinner over a fire. He had been anti–God ever since, and would refer to *The Island of Dr. Moreau,* published when he was 30, as "an exercise in youthful blasphemy."[3]

Moreau became Wells' capricious God figure. He imported animals to his island, and in his laboratory—aka his House of Pain—vivisected these animals (vivisection meaning cutting and experimentation on a *living* animal). The result: Beast Men, whom he taught to obey and fear him. Meanwhile, shipwrecked Edward Prendick became a Christ figure, interacting with Moreau's creatures. They included the Sayer of the Law, who enforced the "Are We Not Men?" litany—a satire on the Ten Commandments, as well as the law in Kipling's *Jungle Books*—and M'ling, the faithful dog man. Prendick described the animal creatures:

The two most formidable Animal Men were my Leopard Man and a creature made of hyena and swine. Larger than these were the three bull-creatures who pulled the boat. Then there was the silvery hairy man, who was also the Sayer of the Law, M'ling, and a satyr-like creature of ape and goat. There were three Swine-men and a Swine woman, a mare-rhinoceros creature, and several other females whose sources I could not ascertain. There were several wolf-creatures, a bear-bull, and a St. Bernard man. I have already described the Ape Man, and there was a particularly hateful (and evil-smelling) old woman made of Vixen and Bear whom I hated from the beginning. She was said to be a passionate votary of the Law....

Moreau died when he pursued a female puma that escaped from his lab, and the two killed each other. Prendick eventually returned to London, but the horrors of the island had taken a toll on him: He feared that all his acquaintances were actually Beast Men, and he escaped society to study astrology.

Note that, while there *were* female beast-people in Wells' novel, there was *no* Panther Woman—nor any idea of mating with a human.

For whatever bitterness regarding God came through in Wells' *The Island of Dr. Moreau,* he had a crusading mission in writing this novel, and it was influential. Two years after the novel's publication, the British Union for Abolition of Vivisection came into being.

Vivisection was still a hot topic over 30 years later:

Saturday, January 16, 1932: Diana Belais, president of the New York Anti-Vivisection Society, announced at New York's Hotel Taft that the society had organized a peaceful army, with reportedly 8365 captains working to stamp out vivisection via the ballot. The Society adopted a resolution to boycott any laboratories that performed vivisections on dogs, and introduced the Vaughan Bill to exempt dogs ("loyal friends of mankind") from vivisection.[4]

Monday, May 23: The scientific community came right back at the anti-vivisectionists at the 126th annual meeting of the Medical Society of the State of New York, held in Buffalo. The delegates unanimously adopted a measure that called the work of the anti-vivisectionists "a menace to public safety and an attempt to strike at the well-being of the community in general." They argued that "these senseless fanatics, bigots and quacks are forever threatening to undo all that has been accomplished in public health, sanitation and hygiene." The Medical Society also pointed out that vivisection on dogs had led to insulin, as well as chest, cardiac, stomach, intestinal and brain surgery.[5]

As for Evolution—in 1932, only seven years had passed since the Scopes Monkey Trial.

How Far Can Hollywood Horror Go?

Meanwhile, in Hollywood, the Big Three horror hits of 1931 had been Universal's *Dracula* and *Frankenstein*, and Paramount's *Dr. Jekyll and Mr. Hyde*, which had opened in Los Angeles on Christmas Eve. As directed by Rouben Mamoulian, Fredric March's Mr. Hyde evoked a sadistic ape, and his scenes with prostitute Ivy (Miriam Hopkins) suggested bestiality. Paramount wanted a horror follow-up, as sexy and violent as its predecessor.

The big question loomed: How far could horror films go? Universal's *Murders in the Rue Morgue*, with Bela Lugosi's Dr. Mirakle hoping (as hinted) to mate a gorilla with a woman, had opened in New York in February and proved only a mild success. MGM's *Freaks*, opening in Los Angeles the same month and featuring real sideshow attractions, had given every sign of being a disaster.

Paramount had a terrific roster of stars—Marlene Dietrich, Gary Cooper, Claudette Colbert, Fredric March, Miriam Hopkins, W.C. Fields, Sylvia Sidney, the Marx Brothers and Mae West. Nevertheless, the lot was bleeding out financially. By April, the loss for 1932 was already a walloping $2,450,211.[6] MGM, "All Out for Sex in 1932," was assured in its market sensuality; Paramount stabbed at it with a bankruptcy-fearing desperation. In fact, Paramount had already showcased an "ape woman," if only briefly in Josef von Sternberg's *Blonde Venus* (1932): Cabaret performer Marlene Dietrich did a burlesque number called "Hot Voodoo," making her entrance in a gorilla suit. (In fact, it was Charles Gemora, Erik of *Murders in the Rue Morgue*, in his ape costume for most of the footage.)

Wednesday, June 1: Nine days after the Medical Society of New York had labeled anti-vivisectionists "quacks," Paramount, having paid $15,000 for the rights to *The Island of Dr. Moreau*, sent a copy of the novel to the Motion Picture Producers and Distributors Association of America (the MPPDA).[7]

Friday, June 3: Col. Jason Joy of the MPPDA, who apparently read the book quickly, personally wrote to Paramount chief B.P. Schulberg: "[F]rankly, I do not see in the story as it now stands enough of the unusual or the plausible, to make it worthwhile following the other pseudo-scientific or horror pictures." Joy added:

> I assume that some thought has been given to the possibility of injecting the idea of crossing animals with humans. If this is the case, it is my opinion that all such thought should be abandoned, for I am sure you would never be permitted to suggest that sort of thing on the screen. The nearest approach to it probably was Murders in the Rue Morgue, *and then, of course there was only a hint of blood transfusion; but even so, wherever there was the slightest suspicion of such mating the idea was rejected....*
>
> I recall also that a picture called Ingagi *got into a lot of trouble, not only because it purported to be an authentic story, but because it suggested that a tribe of African women were mating with apes. It just couldn't be done.*[8]

See Chapter 1 for much more about *Murders in the Rue Morgue* and *Ingagi*.

Despite his reservations regarding bestiality, Col. Joy expressed confidence that Paramount, with its "usual good taste" and "ingenuity," could arrive at a version of the Wells novel that would be "reasonably safe, having in mind, of course, the dangers of gruesomeness, brutality, and mistreatment of animals."

In addition to the novel, Paramount had access to an unproduced play by Frank Vreeland, based on Wells' story and titled *His Creatures*. Eleven writers took stabs at a screenplay. Among them: Joseph Moncure March, who penned the epic poem "The Wild Party" and wrote the screenplay for *Hell's Angels* (1930); Cyril Hume, screenwriter of MGM's *Tarzan the Ape Man* (1932) and *Forbidden Planet* (1956); Garrett Fort, whose name appeared on the credits of both *Dracula* and *Frankenstein*; and Philip Wylie, who wrote the 1930 novel *Gladiator*, one of the main inspirations for the *Superman* comics. (Wylie was later co-author of *When Worlds Collide,* which became a 1951 film.) Fort and Wylie had whipped up an original character, designed to give the movie all the novelty it could possibly need: the Panther Woman. Moreau has created this being in his House of Pain, and wants to mate her with a human.

The sensational Panther Woman role, and the mating concept, was pure (or impure) Hollywood.

Fort and Wylie got a bit carried away. In one of their early adaptations, Moreau beats the half-naked Panther Woman because, rather than mating with a young boy, as Moreau had desired, she'd ripped the boy to shreds. The adaptation also had an unhappy and very gruesome ending: Moreau took Prendick to see his most horrible abomination—a chained monster who had no face. Moreau's fade-out plan: kill Prendick, cut off Prendick's face, and sew it onto the creature.[9]

The final (and much revised) shooting script, dated September 30, 1932, would give credit only to Philip Wylie and Waldemar Young. The latter, the grandson of Brigham Young, had written such Lon Chaney silent melodramas as MGM's *London After Midnight* (1927). Wylie and Young followed Paramount's directive to exalt the Panther Woman.

And, in a macabre precursor to David O. Selznick's 1938 search for the ideal Scarlett O'Hara, Paramount launched one of the most bizarre publicity campaigns in Hollywood history.

The Panther Woman Contest

"Who Will Be the Panther Woman?"
—Slogan for Paramount's publicity campaign, 1932

The mastermind of the Panther Woman Contest was Arthur Mayer, then a Paramount publicist. Mayer later became the manager of New York City's Rialto Theatre, where his "tarting up" the theater marquee and lobby to promote the Universal and RKO horror films of the World War II years became legendary—and won him the nickname "The Merchant of Menace." (See Chapter 13.)

The contest was a sensual mix of Hollywood sexuality and Cinderella fairy tale—tantalizing the aspirants with a trip to Hollywood, 200 Depression dollars a week for five weeks, a stay at the posh Ambassador Hotel, and a role in a movie. The nature of the part, too, certainly had its attractions: One need only review the newspaper fashion advertisements of 1932—the brassieres, the girdles, the hair dyes and bleaches, the ankle-length fashions, the high heels—to imagine the liberation of playing an unbridled Panther Woman.

It was a daring blend of Circe and Aesop's Fables … and its own bizarre way, it was audaciously sexy.

To apply, the contestant was to send a photograph to her local Paramount Pictures exhibitor. There was no charge to enter the contest, but there were 11 requisites. Among them:

- *Each participant in the Panther Woman Screen Opportunity Contest must be not under 17 years of age, nor over 30 years of age, and must be in good health.*
- *Each participant must be not less than 5 feet 4 inches, no more than 5 feet, 8 inches in height.*
- *Each participant must have the written endorsement of two citizens of good standing in the community endorsing her morality.*[10]

The morality clause was ironic, as the hopeful would be playing a bestial creature blasphemously created by a mad doctor, and prime for mating. At any rate, the contest rules went on, saying that no hopeful who had played in a film or professional stage production was eligible; nor was anyone with a relative who worked for Paramount, or a newspaper sponsoring the contest, or a theater hosting it. Also among the rules: The winner of the contest would automatically be under contract to the Paramount Publix Corporation.

As Mayer wrote in his 1953 memoir *Merely Colossal,*

To our amazement, the announcement created a sensation. All over the country, attractive lassies, regardless of rosy cheeks and dovelike features, flooded the offices of the newspapers with whom we were cooperating, to make their bid for this feline short cut to fame and fortune.[11]

As the Panther Woman contest took off, the *Detroit News* ran a July 17 blurb that made *Island of Lost Souls* sound even more enticing:

Nancy Carroll, Myrna Loy, Bela Lugosi, Noah Beery and Boris Karloff—it is among this distinguished company of screen players that some unknown girl will find herself when Paramount begins shooting Island of Lost Souls *August 29.*

Actually, Nancy Carroll, a Paramount star, was in line for the role of Ruth, the

ENTRY BLANK

I hereby agree to conform to all rules and regulations governing the ——————— SCREEN OPPORTUNITY CONTEST, sponsored by the Paramount Publix Corporation to select a suitable personality to portray the role of

"THE PANTHER WOMAN"

—In—

"THE ISLAND OF LOST SOULS"

I have full knowledge and understanding of said rules.

SIGNATURE OF ENTRANT ....

ADDRESS ....

TELEPHONE ....

AGE......................................

We, the undersigned, hereby attest to the moral reputation of the above entrant.

SIGNATURE OF SPONSOR ....

      ADDRESS ....

SIGNATURE OF SPONSOR ....

      ADDRESS ....

In the event of the entrant being under legal age, this entry blank must be signed by parent or guardian.

PARENT OR GUARDIAN ....

      ADDRESS ....

THIS ENTRY BLANK, PROPERLY FILLED OUT, MUST BE AC-COMPANIED BY PHOTOGRAPH OF ENTRANT, AND BOTH MUST BE MAILED OR DELIVERED TO E. E. WHITAKER, MANAGER PARA-MOUNT, BY JULY 22D.

The officials of this contest cannot assume responsibility for the return of photographs submitted by contestants. However, every precaution will be observed for their preservation, and at the close of the contest, contestants may call upon the contest manager in person at the Paramount for the return of their photographs.

An entry blank for Paramount's Panther Woman contest.

heroine, but the other actors at this point were only pipe dreams. The article ran a picture of Bela Lugosi, so the actor pasted the notice into his scrapbook.

Perhaps the best account of the Panther Woman contest came from an actress who participated: Verna Hillie, who in 1932 was an 18 year old living in Detroit. Hillie told me 62 years later:

> *Paramount publicized the Panther Woman contest in every newspaper in every major city in the United States. WWJ Radio in Detroit, for whom I did the* Widow Brown *show, asked me to be in it—and I said "No!" I thought it was demeaning! However, my mother sent my picture in, and the Paramount people contacted me to make a test for the Panther Woman.*
>
> *We filmed the test in Detroit. I'm a blonde, and they put a black wig on me for the test, which had nothing to do with the* Island of Lost Souls *script. We just showed off "dramatic skills"—happy, angry, sad.... Then I appeared at three different theaters in Detroit on three succeeding*

Babes in the Hollywood Woods: The four Panther Woman finalists, left to right, are Lona Andre, Gail Patrick, Kathleen Burke and Verna Hillie (from the John Antosiewicz Collection).

Saturday nights, as one of the 12 finalists; each week they would knock off a few of us. I'd walk across the stage in a bathing suit (and without the black wig) and they'd show the test—it took the place of vaudeville, which played most of the big movie houses in those days. The movie house audience voted, and put their ballots in when they left. There were four of us by the last night, and the audience voted—and I won![12]

During July of 1932, this perverse Panther Woman pageantry played in cities across the country. Audiences flocked to see their hometown lovelies, dreaming of movie fame.

There was a darker, more sinister fascination. Here were these innocents, parading in their bathing suits, in hopes of playing an animal woman, mercifully unaware—or were they?—that they were about to be thrown to the wolves in Hollywood.

There was another brazen undercurrent in the Panther Woman publicity. In 1913, H.G. Wells began a ten-year love affair with author and suffragette Rebecca West—a relationship described as "turbulent." Rebecca's pet name for Wells was "Jaguar."

Wells' nickname for Rebecca: "Panther."[13]

In fact, in 1914, Rebecca bore Wells a son, Anthony West. Anthony's middle name: Panther. One wonders if any of the writers assigned to *Island of Lost Souls* knew about these private matters and mischievously hoped the Panther Woman would provoke Wells—the way Orson Welles' use of "Rosebud" in *Citizen Kane* (1941) would fire up William Randolph Hearst and Marion Davies. Although Wells didn't openly address the matter, he publicly expressed hatred in general for *Island of Lost Souls*.

And so the Panther Woman contest raged, attracting a reported 60,000 applicants. In Chicago, an 18 year old who had large, frightened-looking eyes, who lived with her mother Eulalia at 1243 North Dearborn Street, and who worked now and then as a fashion model, had her commercial photographer boyfriend take a picture of her so she could enter the contest.

What did she have to lose?

The Star

As *Island of Lost Souls* germinated, Paramount prided itself as Hollywood's Sin Capitol. At full baroque blast was Cecil B. DeMille's *The Sign of the Cross*, boasting a genuinely naked Claudette Colbert bathing in asses' milk, a lesbian number called "The Dance of the Naked Moon" and a climactic Roman Games episode. Among the sadistic spectacles delighting Emperor Nero: An Amazon killing a pygmy (and waving his head on her sword) and a gorilla attacking a nude, bound female martyr with flowing platinum blonde hair. Playing Nero: Charles Laughton.

"Laughton manages to get over his queer character before his first appearance is a minute old," *Variety* noted in its review.[14]

Laughton's self-judgment of his facial features—namely, that they resembled an elephant's posterior—might have made him ideal for *Island of Lost Souls,* considering the nature of the show. Audiences loved that face, and over his 30 years as a movie star, it was the face of Henry VIII, Captain Bligh and, with appropriate makeup, of course, the Hunchback of Notre Dame. Ironically, his parents, who ran the Victoria Hotel in seaside Scarborough, England, wanted Charles to follow in their footsteps in the hotel business; he failed there, after various patrons found his face, as they expressed it, "too alarming."

On the stage, Laughton was often a racy revelation. Consider, for example, *A Man with Red Hair*, a melodrama based on the Hugh Walpole novel, that opened at London's Little Theatre on February 27, 1928. Laughton played Dr. Crispin, a lunatic obsessed with pain, who cracks a whip and has a spooky, cadaverous son who seems prophetic of Karloff's Frankenstein Monster. (The actor playing Laughton's son was future *Frankenstein* director James Whale, who was ten years older than Laughton.) During the play, Laughton simulated having a show-stopping orgasm. Whale had to make an entrance immediately afterwards.

"Nobody noticed me," recalled Whale.[15]

Laughton and wife Elsa Lanchester (they wed in 1929; soon afterwards she learned he was homosexual) came to the New York stage to star in *Payment Deferred* (Lyceum Theatre, September 30, 1931, 70 performances), with Laughton as a murderer who buries his victim in the backyard. Lanchester played his daughter. Paramount beckoned and the Laughtons came to Hollywood in the spring of 1932. Paramount didn't have a vehicle ready, so Laughton visited Universal, joining *The Old Dark House*, starring Boris Karloff and directed by Laughton's *Man with Red Hair* "son," James Whale.

On *The Old Dark House*, Laughton displayed his Method acting: Having to appear out of breath in one scene, he ran all over the stage, to be genuinely out of breath. Co-star Gloria Stuart was amazed.

"I can get out of breath," she said over a half-century later, "without moving a muscle."[16]

Sunday, June 19: Over three months before *Island of Lost Souls* started shooting, the *New York Times* announced that Laughton would play the starring role. Meanwhile, Laughton played an insanely jealous husband in Paramount's *Devil and the Deep* (which ends with him about to drown and laughing insanely); he then visited MGM, repeating his stage role in *Payment Deferred* (which ends with him about to be arrested and laughing insanely). Maureen O'Sullivan played his daughter; Elsa, heartbroken that she didn't get that role, soon went home to England. Laughton performed a marvelous cameo in the studio's all-star *If I Had a Million* as a milquetoast employee who, learning he's inherited a million dollars, goes to his boss and blows a raspberry. And there'd been DeMille's *The Sign of the Cross*, with Laughton camping away as a thumb-sucking, epically uncloseted Nero.

At the time the 33-year-old Laughton began *Island of Lost Souls*, none of these films had been released, yet the Hollywood buzz was out: Charles Laughton was an amazing, disturbing, riotously brilliant young actor.

Approaching *Island of Lost Souls*, Laughton, as always, was the exhaustive Method actor, who worked from the "inside" and "outside." How he psyched up as Moreau from the "inside" is lost to the ages, perhaps fortunately, but from the "outside," there were two inspirations. One was a

Charles Laughton, the magnificently blasphemous Dr. Moreau. Here he pleasantly poses on what appears to be a cockeyed cross.

bullwhip, which he'd already mastered in the aforementioned *A Man with Red Hair*. The other was a little devil beard, inspired by a doctor Laughton had visited.

"Dr. Moreau, I presume!" rejoiced Laughton when he saw the medico.

As *Island of Lost Souls'* mad Dr. Moreau, Laughton would be a three-ring circus: blasphemous mad doctor, South Sea Satan, and creepy burlesque comedian—all at a salary of $2250 per week.

The Director, the Co-Stars, the Crowning of the Panther Woman

Originally set to direct *Island of Lost Souls* was Paramount's Norman Taurog who, on November 10, 1931, had won a Best Director Academy Award for *Skippy* (1931), starring his real-life nephew Jackie Cooper. Taurog's specialty was directing children and comedy—making him a strange choice for *Island of Lost Souls*.

Tuesday, September 20: Eleven days before shooting started, *Variety* ran this report:

> Paramount is having trouble injecting comedy into Island of Lost Souls, *fantastic yarn in which a dog's soul becomes a man.*
>
> Original directorial assignment was given to Norman Taurog. Studio took him off, figuring the story wasn't his type. Later, Erle Kenton was assigned. Kenton is also a comedy director, but studio figures he will supply a more subdued type of comedy in his direction.

The idea of a comedy element in *Island of Lost Souls*, even "subdued," sounds ludicrous. At any rate, the new director was Paramount's 36-year-old Erle C. Kenton, who began his career as a Keystone Cop for Mack Sennett. A stout, husky, mustached man, he resembled Teddy Roosevelt—in fact, in Columbia's *End of the Trail* (1936), a saga about the Rough Riders, Kenton *played* Teddy Roosevelt. Directing *Island of Lost Souls*, Kenton would have a "bully" time.

Kenton's right-hand man was Karl Struss, the legendary cinematographer who shared (with Charles Rosher) the first Best Cinematography Oscar for F.W. Murnau's *Sunrise* (1927). Struss had been Rouben Mamoulian's cameraman on *Dr. Jekyll and Mr. Hyde*, and DeMille's on *The Sign of the Cross*. Kenton and Struss enjoyed a mutual admiration: Struss said Kenton had "a greater command of the English language than anyone I ever worked with," and they proceeded hand-in-glove on *Island of Lost Souls*.[17]

On July 31, *the Los Angeles Times* reported that Nancy Carroll and Randolph Scott, both under contract to Paramount, had won the roles of Edward Parker (a name-change from Wells' hero character Prendick) and his true love, Ruth. However, the role of Parker went to Paramount contractee Richard Arlen, a World War I pilot who had done his own flying in the studio's Academy Award–winning *Wings* (1927). For Ruth, Paramount engaged Leila Hyams, whose refined blonde beauty contrasted nicely with the brunette Panther Woman, arousing her jealousy. Earlier in 1932, Hyams had appeared in MGM's notorious *Freaks*, in which she played Venus, the leggy carnival heroine.

Thursday, September 22: Paramount sent Col. Jason Joy of the MPPDA two copies of the "First Yellow Script" of *Island of Lost Souls*, noting the film was to start shooting September 26.

Monday, September 26: Col. Joy responded that the film would be "satisfactory under the Code," but noted:

> With regard to official censorship it is very likely that you will lose the line on Page D-35 in which Moreau says: "Do you know how it seems to feel like God" since a similar line in a recent picture was eliminated by the majority of the boards.[18]

That "recent picture" was, of course, *Frankenstein*, in which Colin Clive had cried triumphantly, "In the name of God! Now I know what it feels like to *be* God!" At any rate, shooting was delayed as the writers did a final polish on the script. They did *not* cut the "feel like God" line.

Hollywood glamorization is in full swing as the Panther Woman finalists pose by "Old Iron-sides," the historic battleship *Constitution*: Gail Patrick, Kathleen Burke, Lona Andre and Verna Hillie.

Meanwhile, as the start of production neared, Paramount selected four Panther Woman finalists. Among them: the aforementioned Verna Hillie. "Oh God, it was thrilling!" remembered Verna, who arrived in Hollywood and sized up her trio of competitors: Red-haired Lona Andre from Nashville, Tennessee, who Verna recalled as "the sex baby" of the bunch; brunette Gail Patrick from Birmingham, Alabama, who Verna discovered to be "ambitious," "calculatingly smart," and "not the warmest creature"; and dark-brown–haired Kathleen Burke from Chicago, a seemingly shy beauty with fawn eyes. On September 5, Burke had just turned 19 years old.

Verna Hillie said:

> [Kathleen] was kind of mysterious—very, very nice, but quite quiet. She was a very friendly girl, but not very outgoing. It really wasn't in her nature to be noticed. She was very poised—and of course, those eyes were marvelous!

In early publicity shots of these virtual babes in the L.A. woods, the foursome looks less like vamps as they do like classmates at a convent school. The Paramount makeup and grooming artists went to work. A winner was yet to be named. Production was to start in only a few days.

Thursday, September 29: Two days before *Island of Lost Souls* was set to begin shooting, the judges of Paramount's Panther Woman Contest announced the winner. The panel was a Who's Who of Paramount directors: Cecil B. DeMille, Rouben Mamoulian, Ernst Lubitsch, Norman Taurog, Stuart Walker … and Erle C. Kenton.

The winner: Kathleen Burke. Apparently, the announcement came with no beauty pageant–style hoopla, but a simple summons to the casting office. As Burke related:

> When Fred Datig sent for me to come to the casting office this morning, I was afraid the news would be disappointing. While he was telling me that I had been selected for the part, I wondered why I didn't scream for joy. Instead I sat there and cried and twisted my handkerchief.[19]

Arthur Mayer was not very gallant in his memoir about Burke, whom he failed to mention by name:

> [T]he final victor was a charming though scarcely talented young woman from Chicago, where, by a peculiar coincidence, Paramount happened to operate more theaters than in any other city. In addition to a complete lack of picture experience, the Champ had one other liability. She resembled a panther as much as Boris Karloff looked like a lamb.[20]

Mayer wasn't entirely accurate. Kathleen Burke definitely had a feline quality, and if she suggested

Kathleen Burke, Paramount's "Panther Woman."

a bit more of a deer than a cat, Paramount had the artists to glamorize her accordingly. Additionally, the studio assigned Stuart Walker (future director of Universal's 1935 *Were-Wolf of London*—see Chapter 5) to coach Burke in developing the slinky nuances and tragic persona of the Panther Woman.[21]

If it's true that there were 60,000 contestants, this infers that approximately 59,999 of the jealous Panther Woman wannabes longed to sink their claws into Burke. Her three finalists sincerely didn't. For one thing, Verna Hillie, Lona Andre and Gail Patrick all received Paramount contracts as well. Also, while the four girls weren't yet worldly, they all were bright enough to sense the darkness as well as the tinsel. They had arrived in Hollywood in what was basically a sexed-up freak show, with the winner challenged to bring bestiality to a horror movie. They surely had hometown neighbors who clucked that the foursome was diving into flames and perdition.

As they spent nights newly settled in Hollywood, the four Panther Women—especially the victorious Burke—likely feared that the naysayers might be right.

The Production Blueprint

Shooting of *Island of Lost Souls* was to start Saturday, October 1. Paramount detailed the budget, schedule and salaries:

Schedule: 28 days.
Budget: $300,000 (a bit higher than the final cost of *Frankenstein*).
Charles Laughton, as Dr. Moreau: Four and a half weeks at $2250 per week—total, $10,125.
Richard Arlen as Parker: $12,083.33 for the production. (Arlen had been at Paramount longer than Laughton, hence the higher fee.)
Leila Hyams as Ruth: $1000 per week for three weeks and five days—total, $3,833.34.
Kathleen Burke as Lota: $200 per week for five weeks—total, $1000 (as promised in the contest).
Arthur Hohl, excellent as the mysterious Montgomery, Moreau's conscience-plagued assistant: $500 per week for four and a half weeks—total, $2,250.
Tetsu Komai as M'ling, the "Dog Man": $250 per week for three weeks and two days—total, $833. The Japanese actor was an eleventh hour addition to the cast; the September 30 shooting script noted the role as yet uncast.
Hans Steinke as Ouran, a Beast Man: Four weeks at $350 per week—total, $1400. Steinke was a wrestler known as "The German Oak."
Harry Ezekian as Gola, another Beast Man: Three weeks and one day at $125 per week—total, $395.83. Ezekian also was a wrestler, with the name of "Ali Baba."
The role of the Sayer of the Law had not yet been cast.

As for the additional Beast Men, Paramount budgeted ten men to be carried on the payroll for three weeks:

- Duke York, a noted stuntman and actor who played King Kala in the 1936 serial *Flash Gordon*, the Leopard Man in the 1940 serial *Terry and the Pirates* (1940), and assorted monsters in Three Stooges shorts.
- "Strongman" Joe Bonomo, who doubled Lon Chaney in *The Hunchback of Norte Dame* (1923) and Charles Gemora in *Murders in the Rue Morgue* (1932; see Chapter 1).

- Otto Lederer, actor–makeup artist who assisted Jack P. Pierce at Universal.
- "Little person" John George, who appeared in the Chaney silents *The Road to Mandalay* (1926) and *The Unknown* (1927), and had bits in the classics *The Black Cat* (1934) and *Bride of Frankenstein* (1935).
- Buster Brodie, a bald character actor who landed a featured role as Moreau's Pig Man.
- Jules Cowles, who played the Beadle in both the 1926 and 1934 film versions of *The Scarlet Letter*.
- Jack Burditte, silent film actor.
- Robert Milasch, who stood 6'6", had been a circus performer; his film career dated all the way back to 1903's *The Great Train Robbery*.
- Julius Graubart.
- As for the tenth, the studio noted to make a call to the Central Casting and Call Bureau. Various extras would be hired for the more populous Beast Man episodes.

Erle C. Kenton, director: five weeks at $750 per week—total, $3750

Karl Struss, cinematographer: four weeks and four days at $400 per week—total, $1,866.66.

Philip Wylie and Waldemar Young, the credited screenwriters: $4400 for Wylie; $10,375 for Young. Young stayed on the script after shooting began. Emjou Basshe worked on the screenplay from September 19 throughout the shooting (and earned $812.50).

Arthur Hohl as Montgomery, Charles Laughton as Moreau, Richard Arlen as Parker, and Beast Men in the background. Notice how Laughton wears his gun.

Makeup: Wally Westmore received a hefty budget for makeup: $250 for the women and $7500 for the men (plus an additional $750 for hairdressing and wigs).

Wardrobe expense: $11,700. Leila Hyams had the top-priced costumes at $225. Laughton's white tropical togs cost $200. The cost for Kathleen Burke's skimpy threads: $25.

Burke was *Island of Lost Souls'* talisman. Her Hollywood dream had come true: She was Hollywood's latest, strangest discovery. Paramount would luridly concoct publicity in praise of the film, sensually selling the role the novice played:

> He took them from his mad menagerie ... nights were horrible with the screams of tortured beasts ... from his House of Pain they came re-made.... Pig-men.... Wolf-women ... thoughtful Human Apes and his masterpiece—the Panther Woman, throbbing to the hot flush of love.

Kathleen Burke, the Panther Woman, was scared to death.

Part Two: The Shoot

> *"He's a black-handed, grave-robbin' ghoul!"*
> —Captain Davies (Stanley Fields) describing
> Dr. Moreau in *Island of Lost Souls*

Catalina Island

Catalina Island is 22 miles off the coast of Los Angeles. The *Island of Lost Souls* company was set there for one week of location work. The principals who went to Catalina: Laughton, Arlen, Hyams and Hohl. Among the featured cast and crew who also came along: Stanley Fields (as the brutal Captain Davies), Hans Steinke and Harry Ezekian as Beast Men (Ouran and Gola, respectively) and Tetsu Komai as M'ling, the dog man. There were other Beast Men as well, and a "surprise" passenger—more on him later.

The company sailed to the location site on a steamer, called SS *Covena* in the film, along with the caged beasts. The steamer hit rough waters, and the animals, sickened by the passage, vomited. The stench was almost overpowering. Erle C. Kenton nearly had a mutiny on his hands.

Still, Kenton was excited and fully in command. As Karl Struss remembered:

> Island of Lost Souls *was an interesting thing. [Kenton] had been a pictorial photographer, and I had met him when I was exhibiting stills in the early '20s. We actually went on a steamer to Catalina and shot the picture on it ... [T]he cages were out on deck. Luckily, we had real fog, which was called for by the script....*[22]

While various sources claim Paramount filmed most of *Island of Lost Souls* on Catalina Island, only the following scenes were scheduled to shoot there:

- Parker's rescue at sea;
- the scenes on the steamer deck;
- the loading of animals onto the sloop;

- the scenes on the sloop deck;
- the landing at Moreau's island;
- Ruth at the pier at Apia, learning of Parker's rescue and later meeting Captain Davies; and
- the final scene in the sea at night, in which Parker, Ruth and Montgomery sail away from the island-in-flames.

Kenton and Struss squeezed every drop of atmosphere out of the Catalina sojourn, where fog and mist set in as they arrived at Moreau's island.[23] A sad note: The pier seen in *Island of Lost Souls*, leading to the island, is about 300 yards from the site where Natalie Wood's drowned body would be found in 1981.

The first of Moreau's creations to enter: M'ling, Montgomery's servant, whose very appearance causes the dogs on board to bark viciously at his unnatural presence. Tetsu Komai wore a canine makeup designed and applied by Wally Westmore, who had applied Fredric March's *Dr. Jekyll and Mr. Hyde* makeup. Westmore flew each morning to Catalina on a seaplane after applying Sylvia Sidney's makeup on *Madame Butterfly*. The shooting script described M'ling:

> *His face is horrible in its abnormalities. His mouth, half-open, shows two even rows of unnaturally large, white, pointed teeth. His face is scarred…. He snarls like an angry dog.*

A close-up of M'ling's ear reveals that it's pointed—and has hair on it. It's *Island of Lost Souls'* first nasty jolt.

Leila Hyams as Ruth, our soon-to-be-imperiled heroine.

A crane on the ship lowers the cages to a waiting sloop, on which we glimpse Laughton's Moreau in a long shot from above—seated, face down, alone, mysterious. Parker and Captain Davies have a disagreement and the captain punches our hero, knocks him out, and tosses him overboard; he lands with a crash on the deck of the sloop. The ship sails away, leaving Parker marooned with Moreau and Montgomery.

Among Moreau's caged beasts was an imposter: The gorilla was actually Charles Gemora, "Ingagi" in person. Indeed, 1932 would be a rip-roaring year for Gemora: Universal's *Murders in the Rue Morgue* (as Bela Lugosi's ape Erik), Hal Roach's comedy short *The Chimp* (as Laurel and Hardy's pet ape Ethel) and Paramount's *The Sign of the Cross* (as the rapacious gorilla in the Coliseum atrocities).[24] Gemora also reportedly worked on *Island of Lost Souls* as a makeup man.

Laughton takes unholy possession of *Island of Lost Souls*. As Moreau, Laughton, with his devil beard and body by Pillsbury, purrs like a cat and suggests he himself is an animal man—perhaps vivisected from a creepy koala bear. Always, he's the ultimate pre-Code star; in these early scenes, Laughton strides about, wearing his pistol and holster directly over his groin.

The location work at Catalina Island soon ended after a feverish week of shooting. Laughton would return to Catalina in 1935 for MGM's *Mutiny on the Bounty*, in which he portrayed the infamous Captain Bligh … and was billed over Clark Gable as Fletcher Christian. The two stars had their professional rivalry, but Gable broke the ice, according to Elsa Lanchester, by taking Laughton as his guest to a Catalina brothel.

"I think that Charles was flattered," recalled Lanchester.[25]

Agoura, Hollywood and the Boudoir of the Panther Woman

The *Island of Lost Souls* company moved to the Paramount Ranch, in Agoura, in the Santa Monica Mountains. Here we see Moreau with Parker, after his arrival on the island, Laughton masterfully cracking his whip at the Beast Men who peer and leer at him from the trees and brush. Neighboring the Ranch, incidentally, was Malibou Lake, where Karloff's Monster drowned Marilyn Harris' Little Maria in *Frankenstein*.

It's on Paramount's Soundstage 9 where we admire Moreau's art deco house—a combination home, zoo, laboratory … and his House of Pain. Creator of the sleek villa: Paramount's legendary set designer Hans Dreier, who won three Oscars—*Frenchman's Creek* (1944), *Samson and Delilah* (1949) and *Sunset Blvd.* (1950)—and had an additional 14 nominations.

Parker remarks on the "strange-looking natives." Among them is the Pig Man, played by Buster Brodie, who was later Jack in the Box in Laurel and Hardy's *Babes in Toyland* (1934) and one of the Wicked Witch of the West's Flying Monkeys in MGM's *The Wizard of Oz* (1939). Brodie wee-wee-wee-ed all the way home with $75 a week for the time he worked on *Island of Lost Souls*.

Moreau is a perfectly charming host, and it appears Parker will depart soon for Apia on Moreau's sloop. But Moreau sees Parker's marooning as Destiny, not accident. What will happen if Parker meets the yet-unseen Panther Woman? Moreau privately asks Montgomery:

> But how will she respond to Parker when there's no cause for fear? Will she be attracted? Is she capable of being attracted? Has she a woman's emotional impulses?

Laughton delicately hints what he has in mind, yet delivers it so implicitly that the censors in Pennsylvania, British Columbia, Quebec and Australia cut those lines upon the film's original release.

The audience gets its awaited peek at the Panther Woman—"Lota" is her name. Moreau calls on her in her lair—or her boudoir. Effectively, we first see her only from the back and in shadow. The doctor tells her that "a man has come from the sea," eventually taking her hand, leading her to the rendezvous.

At length, we see her, head to toe.

At first glance, Kathleen Burke's Panther Woman suggests a Singapore drag queen. Yet almost immediately, her presence and performance spark. Ouran and Gola, Moreau's Katzenjammer Kids (only with raging animal hormones), see her with Moreau and leer at her. Laughton gives her a reassuring little smile as he orders the Beast Men away.

Moreau introduces Parker to Lota. The doctor claims the girl is a "pure Polynesian," and the only woman on the island. "Well, I leave you two young people together!" says matchmaker Moreau.

Lota, shy at first, eventually turns up her vamp act, preening like a cat as Moreau, playing voyeur at the window, watches in fascination. Burke sells the role largely by her eyes … and by a quite remarkable feline presence that makes her at times surprisingly convincing and alluring.

"Just a kid," recalled Richard Arlen of Kathleen Burke over 40 years later. "But beautiful—and she moved like a cat."[26]

Richard Arlen succumbs to the charms of Kathleen Burke's Lota, who in some shots (including this one) evokes a depraved 1960s "love child."

She was, in fact, terrified. After production was finished, *The Pittsburgh Press* published excerpts from what was purported to be a diary Burke kept during *Island of Lost Souls*. Only a few entries went into print, likely edited and pruned by Paramount's publicity department, but they have a ring of truth.

There was this reflection, written on the eve of her first day's shooting:

I wish I could go to sleep. I feel lonesome.

This entry was written the next night:

My first day's work and what a day.
Wally Westmore helped me put on my makeup. Then I got into my costume, a string of beads and a piece of bright painted silk.
Erle Kenton, the director, Dick Arlen, Charles Laughton and Leila Hyams all came up to congratulate me and wish me luck when I walked on the set.
What a thrill it was when Mr. Kenton called "Camera" and I knew that every movement and sound I made was being recorded. I am too quick in my movements. Mr. Kenton has to keep reminding me to take it slowly.

And later:

Ran into my first trouble today, but Dick Arlen tells me that all players have trouble in some scenes. I just couldn't get my scene. Mr. Kenton was very patient. We worked all morning until I was so tired, I hardly could walk. Then Mr. Kenton called lunch and said we would try it again in the afternoon. I had lunch with Sylvia Sidney and Cary Grant. What a thrill that was. And Fredric March and Claudette Colbert sat at the table right next to us....[27]

Dousing Lota's seduction of Parker are screams from the House of Pain. Parker runs to see what became a widely censored scene: He peers into the House and sees Moreau cutting into a screaming man.

"*Get out!*" shouts Moreau.

Chicago, Alberta and British Columbia scissored this scene, and Quebec cut the sound of the screams. Quebec also cut Parker's lines, "They're vivisecting a human being!" and "They're cutting a living man to pieces!"

Parker and Lota run off into the jungle night. Karl Struss masterfully provides a terrific shadow effect of the couple after they pass through a door (Struss also used shadows effectively in *Dr. Jekyll and Mr. Hyde*). Ouran and Gola pursue them to the village of the Beast Men. There, a creature that looks like a tropical werewolf leers at Lota ... and lunges for her.

The creature is the Sayer of the Law, played by a legendary horror star who was a late but unforgettable addition to *Island of Lost Souls*.

Bela Lugosi, "The Sayer of the Law"

As the Sayer of the Law, Paramount had considered contractee George Barbier, a husky 67 year old who, in 1902, had starred as the hunchbacked Quasimodo in the Broadway play *Notre Dame*. (The show had celebrated the 100th anniversary of Victor Hugo's birth.) At this stage of his career, Barbier mainly played windbags.

Friday, October 14: Island of Lost Souls had been shooting for two weeks when Elizabeth Yeaman, one of the film colony's finest reporters (and attractive enough to have been a starlet), ran this report in the *Hollywood Citizen-News*:

Bela Lugosi as the Sayer of the Law, between two Beast Men, cowers from the whip-wielding Moreau. Lugosi appears in hardly any *Lost Souls* stills; one wonders if the still photographers failed to recognize him under all the facial hair.

> *Paramount has decided that Charles Laughton is not enough horror for* Island of Lost Souls... *[The company] has engaged Bela Lugosi of* Dracula *fame for one of the featured roles in this H.G. Wells story. Lugosi will portray the role of herder of the beast men. You see, the story deals with the fanciful theme of a scientist who learns how to transform men into beasts. It doesn't always take a scientist to do that!*

Lugosi added the clipping to his scrapbook, one of a bunch on the film with which he'd fill an oversized page.[28] Newspapers were often tardy in reporting casting news, but the October 14 article—the earliest to report his definitive casting—indicated that Paramount signed Lugosi after shooting of *Island of Lost Souls* began on October 1, and perhaps not even until the company had returned from Catalina. Folklore claimed that Bela accepted the small (but pivotal) Sayer of the Law role to show he could handle heavy makeup—his loss of *Frankenstein* to Karloff was already becoming Hollywood legend. There was, however, a more personal reason why Lugosi took the job.

Monday, October 17: Three days after the *Hollywood Citizen-News* reported his casting, Lugosi declared bankruptcy.[29]

The year of 1932 had been a big year for Bela: the release of *Murders in the Rue Morgue*, the shooting of *White Zombie* and *Chandu the Magician*, a week playing Dracula on stage in Portland opposite *Murders in the Rue Morgue*'s Leon Ames, and a run in a West Coast stage production titled *Murdered Alive*. Yet he now found himself several thousand dollars in debt. He tabulated his assets as $600—which he described as $500 equity in furniture and four suits.[30]

	Dollars	Cents
to Ledger or Voucher.—Names of Creditors.—Residence (if unknown, that fact to be stated). Where and when contracted.— d consideration of the debt, and whether any judgment, bond, bill of exchange, promissory note, etc. and whether contracted as partner ontractor with any other person, and if so with whom.		
importer, clothier Alexander & Oviatt, 6th & Olive, Los Angeles, Calif., goods, wares & merchandise purchased between Sept. 1931 and Aug. 1932,	1000.00	
Fred Bergman, Union Oil Bldg., Los Angeles, Calif., goods, wares & merchandise purchased in Aug. 1932,	175.00	
Dow Limousine Service, Fred Latray owner, 1627 Cahuenga Boulevard, Los Angeles, Cal., for transportation in 1931 and 1932,	318.10	
The Cast, Fred Robertson manager, 6305 Yucca St., Los Angeles, Cal., advertising January to May, 1932,	185.00	
Central Hardware Co., 6673 Hollywood Blvd., Los Angeles, Cal., goods, wares and merchandise purchased from Jan. to Aug. 1932,	143.81	
General Directory, Bank of Hollywood Bldg., Los Angeles, Cal., advertising in 1931,	60.00	
Bonded Tobacco Co., 1183 Broadway, New York, for goods, wares and merchandise purchased in 1932,	59.87	
tailor Eddie Schmidt, 719 S. Flower St., Los Angeles, goods, wares and merchandise purchased in 1931,	235.00	
dentist Dr. Raymond Beebe, Medico Dental Bldg., Los Angeles, Cal., for professional services, in 1931,	60.00	
E. T. Remmen, 119 N. Central, Glendale, Cal., for professional services in 1932,	35.00	
Dr. Maxwell Fields, 1051 Roosevelt Bldg., Los Angeles, Cal., for professional services in 1931,	140.00	
Roth Furniture Co., 8649 Hollywood Blvd., Los Angeles, Cal., goods, wares and merchandise in 1932,	34.15	
Wolf's Market, 8656 Sunset Blvd., Los Angeles, Cal., goods, wares and merchandise purchased in July and August, 1932,	93.77	
Mildred Schneider, 1325 Redondo Blvd., Los Angeles, Cal., for services rendered in May and June, 1932,	118.00	
Pacific Patrol, 1717 N. Highland, for services rendered on June 1, 1932, at Los Angeles, Cal.	5.00	
Mrs. Karl Biehl, 18 W. 71st, New York, N.Y., for room rent in 1926,	150.00	
Mrs. Charles Rowland, c/o Albert Andrews, 154-35 Tenth Ave., Beechhurst, Whitestone, N.Y., for personal loan in 1926,	150.00	
Collector of Internal Revenue, Federal Building, Los Angeles, California; Income tax for 1931,	$ 65.56	
Lulu Schubert, 1215 Lodi Place, Los Angeles, Cal.; Services rendered during two years last past,	700.00	
4　W.W.F. Cavanaugh, c/o Wendell P. Hubbard, 510 S. Spring 5　　St., Los Angeles, Calif. 6　　Any liability of any kind whatsoever, arising out of 　　the execution of that certain lease for one year from 7　　October 21, 1931, between M.T. Willard and Sadie V. 　　Willard, lessors, and Bela Lugosi, the bankrupt here- 8　　in, lessee, covering that certain dwelling house and 　　its appurtenances situated at 2643 Creston Drive, 9　　Hollywood, California, and more particularly describ- 　　ed as Lot 13, Block 5, Tract 7,011, Sheets 1 to 6 in- 10　clusive of Maps, in the office of the County Recorder 　　of Los Angeles County, California; said Tract being 11　sometimes known as "Carlton Terrace", which such lease 　　is purported as having been assigned to the plaintiff 12　in that certain action in the Municipal Court of the 　　City of Los Angeles, County of Los Angeles, State of 13　California, entitled "W.W.F. Cavanaugh, Plaintiff, vs. 　　Bela Lugosi, Defendant", being numbered on the records 14　and files of said Court as No. 301253. Said bankrupt 　　admits that he executed said lease and occupied said 15　premises for a period of said term, but alleges that 　　said lease was cancelled by mutual agreement of the 16　parties thereto and that he thereupon surrendered said 　　premises to the owners thereof.	Undetermined	
17　W.W.F. Cavanaugh, c/o Wendell P. Hubbard, 510 S. Spring 　　St., Los Angeles, Calif. 18　Any liability for rent on basis of month to month 　　tenancy by reason of occupancy of above premises.	Amount owing, if any, undetermined	
Total	$ 3731.06	

Bela Lugosi
Petitioner

An excerpt from Bela Lugosi's bankruptcy papers dated *October 1932* (courtesy of Frank J. Dello Stritto).

Paramount had apparently caught wind of Bela's desperate straits, dropped George Barbier, and signed Lugosi. The deal: $750 per week for a week and one day's work—total, $875 for the picture. It was an insulting fee for a star. It was especially humbling, since Paramount had publicized that newcomer Kathleen Burke was earning $1000 for her work.

Lugosi had little choice. He accepted the part, approaching it with all his usual enthusiasm. He'd give a brilliant, tormented, almost Expressionistic performance that no other actor in Hollywood could have matched—and his first scene would be a show-stopper.

"Are We Not Men?"

The imagery is magnificent: The Beast Men congregation, hurrying from the jungle to partake in the horrific ritual. A bonfire burns, with the creatures gathered around it.

A gong sounds and Moreau appears, saving Lota from the Sayer of the Law's carnal clutches. Laughton appears a god, looming over this fiery pit of Hell, where the demonic beings he's created via vivisection bow and pray before him.

"What is the Law?" demands Moreau, cracking his whip.

"Not to run on all fours," chants the Sayer of the Law. "*That* is the Law. Are we not men?"

"Are we not men?" the Beast Men drone.

Erle C. Kenton filmed this scene on the Paramount Ranch, the night so cold that you can see Lugosi's breath as he speaks. (Or is it Lugosi's cigar smoke? He often inhaled deeply before a scene was filmed.)

Laughton raises his whip with pride and power: "What is the Law?"

"Not to eat meat. *That* is the law. Are we not men?"

The Beast Men repeat the litany.

"Not to spill blood—*that* is the Law. Are we not men?"

There were also extras, and Paramount hired sometimes as many as 25 at a time—earning anywhere from $7.50 to $15 per day. The legend is that Buster Crabbe, Alan Ladd and original-choice-for-Parker Randolph Scott were among the horrid posse, but it's hard to prove or disprove. The hair and makeup are so heavy that Paramount's the Marx Brothers could be down there.

The eerie episode still packs a wallop—*Island of Lost Souls'* magnificently blasphemous High Mass. Lugosi's Sayer of the Law, back-lit by the bonfire, evokes a hairy, rock star–style priest, his horrid hymn echoed by a dope-crazed choir. As such, it's perhaps not surprising that the episode inspired much later musical homages. New Wave band Devo sang "Jocko Homo," with the lyrics "Are We Not Men," on the 1978 album *Question: Are We Not Men? Answer: We Are Devo!* Hard Rock band Van Halen included the song "House of Pain" on its album *1984*.[31]

For the Sayer of the Law and his Beast Men band, the beat truly went on.

"Do You Know What It Means to Feel Like God?"

After the ritual in the jungle, Moreau sends Lota to her lair and merrily gives Parker a grand tour, gesturing with his whip, showing off how he's accelerated Evolution, proud of his giant, tree-sized asparagus stalk. He presents his caged animals, and delivers a line that Quebec would cut:

> *Man is the present climax of a long process of organic evolution. All animal life is tending toward the human form.*

Moreau eventually shows Parker an animal man moaning in the midst of surgery. In the tradition of classic horror, the romantic lead is no match for the star villain, and Arlen—while a good actor—is no match for Laughton as he responds to what he sees in the laboratory:

> **ARLEN** (outraged): *Of all things vile!*
> **LAUGHTON** (super cool): *Mr. Parker, spare me these youthful horrors, please.*

Indeed, Laughton at this point, caught up in his role, becomes increasingly, perversely peculiar: He languishes on an operating table, effeminately crossing his legs, striking a Dietrich pose. Then, in close-up, Laughton delivers this zinger about his Beast Men with the style of a giddy Weimar Berlin cabaret emcee:

> *Oh, it takes a long time and infinite patience to make them talk. [Giggles] Someday, I'll create a woman, and it will be easier!*

Moreau shows his "less successful" Beast Men at work on a treadmill to provide power to the laboratory.[32] Then, with quiet, almost whispered pride, and in a moodily lit close-up, Laughton says *Island of Lost Souls'* most famous line:

> *Mr. Parker—do you know what it means to feel like God?*

As previously noted, the MPPDA suggested this line be cut. Paramount fought for it. On October 3, 1932, Tom Baily of Paramount wrote to Col. Joy at the MPPDA, citing Joy's objection that the line "would be censorable in many spots":

> *It is necessary to the sense of the scene that Dr. Moreau, in his fanaticism, believe that he is the equal of the Creator Himself, inasmuch as the whole theme of the picture is that of the would-be Creator, who is himself destroyed by his fantastic creations. It is very important that we get the equivalent of our line in the picture.*
>
> *I would appreciate it if you would suggest an alteration that would still retain the meaning of the line and pass the more critical boards.*

On October 5, Geoffrey Shurlock of the MPPDA wrote this memo:

> *Discussed this matter with Mr. Baily over the telephone. Our suggestion was that they do not try to juggle words in this case, but use the line in question honestly and sincerely, and let it take its chances with the censor boards.*

The line indeed took its chances—and Maryland, Massachusetts, Pennsylvania, Quebec and Australia cut it. It's intriguing to compare the assured sense of pride and wonder with which Laughton delivers the famous line with Colin Clive's quivering, hysterical delivery of *Frankenstein's* "In the name of God! Now I know what it feels like to *be* God!" It's also perhaps interesting to note that, as teenagers, Laughton and Clive had simultaneously attended Stonyhurst, an all-male Jesuit preparatory school in England. In fact, they were both in the school orchestra—Laughton played the violin, Clive the clarinet.[33]

Two Stonyhurst-educated actors ... two different approaches to delivering a blasphemous line of dialogue.

By now, an epically twisted allegory has formed. Laughton, in his white suit and satanic little beard, is an immaculately evil Lucifer … and Parker and Lota are the jolly Satan's own Adam and Eve. Hollywood has rarely (if ever) come up with so mad a metaphor for the Creation Story (and even long-suffering humanity) as it did with *Island of Lost Souls*. Moreau describes his procreation plan to Montgomery; Pennsylvania, Australia, Quebec and British Columbia cut the dialogue, including the line regarding Parker: "Wouldn't it be a great loss to science if he left for Apia in the morning?"

The next morning, Moreau and Parker find the sloop on which Parker was to sail away has been destroyed. Laughton is all wide-eyed innocence, betraying his guilt to the audience with a smirk and wink.

The great experiment will proceed. If all goes Moreau's way, bestiality will blossom in his tropical Paradise—and a spawn of human male and panther female will come into the light in his jungle Garden of Eden.

Intermission

> If I do any more pictures, I want to get as far away from Panther Women as possible.
>
> —Kathleen Burke[34]

The Fall of 1932—Hollywood Horror was amok.

Boris Karloff was starring in Universal's *The Mummy*, pursuing his nubile reincarnated love (Zita Johann); he was also doing retakes and revisions for MGM's *The Mask of Fu Manchu*, presiding over snakes, crocodiles and spectacular torture devices. At Warner Brothers, Fay Wray was smashing Lionel Atwill's wax face (in Technicolor) in *Mystery of the Wax Museum*, and on her days off, donning a blonde wig to cavort with King Kong at RKO.

A Kathleen Burke autograph (from the Roger Hurlburt Collection).

At Paramount, *Island of Lost Souls* was winning the prize as Hollywood's most sexed-up horror film-in-the-works. Perhaps inevitably, the shocker was taking a toll on the emotions of its makers.

Laughton, enjoying himself, was "charming" on the set, as Richard Arlen remembered. A visitor to the studio, appropriately, was Laughton's friend, British scientist Julian Huxley, grandson of biologist T.H. Huxley, Darwin's major public champion. This movie, however, was getting to Laughton. He was a great animal lover and the very concept of vivisection nauseated him. The hirsute animal men were also greatly disturbing him, and he developed a hair phobia.

"Each horror and monster had more hair than the one before," lamented Laughton. "Hair was all over the place. I was dreaming of hair! I even thought I had hair in my food."[35]

Meanwhile, Erle C. Kenton so got into the spirit of the show that he dressed in a white suit similar to Laughton's and began extravagantly acting out Laughton's role for him.[36] It must have been a sight to see a stocky man resembling Teddy Roosevelt doing a Charles Laughton impersonation. Laughton, meanwhile, bore up with the indignity of a former Keystone Cop showing him how to portray Dr. Moreau.

Keeping to himself was Bela Lugosi, facing such real-life horrors as mistress Lulu Schubert (who publicly referred to herself as his "housekeeper"). Lulu added to Bela's bankruptcy woes by demanding two years' back salary: $700.[37]

Kathleen Burke gave it her all. In interviews, she said she liked malted milks and spinach (not necessarily together). She opined that movie stars are "like other people, but more dressed up." She confessed she found it a challenge to play a scene to "a blinding light or a grinning electrician." She posed for publicity pictures with Laughton, Arlen and Palooka the baby lion. She also claimed, apparently sincerely, that as soon as *Island of Lost Souls* was finished, she was heading for the hills "to go mountain lion–hunting."[38]

Paramount had other plans for Burke. They announced that she would embark on a personal appearance tour to promote *Island of Lost Souls* openings, including a visit to her hometown of Chicago. The idea horrified the starlet:

> *I've never been on the stage in my life, and I know I'm going to be scared to death—trip over carpets, fall into the footlights or the bass drum or something. But, of course, it's an honor, and I'm going to do my best.*[39]

Alas, when genuine trouble erupted on the set, Kathleen was the cause.

Glen Rardin, Kathleen's Chicago boyfriend who had taken the picture she submitted for the contest, came to Hollywood. Rardin was a tall fellow, a former University of Indiana football player, with sleek dark hair and matinee idol mustache. Possibly because he realized how frightened Kathleen was at Paramount, he began following her to work each day, which was against the rules. *The Chicago Daily Tribune*, rooting for its hometown gal and her swain, reported:

> *Miss Burke isn't wearing an engagement ring or making plans to get married in the near future. In return, the studio is laying off of remarks or suggestions to her about not seeing so much of her boyfriend....*
>
> *Rardin's frequent visits to Miss Burke on the set and the couple's meetings after working hours late at night were noted with interest, but not friendly interest, by some of the representatives of the studio and as the movie studios are noted less for their tact and more for their bluntness, it was suggested to Rardin that he stay away from the set, and moreover, that he not see the girl friend for a soda or a midnight snack after working hours, because she might do the morrow's acting assignment better.*

Miss Burke's retort was short and snappy, and Rardin now continues to be welcome around the studio and elsewhere in the young actress' company.[40]

Yet things erupted. Wildly jealous Rardin returned to the set at least one too many times ... and got into a fistfight with Erle C. Kenton!

Paramount encouraged Rardin to go the hell home to Chicago, at least until filming was over, but he remained, raving to Kathleen that Hollywood was a hell-hole, a town of "morons" (his preferred word) and pagans. There was, perhaps, some truth in what he professed during this booming era of pre–Code sensuality. For example, Verna Hillie, now a member of the Paramount lot, remembered:

Charles Laughton? Terrible! Frightening! Laughton was lascivious! The joke at Paramount was, "If you get on the set, and they're not shooting, look at Laughton—because he's got his hands deep in his pockets." And it was true!

"This Time I'll Burn Out All the Animal in Her!"

The moment arrives the audience has been waiting for: the kiss.

The scene begins with all the lush sensuality that was Paramount's trademark. Parker and Lota ... seated by the pool inside Moreau's villa. Rippling water ... beautiful reflections. Lota leans against Parker, like a nestling cat. In one take, Burke's legs slightly part, probably accidentally, definitely provocatively. The shot couldn't appear in the movie, but Paramount made sure to use the eye-opener outtake in the *Lost Souls* trailer.

She all but meows ... and they kiss.

Audiences, of course, know that the All-American hero is smooching with a Panther Woman. Parker doesn't. However, his face contorts. Guilt, because of his engagement to Ruth? Repulsion, because of what he tasted and sensed in that kiss? None of the censor boards cut the scene—odd, in that Parker has just passionately kissed a panther.

Then we see Lota's nails ... becoming claws. Parker's shock ... Lota's humiliation. Arlen, and Burke especially, play this raw realization beautifully. Edward Parker realizes what Moreau had hoped for, and storms off to confront the monster, who he finds calmly sipping tea.

> **ARLEN** (incensed): *Moreau, you don't deserve to live!*
> **LAUGHTON** (calmly): *I beg your pardon?*

Moreau confesses that Lota is his "most nearly perfect creation." Laughton's silky, seductive voice now provides the purring ... "loving, mating, having children ... the possibilities that presented themselves...."

Parker punches Moreau, knocking him to the floor. Pennsylvania, British Columbia, Quebec, Australia and Paramount's 1941 re-release cut Moreau's entire speech.

This is followed by a horrific highlight: Anguished Lota is at her vanity table, with her mirror and perfume bottles, staring in agony at her beast flesh claws. The scene's wicked intensity is still potent, even after 88 years, as Moreau enters with Montgomery and roughly examines her hands. He drags her to her bed.

"The stubborn beast flesh," bemoans Laughton, "creeping back."

But there's hope: Lota is crying. A *human* emotion!

"This time I'll burn out *all* the animal in her!" exults Laughton.

Lota writhes like a trapped animal, backing against the wall, her arms stretched at her side, becoming—was there ever any doubt in this wildly subversive film?—Panther Woman as Christ symbol.

"I'll keep Parker here," rejoices Moreau. "He's already attracted. Time and monotony will do the rest!"

Laughton laughs triumphantly, insanely. Kathleen Burke weeps pitifully, heartbreakingly.

Fade-out.

Ruth's Semi-Strip, Moreau's Unspeakable Plan, and the Censor Cuts Increase

Pig Man spies a couple arriving in a boat: Ruth and Captain Donahue, the latter played by Paul Hurst (best-remembered as the Yankee looter shot in the face by Scarlett O'Hara in *Gone with the Wind*). "One like Lota!" squeals Pig Man of Ruth—except Ruth is a blonde, without any beast flesh creeping back.

Leila Hyams enjoys the distinction of starring in Hollywood's two most notorious pre–Code horrors. As for the aforementioned *Freaks*, she recalled that the Bearded Lady, Olga Roderick, "went Hollywood." When Olga arrived at MGM, her beard was gray; by the time she shot her first scene, she'd dyed the beard black—and marcelled it.

Ruth's arrival, although not on the original schedule for the Catalina location shoot, was obviously filmed there, presumably with Leila Hyams and a double for Paul Hurst in the beautifully photographed long shot. Ouran and Gola get a gander at Ruth, machismo erupts, and they fight. (In the wrestling ring, it would have been "The German Oak" vs. "Ali Baba.") Ouran triumphs.

A stunning visual follows: Laughton's Moreau, in his villa, leaning on what appears to be a cockeyed cross. The superbly composed shot accents Moreau's blasphemy as Laughton appears a portrait of Lucifer himself, casually posing with the apex of Christian iconography. Amazingly, based on the evidence, no censor of the era cut it.

Ruth and Parker reunite, hug, kiss. Ouran gapes lustfully at Ruth. And a new despicable idea lights up in Moreau's mad brain: If Parker won't mate with Lota, maybe Ouran will rape Ruth!

"I may not need Parker," Moreau says casually to Montgomery—a line cut by the British Columbia censor.

A candlelight dinner. Moreau mentions that the natives on the island are vegetarians and don't eat "long pig."[41] Ruth's presence has stirred up the Beast Men in the jungle.

"They *are* restless tonight!" says Laughton who, as Moreau, appears increasingly exhilarated by the danger and its riotous carnal possibilities.

Ruth goes upstairs to bed. She undresses. Hyams performs a candlelight semi-striptease, sitting in her slip, removing her high heels and stockings—a peep-show left alone by the censors. The hot-and-bothered Ouran makes his way up a tree, only to have Australia's censor cut the scenes of him peeking through Ruth's window.

The semi-clad Ruth screams. Parker runs to her rescue and fires at Ouran, who was breaking through the barred window. Ouran flees. Moreau explains to Montgomery his hope that Ouran will attack Ruth. Montgomery protests, "You're insane to even think of it!" The censors in Pennsylvania, Kansas, British Columbia and Quebec agreed: They considered Paramount insane to have these lines in the movie, and cut them.

Parker, Ruth and Captain Donahue decide to flee in the night. Donahue, going ahead to get his crew, shoots a Beast Man who acrobatically manages to die standing on his head. Moreau orders Ouran to kill Donahue, but nobody knew it in Quebec: The censor cut the scene. In the Beast Men's village, the cry arises that Ouran has spilled blood. Lugosi's Sayer of the Law at first tries to keep order, but Ouran insists Moreau *told* him to spill blood (and he had, in lines cut by the New York censor). Blood has spilled. The Law is broken.

Meanwhile, outside the villa, Laughton's Moreau listens to the rising fervor in the jungle, clearly masochistically aroused by the chance of the Beast Men going on a rape and carnage rampage.

"They're more than usually restless tonight!" says Laughton. Then he mischievously asks Parker, Ruth and Montgomery "Where's Captain Donahue?" He smiles. In the shadows, he appears to have his hands in his pockets.

Climax

If Captain Donahue can die, Dr. Moreau can die....

As if from the Abyss, the Pit, the roaring, growling Beast Men arise, hellbent on destroying Moreau's law and spilling his blood. Laughton's Moreau goes to the village to control them—too late. The star is a whirlwind with his whip, but still the monsters he'd created come. In a crowd-pleasing moment, M'ling, the faithful dog, fights to save Moreau. He's savagely slaughtered.

Lugosi's Sayer of the Law, leading the creatures, passionately howls the classic line with unforgettable ferocity:

> "You *made* us in the House of Pain.... *Not* men! *Not* beasts! *Things!*"

"*Things!*" chant the Beast Men, and *Island of Lost Souls* explodes in all its nightmarish power. The horrid chanting, the close-ups of creeping beast flesh, and one of the most livid images of all: a close shot of a beast man's hoof. The creatures light torches, an echo from *Frankenstein*, in which the torch-bearing villagers chased the Monster—here, the Monster is Moreau. The charge against the villa is tremendous, but Chicago moviegoers didn't see it: The censor cut it.

The shots of the "lost souls" scaling the wall provide a quick, infamous blooper: One of the Beast Men sets afire the wig of the Beast Man in front of him. The offender quickly pats out the smoking wig.

Parker, Ruth, Montgomery and Lota flee to Captain Donahue's boat. Ouran pursues them. Lota, realizing it, pursues Ouran. In another crowd-pleasing vignette, Lota leaps from a tree, a hellcat, attacking Ouran with her reverting claws. She kills him, but she's been fatally mauled in the fight.

"You ... go back ... to sea," says the Panther Woman, dying in Parker's arms, having sacrificed herself to save him.

Revolution is amok in the House of Pain. The bloodthirsty Beast Men gang up on Moreau in his laboratory.

"Little knives!" grins Lugosi.

They smash the glass of a case of surgical instruments. The revenge is poetically appropriate: The creatures Moreau created force him onto an operating table—*they* will vivisect *him*! As Karl Struss recalled:

> *I had a subjective camera shot there again, as in* Dr. Jekyll and Mr. Hyde, *when the evil doctor is murdered by the creatures on the island, and he looks up and sees the vivisectional instruments over him in a kind of forest of steel.*[42]

The shot was apparently trimmed from the original release print. Nevertheless, Laughton has one more racy trick up his white coat sleeve. As the Beast Men carve into him, he explodes into rising, perverse laughter ... as if a lover is tickling him in bed ... as if soaring to a sexual climax. Laughton's mad laughter rises to insane ecstasy.

Amazingly, the perverse twist drew no censorship cuts—at least during the original release. But when Great Britain finally passed *Island of Lost Souls* in 1958, after a 25-year ban, the censor cut Laughton's entire death scene.

"Don't look back," says Montgomery as he, Parker and Ruth row away in the night. Dr. Moreau's tropical Garden of Eden-Kingdom of Hell is spectacularly going up in flames, apocalyptically destroying the "lost souls," cremating Moreau's vivisected corpse and Lota's carcass. The music swells triumphantly.

Island of Lost Souls enters into Hollywood Horror legend and lore.

*   *   *

On Halloween, appropriately, the *Chicago Daily Tribune* had announced that Kathleen Burke and Glen Rardin, her pugnacious Chicago boyfriend, had become engaged. As such, "the Panther Woman" finished *Island of Lost Souls* as a bride-to-be. Paramount picked up its option on her contract.

The film wrapped in early November. Bela Lugosi worked extra days beyond his original deal and earned about double the $875 he originally was to receive.

Laughton soon went home to England, starring in *The Private Life of Henry VIII* for Alexander Korda. For that film, he won the 1933 Best Actor Academy Award. He actually deserved a nomination for his Dr. Moreau. However, by the time the Academy made its 1933 choices, Hollywood, and much of the world, considered *Island of Lost Souls* a vile disaster.

Part Three: Promotion, Release and Censorship

> Island of Lost Souls: ...*Three cheers for the foreign countries who have banned this picture, and shame on us for allowing this to be shown anywhere. Words fail me ... putrid.... It actually sickened some of our patrons.*
> —J.J. Hoffman, Plainview Theatre, Plainview,
> Nebraska, general patronage[43]

Thursday, December 8: Twenty days after Fredric March won an Academy Award for Paramount's *Dr. Jekyll and Mr. Hyde*, James Wingate of the MPPDA wrote to Paramount, approving *Island of Lost Souls*. He cordially warned the studio that state censors would likely cut Moreau's "Do you know what it means to feel like God?" Nevertheless, the censor added, "Incidentally, we enjoyed this picture thoroughly, and hope that it will meet with the success which it certainly deserves."

Also on December 8: Erle C. Kenton shot a retake of the scene of Leila Hyams' Ruth with Hans Steinke's Ouran.

December 10: The unsigned critic for *The Hollywood Filmograph*, after seeing a *Lost Souls* preview in Pasadena, published a lengthy, all-hailing review:

> *All that can be done in the way of horror pictures has now definitely been done.* Island of Lost Souls *tops all the rest. It out-Frankensteins* Frankenstein, *and relegates all other thrillers to the class of children's bedtime stories....*
>
> *What the general reaction to this picture will be, one cannot with certainty say. Personally, I am for it 100 percent. In other words, I ate it up and yelled for more.... I should say approximately half of the Pasadena preview audience agreed with me in this stand. The other half divided into two sections. One section left the theatre during the preview, grunting and denouncing. The other remained, hair standing on end, also grunting and denouncing, but fascinated....*
>
> *Charles Laughton ... makes a grand character of Dr. Moreau. Next in line of credit, I would place Kathleen Burke, the much publicized "Panther Woman." In a terrifically difficult role, this newcomer performs with striking charm. ... The leader of the Beast Men, who resembles Jo-Jo, the Dog-Faced Boy of circus memory, is more than ably portrayed by Bela Lugosi, who bellows from behind foot-long hair which sprouts eagerly from his face....*
>
> *Erle C. Kenton did a splendid job of directing....* Island of Lost Souls *is like a nightmare.... There will probably not be another picture like it in a decade.... If you want horror, here is your dish!*

Bela Lugosi added this review to his scrapbook. One wonders how much he knew about Jo-Jo the Dog-Faced Boy (aka Fedor Jeftichew, 1868–1904), who came from Russia to America via P.T. Barnum in 1884, the year Lugosi turned two years old.

Friday, December 23: *Island of Lost Souls* opened at the Roosevelt Theatre in Chicago, Kathleen Burke's hometown. "Mae Tinee," reviewer for the *Chicago Daily Tribune*, wrote of Burke:

> *She hasn't much to do other than crouch and run and open her eyes wide, but she is agile and uncamera-conscious and very well-suited to the part she plays.*

Thursday, December 29: The annual Winter Meeting of the American Association for the Advancement of Science took place in Atlantic City. Dr. William K. Gregory spoke on evolution, sounding as if he were publicizing *Island of Lost Souls*:

> *For untold millions of years, the long line of vertebrates that led toward men were unblushing thieves and robbers. Even now, the human face beneath its smiling mask carries the old mammalian trap set with sharp teeth. Such being the case, it's no wonder that we suffer from grafters, racketeers and gunmen. The wonder is not that so many of us find ourselves in prison, but that any of us have ever learned to keep out.*[44]

Saturday, January 7, 1933: *Island of Lost Souls* opened at the Paramount Theatre in Los Angeles, complete with a stage show. The *Los Angeles Times* critic blasted it as "[h]orrible to the point of repugnance," but praised its atmosphere. As for Laughton: "[Y]ou dare not laugh," wrote the critic; "he might hear you, and then... Well, better not think about that."

The film took in $23,000 in its first (and only) week at the Paramount,[45] where the high had been 1931's *Beloved Bachelor* ($41,000) and the low 1932's *Tomorrow and Tomorrow* ($7,500).

Wednesday, January 11: *Island of Lost Souls* opened at Broadway's Rialto Theatre. *The New York Herald-Tribune* critic wrote that the film had the quality of "a hangover," saluted Laughton, and facetiously claimed he'd never met a Panther Woman before, so he couldn't accurately assess Kathleen Burke's interpretation. Nevertheless, he noted that "her portrayal of the wistful half-woman ... possesses a certain bewildered, sad-eyed quality that manages to be rather touching."

A trade advertisement for *Island of Lost Souls*. Note that the Panther Woman has become the talisman of the movie.

The movie took in $26,100 in its first week at the Rialto,[46] where the recent high had been 1932's *Shanghai Express* ($64,600) and the low a re-release double bill of *Dracula* and *Hell's Angels* ($4500). *Island of Lost Souls* did $14,500 in its second week there, and $12,400 in its third.

Variety, meanwhile, critiqued that the title should be *Island of Lost Freaks* and panned Kathleen Burke: "Girl is too much like a girl."[47]

Paramount canceled the plan to send Burke on a personal appearance tour, probably due to her severe stage fright. Instead, the studio cast her in *Murders in the Zoo*, in which Lionel Atwill, as her insanely jealous spouse, tosses the erstwhile Panther Woman into a pond of lip-smacking alligators. Atwill and Burke also share a very hot pre–Code "love" scene in which, on camera, the wild-eyed Atwill nearly grabs her left breast. In Atwill's clutches, Burke looks and sounds genuinely frightened.

As *Island of Lost Souls* worked its way across the U.S., the state censors, as noted in Part II, had their wicked way with it, making extensive cuts. However, the real outcry would come abroad. *Island of Lost Souls* set off a worldwide censorship firestorm—indeed, the following countries actually banned it! To list the countries in alphabetical order:

- Germany
- Great Britain
- Holland
- Hungary
- India
- Italy
- Latvia
- The Netherlands
- New Zealand
- Singapore
- South Africa
- Tasmania

Its enemies were not subtle: Great Britain, for instance, attacked the film as "Against Nature." H.G. Wells, not surprisingly, despised *Island of Lost Souls* and was delighted by the British ban, which was still in effect when Wells died in 1946 and for 12 years afterward. As he told *Screenland* magazine in 1935:

> *If you want to know, I think* The Island of Dr. Moreau *as a film was terrible—terrible! You can print that, if you want to....*
>
> *...[M]y story was handled miserably. With all respect to Charles Laughton, who is a splendid actor, and to others concerned in the making of this moving picture, ...I must say that it was handled with a complete lack of imagination.*
>
> *The translation from the book to the film was so free that it might almost have been another story. The characters were not true. The horror element, for which I have never particularly aimed, prevailed throughout. No subtlety was used in the creation of the dreadful atmosphere. The whole thing was so ridiculously obvious that I must repeat—it was miserable.*[48]

Arthur Mayer, who masterminded the Panther Woman Contest, claimed 20 years later that the film had been "a resounding dud." This wasn't quite accurate, but the film didn't live up to box office expectations and its worldwide bans certainly limited its profits—if there were any.

The new Production Code came into effect in mid–1934. In 1935, the year of the release of such Code-defying horror classics as *Bride of Frankenstein, The Raven* and *Mad Love,* Paramount wanted to reissue *Island of Lost Souls*, but Joseph Breen refused to permit it, due to the film's "Extreme Horror." In 1941, Paramount tried again, and Breen replied:

> *[T]he blasphemous suggestion of the character, played by Charles Laughton, wherein he presumes to create human beings out of animals; the obnoxious suggestion of the attempt of these animals to mate with human beings, and the ... excessive gruesomeness and horror ... all these tend to*

make the picture quite definitely repulsive and not suitable for screen entertainment before mixed audiences.

Still, Paramount was eager to get the 1941 re-release certificate—so the studio agreed to make 14 (!) deep surgical cuts. They included:

1. Moreau's lines regarding Lota, "*Will she be attracted? Is she capable of being attracted? Has she a woman's emotional impulses?*"

2. Parker's line, "*They're vivisecting a human being!*"

3. Moreau's line, "*Man is in the present climax of a long process of organic revolution. All animal life is tending toward the human form.*"

4. Close-ups of the Beast Man on the table in the House of Pain, and this dialogue:
   MOREAU: *You're convinced that this thing on the table isn't human?*
   PARKER: *Its cries are human.*
   MOREAU: *These are my creations.*

5. Moreau's line, "*Mr. Parker, do you know what it means to feel like God?*"

6. This dialogue exchange:
   MOREAU: *I wonder how much of Lota's animal origin is still alive, how nearly perfect a woman she is. It's possible I may find out, with the aid of Mr. Parker.*
   MONTGOMERY: *You won't have much time if he leaves for Apia in the morning.*
   MOREAU: *Wouldn't it be a great loss to science if he left for Apia in the morning?*

7. The non-italicized portion of Parker's line: "*Those creatures out there in the jungle were horrible enough,* but to have created a thing as tragic as *that girl.*"

8. Parker's dialogue, "*An animal with a woman's emotions, a woman's heartbreak, a woman's suffering.*"

9. Moreau's dialogue: "*Lota is my most nearly perfect creation. I was thinking of taking her as Exhibit A on a triumphal return to London … but I wanted to prove how completely she was a woman … whether she was capable of loving, mating and having children….*"

10. Moreau's line, "*She is human!*"

11. Moreau's dialogue: "*I'll keep Parker here. He's already attracted. Time and monotony will do the rest.*"

12. Moreau's line, "*I may not need Parker.*"

13. What the censor called a "Shortened undressing of Leila Hyams."

14. Montgomery's dialogue: "*You didn't want it to happen, of course? That isn't what you meant when you said that you might not need Parker?*"

Thusly, a vivisected version of *Island of Lost Souls* forlornly haunted movie theaters in 1941.

Part Four: Legacy

In 1981, my wife and I visited Elsa Lanchester at her home in Hollywood. It was the house where Charles Laughton had died of bone cancer on December 15, 1962, and I confess a fanboy thrill at realizing I was in the house where Dr. Moreau had lived with the Bride of Frankenstein.

Ms. Lanchester had been much amused by the censorship troubles of *Island of Lost Souls*, and Great Britain's objection that the film was "against nature."

"Of course, it's against nature," she said. "So's Mickey Mouse!"[49]

As *Island of Lost Souls* had lurked on TV's late shows, in various cut forms, there'd been later film rip-offs and two official remakes.[50] Yet the 1932 version appears secure as the official classic version of H.G. Wells' "exercise in youthful blasphemy."

As for several of the creative forces of *Island of Lost Souls:*

Director Erle C. Kenton directed Universal's *The Ghost of Frankenstein* (1942), *House of Frankenstein* (1944) and *House of Dracula* (1945). His later work included TV episodes of *Racket Squad*, *The Public Defender* and *The Texan*. He died in 1980 at the age of 83.

Cinematographer Karl Struss had a remarkable 40-year career; later credits included *The Fly* (1958) and episodes of TV's *My Friend Flicka*. He died in 1981 at the age of 95. In early 1978, Struss communicated by mail with Richard Bojarski, author of *The Films of Boris Karloff* and *The Films of Bela Lugosi*. Proudly remembering *Island of Lost Souls* as "one of my best photographic achievements," Struss wrote, "Erle Kenton was such a splendid director. ... I see him frequently. He is a brilliant artist." Asked specifically about Lugosi, he recalled the actor as "Splendid." Asked about Kathleen Burke, Struss provided his most vivid memory of the actress: "She handed me the Sixth Annual Golf Tournament Award in 1932, presented by David O. Selznick."[51]

And as for Kathleen Burke: After playing in *Island of Lost Souls*, she appeared in the aforementioned *Murders in the Zoo,* devoured by alligators. The notoriety of both films, the experience of playing off the thespic kinks of Laughton and Atwill, and the doomed-to-die portrayals must have taken a personal toll on Burke. One can also imagine the variety of aberrant fan mail the young actress received after these performances.

On February 25, 1933, she wed Glen Rardin at the San Fernando Mission, but they fought; he said her Hollywood pals were all "Morons" ("Morons Preferred by Panther Woman," read one headline reporting their marital discord), and the marriage fizzled. She stayed a while at Paramount, was memorable as a vamp in *The Lives of a Bengal Lancer* (1935), but left the studio, remarried, had a daughter, and left Hollywood soon thereafter. In 1940, she turned up in New York on the Biblical radio show *Light of the World,* did some stock theatrical work ... then vanished.

The former Panther Woman gave every evidence of trying to cover her beast flesh tracks. She returned to Chicago, married at least once more, and died from emphysema on April 9, 1980,[52] reportedly survived by her husband, daughter and mother. *The Hollywood Reporter*, running a notice on her death, wrote that she had died "in anonymity." Gail Patrick, her former Panther Woman rival, said:

> *The best thing that ever happened to me was not winning as the Panther Woman. I became good friends with Kathleen Burke, and that phrase came to haunt her and ruin her chances for better roles.*[53]

2011: Criterion released a restored Blu-ray version of *Island of Lost Souls*. I was privileged to write and narrate the audio commentary. It was an adventure as Criterion's sources conducted a virtual worldwide search for all the missing lines and shots to present the film as it originally appeared in 1932 before the mutilations began.

*   *   *

November 2018: The "Woolsey Fire" ravaged Agoura, California. In a Hollywood irony, the Paramount Ranch met the same fiery fate as Dr. Moreau's island, but 86 years later.

The ranch, first seeing service in 1927 and long a part of the National Park Service, had been, as previously mentioned, the site of *Lost Souls*' Beast Man village. The village's precise location had, of course, been lost to the ages. Nevertheless, it had been a bizarre treat for a disciple of the film to realize that somewhere on that ranch was the unhallowed ground where Charles Laughton had sounded the gong and cracked his whip, where Bela Lugosi had chanted the Litany of the Law, and where Kathleen Burke had emoted in her $25 costume.

No more.

It had been a site of one of the most haunting scenes of one of the most daring films of Hollywood's pre–Code era. And it was an episode that will always strike visceral responses in its viewers, most of whom have endured their own personal House of Pain … and have survived those long nights when the stubborn beast flesh seems to be creeping back.

Island of Lost Souls

Paramount, 1932. Director, Erle C. Kenton. Screenplay, Waldemar Young and Philip Wylie (based on the 1896 novel *The Island of Dr. Moreau* by H.G. Wells). Cinematographer, Karl Struss. Art Director, Hans Dreier. Makeup, Wally Westmore, Charles Gemora. Sound, M.M. Poggi, Loren L. Ryder. Special Photographic Effects, Gordon Jennings. Music, Arthur Johnston, Sigmund Krumgold. Assistant Director, Russel Mathews. Assistant Cameramen, Paul Cable, Cliff Shirpser, Fleet Southcott. Camera Operators, George T. Clemens, Otto Pierce. Casting, Fred A. Datig. Running time, 70 minutes.

Chicago opening, Roosevelt Theatre, December 23, 1932; Los Angeles opening, Paramount Theatre, January 7, 1933; New York opening, Rialto Theatre, January 11, 1933.

The Cast: Charles Laughton (Dr. Moreau), Richard Arlen (Edward Parker), Leila Hyams (Ruth Thomas), Bela Lugosi (The Sayer of the Law), Kathleen Burke (Lota), Arthur Hohl (Montgomery), Stanley Fields (Captain Davies), Paul Hurst (Donahue), Hans Steinke (Ouran), Tetsu Komai (M'ling), George Irving (The Consul), Harry Ezekian (Gola), Bob Kortman (Mr. Hogan), Buster Brodie (Pig Man), Charles Gemora (Gorilla on Pier), Rosemary Grimes (Samoan Girl), Joe Bonomo, Jack Burditte, Jules Cowles, John George, Julius Graubart, Otto Lederer, Robert Milasch, Constantine Romanoff, Duke York (Beast Men), Schlitze (Furry Beast),* Buster Crabbe, Alan Ladd, Randolph Scott (Beast Men).**

*Not confirmed.
**Not confirmed.

4

"A Sin Against the Holy Ghost!"

Early Drafts, Studio Politics and Censorship
Sagas of *Bride of Frankenstein*

*My son, this is indeed a sin against the Holy Ghost! A female monster! Are
you trying to create a race of devils to make war on God's creatures? They will
breed, these two! You will people the world with monsters!*
—Father Gerard, warning Henry Frankenstein
in John L. Balderston's script for *The Return of Frankenstein*[1]

January to March 1935.

Envy the wide-eyed visitor to Universal City, California, and the set of *Bride of Frankenstein*. Director James Whale, sardonic ringmaster of this three-ring circus of sex, horror and blasphemy, offered audacious attractions a-plenty … such as Karloff's Monster, crucified on a pole in a soundstage forest, the cinema's all-time *outré* Christ symbol.

How, in 1935 Hollywood, was this film ever being made?

Yet imagine, if you will, the irreverent Whale, in an alternate Universal universe, directing the following *Bride of Frankenstein* vignettes. All are from scrapped early drafts as the pre–Code era gave way to Joseph I. Breen, the newly vigilant Code, and the Roman Catholic Legion of Decency:

- The Monster peek-a-booing at a peasant couple making love in their cottage.
- The Monster violently smashing a statue of the Virgin Mary holding the Baby Jesus.
- The Monster, seeking body parts, furtively following a procession of nuns into their convent, causing, in the words of the script, "mad pandemonium."
- The Bride, after rejecting the sobbing Monster, going into a vampy "child bride" act as she tries to seduce Henry Frankenstein.
- The Monster pounding Henry and his wife Elizabeth to death with a giant pine tree branch.

These early drafts came complete with satellite characters, ranging from the lesbian circus couple of Emma (a lion tamer) and Fifi (a giantess), to Father Gerard, a devout priest who tried to perform an exorcism of blasphemous Henry Frankenstein.

Bride of Frankenstein, before and after its production, was a lightning rod for a censorship firestorm. Yet there was another aspect: The film came to pass during an explosively bitter civil war at Universal City, as Carl Laemmle Sr. stabbed Carl Laemmle Jr. in the back in as shocking an act of figurative filicide as the film colony had ever seen.

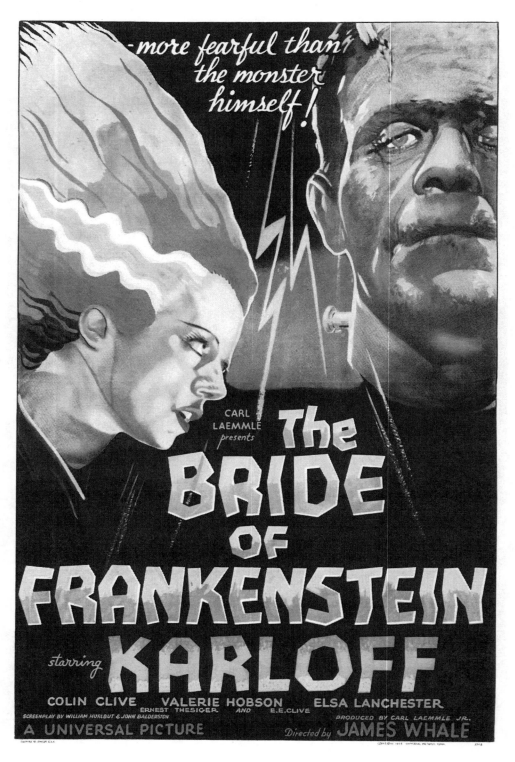

Poster for Universal's *Bride of Frankenstein*, 1935 (from the Jim Clatterbaugh Collection).

A candid shot of Boris Karloff, director James Whale, and cinematographer John J. Mescall, ready to go outrageous on *Bride of Frankenstein* (from the Jim Clatterbaugh Collection).

It's frightening to think how close things came to an eleventh hour aborting of what is largely considered the Golden Age of Horror's beloved masterpiece.

Part One: Pre-Production

We suggest this tag of the baby wetting its diapers ... should be modified under the vulgarity clause of the Code.
> —James Wingate, Association of Motion Picture
> Producers, letter to Universal regarding the script
> of *The Return of Frankenstein*, July 28, 1933

Evolution and Early Drafts

Thursday, June 1, 1933: It was a bad day for Universal: The Monster walked out.

After the sensation of *Frankenstein* in 1931, and his macabre triumphs in *The Old Dark House* and *The Mummy* in 1932, Karloff left the lot. Reason: the studio's refusal to pay the promised salary increase from $750 per week to $1250. Ruling this crazy mountain kingdom in the San Fernando Valley: Carl Laemmle Sr., Universal's 66-year-old founder, and Carl Laemmle Jr., its 25-year-old "Crown Prince." They'd exalted the star as "Karloff the Uncanny" on posters for *The Mummy* ... and, battered by the 1932 Depression loss of $1,250,283,[2] had pinned hopes for survival on an eventual sequel to *Frankenstein*.

Such a film without Karloff was unthinkable. Within 48 hours of his walk-out, the studio reported a "two-month leave of absence" for the star as negotiations opened for a new contract.

Monday, July 10: Harrison Carroll reported in the *Los Angeles Evening Herald Express*:

> *One of the outstanding monsters of last year's horror pictures is to roam again. Universal has signed Boris Karloff to make two films, the first to be* The Return of Frankenstein.... *He receives from the new deal a salary increase and plenty of time off to make pictures at other studios.... Production of the picture probably will entail the return of Colin Clive from London to play his original role....*

A looming problem for the *Frankenstein* sequel: a workable script. Robert Florey, who had originally adapted *Frankenstein* and had hoped to direct it before James Whale claimed it, tried to jump back on the bandwagon, submitting *The New Adventures of Frankenstein—The Monster Lives!* just after the original film was released. Universal rejected it.

Tuesday, July 25: Tom Reed, Universal writer whose credits included James Whale's *Waterloo Bridge* (1931) and contributing to the screenplay for Robert Florey's *Murders in the Rue Morgue* (1932), completed his script for *The Return of Frankenstein*. The scenario: The Monster escapes the burned mill; Henry Frankenstein marries Elizabeth, and the couple have a baby boy. Meanwhile, the Monster spies on a peasant family, and learns to read and speak. While hunting a wolf in the mountains, Henry meets his Monster, who demands a mate. To force Henry's cooperation, the Monster kills Henry's father and threatens to murder Elizabeth and their son. Henry begins stealing bodies from morgues and railroad accidents, and when his experiment fails, he tells the Monster he'll steal no more corpses.

The Monster then kills Elizabeth.

Frankenstein revives the Mate, who stirs to life, as horrific as the Monster himself. Climactically, Frankenstein uses "high-powered voltage" to zap the Mate and Monster. The latter drags Frankenstein into the electrical path; Monster, Mate and Monster Maker all perish.

Friday, July 28: James Wingate, of the Motion Picture Producers and Distributors Association of America (the MPPDA), which enforced the—at that time—very lax Production Code, responded to the script for *The Return of Frankenstein*, writing Universal executive Harry Zehner that it was "basically satisfactory," but advising "caution" regarding "gruesomeness."[3] Wingate also listed several "minor items" for deletion, including the expressions, "Thank God!" "God" and "Great God!" As for a scene in which the Monster ogled a peasant lass named Hertha as she swam in a lake, Wingate wrote:

> *Scenes E-14, E-20 and E-22: In this sequence, the girl should have some clothing on, to avoid being completely nude, under the Code.*

As for the Mate, Wingate added:

> *Scene I-6: Care will be needed with this scene of the creation of the female monster, to avoid any undue exposure.*

Wingate also made the aforementioned complaint about the baby and wet diapers; as a complete Tom Reed script isn't currently available, this "tag" remains a mystery.

At any rate, the project fell into limbo. James Whale disdained it, opining, "They've had a script made for a sequel, and it stinks to heaven." Junior Laemmle said that Kurt Neumann would direct it.

Wednesday, August 30: Karloff boarded a train to Arizona and its 119-degree sand dunes to play the religious lunatic Sanders in RKO's *The Lost Patrol*, directed by John Ford.[4] The role provided him a wildly baroque death scene: Having gone deliriously mad, he marches up a dune amidst Arab gunfire, scantily clad and carrying a makeshift cross, as if he's Christ going to Calvary.

Meanwhile, Junior Laemmle let loose two writers to adapt new and separate treatments for *The Return of Frankenstein*: Philip MacDonald[5] and Lawrence G. Blochman.

MacDonald had written the story "Patrol" on which *The Lost Patrol* was based. He concocted a story about Frankenstein creating a death ray and hoping to sell it to the League of Nations. The death ray resurrects the Monster, buried in the ruins of the burned windmill. The audience was to see a "moving thing" at the charred edge of a fallen mill beam:

> *The camera goes closer; the moving thing is a frightful travesty of a human arm. It is flecked white and black, the white being islands of unharmed flesh surrounded by the blackness of burning....*
>
> *Again, our viewpoint changes; to one further away. The rotting debris beneath the second beam seems imbued with life. It is moving.... Mercifully, we cannot, in the queer light of the ray, see very clearly. But we see enough. We see the half-burnt, half-mouldered form of the Monster....*

When Frankenstein learns that Elizabeth (his wife, and the mother of his son) is actually in love with her former swain Victor Moritz (played by John Boles in the 1931 film), he decides to kill himself, but first uses the death ray to kill the chained (and, in this version, mute) Monster. ("A frightful convulsion passes over the figure and then there seems to rush out of it a vivid, blinding flash...").

"I am sorry," Frankenstein says to the dead Monster. "My fault. All my fault." Then he himself walks into the death ray, leaving Elizabeth free to marry Victor. No "Mate" appeared in the treatment.

Blochman, a prolific detective storywriter, whipped up a far more sensational tale. Henry Frankenstein and Elizabeth are traveling incognito through the hills of Europe as puppeteers in a carnival, their puppets enacting the death of the Monster. The Monster shows up, lugs Frankenstein into the woods to a moonlit waterfall, and reveals to him the corpse of a young woman in the water. The implication: Create me a Mate, or this is what will happen to Elizabeth.

The pre–Code treatment has a dash of MGM's *Freaks*: its carnival repertoire includes Arnaldo, a sinister-looking magician; Sari, his assistant, a "shapely blonde" in pink silk tights who is carrying Arnaldo's child; and Siamese twins Meta and Greta. Then there's Emma and Fifi:

> *We see Emma, the lion tamer, a masculine looking woman with the shadow of a mustache on her upper lip, putting her arm affectionately around Fifi, the giantess. In the same tone she uses to address her lions, she boasts of how she beats her husband into submission whenever she sees him in Bratislava. Her tone is more tender as she tells Fifi of her general contempt for all men....*

Frankenstein agrees to create a female creature. The Monster raids funeral parlors for body parts. Also: "We see him following a bevy of nuns into a convent, converting the cloistered quiet into mad pandemonium."

One yearns to see how James Whale would have directed *that* episode!

Frankenstein hooks his wagon lab to a power line; a short circuit erupts and the Mate comes to life but, due to the short circuit, won't live long. The Monster, oblivious, passionately grabs her and runs off into the woods to commence the honeymoon. When she expires, he comes a-roaring back to the carnival:

> We see the Monster on a maniacal rampage, smashing windows, pulling doors from wagons, and uprooting tent poles. He finds the giantess and drags her by her hair past the animal cages. When Emma tries to interfere, the Monster drops the giantess, strangles the lion tamer, and, howling insanely, tears open the cages of the animals one by one....

This sets the stage for a climactic battle: Monster vs. lion. As the carnival folk watch in horror and the sexton rings the village church bell, the two creatures fight ... and "the lion triumphs." Henry and Elizabeth, free of the Monster, approach sunny Bratislava in their wagon.

The Blochman script had richly outlandish possibilities. In one scene, the Monster "laughs crazily" as he pounded out the same note over and over on a carnival calliope. Later, when he demanded Frankenstein create a Mate for him, the Monster made "queer sounds, like the purring of a cat." However, Universal presumably failed to take either of these treatments seriously; no full script evolved from either scenario.

Friday, September 22: John Ford completed location work on *The Lost Patrol*. When Karloff reported back to Universal, the studio still had no vehicle prepared for him. The Laemmles eventually loaned him to 20th Century to play anti–Semitic Count Ledrantz in the George Arliss epic *The House of Rothschild*.

Friday, November 17: Universal's *The Invisible Man*, starring Claude Rains, directed by James Whale, and scripted by R.C. Sherriff, opened at Broadway's Roxy. It was another horror hit.

Wednesday, February 28, 1934: Universal began shooting *The Black Cat* starring, as the credits proclaim them, KARLOFF and BELA LUGOSI.[6] Edgar G. Ulmer passionately directed this perversely silky saga of Satanism and necrophilia. This time the censor warned Universal on 20 points—especially the climax, where Lugosi skinned Karloff alive on a rack.[7]

Censorship was changing profoundly in Hollywood. Now leading the charge for the Production Code Administration (PCA, the strict enforcement arm of the MPPDA) was 43-year-old Joseph Ignatius Breen, a Catholic former journalist. Allied with the Catholic Church's Legion of Decency, Breen had vowed to scour what he called the "perverts" and "Paganism" of Hollywood.[8]

The facts of life were about to morph in the movies ... and set the stage for a bloody battle over the content of *The Return of Frankenstein*.

Sin City Universal

> *Cum grano salis.... Brutem fulmen.*
> —Boris Karloff, reciting the Latin prayers
> of the Black Mass in *The Black Cat* (1934)

Hollywood had sensually indulged itself in the pre–Code era. Waiting in the wings in early 1934 were Paramount's *The Scarlet Empress*, starring Marlene Dietrich as Catherine the Great as sex dominatrix; Warners had *Madame DuBarry*, boasting Dolores del

Rio as King Louis XV's mistress (here with a Mexican accent). Breen had battled both studios long and hard over these sex biopics, and it appeared the Catholic Church's Legion of Decency would spank both Dietrich's Catherine and del Rio's Madame with its big paddle: the dreaded "Condemned" rating.

A Catholic who knowingly attended a "Condemned" film was endangering his eternal soul. Tens of thousands had decided it wasn't worth it. Vigilante fervor was afire. Universal lacked a Dietrich or a del Rio, but "Uncle Carl" was worried nonetheless over Junior's selection of entertainment.

Thursday, May 3: The Black Cat premiered at Hollywood's Pantages Theatre, with Karloff and Lugosi present for the festivities. Junior Laemmle and Edgar G. Ulmer had ignored virtually all of Breen's 20 cuts, including the cockeyed cross looming over the altar of satanic high priest Karloff, and Lugosi skinning Karloff alive. Indeed, the skinning took on a blasphemous savagery: Karloff resembled the Devil in *The Black Cat*, and hanging on the rack, he evoked Lucifer Crucified.

For some mysterious reason—maybe because it was "only" a horror film—Breen had passed *The Black Cat*, and by some wacky miracle, it escaped the Legion's "Condemned" rating.

Friday, May 11: A big day at Universal. The studio awarded Karloff a new contract (*The Black Cat* had completed his two-picture pact), and James Whale started directing *One More River*.[9] Based on the John Galsworthy novel, the script concerned a sex sadist (Colin Clive) who beat his wife (Diana Wynyard) with a riding whip. Breen had responded with a storm of protests. Universal paid lip service; Whale cavalierly proceeded to shoot the film as he desired.

Tuesday, May 22: Variety panned *The Black Cat*'s skinning alive scene as "a truly horrible and nauseating bit of extreme sadism." This wasn't the type of publicity "Uncle Carl" wanted for Universal. Local censor boards attacked the movie with cuts and trims.

Thursday, June 14: "War Against Indecent Motion Pictures Taking Shape in Form of Catholic Boycott," headlined *The Baltimore Sun* with film critic Donald Kirkley writing:

> *A storm is brewing in this land and when it breaks in full force, certain Californians may be surprised and pained by its unprecedented fury.*

Sunday, June 17: "Film Producers Are Shaken by Widescope of Clean-up Effort" headlined *The Washington Post* with Edwin Schallert writing: "Hollywood is in the midst of the most serious crisis in its history." On the same date, 50,000 Catholics in Cleveland took the Legion of Decency pledge and threatened a "film boycott."

Tuesday, June 19: John L. Balderston, whose name had already appeared on the screen credits of *Dracula, Frankenstein* and *The Mummy,* turned in a revised script for *The Return of Frankenstein*. With Balderston's track record and input, Universal's Frankenstein sequel was finally on its way.

Maybe.

The John L. Balderston Script

> Monster *(astonished)*: God loves—me? *(He demands eagerly and violently beating his breasts)* Loves Frank-en-stein?
> —The Monster, just before his death in John L. Balderston's
> script for *The Return of Frankenstein*

Wednesday, June 27: Having produced *The Black Cat* about devil worship, now completing *One More River* about sex sadism, and with *The Return of Frankenstein* in fresh script form, Junior Laemmle launched *Imitation of Life*, based on Fannie Hurst's best-selling novel about the tragic friendship of a white woman and a black woman. The film started shooting this day, starring Claudette Colbert and Louise Beavers, with John Stahl directing. The budget: a walloping (for Universal) $565,750.[10] Controversy over the material abounded.

Monday, July 2: Universal began *Gift of Gab*, Karl Freund directing.[11] During the shoot, Karloff, in a black cape, top hat and fright wig, and Bela Lugosi, in a rakish cap and outfit, appeared briefly with other Universal actors as guest stars in a comedy skit.[12]

Tuesday, July 17: Breen, seeing the work print of *One More River*, demanded 30 cuts(!) before he'd grant a release certificate.[13] Meanwhile, James Whale, pleased that Universal had allowed him to direct *One More River*, had reconsidered directing the *Frankenstein* sequel.

Some features of the John L. Balderston script:

Prologue: Balderston provided the first draft of the opening whimsy in which Mary Shelley discusses her novel with Percy Shelley and Lord Byron.

Man of God: The script presented Father Gerard, the village priest, who wants to save Henry Frankenstein's ravaged soul.

Talking Monster: Balderston used Tom Reed's idea (which had originally been Mary Shelley's idea) of the Monster hiding near the cottage of a family—husband Eric, wife Hilda, child Hertha, and Eric's old, blind grandfather. It's here that the Monster learns to speak; he also learns about physical love by spying on Eric and Hilda while the couple is in bed (this was "Hollywood," not "Shelley"). The Monster hopes to befriend the family, but when little Hertha sees the Creature's visage and screams, the Monster goes berserk with an axe and wrecks the cottage, including a plaster statue of the Virgin Mary holding the baby Jesus.

Pleas for a Mate: The Monster calls himself "Frank-en-stein," and implores his creator:

> *Every man—every beast—has mate. Only Frank-en-stein alone.... Men will hate her as they hate me—but she not hate me, she not afraid. She love me, I love her.... You make her, I take her with me, far from all men—in mountains where no man live—in woods she live with me—we will never kill—never see you or any men again—no more hate—only love!*

Exorcism: As Frankenstein brings the Bride to life, Father Gerard devoutly tries to exorcise Henry, intoning Latin prayers ("*Retro me, Sathanas!* ...").

Monster Honeymoon: The Monster, as he promised, takes his Bride (described, incidentally, as wearing "a simple white garment that falls to her feet" and having a "cascade" of hair that "ripples down over her shoulders to the waist") to a cave ... but she too rejects him, screaming at his face and touch. He storms off, sobbing, and the Mate makes her way back to the laboratory, where she only has eyes for Henry: "She smiles, she gives a little rippling laugh of happiness, she holds out her arms to him..."

Apocalyptic Redemption: The scorned Monster, furious, breaks into the laboratory and with a branch from a pine tree, kills Henry and Elizabeth. Then he grabs his Mate and breaks her neck. Father Gerard sympathizes with the Monster:

> **Father Gerard:** *You sought among men for love and you found only hate. God is love! God loves you!*

Monster (*astonished*): *God loves—me? (He demands eagerly and violently beating his breasts) Loves Frank-en-stein?*

Father Gerard: *Yes. God loves even Frankenstein. Ask him to forgive your sins, to bring you peace.*

The Monster falls to his knees, looks up through the skylight at the storm, and clasps his hands:

Monster: *God ... love ... peace.*

There follows a great explosion of lightning and thunder, destroying the lab ... and killing the Monster. Father Gerard, unhurt, is "on his knees, lifting up his joined hands to Heaven." THE END.

Tuesday, July 24: As Whale made cuts and filmed retakes for *One More River*, desperately preparing it for a July 27 preview in Santa Barbara, Breen responded to the Balderston script for *The Return of Frankenstein*:

Throughout the script there are a number of references to Frankenstein and by Frankenstein which compare him to God and which compare his creation of the Monster to God's creation of man. All such references should be deleted or changed in a manner which will avoid all possible objection. You may find that the substitution of the word "creator" or another of the same meaning will satisfactorily overcome any difficulty.

Other Breen warnings:

Scene G-20: Care should be taken in the struggle between Father Gerard and Henry to avoid any objectionable rough treatment of the Priest.

Scene D-23: The love scene between Hilda and Eric which is watched by the Monster should be changed to avoid the obvious inference that the Monster is watching the beginning and culmination of a physical affair between two people. We suggest a revision to make this scene an unsuggestive, unobjectionable and harmless picture of the pure and innocent affection felt between simple folk for each other. This will eliminate Eric taking down Hilda's hair, any scene of undressing or suggestion of it, the kiss, and the action of falling back on the bed....

Scene D-39: We suggest that there be no evidence that the figure of the Virgin and Child is smashed in this scene.

Scene F-26: The Monster's use of the word "mate" should be dropped in this scene. All material which suggests that he desires a sexual companion is objectionable. We suggest that you substitute the word "companion" in this dialogue or some synonym for it.

At any rate, Balderston had added or refined aspects of the script that would be major features of the final film, including the prologue, the Monster learning to speak, and the tragically ironic rejection of the Monster by his Mate. Whale, nevertheless, instinctively felt the script needed something more.

Friday, August 3: *Imitation of Life* was still shooting at Universal. Breen wrote in a report to Will H. Hays, founder of the Production Code, about the film:

The danger point in this story is the handling of the Negro question, and we have had several conferences with the studio. They are going ahead with its production and are thoroughly aware of our fears in the matter. We have advised them definitely, however, that the element of lynching would, we believe, be entirely unsuitable for screen presentation, and that we would not pass the picture if it were in.[14]

Thursday, August 9: *One More River* opened at New York's Radio City Music Hall and Hollywood's Pantages Theatre. It received excellent reviews.

Friday, August 17: Breen sent Universal a letter with catastrophic news: Despite the cleanup job on *One More River*, the Legion of Decency had slapped it with its "Condemned" rating. Box office would surely suffer.

Wednesday, September 26: The Los Angeles Dioceses' Bishop John J. Cantwell, who had been working closely with Breen, met in Vatican City with Pope Pius XI. Bishop Cantwell discussed the censorship issue and said the Pope was aware that "many pictures hitherto were destructive to the principles of Christian morality."[15]

The studios were in turmoil. By the end of 1934, the Legion of Decency had condemned over two dozen films, including the aforementioned *The Scarlet Empress* and *Madame Du Barry*. Even lowly Monogram drew the Legion's wrath: The John Wayne-Gabby Hayes 54-minute western, *West of the Divide,* got a "Condemned" certificate.

"Uncle Carl" Laemmle was aghast. Devil worship? Sex sadism? The "Negro question"? Condemnation from the Catholic Church? What had Junior done to the studio Uncle Carl had founded? Had Karloff and Lugosi bewitched his son? Had that British pagan James Whale warped his mind? Why did Junior produce films such as *The Black Cat, One More River* and *Imitation of Life*? And why, *Gott im Himmel*, did they ever make horror pictures ... and why plan one now with a *Mate* for Frankenstein's Monster?

Had Laemmle Sr. created his own Frankenstein's Monster?

If so, should he destroy that monster, even if he was his only son?

Father-Son Fallout

Fall, 1934. Laemmle Sr. was still reeling from the recent developments at his studio. *One More River,* despite excellent reviews, would probably fail to recoup its cost due to its "Condemned" rating. *Imitation of Life* finally wrapped September 11, after 23 days of retakes; the final cost was $664,587.45 ($98,837.45 over budget). And a new Frankenstein film was now definitely in the planning stages. The "Crown Prince," as evidenced by his battles this year with Joe Breen, was making Universal City, in his father's eyes, a spawning ground of controversy, horror and perversion.

Then came news that ultimately would shock Hollywood.

Friday, September 28: *Variety* reported on page one that Junior Laemmle would leave in October on a "story and writing-acting talent hunt." He was to be gone for three months. His itinerary: Italy, Egypt, Algiers, Palestine, Greece, Hungary, Czechoslovakia, Austria, Switzerland, France and England as Universal's ambassador.

Sunday, October 7: Universal's fiscal year ended with a profit of $238,000.[16] Junior must have been doing something right.

Friday, October 19: Uncle Carl, his daughter Rosabelle, and her husband, 31-year-old Universal producer Stanley Bergerman (producer of *The Mummy*) hosted a farewell party for Junior at Dias Dorados, the Laemmle estate in Benedict Canyon.[17] Jean Harlow, Claudette Colbert and Irene Dunne were there to wish Junior *bon voyage*. Also among the guests: Irving Thalberg, Howard Hughes, Frank Capra, Karl Freund, Rouben Mamoulian, Lewis Milestone, William Wyler, Margaret Sullavan, William Powell, Josephine Hutchinson, Billie Burke, Edward G. Robinson, Paul Lukas, Joe E. Brown and Anne Darling. Significantly present, in light of things to come: Joseph Breen, Henry Hull, Stuart Walker and James Whale.

Tuesday, November 6: Junior arrived in New York City on the *Santa Rosa* steamship, having made his way east via the Panama Canal and Havana. The censorship travails were still hot and heavy, and the *New York Times*, interviewing Junior, reported:

> *Mr. Laemmle expressed the opinion that the film crisis due to the hostility of certain church groups had passed, as features which had caused the hostility had been eliminated from all worthwhile pictures.*[18]

It was a strange remark, considering that *The Return of Frankenstein*, which Junior had personally spearheaded toward production, would start shooting during his sojourn, power-packed with all variety of subversive subtext. Perhaps Junior had not even read the script.

At any rate, Laemmle Sr. ran Universal in Junior's absence, creating a sinister atmosphere of canceled plans and scuttled projects. "Uncle Carl" appointed son-in-law Stanley Bergerman, whose production of *Great Expectations* had previewed in early October, to replace Junior as Universal's executive producer. When Junior learned of these palace intrigues, the notorious hypochondriac responded in character: He "was taken ill."[19]

Friday, November 23: It was Boris Karloff's 47th birthday. Junior was set to sail this day for Europe but, doing poorly, he missed the ship and stayed in New York.

Tuesday, November 27: *Imitation of Life* premiered at the Hollywood Pantages Theatre, with Laemmle Sr. present for the festivities. The film became a big holdover hit in Los Angeles and New York, and later received a Best Picture Academy nomination.

Meanwhile, Laemmle Sr. and Bergerman made it clear they wanted to create a new Universal as far as product was concerned, dedicated primarily to family fare. At the same time, James Whale was turning all his sardonic energy to *The Return of Frankenstein*.

Indeed, Whale had found the ideal ally in preparing the script: William J. Hurlbut. Hurlbut had worked on the rewrites of *One More River* (scripted by R.C. Sherriff) and was the only credited writer (besides Fannie Hurst) on *Imitation of Life*.

The 56-year-old Hurlbut had experience in dramatizing off-kilter "Brides." On March 30, 1926, his play *Bride of the Lamb* had opened at New York's Greenwich Village Theatre. Alice Brady (later an Academy Award winner for *In Old Chicago* [1938]) played Ina, a neurotic, sex-charged housewife who falls under the spell of a blood-and-thunder revivalist preacher named Albaugh. She throws herself at Albaugh, who flees. Brady's Ina, alone, launches into a passionate Act II finale soliloquy:

> *Our Father in heaven—Blessed Jesus—Thy Son—Take me—take me—Amen—Jesus walking in light—Jesus the Son—take me—fill me—Thy blood—wash me in the blood—Praise God the Lamb—the blessed Lamb—the Son of Man—Jesus the Lamb—bathe me in the fountain of the Lamb—Thy Bride—beautiful Jesus—strong in spirit—strong—take me into Thy arms—Jesus my bridegroom—my bridegroom—Fountain of blood—fountain of love—fill me—spray over me— Thy love—fill me—fill me—Take me—bridegroom—bridegroom....*

She followed with an on-stage orgasm:

> *She falls back in a paroxysm, twisting, shuddering on the floor. Gradually she quiets and lies inert, tremors racking her at moments....*

At which time the Reverend Albaugh returns to the room. Ina utters "a low moaning cry" of "ecstasy," and they make love on the floor as the Act II curtain falls.

Come Act III, Ina kills her "drunken sot" husband, poisoning him with shoe polish(!) ... and Albaugh's wife, missing the past 18 years, shows up and reclaims her errant spouse. Ina goes insane. The delirious finale: Ina invites her neighbors, and Albaugh, to her home, appearing as a bride. The sheriff and the coroner are there too.

Ina: *Oh, pardon me—just a moment. I forgot you haven't met my intended! (She smiles a proud, happy, humble smile and indicates an imaginary figure at her side.)*
    Let me introduce the bridegroom—Mr. Christ. Oh, I am such a proud and happy girl!

At which time the sheriff takes Ina by the arm. They walk to the door, Ina taking the measured steps of a bride, humming the wedding march: "Tum-tum-te-tum—tum-tum-te-tum…."[20]

Bride of the Lamb was a sensation, and ran 109 performances.

*   *   *

Friday, November 30: Lillian Russell, a secretary at Universal who dealt directly with the censorship office, sent Joe Breen a working script for *The Return of Frankenstein*, which "will be put into production by Mr. James Whale, in the near future." The script was a patchwork job of various previous scripts (including some dabbling by Whale's friend and often-collaborator R.C. Sherriff as well as contributions by Edmund Pearson). This working script was such a patchwork that Russell apologized for its "untidy condition."

Despite all the writers and contributors throughout the genesis of various scripts, the onscreen credits would ultimately read: "Suggested by the original story written in 1816 by Mary Wollstonecraft Shelley and adapted by William Hurlbut and John Balderston."

The Final Script

> *Long shot … an imposing monument … night … set against the sky—a huge Christus. The Monster comes upon it suddenly in the dim light, he sees it as a human figure, tortured as he was in the wood. He dashes himself against the figure, grappling with it. The figure is overturned. He tries to rescue this figure from the cross….*
>
> —From William J. Hurlbut's version of the script
> for *The Return of Frankenstein*

When William Hurlbut came on board, he and Whale had cast out Balderston's Father Gerard, and had given the heave-ho to the love-making peasants, but had added Dr. Pretorius—a blasphemous wizard, and an ideal role for Whale crony Ernest Thesiger. Hurlbut had also provided Pretorius' Lilliputian people in glass jars, the old holy Hermit (a revision from the blind grandfather of earlier drafts), the hysterical maid Minnie (a colorful part for Whale's friend Una O'Connor) and, most bizarrely, an affinity between the Monster and the Christ.

Saturday, December 1: Junior was set to sail this day on the Italian liner *Rex*, bound for the Mediterranean. He missed the ship again. "Carl Laemmle Jr. Halted by Medic from Sailing," headlined page one of *Variety*. The blurb noted that he might sail in "about ten days" if he recovered from his "flu attack."

Junior kept hearing from his allies at Universal about his father's appalling behavior. It was clear that Laemmle Sr. and Bergerman wanted a kinder, gentler Universal, with a squeaky-clean content.

Monday, December 3: Boris Karloff guest-starred on radio's *NBC Shell Show* in Ibsen's *Ghosts*. Considering the climax of the play finds a mother wondering if she should

Karloff's Monster embraces a graveyard statue of a bishop, then topples it. In the graveyard scene in the original script, the Monster approaches a figure of the crucified Christ and tries to help him off the cross. Breen said no way. Whale opted for the toppled bishop (from the Jim Clatterbaugh Collection).

euthanize her insane-from-syphilis son, the broadcast script must have faced censorship troubles too.

The same day: The *Variety* news squib "Ultimatum by Breen" alerted readers to the fact that Breen had demanded that MGM, *the* most powerful studio, do major rewrites and retakes on *Forsaking All Others*, starring Clark Gable, Joan Crawford, Robert

Montgomery and Frances Drake. If not, there would be no (as *Variety* expressed it) "Hays Office purity certificate" and *Forsaking All Others* would miss its Christmas Day opening at New York's Capitol Theatre. MGM complied.

Wednesday, December 5: Breen responded to the *Return of Frankenstein* script. He was "happy to report that it seems to meet the requirements of the Production Code," but sought a number of modifications:

> One of the principal elements which we believe needs further attention is the number of killings which the present script indicates. We counted ten separate scenes in which the Monster either strangles or tramples people to death—this, in addition to some other murders by subsidiary characters. In a picture as basically gruesome as this one, we believe that such a great amount of slaughter is unwise....
>
> In a story of this particular flavor, care must also be used to avoid any suggestion of irreverence, particularly with the use of the name God.... Your studio is, of course, only too well aware of the difficulty which attended the release of the first Frankenstein picture in a great many parts of the world ... based principally on the two elements of undue gruesomeness and an alleged irreverent attitude on the part of some of the characters, particularly wherever they even suggested that their acts were paralleling those of the Creator....

Breen itemized the script sensitivities:

- The dialogue of Mary Shelley, Lord Byron and Percy Shelley in the prologue, with such lines as Mary's "We are all three infidels, scoffers at all marriage ties," "should be modified," according to Breen.
- Minnie's line at the windmill, about the Monster's "entrails" having caught fire, "may be offensive to mixed audiences."
- The rat who watches the Monster rise from the windmill prompted Breen's comment, "[S]uch a portrayal has in the past proved offensive to mixed audiences."
- Lines such as Frankenstein's "It was like being God" and Pretorius' "...as they say, in God's own image," were "somewhat blasphemous."
- In the scene of the miniature mermaid, the moviemakers should "avoid any improper exposure."
- Pretorius' "If you are fond of your fairy tales" was "a derogatory reference to the Bible."

And while the crucifixion scene apparently got past Breen, he did object to the episode in which the Monster tries to rescue the crucified Christ figure from a grave marker: "You should omit the figure of the statue of the Christ from this scene, substituting some other type of monument."

Friday, December 7: James Whale discussed the script for *The Return of Frankenstein* with censors Iselin Auster and Geoffrey Shurlock at the Breen office. Later in the day, Whale wrote to Breen, claiming he would deal with the troubles "in the following manner":

> 1. *The killings will all be minimized in the photographing of the scenes, most of them being in one little sequence to describe the reign of terror, and the whole of the film on this will be very short.* (There would be killings throughout the movie.)
>
> 2. *On Page A-5: Instead of "We are all three infidels, scoffers at all marriage ties,"* suggest, *"We are all three skeptics, scoffers at all normal ties."* (These lines do not appear in the release print.)

3. *On Page A-12: I suggest changing the word "entrails" to "insides."* (Una O'Connor says "insides" in the movie.)

4. *On Page A-16: I suggest that instead of the rat that a bat or an owl be substituted.* (It was an owl in the release print.)

5. *On Page B-7: Instead of "It was like being God," I suggest, "It was like being the Creator Himself."* (Colin Clive does not say either of these lines in the film.)

6. *On Page B-20: Instead of "as they say, in God's own image," I suggest, "As we say, in God's own image," omitting the derision implied.* (Ernest Thesiger says "we" in the dialogue.)

7. *On Page B-25: The mermaid will have impossibly long hair almost enveloping the body.* (She did.)

8. *On Page B-28: Instead of "If you are fond of fairy tales," make it, "If you are fond of your scriptures."* (Thesiger's line became "If you like your Bible stories.")

9. *On Page F-8: Although the scene, including the figure of Christ on the Cross, as I explained to Mr. Shurlock, was meant to be one of supreme sympathy on the part of the Monster as he tries to rescue what he thinks is a man persecuted as he was himself some time ago in the wood ... if you still find this objectionable, I could easily change it to the figure of death.* (The Christ on the Cross monument remained in the graveyard, as did the Figure of Death; but the Monster toppled a towering statue of a bishop.)

Whale also addressed the censors' concern about the "alleged irreverent attitude":

It is pointed out in various places throughout the story that the whole picture is a moral lesson. First, Mary Shelley herself in the "A" Sequence says: "The publishers did not see that my purpose was to write a moral lesson—the punishment that befell a mortal man who dared to emulate God." Also, Elizabeth in "B" Sequence says: "No one is meant to know these things—it is blasphemous and wicked," and finally the destruction at the end is sufficient warning to anybody, I should think.

Meanwhile, Universal City remained all politics and intrigue as Laemmle Sr. and Stanley Bergerman plotted to wreck the Laemmle Jr. regime. Junior was personally producing *The Return of Frankenstein*, but with him in exile from the studio—perhaps for good—the film was at the mercy of his father (who hated horror films) and brother-in-law (who hated Junior).

In this toxic ambience, *The Return of Frankenstein* might have lacked the resources to become what Whale wanted it to be. It was possible Laemmle Sr. and Bergerman would scrap the film altogether.

Monday, December 10: Harrison Carroll, in the *Los Angeles Evening Herald Express*, reported that Junior had received "a good offer" from another studio, adding:

The young boss of Universal says he is going to Europe but still hangs on in New York, where he is running up record telephone bills talking to the coast. It's a pretty general rumor that Junior is none-too-pleased with the developments at Universal since he left on his holiday. Worn out as he is, he may let them be until his return from Europe, but many of his pals are predicting an early return to the studio....

Monday, December 17: It all came to a head when *Variety* ran this page one headline:

U Bids for Joe Breen
Hays Purity Sealer Urged as Story Chief

It was a shocker: Breen, who battled the studios all through 1934 regarding sexual and moralistic content, would—if he accepted the job—select all future story material at

Universal! The strategy was clear: With Joe Breen as story editor, films such as *The Black Cat*, *One More River* and the impending *The Return of Frankenstein* would never get a green light for development.

Thursday, December 20: Jimmy Starr wrote in the *Evening Herald Express*:

> *A new bombshell exploded on the Universal lot, and the fires flamed for another shake-up—not an uncommon inter-office blast at this particular studio....*
>
> *Unfortunately, or maybe it is most fortunate (for Universal), Junior was taken ill in New York and missed his steamer. Since Junior's departure, Carl Laemmle Sr. has had full sway of the studio operating reins, and dissatisfaction has loomed among the ranks of associate producers, directors and story department heads.*
>
> *The latest development: Junior Laemmle is definitely foregoing his vacation to return to the studio and rearrange studio matters (which he hopes will "stay put")....*

Friday, December 21: "Breen Declines Laemmle Offer," *Variety* announced. Breen had decided, as *Variety* expressed it, "not to desert the morality ship which he had been navigating successfully since its launching."

The same day: Junior started his train trip back to California.

Monday, December 24: Junior Laemmle arrived in Los Angeles, ready to take on his father and brother-in-law and protect his job and his interests. Laemmle Sr. was the studio's president, and Bergerman its executive producer, but Junior still had his loyal allies—including James Whale. At any rate, there was little Yuletide peace and goodwill this Christmas Eve at Universal, but with Junior back, the *Frankenstein* sequel was safe.

Breen, a sincere and determined man, was not a petty or spiteful one. Nevertheless, with his overall concern about Hollywood, he must have felt a certain caution about *The Return of Frankenstein*'s prodigal talent force. Karloff, having played the Frankenstein Monster, the resurrected Mummy, and *The Black Cat*'s Luciferian high priest, was the screen's most sacrilegious presence; he'd also played Calvary-esque death scenes in *The Lost Patrol* and *The Black Cat*. (Why Breen let this get by in those two films, as well as allowing the Monster's crucifixion episode in the *Return of Frankenstein* script, is baffling.) Whale had already defied Breen on *One More River*; he also lived openly with a male lover, producer David Lewis. Colin Clive, by all reports, was a severe alcoholic; Junior Laemmle, a capricious playboy.

And so it went.

Aware, of course, that he could legislate screen content but not off-screen morality—and in all fairness, there's no evidence he wanted to—Breen continued to keep a careful eye on the Monster sequel.

Wednesday, January 2, 1935: *The Return of Frankenstein* began shooting.[21] The title quickly changed to *Bride of Frankenstein*—promising a sexual twist.

Part Two: The Shoot

> *In the mysterious hocus-pocus surrounding the making of* Bride of Frankenstein, *Universal is duplicating the build-up it gave Boris Karloff in the original* Frankenstein. *Star is not permitted outside his dressing room or off the set unless encased in a scrim head sack, like a hangman's cap.... Two cops are*

always at Karloff's side, fending off the curious and blocking out visitors to the set. Karloff gets to the studio at five a.m. and requires until noon to put on makeup.

—"Hollywood Inside," *Variety*, January 14, 1935[22]

Controversy

Tuesday, January 8: Jimmy Starr reported in the *Evening Herald Express* that things had "cooled down" at Universal: Laemmle Sr. remained in charge, Bergerman retained his executive producer job, and Junior Laemmle, now second vice-president of Universal, would produce "six super-special films" in 1935.

"And once more the little dove of peace sails over Universal," wrote Starr, "and everybody is happy!"

Well, not really. Enmity between Junior and Bergerman was severe, especially now that Bergerman was preparing his own horror show, *WereWolf of London*, which would begin shooting January 28 (see Chapter 5).[23] For all of Bergerman's aspirations for Universal "family" entertainment, the horror genre had paid off for the studio, and he'd have been foolish to disregard it entirely. Also, Bergerman's *WereWolf of London* would be a challenge to Junior's *Frankenstein* sequel.

Thursday, January 10: Eight days after *Bride of Frankenstein* started shooting, Universal completed the film's production pages. The budget was $293,750. (*Frankenstein*'s final cost had been $291,129.13.) The front office was demanding that lightning strike twice at virtually the same price. At any rate, the cost far exceeded the budget for *WereWolf of London* (only $159,000). This, too, probably angered Bergerman.

Needless to say, Whale approached the Monster show with a good cigar, sly humor, unbridled audacity, four p.m. tea breaks, and a certain fetishism. Anne Darling, who played the shepherdess whom the Monster saves from drowning, was surprised when the director commanded:

"Let me see your panties."

It was a shocking demand, not only due to its intimacy, but because Darling's shepherdess costume went all the way down to her shoes and there was no chance her panties would show. She shyly pulled up her skirt and showed Whale, as she would recall, her "white lacy panties."

"No, no," said Whale. "You must wear *black* lacy panties."

Whale didn't send her to a dressing room. Instead, he dispatched a go-fer to Wardrobe to fetch a pair of black lacy panties. He then ordered members of the crew to surround Darling (presumably with their backs to her) as she changed panties on the set.[24]

As Whale might have said, "It's all part of the ritual." It was certainly all part of *The Return of Frankenstein*'s spiky atmosphere. Whale demanded that Valerie Hobson wear no lingerie under her satin dress as Elizabeth.[25] Elsa Lanchester wore nothing at all under her Bride shroud. Whale later told Curtis Harrington about Elsa, in full Bride makeup by Jack P. Pierce and flowing gown, flashing set visitors, proving she was a natural redhead.[26] Lanchester, as Mary Shelley, also gave several generous views of the tops of her breasts, coyly peeking over her gown, which cinematographer John J. Mescall lovingly captured.

Whale even got brazen with Pretorius' miniature mermaid. Playing the role: 1932 Olympic gold medal winner Josephine McKim, who doubled Maureen O'Sullivan in the nude swimming scene in MGM's *Tarzan and His Mate* (1934). McKim, surely at Whale's directive, wore a black evening gown–mermaid costume and long blonde wig, its tresses waving in the water. We see only a glimpse of this siren, but the voluptuous effect is quite remarkable.

It was a mad morality play: Colin Clive, a jittery, tormented Frankenstein; Valerie Hobson, an angelic Elizabeth; Ernest Thesiger, a satanic Pretorius. There was the giant statue of a bishop that Karloff's Monster angrily overturned in a cemetery ... and of course, unforgettably, the Monster's torture in the forest, which was Karloff's third onscreen crucifixion in less than a year and a half.

Then, of course, there was the "gay subtext" of the film—notably in Thesiger's dry insinuations. In his book *The Monster Show*, David J. Skal wrote how Pretorius "swept into Henry Frankenstein's bedchamber, bitchily banishing the young man's bride and tempting him with the promise of an alternative way to create life."[27]

The original cut had a brief, bloody subplot: Dwight Frye, the hunchbacked dwarf Fritz of *Frankenstein*, here played Karl, the village idiot, who takes advantage of the Monster's wrath to strangle and rob his Uncle and Auntie Glutz, and blame it on the Monster. Whale so enjoyed Frye's grotesqueries that he'd combine two roles in the film for him: Karl and *Fritz*, the lab assistant, whom the Monster would hurl off the tower roof.

Indeed, at times, the film was almost cruel in its daring. As scripted and filmed, the Monster's rampage through the village coincided with the Holy Communion Day for a group of little girls, all in white dresses. One of the children dies violently in the mayhem—a fatality only glimpsed in the released version. However, a surviving still of this scene showed the aftermath of this atrocity all too clearly: the little girl's "corpse," mourned by her mother and horrified friends, the child liberally smeared with prop blood.

Whale posed on the set with the stars. At no time did he taunt or tantalize a visitor with coy allusions to his own daring vision. He never said, for example:

- "Isn't Boris a hoot, playing Jesus up on that pole?"
- "You rather expect Valerie to grow archangel wings and fly away any moment, don't you?"
- "Isn't Thesiger a riotous old bitch?"
- "Do stay a while, and see Elsa's little peep show."

No, Jimmy Whale created his horror show without any obvious grandstanding. For example, David Lewis, who lived with Whale at this time, later claimed that Whale, a very private fellow who would have been "horrified" by modern-day Gay Rights Parades (or so opined Lewis), never intentionally injected homosexual subtext into *any* of his films.[28]

Perhaps Whale was devoted to showcasing his own personality in *Bride* ... the movie is simply *him*. Yet *Bride of Frankenstein* played so wickedly with sex, religion and conventional morality that surely Whale rejoiced in its mockeries. All the while, Junior Laemmle indulged him.

The studio did proceed with caution at least in one area. For decades, horror fans have debated whether Universal ever intended for Frankenstein to use Elizabeth's heart for the Mate. On February 9, 1935, in the midst of shooting, Geoffrey Shurlock sent this memorandum to Breen:

Lillian Russell called about the proposed sequence dealing with grafting of heroine's heart onto female monster. I suggested that the script was already top-heavy with gruesome elements and expressed fear that any further exaggeration along this line might make the finished picture unacceptable screen fare. Miss Russell indicated that the studio was not at all committed to the idea themselves.

The idea was scrapped.

Tuesday, February 12: Universal premiered *The Good Fairy*, starring Margaret Sullavan. Both of *Bride of Frankensteins'* "Brides," Elsa Lanchester and Valerie Hobson, attended.

Tuesday, February 19: After this day's work on *Bride of Frankenstein*, the production shut down to await O.P. Heggie's availability to play the Hermit. Come Heggie's arrival, the Monster wept, "Ave Maria" played, the crucifix glowed on the wall.

Thursday, March 7: The film wrapped up. As originally shot, Clive's Frankenstein climactically died in the exploding lab, along with the Monster, the Bride, Pretorius—and even the seraphic Elizabeth.

Friday, March 15: Word leaked: Carl Laemmle Sr. was seriously considering selling Universal to Warner Bros.[29] The price: $9,000,000. Laemmle Sr. would receive five to six million; the rest would cover Universal's debts.

Saturday, March 16: Rumor spread that Laemmle Sr. wanted a larger payment, plus guaranteed long-term contracts for Junior Laemmle, Stanley Bergerman and other relatives. Warners yanked the offer.

That night: Amidst all this uncertainty about its future, Universal City celebrated its 20th anniversary.[30] Twenty-two hundred revelers joined the party on the Phantom Stage, where Wilfred North read a poem honoring the dead who had once worked there. Among them: Lon Chaney, who died in 1930. Placing flowers on the stage: Lon Chaney Jr. If Karloff, Whale or Bela Lugosi were at the festivities, the news accounts didn't mention them.

Wednesday, March 20: As shooting began on the Karloff-Lugosi film *The Raven*, the PCA's Iselin Auster and Geoffrey Shurlock reviewed *Bride of Frankenstein*. The next day, Shurlock reviewed it again, with three other censors.

Saturday, March 23: Joe Breen himself responded. The news was dire.

Pre-Release

> As you know, we have given much serious thought to your production The
> Bride of Frankenstein, *and as I have indicated to you, we are gravely concerned about it....*
>
> —Joseph Breen, letter to Harry Zehner,
> Universal Studios, March 23, 1935

Yes, there was "grave" concern—probably no pun intended. The only hope for the film getting a release certificate was what Breen called "careful and intelligent editing."

Monday, March 25: Universal hosted a conference attended by Breen, Whale, Junior Laemmle and Zehner. They discussed the one dozen eliminations Breen demanded. Breen sincerely believed he was being helpful, noting "[I]t is our considered unanimous judgment here that these eliminations will very materially help your picture from the general standpoint of entertainment." He was also trying to save the film "mutilation" by various state censor boards.

Here were "The Big 12" censorship issues, and Whale's response:

Mary Gordon as Little Maria's mother (or maybe her grandmother?) is about to be killed by the Monster, just moments after her husband Hans died at the Monster's hands. Breen wanted both scenes cut; Whale refused (from the John Antosiewicz Collection).

1. *Delete all the offensive "breast shots" in reel one.* (Whale agreed.)

2. *Delete the shots of the Monster in the pool actually drowning Hans.* (Whale trimmed the scene, but the episode remained.)

3. *Delete shots of the Monster actually pushing Hans' wife into the cistern.* (Whale refused.)

4. *Delete the shots of the little girls coming out of church in their white dresses and discovering the body of the little child lying on the ground.* (Whale refused.)

5. *Delete the shot of the mother carrying the child's dead body in her arms.* (Whale agreed.)

6. *Delete the shot of the bloody hands of the Monster in the Hermit's hut.* (Whale refused.)

7. *Delete entirely the sequence of the idiot nephew strangling his uncle.* (Whale cut the entire subplot.)

8. *Delete the close-up shot of the Monster as he falls, crashing the lid of a coffin and later seems to fondle the head of the corpse.* (Whale refused.)

9. *Delete the footage showing the entrance of Dr. Pretorius into the vault accompanied by the two men and all their talk about the young girl, the action of opening the casket, etc. Our idea here would be that you cut from the shot of the Monster prowling about the vault, to the shot of Dr. Pretorius eating and drinking from the table made of a coffin.* (Whale refused.)

10. *Cut the entire sequence of the deserted street and the murder of the woman by the half-wit* [Frye as Karl]. (Whale trimmed it, but the episode remained.)

11. *Cut the shot of the heart being taken from a jar with forceps.* (Whale cut away from the heart as it was being removed from the jar.)

12. *Cut the shot of the Monster throwing the man* [Frye as Karl] *over the roof.* (Whale refused.)

All the while, Whale played it cool. He gave an interview to England's *Picturegoer Weekly*, who called him "one of the most charming of men" and quoted Whale on the essence of *Bride of Frankenstein*:

> In the filming of such a picture as Bride of Frankenstein, *which I have just completed, and in which is depicted the actual creation of a human being, the whole story must be so built up as to implant one all-important thought in the minds of the audience. They must accept the one premise that life can be created. And the story must be so fashioned that, in spite of themselves, they are so carried away that they believe it implicitly—at least, for the time that it takes the picture to unfold. That is the whole secret.*[31]

The film had other "secrets," although in several cases, it would take decades for audiences to catch up and discover them.

Saturday, April 6: *Bride of Frankenstein* previewed at Warners Beverly Theatre, complete with Franz Waxman's brilliant musical score.

Monday, April 8: *Variety* published its rave review:

> This tops all previous horror pictures in artistry and popular entertainment, and credits Carl Laemmle Jr. with a smash hit.... Daring sex implications have been carefully handled within limits of censorship and good taste and spell one of the excellent showmanship qualities of the picture....

The same day: Iselin Auster noted that he gave Harry Zehner approval to make several changes in *Bride of Frankenstein*: (a) lengthen the scene with the shepherdess to "protract the suspense" ("It is understood that this scene will, in no sense, have a sexual connotation"); (b) lengthen the scene in the jail to show the jailers roughly treating the Monster; and (c) add a scene of the Monster stalking Elizabeth before he kidnaps her. This implies that Whale was adding bits of previously trimmed film, or (more likely) shooting retakes.

Whale also made trims for pace, cutting an episode in which the Burgomaster (E.E. Clive) presided at a coroner's inquest—interrupted by the Monster. He added a scene in which the Monster comes upon a band of Gypsies dining by their campfire at night, scaring them off, including the Old Woman (Elspeth Dudgeon) who caws about her food, "Where's the pepper and salt? We got no pepper and salt!"

Thursday, April 11: The Breen Office watched *Bride of Frankenstein* again.

Monday, April 15: Joe Breen reluctantly gave *Bride of Frankenstein* Code Certificate No. 768. With it, however, came an ominous warning:

> It might be well for you to advise your office in New York to be on the lookout and be prepared for considerable difficulty with the political censor boards. It is the kind of picture which is acceptable under the letter of our Production Code, but very dangerous from the standpoint of political censorship.

The same day: *Universal Weekly*, the studio's in-house promotional publication, offered a variety of nursery rhyme–style jingles in praise of *Bride of Frankenstein*, the following one inspired by the Female Monster's rejection of the Monster:

"Where are you going, my Monster Maid?"
"I'm going a-wooing, Kind Sir," she said.
"May I go with you, my Monster Maid?"
"You may go to the devil, Kind Sir!" she said.

*   *   *

At the eleventh hour, Whale added a happy ending, bringing Karloff, Colin Clive and Valerie Hobson back for a reshoot: The Monster allows Frankenstein and Elizabeth to escape before exploding the tower:

"Go! You *live*! Go!"

The final cost: $397,023.79, which was $103,273.79 over budget. The shooting days: 46, which was ten days over schedule.

Part Three: The Release and the Impact

Nobody knows what that Monster created jointly by Mary Wollstone-craft Shelley, Baron Frankenstein, Boris Karloff and Universal Studios will

An example of how movie theaters played up the sexuality of *Bride of Frankenstein* (from the Jim Clatterbaugh Collection).

do next. In Bride of Frankenstein, *at Keith's Theatre, he's a coy nightmare, by turns clumsily comical, slightly obscene, insanely murderous, childishly pathetic....*

—Donald Kirkley, review of *Bride of Frankenstein*,
The Baltimore Sun, May 3, 1935

Friday, April 19: *Bride of Frankenstein* opened, spectacularly, in San Francisco, Portland and Chicago. It was Good Friday, and on this commemoration of Christ crucified, the opening day-night crowd beheld Karloff's Monster ... crucified.

Saturday, April 20: *Bride of Frankenstein* opened at the Hollywood Pantages.

Monday, April 22: Universal proudly displayed telegrams in *Variety* from the exhibitors, including:

- San Francisco: "*Bride of Frankenstein* Broke All Box Office Records Orpheum Theatre Saturday.... Positive Sensation."
- Los Angeles: "Opening *Bride of Frankenstein* Biggest Business Since Pantages Reopened Two Years Ago.... Expect Record Run."

The Same Day: In the wake of Junior Laemmle's *Bride of Frankenstein* triumph, Stanley Bergerman erupted in spite and jealousy. He'd refused to green light any of Junior's future productions, and Laemmle Sr., realizing he'd created a new monster, demanded that Bergerman work with Junior. Bergerman refused and exited Laemmle's office.

Tuesday, April 23: Rumors spread that the volcanic success of *Bride of Frankenstein* would cause Laemmle Sr. to demote Bergerman and replace him with Junior. Bergerman, hearing the buzz, tendered his resignation and walked out of Universal altogether.[32] (For more on Bergerman, see Chapter 5.)

Meanwhile, *Bride of Frankenstein*'s openings were so solid that Laemmle Sr., who had toyed with ideas of selling Universal, now insisted that his studio was not for sale.

Tuesday, May 7: Trouble. Paul Krieger, branch manager of Universal's Cincinnati exchange, wrote to Sydney Singerman of the Program Department in Universal's home office, with bad news: The Ohio censor had ordered nine cuts in *Bride of Frankenstein*, which Krieger felt were "very drastic and very harmful to the success of this picture." They were:

- The Monster drowning Hans in the windmill cistern.
- The Monster throwing Hans' wife into the cistern.
- Hans' wife falling over the mill wheel and into the water.
- The Monster pushing a rock off a peak in the forest, crushing the men below.
- The mother finding her daughter Frieda murdered.
- Pretorius' words after the Monster kidnaps Elizabeth: "Nothing, that is, except what *he* demands."
- Karl abducting the girl in the street.
- The Monster throwing Karl from the tower.
- The following shot of Karl falling from the tower.

These cuts had a back story. Krieger wrote that "on account of immediate Cleveland bookings," he had to rush the primary censor, Dr. Skinner, to review it. Skinner had begged off, "unusually busy with legislative matters," but finally agreed to watch it after Krieger argued about "money that would be lost in newspaper advertising."

Universal's sensational (and sensual) selling of *Bride of Frankenstein* included this come-hither publicity shot of Valerie Hobson.

"It is my opinion," wrote Krieger, "that [Skinner] was not in the proper frame of mind to do justice to the picture."

Wednesday, May 8: *Variety* reported that *Bride of Frankenstein* (and its stage show) was the "Smash of the year" at Pittsburgh's Alvin Theatre; that at Detroit's Fox Theatre, where it also played with a stage show, it "should crash through for plenty"; and that the film was "socko" at Baltimore's Keith's Theatre.

The same day: Joe Breen wrote to Will Hays about Ohio's nine *Bride of Frankenstein* cuts. Universal had written to Breen, asking him to intercede, "inasmuch as we feel sure these deletions materially hurt the box office value of this production." Breen pointed out to Hays:

> When the finished picture was first presented to us, we told the studio that it was unacceptable, and succeeded in getting them to make a number of eliminations.
>
> At the time these discussions were held, we pointed out to Messrs. Laemmle Jr., Whale, the director and Harry Zehner, that censor boards pretty generally would delete a number of the shots which, while acceptable under the letter of the Code, were definitely dangerous from the standpoint of political censorship. All three of the Universal executives waved aside our decision in the matter and told us they were willing "to take a chance" on these eliminations.
>
> Curiously enough, of the (9) eliminations ordered by the Ohio Board, (6) of them—definitely— were eliminations which we warned the studio would be made.

Breen, fired up, drove home his point:

> The point in this whole discussion is this: What responsibility, if any, have we to defend a picture before political censor boards, where the studio deliberately refuses to accept our counsel in the matter and decides to risk mutilation?

Breen did intercede. Ohio reconsidered and eventually made only three cuts: the scene of the murdered child, Pretorius' line "Nothing, that is, except what *he* demands," and (a new one) Karl's line (regarding the human heart), "It was a very fresh one!"

Thursday, May 9: The Monster takes Manhattan: *Bride of Frankenstein* played a preview on this night at Broadway's 5886-seat Roxy Theatre, to a standing-room-only crowd. The film officially opened at the Roxy the next day, with a stage show: Teddy "Blubber" Bergman (later know as Alan Reed, and still later the voice of Fred Flintstone); the Gretonas, high-wire acrobats; and the Gae Foster Girls, dressed as "Silver Amazons." The highlight: "Eleta Dayne is shot from a cannon in a short white skirt and brassiere."[33] The film performed powerfully at the box office all weekend, and on Sunday, broke a house record.

Wednesday, May 15: *Variety* reported: "Among the new arrivals on Broadway, *Bride of Frankenstein*, at the Roxy, is grabbing the business. It is so far outdistancing everything else there is no comparison." The trade paper predicted an "easy $45,000," noted a holdover for a second week, and expressed hopes for a third.

However, there was a drop-off. *Bride of Frankenstein*'s first week at the Roxy actually tallied $40,500[34]—a solid figure, but failing to break the recent $42,600[35] of *Imitation of Life*. The second week took in $25,200.[36] There was no third week. There had been and would be similar box office situations for *Bride of Frankenstein* around the country; word of mouth wasn't entirely good. Clearly, the mix of Gothic horror and subversive humor wasn't everybody's four p.m. cup of tea.

The film ran into minor censorship troubles in other states and territories. Pennsylvania cut Pretorius' line, "In God's own image," as did Quebec. Alberta cut the scene of the Monster and the shepherdess, Karl's "It was a very fresh one!," Karl's death scene, and these lines from the grave-robbing episode: "How old was she?"; "Nineteen years, three months"; "Pretty little thing in her way, wasn't she?"; "I hope her bones are firm."

British Columbia slapped the film with an Adult Permit. Japan's cuts ran a full two pages, including the prologue flashbacks and the scene in which Pretorius uses tweezers to put his miniature King Henry VIII back in his bottle ("Reason for deletion—making a fool out of a king"). Singapore's censor was the first to cut the Monster's crucifixion, listing the scene as the "lynching of the Monster"; the censor made several other deletions, including the Monster knocking over the bishop statue.

Sweden made over two dozen cuts. Among them were Elizabeth's hysterics as she tells Frankenstein of her vision, the crucifixion, Karl's death scene, and even "close picture of the Bride and the Monster." Hungary rejected the film: "Because picture portrayed crimes and acts of a monster called into being through scientific experiments." Palestine and Trinidad also rejected it.

Perhaps the major news came from China. On March 3, 1936, the Breen Office noted this deletion: "Scene showing the Monster in crypt of the graveyard, where the face of a woman has been uncovered when he staggers against the coffin, causing the lid to open, and where he passes his hand over said face, has been eliminated." Added parenthetically: "This was done by the International Censors." Word was spreading that this scene evoked "necrophilia"—a quite sensational charge that somehow had escaped *The Black Cat*, although Karloff in that film had preserved young female cadavers in glass caskets, leering at them while stroking his cat! Note that this was a *Bride* scene that Joseph Breen originally had wanted to cut. At any rate, this accusation, piled upon censorship wrath against other 1935 shockers such as Universal's *The Raven* and MGM's *Mad Love*, would inspire the British ban on horror.

The Monster tenderly gazes at a female corpse. The International Censor interpreted this scene as "necrophilia." (From the John Antosiewicz Collection).

Incidentally, China's Nanking Censorship Board also removed the Monster murdering Hans and his wife, the scene with the shepherdess, and Pretorius' order to Karl to kill a woman for her heart.

Bride of Frankenstein played the cities and hinterlands in the United States and abroad. In March 1936, the Laemmles lost Universal to new management, and neither Laemmle Sr., nor Laemmle Jr., would ever produce another picture. Father and son

Breen asked for the deletion of the scene in which the Monster hurls Karl from the top of the tower, but Whale refused to sacrifice it (from the John Antosiewicz Collection).

would die 40 years to the day apart—Senior on September 24, 1939, Junior on September 24, 1979.

In 1937, Universal determined that *Bride of Frankenstein* had earned a profit of $166,000[37]—a very good figure, but hardly in the class of the original 1931 film. Also, in 1937: Colin Clive died of alcoholism and consumption; James Whale fell into disfavor at the "New" Universal; Elsa Lanchester, Ernest Thesiger and Valerie Hobson were all back in England; and Boris Karloff, dropped by Universal and working at Warner Bros., told reporter John Dunlap (*Cleveland Plain Dealer*, June 6, 1937):

> *Yes, I'm sure Frankenstein is dead and will rise no more. What else could they do for him? He started to talk this last time. He spoke only simple child-like words, I know. But it would be fatal to carry on with Frankenstein. They would have him speaking perfect English now, and then where would your character be?*

Part Four: Aftermath and Legacy

> *It should be a helluva downer, but Whale's story—and, more importantly, Karloff's performance—generates a greater realization. I walk out of* Bride *knowing that everyone feels misunderstood. Everyone is in need of a friend who both accepts and "gets" them. There are many times in life when we don't have such friends, but that's a sad fact mitigated by our unity in longing. Anyone who really pays attention to* Bride *identifies with the creature. In one of the single finest performances ever captured on film, Karloff represents all of our longing, all of our simple joy, all of our optimism....*
> —Patrick McCray, "*Bride of Frankenstein*," *Monster Serial*[38]

So, *Bride of Frankenstein* became a classic—perhaps horror cinema's *greatest* classic—born of studio wars, censorship and a director devoted to a vision. Whale's bravura shines, and the film is surely his masterpiece. The calculated blasphemy, the gay subtext ... all are there to admire, to enjoy—if one's inclined to do so. One marvels at Whale's supreme magic act that conjured all this audacity in a 1935 film.

Yet oddly, this doesn't provide the lion's share of the film's power.

In October 2012, as part of Universal's 100th birthday celebration, the studio released *Frankenstein* and *Bride of Frankenstein* to theaters. My wife Barbara and I attended a screening in Abingdon, Maryland. It was, of course, a pre-sold audience: most of the approximately 150 people there surely had seen both films, probably many times.

Nevertheless, the response was very intriguing.

Frankenstein drew respectful silence. *Bride of Frankenstein* was the crowd-pleaser, getting lots of laughs ... and in all the right places. Una O'Connor, frequently panned today for her over-the-top hysterics as Minnie, was a big favorite. Dwight Frye's mugging and line delivery as Karl ("It was a very *fresh* one!") also got great audience reaction. The old Gypsy's "pepper and salt" line got one of the biggest laughs I've ever heard in a theater.

Ernest Thesiger's Pretorius, on the big screen, seemed to come across to the crowd as more creepy than funny, but landed a few snickers. You could feel the audience's palpable excitement as Elsa Lanchester's Bride appeared, heralded by Franz Waxman's wedding bells.

Yet the true powerhouse was Karloff.

As the villagers raised Karloff's Monster crucified, the effect wasn't that of the Hollywood "pagan" director mocking Calvary by placing the soulless Monster in the place of Jesus Christ. Karloff had given the Monster such compassion and beauty that the Christ symbol imagery, admittedly odd, actually suited the show.

When the Hermit scene came, one boor in the crowd guffawed (he'd obviously seen Mel Brooks' *Young Frankenstein*) and suffered the humiliation of a hundred people hushing him. Whale might have been going for irreverence, but Karloff rose above it: He was heartbreakingly brilliant.

And so it went, Whale offering a subversive, blasphemous burlesque, Karloff constantly, magnificently transcending it, making the horror film truly a Passion Play. Indeed, perhaps the lasting magic of *Bride of Frankenstein* is the star's one-upmanship of his director … and maybe it's why Whale, realizing this would happen, had pushed this quirky alchemy so perilously to the limits.

It's now, and ever shall be, one of the profound miracles of the Movies.

Bride of Frankenstein

Universal, 1935. Producer, Carl Laemmle Jr. Director, James Whale. Screenplay, William Hurlbut, from an adaptation by Hurlbut and John L. Balderston. Suggested by the original story written in 1816 by Mary Wollstonecraft Shelley." Photographer, John J. Mescall. Music, Franz Waxman. Art Director, Charles D. Hall. Photographic Effects, John P. Fulton. Orchestra Conductor, Bakaleinikoff. Editor, Ted Kent. Make-Up Artist, Jack P. Pierce. Special Electrical Properties, Kenneth Strickfaden. Sound Recorder, Gilbert Kurland. Assistant Directors, Harry Menke and Joseph McDonough. Shooting Title: *The Return of Frankenstein*. Running time, 75 minutes.

Los Angeles opening, Hollywood Pantages Theatre, April 20, 1935. New York opening, Roxy Theatre, May 10, 1935.

The Cast: Boris Karloff (The Monster), Colin Clive (Henry Frankenstein), Valerie Hobson (Elizabeth), Ernest Thesiger (Dr. Pretorius), Elsa Lanchester (Mary Wollstonecraft Shelley/The Monster's Mate), Gavin Gordon (Lord Byron), Douglas Walton (Percy Bysshe Shelley), Una O'Connor (Minnie), E.E. Clive (The Burgomaster), Lucien Prival (Albert—Chief Servidor), O.P. Heggie (The Hermit), Dwight Frye (Karl), Reginald Barlow (Hans), Mary Gordon (Hans' Wife), Anne Darling (Shepherdess), Ted Billings (Ludwig), Gunnis Davis (Uncle Glutz), Tempe Pigott (Auntie Glutz), Neil Fitzgerald (Rudy), John Carradine (A Hunter), Walter Brennan (A Neighbor), Helen Parrish (Communion Girl), Edwin Mordant (The Coroner), Lucio Villegas (Priest), Brenda Fowler (A Mother), Sara Schwartz (Marta), Arthur S. Byron (Little King), Joan Woodbury (Little Queen), Norman Ainsley (Little Bishop), Peter Shaw (Little Devil), Kansas DeForrest (Little Ballerina), Josephine McKim (Little Mermaid), Billy Barty (Little Baby), John Curtis, Frank Terry (Hunters), Rollo Lloyd, Mary Stewart (Neighbors), Frank Benson, Ed Peil Sr., Anders Van Haden, John George, Grace Cunard, Maurice Black, Peter Shaw (Villagers), Marilyn Harris (Little Girl in Forest), Monty Montague, Peter Shaw (Doubles for Thesiger), George DeNormand (Double for Barlow).

5

"It's the Devil ...
Creeping Out of Hell"

WereWolf of London

[I]f this story is photographed in a fashion to create nervous shock among women and children, it might be held up as contrary to the good and welfare of the industry.

> —Censorship dictate regarding *WereWolf of London*, 1935[1]

Well, believe it or not, I am not crazy.... I have even been asked, seriously, if I had not sometime been incarcerated in an asylum. Such is not the case, I assure you.

> —*WereWolf of London* makeup artist Jack P. Pierce, discussing his horror creations, 1935[2]

I don't want to look like Jack Pierce's teddy bear!

> —Henry Hull, star of *WereWolf of London*, 1935[3]

*   *   *

It was, in a way, *Frankenstein Meets the Wolf Man*, more than seven and a half years before that film began shooting.

Universal City, California, late January through mid–February 1935: For several wildly colorful weeks, *Bride of Frankenstein* and *WereWolf of London* shot simultaneously. Boris Karloff's Monster and Henry Hull's lycanthrope romped unleashed, against a raging in-house studio civil war that made Universal, for a time, Hollywood's most violently disruptive lot.

Of course, *Bride of Frankenstein* had the edge on studio resources. Yet *WereWolf of London* (with the capital *W* in the middle of *WereWolf* in the title) was a distinctive dark horse contender. Packed with wildfire talent, the film starred Henry Hull, a powerhouse star of the Broadway stage; boasted a screenplay by John Colton, one of the most prodigal playwrights of the American theater, and let loose a new Universal monster. Its demonic visage would spark a bitter battle between Hull and makeup legend Jack P. Pierce.

The two films would enter Universal mythology in entirely different ways. *Bride of Frankenstein* became the studio's All-Time Greatest Horror Classic; *Werewolf of London* became....

What?

Poster for *WereWolf of London* (Universal, 1935). Note that leading lady Valerie Hobson dominates the image.

- An inferior early stab at the werewolf legend, that later fully bloomed in 1941's *The Wolf Man* with Lon Chaney Jr.?
- A thinking person's lycanthropic tragedy, with more sublime undercurrents and metaphysics than the later Chaney movie?
- A groundbreaking, gay subtext fable (as some revisionists have professed) of two homosexual werewolves … destined to find each other under a full moon in Tibet?

Dysfunctional family: Carl Laemmle Jr., Carl Laemmle Sr., Rosabelle Laemmle Bergerman (Laemmle Sr.'s daughter and the wife of Stanley Bergerman), and Bergerman.

The film tosses out a variety of fascinating questions, perhaps only answerable in the eyes of the beholder:

- Did Warner Oland, as Dr. Yogami, rate his huge payday for this one film, an amount that could have hired Bela Lugosi for *two* films?[4]
- Does Valerie Hobson, as Hull's wife Lisa, deserve the rap she's received as the Golden Age horror heroine you love to hate?
- Do the drunken Cockney hags Mrs. Whack (Ethel Griffies) and Mrs. Moncaster (Zeffie Tilbury) deliver the best comic relief in Universal Horror?
- Does the episode in the zoo, with the nasty floozie slaughtered by the WereWolf, deserve a prize for its audacity in censor-ridden Hollywood?
- Was it a good directorial choice for Stuart Walker to have shot Hull's climactic death scene upside-down?
- Does the 1935 film actually complement, in a profound way, the 1941 film?

The 87-year-old *WereWolf of London* still howls mournfully at the moon, the beast baying for a full production history, an examination of the cuts and alterations between script and release, and long-awaited proper placement in the Universal Horror canon.

Part One: Pre-Production

Politics at Universal City

Carl Laemmle Jr., who was within a hairline of leaving Universal, because of serious friction with his Dad, will stay on as a production unit head (his title will be second vice-president) ... Stanley Bergerman, Laemmle in-law, is out of the company.

—Ed Sullivan, *Broadway*, January 8, 1935

It had been as viciously shocking a stab in the back—inflicted by father to son—as Hollywood had ever witnessed.

To recap the events, as detailed in the preceding *Bride of Frankenstein* chapter:

1. In the Fall of 1934, Junior Laemmle left Hollywood for New York City to sail to Europe and Africa to promote Universal product and find new stars.

2. After his departure, his father Carl Sr., Universal's founder-president—unhappy with Junior's sex and horror films—moved his son-in-law, Stanley Bergerman, into Junior's executive producer post.

3. Junior, learning of the betrayal in New York, collapsed and missed his ship—twice.

4. Laemmle Sr. and Bergerman plunged Universal into chaos, with vague plans to transform it into a fount of family-friendly entertainment.

5. Laemmle Sr. actually offered the post of story editor to Production Code czar Joseph Breen, who declined.

6. Junior vowed to return with a vengeance and regain control.

Despite Ed Sullivan's report that Bergerman was "out of the company," the son-in-law was still operating as Laemmle Sr.'s hatchet man. As Junior came back to oversee *Bride of Frankenstein*, Bergerman assembled his own horror production to compete.

The title: *WereWolf of London*.

The Script Writer

> *Yes—yes—all—all I survived—whippings with hippo hide when I was stubborn.... I survived! I survived it all! Hate helped me—black gods helped me—Hell and the Devil helped me—I lived!—I lived!*
> —Mother God Damn in John Colton's play *The Shanghai Gesture*

Stanley Bergerman passed the actual reins of production of his lycanthropic tragedy to Robert Harris. Harris had associate-produced *Daughter of the Dragon* (Paramount, 1931), which had featured Warner Oland as Fu Manchu. Harris would also receive credit for *WereWolf of London*'s original story.

However, in its calculated twists and quirky nuances, the *WereWolf of London* script had John Colton's name figuratively written all over it.

Research Colton and you'll likely find sagas of his homosexuality—and how in the early 1930s he shared a house at 12824 Sunset Boulevard with writer Mercedes de Acosta, the lesbian lover of neighbor Greta Garbo.[5] Few in Hollywood cared. Such lavender trivia raises much more of a stir in these "enlightened" times than it did over 85 years ago.

At any rate, Colton's life was colorful. Born on New Year's Eve 1887 in Minneapolis, he went at the age of seven weeks to Japan, where his father purchased art work for the House of Vantine, an importing firm. John spent his first 14 years in Japan, and said his earliest memory was his parents leaving him at a tea house as they went to a dance. Colton awoke looking up at a bevy of geisha girls, who'd all come to coo at the first Caucasian baby they'd ever seen. At the sight of them, Colton claimed, he'd "screamed in terror."[6]

Tuesday, November 7, 1922: *Rain* premiered at Broadway's Maxine Elliott's Theatre. Colton and Clemence Randolph had dramatized W. Somerset Maugham's novella in praise of Miss Sadie Thompson, an alluring prostitute in a port in Pago Pago, driving the fiery Reverend Davidson to Act III madness. A legendary triumph for actress Jeanne Eagels, the play was the last word in racy sex melodrama. It ran over 700 performances.

The 34-year-old playwright was clearly on the side of the sinner: Colton flamboyantly revealed his flair for dramatizing sensual (and sometimes monstrous) women who dominated (and usually destroyed) men.

Monday, February 1, 1926: Colton topped himself with *The Shanghai Gesture*, an uber-melodrama that opened at Broadway's Martin Beck Theatre. Florence Reed starred as Mother God Damn, the revenge-craving Dragon Lady Madame of Shanghai's most wickedly opulent brothel, where her prostitutes sing in cages. At one point, a character accuses Mother God Damn of witchcraft. Her response:

> *No—not witchcraft.* (Smiles—pauses—then ironically) *Rather let us call it—bitchcraft.*

During the play, Mother God Damn horrifically avenges herself on the man who betrayed her in her youth. A Roaring '20s sensation, *The Shanghai Gesture* enraptured the flappers and ran for 206 titillating performances.

Playbills for two of John Colton's plays: *The Shanghai Gesture* **(left, a Broadway sensation in 1926) and** *Saint Wench* **(a Broadway disaster in 1933).**

Rain became a silent film, 1928's *Sadie Thompson*, starring Gloria Swanson as Sadie (Swanson also produced) and Lionel Barrymore as the Reverend Davidson. At MGM, Colton did two silent films with Greta Garbo, 1928's *The Divine Woman* and 1929's *Wild Orchids*. The big scene in *Wild Orchids*: Garbo passionately dreaming that a Javanese prince (Nils Asther) is whipping her. *Wild Orchids* was originally titled *Heat*, but MGM changed it after visualizing the marquees: Greta Garbo in *Heat*.

For Colton, however, things began to come undone. He worked on a script for MGM's *Rasputin and the Empress* which was discarded (see Chapter 2). United Artists released the first talkie film version of *Rain*, starring Joan Crawford and Walter Huston, in 1932. It lost $197,786.[7] Meanwhile, Colton had a dream play in his head. It opened at Broadway's Lyceum Theatre on Monday, January 2, 1933.

The remarkable title: *Saint Wench*.

Colton had written it as a 17th-century "miracle play." Helen Menken starred as well as produced. The story: A blonde hellcat marries a saint, eventually saps his powers, and becomes herself a miracle worker while her husband becomes powerless. It was a Colton play all the way: a voluptuary overcoming a man's power and reigning triumphant as a saint, no less. But *Saint Wench* fell in flames after 12 performances, losing Colton a chunk of his own money.

"Helen Menken is now vowing she is through with the stage," wrote *Variety*. "Helen had some money in it, too."[8]

Thursday, April 27, 1933: Colton rebounded quickly, having found a new infamous female to dramatize sympathetically: His new play, *Nine Pine Street*, starring Lillian Gish, opened at New York's Longacre Theatre. The *New York Times* review's headline the next day said it all: "Miss Lillian Gish, as a Reincarnation of Lizzie Borden, appears in *Nine Pine Street*." It expired after 28 performances.

Colton's plays by now had exalted a Pago Pago prostitute, a Dragon Lady Madame, a Renaissance era "wench" who works miracles, and an axe murderess. Audiences of the 1920s and '30s loved their "complicated women," but Colton had gone delirious. After *Rain's* flop, two Broadway bombs and a failed 1934 lawsuit to free himself from an agent, Colton signed with Universal to write the *WereWolf of London* screenplay.

Whatever his feelings about penning a horror movie, Colton was aware he was crafting a starring role for a true dynamo of the American stage.

Henry Hull, star of Broadway and Universal Pictures, circa 1934 (from the Cortlandt Hull Collection).

The Star

> *They ain't going to lay me in no corn crib.... My pa was laid in the corn crib before they buried him and the rats ate off half his face. You can't let them do that to me!*
>
> —Henry Hull, as Jeeter Lester in *Tobacco Road*, 1933

"I was practically born in the theater," Henry Hull said late in life.[9] His father had been a drama critic; his brother Shelley an actor; his sister-in-law, Josephine Hull, would star in both the Broadway and film versions of *Arsenic and Old Lace* (Aunt Abbey) and *Harvey* (Veta Louise Dowd Simmons). As for Henry's wife, she was actress Juliet van Wyck, the granddaughter of John C. Fremont (1813–1890); his adventures as a frontiersman and soldier won him the nickname "The Pathfinder."

The Kentucky-born Hull, a natural-born barnstormer, was a stage star for David Belasco, "the Bishop of Broadway" (Belasco dressed the part in black suit and white

The climax of the Broadway play *Lulu Belle*, produced and directed by David Belasco in 1926: Henry Hull's George kills Lenore Ulric's Lulu Belle. Both stars played their roles in blackface (from the Cortlandt Hull Collection).

clerical collar). Hull, 20, starred for Belasco in a 1911 company of *The Nigger*—displaying his acting and makeup virtuosity by playing both the title role, an escaped slave, *and* the white sheriff who pursues him. For a brief while, Hull departed acting and tried his luck as a gold prospector, but soon came back to the stage—appearing, appropriately, in Broadway's 1916 *The Man Who Came Back*. His wife Juliet appeared in this play as well.

Hull acted in over a dozen silent films including 1917's *Rasputin, the Black Monk* (Montagu Love played Rasputin, Hull played Kerensky), but he was at his best on the boards. Among his Broadway credits was the original 1922 production of the spooky melodrama *The Cat and the Canary*. That play's success, and that of *The Bat*, inspired what's been called the first "old dark house" movie, D.W. Griffith's *One Exciting Night* (1922)—*also* starring Hull!

Tuesday, February 9, 1926: Lulu Belle, produced and directed by Belasco, premiered at the Belasco Theatre. It was a three-hour saga of a black, Charleston-dancing floozy, who sleeps her way from Harlem to a Paris boudoir. Come the last act, Lulu's early and scorned lover, black barber George Randall, vengefully strangles her in her French bed.

Playing Lulu Belle and George, in blackface: Lenore Ulric and Henry Hull, respectively.

Belasco defended protests of racism by pointing out that the play paid 93 black actors, 21 of whom had speaking parts. At any rate, Hull's climactic strangling of Ulric was both a crowd-pleaser and a crowd-shocker. *Lulu Belle* ran 461 performances.

Thursday, November 13, 1930: Hull played Baron von Gaigern, the dashing lover-thief in the play version of Vicki Baum's *Grand Hotel* at New York's National Theatre. When MGM made the all-star film version, which won the 1932 Best Picture Academy Award, John Barrymore portrayed the baron.

Monday, December 4, 1933: "*By God and by Jesus!*" swore Henry Hull (time and again) as the epically ornery Jeeter Lester in the play *Tobacco Road*, that opened this night at Broadway's Masque Theatre. The play, by Jack Kirkland, was based on the Erskine Caldwell novel. *Variety* opined:

> Too much dirt…. Georgia crackers in the play spend their time in farming and sex, and there is little farming…. Henry Hull is outstanding … his performance gives the play some fascination…. Tobacco Road *is drama, but doubtful for Broadway.*[10]

Hardly. *Tobacco Road* became one of the historic hits of the American theater, tallying 3182 performances, closing in 1941 after running almost seven and a half years! Hull, however,

Henry Hull's most famous performance: Jeeter Lester in the play *Tobacco Road*, which was first produced on Broadway in 1933 (from the Cortlandt Hull Collection).

On the left, Jack Pierce making up Henry Hull as the old Magwitch in Universal's *Great Expectations* (1934). On the right is Hull made-up as Magwitch at a younger age in the film. Hull later refused to pose with Pierce during the shooting of *WereWolf of London* (from the Cortlandt Hull Collection).

headlined *Tobacco Road* for only six months. Universal signed him to a star contract, calling for three pictures and a total of $30,000.

The role awaiting Hull at Universal was Magwitch, the ominous convict of *Great Expectations*, produced by Stanley Bergerman and directed by Stuart Walker. The part called for considerable makeup, and Jack P. Pierce proudly posed with Hull to show off the final result. When *Great Expectations* previewed in October, *The Hollywood Reporter* headlined, "Florence Reed and Henry Hull Superb." (Reed played *Great Expectations*' eccentric Miss Havisham; she had, as noted, also portrayed Mother God Damn in John Colton's play *The Shanghai Gesture*.)

Come December, the workforce at Universal was blessed to live in interesting times:

Monday, December 10, 1934: The studio began shooting *Transient Lady*, a saga of a Southern lynch mob, starring Hull as a politico in age makeup. The leading lady was Frances Drake (later in *Mad Love* and *The Invisible Ray*), seen in *Transient Lady* on roller skates. The director was Edward Buzzell.

Friday, December 14: *The Los Angeles Examiner* presented its Gala Christmas Benefit Show at the Shrine Auditorium. It featured such stars as Clark Gable, Jeanette MacDonald and Bing Crosby. Among the stars representing Universal: Boris Karloff, Gloria Stuart and Henry Hull.

Friday, December 21: The day after *Variety* headlined Universal's amazing and appalling offer of the story editor job to Joe Breen, *The Hollywood Reporter* noted that the studio would produce *WereWolf of London*. Kurt Neumann, the one-legged émigré friend of the Laemmles who had directed *Secret of the Blue Room* (1933), was to direct, and the stars were to be Henry Hull ... and Bela Lugosi! Lugosi would portray the lycanthropic Yogami, described thusly in the script:

> *There is something strange and lonesome and wistful about him ... a snake yearning for the hearth....*

Monday, December 24: Junior Laemmle arrived back at Universal City, gunning for bear. He would personally produce *Bride of Frankenstein,* set to start shooting January 2, 1935. Stanley Bergerman, meanwhile, had *WereWolf of London* in the nebulous works, dreaming it would upstage and out-perform Junior's long-awaited *Frankenstein* sequel.

First, Bergerman's project had to face the wrath of the Production Code Administration (PCA).

The Production Code

> *At the conclusion of the picture, where Glendon is shot and killed by the head of Scotland Yard, they expect to return to the morality theme through his dying confession to his wife that he knew he had violated the laws of God and man and that his death was a deserved one.*
> —Letter to Universal Studios from John Stuart,
> Production Code Administration, regarding
> the *WereWolf of London* script, January 15, 1935

Wednesday, January 9, 1935: Universal executive Harry Zehner submitted two copies of the *WereWolf of London* script to the PCA. *Bride of Frankenstein* had just waged (and was still waging) bloody war with Joe Breen, as horror films were a red flag for Code concerns.

Tuesday, January 15: John Stuart of the PCA met with Robert Harris, active producer of *WereWolf of London*, as well as Zehner and the studio's in-house censor liaison, Lillian Russell. In a memorandum dated that day, Stuart addressed the aforementioned "laws of God and man" climax, that would drive home the film's "morality theme." He also wrote that the Universal folks had agreed that "the whole story will be photographed discreetly":

> *We made clear that there was nothing in the script specifically contrary to the Code, except one characterization of a soliciting prostitute which later will be modified to make the woman a beggar.*
> *We suggested, however, that if this story is photographed in a fashion to create nervous shock among women and children, it might be held up as contrary to the good and welfare of the industry. Both Mr. Zehner and Mr. Harris assured us that they were cognizant of this danger and would do everything to avoid it....*

This was a rather ominous warning. What followed was a shocker:

> *They will not show on the screen the actual transvection of Glendon from man to wolf and will eliminate repulsive physical details.*

The PCA had demanded Universal *not* show the "transvection" of man to wolf—which was the whole point of *WereWolf of London*!

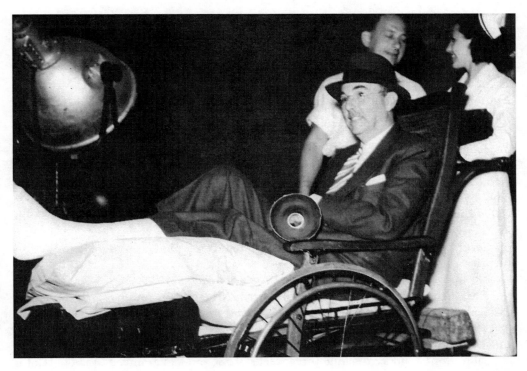

A rare photograph of director Stuart Walker, directing a Universal promotional film shortly after completing *WereWolf of London*. He'd recently suffered a leg injury (from the John Antosiewicz Collection).

A New Director, a New Co-Star, and the Production Blueprint

A lost soul, perhaps...
—Warner Oland as Dr. Yogami,
WereWolf of London

As production neared, Kurt Neumann was shifted to another project. *WereWolf of London's* new director: Stuart Walker.

Gray-haired, mustached, bespectacled, and publicizing himself as 46 years old (he was 54), Walker had been a New York stage producer, director, writer and manager of his own Walker Portmanteau Theatre. He came to Universal from Paramount, where he directed such films as *The Eagle and the Hawk* (1933), a First World War aerial combat saga, starring Fredric March, Cary Grant and Carole Lombard. While at Paramount, Walker earned an offbeat distinction: He personally coached Kathleen Burke, winner of *Island of Lost Souls'* Panther Woman Contest, for her sexy, slinking portrayal (see Chapter 3).

John Stahl, James Whale and William Wyler were Universal's prize directors, but Walker was doing nicely, coping with the studio's eccentricities and delivering very respectable product. On December 17, he completed the splendidly atmospheric *Mystery of Edwin Drood*, starring Claude Rains as opium-addicted choir-master John Jasper. Like Whale, Walker also enjoyed Universal's protection: He was a homosexual who had adopted his young lover—a not unusual custom in those closeted times.

Stanley Bergerman was clearly pleased with Walker's talent—*WereWolf of London* would be their third film together (after *Romance in the Rain* and *Great Expectations*, both 1934).

As production approached, Bela Lugosi, whose deal with Universal was non-exclusive, had accepted an offer from MGM: *Mark of the Vampire*, directed by *Dracula*'s Tod Browning. The film, with Lugosi co-starred as pseudo-vampire Count Mora, had begun shooting January 12 on a 24-day schedule. This made Lugosi's availability for *WereWolf of London* problematic

Friday, January 25: Universal, determined to cast with showmanship, announced in *The Hollywood Reporter* that it had engaged Warner Oland for the role of Yogami. Oland had played Fu Manchu in three Paramount films, and was then popular as Fox's Charlie Chan. Oland had a powerful screen presence and his casting as Yogami appeared promising. It was also potentially troublesome; Oland was a severe alcoholic. Indeed, *WereWolf of London* now had a new and sad similarity to *Bride of Frankenstein*—where Colin Clive's tragic alcoholism was a concern of the company.

Saturday, January 26: Universal completed *WereWolf of London*'s production blueprint[11]:

The budget: $159,000. (*Bride of Frankenstein*'s budget: $293,750.)

The schedule: 20 days. (*Bride of Frankenstein*'s schedule: 36 days.)

Salary for Henry Hull as Glendon: $2750 per week for four weeks, plus $1375 for what the budget sheet called "trick shots"—total, $12,375. (Karloff's salary on *Bride of Frankenstein* was $2500 per week for five weeks—total, $12,500.)

Salary for Oland as Yogami: Three weeks' work and a guaranteed $12,000. (Colin Clive, officially the second lead on *Bride of Frankenstein*, was set at $6000.)

Salary for Valerie Hobson, as Lisa: $250 per week for three weeks total, $750. (She had been earning $200 weekly on *Bride of Frankenstein*, and would act in both films simultaneously.)

Salary for Lester Matthews as Lisa's true love, Paul Ames: $600 per week for four weeks, total $2400.

Salary for Spring Byington as Miss Ettie: $750 for two weeks, total, $1500. Universal would also pay for her transportation from New York.

Salary for director Stuart Walker: A flat $12,500. (James Whale's projected salary for *Bride of Frankenstein*: $15,000.)

Salary for producer Stanley Bergerman: a flat $5000. (Junior Laemmle's salary for *Bride of Frankenstein*: $5,906.25.)

Salary for John Colton: $5808.30. (The other writers listed: Edmund Pearson, $1000; Harvey Gates, $1,166.65.) The story cost of $2000 presumably went to Robert Harris (who also received a $1000 bonus on the film).

Saturday, January 26: Lillian Russell sent Joseph Breen a revised script of *WereWolf of London*, noting, "There are two more sequences being written which will be forwarded to you the minute they reach this office." There was no time to spare: The film was to start shooting in two days.

Monday, January 28: Breen, having read the revised script, responded that he was glad to see that the studio had "eliminated the prostitution angle," but was upset that the script still presented Glendon's man-to-wolf transformation. Breen wrote:

> We note that Scene D-94 Page D-8 directions "And before our eyes we feel the horrible phenomena of transvection as man merges into wolf." We note the same directions in Scene F-15 on Page F-7. In consequence, I remind you again of our conference on Jan. 15th.

Universal still faced a man-into-werewolf movie in which, according to Breen's decree, the studio couldn't show a man turning into a werewolf. On the same day Breen repeated this warning, shooting began on *WereWolf of London*.

Part Two: The Shoot

"Without fools, there would be no wisdom. *Pax Vobiscum!*"
—The priest (Egon Brecher) in the opening
episode of *WereWolf of London*

Who's "The Muscle"?

Fade In: The Weird Fastnesses of Tibet—(Night)—Jagged mountains in background—a strange moonrise throwing the scene into sharp bas relief ... it all looks like an illustration from Dante's Inferno.

John Colton's script captured the opening of *WereWolf of London*: A full moon, above a valley in Tibet. Actually, we're at Vasquez Rocks, located in Agua Dulce, 43 miles north of Los Angeles. The area had already served Universal nicely as the Borgo Pass mountains, glimpsed early in *Dracula*.

Henry Hull makes his entrance as Dr. Wilfred Glendon, bedeviled botanist. Often over-the-top in movies (ever see him in 1939's *Jesse James*?), he's subdued here. Perhaps he's eschewing the star presence of Karloff or Lugosi in pursuit of credibility—and, in the first scenes, likability—as he seeks the mariphasa lumina lupina flower, which takes its light from the moon.[12]

The Breen Office had written:

[T]hey expect to introduce a morality note of sorts by introducing an aged missionary in the first scenes where Glendon and his assistant are seeking the moon flower.... This missionary is to say that the violation of beliefs or superstitions always brings trouble.

Playing the camel-riding missionary (very well) is Egon Brecher, who had recently portrayed the sinister majordomo in the Karloff-Lugosi *The Black Cat*. Glendon's Asian workforce fears the missionary is a demon from the forbidden valley, and they run in terror. The holy man says that Glendon and Renwick (a young friend of Glendon's along for the trip, played by Clark Williams) are the first white men he's seen in 40 years. Asked about the flower, the priest intones:

There are some things it is better not to bother with.... I've never been into that valley, and I've never known a man to return from it.

Cinematographer Charles Stumar, who so mystically filmed *The Mummy*, captures the atmosphere masterfully. Publicity rarely embraced a cameraman, but *The Boston Globe* reported:

Numerous night and day scenes in the picture were shot at Vasquez Rocks.... Stumar found that the natural shadows of the rocks were too light for the eerie effects desired in the night scenes.

So, he made his own moonlight and shadows. Sheet iron was scalloped by powerful shears into jagged edges and set along the rocks where Hull was to act. Powerful blue-white lamps playing behind these screens threw the necessary jet-black shadows and created a silvery blue-green glow, richer than moonlight. In a way, this was a synthetic effect. But it happened to be truer to the story than nature itself, which made it good camerawork.[13]

Of course, Glendon and Renwick defy the priest's warning, venturing into the valley—under a full moon. Glendon sees the flower and moves to take it. The script described the first werewolf attack:

Spectral shadow of wolf slinking against misshapen walls.... Two gleaming eyes peer out from a shadowy body which quivers preparatory to leaping.... CAMERA SHOOTING over Glendon's shoulders as wolf charges. Together they fall into the floor of the little valley.... Wolf's teeth locked on Glendon's arm.

Glendon stabs the wolf with his knife. "There is something almost human in the horrid sound of his snarling and whining," noted the script. The wolf crawls away, the script detailing this "trick shot":

As the moon goes behind a cloud, the figure of a hairy man seems to materialize from the wolf and merge into the black shadows....

In the release version, the wolf attacking Glendon, a genuine wolf in the script, is a werewolf, revealing only his eyes and top of his head. There's no shadow of a wolf, and the wide-eyed, blondish, peek-a-booing werewolf looks as if he escaped from the Pixie Puppet Theatre. Additionally, the attack itself appears to have been shot (or re-shot) on a soundstage, not on exterior.

Apparently, it was. The reason? Censorship. Joseph Breen had apparently been voicing definite ongoing concern about anything to do with wolves. In a February 9, 1935, letter to Breen, Harry Zehner wrote:

(Quoting from Mr. Robert Harris) We have gone to the utmost limit to comply with the wishes of Mr. Breen [on] WereWolf of London *... even going to the extent of re-shooting the prologue which had been shot before we had promised you there would be no wolves in the picture and, on our own volition, even eliminating the shadows of wolves. I mention this in evidence of our good faith..."*

As production began, there was jostling, as there was on most films, as to who was "the muscle," the movie's most dynamic power figure. On *Bride of Frankenstein*, of course, it was James Whale; Karloff fought a spirited but losing battle to convince Whale to scrap the idea of the Monster's dialogue. As *WereWolf of London* started on location, the "muscle" was neither Stuart Walker (whom Valerie Hobson found "rather weakish, but awfully nice"), nor Henry Hull (despite his carrying clout in his third film for Universal).

It was Jack P. Pierce.

In 1935, Pierce was at his peak. He could also be prickly. Elsa Lanchester told me that, on *Bride of Frankenstein*, Pierce "thought he was a god, who *made* these people."[14] Pierce relished being Universal Horror's genius behind the curtain. And as *WereWolf of London* started, the *New York Times* awarded Pierce the lion's share of coverage:

This practitioner of occult rites, before whom strong actors tremble, is Jack Pierce, half-man, half-plasterer....

There are shaggy Bactrian camels at Vasquez Rocks, fifteen Chinamen in quilted coats and a turbaned Buryat, all members of Director Stuart Walker's troupe, but Pierce is the center of attraction for all the players and staff. A wry, irascible-looking little chap, with black mustache and steel-rimmed spectacles, he looks precisely like a German scientist. Especially is this so when, attired in his white surgeon's tunic worn over a sweater, he is busy doing unprecedented things to the visage of homo sapiens. He thinks nothing of grafting a wolf's head over the bland, celestial features of Warner Oland before breakfast on the desolate location on any of these clear mornings.[15]

The reference to Oland was significant: it appeared that, as originally shot on location, Pierce made up Oland as the hairy creature glimpsed in the shadows after attacking Hull. Theory: After censorship troubles caused the attack scene to be reshot on a soundstage, Pierce hastily substituted the less wolf-like, more werewolf-like lycanthrope (probably a stunt man) glimpsed in the release version.

At any rate, the *New York Times* article detailed Pierce's work on the "monster" and "monsterette" of *Bride of Frankenstein*, referring to him as "the Machiavellian cosmetician" and concluding:

Frankenstein Pierce does not perform his experiments in an ancestral castle but in a tiny white-walled cubby hole at Universal City. This, nevertheless, is a far more fearsome spot than any gloomy dungeon to movie players. It is here that Henry Hull will acquire a wolf's head in addition to his hirsute hands when Stuart Walker brings his Thespians back from the wilds in two weeks. Hull will be a lone werewolf from Vasquez Rocks, and when he falls into Pierce's clutches it will be his night to howl.

The *WereWolf of London* tea party. Left to right: Clark Williams as Hugh Renwick, Valerie Hobson as Lisa Glendon, Spring Byington as Aunt Ettie, and Henry Hull as Dr. Wilfred Glendon. The dog, in the script, was named Sappho (from the John Antosiewicz Collection).

Hull had no plans to "fall into Pierce's clutches." A fight for dominance was soon to erupt, adding to the tensions of *WereWolf of London*.

"Pretty Lisa"

Back at Universal City, *WereWolf of London* presented a Botanical Society tea party episode outside of Glendon's London greenhouse laboratory.

It also introduced one of the film's more subtle horrors.

Glendon's in his lab, studying the mariphasa plant he has imported to London, hoping to make it bloom via artificial moonlight. Enter his wife Lisa—played by Valerie Hobson. "Wilfred, Wilfred, what *are* you doing?" she asks, casting her eyes heavenward as he peeks up at her through a periscope in his greenhouse cellar. Glendon emerges and Lisa laments:

> *Dear old bear—Nothing interests you any more except your moldy old secrets in there—not even your wife.*

In her First Holy Communion–style dress, an Easter bonnet of a hat, and an ultra-vain manner, the 17-year-old Hobson instantly evokes the title of John Colton's recent disastrous Broadway play: *Saint Wench*. *The Christian Science Monitor*, after catching a *WereWolf of London* preview, summarized the film thusly: "Henry Hull [as] a Jekyll and Hyde person whose taking-off leaves his wretched wife free to marry the man she long has loved...."[16]

"Wretched" indeed; for many fans, Hobson's Lisa gives chills as the Golden Age of Horror's Leading Lady from Hell. After all, the Irish-born Hobson played a role fashioned by the artistically complex John Colton, who had dramatized Sadie Thompson and Mother God Damn. It was largely in the writing, and apparently Hobson, a perceptive performer, picked up on the kinks and quirks Colton had sprinkled into her role. Director Walker presumably saw the danger of this Colton-esque female, and trimmed (or later cut) several of Hobson's more arch lines, including:

> *Some women are Cleopatras—they wiggle—some are Penelopes—they wait—I'm a waiter.*

At the tea party, Lisa chats with her aunt, Ettie Coombs (Spring Byington), who carries her small dog and prattles away; Lisa also re-acquaints herself with a former beau, Capt. Paul Ames, aviator, played by Lester Matthews. The British actor (who would soon be the romantic leading man of *The Raven*) has charm and likability, despite the toupee and foppish mustache. At her first sight of him, Lisa tosses her girdle in the air (figuratively), so glowing in Paul's presence (while glowering in Glendon's) that the reawakened attraction plays as a calculated torment to her husband.

"We get the start of his jealousy here," noted the script of Glendon, underlining the direction.

Hobson, in a 1989 interview with the author, recalled that Universal was

> *very hopeful that Hull, who had starred in the stage hit* Tobacco Road, *was going to be a great star. He was, of course, a very good and powerful actor, but he didn't photograph very well—he had a snub nose, which is never good for a leading man, and he never really made it. So, I think they were rather disappointed in that.*[17]

Hobson had been having much more fun on *Bride of Frankenstein*, where she adored

Karloff and respected Whale. For a time, she worked on *both* films, trading the arch-angelic wig she wore in *Bride* for the flamboyant bonnet she affected in *WereWolf*.

Colton, meanwhile, had imagined a spectacularly vile way to comment on the char-acter of Lisa.

The Giant Madagascar Carnalia

During the greenhouse tea party episode—where one of the guests, Mrs. Char-teris (Maude Leslie), says the remarkable line "I simply jitter to go to Java"—*WereWolf of London* originally presented a horror vignette that would be excised—and would have delighted fans of sexual subtext.

Shortly after Lisa's entrance, significantly, the film introduced "the Giant Mad-agascar Carnalia," a monstrous man-eating plant, identified in the film as a female of the species. Such a plant truly exists—sort of: the Giant Madagascar Carnelian, aka the Man-Eating Tree of Madagascar. As the script related:

> Above the din can be heard the thin frightened screaming of a child....
> The Giant Madagascar Carnalia, a pink fleshy-looking plant, in appearance rather like an octo-pus, is waving its tubular leaves in wild agitation. One of these snakish tentacles has reached out over the railing and is grasping a little boy of four or five around the middle. A short distance off, someone is holding the child's hysterical mother....

Prophetic of Audrey II in *Little Shoppe of Horrors*, the monstrous plant wanted to eat the child! Noel Kennedy played the boy, and Helena Grant acted the distraught mother. Note Colton's script changed the plant's name from Carnelian to Carnalia, as in *carnal*, and ended the name with a Latin "a," making it female. Also, read on how the always-audacious Colton none too subtly presented the "pink, fleshy" Giant Madagas-car Carnalia as a monstrous, devouring vagina, with giant octopus tentacles, as Glendon attacked the plant with a hat pin:

> [He] stabs sharply at the ugly mouth-like opening in the middle of the plant ... thrusts the pin into the plant's head. A spurt of black-looking juice spurts upward.

Cut to:

> Group of Onlookers. They are holding their noses or bringing handkerchiefs to their faces. It is evi-dent a noisome smell which has effluviated from the plant's wound....

The plant's tentacle quivered, and loosened its grip on the boy. Glendon told the child:

> There—there—poor Madagascar Carnalia was hungry, that's all! Lucky for you—you were rather too big a spoonful for her to manage.

The release version resumes after this deletion: We glimpse in the background the upset mother comforting her rescued son, as Hawkins, Glendon's assistant (played by J.M. Kerrigan in a straw boater), feeds the grotesque plant a live frog, dropping it into the hungry cavity. The excised episode would have established Glendon as a hero, provided a sideshow horror sequence prior to the werewolf transformation, and—perhaps—sugges-tively presented the giant Madagascar plant as a Carnalian counterpart to Lisa.

A sly subterfuge on Colton's part? Based on his previous works, definitely maybe.

Hobson apparently (and fortunately) saw no such symbolism in the film's "spurting," "noisome" and "effluviating" Giant Madagascar Carnalia. Publicity in 1935 claimed Universal had a live specimen of the Giant Madagascar Carnelian, kept locked up in a warehouse on the lot, and fed it frogs and mice once a day: "[I]f its feeding is neglected, it becomes terribly agitated and fastens its long tentacles about whatever is near."[18] Hobson claimed, however, that the plant in the film was a fraud:

> *I remember the animal-eating plant in* WereWolf of London *… a perfectly ordinary thing, in fact, made of plastic, a bird-eating thing that opens its mouth and catches a thing…. It was only there to try to be frightening, and it didn't frighten anybody!*

"Dr. Yokohama" and Lycanthropes in Love (?)

> *In Tibet once—but—only for a moment—in the dark.*
> —Warner Oland, WereWolf of London

This tea party episode also introduces Warner Oland as Dr. Yogami. The script described him as "a swarthy Oriental-looking man," which indicates that Colton was aware of Oland's casting as he finalized the script. Oland gets a great opening line as a party guest, described by a John Bull–type, voices disgust at the Giant Madagascar Carnalia:

JOHN BULL–TYPE: *Fancy, bringing a beastly thing like that into Christian England!*
YOGAMI: *Nature is very tolerant, sir. She has no creeds!*

Oland's performance is either doom-laden, or lugubrious—audience response over the decades differs. The star might have been going for sadness, a melancholia likely inherent in lycanthropes; or, he might have been sluggish in this case in his acting, even under the influence of alchohol.[19] One can imagine the zest Lugosi would have given the performance (and overall film) had he been available to play Yogami.

Of course, Yogami—whom flibbertigibbet Aunt Ettie, refers to time and again as "Dr. Yokohama"—has tracked Glendon from Tibet to get the mariphasa:

GLENDON: *Have I met you before, sir?*
YOGAMI: *In Tibet once—but—only for a moment—in the dark.*

As the tea party concludes, Lisa has another memorably bitchy moment. Paul has recognized her unhappiness:

PAUL: *Won't you tell an old pal how to help?*
LISA: *Um-hmm.*
PAUL: *How?*
LISA: *Shut up.*

Meanwhile, Yogami tries to convince Glendon to allow him to see the mariphasa, and provides Glendon a lesson on lycanthropy, for which the plant is an antidote. Glendon scoffs, but Yogami insists that in London "at this very moment, there are two cases of werewolfry known to me":

GLENDON: *And how did these unfortunate gentlemen contract this … this medieval unpleasantness?*
YOGAMI: *From the bite of another* werewolf.

At which time, Oland touches Hull's arm. The simple gesture makes perfect sense: He's indicating the wound that he, Yogami, in werewolf form in Tibet, inflicted upon

Glendon. However, vocal "revisionist" viewers out there have their own spin on that gesture: Yogami touches Glendon because he's gay. He fell in love (or at least "lust") with Glendon in Tibet, where his attack was a virtual rape. The claim is that the horror angle is a metaphor, whipped up by homosexual writer Colton: Love is in bloom, along with the mariphasa lumina lupina.[20]

Frankly, the Giant-Madagascar-Carnalia-represents-Lisa's-genitalia interpretation makes considerably more sense.

Incidentally, Colton did sprinkle at least one apparently deliberate homosexual reference into *WereWolf of London*: The script referred to Miss Ettie's dog as "Sappho" (Sappho was an ancient Greek poetess from the isle of Lesbos). The dog was never addressed as such, however, in the release version.

"Transvection"

In the lab, Glendon has created artificial moonlight to try to fool the mariphasa into opening. Triumphant as a bud opens, he's nevertheless shocked to see his hand has become hairy. Juice squeezed from the mariphasa restores his hand to normalcy. Yogami returns to Glendon's home and begs for two mariphasa blossoms—this night is a full moon. Glendon refuses. Yogami informs him that the mariphasa is only a temporary antidote, not a cure, for lycanthropy, and caps the episode with the film's most memorable line:

> But remember this, Dr. Glendon: The werewolf instinctively seeks to kill the thing it loves best.

As for "the thing it loves best": Lisa appears in Glendon's library, where he's studying a book's illustration of "Transvection of Man into Werewolf." Paul, of course, is tagging along with her, both of them heading for Aunt Ettie's party. After Paul leaves the room, Glendon apologizes for his recent brusque behavior and kisses his wife passionately.

Lisa stands there like a vertical corpse. "Good night, my darling," he says. She glares at him, arms limp at her side. Without a word, Lisa strides away to go to the party with Paul.

Ouch!

In this episode in the original script, Glendon had hair sprouting on his face on this "night of a glorious full moon." He was in a stage between human and lycanthrope, "hair creeping down on forehead and definite growth of beard." He kept the room darkened to hide his hairiness; he bid Lisa a tender good night, but didn't kiss her. A Dr. Phillips visited to examine Glendon's hirsute state.

"I just shaved before dinner, too," lamented Glendon.

The release version scrapped the transitional sprouting, as well as the character of Dr. Phillips. It also differed from the script in presenting the first full "transvection":

> Moonlight streaming through window, strikes him directly. As this occurs the cat leaps from Glendon's lap and backs away, spitting.... Its fur bristling, spitting at Glendon.
> Med. Close Shot—Glendon staring at cat. Suddenly he gives a wild laugh and starts for cat.
> Long Shot—As animal scrambles around room, Glendon trying to catch it.
> Med. Shot—As cat leaps through open window. Glendon's laughter is grisly, hellish. Suddenly he jumps out of window after cat....
> Traveling Shot—Garden—As Glendon runs through gardens, dodging the direct shafts of the moon, keeping to the shadows....

A candid shot: Henry Hull and Lester Matthews both woo Valerie Hobson between scenes of *WereWolf of London* **(from the Cortlandt Hull Collection).**

> *Med. Close-up—Glendon—Moonlight streaming down on him.... Now the moonlight strikes him full ... and before our eyes we see the horrible phenomena of transvection as man merges into wolf! He leaps from the laboratory.*

The toned-down release version presents no "grisly, hellish" laughter, and no jumping out a window. Glendon, *sans* hairy face, does spook the cat, who spits and claws before running away. Then he rises, walks through the house, and as he passes columns, we see the transformation of man into werewolf, seamlessly staged by the John Fulton unit. The trick, in a nutshell: Photographing Hull (on a treadmill) in various stages of makeup against black velvet, with the columns matted into the scene later.

Glendon-as-WereWolf rushes to the lab to get the blossom antidotes. Someone has stolen them: Yogami!

Thus, Universal's new monster—a diabolic hybrid of wolf and devil—stunned the public.

Jack Pierce's latest triumph? Hardly.

Hull Versus Pierce

As *The New York Times* reported in its visit to Vasquez Rocks, Pierce, basically the unseen star of *WereWolf of London*, was soon to startle the world with his new makeup creation.

"'Ogre' Henry Hull Uses Weird Make-up in Film Thriller" was a *Los Angeles Times* headline on May 18, 1935, the day *WereWolf of London* opened at Hollywood's

Pantages Theatre. The story gave a very different account of who deserved praise for the makeup:

> *Henry Hull had no idea what a werewolf looked or acted like when he was assigned to play the title role in* WereWolf of London*.…*
>
> *Six weeks of private research in four languages taught Hull a lot about this legendary monster. He found out more while inventing and putting on the weirdest makeup he has ever worn in all his years of experience with makeup, including those in* Tobacco Road *and* Great Expectations.
>
> *Production officials left Hull entirely on his own resources to prepare his werewolf role.…*
>
> *From Colton's script and twenty-five research books…[Hull] began planning his makeup by using portrait photographs of himself. On these photographs he drew in pen and ink the facial changes wanted to look like a werewolf and then made up his face as he would if he were to act the role on the stage. In this make-up he went to see Jack Pierce, cosmetician.*
>
> *"Here's the way I want to look," he told Pierce. "Now fix me up to look like this on the screen."*

It was clearly a calculated insult to Pierce—Hull taking the full credit for designing the werewolf makeup, and Pierce reduced to a technician, following Hull's orders. By the time the *Los Angeles Times* ran the story, the news of Hull's creation had been circulating for nearly three months. On February 20, three days before *WereWolf of London* completed shooting, *Variety* ran this notice headlined "PINCH-FACING":

> *When Universal's makeup department couldn't make a face horrible enough for Henry Hull after a week's experimenting, the actor himself devised the wolfish mask he wears in* WereWolf of London.

Henry Hull, lunching in the Indian Room of Universal's commissary during the *WereWolf of London* shoot. His companion is starlet Phyllis Brooks; Universal publicized her as a candidate to play the Bride of Frankenstein (from the John Antosiewicz Collection).

On February 26, three days after *WereWolf of London* wrapped, *Variety* re-ran the story, now titled "My Fright Wig!" The blurb also reported that Hull created his own "lupine mask" because "no one in Universal's makeup department had sufficient imagination to create a horrible enough phiz" for the actor.

In fact, Pierce *had* created a werewolf makeup for Hull, similar to what he would later use on Lon Chaney Jr. in 1941's *The Wolf Man*. Hull had refused to wear it.

As far as Pierce was concerned, this was basically blasphemy at Universal.

Universal legend and lore would paint Hull as a ham actor with too much vanity and too little patience to submit to Pierce's brilliantly conceived makeup. Actually, Hull had good reasons to object. At the 2019 Monster Bash convention in Mars, Pennsylvania, Cortlandt Hull, Hull's great nephew and creator of the acclaimed "Witch's Dungeon" exhibition in Connecticut, spoke with me about *WereWolf of London*:

> During my Uncle Henry's later years, I used to visit him at his farm in Kent, Connecticut, and pester him constantly with questions about WereWolf of London! *Regarding the makeup, he said that at two points in the script, Glendon is recognized as the WereWolf—Valerie Hobson recognizes him, and so does Lester Matthews.*
>
> "How could they recognize me," Uncle Henry said, "if I'd worn that original makeup ... and looked like Jack Pierce's teddy bear?"

Pierce, of course, hit the roof. Star and makeup-artist had a showdown. As Cortlandt Hull related:

> Uncle Henry said that Pierce was Universal's "golden boy" as far as anything dealing with makeup was concerned. He saw Uncle Henry as an upstart! Henry, who could be stubborn, sent a memo to Carl Laemmle Jr. Laemmle agreed with Henry and sent a memo to Pierce, saying so.

Now Stanley Bergerman was outraged. *He* was *WereWolf of London*'s producer—not Junior! Considering the Junior vs. Stanley enmity, this caused another firestorm. Hull had likely gone to Junior because Junior had offered him his Universal contract. Also, Junior was a Universal vice-president. This out-trumped Bergerman's post as executive producer.

Junior gave Hull the freedom to employ his own makeup.

Hull had an excellent point regarding the recognition factor. Also, the devilish, bestial and demonic makeup he conceived chillingly suited a line of dialogue spoken by Dr. Yogami: "The werewolf is neither man nor wolf, but a satanic creature, with the worst qualities of both."

Jack Pierce took it badly. Very badly. He agreed to apply Hull's makeup so to refine it for onscreen effectiveness but, as Cortlandt Hull says, "Pierce refused to have any pictures taken with Uncle Henry during the makeup application." Additionally, Pierce sculpted heads of Hull to use in transformations, which Hull felt was a deliberately spiteful action so that Pierce wouldn't have to work with Hull on the transvection scenes.

Bela Lugosi and Henry Hull had defied the great Jack Pierce: Lugosi on *Dracula* and the test for *Frankenstein*, Hull on *WereWolf of London*. Universal Mythology would see that both men paid for it.[21]

Party-Crasher

Aunt Ettie's home is identified as being located near London's Whitechapel, the notorious hangout of Jack the Ripper. Among the guests is Scotland Yard's chief, Sir Thomas

Forsythe, played by Lawrence Grant. The Britisher was a familiar face in horror films; Karloff subjected him to the "torture of the bell" in 1932's *The Mask of Fu Manchu*, and he later played the burgomaster in 1939's *Son of Frankenstein*, among others.

During the party, the guests hear a howl outside, providing Oland's Yogami one of his best lines: "A lost soul, perhaps…"

Glendon-as-WereWolf scales a wall, creeping into a bedroom where Ettie, "over-served" at her own party, is passed out on the bed. (In this WereWolf's-point-of-view shot, the shadow of the WereWolf is seen cast on the wall above the bed; it shows that the shadow-caster is wearing a very different wolf-man mask or makeup.) The script's reason for this "home invasion": Lisa has covered Ettie with her wrap, and the WereWolf is tracking the scent of Lisa.

"The creature throws back his head and yowls at the moon," wrote Colton, and as the script describes it:

> SHADOW OF WOLF *suddenly materializes into werewolf (Glendon) standing over Miss Ettie. He lifts folds of cloak—smells it—peers into Miss Ettie's face, just as she awakens. Werewolf leaps away and jumps out of window. On the wall we see shadowgraph of wolf leaping—Miss Ettie begins to scream.*

In the film, the WereWolf never appears in actual four-legged wolf form—clearly forbidden by Breen. The smelling of the cloak was a nice, suggestive, bestial touch, but it's not in the release version either. Breen didn't specifically object to it, but perhaps Universal felt it was "borderline."

At any rate, the bloodlust is on Glendon's WereWolf—he seeks a kill!

The Alms Beggar–Streetwalker

Hull's WereWolf prowls the streets, looking rather smart in cap, scarf and jacket—an outfit that seems strange in retrospect after seeing Chaney Jr.'s far less dapper Wolf Man. Glendon's first victim: a streetwalker.

Joseph Breen had immediately pounced on this scene. Colton, likely under protest, changed the streetwalker to "a little beggar," a female one. In the script, she approached the WereWolf, who, in shadow, appeared like a man in his peaked cap.

> *I could do with a cup of coffee, mister, if the same is favorable to you…. Just a penny, mister….*

The WereWolf revealed his face in the street's gas lamp, she ran, he chased her, she screamed … Fade Out. Nevertheless, Breen and his cronies picked up a scent that Universal still wanted to go for sex in this episode—and indeed, the film's associate producer Robert Harris clearly wished to suggest she was a prostitute. On January 30, Harris wrote to Breen, his desperate effort to persuade Breen that the alms-beggar *wouldn't* suggest a prostitute becoming almost comical:

> *Mr. Walker, the director, has promised to shoot this scene with his usual taste and discretion. The writer further explained that the girl, being of the lower class, is wearing a skirt which is not too lengthy, possibly having shrunk when she herself washed it, being quite without money to send it to be regularly cleaned, and carried a handbag such as is carried by millions of respectable women today, large enough to hold the miscellaneous vanities which women carry today.*

So, how did Walker shoot the episode? The film engaged actress Amber Norman, whose credits included the role of "the Vamp" in *A Briny Boob* (1926) and "A Streetwalker" in *Love and the Devil* (1929). As this "alms-beggar," Norman wore a black beret over Jean Harlow platinum blonde hair, sported a short, snug skirt, provocatively sashayed through a back lot village archway—Goose Lane, as the movie referred to the locale—and saw the WereWolf.

As she ran away screaming, it was all too clear that the WereWolf would be dining on hooker.

The Wrath of Lisa

The script continued with dialogue cut from the film: "It has the look of a Ripper atrocity," said a policeman aide. Also, Glendon and Lisa originally had an important scene, Glendon suggesting that Lisa would never have married him if Paul Ames hadn't gone to America:

> GLENDON: *What made you marry me, anyhow?*
> LISA (with a tremulous little laugh) *What made Desdemona marry Othello?*
> (puts her handkerchief to her eyes and dabs a tear away)
> *When you talked to me of all the strange places you've been—Abyssinia—Samarkand—*
> *Timbuctoo—I—I couldn't resist you.*

The dialogue explained a lot, and the Othello-Desdemona reference was effective, as we all know what Othello did to Desdemona. The cut was unfortunate. Remaining is the scene where Lisa, in her beret and riding togs, prepares to venture on a moonlight horse ride with Paul. She invites Glendon to join them, but he can't due to the full moon. He begs the angry Lisa not to ride. She refuses.

> GLENDON: *…then promise me that you'll get back here before the moon rises—promise me that.*
> LISA: *I'll promise you nothing of the sort—I shall ride tonight, tomorrow night, the next night—in fact, every night there's a moon. Come, Paul.*

It appears Lisa will be the next victim. Indeed, many viewers at this point probably *hope* Lisa will be the next victim.

Instead….

Two Hags, a Massage Shop, and "Probed in a Vital Spot"

WereWolf of London fully springs to life come the Whitechapel dive[22] and the redoubtable duo of Mrs. Whack and Mrs. Moncaster, played with British Music Hall high spirits by, respectively, 55-year-old Ethel Griffies and 71-year-old Zeffie Tilbury.

These gin-guzzling, tripe-eating hags who run afoul of the WereWolf provide terrific comedy relief, in the grand (if less delirious) manner of Una O'Connor in Whale's *The Invisible Man* and *Bride of Frankenstein*. The script originally offered this exchange:

> MRS. MONCASTER (RESPONDING): *It's a treat to see you, Mrs. Whack—(drinks)—How's your daughter?*
> MRS. WHACK: *My daughter has a position in the West End now.*
> MRS. MONCASTER: *You don't say?*
> MRS. WHACK (PROUDLY): *She's assistant in a massage shop.*
> MRS. MONCASTER: *Um! Pleasant work, I hear—if you can get it….*

Mrs. Whack (Ethel Griffies) and Mrs. Moncaster (Zeffie Tilbury)— *Were Wolf of London*'s comedy relief.

Joseph Breen demanded this dialogue be cut, claiming in a January 28 letter to Universal that the exchange was "a play on a well-known dirty British story."

A bit later, Glendon shows up, wanting a room to lock himself up in on this full moon night. Mrs. Moncaster leads him into the street, past a coster's vegetable cart, pulled by a horse that the script describes as "so old and woebegone it looks more like a bird than a horse." As Glendon passes it, the horse, picking up his unholy vibe, "dashes down the street, scattering vegetables and cart wheels in every direction."

Mrs. Moncaster (aghast): *Lor! What do you make of that? I've known that animal fifteen years and never seen it move a muscle without it was probed in a* vital spot—

Colton had underlined "vital spot," and Breen, in the aforementioned letter, suggested its elimination—as it "is likewise a play on a well-known British dirty story." Out went the coster, cart, horse and "vital spot" line.

Yet even with the cuts, the dialogue crackles in this episode, as *WereWolf of London* finally achieves its stylized level. Remaining in the movie, with few words changed from the original script, Mrs. Moncaster asks Glendon if he's a "single gentleman," and he replies, with irony and melancholy:

Singularly single, madam—more single than I ever realized it possible for a human being to be....
   Glendon asks ("with grim facetiousness"): *What would you say, if I were to tell you it was possible for a man to turn into a werewolf?*

"*I'd say*," coyly giggles Mrs. Moncaster, "*I was Little Red Riding Hood!*"

She leads him to the room, with a quite extraordinary soliloquy about her husband, whom she hasn't seen in 20 years, since he ran away to Australia:

What a man he was! Used to come home from his work all portered up—hit the baby with the plate—throw the gravy in the grate—spear the canary with a fork—and then with his heavy hobnail boots, black and blue me from head to foot—and all because I forgot to have crackling on the pork.

There followed in Colton's script a highly dramatic scene, worthy of one of America's greatest emotional actors. Henry Hull, locked in the shabby room, was to see the moonlight streaming through the window, then *crawl* to the window, praying: "Don't let this happen to me. Father in Heaven, don't let it happen to me again...." He was then to beat the floor, choke and say with "terrifying realization":

I know. It isn't God. God doesn't let such things happen. It's the devil. It's something creeping out of Hell. God has nothing to do with it. It's man—poor pitiful man—who cannot bear the face of God.

   (moans—grovels)

Some must win—some must lose—It's the Law—but why must I be lost that others may learn? Why, God, why?

Colton noted in the script that he planned to expand this soliloquy, in which Glendon prayed he'd not escape the room and harm Lisa. As it is, the release version contains only the beginning of the speech, then ends with his prayer that Lisa be unharmed. The lines and physical torment were either never filmed or cut before release. It would have been a *tour de force* for Hull.

We see Glendon transform in the film, very effectively. With "a baying moan" (supposedly his howl was an audio mix of Hull and a timber wolf), he smashes through the second-floor window. Hearing the howl, Mrs. Moncaster approaches the room. Mrs. Whack joins her, and suggests that Mrs. Moncaster peep through the keyhole. But as she does, Mrs. Whack, "with an evil grin, leans forward and clips her suddenly in the jaw." Mrs. Moncaster passes out, and as the script details:

Triumphantly, Mrs. Whack takes key from her limp hand—inserts it in keyhole and opens Glendon's door—a grin of ghastly coquetry on her face. She fluffs her scraggly locks, twitches her skirt, enters.

Her plan, obviously, is to seduce Glendon, but Mrs. Whack sees the smashed window, "emits an unholy yell" and "[l]ifting her skirts, she scurries away like a frightened old rabbit." Alas, the release version minimizes Mrs. Whack's "ghastly coquetry" and rabbit-like scurrying.

The Floozy in the Zoo

There follows the horror highlight of *WereWolf of London*: the zoo episode.

Alf (Jeffrey Hassel), "a good-looking young watchman," goes to a zoo gate this moonlit night and admits Daisy (Jeanne Bartlett[23]), described as "flaunting, common, but wickedly pretty." The wolves in the zoo are baying. Walker gives us a lingering rear-view of Daisy's snug dress, her derriere straining against it, before she vamps Alf in the moonlight:

> **DAISY:** *Wolves is nothing to me. Give me a nice kiss, Alf....*

> They kiss:.

> **ALF:** *I hadn't ought to do this—me with a wife and kids....*
> **DAISY:** *But you don't love your wife and your kids—you love me.*

Glendon-as-WereWolf appears, in his jaunty cap, and sees a restless wolf in its cage. "Glendon laughs," reads the script. "It is not pretty laughter." Also, in the script, in

As originally scripted, Henry Hull spoke as the WereWolf, and told this wolf in the zoo, "You poor thing. I'll set you free..." (From the John Antosiewicz Collection).

lycanthropic form, he *talked* to the caged animal in a guttural wolf whisper: "You poor thing. I'll set you free if you like—I'll set you free...."

Glendon uncages the wolf and turns his face to the moon. "He is laughing the laughter of hell," reads the script. Daisy, meanwhile, in the release version, is pretty devilish herself, snapping at Alf:

> **Daisy:** *Oh, what a fool you are. A young fellow like you tied to a white-faced, whimpering scarecrow of a woman. You're going to leave her and come with me, ain't ya?*
> **Alf:** *Maybe.*

Glendon eavesdrops on this seduction, his face "distorted with rage": Alf goes off to check on the baying of the wolf. Daisy, "triumph in her eyes," sits on a bench, takes out a compact mirror and refreshes her makeup. In her mirror, she sees the approaching Were-Wolf. She unleashes "a cascade of piercing screams" as she runs as fast as her high heels can take her into the shadows.

The WereWolf of London follows and slaughters her.

Although Walker, under pressure to be discreet, toned down the episode—no talking WereWolf, no "laughter of hell"—the scene's mix of sex and horror delivers. Apparently shot actually at night, and presumably at Universal's old zoo, it's one of the most underrated shock sequences in Universal Horror. With Joseph Breen so uptight about wolves, a prostitute and British dirty story zingers, it's amazing this episode was filmed at all. The censor likely allowed it because it climaxes with the WereWolf mutilating the floozie, hence the title horror playing on the side of the Angels.

This part of the film ends up back at the Whitechapel room, with Mrs. Moncaster and Mrs. Whack sitting on the stairs outside it, the two of them drunker than ever, reflecting on Glendon's exit:

> **Mrs. Moncaster:** *Vanished as if he was air.*
> **Mrs. Whack (with a cackle):** *He must have been a 'airy man!*

Scripted but unfortunately missing in the film was this lament from Mrs. Moncaster: "*Tears up the bed—smashes me window—leaves me rooms smelling like a kennel!*"

They hear him howling in the room—he's back. Both ladies get a peek at the Were-Wolf through the keyhole, and flee down the stairs:

> **Mrs. Moncaster:** *We seen something better left unsaid to the police ... they might say we been drinking.*
> **Mrs. Whack:** *Mebbe we have?*

The Monk's Rest

On February 11, 1935, two weeks after the film began shooting, John Colton finished writing the sequence that began the day after Daisy's murder. The scene, set in Col. Forsythe's outer office at Scotland Yard, presented on its first page a line that bothered Joseph Breen: A detective says, "I just left old Forsythe ... he's jumping up and down, blowing bubbles with his spit."

And then ... he "illustrates." Breen wrote (February 12, 1935):

> *The story requires for its essential points so much of unpleasantness that we recommend you eliminate as unnecessarily vulgar the last five words of the detective's speech..., "blowing bubbles with his spit."*

The line was changed to "Old Forsythe's bobbing up and down like a balloon that can't land."

Dr. Yogami visits Forsythe's office. Forsythe believes that Daisy's killer is the escaped wolf from the zoo, but Yogami tells him about Glendon's mariphasa flower and cautions him of lycanthropes on the loose:

> I warn you, sir, unless you secure this plant, and discover the secret of nurturing it in this country, there will be an epidemic that will turn London into a shambles!

Glendon travels into the countryside, to Faldon Abbey, to lock himself away for the night. Greeting him is the caretaker, Timothy—played by Reginald Barlow. (Barlow was given this role after Universal scrapped the character he was originally set to play: Dr. Phillips, who examines Glendon.[24]) Timothy gives exposition that this was Lisa's home and that Glendon had courted her here when her parents were alive. Glendon proposes he stay the night in the Monk's Rest, an old room high in the estate. Timothy warns that it "ain't been opened for years."

Timothy, at Glendon's command, locks him in the room. "Keep that door locked till dawn," he orders. Lisa is riding with Paul in his open car through the same countryside this night, and they visit Faldon Abbey, where they played as children. After telling Paul there's no hope for their romance, she nevertheless proceeds to flirt, giggle and lead him on a chase across the grounds where they'd once hunted for bird eggs, and where he'd once proposed to her.

Watching from his room up in the tower: the transformed WereWolf (the man-to-wolf vexation done by Jack Pierce on the profile of a Henry Hull head sculpture). The WereWolf leaps from the window, lunging toward Lisa. In the script, he says, "Lisa.... Lisa," but he remains silent in the release version. She collapses and he attacks Paul.[25] Paul battles the beast (fortunately without being bitten) and rescues Lisa, still unconscious. The scene concluded in the script with a revived Lisa saying this significant dialogue, missing from the film: "What a horrible thing ... it called me by my name."

The highlight of the episode: Valerie Hobson's magnificent scream—although even here, her Lisa is a bit off-putting: Her mouth is so wide-open and her teeth so pronounced that she evokes *The Snake Lady of London*. As Hobson told me:

> I remember some of the publicity that went out—that I was "the new Fay Wray." Is anything sillier than that? To begin with, she was marvelous-looking, Fay Wray, and a great star. Perhaps I could scream *better* than she could, so I did a lot of screaming!

Indeed, Universal, proclaiming that Valerie Hobson "has literally screamed her way to success," hailed her as the "lovely lady of the vociferous tonsils."[26]

The Climax

WereWolf of London stays in high gear for its climax. Paul's convinced that Glendon is the WereWolf. We learn that Yogami has committed a lycanthropic murder at his hotel—the victim, his chambermaid. A Scotland Yard aide has a vivid line: "The place smelled like a kennel when we came in—you can still notice it, sir."

Yogami creeps into Glendon's lab, just as Glendon succeeds with his moon-ray machine in making the mariphasa bloom. Glendon discovers him. As scripted, the dialogue was dynamite:

YOGAMI: *There is enough blood in that flower to save us both if it blooms in time.*
GLENDON: *No, Yogami. There isn't room on all the planet for both of us—You brought this thing on me.*
YOGAMI: *In Tibet—in the dark. I brought this thing on you.... You had gone to a place you had no right to.... You meddled with Hell, Glendon.... What happened was no fault of mine.*
GLENDON: *I'm going to kill you, Yogami.*
YOGAMI: *Let us fight this thing together, Glendon. ...[T]wo men against all the forces of blackness ... two beings against Satan himself.* (pointing) *Look—look—one little flower has begun to bloom!*

In the script, both men fight for the flower. The blossom falls to the floor, and Yogami, aware he can't get the blossom, spitefully stamps on it. There originally followed a remarkable effect. As the script described it:

> *The flower dies with an agonizing cry. A ray of moonlight shoots from the dead flower to the moon ... the soul of the flower returned to its final resting place.*

It would have made for a striking moment—metaphysics, cinematically pollinating with science fiction ... yet it was apparently never shot. Additionally, the full-blooded dialogue quoted previously is reduced to two lines:

GLENDON: *Yogami.... You brought this on me ... in Tibet!*
YOGAMI (**trying to escape with the mariphasa blossom**): *Sorry I can't share* this *with you!*

Glendon transforms into the WereWolf. He rakes Yogami's face, leaving claw marks,

Climactic battle of the WereWolves: Oland vs. Hull (from the John Antosiewicz Collection).

and strangles him to death. The free-for-all finale finds Glendon's WereWolf escaping the lab, leaping onto Paul from the roof, and crashing into the house. Ettie faints, the WereWolf stalks Lisa, and in the script, talked:

Glendon (guttural tone): *Lisa…. Pretty Lisa … soft and dead in my arms.*

Again, the WereWolf doesn't speak in the release version—but Lisa *does* recognize him. "*It's Lisa. Don't you know me?*"

As the beast stalks her up the staircase, Col. Forsythe arrives and fires a bullet (not a silver one) into Glendon. He falls down the stairs. The script had him slowly transform back into Glendon, and say:

Glendon: *Thanks for the bullet, Forsythe. There was no place left on earth for me.*

Glendon then looked at Lisa and Paul, saying:

In a moment, I shall know why all this had to be. Goodbye, Lisa—be happy.

And he died. The release version altered the scene: Glendon *remains* in WereWolf form as he dies and speaks his final words:

Thanks for the bullet—it was the only way.

Walker shot the scene strangely: He filmed it with Hull on the floor, angled so his head is *upside-down* onscreen, as he says:

In a… in a few moments now … I shall know why all this had to be. Lisa—goodbye. Goodbye, Lisa. I'm sorry I – I couldn't have made you—happier.

He dies and it's now, in death, that the WereWolf reverts to human form. Again, it's not Hull, but one of the Hull sculptures made by Pierce. Pierce had remained vengefully spiteful to the last.

The script of *WereWolf of London* originally ended with a comic finale for Mrs. Moncaster and Mrs. Whack, the former about to be photographed as "the lady that lodged the werewolf." Mrs. Whack protests it was *she* who saw him first. When six bottles of gin appear from the corner pub, Mrs. Moncaster jumps to protect them as Mrs. Whack poses for the picture.

THE END

In the release version, neither of the harridans is in sight. We see a plane flying and we assume it's Paul, taking Lisa back to America with him. The Universal globe appears with its familiar plane circling it.

THE END

*   *   *

WereWolf of London wrapped on Saturday, February 23, four days over schedule. *Bride of Frankenstein*, that had so overshadowed it, resumed shooting after *WereWolf* was finished, as O.P. Heggie reported to Universal and Whale shot the Monster and Hermit episode.

There'd been plenty of time for the two companies to interact, and Cortlandt Hull relates:

Universal was shooting WereWolf of London *and* Bride of Frankenstein *at the same time and on adjacent soundstages. Since Valerie Hobson was acting in both films simultaneously, there was a tunnel-like causeway between the two stages so she could easily get from one set to the other.*

Well, Uncle Henry and his wife were friends with Boris Karloff, and his wife (my aunt) came to visit him at Universal one morning. She ended up on the Bride of Frankenstein *set by mistake, and a stage hand directed her to the tunnel leading to the* WereWolf of London *set. It was a gloomy tunnel, lit by single hanging bulbs overhead. As my aunt was making her way, she heard this loud "clump, clump, clump, clump" ... and around the corner comes Boris Karloff, in full Frankenstein Monster makeup, smoking a cigar!*

"Good morning, Mrs. Hull!" Karloff said cheerfully, and gave a little bow. Boris had visited the WereWolf of London *set to say "Hello" to my Uncle Henry. It was a shock for my aunt to meet this towering, cigar-smoking Monster, greeting her personally in the tunnel!*

Part Three: Post-Production, Release, Reviews and Box Office

Henry Hull [is] disguised so that his own mother would not hesitate to let him have both barrels. This is a pretty valiant bit of gooseflesh melodrama in the Jekyll and Hyde tradition....

—*The New York Times,* May 19, 1935

Wednesday, February 27, 1935: Four days after the completion of *WereWolf of London, The Los Angeles Times* announced that Henry Hull would star locally in a stage production of *Tobacco Road.* Hull had completed his three-picture deal at Universal, apparently checking off the lot almost immediately. One guesses that Jack Pierce wasn't sad to see him go.

Wednesday, March 6: Carl Laemmle (presumably Senior) sent out a memo to Universal at large, along with a two-page synopsis of *WereWolf of London,* announcing a contest:

... Because I believe that a real outstanding box office title means everything to the success of this or any other picture, Universal will pay fifty dollars ($50.00) to the individual submitting the best title for the attached story.[27]

Among the many studio employees who entered the contest: Carla Laemmle, Uncle Carl's grand niece, who'd played a coach passenger in *Dracula* and whose 12 suggestions included *Moon Magic* and *Moon Madness.* David Boehm, who got solo screenplay credit on *The Raven,* was quite adamant about his title suggestion: "[T]he only title for your new horror picture is WEREWOLF—Not 'The' WEREWOLF, just WEREWOLF." Carolyn Wagner of the publicity department suggested *It Happened at Night,* which sounds suspiciously like 1934's Academy Award–winning Best Picture *It Happened One Night.* Elizabeth Miller of the Stenographic Dept. came up with 70-plus titles, including *Satan Astride the Moon.*

Additionally, Robert Harris, the film's producer, sent six suggestions, including *Moon Over Tibet*; Charles Stumar, the film's cinematographer, included *Murder in the London Zoo* among his eight entries; and Valerie Hobson herself sent in nine titles, including *When the Devil Hates* and (my personal favorite) *Oh! Fatal Flower.*

Nobody won the $50. The title remained *WereWolf of London.*

Karl Hajos added the *WereWolf of London*'s moody musical score, peppering it with classical selections previously used in *The Black Cat*. Universal officially tabulated the final cost: $195,393.01, which was $36,393 over budget (and almost precisely half the final tab of *Bride of Frankenstein*).

Monday, March 18: Henry Hull opened at the Belasco Theatre in Los Angeles in *Tobacco Road*. The *L.A. Times* reported five days later that he'd "won the unanimous praise of first-night critics," and that the play was so successful that it was playing nine performances a week rather than the usual eight.[28]

Wednesday, March 20: Universal began shooting the new Karloff-Lugosi vehicle, *The Raven*.

Friday, March 22: *WereWolf of London* played for review by the Breen Office.

Saturday, March 23: Joseph Breen wrote to Universal, officially demanding the excision of "the shot in which Yogami's face is shown scratched and dripping blood, and second, the actual strangling of Yogami." Trusting Universal would comply, he enclosed the Association's certificate. Universal cut the action to which Breen objected, but the clawing of Yogami's face appeared in the film's trailer.

Actually, the minimal cuts were a break for *WereWolf of London*. The same day, Breen wrote to Universal, suggesting *Bride of Frankenstein* receive 12 cuts.

Saturday, April 20: *Bride of Frankenstein* opened at the Hollywood Pantages Theatre.

Monday, April 22: Stanley Bergerman refused to green-light any Junior Laemmle productions for Universal's 1935–1936 season. When Laemmle Sr. demanded that Bergerman change his mind, Bergerman stormed out of Laemmle Sr.'s office.

Tuesday, April 23: Learning of *Bride of Frankenstein*'s success—and fearing his father-in-law would replace him as executive producer with Junior—Bergerman departed Universal.[29]

Wednesday, April 24: *Variety* reported that Stuart Walker "has been graduated to an associate producer" at Universal.[30]

Friday, April 26: Three days after its producer walked out, there was a preview of *WereWolf of London*. *Variety* reported the next day:

> Here's a horror picture, which, due to expert casting and direction, should attract those who are not 100 percent creep and chill fans.... WereWolf *will be able to hold its own with the best chillers....*

Tuesday, April 30: *Variety* reported that Bergerman would return to Universal to supervise his two final films, *Lady Tubbs* and *Sing Me a Love Song*.[31]

Thursday, May 9: Another battle between *Bride of Frankenstein* and *WereWolf of London* ended in *Bride*'s favor: New York's Roxy Theatre (5886 seats) and Rialto Theatre (1960 seats) both wanted to show *Bride*. The Roxy won—and the Rialto got *WereWolf* as a consolation prize. It opened there on May 9, the same night *Bride* played a special preview at the Roxy (where it officially opened the next day). As it was, *WereWolf of London* became the final film to play the original Rialto, which had a date the following week with the wrecking ball. The *New York Times* called the film "a fitting valedictory for the old Rialto, which has become melodrama's citadel among Times Square's picture houses."[32]

Bride of Frankenstein and *WereWolf of London* played Broadway simultaneously, but there was no real competition. The first week's take for *Bride* was $40,500; for *Werewolf of London*, $12,000.[33]

Saturday, May 18: *WereWolf of London* opened at Hollywood's Pantages Theatre, almost a month after *Bride of Frankenstein* had reigned there. Henry Hull, meanwhile, was still starring in *Tobacco Road* on stage in L.A.

Wednesday, May 22: Variety ran an interesting report on *WereWolf of London*'s engagement at San Francisco's Orpheum Theatre:

> *Doing good biz ... pulling same class as* Bride of Frankenstein, *but pub [sic] is going out liking the pic, where they panned* Bride of Frankenstein.

Sunday, June 2: The Hartford Courant reported that Henry Hull's 15-year-old son, Shelley, had attended a showing of *WereWolf of London* at Loew's Theatre in Hartford, Connecticut. "Gee, Dad's swell!" exclaimed Shelley, a student at the Loomis Institute in Windsor. Shelley went on:

> *This is the best picture Dad has ever done. Of course, it's different from acting on the stage. Acting before a camera must be like a rehearsal. Oh, no! Dad doesn't like Hollywood. He says he likes to get away from there just as soon as he can. He likes the stage much better.*[34]

Meanwhile, censors around the world chimed in. Ontario deleted views of Glendon choking Yogami, and the close-up views of Glendon's wolf face after he was shot (which would have also eliminated his closing dialogue, including the profound "I shall know why all this had to be"). Singapore reduced the sound of screams, eliminated "scene of girl soliciting at the Zoo," and cut the strangling scenes. Holland rejected the film "[b]ecause of degrading effect on the public." *The China Press* ran this June 4, 1935, headline: "*WereWolf of London* Banned as Film Here."

The film got a warmer welcome in London, where it played the Capitol Theatre. "A rip-roaring shocker of the first order," wrote *The Observer*.[35]

It was Jack P. Pierce who got the last word, at least temporarily. In a feature titled "Genius in a Rouge Box," published in *The Daily Boston Globe* (October 20, 1935), he took bows for the makeup in *WereWolf of London*:

> *I don't rely on imagination alone. I do exhaustive research. When I have learned the type of character to be presented, I read every book I can get my hands on containing descriptive passages of that type. Nothing is impossible for make-up. I can make any man unrecognizable on the street in broad daylight.*

Pierce detailed how he applied the transformations in *WereWolf of London*, but stopped short of claiming he'd actually designed the makeup.

Generations will read that Hull was too arrogant to submit to Pierce's artistry. The oft-repeated tale appeared yet again in a British horror magazine in 2019.

Part Four: Eclipse and Legacy

> *Even a man who is pure in heart....*
> —From *The Wolf Man*, 1941

WereWolf of London, of course, faced eventual eclipse by Universal's *The Wolf Man.* A comparison of the two films could make for another full chapter, but the later film benefits from Curt Siodmak's wonderful Gypsy mysticism, Jack Pierce's genuinely frightening original werewolf makeup, a great featured cast and, of course, Lon Chaney Jr.'s strangely affecting Everyman portrayal of the title role. The film remains the iconic classic on lycanthropy.

Yet … *WereWolf of London* is not the misfire that conventional wisdom too often claims it to be. Indeed, in several vital ways, *WereWolf of London* tops *The Wolf Man*. Hull's satanic makeup, in its own "lost soul" way, is at least as effective as Chaney's almost bear-like visage. Valerie Hobson's Lisa Glendon is as intriguing as Evelyn Ankers' Gwen Conliffe. Hobson—destined for stardom in England—gets bonus points for playing her *soignee* ball-buster role as bitchily as it's written, while still delivering the requisite beauty and charms of a Classic Horror heroine. The sexy, sinister atmospherics in the zoo with the doomed Daisy, and the near-slapstick in the Whitechapel pub, enlivened by the uproarious Mrs. Moncaster and Mrs. Whack, are terrific. And we *do* see the moon— which is somehow absent from *The Wolf Man*.[36]

Perhaps most effectively, Hull's Wilfred Glendon is *aware* of the satanic forces that are destroying him, and recognizes them as such, while Chaney's Larry Talbot is *confused* by them. This is a major point in the former film's favor.

WereWolf of London is one of many horror films (and films in general) with a giant "If" attached to it. *If* the Breen Office hadn't scared Universal into pulling its punches. *If* Stuart Walker had more passion as a director. *If* Bela Lugosi had played Yogami instead of Warner Oland. *If* more of the metaphysical dialogue had stayed in the script.

Most of all, *WereWolf of London* might carry more impact today *if* Henry Hull, as one of the American theater's great blood-and-thunder performers, had played the role unleashed from movie "technique" and gone full-throttle. If he'd thrown himself into the part, "crawling" on the floor as he prayed, "laughing the laughter of Hell" as he set free the wolf in the zoo … indeed, had he given full release to the WereWolf's terror and horror, the performance might have been a classic for the ages.

* * *

A final word about two of the prime movers of *WereWolf of London*:

John Colton wrote the screenplay for Universal's Karloff-Lugosi film *The Invisible Ray* (1936), which possessed the usual Colton quirks. Karloff, as Dr. Janos Rukh, is married to a foxy woman (Frances Drake), whom he can't touch (or, as hinted, with whom he can't have sexual relations). The melodrama tingles with this errant sexuality. The wife remarries after thinking her husband is dead; the ex-husband, literally glowing with Radium X poisoning, vengefully stalks her, and he's about to kill her by touching her. However, he can't do it. The wife survives, embraced by her new husband, while Rukh dies, a fireball.

Tormented by an alluring wife, Karloff's Janos Rukh is a virtual pin-up boy for the John Colton mystique.

In 1941, United Artists released a film version of Colton's play *The Shanghai Gesture*, directed by Josef von Sternberg. Ona Munson (*Gone with the Wind*'s Belle Watling) played Mother God Damn (renamed Mother Gin Sling). The film, naturally picked clean by the Production Code, was a stylistic triumph, perhaps most enjoyed today by audiences who swoon over the sets and Munson's exotic wigs. Colton wrote the play *Under Capricorn*, which became an Alfred Hitchcock film in 1949, starring Ingrid Bergman as an alcoholic fighting insanity. By the time it was released, Colton had been dead for nearly three years. Cursed with a weakness for divas, he had become close to an actress named Madam Barry Orlova,[37] suffered three strokes, and died in Gainesville, Texas, on

December 26, 1946, at the age of 58. He was cremated in Dallas and his ashes sent to his brother Marcus in Los Angeles.[38]

And as for Henry Hull ... he had a long career on Broadway (e.g., he played Edgar Allan Poe, creating and applying his own makeup in *Plumes in the Dust*, 46th Street

Cortlandt Hull poses with his figure of his Uncle Henry as the WereWolf of London. Cortlandt created the famed Witch's Dungeon attraction, which has recently relocated to Plainville, Connecticut (from the Cortlandt Hull Collection).

Theatre, November 6, 1936, 11 performances): in films (he played a magician in Tod Browning's last film, 1939's *Miracles for Sale*, which promoted Hull as "The New Lon Chaney"): and on TV (including playing "Gramps" in "On Borrowed Time" on *The Ford Theatre Hour*, June 30, 1950). In 1964, Hull, living on his farm in Old Lyme, Connecticut, spoke to a reporter about *WereWolf of London* having appeared on the late show, saying he'd watched the first part, then gone to bed. "It was a pretty good get-up, wasn't it?" said Hull. "Jack had a special talent for turning men into freaks."[39] The testimony to Jack Pierce (still alive at the time) was a bit surprising, considering the circumstances at Universal in 1935.

In the early 1970s, *Famous Monsters of Filmland* magazine offered to forward fan letters to Hull, the inference being that the aged actor felt forgotten. After the death of his wife Juliet in 1971, Hull went to live with his daughter in Cornwall, England. He died there on March 8, 1977, at the age of 86. His ashes came back to America, buried with his wife in the plot of Juliet's grandfather, the famed John C. Fremont, in Rockland Cemetery, Sparkill, New York, above the west bank of the Hudson River.[40]

* * *

Henry Hull's anguished Dr. Wilfred Glendon, with his dying words, "In a few moments now ... I shall know why all this had to be," has earned a special niche amidst the Universal Goblins. He's rather the "goth" patron saint of all those who daily ask themselves, regarding things trivially inconsequential or heartbreakingly grave....

"Why did all this have to be?"

As such, imagine the climax and finale of *The Wolf Man*—Lon Chaney's Lawrence Talbot, dead in the foggy forest, transforming before the eyes of his father who killed him, leaving his mortal coil ... finding himself in the Afterlife. His mother is there, and his brother, who died in a hunting accident. Then the figure of Wilfred Glendon appears, looking with deep empathy into Talbot's eyes.

"I'm going to explain to you, Larry," says Glendon gently, compassionately, "why all this had to be."

Larry Talbot's eyes glisten.

"But first, my boy," says Glendon, "I'm afraid we're sending you back down there for four sequels ... and the last one will be with Abbott and Costello."

WereWolf of London

Universal, 1935. Executive Producer, Stanley Bergerman. Associate Producer, Robert Harris. Director, Stuart Walker. Screenplay, John Colton, based on a story by Robert Harris (Harvey Gates, Robert Harris and Edmund Pearson, uncredited). Cinematographer, Charles J. Stumar. Art Director, Albert S. D'Agostino. Musical Score, Karl Hajos. Musical Supervision, Gilbert Kurland. Special Effects, John P. Fulton. Editor, Russell F. Schoengarth (Milton Carruth, uncredited). Supervising Editor, Maurice Pivar. Makeup Artists, Jack P. Pierce, Armand Triller. Hair Stylist, Mary Dolor. Assistant Directors, Charles S. Gould, Phil Karlson. Special Effects Assistant, David S. Horsley. Assistant Cameraman, John J. Martin. Property Master, Robert Laszlo. Script Clerk, Jean Raymond. Running time, 75 minutes.

New York opening, Rialto Theatre, May 9, 1935. Los Angeles opening, Hollywood Pantages Theatre, May 18, 1935.

The Cast: Henry Hull (Dr. Wilfred Glendon), Warner Oland (Dr. Yogami), Valerie Hobson (Lisa Glendon), Lester Matthews (Captain Paul Ames), Lawrence Grant (Sir Thomas Forsythe), Spring Byington (Miss Ettie Coombes), Clark Williams (Hugh Renwick), J.M. Kerrigan (Hawkins), Charlotte Granville (Lady Forsythe), Ethel Griffies (Mrs. Whack), Zeffie Tilbury (Mrs. Moncaster), Jeanne Bartlett (Daisy), Egon Brecher (Priest), Reginald Barlow (Timothy—Faldon Abbey Caretaker), Amber Norman (Prostitute), Jeffrey Hassel (Alf—Zoo Guard), Joseph North (Plimpton—Glendon's Butler), Harry Stubbs (Officer Jenkins), Herbert Evans (Detective Evans), Tempe Pigott (Drunk Woman), Connie Leon (Millie—Yogami's Maid), Eole Galli (Prima Donna at Party), Boyd Irwin (Hotel Manager), Maude Leslie (Mrs. Charteris), William Millman (John Bull), David Thursby (Photographer), J. Gunnis Davis, George Kirby (Detectives), Roseallo Novello (Maid), James May (Barman), Dick Gordon, Edmund Mortimer (Party Guests), Louis Vincenot (Head Coolie), Wong Chung, Beal Wong (Coolies), Helena Grant (Mother), Noel Kennedy (Boy).

6

Procuring *Mad Love*

*I'm really a very mild person, and yet, at the preview of this picture when I
came out, they didn't come up to me for autographs ... everyone ran away
from me.*

> —Curtain speech written for Peter Lorre, to be delivered
> at personal appearances with *Mad Love*, 1935[1]

Lorre's shaven head seems to expose a naked soul full of macabre lusts....
> —*Mad Love* review, *Daily Variety*, June 27, 1935

...one of the most completely horrible stories of the year....
> —*Mad Love* review, *Time* magazine, July 22, 1935

*... Clever makeup men experimented for some time before they succeeded in
getting my hands to look sufficiently horrible.... Two hours each morning; at
the end of which my hands looked terrible, and felt much worse!*
> —Colin Clive, *Film Weekly*, August 16, 1935

*Terrible.... I had more walkouts on this picture than I ever had before on all
the rest of the other pictures I ever ran in the history of the theater....*
> —The manager, Coliseum Theatre, Annawan,
> Illinois, *Motion Picture Herald*, November 16, 1935

*[Peter Lorre's] marbly pupils in the pasty spherical face are like the eye-pieces
of a microscope through which you can see laid flat on the slide the entangled
mind of a man: love and lust, nobility and perversity, hatred of itself and
despair jumping out at you from the jelly.*
> —Graham Greene, *The Spectator*, August 9, 1935

It was 1935, and the water tower at MGM was as ugly as ever.

There was an increasing artifice among the studio's "More Stars Than the Heavens."
Clark Gable now wore dentures; his teeth had been extracted while he was ill during
the shooting of 1933's *Dancing Lady*.[2] Jean Harlow's platinum mane was now a wig; her
weekly Sunday bleachings with peroxide, Lux Flakes, Clorox and ammonia had left her
balding.[3]

Yet Metro-Goldwyn-Mayer had only risen in glorious ascendancy as the most prodigious film studio in the world. Leo the Lion roared defiance at any and all Hollywood
rivals, more proudly than ever before, and with good reason. The studio's 1934 profit had
tallied a staggering $8.6 million. Its nearest competitor: Darryl F. Zanuck's newly formed
20th Century Pictures, with a profit of $1.3 million.[4]

As studio patriarch, Louis B. Mayer could proudly behold his bevy of Metro stars
every noon in the commissary. Garbo, starring in *Anna Karenina*, lunched in private,

A window card for *Mad Love* (MGM, 1935).

of course, but Gable and Harlow breezily dined here. Joan Crawford. Jeanette MacDonald, whom Mayer openly adored. Lionel Barrymore, whom he continued to admire. The Marx Brothers, who would start *A Night at the Opera* in a few weeks. Johnny Weissmuller, who would begin a new Tarzan picture that summer.

Indeed, the MGM commissary might present anyone and everyone from Charles Laughton, at that time co-starring with Gable as Captain Bligh in *Mutiny on the Bounty*, to the leggy showgirls, capering in the prematurely titled *Broadway Melody of 1936*.

This spring day, there were two strange, striking interlopers. One was the short,

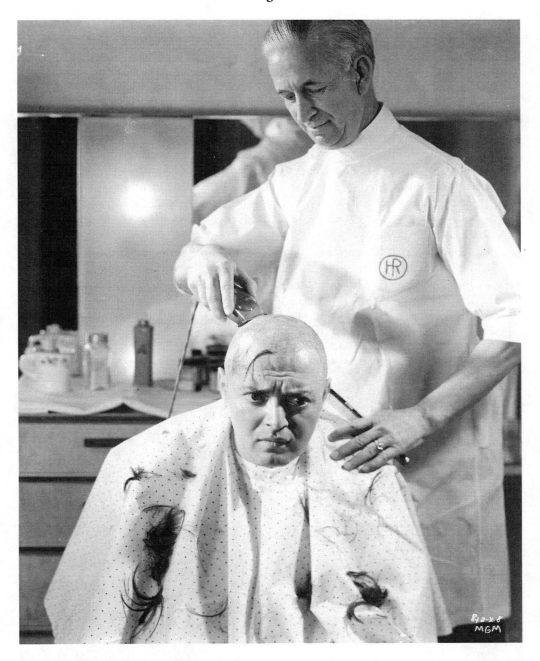

Lorre surrenders his hair for *Mad Love*. Leading lady Frances Drake recalled that he insisted they first meet pre-haircut, so she wouldn't think he was actually bald.

chubby Hungarian actor renowned for the German film *M* (1931), in which he'd played a child killer who kept his victims' shoes. He was Peter Lorre, making his U.S. debut in MGM's horror melodrama *Mad Love*. The makeup department had shaved his head totally bald for his mad doctor role, and he disturbingly resembled a jack-o'-lantern, with real (and enormous) eyes. Also decidedly peculiar was a gaunt British actor who'd played

Henry Frankenstein in Universal's *Frankenstein* (1931) and the recently released *Bride of Frankenstein*. He was Colin Clive. In *Mad Love*, Lorre has transplanted onto Clive's wrists the hands of a knife murderer. Clive wore a hand makeup of livid scars and stitches, worthy of his Universal creations: Karloff's Frankenstein Monster and Elsa Lanchester's Bride.

Then there was *Mad Love*'s ethereal leading lady, Frances Drake. Her makeup this day was strangely "waxy," and for good reason: She was playing her own wax dummy in *Mad Love*—a life-size sex doll that Lorre's Dr. Gogol lovingly keeps in his home.

Joseph Breen of the Production Code Administration had personally addressed Mayer regarding Lorre's *Mad Love* character perfuming and fondling the wax figure. A guillotined head, refastened to a body in a laboratory! Surgical amputations! Knife killings! Horrible! Mayer preferred MGM to be a dream factory, not a haunted house. Yet horror was part of Metro's 1935 program, and this film, the studio boasted, would top all previous screen shockers.

Mad Love had real-life darkness behind the curtain. Lorre was battling drug addiction.[5] Clive was fighting alcoholism.[6] Among the morbid ironies in *Mad Love*'s legacy: When Clive died in 1937, Lorre was one of the pallbearers. Mayer, of course, couldn't foresee this, nor could he imagine that *Mad Love* would be 1935's toxic horror overdose … responsible, perhaps more than any other melodrama of that milestone year, for the temporary entombment of the Horror Film.

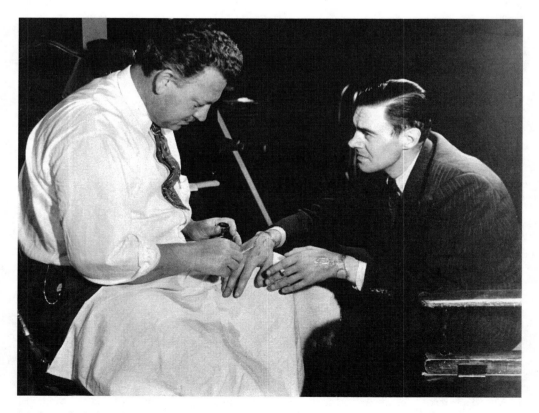

Mad Love's Colin Clive, cigarette in hand, endures a makeup man creating his scarred hands. The highly strung Clive despised the makeup and *Mad Love* itself.

Frances Drake (left) as Yvonne, poses for this publicity picture with the wax Yvonne.

Part One: The Background

The Property

Three months previously:

Wednesday, February 20, 1935: The same day that Tod Browning wrapped MGM's *Mark of the Vampire*, starring Lionel Barrymore, Bela Lugosi and Lionel Atwill, Lucile

Sullivan, a reader in MGM's Story Department, submitted a one-page summary of *The Hands of Orlac*, by Maurice Renard. Sullivan's appraisal:

> *This seems to be enough off the beaten track to make a gruesome and dramatic picture. It has suspense and the final revelation is wholly unexpected. Stock characters but the story can stand on its own feet.*[7]

The basic story: Stephen Orlac, famed piano virtuoso, suffers severe damage to his hands in a train wreck outside Paris. His beautiful wife Rosine is fearful for his hands, and a famed surgeon, Dr. Cerral, saves them. Orlac can no longer play the piano, and is hounded by nightmares, so Rosine calls upon aged Chevalier de Crochans, "a bizarre old spiritualist and painter of souls." De Crochans lives with Edouard Orlac, Stephen's father, who has never forgiven his son for not following him into law and now is a psychic as well. Crochans keeps a life-size puppet which supposedly can contact the spirits of the dead.

De Crochans is murdered, it appears, by his puppet. Edouard Orlac is murdered too, and the dagger in his heart bears the fingerprints of Vasseur, a murderer guillotined on the day of Orlac's train accident. Orlac, losing his sanity, believes that Dr. Cerral had amputated his hands, grafted Vasseur's hands onto him … and that he, Orlac, has killed his own father. Meanwhile, a blackmailer dogs Orlac, claiming that he's the guillotined Vasseur, and that an assistant to Dr. Cerral has resurrected him by grafting his severed head back upon his body. Come the ending, the back-from-the-dead "Vasseur" is revealed to be a phony medium, guilty of all the deaths blamed on Orlac. The dead Vasseur is innocent … and Stephen Orlac does not have a killer's hands. (There had already been a 1924 Austrian film version, *The Hands of Orlac*. It had reunited the star [Conrad Veidt] and director [Robert Wiene] of 1920's *The Cabinet of Dr. Caligari*.)

The story had potential. The major twists to come at MGM would make the surgeon the true monster of the show … and there would be no happy ending. Orlac would indeed have an executed murderer's hands.

The Adaptors

First to tackle a new adaptation of Renard's story at MGM's Culver City plant was the duo of Karl Freund and Guy Endore—Freund a native of Bohemia, Endore of Paris.

The 45-year-old Freund, nicknamed "Papa," weighed close to 300 pounds and wasn't tall. He was a legendary cinematographer, whose camera had embraced Paul Wegener's *Der Golem*, Brigitte Helm's "Evil Maria" of *Metropolis*, Bela Lugosi's *Dracula* and the ardent ape of *Murders in the Rue Morgue* (see Chapter 1). Freund had conceived the heartbreaking "butterfly" ending for *All Quiet on the Western Front*, and had filmed it (Arthur Edeson was the film's official cameraman). Freund became a director on Universal's *The Mummy* in 1932, a beautifully visual film that romantically exalts Karloff's Imhotep as a time-traveling lover as much as an amok mummy. As the late great William K. Everson wrote, *The Mummy* reigns as "the closest that Hollywood ever came to creating a poem out of horror."[8]

MGM wooed Freund away from Universal, and *Mad Love* would be his first film for his new studio. He was determined to make it distinctive—and disturbing.

As for Guy Endore, the 34-year-old novelist had written the 1933 best-seller *Were-Wolf of Paris*, which became a No. 1 *New York Times* best-seller. The saga in summary:

Sgt. Bertrand Caillet, court-martialed in 1871, was born on Christmas Eve; his mother was an adolescent girl, his father the priest who raped her, and these factors presumably contribute to Caillet's lycanthropy. He attacks a prostitute, has sex with his mother and, during the Franco-Prussian War, meets a masochistic lover named Sophie who sympathetically allows him to suck her blood. Both Caillet and Sophie commit suicide and eight years later, when Caillet's grave in Paris is opened, a body of a "dog" is found.

Endore had been one of several writers who contributed to the scripts for MGM's *Mark of the Vampire* and (uncredited) to Universal's *The Raven*. He and Freund were a powerhouse team for *Mad Love*.

Thirty-six-year-old John Considine Jr., associate producer of MGM's 1933 mega-hit *Dancing Lady*, took over as producer. He simultaneously produced *Broadway Melody of 1936*, which became one of the four MGM Best Picture Academy Award nominees for 1935.

Considine and company were determined: *Mad Love* would be a sensation!

The First Treatment

Tuesday, March 12: Five days after Universal completed *Bride of Frankenstein*, four days before MGM started shooting *China Seas*, starring Gable and Harlow, and eight days before Universal began *The Raven*, starring Karloff and Lugosi, Freund and Endore submitted a 25-page "Incomplete File Copy" for *Mad Love*. The first page described a "close-up of a pair of eyes," and as the camera drew back, a "wicked, malicious face" behind iron bars:

> As CAMERA DRAWS BACK FURTHER *the face is seen to belong to a ticket seller at the box office of a theatre exclusively devoted to horror plays.*
> GIRL'S VOICE (off scene): *But you know I have a weak heart.*
> TICKET SELLER: *Madame, we have a trained nurse in attendance.*

The scene evokes Paris' Grand Guignol Theatre. "Madame Yvonne" is the star performer, giving her farewell performance in a play entitled *The Torture Fiends*. The *Mad Love* treatment presented its star trio: the brilliant surgeon "Professor Lebri," an obsessed fan of Yvonne's, who attends the play nightly ("type of Charles Laughton," noted the writers); Yvonne, "clad only in a sketchy costume" (the treatment suggested MGM's blonde Virginia Bruce for the role); and Stephen Orlac, Yvonne's pianist husband, playing a concert in Lyon that evening ("Freddie March type," noted Freund and Endore).

The scenario goes basically the way of the actual film: Lebri pays a call on Yvonne backstage and senses her revulsion; Orlac boards a train and sees the police with Rollo, a circus knife thrower who killed his own father, en route to the guillotine the following dawn. Yet the treatment had several surprises for fans of the release version—and, as a horror scenario, was almost deliriously racy and grim. For one thing, Freund and Endore originally made much more of the train wreck. A bonfire illuminates the wreckage on a rainy night as Yvonne searches for Stephen:

> *Sees foot protruding from debris—shouts "Stephen!" but when dug up, it proves to be another man. He is dead. Yvonne exclaims—"Thank God!" But is then ashamed of herself, for dead man's wife is there and throws herself on body. Someone informs her that many victims have already been taken to baggage room. She runs there. Baggage of all kinds has been pushed aside. Wounded—dying—dead are there on floor in dimly-lit room.*

Nuns—doctors—officials—volunteers—relations rush in every direction. There is moaning, weeping, shouting. It is a ghastly morgue. One woman, unable to bear her grief, goes mad—tears clothes—screams—laughs—capers about wildly. She has to be dragged away....

There was also, crucially, an episode *à la Frankenstein* in which Lebri, with police permission and the help of his assistant Dr. Maurice, plans to revive the guillotined Rollo because he believes the man innocent of the murder charge:

Dissecting room. Professor and assistant busy over dissecting table. A vast conglomeration of glass pipes, tubes, retorts, alembics, electric wires and coils, machinery of all kinds is connected with the body.

> **PROFESSOR LEBRI:** *The head pump. Is it ready? Start it! Now the artificial respiration.*
>
> DR. MAURICE OBEYS. THE MACHINERY WHIRS, SPITS ELECTRIC SPARKS. COLORED LIQUIDS GURGLE THROUGH THE TUBES.
>
> CUT TO: *Body of Rollo on dissecting table, his guillotined head fastened by means of straps and iron braces to the trunk.*
>
> CUT TO: *Dials registering, machinery in action etc.—final burst of sparks, liquids bubbling over etc. then CUT to Rollo's dead face and to Professor and Maurice watching intently.*
>
> CUT TO: *Rollo's eyes opening slowly. The Professor and his assistant exult but their joy is short-lived, the eyes close—and won't open again despite the efforts of Professor.*
>
> **PROFESSOR LEBRI:** *We need a better bracing for the head. I want you to arrange for the construction of a hood that will cover the whole head and neck down to the shoulders. Then we'll try again. We've got to succeed.*

Perhaps the most startling aberration in the March 12 treatment is Lebri's little secret: He keeps a life-size wax "Yvonne" in his boudoir. In the release version, the mad doctor (renamed Gogol) buys a wax figure of Yvonne from the theater and installs it in his house, but the concept is far more developed in the treatment. In fact, when Yvonne rejects his gift of a diamond bracelet, Lebri gives the bracelet to his wax dummy:

Professor Lebri goes upstairs, opens heavily carved oaken door, enters boudoir charmingly furnished in gayest French style—discreet lamps, lacy curtains, expensive objets d'art. On a chaise lounge lies a woman—absolute double of Yvonne—in silk and lace negligee. Professor kneels before her.

Professor fondles hair of Yvonne's double, bends down to kiss her. On the wrist of her arm, which droops, relaxed, over edge of couch, is visible the diamond bracelet.

After Lebri "saves" Orlac's hands, Yvonne says, "I'll never be able to repay you, Professor," and Lebri asks as payment the secret mixture of her perfume. She writes it down for him, and the scene dissolves to:

Paper in hands of clerk over showcase. CAMERA DRAWS BACK revealing luxurious perfume shop furnished in glittering modernistic style.

> **CLERK (TO PROFESSOR):** *Yes Monsieur, I'll have the order filled at once.*
>
> LAP DISSOLVE TO: *lingerie shop with displays of silk stockings, and dainty feminine underthings. Professor receives package, pays and leaves.*

Shortly later, the scene presents "LADY's BOUDOIR," where we see a pair of legs, seated in a wheelchair; they are the apparently pliable legs of the Yvonne wax figure, and Francoise, the doctor's drunken old housekeeper who keeps a pet cockatoo, is "groaning" as she kneels to pull the stockings up "Yvonne's" wax legs. Meanwhile, Lebri, in his room, is wearing a silk dressing gown and "combing his beard in front of mirror." Cut to the dining room, where Francoise pushes in the wheelchair, in which is seated the wax Yvonne in "a low-cut evening dress," the cockatoo perched on the wheelchair.

Professor Lebri (approaching her): *Cherie, I'm sorry I'm late. I had another hectic day. (He kisses top of her head)*

He toasts the wax woman with a champagne cocktail—but it's not over yet. There follows a scene in Lebri's drawing room. Wax Yvonne, "now clad in Oriental evening wrap," sits at the piano. "Professor Lebri," reads the treatment, "is dabbing perfume at lobes of her ears with stopper of perfume bottle." He turns on a mechanism that makes the piano play automatically, the illusion that Yvonne is playing it.

"Now everything is perfect—perfume, too," wrote Freund and Endore.

The *Mad Love* treatment ended on page 25, with Francoise breaking in on this aberrant interlude and Lebri shoving her out the door. "Get out, you drunken idiot … before I kill you!" he roars, then apologizes to Yvonne for losing his temper.

Would any of this story have had a chance in Hell of getting past Joseph Breen and the Production Code Administration?

Censorship

Friday, March 22: Ten days after Freund and Endore submitted their *Mad Love* treatment, MGM previewed *Mark of the Vampire* at the Uptown Theatre in Los Angeles. It was hardly a night of triumph. "Well, I don't think this movie will *hurt* you," a publicist comfortingly told Carroll Borland, who played vampire Luna, after the preview.[9] Metro, aware of the static pace, would desperately cut 14 minutes before release, reducing the film to a bare-bones 61 minutes, a barely allowable length for an "A" picture.

It appeared, based on *Mark of the Vampire*'s preview, that MGM might have fumbled the horror ball again. Could *Mad Love* carry on the charge?

Monday, April 8: Story conferences began on *Mad Love*. John Considine Jr. met with Freund, Endore and P.J. Wolfson—the last having been a contract writer on MGM's *Dancing Lady* (1933) and the recent Jean Harlow musical *Reckless* (1935). They adjusted various lines and business, including cutting the name of the Grand Guignol Theatre. The same quartet met again on April 10; Considine and Wolfson had further conferences on April 11 and April 12. Developed in that time was the role of MacDonald, a breezy reporter, to provide comic relief.

Friday, April 12, Saturday April 13, and Monday, April 15: A new "Temporary Incomplete File Copy" script came together—87 pages, polished by Wolfson. The big sex and horror episodes of the treatment were in place, although there was still no climax; the script ended with a big showdown between Lebri and Yvonne, in which he poured out his love and she responded, "Pity! You disgust me too much even for that!"

One unusual alteration: The play presented in the opening was not *The Torture Fiends*, and the exhibit in the theater foyer was not Yvonne on the rack:

> *In the center stands a wax figure of a beautiful woman. The woman stands erect, a scornful look on her face. At her feet kneels a wax figure of a man. He is bent in grief and supplication, his arms flung around her, his head on her feet. The woman wears a bed jacket and nightgown. The tableau stands on a pedestal. A card in front of it reads:*
> Beyond, *with Madame Yvonne. Last Time Tonight.*

In the playlet, Yvonne has become hysterical after her husband has tried to make love to her—she's committed adultery with another man, whom she still loves. She paces "up and down like a caged tigress," proud of her sins, scorning her husband, vowing she'll leave him. She falls asleep. He closes the windows:

> *Moon beams eerily light up the room. There is a large fireplace with a large gas heater in it. Bending down, the man turns on the gas…. He bends over and kisses his sleeping wife, then seats himself on the floor, leaning his head against the couch near his wife's hand. The escaping gas continues to hiss.*

The writers had opted out of the Grand-Guignol torture-on-the-rack in favor of a sadistic wife, a masochistic husband, and a suicide-murder.

Monday, April 22: Two days after Universal's *Bride of Frankenstein* had its smash opening at the Hollywood Pantages Theatre, Joseph Breen wrote to Louis B. Mayer regarding the temporary script for *Mad Love*. Although Breen opined that the basic story was "acceptable under the provisions of our Production Code," he provided about two and a half pages of concerns, including the new "Yvonne" playlet:

> *[Y]ou will have to be very careful merely to suggest, and not actually to play the scene as set forth in your script. Despite the fact that this is really the part of a play, it may be classified by political censor boards as "details of crime," which may readily be imitated, and, as such, may be deleted from your picture.*[10]

Breen went on with various warnings: "[T]he intimate parts of the body—male or female organs and the breasts of women—are to be fully covered at all times." … "[D]o not overplay the drunkenness of the servant, Francoise." … "[T]he scene showing the railroad wreck, should be merely suggested, and should be handled to get away from any suggestive horror." Of course, Breen was most concerned about the doctor's waxy Yvonne sex doll:

> *In all the business between the professor and the wax figure which he has in his combination sitting room and boudoir, you will have to exercise great care so that there will not be the slightest suggestion of perversion. The professor should not at any time handle or fondle the figure, and it might be well, also, to cut down as much as possible the spraying of the perfume. This kind of action is dangerous material from the standpoint of public entertainment for mixed audiences, and the less suggested about it, the better all around.*

As for the laboratory scene, with Rollo's decapitated head, Breen was fairly restrained:

> *The laboratory business in scene 84 will likewise, have to be handled with extreme care to prevent its becoming too gruesome, too shocking, and too horrifying.*

Time was running out for alterations: The film was set to start shooting in two weeks.

The Dream Team

Tuesday, April 23: There had been talk that *Mad Love* would star Claude Rains. However, on this day, the day after Joseph Breen wrote his *Mad Love* concerns to Louis B. Mayer, *The Hollywood Reporter* announced big news: Peter Lorre would star in *Mad Love*, his U.S. debut.

As noted, Lorre had won worldwide fame in 1931's *M*, directed by Fritz Lang. Always a raconteur, Lorre enjoyed telling the story that a mob had recognized him as "M" one night in Berlin and angrily pursued him down the street! He had starred in Germany's science fiction epic *F.P.1 Antwortet Nicht* (1932), produced by Ufa, and in Britain's *The Man Who Knew Too Much* (1934), directed by Alfred Hitchcock. He and his wife, actress Celia Lovsky, were now in Hollywood, where Lorre was under contract to Columbia. The émigrés lived at 326 Adelaide Drive, above the Pacific Ocean.[11]

Lorre's *Mad Love* casting was complex. Columbia had no film prepared for him, and wanted to loan him to MGM so not to lose money on their investment. Lorre had agreed to go if Columbia promised to produce *Crime and Punishment*, with Lorre as Raskolnikov and Josef von Sternberg as director. At any rate, it was a *coup*: MGM had an internationally acclaimed character star making his Hollywood bow in *Mad Love*.

Wednesday, April 24: John L. Balderston reported to MGM, in the words of *The Hollywood Reporter*, to "polish up dialogue" for *Mad Love*. He was the man for the job: His name had appeared on the play *Dracula*, plus (among other films) *Frankenstein*, *The Mummy*, *Bride of Frankenstein* (see Chapter 4) and *Mark of the Vampire*.

A portrait of Peter Lorre, dated 1935.

Friday, April 26: Paramount dispatched Frances Drake to MGM to play Yvonne in *Mad Love*—replacing originally announced Virginia Bruce. Drake was a foxy Hollywood vamp. She was previously loaned to MGM for the Clark Gable–Joan Crawford–Robert Montgomery 1934 Christmas release *Forsaking All Others*, where she played a temptress wearing a high-collared black cape that looked as if it was borrowed from Bela Lugosi.

"Oh, I'm such a *bitch* in that, aren't I?" she'd proudly recalled of *Forsaking All Others* over 50 years later.[12]

Posterity will acclaim Frances Drake, both for *Mad Love* and Universal's Karloff-Lugosi vehicle *The Invisible Ray* (1936), as one of the Golden Age of Horror's top Scream Queens.

Wednesday, May 1: "Clive Wary," headlined *Variety*, noting:

> Colin Clive goes to Metro for featured spot in Mad Love…. Picture is third horror thriller for Clive, who was in two Frankenstein *features at Universal, and sustained injury while working in each. Player is trying to anticipate what will happen on Metro picture.*

Clive was hurt tussling with Karloff on the original *Frankenstein*, and fell down stairs during the shooting of *Bride of Frankenstein*. The highly strung actor was a natural for the tormented Stephen Orlac.

With the casting of Lorre, Drake and Clive, *Mad Love* had a dream team trio of stars.

Also on May 1: Balderston, who had restored the original opening playlet with Yvonne branded on the rack and had finessed the episode, wrote an MGM Inter-Office Communication to Joseph Breen, noting:

> *The little horror playlet, scenes 11 to 25 inclusive, will be played for burlesque, not horror, as is indicated by the climax, scenes 22–25, and direction will be careful to avoid making the scene on the stage seem real or showing anything offensive.*

As for scenes 22–25: As Yvonne unleashes a "wild scream" onstage, a man in the audience "leaps up screaming, 'Stop! Stop!'" The man falls on the floor in the aisle in a simulated faint as a nurse on duty runs down the aisle to him, followed by two ushers— one dressed as a vampire, one as a devil. After the playlet, we see the man in the lobby with the nurse, who is laughing:

> **Nurse:** *Your scream was better than Yvonne's.*
> **Man:** *I put on a bit extra for the last night. The best thing in the show, and they only pay me 20 francs.*

Alas, the bit—an apparent jab at the on-duty-nurse and screaming patrons Universal engaged for showings of *Frankenstein*—didn't appear in the release version.

Also, on May 1: Balderston submitted his polished script-so-far for *Mad Love* ... only 21 pages. The next day, MGM sent the pages to Joe Breen for approval. Balderston continued working on the script at least until May 22, 16 days after shooting begins. Aware

On the rack: Frances Drake's Yvonne performs the horror playlet in *Mad Love*.

of Breen's objections, Balderston toned down the bits with Yvonne's wax figure (no dressing it up in lingerie and silk stockings, for example), but did enjoy spicing up the script with in-jokes related to other horror films. For example, late in the film, drunken Francoise sees the real-life Yvonne and thinks the wax statue has come to life—and screams, "It's come alive!" The line resembled, of course, Colin Clive's infamous cry of "It's alive!" in *Frankenstein.*[13]

Meanwhile, MGM cast the featured roles with contract players. Ted Healy, who split from his backup comics, the Three Stooges, was cast as Reagan the reporter (formerly named MacDonald). Isabel Jewell, diminutive platinum blonde actress who frequently played floozies, signed on as Marianne, a flirtatious Parisienne thief. Ian Wolfe acted the role of Henry Orlac, Stephen's wretched father.

Edward Brophy was set as Rollo, the guillotined knife thrower. Before shooting began, MGM measured Brophy for "an iron mask which will sheath his head during most of the production of *Mad Love.*" This related to the previously quoted script treatment, which noted that the mad doctor wanted "the construction of a hood that will cover the whole head and neck down to the shoulders" to fasten the headless body.

The reason for the seemingly oddball casting of bald, chubby Brophy, usually a comic actor, becomes evident in *Mad Love*'s last act: He basically resembles Lorre's Gogol! Also, Brophy had portrayed one of the Rollo Brothers in MGM's 1932 *Freaks* (one wonders if he was supposed to be the same character, thus the ultimate homage to an earlier horror movie).

Chester Lyons, cinematographer of MGM's beautiful *Sequoia* (1934), was chief cameraman. Karl Freund planned to borrow Gregg Toland from Samuel Goldwyn for special scenes.

The Hollywood Reporter promised that the "highlight and extra kick" of *Mad Love* would be "the resuscitation of a dead man." Meanwhile, Freund and Lorre psyched up for *Mad Love* in a peculiar way: They sat through two major operations at Los Angeles' Lutheran Hospital in order to soak up "atmosphere."[14]

Part Two: The Shoot

Creating monsters is good fun in fiction, but scientists and biologists should thank their stars that it's never occurred in real life.
                    —Colin Clive, *Los Angeles Times*, May 13, 1935

Good Fun...?

Monday, May 6: Mad Love started shooting. The same day, *The Black Room*, starring Boris Karloff in dual roles as good and wicked medieval barons, began at Columbia.

The budget for *Mad Love*: $217,176.53.[15] The shooting schedule: 24 days. This was about $8400 more than the budget of *Mark of the Vampire*, and the same number of filming days. A female reporter for *Silver Screen* magazine wrote:

Out on the Metro-Goldwyn-Mayer lot, Culver City's pride and joy and as merry a studio as you may find in the whole Hollywood colony … they are making a horror picture that will doubtless end all horror pictures.

From the time of Chaney down through Karloff, productions of this type have been promised.… That was before an inoffensive-appearing Hungarian by the name of Peter Lorre arrived on the scene.[16]

The major attraction on the *Mad Love* set, of course, was Lorre. Andre Sennwald, a 28-year-old *New York Times* film critic, visited Hollywood during the eventful summer of 1935. He paid a call to the *Mad Love* set and observed Lorre between scenes, smoking a cigarette and tossing off dark witticisms on a variety of topics.

On his emigration from Germany: "The country was too small for two such monsters as Hitler and myself."

On children: "I hate child actors." (He appeared to mean it, according to Sennwald.)

As for *M,* he had a virtual stand-up routine regarding his notoriety. Among them was the saga of a man in Munich so disturbed by Lorre's chilling performance that he suffered a heart attack. Lorre told Sennwald that he had to restrain his press agent from issuing a release boasting about the incident.[17]

Frances Drake, agog over Lorre, told me in 1986:

Little Peter Lorre was charming, and so cute.… He had to meet me before he had his head shaved, to show me that he had hair. And lots of it.… But he was rather naughty. If your scene was going

Peter Lorre's "ellipsoidal" profile vs. Frances Drake's favored left side as Gogol and Yvonne have an emotional showdown.

Frances Drake in all her pre–Code glory in *The Trumpet Blows* (Paramount, 1934). Drake had a harrowing real-life knife experience while making this film.

very well, he'd suddenly say, "Don't you know me? I'm your little Peter!" You know, he didn't want you to be too good!

Mad Love's leading lady had already had a frightening Hollywood experience with knives. During the shooting of Paramount's *The Trumpet Blows* (1934), Drake met Steve Clemente, who told her that he had once had a knife-throwing act in a circus. Clemente asked Drake if she would pose for him if he came to the set with his knives. Drake politely agreed, never thinking it would actually happen:

> *My dear, he brought the knives! So, during the lunch hour, outside, he said, "I'm all ready—you stand there," and he was going to outline my head if you don't mind, with the knives! I thought, "I'll trust this man, I'm sure he's all right," and I felt I should do it because I said I would. So, he said, "Let's do the profile first," and I said, "That's a good idea," and as I was standing there, he did the profile. Then he said, "We'll do your front face." So he threw a knife, about six inches from the face. Just then, the director, Stephen Roberts, appeared, and he said, "You stop that at once. I don't care what you do when the picture's finished—but not during the picture!"*
>
> *Well ... it turned out that this knife-thrower had killed his wife in his act—and that's why he had to stop. Of course, he didn't mean to—but he didn't tell me that before!*

Colin Clive also had a real-life hook to his *Mad Love* role. Born to a military ancestry, Clive had the boyhood dream to join the British Cavalry in India. A horse fall at Sandhurst, England's Royal Military Academy, had ended his hopes of becoming a Bengal Lancer. The actor must have related to Orlac's injury, which shattered the character's musical career.

The chain-smoking star trio got along nicely, and the work was impressive. The atmosphere on the Metro lot was exciting: *Broadway Melody of 1936* started shooting April 29, one week before *Mad Love* commenced, and starred tap-dancing marvel Eleanor Powell. *Mutiny on the Bounty* began filming May 8, two days after *Mad Love*'s start, and pitted Clark Gable's Fletcher Christian vs. Charles Laughton's Captain Bligh. *Mutiny on the Bounty* won the 1935 Best Picture Oscar.

Hollywood history was epically alive at MGM, and in the midst of it, *Mad Love* aspired to be the "horror picture that will doubtless end all horror pictures."

Yet the film had a major problem: Karl Freund, a genius as a cinematographer, was a sadist as a director. He had behaved abominably on *The Mummy*. The topper on that film: Ordering leading lady Zita Johann into an arena with lions for a Christian martyr reincarnation episode that was ultimately cut from the film. Everyone else on the crew was protected from the lions except Zita, and the corpulent Freund directed the episode from his own personal cage.

"A very large one," recalled Johann, who late in life referred to Freund as "that pig."[18]

Now, on *Mad Love*, Freund indulged himself with camera wizardry, bullying Chester Lyons and Gregg Toland (cinematographer on 20th Century's 1935 *Les Misérables*, in which Frances Drake had played the self-sacrificing Eponine). He basically ignored his actors. Drake remembered:

> Mad Love *was a bit difficult.... Director Karl Freund kept wanting to be the cinematographer at the same time—and Gregg Toland was a marvelous cameraman! He was such a dear little man, sort of slender, and he looked rather hunted when this wretched big fat man would say, "Now, now, we'll do it this way!"*

The actors could fend for themselves, of course, and did. Producer John Considine Jr., supervising *Broadway Melody of 1936* at the same time as *Mad Love*, decided to take on the additional responsibility of being *Mad Love*'s uncredited director. As Drake remembered, the stint didn't last long:

> *You never knew who was directing. The producer was dying to, to tell you the truth, and of course, he had no idea of directing. Finally, I said, "Look here, we've got to have one director, because we're all going mad."*

Between scenes: Karl Freund (seated in sunglasses) directs the guillotine episode. Standing from left: Ted Healy, Henry Kolker and Peter Lorre.

That Englishman, Colin Clive, would go to sleep. He'd pay no attention to anybody—it was too sweet! He didn't care who was directing, he didn't give a damn. He was such a good actor he didn't need it, perhaps!

The show went on, despite "Papa" Freund's half-hearted direction and bellicose ways. Adding to the tension was the fact that John Balderston was still writing the script.

On a soundstage where "M" and "Dr. Frankenstein" co-starred, things eventually darkened.

There was, for example, Colin Clive's genuine and barely controlled hysteria over the stitched-on-hands makeup he wore as Orlac. Usually reserved with the press, Clive gushed to *Film Weekly* so vehemently about *Mad Love* that the journal would headline the feature, "I Hate Horror Films." Clearly anguished by his role, he ranted most bitterly about the two-hour makeup for his "transplanted" hands:

The finger joints were built up; the hands had to be almost a quarter larger than normal size. Then, around the wrists, where the surgeon had supposedly grafted them on to their new "foundation," ghastly scars were created.... I know that my hands were first stained with something green; then with something blue and then with something white. Meanwhile, the knuckles and palms were built up and coarsened with some kind of wax, over which new skin was laid. The wrinkles in the joints were picked out with innumerable exaggerations traced with an ordinary lead pencil.

The experience of viewing one's own hands in this condition was in itself a shock. Often, I felt quite sick, and the real hands underneath this awful disguise ached with some unaccountable form of irritation. All day and every day, I felt that I would give almost anything to be able to wash away the whole ghoulish mess and forget the rest of the picture!

Frances Drake knew about Clive's offscreen torment:

Colin Clive was a great drunk, you know—a pity. No problem on the set, he always knew his lines, and everything was fine; he didn't appear drunk at all. But I remember once we were at a party about six or seven in the evening, and he was in the garden, and he was sitting on a little straight-backed chair. And we were all having a drink. The back of the chair sank slowly down, and he lay there with his head in a flower bed, drinking his drink—and nothing fazed him! Absolutely amazing!

As for Peter Lorre, he was fighting drug addiction, which also plagued his wife Celia. Not long after *Mad Love*, October 21, 1935, Lorre and Celia embarked on the *Santa Fe Chief* to begin a trip for Europe aboard the *Berengaria*. Traveling with them was writer-director Billy Wilder, whom Lorre had known since his days in Berlin and Vienna. As Stephen D. Youngkin wrote in his acclaimed biography *The Lost One: A Life of Peter Lorre*, Celia approached Wilder on the train, desperate that Lorre's "medicine" had "broken" and asking Wilder to wire ahead for a doctor at the next stop to provide Lorre's prescription. Wilder recalled:

Then I went back to the compartment and Celia was trying to calm Peter down, hold him down. He was in excruciating pain and absolutely suicidal. If he would have been able to open the window, he would have thrown himself out of the train, so we pacified him....

The doctor refused to provide the medicine at the train stop—the prescription was for morphine. The train trip resumed:

The train started again, and again we had to calm down Peter and it was not an easy task. He was just like a madman. Then Cilly [Celia] and I decided to send a wire to the next stop which was Albuquerque, to have an ambulance ready for him. There was indeed an ambulance. And there were two nurses and a doctor. It was a Catholic hospital [Saint Joseph's] and we got him off the train with Cilly and their luggage. And I went on because I knew the man needed hospital attention.

Wilder was amazed, after boarding the *Berengaria*, to find Lorre and Celia aboard, calm and convivial. "Peter had been provisioned by the nuns at the hospital," said Wilder. "Naturally, he charmed them all."[19]

For damaged souls such as Lorre and Clive, the attempt to create this horror film of all horror films must have seemed trite. Professionals, they nevertheless give it their all. In the film, a mad doctor transplanted a bit of a man's soul into a patient by grafting on the dead man's hands. Lorre and Clive appeared to be grafting a bit of their own souls into *Mad Love*.

The Cut and Altered Scenes

As *Mad Love* is so familiar to horror fans and the DVD easily available, there's no need to devote many words to the film's major sequences. Rather, we'll proceed describing alterations in the script, and cut and altered scenes.

1. The laboratory scene, dated May 22. This was the "mad lab" centerpiece of *Mad Love*, with dialogue between Lorre's Dr. Gogol and Keye Luke's Dr. Wong:

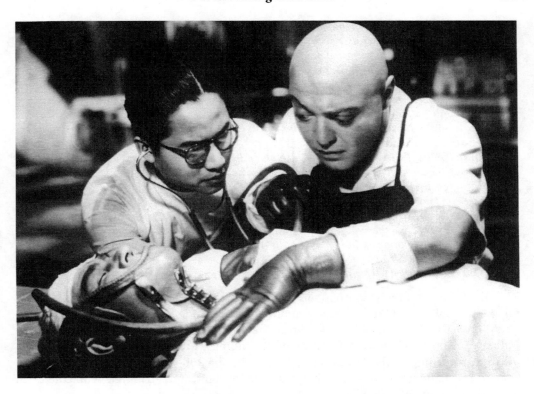

A scene from what was filmed as *Mad Love*'s spectacular horror centerpiece: Dr. Wong
(Keye Luke) and Dr. Gogol (Peter Lorre) fasten the head of guillotined knife murderer Rollo
(Edward Brophy) back onto his body by means of a brace to restore him temporarily to life. The
sequence was cut before the film's release.

> *INT. GOGOL'S LAB Fitted up with glass pipes, tubes, wires, coils, all the appliances of scientific experiment. CAMERA PANS SLOWLY around until it sights Gogol and Wong in center of room. In front of them, on table propped against wall, is body of Rollo. His head is fastened by means of straps and iron braces to trunk.*
>
> *A glass tube is in his neck. This is attached by long rubber tube to beaker which holds blood fluid, under which gas flame is burning. A sort of bellows is connected to the beaker.*
>
> *Both men are very sure in their movements, but Gogol is laboring under suppressed excitement; Wong, calm and self-possessed*
>
> **Gogol:** *Ah. But the great artery! That is the crux. Now—if I can pump blood through the severed artery, what will that prove, Wong?*
>
> **Wong:** *That you have done the impossible.*
>
> **Gogol:** *(working fervently at the beaker, seeing that tubing leading to body is all right) Why? It's been done with rabbits, with dogs, same thing—ready?*
> *(turns stop-cork in tubing near beaker)*
> *You've forgotten the music—you know I always must have music at the crisis.*
>
> *Wong goes to the phonograph, starts it, it begins to play Bach, and continues throughout the whole scene. Wong turns back to Gogol.*
>
> **Gogol:** *Now go ahead—and gently with those bellows, Wong!*
> *Wong gently presses the bellows.*
> *CLOSE SHOT—BEAKER CONTAINING BLOODLIKE FLUID The fluid slowly begins to sink in the beaker. Cry of joy from Gogol.*
> *MED. CLOSE SHOT—GOGOL—WONG—CORPSE*

GOGOL: *(watching eagerly) That's enough!*
    Wong leaves bellows, crosses over, puts his stethoscope against chest of dead man.
WONG: *(for the first time, excited. Raises his head) The heart! It beats!*
GOGOL: *(laughs) Fooled you that time, Wong. But your bellows did pump blood back into the heart—and through that severed artery! If we can join the severed ends—don't you see?*
WONG: *(with reverence in his voice) I see, master. For the moment, I even thought—*
GOGOL: *Ah, yes, someday we can do even that!*
WONG: *(shrugs his shoulders) It would be a pity.*
GOGOL: *To defeat death—a pity?*
WONG: *(smiling) How foolish you Occidentals are! Life is only a preparation for death.*
GOGOL: *The day will come when man can stay alive as long as he wills!*
WONG: *(gently, with a remote sort of pity) Then he will learn to* will *death. For what is life? We seek and do not find—power—riches—we seek love, and are left with empty arms.*
GOGOL: *Come, Wong, there is no time to lose. That secondary suture we did on the pneumo-gastric nerve and the hypoglossal was difficult and now we have seen that it is possible to re-establish circulation of the blood. There is still work to be done on the phremic nerve, but for the present our dead friend here must serve us in another way.*
    The two men turn to corpse, start lifting sheet.

The purpose of reviving Rollo temporarily is to get the blood flowing into his hands for the transplant. MGM apparently mounted the episode with considerable expense. On May 29, *The Hollywood Reporter* wrote that Metro had borrowed "an ultraviolet ray diffuser" from the California Institute of Technology, presumably for this scene. The diffuser, according to the blurb, reportedly emitted a 200-degree flash on the set. The camera and all microphones were shielded from the light, and "all players with gold teeth warned out of range."

    2. A scripted episode preceding the Orlac Meets Gogol-Rollo showdown scene presented a Street Fair in Montmartre, with a merry-go-round, show booths, a shooting gallery and a Punch and Judy show. There's a knife thrower, hurling knives around his female partner's head. From the script:
    There are two other human figures drawn on board placed alongside of girl. The girl is protected from inexpert throwers by a wooden partition."
    The knife-thrower calls to the crowd as he throws the knives, "Try your skill, ladies and gents—You see how easy it is—six knives for fifty centimes—win a prize!" Orlac walks up to the platform, "fascinated":
    CLOSE SHOT—STEPHEN: As his phobia creeps over him, and he sees what is going on. He edges up to the platform, and, as if in spite of himself, reaches over his hand and fondles the knives on the tray. Knife-thrower, having just thrown a knife, turns to pick up another. Sees Stephen.
    Knife-thrower: *Fancy yourself, friend? Only 50 centimes!*
    Stephen picks up large knife, weighs it in his hand, pulls it back behind his shoulder, as if about to throw it. Knife-thrower recognizes the professional gesture.
    Knife-thrower: *You've done it before! Here's an old hand! Come up and show 'em what you can do!*
    CLOSE SHOT—STEPHEN: Holding knife, struggling with desire to throw knife. He conquers impulse, puts knife down, like an unclean thing, and walks away out of shot.

The Call Bureau Cast Sheet for *Mad Love*, which lists all actors who worked on the film, does not list the knife-thrower or his female partner, which indicates that this episode was probably not shot.

3. As for Marianne, played by Isabel Jewell … she was "a street girl," a thief who vamped Ian Wolfe's Henry Orlac in order to rob his jewelry shop.

EXT. ORLAC JEWELRY SHOP—NIGHT: Orlac Sr. with a street girl, Marianne, holding her by arm, enters.

Orlac Sr.: *My shop.*

Marianne: *So, you weren't lyin'. Jewels—all yours.*

Orlac Sr.: *(fumbling with latchkey) Come inside a minute.*

Marianne: *No, I couldn't.*

Orlac Sr.: *I've got the prettiest little bracelet in my safe. (fondles her arm)*

She pretends to hesitate, and he unlocks the door.

Marianne: *Well, just for a minute.*

He enters shop first. Marianne's hand, as she enters, skillfully fixes catch on lock so door can be opened from without. As she does so, looks up street.

LONG SHOT—STREET: An Apache standing in shadow on a corner, watching her. He makes a slight signal to her, with his hand.

INT. SHOP—ORLAC'S PRIVATE OFFICE—Door is open and a little light penetrates through shop from the street. We see Orlac's shadowy back as, on one knee, he twirls dials of the safe.

EXT. SHOP—As a shadowy outline forms and grows larger as someone approaches the window. It slinks back into an alleyway.

EXT. STREET—As a gendarme on a bicycle pedals quietly past.

EXT. SHOP—As the shadow begins to emerge slowly from the alleyway.

INTERIOR ORLAC'S OFFICE—As Orlac swings wide the safe and twirls the combination of the inner door. He gets it open and pulls out a tray of jewels. There is a faint noise—as of door gently opening and closing. Orlac looks frightened. He begins putting the tray back in the safe. Suddenly his face contorts with pain. He stiffens erect, draws in a grating, choking breath, his eyes stare, his mouth is agape, gasping. Slowly he falls forward, dragging some silver plate with him. Screams from girl, stifled, as though hand were clapped over her mouth.

CLOSE SHOT ORLAC—Sprawled on floor, knife in back.

The actual killer of Orlac Sr. is Gogol, who has thrown a knife into the lecher's back and wants to convince Stephen Orlac that he's killed his own father.

4. The classic scene of *Mad Love* is the episode in which Gogol hopes to drive Orlac hopelessly insane by disguising himself as the dead Rollo and convincing Orlac that he (Orlac) has Rollo's knife-throwing hands. The scene, dated May 13 by Balderston, differed in several key ways from the scene as

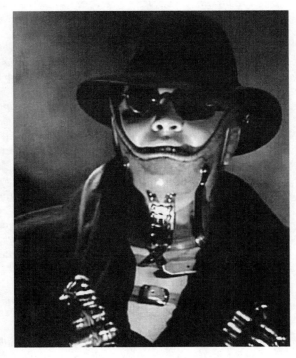

One of the most chilling scenes in Classic Horror: Lorre's Dr. Gogol poses as the decapitated Rollo, his severed head braced back on his body, and his amputated hands replaced by metal appendages … all designed to drive Orlac mad.

it appeared in the film, as noted by [brackets for deletions] and (NOTES for changes and additions):

EXT. PARIS—EVENING—IN THE WORST SLUMS—Half broken-down wall, foul-looking warrens. We see Stephen walking along apparently looking for an address....

INT. DIMLY LIT CORRIDOR: Stephen comes down hall, stops at the second door [and knocks]. [Rasping Voice: Come in.]

Stephen opens door and enters.

INT. DINGY ROOM—[lit only by coal fire burning in grate] (NOTE: in the movie, there is no fire but there is a lamp on the table), *flickering shadows on the walls. Backed away from light is Gogol-Rollo, wrapped in cloak. [Between him and door is small cheap plain wood table.]* (NOTE: Gogol-Rollo is seated at the table instead of standing with the table between him and the door.)

STEPHEN: *Was it you who telephoned me to come [to this foul hole]?* (NOTE: Stephen says "here" instead of bracketed words.)

GOGOL-ROLLO: *(rasping voice) Yes.*

STEPHEN: *You said you can tell me the truth—about my hands.*

GOGOL-ROLLO: *[(gives inhuman laugh)] They [do things]—throw knives[, don't they]?*

STEPHEN: *How do you know that?*

[GOGOL-ROLLO ADVANCES. WE NOW SEE A CAPE IS THROWN OVER HIS HEAD; COMPLETELY MUFFLING HEAD, SHOULDERS AND HANDS.]

[GOGOL-ROLLO: Hold out your hands.]

[STEPHEN HOLDS OUT HIS HANDS INTO THE FIRELIGHT.] GOGOL-ROLLO LIFTS CLOAK FROM HIS HANDS AND STICKS THEM FORWARD. THEY ARE MADE OF STEEL, LIKE ROBOT'S.

GOGOL-ROLLO: *I have no hands. Yours, they were mine, once.*

STEPHEN: *I knew it! He lied!*

GOGOL-ROLLO: *And so, when you knifed your father in the back [tonight]* (NOTE: Gogol-Rollo says "last night" instead of "tonight"), *you killed him with* my *hands.*

STEPHEN: *Killed my father—no—I threw a knife at him yesterday, but...* (NOTE: Stephen has additional dialogue: "Last night ... no ...")

[GOGOL-ROLLO: That was yesterday. Your aim tonight was better.] (NOTE: Gogol-Rollo says "You remember now?" instead)

STEPHEN: *(already driven half-insane by this) [Did I...could I...I remember nothing—after the knife thrower at the street fair.]* (NOTE: Stephen says instead: "No. Since I left Dr. Gogol, I can't remember anything.")

Suddenly Gogol-Rollo's steel claws clumsily pull knife from beneath his cloak and jams it into the wooden table. [Stephen backs away from the knife. Gogol-Rollo picks it up and tosses it across the table.]

GOGOL-ROLLO: *Pick it up. [You want to. I know you do; I know my hands.]*

[(Stephen, as though half-hypnotized, picks it up.)]

Feel the balance. [A lovely blade. It's yours—come in handy—] (NOTE: Gogol-Rollo says instead: "use it") *when they try to arrest you.*

[As in a trance, Stephen puts it into his pocket.] (NOTE: Stephen holds the knife through the rest of this scene.)

STEPHEN: *(hoarsely) Who are you?*

[Again that laugh.]

GOGOL-ROLLO: *[I killed my father too.] I am—Rollo—the knife-thrower.*

STEPHEN: *(in a whisper) Rollo died on the guillotine.*

GOGOL-ROLLO: *Yes[, but he came back]. That Gogol [—black magic—he put my hands on you; he put my head back here.]* (NOTE: Gogol-Rollo says instead: "They cut off my head. But that Gogol he put it back—here.")

[(touches his head)]

Gogol steps toward into light and pulls his cape away to reveal a head wearing hat pulled down over forehead, black mask over eyes, and a curious steel and leather brace around his neck. This is the same steel brace we saw on Rollo during the experiment in Gogol's lab. As Gogol calculates, this culminating horror drives Stephen quite out of his head. Looks at apparition and begins to laugh. His laughter rises. Flees from the room, still laughing.

In the release version, Lorre saved the "inhuman laugh" for the revelation where he appeared to be Rollo with his head braced atop his neck. It's incredibly startling, as if a wheezing exorcised devil has escaped from Gogol's body. Strangely, Clive, while acting with intensity, chose to underplay the scene; there's no rising laughter as Orlac flees the room. Perhaps Lorre and Clive (and Freund, if he bothered to get involved) felt one blast of mad laughter was enough; at any rate, the scene is a classic and still packs a powerful punch.

5. Later in the script, in the Prefect's Outer Office, there is a scene involving Marianne and the Apache (played by Harold Huber). They have been arrested after the murder of Stephen Orlac's father:

Outer door opens, and detective pushes in Marianne and Apache, handcuffed together. Girl, like a spitfire, turns on the Apache. Nobody can get in a word while she screams....
Marianne: *(screams) He did it—I'm innocent—We agreed to rob the old man—but I never knew he meant to kill him!*
Apache slaps the girl across the mouth to keep her quiet....
They've been arrested after attempting to pawn Orlac's jewels.

Some *Mad Love* posters went out with Isabel Jewell's name prominently displayed, indicating her deletion from the film was a late-in-the-game decision.

*   *   *

Of course, *Mad Love*'s finale flows deliriously; as scripted, Lorre's Gogol returns home, laughing triumphantly and insanely at the success of his Rollo masquerade. Drake's Yvonne is hiding in Gogol's house, watching as he cackles and grotesquely strips off his neck brace like a fat witch struggling out of her corset. As she tries to save herself by posing as his wax statue, Gogol serenades her at the organ. The pet cockatoo flies, and scratches Yvonne's face.

She screams ... and there's blood on her cheek.

"Galatea!" rhapsodizes Gogol. "I am Pygmalion.... You came to life in my arms.... Galatea! Give me your lips!"

However, a phantom voice tauntingly sounds in the chamber: "Each man kills the thing he loves.... *Each man kills the thing he loves....*"

The line is a paraphrase of the ominous warning from *WereWolf of London*, "The werewolf instinctively seeks to kill the thing it loves best." Gogol carries Yvonne to a couch and starts strangling her with her own hair as he recites:

> *In one long raven string I wind,*
> *Three times her little throat around*
> *And strangle her. No pain feels she*
> *I am quite sure she feels no pain.*[20]

The police crash into the house with Orlac. The door to the chamber is locked, but Orlac can see through a window in the barred door.

"He's killing her!" cries Clive's Orlac—and fatally throws a knife, with the skill of Rollo the knife thrower, into Gogol's back.

The men break into the room. Orlac takes Yvonne in his arms, which still have Rollo's hands. And the film fades out with the chilling question:

Will Stephen Orlac, with his knife-murderer hands, eventually "kill the thing he loves"?[21]

*   *   *

Tuesday, June 4: A Tale of Two Cities started shooting at MGM. It too, of course, had a guillotine.

Saturday, June 8: MGM completed *Mad Love*. It ran one week over schedule

Dimitri Tiomkin, future multiple Oscar winner, scored *Mad Love* quite non-intrusively. A highlight: the "very modern music" (as Gogol derisively calls it) that Orlac plays, that sounds like a satanic boogie-woogie.

Final cost: $261,000—more than $40,000 over budget.[22]

Part Three: Promotion, Censorship, Release and Impact

> *"THE THING" ... demanded—love.*
> —MGM's *Mad Love* publicity manual

Since MGM had high hopes for *Mad Love*, the studio's master publicist, Howard Dietz, began a marketing campaign while it was still shooting, the manual dated May 29, 1935. At the time, MGM was planning to change the title to *The Hands of Orlac*.

The manual started off hailing Lorre as "Dynamic Star of *M* and *The Man Who Knew Too Much*"; Frances Drake, her name below the title, was "The Luscious Beauty of *Forsaking All Others*."

As for "Exploitation," there were various ideas:

Knife Thrower As Ballyhoo:
If you can get an expert knife thrower you have an ideal ballyhoo for the picture, used either in the lobby, on the streets on a ballyhoo truck, or in a store window or other prominent location.... If your performer works with a human target, particularly a pretty girl, you have the real thing in ballyhoo.

Then there's:

Street Ballyhoo Using Tall "Undertaker"
Find the tallest, thinnest man in town, dress him in black clothes to suggest the comedy idea of an undertaker, and let him wear a high black hat, with the long black hair of a wig extending down on his shoulders.
Give him a small handbag or case bearing the following wording:

> *Don't Stop Me!*
> *Something Happened At*
> *Loew's State Theatre....*
> *It's Horrible!*
> *It's* The Hands Of Orlac

Metro also decided to do something "different" with the trailer. "PETER LORRE— WHOM CHARLIE CHAPLIN CALLS 'THE GREATEST LIVING ACTOR,'" headlined the screen, then showing Lorre (with hair) relaxing at home, draped in a chair, a large dog beside him. An attractive woman in a negligee and on a lounge somehow had his phone number, called him to express her admiration, and asked about his new picture. There followed such clips as Lorre laughing madly in his "Rollo" mask, Frances Drake on the rack, and a close-up of Clive, beneath which reads, "COLIN CLIVE—'Doctor Frankenstein.'"

Wednesday, June 26: MGM previewed *Mad Love* at the Alexander Theatre in Glendale. The next day, *The Hollywood Reporter* and *Daily Variety* ran reviews. Both praised the star, the *Reporter* hailing, "Lorre triumphs superbly in a characterization that is sheer horror." *Daily Variety* clocked the print at 82 minutes.

Monday, July 1: The Film Daily reviewed *Mad Love*, headlining, "Strong Horror Melodrama Hits High Spot in Its Class with New Twists and Expert Production":

> *Peter Lorre, who is just about tops in the thriller-chiller sort of thing, makes his American film debut in one of the most fantastic horror numbers ever presented....*

The review noted, "A number of new elements are introduced, one of them being the bringing back to life a man, whose head has been severed from his body, so that his hands may be grafted onto another body." *The Film Daily* gave *Mad Love*'s running time as 83 minutes.

Wednesday, July 3: The Breen Office reviewed *Mad Love*. On July 5, Breen wrote to L.B. Mayer:

> *We have requested the deletion of the shots of the murderer being tipped forward into the guillotine, as unduly gruesome. The cutter who accompanied the picture assured us this change could and would be made. With this understanding, we take pleasure in enclosing herewith the Association's certificate No. 1034.*

Mad Love got off far more easily with Breen than had *Bride of Frankenstein*. Yet here entered a mystery: Some time between the preview in late June and the release in July, MGM decided to make cuts in *Mad Love*—*14 to 15 minutes* of them. They included, as noted, the Rollo head-strapped-to-body laboratory episode (the film's horror centerpiece), as well as Isabel Jewell's entire performance as Marianne the thief. By the time the Metro editing department made all the surgical amputations, *Mad Love* ran 68 minutes.

Added to the attraction was this recorded prologue, which will strike some horror fans as strangely familiar:

> *Ladies and gentlemen, Metro-Goldwyn-Mayer feels that it would be a little unkind to present this picture without just a word of friendly warning. We are about to unfold a story which we consider one of the strangest tales ever told. We think it will thrill you. It may shock you. It might even horrify you. So, if any of you feel that you do not care to subject your nerves to such a strain, now is your chance to—well, we've warned you.*

It was, almost word for word, the same speech Edward Van Sloan delivered before the credits of *Frankenstein*. Presumably, John L. Balderston intended it as an in-joke. One guesses it came without the permission of Universal. It eventually went missing from *Mad Love*.

Monday, July 22: Time magazine reviewed *Mad Love*, two days before the Hollywood opening. "[O]ne of the most completely horrible stories of the year," judged *Time*.

It praised Lorre and his flair for "suggesting the most unspeakable obsession with the roll of a protuberant eyeball, an almost feminine mildness of tone, an occasional quiver of thick lips set flat in his cretinous ellipsoidal face." The review also noted the film's chillingly downbeat ending:

> *Even the music that bursts forth for the lovers' reunion has chilling overtones, for nothing has been done about the hands of Orlac. They still, as he clasps his wife to his breast, are the hands of the guillotined knife-thrower.*

Tuesday, July 23: Edgar Allan Woolf, an MGM contract writer, completed what was titled "Curtain Speech for Mr. Peter Lorre":

> *I really am not half as terrible as I appear in my pictures. In fact, though you may not believe it, I have never really killed anyone in all my life....*
>
> *Making this picture here in America has been a real pleasure to me. Everyone has been so nice and kind to me—Mr. Considine, the producer, Miss Drake, Mr. Clive, Mr. Healy—all of them made me feel as if I weren't mad at all.*
>
> *In fact, there was only one thing which disconcerted me and that was having to have my head shaved every morning. The first morning the barber, as he shaved me, looked at me as if he thought I were just a little eccentric. The second morning, as if he knew I were a little eccentric; and the third morning, as if I were really crazy.*
>
> *But all that I have been through is nothing if you really like the picture. I am hoping that you do, because I am anxious to stay here in America and make many more, and, in the words of a song I've heard here in your lovely country—"It All Depends on You."*

Wednesday, July 24: *Mad Love* opened at the Hollywood Pantages Theatre, where 1935's top horror films had played. On the bottom half of the double bill was Universal's *Manhattan Moon*. The curtain speech infers that Lorre was on hand for the opening, although there are no reports confirming it.

Friday, August 2: *Mad Love* opened at New York's 5886-seat Roxy Theatre. The stage show boasted Freddy Mack, the Gae Foster Girls and others. Andre Sennwald of *The New York Times,* who had met Lorre on the set that summer, wrote, "*Mad Love* is frequently excellent when Mr. Lorre is being permitted to illuminate the dark and twisted recesses of Dr. Gogol's brain."[23]

The attraction stayed at the Roxy one week and took in $24,800[24]—not bad, but about 60 percent of what *Bride of Frankenstein* earned in its first week at the Roxy in May.

The real excitement awaited in Great Britain.

August 7: *Mad Love*, titled *Hands of Orlac* in England, had a trade show at London's Prince Edward Theatre. *Today's Cinema* two days later called the film "[f]irst class entertainment of its type. *Hands of Orlac* may not prove to the taste of patrons. Not a film for the squeamish." It wasn't strong enough criticism for Edward Shortt, president of the British Board of Film Censors. He was dedicated to "family entertainment"—which *Mad Love–Hands of Orlac* definitely was not.

The controversy nudged noted British author Graham Greene to write in *The Spectator* (August 9, 1935):

> Hands of Orlac *is one of those horror films that Mr. Shortt, the head of that curious body of film censors rumoured to consist of retired Army officers and elderly ladies of no occupation, has declared his intention of banning.... Guiltily I admit to liking* Hands of Orlac *because it did make me shudder a little ... and because Herr Karl Freund's romantic direction did "put across" the agreeable little tale of how the dead murderer's fingers retained a life of their own.... It would have been a thousand pities, too, if Mr. Shortt's rigid good taste had prevented us enjoying the*

performance of Mr. Peter Lorre as Dr. Gogol. Mr. Lorre, with every physical handicap, can convince you of the goodness, the starved tenderness, of his vice-entangled souls....

Rather than ban the film, Shortt approved its release after a mutilation by the censor board, which made over *30* cuts:

- Extensive cuts of the playlet and torture scenes
- Eliminations of close shots of the guillotine
- Trims in the execution of Rollo (nine cuts in that sequence)
- The sound of anesthesia
- Old Orlac's line to Stephen regarding Yvonne, "Her pay may be small, but she could supplement her earnings, eh?"
- Modification of operation scenes (Reel 5)
- Modification of Gogol strangling Yvonne

"CENSOR BOARDS ON VIVISECTION SPREE, CRACK DOWN ON FOUR HORROR OPERAS," headlined *Variety* on September 4. The four films were *Mark of the Vampire*, *WereWolf of London*, *The Raven* and *Mad Love*. "English censors went after *Mad Love* hot and heavy," the story reported, "and before they were through, 20 [*sic*] scenes fell by the wayside and every reel but one felt the heavy touch of the morals squad."

Back in the U.S., the Pennsylvania censor made extensive cuts, including the torture playlet's hot poker, much of the guillotine sequence, and a "close-up of Gogol's hands actually strangling Yvonne with her hair."

Hungary, Finland, Austria and Palestine rejected *Mad Love*. U.S. exhibitors weren't happy, as indicated by this report from William A. Levee, manager of the Suffolk Theatre in Long Island, New York, to *Motion Picture Herald*:

The producers must have been mad to even attempt such a piece as this. This is certainly a black eye for MGM... Mad Love *is the picture that makes a manager want to hide from view when the cash customers leave the theatre.* Mad Love *will do more harm to the industry than a thousand ministers of good-will can undo or hope to undo.* Mad Love *is the type of picture that brought about censorship.*[25]

"One of the worst pictures I have ever shown," agreed Phil Billiet of the Coliseum Theatre in Annawan, Illinois. "Absolutely nothing to it ... the plot is impossible and there were altogether too many horror scenes."[26]

Business was big in at least one city: Boston. Loew's State Theatre, and Loew's Orpheum Theatre, Metro's flagship movie houses, actually wanted no part of *Mad Love* and let it go to their rival theater, Keith's. The Keith's strategy for wooing crowds: Present *Mad Love* along with an in-person gig by a famed fan dancer. As *Variety* reported:

Keith's Boston is rushing 'em in, with Sally Rand on the stage and Mad Love *on the screen. First time in several seasons that a Keith house has run a Metro pic, but the Loew's houses had no yen for the horror special, and let it go to the opposition. Shapes up like $30,000 for the Keith spot, due in no small part to a boom-boom advance campaign and rah-rah publicity on opening days of the show, stressing the city censor's no-like for nudity.*[27]

Mad Love had exploded in MGM's face. The box office was astoundingly bad. The total worldwide rental: $364,000. The final loss: $39,000.[28] Universal's *The Raven*, also panned and slammed by the critics and censors, actually had a smaller worldwide rental than *Mad Love*: $335,000. However, *The Raven* cost only $118,000, and therefore registered a $72,000 profit.[29]

In *Mad Love*'s wake, one might have made a case for a "*Mad Love* Curse." For example:

Chester Lyons, *Mad Love*'s cinematographer, died of a heart attack on November 27, 1936, while shooting 20th Century–Fox's *Fair Warning*. Lyons was 51.

Colin Clive, *Mad Love*'s Orlac, died of consumption and alcoholism on June 25, 1937. Among his final torments was fear he would have a leg amputated—which conjures up *Mad Love*. Peter Lorre was one of the pallbearers at Clive's funeral at the Edwards Brothers Colonial Mansion mortuary in Los Angeles on June 29. Clive was 37.

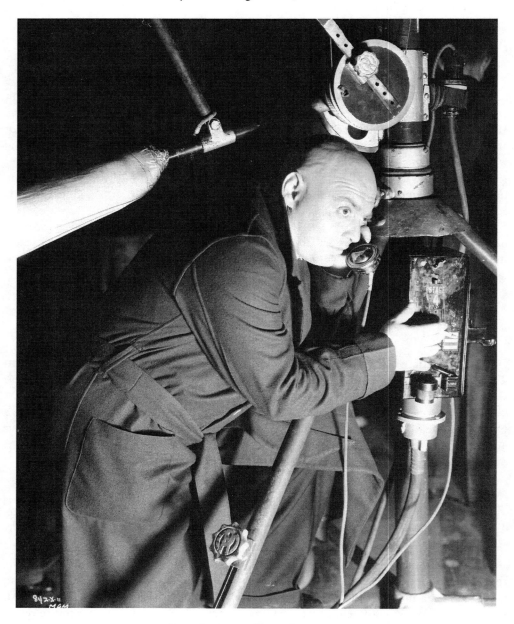

Peter Lorre on the *Mad Love* set.

Ted Healy, *Mad Love's* Reagan, died on December 21, 1937, following a severe beating at the Hollywood Trocadero night club. Healy had been roisterously celebrating the birth of his baby son. Suspects ranged from Albert "Cubby" Broccoli, later producer of the James Bond films, to MGM's own Wallace Beery. The coroner nixed the scandal by ruling that Healy died due to alcoholism.[30] Healy was 41.

At any rate, Peter Lorre, who became one of the cinema's great character stars, appeared immune from any such "curse." He appeared in many movies including several in 1964, the year he died (March 23).

Karl Freund, who returned to cinematography, won an Oscar for MGM's *The Good Earth* (1937), and was later a pioneering TV cameraman for *I Love Lucy* and other Desilu product. He died May 3, 1969, a legend unknown to basic Hollywood fans, but certainly respected by the knowledgeable ones.

As for Frances Drake ... if the *Mad Love* curse eventually overtook her, it took more than 64 years to do so. Having retired from films in 1942, she was the widow of the Hon. Cecil John Arthur Howard, wealthy British royalty; he died in 1985. She lived resplendently at 1511 Summitridge Drive, high in Beverly Hills. When I met her in 1987, she was still slender, funny and charmingly vain (she positioned herself beside me for a photo to show her "best side"), with a mane of silver hair, a love of animals ... and a cigarette addiction. In 1992, she married David Brown a much younger property owner and "friend of the family."

In January 2000, Frances, probably 91 years old (she was always secretive about her age), lit a cigarette in her Beverly Hills aerie, away from the watchful eye of a now-tending nurse. The former star caught afire and died several days later. I was touched and honored that the program for her funeral, January 26, 2000, at the Hollywood United Methodist Church, included part of the tribute I'd written to her years before in *Films in Review*. Drake is buried in Hollywood Forever Cemetery, near the lake.

*   *   *

Of the Great Horror Classics of 1935, does *Mad Love* top them all?

If put to a vote, *Bride of Frankenstein* would likely be the "topper." And this brings us to an analysis of *Mad Love*, and Karl Freund's directorial approach.

One can describe Whale's approach to *Bride of Frankenstein* as irreverent, theatrical and wildly stylistic. As far as cinematography goes, John J. Mescall provided a far more virtuoso display, capturing startlingly haunting close-ups of Karloff's Monster and Elsa Lanchester's Bride ... as well as stark studies of Colin Clive's Frankenstein, Ernest Thesiger's Pretorius, and even Valerie Hobson's Elizabeth. One imagines how Whale and Mescall would have handled, for example, *Mad Love's* Grand Guignol playlet ... and how they would have exalted Frances Drake's Yvonne.

On *Mad Love*, however, Freund and the two cinematographers—counting Freund, the *three* cinematographers—tend to avoid *Bride's* flash. There are some marvelous shots in *Mad Love*, and Gogol talking to his reflections (and them talking back) in the operating room is bravura cinema.

Yet Freund's dominant approach to *Mad Love* is—to use a single word—clinical.

The script is indeed an overdose, and Freund likely figured that if he added too much to a movie that presented a woman being branded by a hot poker, a guillotining, a decapitated head reattached to its body, stitched and scarred transplanted hands, knife-throwing, a sexy wax figure, a cockatoo, a truly horrific disguise, unbridled

A candid shot on the *Mad Love* set: Colin Clive (appearing a bit more pleasant), Frances Drake and Karl Freund (seated and pointing).

insanity, and the villain playing the organ before nearly strangling the heroine to death with her own hair—plus the bevy of John L. Balderston in-jokes—the entire film would have become a ridiculous hoot. As such, Freund's approach to *Mad Love* is that of an tour guide, calmly escorting us to see chamber after chamber of horrors—rather like those costumed but polite ushers on duty at the Grand Guignol Theatre early in the film.

Just so, Dimitri Tiomkin's minimalist musical score leaves the film with a certain nakedness. Again, this appears a deliberate decision—no epic score, *à la* Franz Waxman's *Bride of Frankenstein*, to chill the spine. Isn't that creepy catalogue of horrors in *Mad Love* enough without the punctuation of music?

Freund's work on *Mad Love* actually gets credit for its lack of ego. James Whale appeared eager to showcase his own personality in *Bride of Frankenstein*, and Tod Browning was anxious to trot out his favorite vampire atmospherics (including armadillos) in *Mark of the Vampire*. Freund was possessive of the camera on *Mad Love*, but he used it with restraint, leaving the trio of stars alone to provide the soul of the movie. Lorre's brilliant, Clive's excellent, and Frances Drake deserves the bouquet Danny Peary tossed her in his book *Guide for the Film Fanatic*: "[O]ne of the strongest, most intelligent women in the horror cinema."[31]

* * *

A final story about *Mad Love*.

Sunday, January 12, 1936: *The New York Times* ran a column by the aforementioned film critic Andre Sennwald. The title: "Gory, Gory Hallelujah." Sennwald wrote:

> *Hollywood has been treating us to emotional horror orgies. … As the cinema sadists tortured their victims in relentless close-ups, we have shuddered, cringed, bitten our mouths, dug fingernails into our flesh, and perhaps slipped back to see the film over again.*

Sennwald's column primarily concerned major releases … and *not* horror films. He called MGM's *Mutiny on the Bounty* 1935's "prize collector's item," noting, "The most morbidly exciting moment in that odyssey of pain occurred when Captain Bligh ordered the corpse flogged." He alluded to the lit bamboo shoots under Gary Cooper's fingernails in *The Lives of a Bengal Lancer* … the guillotine that decapitated Ronald Colman in *A Tale of Two Cities* … the lynch mob that hanged Brian Donlevy in *Barbary Coast* … and more. However, the young critic mentioned only one horror film.

> *Possibly you recall the fascinating facial contortions of Peter Lorre in* Mad Love *when he sat in a box at the theatre des horreurs and drooled with satisfaction as he watched his lady broken upon the rack.*

It was quite a distinction for *Mad Love*. To have been signaled out by Sennwald in a year that had offered such films as *Bride of Frankenstein, Mark of the Vampire, WereWolf of London* and *The Raven* was truly a coup.

"If the trend continues during 1936," wrote Sennwald, "you may expect some interesting experiences in the cinema."

Sennwald's "Gory, Gory Hallelujah" appeared in the Sunday, January 12, 1936, *New York Times* on page 10. It was published posthumously. On the same edition's page one was this headline:

"Andre Sennwald, Times Film Critic, Killed As Explosion Wrecks West End Av. Home."

The explosion had erupted at 12:50 a.m. in Sennwald's top floor quarters of a 17-story, 106-family apartment building located at 670 West End Avenue in New York City. The *Times* reported:

> *The blast was so terrific that it blew away the outer walls of the apartment, hurtling the debris into an inner courtyard. The inside walls of the apartment were knocked down and the roof sagged in. The adjoining eight-room apartment … was badly damaged. The water tank on the roof was ripped open and water poured into the building.*

Sennwald's body, clad in pajamas, was found in the kitchen. His wife was not at home at the time of the explosion, but arrived with her sister shortly afterwards, and police detained them in the lobby. There were no other injuries. The investigators and assistant medical examiner determined that gas had escaped from the stove in Sennwald's kitchenette and had been ignited by "a spark from the electric refrigerator motor."

It was noted that Sennwald was suffering from severe iritis, an inflammation of the iris of the eyes, which threatened his sight. The death was listed as "probably suicidal," the suspicion being that Sennwald had tried to gas himself to death. The explosion had been an accidental result.[32]

The curse of *Mad Love*?

Probably not, but it does make one wonder.

Mad Love

Metro-Goldwyn-Mayer, 1935. Producer, John W. Considine Jr. Director, Karl Freund. Screenplay, P.J. Wolfson and John L. Balderston, based on an adaptation by Guy Endore, from Florence Crewe-Jones' translation-adaptation of Maurice Renard's novel *Les Mains d'Orlac*. Uncredited Contributing Writers, Leon Gordon, Edgar Allan Woolf, Gladys Von Ettinghausen, Leo Wolfson. Cinematographers, Chester Lyons and Gregg Toland. Music, Dimitri Tiomkin. Musical Director, Oscar Radin. Recording Director, Douglas Shearer. Art Director, Cedric Gibbons. Associate Art Directors, William A. Hornig and Edwin B. Willis. Wardrobe, Dolly Tree. Editor, Hugh Wynn. Organ Music Composer, David Snell. Makeup, Norbert A. Myles. Assistant Director, Dolph Zimmer. Dialogue Director, John Langan. Alternate Titles: *The Mad Doctor of Paris* and *The Hands of Orlac*. Running time, 68 minutes.

Los Angeles opening, Hollywood Pantages Theatre, July 24, 1935. New York opening, Roxy Theatre, August 2, 1935.

The Cast: Peter Lorre (Dr. Gogol), Frances Drake (Yvonne Orlac), Colin Clive (Stephen Orlac), Ted Healy (Reagan), Sara Haden (Marie), Isabel Jewell (Marianne), Edward Brophy (Rollo), Henry Kolker (Prefect of Police Rosset), Harold Huber (Thief), Keye Luke (Dr. Wong), May Beatty (Francoise), Ian Wolfe (Henry Orlac), Charles Trowbridge (Dr. Marbeau), Robert Emmett Keane (Drunk), Clarence Hummel Wilson (Piano Man), Billy Gilbert (Man on Train with Dog), Murray Kinnell (Charles), Edward Lippy (Pierre—Henry Orlac's Clerk), Sarah Padden (Mother), Cora Sue Collins (Child Patient), Edward Norris, Mary Jo Mathews (Couple Outside Horror Show), Frank Darien (Lavin—Waxworks Proprietor), Rollo Lloyd (Varsac—Fingerprint Expert), Nell Craig (Nurse Suzanne), Maurice Brierre (Taxi Driver), Julie Carter (Nurse), Hooper Atchley (Conductor), Sam Ash, Christian Frank, Robert Graves, Roger Gray, Earl M. Pingree (Detectives), George Davis (Chauffeur), Otto Hoffman (Blind Man), Mark Loebell (Prince in Horror Act), Ramsay Hill (Duke in Horror Act), Carl Stockdale (Notary in Horror Act), Al Borgato (Doorman), Harvey Clark (Station Master), Alphonz Ethier (Fingerprint Man), Russ Powell (Gendarme), Jacques Vanaire (Police Broadcaster), Matty Roubert (Newsboy), Rolfe Sedan (Gendarme Directing Traffic), Michael Mark (Official at Guillotine).

Unholy Royalty

Universal's *Tower of London*

Tower of London ... might have been written by Bill Shakespeare after a joust at the Mermaid Tavern with Boris Karloff and Fu Manchu.

—George E. Phair, "Retakes," *Variety,* November 18, 1939

Well, in 2012, they finally dug up the old devil.

The skeleton, with a spine curved like an "S" and a skull with two severely lethal injuries, was that of Richard III, who died at the Battle of Bosworth Field in 1485, and whom Shakespeare poetically described in his 1591 play as that "foul lump of deformity." The infamous "Crookback" had been resting all these centuries in Leicester on a site that had once been Greyfriars Friary Church—but was now a parking lot.

On September 12, 2012, a research team of anthropologists removed the remains.[1] On March 26, 2015, there was a funeral service at Leicester Cathedral, where Richard III now lies in an ossuary.[2] The "bottl'd spider" (Shakespeare again) had finally been interred with pomp and circumstance, almost 530 years after his death.

One fancifully imagines Richard's Ghost celebrated properly with a vengeful world tour.

Perhaps he visited the Tower of London where he allegedly perpetrated the assassination of 12-year-old Edward V and his nine-year-old brother Richard of Shrewsbury, thus bloodthirstily claiming the throne.[3] Maybe he dropped by Holy Trinity Churchyard in Stratford-upon-Avon, desecrating the resting place of Shakespeare with an atrocity of choice. Possibly he visited Westminster Abbey and profaned the tomb of Sir

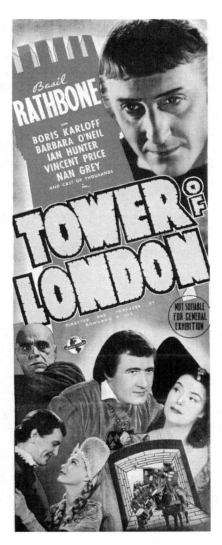

An insert poster for *Tower of London* (Universal, 1939).

Laurence Olivier (who played him so diabolically in his 1955 film version of Shakespeare's play).

And mayhap Richard's vengeful specter visited Universal City, California ... to despoil the back lot site of 1939's *Tower of London*.

It was arguably the most indelicate of the Richard III movies, instantly impressive today due to its Unholy Trinity of horror powerhouses: Basil Rathbone as a bloodthirsty Richard, Boris Karloff as the monstrous executioner Mord, and Vincent Price as the simpering Duke of Clarence. If ever Richard had spun in his Leicester grave, it was during the blistering midsummer shoot of this mad melodrama, an eerie extravaganza that boasted a beheading, a drowning in a wine vat, the killing of two young boys, two big, gory (for the time) battle scenes, a bombastic musical score lifted from *Son of Frankenstein*, a bevy of torture instruments almost a match for those in MGM's *The Mask of Fu Manchu*, and virtually all the sadism and bloodletting that could escape the 1939 censors.

Of course, if Richard III's ghost did visit 2015 Universal, he found that the Tower, a venerable site of the Universal back lot for nearly 50 years, was long-gone—razed in the late 1980s to make room for the *Earthquake* ride.

Yet another indignity.

Part One: Pre-Production

Two Lees but Alas, Only One Rathbone

> *Crookback. Dragfoot. Misfits, eh?*
> —Basil Rathbone as Richard,
> talking to Boris Karloff as Mord about
> their respective deformities in *Tower of London*

It was, poetically, a production seemingly cursed with troubles.

Saturday, August 13, 1938: Rowland V. Lee, director of such films as *Zoo in Budapest* (Fox, 1933) and *The Three Musketeers* (RKO, 1935), began shooting Universal's *Service De Luxe*.[4] He had signed a producer-director contract with the studio and his first film here was this screwball comedy starring Constance Bennett and, in his film debut, Vincent Price. M.F. Murphy, whose job was to troubleshoot Universal productions and report weekly to the front office, wrote precisely five weeks later, September 17, 1938:

> *With all credit to Rowland V. Lee, this picture finished up Thursday, September 15th, and can be considered the most commercially handled big picture we have had on this lot in many years. The total shooting period consumed 27 days.... We figure the probable final cost will run to approximately $350,000—this being $25,000 under estimated budget.*

Meanwhile, Basil Rathbone, whom audiences had been hissing the past spring and summer as the villainous Sir Guy of Gisbourne in Warner Bros.' Technicolor *The Adventures of Robin Hood*, came to Universal. Lee had directed the popular actor in the British *Love from a Stranger* (1937), in which Rathbone played a ravingly mad wife-slayer with an escalating, bravura intensity. Lee saw Rathbone as *his* star. As a team, he hoped they would do big things together at Universal.[5]

Wednesday, November 9: Lee started shooting *Son of Frankenstein*. Rathbone played the title role, Boris Karloff was the Monster, Lugosi acted old Ygor, and Lionel Atwill portrayed one-armed Inspector Krogh. Lee and his writer Wyllis Cooper virtually made up the horror saga day to day. M.F. Murphy, who so admired Lee's efficiency on *Service De Luxe*, wailed in his production report about the $420,000 final cost (about $120,000 over budget) and the 46 shooting days (19 days over schedule). Lee finished at 1:15 a.m. on January 5, 1939, and Universal released the horror epic only eight (!) days later.

Tuesday, March 14, 1939: Lee started *The Sun Never Sets*, a purple paean to the British Empire. The heroes were Rathbone (who, since *Son of Frankenstein*, had played Sherlock Holmes for the first time in 20th Century–Fox's *The Hound of the Basker-villes*) and Douglas Fairbanks Jr. The villain

Basil Rathbone as Richard III in *Tower of London*.

(an ant-studying madman, hellbent on starting a world war) was Lionel Atwill. Shooting began with only 30 pages of revised final script. It wrapped up May 3. Lee announced the film needed a prologue and montage sequence, and resumed shooting May 10. Final cost: $586,000, more than $60,000 over budget.

All of which indicates that Rowland V. Lee had become rather a problem child at Universal.

Lee was a talented director who daubed the screen with lavish production value; *Son of Frankenstein*, for example, has a wonderful fairy tale aura. Universal had always excelled at melodrama, and Lee appeared destined to launch such studio fare into a new, prestigious realm. Yet, after his good behavior on *Service De Luxe*, he became prone to running wildly over schedule and budget, and believing he could produce and direct a movie without a fully prepared shooting script.

This was dangerous at Universal, which was dreaming of its first profitable season in several years.[6]

Monday, April 17: As *The Sun Never Sets* was shooting, *Variety* headlined, "U Adds $5,000,000 This Year on Big Schedule." Announced in the report was *Tower of London*. The producer-director: Rowland V. Lee. The star: Basil Rathbone.

Tuesday, June 20: *Variety* ran this item:

> *Universal has the world's easiest casting job in* Tower of London. *For executioner—Boris Karloff.*

Wednesday, June 21: "Give 'em the Axe," headlined *Variety*:

> *Rowland V. Lee gets the directing chore on Universal's* Tower of London, *with Basil Rathbone as Richard III and Boris Karloff as the executioner. Picture rolls about Aug. 1.*

Tower of London **producer-director Rowland V. Lee tends to Nan Grey, here disguised as a chimney sweep.**

Richard III was an ideal role for Rathbone. Hollywood had only offered the public Richard once before: John Barrymore, carrying a severed head atop a mountain of corpses, delivering Shakespeare's *Richard III* soliloquy in an episode of Warner Bros.' *The Show of Shows* (1929):

> *Why, love forswore me in my mother's womb...*
> *She did corrupt frail nature with some bribe*

To shrink mine arm up like a wither'd shrub;
To make an envious mountain on my back,
Where sits deformity to mock my body....

Meanwhile, Mord, the tower executioner, was a made-in-Heaven (?) role for Karloff. Since *Son of Frankenstein*, Karloff's stardom had spiked, and on April 17, Alta Durant, in her *Variety* "Gab" column, had run this amusing news:

Fans [are] no longer willing to take Boris Karloff straight since horror makeup reached new high in Son of Frankenstein ... 500 autographed photos of thesp[ian] showing natural rather than monster mien having been returned by recipients in last three weeks ... with requests for art showing him as public rather than Hollywood knows him.

Writing the *Tower of London* script, meanwhile, was Lee's brother, Robert N. Lee. He was a prolific screenwriter who shared an Academy nomination with Francis Faragoh[7] for their adaptation of W.R. Burnett's *Little Caesar* (Warners, 1930). Universal even planned to erect a facsimile of the Tower of London on the back lot. Then, as production approached in July of 1939, there loomed a major problem:

Rathbone was overbooked.

First of all, Rathbone was busy this June at 20th Century–Fox, filming *The Adventures of Sherlock Holmes.* Universal had scheduled him for *Rio*, a saga in which he portrayed an escapee from a French penal colony. Meanwhile, RKO had baited Basil with what the actor saw as a "dream" role: Frollo, the wicked chief justice of *The Hunchback of Notre Dame.*

Indeed, as the July 6 shooting date for *Hunchback* came near, *The Hollywood Reporter* listed Rathbone in that film's cast list, along with Charles Laughton as Quasimodo and Maureen O'Hara as Esmeralda. Then, supposedly, came *Tower of London*, which would also conflict with *Hunchback*'s shooting schedule.

Although Rathbone could hardly voice his feelings publicly— and probably didn't want to offend his friend Rowland Lee—he surely preferred to clear the deck to do *Hunchback.* It was to be one of 1939's biggest productions, a $1.8 million spectacular. The combined costs of Universal's *Rio* and *Tower of London* wouldn't tally half of what RKO would invest in *Hunchback.* Also, Frollo, the anguished, black-robed zealot, "bewitched" by Esmeralda, climactically trying

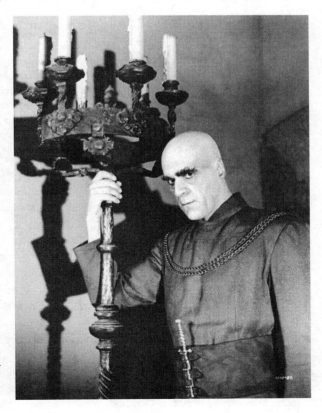

Boris Karloff as Mord, *Tower of London*'s bald, bow-legged, club-footed executioner.

to kill her and Quasimodo, would likely be the richest film "villain" role Rathbone had ever played. Frollo might have been more dimensional than "Crookback" Richard.

Universal and RKO tried to arrange a schedule by which Rathbone could make both *Rio* and *The Hunchback of Notre Dame*. It would be a daunting challenge, no doubt exhausting for the star, but Rathbone was eager to make it happen.

Casting and Censorship Travails

> *Scene 232: We recommend that the business of Edward rubbing the hump-back of Richard be eliminated, as it is apt to give offense to people suffering from physical deformities….*
>
> —Letter to Universal from Joseph Breen,
> Production Code Administration, July 27, 1939[8]

Saturday, July 8: Two days after *The Hunchback of Notre Dame* began shooting, *Variety* headlined, "Rathbone May Leave *Hunchback* for *Rio*":

> *Overlapping assignments probably will take Basil Rathbone out of RKO's* Hunchback of Notre Dame *in favor of Universal's* Rio *slated to start next week. Both studios have endeavored to work out schedules to accommodate, but prospects for Rathbone in* Hunchback *yesterday seemed to have gone glimmering.*

Wednesday, July 12: Louella Parsons reported in the *Los Angeles Examiner:*

> *The most unhappy man in Hollywood for a few days was Basil Rathbone, who wanted to play the Chief High Justice in* The Hunchback of Notre Dame *more than he ever wanted to play any part. He said he had never signed any contract with Universal, but that he had promised to do* Rio *providing the script was satisfactory. Universal had already sold the [upcoming] picture with Rathbone and Sigrid Gurie to the exhibitors, and if Basil had stepped out, it would have meant a terrific loss. Cliff Work [Universal's production chief], who is a diplomat, appealed to Rathbone on that basis, never mentioning a lawsuit. So, rather than put the film company in the middle, he agreed to forget the RKO offer. That's why Sir Cedric Hardwicke was put into Rathbone's role.*[9]

Hardwicke was a good choice for Frollo, having just played Mr. Brink, aka "Death," in MGM's *On Borrowed Time*. Ironically, while Rathbone had portrayed Wolf von Frankenstein in 1939's *Son of Frankenstein*, Hardwicke would play his brother Ludwig in 1942's *The Ghost of Frankenstein*.

Thursday, July 20: Universal began shooting *Rio*. His co-star Sigrid Gurie was a Samuel Goldwyn discovery promoted as an Aphrodite from Norway. (The truth would come out in the early 1940s that she was actually born in Brooklyn.) John Brahm (fated for 1944's *The Lodger*) directed. M.F. Murphy soon predicted that *Rio* would likely extend beyond a 30-day schedule and approximated $450,000 budget.

Meanwhile, *Tower of London* was set to start shooting come early August. If *Rio* ran into late August, this meant Rathbone would, as feared, be unavailable for *Tower of London* as well.

Lee, deeply disappointed, decided he better consider a new Richard III.

On July 18, Paramount's *Beau Geste* had a gala premiere at Los Angeles' Carthay Circle Theatre, and Brian Donlevy was a sensation as the Foreign Legion's scar-faced Sgt. Markoff.[10] Lee decided to test Donlevy for Richard III. It was a bit daunting to imagine Donlevy (who never played a medieval role in his 90-plus films career) in

15th-century wig and a hump on his back, lurking as Richard III; nevertheless, the actor was game.

Thursday, July 27: As Lee fretted over casting Richard III, Joseph Breen responded to the incomplete first draft *Tower of London* script, dated July 24, 1939. He listed 19 areas of concern, among them:

- *Scene 2: Please avoid gruesomeness as to these instruments of torture....*
- *Scene 6: Here and elsewhere, King Henry VI is referred to as an "imbecile," and in other parts of the story he is characterized as being insane. You will have in mind that the British Board of Film Censors deletes regularly scenes of insane persons....*
- *Scene 10: Here and elsewhere, please be sure that the sex organs of the baby are not exposed where he is being bathed.*
- *Scene 65 et seq: These scenes indicating the execution will need careful handling to avoid gruesomeness and possible deletion by political censor boards....*
- *Scene 232: We recommend that the business of Edward rubbing the humpback of Richard be eliminated, as it is apt to give offense to people suffering from physical deformities....*
- *Scene 240: Please minimize this drinking, and eliminate the "burps."*

Saturday, July 29: George Phair wrote in his "Retakes" column in *Variety*:

> Universal is cooking up something extra-special in the horror line. How would you like to meet Boris Karloff and Brian Donlevy in "The Tower of London" on a foggy night?

As trade journals rarely mentioned name players testing for roles until after they were cast—or it was fairly certain that they would be cast (actresses who tested for Scarlett O'Hara had been an exception)—the indication, therefore, was that Brian Donlevy just might become Universal's Richard III.

Friday, August 4: Six days after Phair's notice, *Variety* reported that Lee had cast Nan Grey and Barbara O'Neil in *Tower of London*'s "top femme roles." Grey (who played the victim of Gloria Holden's lesbian-tinged attack in Universal's 1936 *Dracula's Daughter*) would play Lady Alice, the heroine; O'Neil (who just portrayed Scarlett O'Hara's mother in *Gone with the Wind* and had been one of the leading ladies in Lee's *The Sun Never Sets*) would play Queen Elyzabeth (as the film's credits spell it). The same *Variety* notice wrote that Lee had cast George Sanders and John Sutton. Sanders was to enact Edward IV, Richard's compatriot in crime; Sutton would play the heroic John Wyatt.

The news in this notice was definite: These actors would appear "in support of Basil Rathbone and Boris Karloff." Lee had decided that Rathbone was indispensable to *Tower of London* and to work around his schedule however necessary.

The final cast roster of *Tower of London* created a whirlwind of actor changes, affecting several studios:

- Sir Cedric Hardwicke had been committed to playing a British officer in RKO's Revolutionary War saga *Allegheny Uprising*, before replacing Rathbone in *The Hunchback of Notre Dame*.[11] Therefore, George Sanders left *Tower of London* and came to RKO to replace Hardwicke in *Allegheny Uprising*. Universal retained a call on Sanders and later cast him in James Whale's *Green Hell*, which began shooting at Universal on August 21.
- Ian Hunter, borrowed from MGM, played (very well) Sanders' vacated role of Edward IV.

Between scenes, left to right: Royal "brothers" Vincent Price, Ian Hunter and Basil Rathbone.

- Brian Donlevy, who also appeared in *Allegheny Uprising* as a heavy, fulfilled his Universal commitment as the villain in the Marlene Dietrich–James Stewart Western *Destry Rides Again,* which started shooting September 7.

Basil Rathbone had to work in *Tower of London* as he was finishing *Rio*. Vincent Price, cast as the Duke of Clarence, was required to go back and forth between *Tower of London* and *Green Hell*.

Still, all looked promising. Maybe.

There was plenty of *Tower of London* showmanship. Jack Pierce provided Karloff with a nightmarishly vivid "Mord" makeup—a shaved head, a club foot, and eyebrows that resemble engorged caterpillars … approaching to mate.

And, magnificently, there was the Tower: a foreboding 75' tall fortress, looming above a back lot lake. Set designer Jack Otterson designed the edifice, so Universal claimed, after examining the Tower's original blueprints. In some ways, the Tower was a more impressive set than RKO's *Hunchback* Notre Dame Cathedral, which stood on the flats of the RKO Ranch in Encino (and without the two towers that would be matted in to complete the effect).

Wednesday, August 9: Joseph Breen, having reviewed the supposedly "revised" *Tower of London* script, testily wrote to Universal that it still included material he had ordered deleted—including the gruesomeness of the torture instruments, Henry VI being referred to as an "imbecile," the possible exposure of the bathed baby's sex organs, and the gruesomeness of the execution.

Friday, August 11: *Tower of London* began shooting, with an estimated budget of $490,000, a schedule of 36 days, and an incomplete script. For a movie of this historical and "epic" nature, the lack of a finished script was a major handicap. Nevertheless, Lee and his brother Robert claimed they knew where they were heading, and there was guarded optimism.

"While it is somewhat early to make predictions," wrote M.F. Murphy the next day, "we feel, if encountering any sort of good luck, it will be quite possible to finish up within just a few days of this schedule."

Part Two: The Shoot

> *"I've never killed in* hot *blood!"*
> —Boris Karloff as Mord, begging
> Basil Rathbone's Richard III to allow
> him to go into battle, *Tower of London*

"Ensure the Thrust and Bless the Wound"

It was hot this summer in the San Fernando Valley—very hot.

As temperatures soared, *Tower of London* won plenty of attention at Universal City. Basil Rathbone was a sly, beguiling serpent of a Richard, his "Crookback" wearing a very modest "hump," the real deformity the one in his soul. He acted with a splendidly vile majesty, royally wicked in speech and action. At one point, he sent Mord into an alcove to kill the senile old king (Miles Mander) as the graybeard was praying, Richard handing the executioner a dagger that resembles a cross.

The blasphemous weapon will, Richard promised, "ensure the thrust and bless the wound."

The star ran back and forth from *Rio* to *Tower of London,* changing from the

"I've never killed in hot blood before!": In one of *Tower of London*'s best moments, Karloff's Mord begs Rathbone's Richard to allow him to join the battle.

contemporary hairpiece and wardrobe he wore in the former to the 15th-century Richard wig, silk tights and leather shoes that adorned him in the latter.

"I know now," joked Rathbone, "what it's like to be a glamour girl!"

The wig, which photographed silvery in the black-and-white film, was actually reddish blonde. It earned Rathbone a nickname on the Universal lot: "Harpo."[12]

Then there was Karloff as Mord—gaunt, deformed, a totally bald head, a sinister smile, loping about on his club foot, carrying an executioner's axe almost as tall as he was. As Frank S. Nugent wrote in the *New York Times* that December in his review of *Tower of London*: "Karloff can't be taken seriously—else he would drive one insane of fright...."[13]

In a nicely perverse touch, "Dear Boris" went through most of *Tower of London* wearing dark tights, which were curiously fetching with his mini-skirt of a tunic and built-up shoes. In retrospect, he rather evokes a horrid Haight-Ashbury hippie chick of the late 1960s who had shaved her head.

"There, my pretty," leers Boris' Mord as he captured John Sutton's fey hero Wyatt. "Let that be a lesson to you. Don't try to escape from old Mord!"

Amused by his own shaved head, "Dear Boris" revealed a bizarre sense of humor: He decided it would be fun if he shaved the head of his nine-month-old daughter Sara Jane, so they could be "baldies" together. Unfortunately, he proceeded without clearing the idea with his wife Dorothy.

"Boris, how *dare* you!" wailed Dorothy.[14]

Vincent Price, as the Duke of Clarence, scented his foppish role with a whiff of lavender with which he perfumed several later film characters; if there had been Gay Pride parades in 15th-century England, one can easily imagine Price's Clarence straddling the lead horse. He also wore a droopy left eyelid (courtesy of Jack Pierce) to accentuate the sinister. It's intriguing that Price (who had wed actress Edith Barrett in April 1938) had been previously engaged to Barbara O'Neil, who was a wide-eyed eyeful as *Tower of London*'s spirited Elyzabeth. The more prurient might well wonder how many lunches "Vinnie" and Barbara enjoyed together in the Universal commissary during the shoot.

George Robinson, cinematographer of Lee's previous three Universals, was cameraman again.[15] He enjoyed the film's pictorial flair. According to the *New York Daily News*' *Tower of London* review, "[Robinson] gives every indication of having apprenticed on Dante's *Inferno*."

Monday, August 21: Columnist Harrison Carroll wrote in the *Los Angeles Evening Herald Express*:

> *For drama, Hollywood sound stages have offered nothing recently to top the scene in* Tower of London, *where Basil Rathbone, as Richard III, sat in a royal box and watched executioner Boris Karloff chop off the head of a young man whom the tyrant had condemned to death.*
>
> *It took all day to photograph the grimly realistic scene and by the time it was over, impressionable Rathbone was ready to collapse from nerves.*
>
> *He had a special reason. The actor portraying the executioner's victim was his 25-year-old son, Rodion Rathbone.*

Rodion had previously acted in the World War I aviation drama *The Dawn Patrol* (1938), in which his father had co-starred with Errol Flynn; Rodion played a green recruit who became the newest "lamb to the slaughter." This and *Tower of London* were his only two films.

Tuesday, August 22: Harry Mines of the *Los Angeles Daily News* reported on his visit to Universal:

> *By far the most exciting point of interest is the ghastly set where Boris Karloff, new horror makeup to his credit, plots further chills for avid fans in his role of the executioner in* Tower of London....
>
> *For his role Karloff has had his head completely shaved, his ears pinned back to his head, a hump put on his nose and wears a club foot. His disguise is arranged so as to accentuate the superhuman strength of the man.*

Friday, August 25: *Variety*'s Alta Durant, in her "Gab" column, wrote words that, considering the very hot weather, seem to prophesy possible disaster:

> *PRE-DAWN procession of 450 extras trekked out to Universal this morning in answer to 4 A.M. studio call ... [S]tars of* Tower of London *fared no better as studio ... in search of realistic battle scene which necessitated foggy dawn brawl ... ordered 6 a.m. shooting near Tarzana ... [The film] has all players wearing chain mail and armor ... [M]akeup department demanded two hours to stuff players into suits and fit wigs ... [P]lans are for washing up battle scene in one day's shooting.*

The result was a debacle. As M.F. Murphy bemoaned in his August 26 *Tower of London* studio report:

> *We are greatly concerned over the cost of this picture.... We encountered a very serious setback yesterday with a crowd of 300 extras who left the studio at 4:00 a.m. to work at a nearby ranch*

The extras in *Tower of London* were, in the words of the writer of a studio production report, "unruly, uncooperative, and destructive…" and proved a setback for the production.

location. Difficulties with a special fog effect which we could not control because of wind, the breakdown of a pump when we switched to a rain sequence, a particularly hot day, plus a group of unruly, uncooperative, and destructive extras clothed in helmets and armor, all added to make this one of the most unsuccessful days we have had with a large crowd of people in many years.

      Tuesday, August 29: *"Extras Refused Work After Alleged Sabotage,"* reported a page-one *Variety* headline:

Fifty of 200 extras working in battle scenes for Universal's Tower of London *were removed from callback list yesterday after protest had been filed with Screen Actors Guild over asserted lack of cooperation by players.*

      Rowland V. Lee, producer-director in charge of picture, notified Antrim Short, SAG representative, that big percentage of players were not cooperating although they were being paid above Guild scale. Was claimed many of them tossed away equipment, including spears, helmets and cordage breast plates during shooting of important scene.

      Studio officials claimed property truck which followed shooting was piled high with equipment that had been discarded by "soldiers" during march up hill to battle scene. Was said action interfered with shooting schedule and lowered morale of entire company.

      Executives pointed out extras were receiving $11 day, although SAG scale for soldiers is only $8.25 with uniform furnished. Pay was tilted, officials said, because task was difficult, "soldiers" being required to wade stream. Was understood that by paying above scale, company expected to get more experienced players who would be willing to cooperate during shooting.

The *Variety* article intimated that the problems were encountered on both Friday, August 25, and Saturday, August 26, and that Universal had "ironed out" the problem Monday "after approximately 50 of extras were removed and others substituted." The story went on:

> *Film executives pointed out last night it was such action as that which was causing companies to go outside SAG zone to shoot important battle and crowd scenes. Situation is being investigated by SAG, and if evidence warrants, players who were reported will be called before trial board where conviction might result in indefinite expulsion.*

There were other problems:

With Rathbone needed for both *Rio* and *Tower of London*, *Rio* had to trim its script's closing scenes.

Meanwhile, distraught over costs on *Tower of London*, Murphy suggested the front office cut its St. John Chapel scene, in which, via the chicanery of Richard, two children of royal blood marry: five-year-old Donnie Dunagan (from *Son of Frankenstein*) as the Baby Prince and seven-year-old Joan Carroll as little Lady Mowbray. Murphy argued this would cut $10,000 from the budget. "While this carries a certain air of pageantry and color," he wrote, "as far as production values go, and although the sequence may be historical, it definitely has no bearing or development on the story...."

Lee disagreed.

Friday, September 1: Hitler invaded Poland. Anxiety overtook the world. Naturally, the *Tower of London* set was no exception.

Saturday, September 2: *Rio* finally completed shooting. M.F. Murphy freshly assessed *Tower of London*: "While the results of this production look unusually big and particularly promising, the progress is far from our schedule plans...."

The film was four days behind schedule, would probably take 42 days to complete rather than 36, and Lee had won the battle about retaining the St. John Chapel episode. The sight of Master Dunagan and little Miss Carroll getting married is one of *Tower of London*'s most vivid episodes, both funny and shocking as the kiddies take their marriage vows.

"Ah will," promises Dunagan in his Texas accent, the two words—due to the incongruous drawl—among the film's most memorable. In a 2004 interview with the author, Dunagan chuckled about his royal casting.

"I was Junior Redneck no. 1!" he laughed.[16]

Dunagan, who "had a ball" on *Son of Frankenstein*—going for ice cream with Rathbone, playing checkers for quarters (and winning!) with Karloff—recalled that Rathbone wasn't always in comparable high spirits during *Tower of London*:

> *I think Basil Rathbone was responsible for me being in* Tower of London. *He was angry that they kept cutting scenes out of the script. Not angry like rednecks get angry—he was a gentleman, always—but he was disturbed about the script.*

Donnie remembered Karloff, whom he affectionately called "the Giant" after *Son of Frankenstein*, talking about the war on the horizon:

> *Mr. Karloff made some remarks that I paid attention to, when we were sitting there, in different places with other adults. He was talking to some people who had European backgrounds, and he was very, very concerned about the recklessness, callousness and stupidity—he had great enunciation!—of politicians and senior people ... how this thing was going to blow up, and involve everybody for a long, long time.*

Basil Rathbone holds hands with Donnie Dunagan and Joan Carroll. The ceremony showing the children's arranged marriage is one of *Tower of London*'s most memorable episodes.

Somebody said, "No, it'll be over in a month." And he scolded them! Oh, he had his homework done! He was rattling off places, geo-political places in Central Europe, places that I wouldn't have known at the time if they fell on me.

Mr. Karloff was extremely sensitive to what was happening, and he kept talking about the poor and defenseless people, who couldn't protect themselves against what he perceived, and what ended up being ... World War II.

Events Heat Up

You mention a word of this outside these walls ... I'll tear your tongues out!
—Boris Karloff as Mord, Tower of London

War was looming, but the stars were professionals, and high spirits were necessary for morale on a movie, especially one with a runaway budget, hot wigs, heavy costumes, corseted actresses and brutally hot weather.

Karloff makes friends between scenes with Universal attraction "Baby Sandy."

September 8: *Variety*'s Alta Durant reported in her "Gab" column that Baby Sandy, Universal's 20-month-old star, had met Karloff:

> [*Karloff*] *in hideous executioner's costume for* Tower of London *initially scared babe but Karloff's shaven pate attracted gurgling youngster … followed Karloff's treating kid to ice cream and friendship was clinched with "heavy" feeding youngster … [B]abe's cry came when she was taken off Karloff's lap and back to own set.*

September 12: Work continued on shaping and completing the script, with material sent for approval to Joseph Breen. On this day, Breen wrote to Universal:

> *We regret to report that Scenes 386, 387, 392 and 394 are* unacceptably *gruesome as to the torture and tortured condition of Wyatt. The torture should be suggested rather than shown….*

Vincent Price loved telling the story of his terrific *Tower of London* demise: drowned in the vat of malmsey wine by Rathbone and Karloff. The wine Rathbone and Price quaffed down in the drinking duel was actually Coca-Cola. As for the wine vat, Price told *Cinefantastique*:

> *Boris and Basil, knowing I was new to the business, thought it was great fun to throw everything into that vat of wine—which was actually just water—old Coca-Cola bottles, cigarette butts, anything they could find to dirty it up. They knew at the end of the scene I had to get into it! They had fixed a handrail at the bottom of it, so I could dive down and hang onto it. I had to stay under for a full ten counts, and then I was yanked out by my heels. When I came out, I got a round of applause from the crew, but I was disappointed not to see Boris and Basil. Then a few minutes later, they reappeared. They congratulated me for playing the scene so well for a newcomer—and then they presented me with a case of Coca-Cola!*[17]

The drinking duel: Rathbone vs. Price.

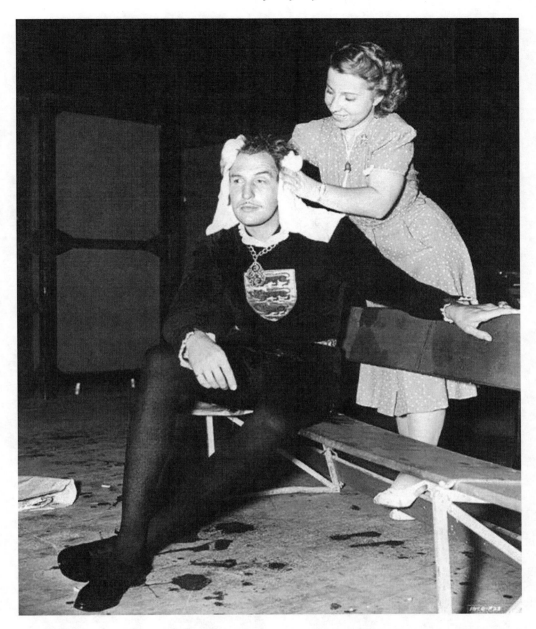

An assistant on the set dries off Vincent Price after his "drowning" in the vat of malmsey wine.

Price would play Richard III himself in the Roger Corman–directed 1962 *Tower of London.*

Saturday, September 16: Murphy reported:

Considering the type of work this company has been doing during the past week, they have made very good progress, averaging better than three pages each day. To accomplish this, they have worked beyond the usual 6 p.m. each evening and two nights as late as 7:30 without dinner. We have concentrated on Karloff during this week and will succeed in finishing his role tonight, thereby eliminating $3,750.00 weekly from the payroll.

Marlene Dietrich in her robe and Basil Rathbone in his undershorts cool off in the rain after a scorching Los Angeles heat wave. Dietrich was starring in Universal's *Destry Rides Again* at the same time Rathbone was making *Tower of London*.

Monday, September 18: The official top temperature this week was 107.2 degrees, although there were reports that Burbank had registered 117 degrees, while Universal had reportedly hit 130.

Thursday, September 21: *Variety* wrote that, due to the record heat, Charles Laughton had lost six pounds in a single day while playing the Hunchback at the RKO Ranch. The trade paper also reported that, on the saloon set of *Destry Rides Again*, Universal had "attached kegs of real beer to spigots, and told cast and crew to help themselves. Free beer has been assured until thermometers do about face."

Lee cancelled *Tower of London* exterior shooting. His progress on stage sets that week, according to Murphy, was "consistently good."

Sunday, September 24: As the rains finally came, Carl Laemmle Sr., Universal's founder, who had lost the studio to usurping new management in 1936, died of a heart attack.[18] He was 72. The funeral was Tuesday, September 26. All Hollywood studios observed two minutes of silence, and then work continued, including on *Tower of London,* which carried on behind schedule.

Finishing Touches

The rain cooled off Universal. Hedda Hopper wrote that the "funniest sight of the week" was Rathbone, taking a break from the *Tower of London* set and joyously running about in the rain "in his shorty shorts."[19] Based on a photo, he was apparently wearing his boxer shorts. Accompanying him in his romp in the rain: *Destry Rides Again*'s Marlene Dietrich, sporting a short dressing robe.

Wednesday, October 4: Production unofficially closed on *Tower of London* after 46 days of shooting—ten days over schedule. Estimated final cost: $533,000.

But it wasn't over yet. There were still scenes to be shot of beggars ("no members of the cast—all extras and bit players," reported Murphy). Also, due to the farrago with the battle scenes, Lee knew he needed to embellish the sequences. His original plan, as Murphy wrote: "Small groups of soldiers against process plates."

Tuesday, October 17: *Variety* reported:

Adds for Tower

Principals in Universal's Tower of London, *which Rowland V. Lee produces, were recalled yesterday for day's shooting of added scenes. Basil Rathbone, Boris Karloff, John Sutton and Nan Grey check back on lot this morning.*

Lee had realized that anonymous soldiers against process plates wouldn't save the day; much more was necessary. The embellishment job went to Ford Beebe, director of such Universal fare as the 1939 Bela Lugosi serial *The Phantom Creeps*. In March 1978, eight months before he died, Beebe wrote a letter to *Films of Bela Lugosi* author Richard Bojarski, recalling *Tower of London*. The letter is now in the archives of collector John Antosiewicz, who graciously shared its content:

Rowland V. Lee was a splendid director, but his forte was not what we know as "action" films. Fortunately, he knew this and when he saw the first cut of Tower of London, *he was the first to realize that its battle scenes lacked action. So, he appealed to Martin Murphy, the production manager, to find one who could supply what the film lacked; and since I had been making nothing but action pictures for most of my life, Murphy suggested that he turn the job over to me.*

So, we met and Lee told me to go to the limit, that expense was no problem. "Just look at the film," he said, "and do anything you choose to do to liven up the battle scenes." It turned out to be one of the most enjoyable assignments I had ever had. The studio gave me everything I asked for, the best stunt men, and at the suggestion of my assistant (Charlie Gould), they gave me half a dozen horses clad in armor. The crew and I had a field day! They even let us work with a number of the actors to add a touch of reality to the stunts—Basil Rathbone, Boris Karloff and Ralph Forbes—and they all cooperated beautifully.

Beebe specifically remembered "Mord":

As for Karloff.... To me the strangest bit about him is that of all the heavies in the business, it would have fallen to Boris to play the heaviest roles. In my experience I have never worked with a man who was so essentially gentle and so courteous as he. What made it even more astounding was that it was not the courtesy of a man of his standing ... trained to be so. It was a courtesy that was an inherent part of the man's character. He was not acting it; he was living it, and a greater compliment I cannot conceive of.[20]

Saturday, October 21: Murphy wrote:

Since last Tuesday (October 17), we have been shooting additional scenes for this picture and encountering great difficulties in obtaining the various members of the cast at present occupied in other productions. Lee will finish up all his work tonight. Ford Beebe, shooting a second unit for the past two days, will finish his work on Monday—all of this making a total shooting period for Lee of 51 days and in addition to three days of second unit work. We figure these additional scenes will cost approximately $25,000 and our probable total final cost on the picture will run approximately $558,000....

Also on October 21: Bruno David Ussher[21] wrote a feature article about *Tower of London*'s music in *The Los Angeles Daily News*:

Universal studio and musical director Charles Previn have managed to do something new. The background music for the Tower of London *film consists entirely of ancient English music, played on pre–Elizabethan instruments, in accordance with the historic character of* Tower of London, *the Rowland Lee production....*

The article quoted Charles Previn:

I have been as faithful musically as producer Lee has been with settings and costumes. For instance, we have not used a single trombone, because that instrument was non-existent in the 15th century.
The music is not "under-scoring" in the usual sense, but background music establishing the feeling of the period....
It's the feeling of historic reality after which Rowland Lee, the producer, and his brother, Robert Lee, have striven, and I think Frank Skinner and I have done the same musically.

"The effect is quite captivating," wrote Ussher, "and the archaic tone color and harmonization sound 'grave and sweet,' as one of the poets of those early Tudor days describes the music of his time."

Friday, November 3: Universal hosted the first preview of *Tower of London*. Presumably it was not an overwhelming success, and M.F. Murphy wrote the next day, "We believe a musical score will help this show considerably...." The "grave and sweet" music created by Skinner and Previn had clearly laid an egg, at least with Universal's studio executives. Hans J. Salter, Previn's associate on the film, remembered:

I remember Tower of London *very well ... we used harpsichord and flutes and viola da gambas—all those old instruments. But when we went to the preview with this, it didn't work out. The executives were somehow startled. They didn't like it. They couldn't make heads or tails out of that sound. I think I had orchestrated some of that old music for strings and harpsichord, and I think I wrote a few sequences, too, in that style. It was a good idea, but it didn't work. So, after the preview, all this music was replaced by some other music, and some of it was from* Son of Frankenstein.[22]

Actually, music such as Salter described does appear here and there in the film—including the scene that climaxes with the murder of the two young princes in the tower.

Saturday, November 4: The morning after the preview, Messrs. Metzger and Houghton of the Production Code Administration reviewed *Tower of London* at Universal City. They listed nine areas of concern:

- The torture scene in the Tower.
- The scene of Mord lifting his axe, and the sound of the axe descending on the block.
- The "gruesome shot" showing Richard shoving sword through the body of Wales.
- Latin prayers at the marriage ceremony in the church. (This was a problem in England.)
- The "gruesome scene" of Mord lashing Wyatt—"prolonged torture."
- Close-up bosom shots. (Undue exposure of breasts.)
- Sound of axe descending in execution scene.
- Scenes of falling horses, and horse lying on ground facing camera, during battle. (This was cited as a problem in England.)
- Scene of man pulling sword out of his body—"gruesomeness."

What had emerged from all the casting, production and censorship mayhem? The result was a mixed bag, but the film definitely had its points. Twelve effective moments from the film:

1. *Meet Mord:* A hellish hoot of an introduction, as we see Karloff's Mord in his torture chamber, sharpening his axe with a raven perched on his shoulder. "Razor sharp!" he exults.

2. *The Execution of Lord DeVere:* Morbid pomp and pageantry as Rodion Rathbone's Lord DeVere proceeds to his death, with a tolling bell and many extras. Nice touch: DeVere, tipping the executioner, giving the hooded Mord the smallest of coins with the words, "Do your worst." Karloff spits on the coin and tosses it. Fadeout shot: Rathbone grinning.

3. *Rathbone's Puppetry:* Throughout the film, Richard slyly peeks at his closet of doll-like figures, all representing the powers-that-be who stand between him and the throne. He tosses the puppets representing his latest victims into the fireplace.

4. *The Battle Scenes:* Despite those 50 jackass extras, the rainy battle of Tewkesbury and the foggy climactic fight at Bosworth Field are both loud, nightmarish, and look almost Expressionistic with the dark figures and their weapons on the hill and horizon. They aren't all they should be, but Ford Beebe's eleventh hour work clearly saved the day.

5. *The Marriage Scene of the Two Children:* One of *Tower of London*'s prize sequences. A singing choir of altar boys, the stunning entrance of the two children, Joan Carroll taller than Donnie Dunagan, the straight-faced crowd…. Thank Heavens Lee fought Universal not to cut the episode!

6. *The Drowning of Clarence in the Malmsey Vat:* Truly a highlight, with Price's wild-eyed, boisterous laughter as he thinks he's won the drinking contest. Nice touch: Price reaching over and spitefully rubbing Rathbone's hump (despite Joseph Breen's

admonishment to eliminate any hump-rubbing). Another nice touch: that huge splash that soaks Rathbone as Karloff slams down the vat lid on poor Price.

7. *Mordant Humor*: At one point, Mord, while chatting with a minion, opens his iron maiden. A bleeding figure—corpse?—falls out. Mord barely notices, leaves the victim on the floor, and runs off to perform some new perfidy.

8. *Torture*: Mord at work is a force of nature: We see Karloff torturing John Sutton's Wyatt with whip, red-hot pincers and the rack. Strong stuff for 1939.

9. *Wyatt's Escape*: Cinematographer George Robinson captures Wyatt escaping down the Tower's face at night, the lake water shimmering on the wall, with a Romantic storybook charm.

10. *Mord's Conscience*: Karloff gets peculiar dimension into his role as he can't bring himself to carry out Richard's directive to kill the teenage princes in the tower. He recruits other killers, and then watches the murders, his face a mix of repulsion and fascination.

11. *Richard's Aftermath*: His death scene isn't much, but there's the nice barbaric touch of Richard's corpse, hooked to a horse, dragged off the battlefield as his enemies shout and spit at the cadaver—the corpse destined, at least temporarily, for the Leicester parking lot.

12. *Mord's Demise*: Finally allowed to kill in "hot blood" at Bosworth Field, Karloff's Mord sees Richard dead on the battlefield, killed by Ralph Forbes' Henry Tudor. "You're a god to me," Mord had told Richard early in the film. Now, in a God-Is-Dead panic, Mord flees, battles a pursuing Wyatt, suffers a hacking, falls into a tree that hangs from the edge of a cliff, and both Mord and the tree tumble down the cliff. In a vivid irony, Karloff's Mord dies screaming. Angelic music plays in celebration.

A bonus thirteenth fine moment: After Mord asked to accompany Richard to the Battle of Tewkesbury, and been rather brusquely denied, we see the bandy-legged executioner, sadly watching the soldiers riding and marching off to glorious battle, as he slowly stalks back through an archway, alone and seemingly heartbroken. It's a weirdly sad vignette, reminding us what a splendid actor Boris Karloff was.

A real star of the show is the Tower itself. It later appeared in too many films to mention, but just one here: It's Karloff's "Mad Doctor" castle in 1944's *House of Frankenstein*, where Glenn Strange's Monster throws J. Carrol Naish's Hunchback (actually his double, Billy Jones) through a skylight, and he topples from the Tower roof for a crowd-pleasing demise (see Chapter 11).[23]

Monday, November 13: The PCA issued *Tower of London* release certificate No. 5819. Lee had apparently refused to eliminate the Latin prayers (which the MPPDA figured the British Board of Film Censors "will probably delete"), some of the torture scenes (which the PCA expected might be cut by "some political censor boards"), and the scenes of the horses falling in the climactic battle ("the British and Canadian Censor Boards will probably delete").

Thursday, November 16: *Tower of London* previewed at the Alexander Theater in Glendale. *Variety*, aware of Universal's troubles with the film, was a bit extravagant in its review the next day:

> [A] horror picture designed to end all horror pictures ... while Tower *is a chiller in the fullest sense of the word, it is something more....* It is a parade of pageantry and trappings as they actually existed in medieval times. It is a gripping cinematic offering, and, above all, a highly entertaining one....

In this shot, we get a good view of the magnificent Tower of London set that Universal built on its back lot. It survived for many years (from the John Antosiewicz Collection).

Production and directorial achievements of Rowland V. Lee will zoom his professional stock to a new high, while the brilliant portrayal of his star, Basil Rathbone, definitely makes the latter a contender for Oscar consideration....

Boris Karloff, heading the support as Mord, misshapen chief executioner and tool of Rathbone, never has had a role so befitting his talents for silver-sheet gruesomeness. Beside it his previous Frankenstein characterizations are dwarfed....

So, with a new musical score and about six minutes of late cuts and edits, *Tower of London* tallied a final cost of approximately $577,000. Average cost of a Hollywood feature film at this time was approximately $300,000.[24]

Saturday, November 18: Bruno David Ussher took note of the new musical score, writing that the original music by Frank Skinner and Charles Previn was

> lovely, bright, and suitably melancholic....
> But in the finished film version little of this historically so atmospheric music was left and most of it dubbed so low as to be nearly inaudible at times.... Instead, the score is now a mixture in which conventional music of the Frankenstein horror, bugle and battle music predominate.

Friday, November 24: "RKO After Rowland Lee as Producer-Director," reports a page one *Variety* headline.

> Rowland V. Lee is being dickered by RKO on producer-director deal. He returns Monday from Palm Springs, where he has been since preview of Tower of London, final picture under his Universal contract.

Part Three: The Release

Thursday, December 7: Universal, eager to give the film a splashy L.A. opening, presented *Tower of London* at Hollywood's 3595-seat Paramount Theatre, with Glen Gray and his Casa Loma Orchestra live on stage. Erskine Johnson critiqued it in the *Los Angeles Daily News*:

> It's all pretty strong and morbid stuff, but if you like that sort of thing, you'll find it good melodrama. There is some fine acting by Rathbone, as No. 1 plotter for the throne, Karloff as the sinister chief executioner and Barbara O'Neil.... The battle scenes, too, are exceptionally well-staged.... The wine "duel" between Rathbone and his younger brother, Vincent Price, is probably the best sequence in the film, and provides its only bit of comedy....[25]

The show played a week. *Variety* reported the take: "Nothing to get excited about at around $15,000."[26]

Monday, December 11: *Tower of London* opened at New York City's Rialto—and was a smash hit. Two days later, *Variety* reported:

> Opened sensationally Monday (11) and should have a big week of around $14,000, kickoff being $2300. This is the biggest Monday this small-seater has ever had, which is all the more remarkable in view of the time of the year it's done. House ran 10 full shows, grinding a total of 21 hours.[27]

Tower of London actually hit over $15,000 at the Rialto, the second-best week the theater ever had, and was held over.[28]

Friday, December 15: Tower of London enjoyed big ballyhoo as it opened at the 2680-seat Warfield Theatre in San Francisco. Appearing on stage in person: its stars Karloff, Nan Grey and John Sutton, hosted by Mischa Auer—and featuring, as a bonus, Bela Lugosi!

It sounded terrific ... but there was at least one disappointed patron. B.J. Smith wrote a stinging letter about the show to the editor of *Variety*, which published his lament on January 10, 1940:

The recent personal appearance of five Universal players in conjunction with the opening of Tower of London *at the Warfield Theatre here stands as a glaring example of poor showmanship. Described at the opening by the m.c., Mischa Auer, as "just a little something we knocked together on the phone on the way here—confidentially, it stinks," the show lived up in every way to Auer's statement.*

Actually, "Confidentially, it stinks" was a paraphrase of Auer's line as the ballet teacher in Frank Capra's *You Can't Take It with You*, Columbia's Best Picture Oscar Winner of 1938. Nevertheless, Smith wrote of the Universal contingent, "Equipped with poor material and in one case with none at all, it would seem that the picture might have had a better chance without their efforts." Then he itemized the ways the show did indeed "stink":

- Mischa Auer "offered two or three Hollywood jokes that the audience applauded out of politeness."
- Then Auer introduced John Sutton, "a personable young man who stooged a minute or two" for Auer. Then Sutton walked off stage, "holding his belly." As Smith added, "We can understand that."
- Then came Karloff, who as Smith reported, "Got a big hand." Smith wrote that Karloff "proceeded to dish out a lot of 'up the years from the Majestic to the Warfield,'" which presumably means that Boris told old theater stories, maybe about his struggles as an actor. Karloff also pleased the crowd by saying that he had "overheard there's a better than even break" that the San Francisco Fair of 1939 would reopen in 1940.
- Bela Lugosi followed. Unfortunately, Smith didn't describe what Bela precisely did; he merely wrote that he "tried hard for a while."
- Finally, Bela introduced Nan Grey, who drew the sharpest criticism from Smith: "a great disappointment indeed. She is of the hand-kissing, arm-flinging, I-love-you-all-my-public variety."

As Smith concluded, "All this might appear to be offset by the fact that the show was packed from noon 'til midnight by one pushover audience after another, mostly kids." At any rate, *Variety* called *Tower of London* San Francisco's "best bet" that week, and predicted it would take in a "nice" $14,000.[29]

Meanwhile, *Tower of London* racked up its share of local censor board deletions.
Ohio:

In torture room, where Wyatt swinging at arm's length by thumbs is being flogged, allow only one scene of flogging where Mord first strikes at him with whip and sound of lash....

Pennsylvania:

Eliminate views where Mord sits on vat and where Richard leans against side and both listen to drowning gasps and bubbles of Clarence.
Eliminate views where Wyatt plunges sword through body of Mord, before body goes over cliff.

New Zealand:

Reduction of view of prisoner being whipped.
Reduction of view of victim on torture rack.
Eliminations of screams of Princes (leaving in preceding action).
Reduction of view of body of slain King being dragged behind horse.

At the box office, *Tower of London* performed sporadically.

January 3, 1940: Variety headlined "Hollywood Toppers" on page one, listing 1939's biggest grossers from the major studios. Universal's list:

- *That Certain Age* (a Deanna Durbin vehicle, actually released in the fall of 1938, directed by Edward Ludwig)
- *When Tomorrow Comes* (starring Irene Dunne and Charles Boyer, directed by John Stahl)
- *You Can't Cheat an Honest Man* (W.C. Fields and Edgar Bergen & Charlie McCarthy, directed by George Marshall)
- *East Side of Heaven* (starring Bing Crosby, directed by David Butler)
- *Three Smart Girls Grow Up* (another Durbin, directed by Henry Koster)
- *Destry Rides Again* (Marlene Dietrich and James Stewart, directed by George Marshall)

None of Rowland V. Lee's four Universal films made the studio's "Topper" list. Nevertheless, with *Son of Frankenstein* and *Tower of London*, Lee had bequeathed Universal two of its most majestic melodramas.

Part Four: Legacy

[Boris Karloff was] *one of the few (very select) of my Hollywood life I'd even care to mention. Boris came into it early on—my second or third film,* Tower of London, *and he and Basil Rathbone introduced me to a kind of joyousness of picture-making I too seldom encountered in the hundred films that came later....*

—Vincent Price, letter to Cynthia Lindsay,
author of *Dear Boris* (1975)[30]

Tower of London has its problems. Lee never excelled at pace. Rathbone has a less than stellar demise, killed in a climactic, sadly perfunctory sword duel with Henry Tudor (Ralph Forbes); he deserved a far more bloodthirsty comeuppance. (See Sir Laurence Olivier's chillingly violent death throes in his *Richard III* as an example of how an epic villain *should* die!)

Critically, the film suffers from an unwieldy script, often verbose and poorly constructed. A carefully prepared scenario, polished *prior* to the start of shooting, would have helped immeasurably.

Of course, it's Golden Age horror fans who will most appreciate *Tower of London*. There are many familiar faces and forms to enjoy: Rose Hobart (from 1931's *Dr. Jekyll and Mr. Hyde*) as Anne Neville; Leo G. Carroll (*Tarantula*) as the faithful Hastings; Lionel Belmore (from 1931's *Frankenstein*) as Beacon, a florid old attendant, who announces demises; Harry Cording (from 1934's *The Black Cat*) as one of the men who slay the princes in the Tower; and Michael Mark (Ludwig in *Frankenstein* and Neumüller in Lee's *Son of Frankenstein*) lurking in background shots. The *Son of Frankenstein* musical score works effectively.

Best of all, there's Rathbone, Karloff and Price, 24 years before they reteamed (and with Peter Lorre)—uproariously—in American-International's *The Comedy of Terrors*.

As for Rowland V. Lee … he directed only four more films. *The Son of Monte Cristo* (UA, 1940) was a handsome and enjoyable costume mini-epic, starred Louis Hayward, Joan Bennett and, as the villain, George Sanders. It was a sequel to Lee's *The Count of Monte Cristo* (UA, 1934), and both films were produced by Edward Small. *Powder Town* (RKO, 1942) was a potboiler about a stolen explosive and starred Edmond O'Brien and Victor McLaglen. *The Bridge of San Luis Rey* (UA, 1944), based on the Thornton Wilder novel (why did the five people who died when a footbridge fell between Cuzco and Peru, happen to be there at that moment?), boasted such players as Louis Calhern, Nazimova and Akim Tamiroff and was a success. It was independently produced by Motorola owner Benedict Bogeaus, as was *Captain Kidd* (UA, 1945). *Captain Kidd* starred Charles Laughton in the title role and, although the film was popular, the story (by Robert N. Lee) was poor and Rowland Lee battled with Bogeaus.

Robert Lee never wrote another film and Rowland Lee never directed one.

Rowland Lee owned a ranch, Farmlake, since 1935.[31] It overlooked the Chatsworth Reservoir, and many filmmakers used it as a location, including Alfred Hitchcock for the carnival episode on *Strangers on a Train*. In 1959, Lee came back to produce and co-write (with Howard Estabrook) the screenplay for *The Big Fisherman,* based on the Lloyd C. Douglas religious novel. Frank Borzage directed, Howard Keel starred as Peter the Apostle, and the three-hour film flopped, soon forgotten in a year that saw the release of *Ben-Hur*.

Robert N. Lee died in Hollywood on September 18, 1964, age 74. Rowland V. Lee died in Palm Desert, California, on December 21, 1975, age 84. Robert's ashes are interred in the Freedom Mausoleum at Forest Lawn, Glendale; Rowland's ashes are also interred at Forest Lawn, in the private Garden of Memory.[32]

*   *   *

One-third of a century after *Tower of London*, Vincent Price participated in another malmsey vat murder, but this time from the other side of the lid: In the black-comic horror *Theater of Blood* (1973), he plays a mad Shakespearean actor serial-killing the critics who panned him—and he joyously presides as his minions force critic Robert Coote into a malmsey vat, as in the Bard's *Richard III*.

As Price wrote, there was also a "joyousness" in *Tower of London*, amidst the star villains. Rathbone may well have been unhappy with certain aspects of the production, but he was a supreme professional and he, Karloff and Price play-act their medieval monsters with schoolboy high spirits. This happy camaraderie made palatable the beheading, the torture rack, the marriage and killing of children, and the tedious pitfalls of the production of this medieval melodrama, that straddles, sometimes painfully, horror film and historic spectacle.

So … with Richard III's skeleton honorably interred, *Tower of London* might take on a new respectability … or perhaps, notoriety. In its star trio, the film boasts a boisterous Hollywood Horror Royalty—and a command performance encore is perhaps in order for all who pay homage in their realm.

At any rate, this *Tower of London* chapter is dedicated to that triumvirate, as well as the real-life, recently honorably interred Richard III whom, we hope and trust, was hardly the "hedgehog," "poisonous bunch-back'd toad," "abortive rooting hog," and other sinister soubriquets Shakespeare had devised for him.

To you, sirs!

The real Tower of London, as it appeared in 2019 (photograph by the author).

Tower of London

Universal, 1939. Producer and Director, Rowland V. Lee. Original Screenplay, Robert N. Lee. Cinematographer, George Robinson. Musical Director, Charles Previn. Orchestrations, Frank Skinner. Art Director, Jack Otterson. Associate Art Director, Richard H. Riedel. Editor, Edward Curtiss. Set Decorator, Russell A. Gausman. Gowns, Vera West. Assistant Director, Fred Frank. Technical Advisors, Major G.O.T. Bagley, Sir Gerald Grove, Bart. Sound Supervisor, Bernard B. Brown. Sound Technician, William Hedgcock. Second Unit Director, Ford Beebe. Makeup Artists, Jack P. Pierce, Otto Lederer, Sam Kaufman. Visual Effects, Jack Cosgrove, Russell Lawson. Fencing Master, Fred Cavens. Camera Operator, Edward Colman. Background Photographer, Henry Schuster. Process Photographer, George J. Teague. Running time, 92 minutes.

Los Angeles opening, Paramount Theatre, December 7, 1939. New York opening, Rialto Theatre, December 11, 1939.

The Cast: Basil Rathbone (Richard III), Boris Karloff (Mord), Barbara O'Neil (Queen Elyzabeth), Ian Hunter (King Edward IV), Vincent Price (Duke of Clarence), Nan Grey (Lady Alice Barton), Ernest Cossart (Tom Clink), John Sutton (John Wyatt), Leo G. Carroll (Lord Hastings), Miles Mander (King Henry VI), Lionel Belmore (Beacon), Rose Hobart (Anne Neville), Ronald Sinclair (Boy King Edward), John Herbert-Bond (Young Prince Richard), Ralph Forbes (Henry Tudor), Frances Robinson (Duchess Isobel), G.P. Huntley (Wales), John Rodion (Lord DeVere), Walter Tetley (Chimney Sweep), Donnie Dunagan (Baby Prince), Joan Carroll (Lady Mowbray), Ernie Adams (Thirsty Prisoner),

Reginald Barlow (Sheriff), Georgia Cane (Dowager), Harry Cording (Lead Murderer of the Children), Nigel de Brulier (Archbishop at St. John's Chapel), Martin Faust (Dighton), Jean Fenwick (Lady-in-Waiting), John George (Spy), Robert Greig (Friar Cautioning John Wyatt), Holmes Herbert, Murdock MacQuarrie, Charles Miller, Arthur Mulliner, Claude Payton (Councilmen), Colin Kenny (Soldier), George Lloyd (Moat Guard), Michael Mark (Henry VI's Servant), Francis Powers (Priest), C. Montague Shaw (Majordomo), Ivan F. Simpson (Anne's Protector).

8

"A Madman's Dream"

Dr. Jekyll and Mr. Hyde (1941)

Yes, dance—dance and dream. Dream that you're Mrs. Henry Jekyll ... danc-
ing with your own butler and six footmen! Dream that they've all turned into
white mice and crawled into an eternal pumpkin!
                                        —Spencer Tracy's Mr. Hyde, as he strangles
                            Ingrid Bergman's Ivy in *Dr. Jekyll and Mr. Hyde* (1941)

Thursday, August 7, 1941.

Inside Broadway's Astor Theatre was Dr. William Moulton Marston, inventor of the lie detector and creator of the comic book heroine Wonder Woman.[1] Also present were several hundred young women, ages 16 to 25. They were there to watch 20 minutes of selected scenes from MGM's new feature *Dr. Jekyll and Mr. Hyde*, while Dr. Marston measured their reaction on what he called his Emotional Response Machine.

Marston had a nickname for this apparatus. The man who created the lie detector called his new machine "the Hyde detector."

There were "variographs," "blood pressure cuffs" and "pneumographs," as the ladies beheld Spencer Tracy's wild-eyed Hyde on the Astor's screen, inflicting his censor-defying sadism on the two leading ladies: Ingrid Bergman as Ivy, the barmaid, and Lana Turner as Beatrix, the fiancée. As *Motion Picture Herald* reported it, the "experiment" seemingly had vestiges of sadism itself:

> *At the Astor Theatre laboratory, Dr. Marston and his associate, James Edmund Boyack, corralled*
> *blondes, brunettes and redheads, two at a time, strapped the aforementioned "cuffs" and "pneu-*
> *mographs" to their ankles and chests, respectively, and let female emotions take their course as Dr.*
> *Jekyll and his fiancée and Mr. Hyde and his girl-friend took over the screen. All this while, another*
> *little trick called a "stylus" was supplying a trail of red ink on a long stretch of graph paper ema-*
> *nating from the "Hyde detector."*[2]

The MGM press agents reported, "Blondes are most submissive to male aggressive-ness, and redheads least so." Photographers had a field day snapping pictures of the young women "cuffed" and "strapped," gazing wild-eyed at the screen.

"The experiment," proudly announced Metro afterwards, "was a grand success. Science was promoted and so was *Dr. Jekyll and Mr. Hyde.*"

The bondage sideshow was just one of the frolics promoting *Dr. Jekyll and Mr. Hyde*. Tracy already had two Oscars. Ingrid Bergman and Lana Turner were two of the most alluring actresses in Hollywood. Although Joseph Breen had tried to housebreak the pro-duction's sensationalism, word was out that MGM had outfoxed the censorship czar and

Poster for *Dr. Jekyll and Mr. Hyde* (MGM, 1941).

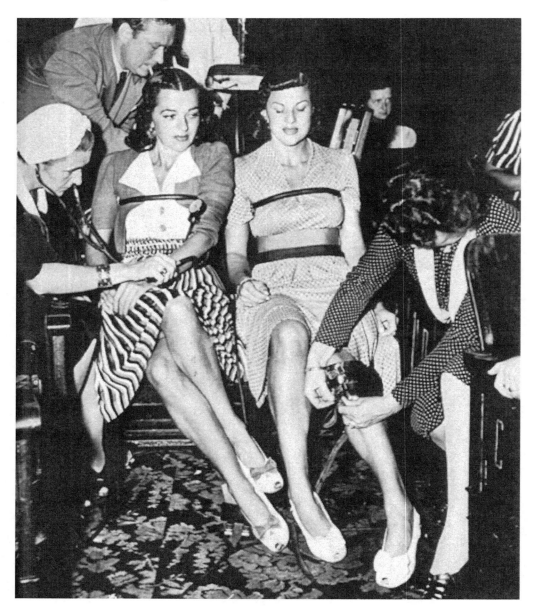

As publicity for *Dr. Jekyll and Mr. Hyde*, ladies submit themselves to the "Hyde Detector" experiment to measure their emotional reaction to Spencer Tracy's Hyde. Its inventor was Dr. William Moulton Marston and, as this picture suggests, one of his inspirations was bondage.

that the new film version of Robert Louis Stevenson's 1886 novella almost amounted to an "Adults Only" *Dr. Jekyll and Mr. Hyde*. There was even a Marquis de Sade–esque fantasy dream where Tracy, as a charioteer, lashed "steeds" Bergman and Turner. The film, by all early accounts, was a sexed-up epic of Good vs. Evil, a two-hour-plus super-melodrama, beginning and closing with a choir singing the 23rd Psalm, beautifully scored by Franz Waxman. And directing the show: Victor Fleming, an Oscar winner for *Gone with the Wind*!

The Hollywood Reporter, having seen a trade show screening, asserted that to see the film was "to indulge in an emotional binge." Expectations were very high. As humorist George E. Phair wrote in *Variety*:

> *They tell us the fans will be goggle-eyed*
> *At* Dr. Jekyll and Mr. Hyde.[3]

Dr. Jekyll and Mr. Hyde had spun off into becoming a bizarre tragedy—a saga of an addict–sex sadist and his victim, basically masquerading as a horror film. It was, for 1941, a remarkably audacious interpretation, amok at a studio where Greer Garson struck noble poses and Mickey Rooney portrayed Andy Hardy. This *Jekyll and Hyde,* with its angelic choirs and Freudian nightmares, would play as a virtual self-crucifixion, with the five wounds being Faith, Sadism, Addiction, Bondage and Blasphemy.

No wonder the alcoholic, Roman Catholic Spencer Tracy acted it in a state of agony.

Part One: Pre-Production

The Ghosts of Hyde's Past—and Future

Monday, May 9, 1887: A year after the publication of Stevenson's novella, Richard Mansfield, 29 years old, first played *The Strange Case of Dr. Jekyll and Mr. Hyde* at the Boston Museum. Thomas Russell Sullivan had written the play, creating the concept of the "good woman" and "bad woman" in Jekyll's life. Mansfield's on-stage transformation frequently caused females in the audience to faint and, during an 1888 engagement in London, inspired suspicion he was Jack the Ripper.[4] Mansfield regularly revived the play until his death in 1907.

Film versions started sprouting in 1908. The most notable two:

Sunday, March 28, 1920: John Barrymore, 38 years old, starred in *Dr. Jekyll and Mr. Hyde,* produced by Paramount–Famous Players Studio in New York; it opened this day at Broadway's Rivoli Theatre. Barrymore was a genuinely beautiful Jekyll and a truly horrific Hyde. Inspiring his Hyde interpretation: a red tarantula Barrymore admired in a zoo.[5] His transformation scene was acrobatic, as he contorted his face into Hyde: After a camera cut, he affected a conical skull, scraggly wig and skeletal fingers. John Stuart Robertson directed, Martha Mansfield was Jekyll's fiancée, and Nita Naldi was the temptress. Barrymore's portrayal was one of the greatest performances of the silent screen; arguably, it was *the* greatest.

Barrymore's self-assessment: "All I did was put on a harrowing makeup, twist my face, claw at my throat, and roll on the floor. That, the critics said, was acting. And, may my worthy ancestors forgive me, I began to agree with them!"[6]

Thursday, December 24, 1931: Fredric March, 34 years old, starred in *Dr. Jekyll and Mr. Hyde,* produced by Paramount in Hollywood, opening this Christmas Eve at Los Angeles' Paramount Theatre. March was a matinee idol of a Jekyll, and a sadistic, talking chimpanzee of a Hyde. "He is like a kitten, a pup, full of vim and energy," said Rouben Mamoulian, who directed the show in a frenzy of pre–Code stylistics. March's ape-kitten went savage on his fleshy tart mistress Ivy (blonde Miriam Hopkins). He also brutally beat to death the father of Jekyll's fiancée Muriel (brunette Rose Hobart). Cinematographer Karl Struss made the transformation happen by "using a red filter on strong red makeup, so that when you photographed red with a red filter, the object was white."[7]

On November 18, 1932, March won the Academy Award for *Dr. Jekyll and Mr. Hyde*. As he had defeated Wallace Beery (of MGM's *The Champ*) by only a single vote, Beery got an Oscar too. March, in his acceptance speech, praised makeup man Wally Westmore as being "responsible for the greater measure of my success."[8]

*   *   *

Jump ahead to a different Oscar night, over seven years later:

Thursday, February 29, 1940: A surprise: Robert Donat, British star, won the 1939 Best Actor Oscar for MGM's *Goodbye, Mr. Chips*. The 34-year-old Shakespearean-trained actor defeated favorites Clark Gable of *Gone with the Wind* and James Stewart of *Mr. Smith Goes to Washington*. Donat was home in England (where *Goodbye, Mr. Chips* was produced). Announcing Donat's victory: Spencer Tracy.

Monday, March 11: "Donat Gets *Jekyll*," headlined page one of *Variety*:

> *MGM has bought* Dr. Jekyll and Mr. Hyde *from Paramount as a starrer for Robert Donat. Price is understood to be around $30,000.*

MGM had chosen to downplay the price paid to Paramount. *Motion Picture Herald* gave the price as $125,000, which is supported by studio records.

Tuesday, March 19: Richard Halliday of Paramount sent MGM the following material from Paramount's archives[9]:

- a synopsis of Stevenson's story,
- a synopsis of a stage play by Luella Forepaugh and George F. Fish,
- a synopsis of the continuity of the 1920 Barrymore version,
- the scene and title outline of the 1920 film, and
- the sequence synopsis of the 1931 version.

Other records indicate that MGM also received Paramount's complete script (July 20, 1931) and complete screenplay (August 7, 1931) by Percy Heath and Samuel Hoffenstein, as well as the release dialogue script (December 29, 1931).

This was quite a haul of intellectual property, and it came along with an unpublicized condition. MGM got the green light to take control of Paramount's prints of the 1931 *Dr. Jekyll and Mr. Hyde*—thereby eliminating any chance of Paramount re-releasing its film to compete with, or show up, MGM's new version.

Monday, April 1: John Lee Mahin, Metro contract writer, Oscar-nominated for *Captains Courageous* (1937), tackled the new screenplay.[10] MGM planned to produce the film in Great Britain. (Donat always fought coming to Hollywood.)

Monday, April 29: Mahin's first draft script was complete. The new script "aped" Paramount's 1931 version, and even included an episode of some controversy from the earlier film. A still from that picture showed Fredric March's Hyde, in tux, cape, and top hat, trampling a child. Mamoulian claimed in later years that it was merely a publicity shot. Nevertheless, the episode (which actually had come from Stevenson's novella) reappeared in Mahin's 1940 script, which suggests it actually did appear, if not originally in the 1931 film, at least in its script. A section of Mahin's script detailed Hyde setting out in the night to find Ivy at the Palace of Frivolities Music Hall:

> We hear music and singing coming from the inside. WE DOLLY IN as Hyde's skulking, scurrying figure approaches the entrance. A little ragged girl, begging, approaches him:
>
> **Little Girl:** *Can you spare a copper—?*
>
> **Hyde:** *Out of my way!*
>
> With a literal growl, he actually tramples over her. She screams with pain. A small thin man jumps in front of him, scared at his expression, but resolute.
>
> **Thin Man:** *Whatcha mean … that's my kid!*
>
> **Hyde** (raising his cane): *Agh! Why you—!*
>
> But he stops, as another man large and burly, steps up to him. Others crowd around. The little girl hugs her father, crying.
>
> **Burly Man** (threatening, slow): *Better give her somethin', mister.*
>
> **Hyde** (after a second's hesitation, looking about at crowd): *This is to bury her with!*
>
> He flips a coin in the air, and ducks into the entrance. The burly man catches it, and all look at him.
>
> **Thin Man:** *'Struth! 'Alf a jimmy-o'-goblin!*
>
> **Burly Man** (looking after Hyde): *He'd have to be rich with a mug like that. He weren't born—he was hatched!*

Production Plans and a New Star

MGM set *Dr. Jekyll and Mr. Hyde* to start shooting in May, then delayed it to June. The War was making production in England seriously problematic. Donat meanwhile toured England and Scotland in Shaw's *The Devil's Disciple.*

Wednesday, July 24: "The Old Two-Timer Back," headlined *Variety*:

> Dr. Jekyll and Mr. Hyde, *originally slated for production by Metro in London, is being shifted to the Culver City plant, with Victor Saville producing on a $1,000,000 budget. Robert Donat, held in England by the war, will be replaced by an American star, whose name is still under cover.*

The American star was Spencer Tracy. Revered for his back-to-back Academy Award–winning portrayals of Manuel the fisherman of *Captains Courageous* (1937) and Father Flanagan of *Boys Town* (1938), the 40-year-old Tracy was Hollywood's most respected male star. While John Barrymore had always appeared half-mad anyway, and Fredric March had a Barrymore-esque flamboyance, Tracy was a naturalistic player with an aversion to showboat dramatics and heavy makeup.

Nevertheless, the challenge of playing Dr. Jekyll and Mr. Hyde took hold of him. In her 1991 book *Me: Stories of My Life*, Katharine Hepburn quoted Tracy:

> *Believe it or not, when they first mentioned* Jekyll and Hyde, *I was thrilled. I had always been fascinated by the story and saw it as a story of the two sides of a man. I felt that Jekyll was a very respectable doctor—a fine member of society. He had proposed to a lovely girl and was about to marry her. But there was another side to the man. Every once in a while, Jekyll would go on a trip. Disappear. And either because of drink or dope or who knows what, he would become—or should I say turn into?—Mr. Hyde. Then in a town or neighborhood where he was totally unknown, he would perform incredible acts of cruelty and vulgarity. The emotional side of Jekyll was obviously extremely disturbed. The girl, as his fiancée, is a proper lady. But as his fantasy whore, the girl matched his Mr. Hyde. She would be capable of the lowest behavior.*
>
> *The two girls would be played by the same actress; the two men would be me.*

Hepburn added, "Oddly enough, when he had this notion, I was the girl he had in mind. At this time, we had never met. It still seems the most fascinating idea to me…."

It was fascinating, but also perilous. Tracy was an alcoholic. Playing a Jekyll-Hyde in which the elixir was "drink or dope" had the danger of hitting too close to home for the actor. Makeup artist Frank Westmore recalled Tracy when he was previously under contract at Fox:

> [He] went on such a drunken rampage that he had to be locked inside a huge studio soundstage…. Before he reached the blessed state of unconsciousness, he tore down the sets and systematically smashed thousands of dollars' worth of lights.[11]

Tuesday, November 12: Joseph Breen wrote to Louis B. Mayer regarding the proposed

Spencer Tracy's Dr. Jekyll … under the shadow of Mr. Hyde.

script for *Dr. Jekyll and Mr. Hyde*. Although Breen noted that the script was, "of course," passable—it was, after all, based on Stevenson's classic—he detailed "certain minor items that are not acceptable."[12] His list ran nearly three pages. Among the cautions and objections:

- *Page 33: Great care will be needed with the characterization of the girl Ivy, to avoid characterizing her as a prostitute.*
- *Page 38: This scene of the girl taking off her stocking must be done inoffensively, and without any undue exposure. Please also do not over-emphasize the garter in this scene.*
- *Page 39: This action of the girl falling back on the bed and swinging her bare leg, must be changed, as suggestive.*
- *Page 48: Please do not overplay the garter in this scene.*
- *Page 49: Omit the non-italicized words in the expression "the little white-breasted dove."*
- *Page 50: Please avoid undue brutality in the scene where Hyde tramples on the girl.*
- *Page 56: The dialogue that ends this scene, beginning "I'm hurting you because I like to hurt you," and running to the fade-out, is unacceptable, by reason of containing a definite suggestion of sadism. Any such flavor is forbidden by the Code. This scene will therefore have to be entirely rewritten.*
- *Page 65: Great care will be needed with scene 151, to avoid any suggestion of rape. Any such flavor will render the scene unacceptable.*

- *Page 81: Great care will be necessary with scene 165, where Hyde strangles Ivy, to avoid undue gruesomeness. This is particularly important, as regards any sound effects.*

As these items note, the new script closely followed the 1931 version. As for the "garter" scene, for example, the 1931 *Jekyll and Hyde* had Miriam Hopkins' Ivy doing a virtual striptease in her bed, flirtatiously tossing her garters at Fredric March's wide-eyed Jekyll.[13] Sadism romped in the 1931 film. Breen vowed it wouldn't in the 1941 version.

MGM had other ideas on the subject.

Tuesday, November 2: "Spencer Tracy Gets Lead in *Dr. Jekyll and Mr. Hyde*," headlined the Cinema page of *The New York Times*. Douglas W. Churchill reported from Hollywood that the horror story "will go before the cameras as soon as Tracy finishes his *Men of Boys Town….*"

Victor Fleming, tall, silver-haired, 52 years old, had helmed such MGM Hall of Fame hits as *Red Dust, Captains Courageous* and *Test Pilot,* the last two with Tracy. His lasting fame, however, had come in 1939 when he directed both *The Wizard of Oz* and *Gone with the Wind*—winning the 1939 Best Director Oscar for the latter, although he directed only approximately 45 percent of the troubled extravaganza.[14] Hollywood regarded him as a "man's man" of a talent.

"Victor Fleming," wrote film historian Scott Eyman, "directed with his genitals."[15]

A candid shot of Victor Fleming, director of *Dr. Jekyll and Mr. Hyde,* with the film's co-stars Ingrid Bergman and Spencer Tracy.

For all his machismo, Fleming was a sensitive man who began films with stomach aches and had trouble controlling his hair-trigger temper. According to John Gallagher in *Films in Review*:

> *During a scene with Cowardly Lion Bert Lahr on the set of* Wizard, *young Judy Garland had a severe case of the giggles that turned into hysterical laughter. Fleming slapped Judy across the face and sent her to her dressing room.*[16]

On *Gone with the Wind*, Fleming had suffered a breakdown and reportedly contemplated suicide. Clark Gable claimed that *GWTW* had taken a year off the director's life. On Oscar night, Fleming, bitterly believing producer David O. Selznick had hogged the glory, claimed illness and skipped the ceremony.

At any rate, with the news that Tracy and Fleming were reteaming, *Dr. Jekyll and Mr. Hyde* became overnight one of 1941's most eagerly awaited films.

Saturday, November 30: John Lee Mahin submitted what the studio referred to as a "Complete OK Script." The script, however, was hardly in a "Final" form. MGM engaged John L. Balderston, whose name appeared on the credits of such horror classics as *Dracula*, *Frankenstein*, *The Mummy*, *Bride of Frankenstein* (see Chapter 4) and *Mad Love* (see Chapter 6), to troubleshoot and revamp the script.

Wednesday, December 11: Frederick Browne, of Long Island, New York, formerly a producer, director and general manager for the late Richard Mansfield's *Dr. Jekyll and Mr. Hyde*, had already written to Tracy, "As it was played by Mr. Barrymore and Mr. Fredric March, it was not the correct version and the theme was entirely wrong." Now he wrote again, this time to the new film's producer Victor Saville:

> *… There are a great many angles to the real scientific and mystery interest which I am very familiar with and the makeup that Mr. Mansfield used was a complete secret; as I had access to his dressing room during the progress of the play, I am perhaps the only one that really knows the formula…. I am sure that the intimate knowledge of the subject that I am familiar with could be of valuable assistance to you in the artistic and mysterious final product….*

Saville politely declined Browne's offer.

Monday, December 16: Tracy dined with Saville, Fleming, and John Lee Mahin, and the quartet watched John Barrymore's *Dr. Jekyll and Mr. Hyde*.[17] Impressed by Barrymore's first transformation *sans* makeup, Tracy decided he too wanted to play Hyde via facial contortion.

Wednesday, December 18: MGM had engaged Ingrid Bergman for the "Good Girl" in *Dr. Jekyll and Mr. Hyde*, borrowing her from David O. Selznick, but had yet to announce her casting as Beatrix. Bergman, already on the Metro lot on loan-out for *Rage in Heaven*, decided that, as far as *Jekyll and Hyde* went, she would prefer to break type and play Ivy. On this day, she tested for the role, with Edward Ashly playing Jekyll. The scene: Ivy comes to Jekyll and shows him that Hyde has whipped her:

> *I need help, I tell you! I can't stand it any more! It's Hyde, sir. … He ain't human, he ain't. He's a beast! He won't let me go, sir, and I'm afraid—I'm afraid of running away. I can't bear it any more! …*

Bergman was heartbreaking in the test. MGM seriously considered her for Ivy.

December 19: *The Hollywood Reporter* wrote that Susan Hayward, on contract to Paramount, was testing for the "femme lead" in *Jekyll and Hyde*.[18] Presumably she was testing for Beatrix. Other reports claimed that Patricia Morison, also on contract to Paramount, was testing for the film, likely as Beatrix. At any rate, MGM engaged neither Hayward nor Morison, and the role of Beatrix would remain un-cast for seven weeks.

Thursday, December 19: *Variety* wrote that *Jekyll and Hyde* would roll at MGM starting January 2, 1941, and that Karl Freund (see Chapters 1 and 6) and Paul Vogel were working with makeup artist Jack Dawn "on special makeup tests."

Friday, December 20: John L. Balderston, having read Mahin's script, wrote to Saville, praising Mahin's overall adaptation (that began in a church) and making a major suggestion:

> *Rewrite the dialogue where Jekyll sets forth the nature of the problem, the dual nature of man, the existence of Plato's two souls, the good and the bad, as indicated in his famous metaphor about the soul as a charioteer driving two horses, the good horse and the bad horse. I think that metaphor could be condensed in one speech that would light up the whole picture. It's one of the greatest passages in all literature, and Stevenson once said it gave him the idea for the book, and when asked why he didn't put it into the book replied he didn't want people to give Plato the credit but preferred to hog it for himself....*

Balderston added, probably humorously, that Plato "is in the public domain." MGM would take Balderston's idea, and eventually develop it in a racy way no one at this time anticipated.

Monday, December 23: As reported in James Curtis' 2011 *Spencer Tracy: A Biography*, the star performed a screen test as Hyde, with subtle facial contortions.[19] When Tracy saw the test the next day, he was so humiliated by his attempt that he completely lost all his once-considerable enthusiasm for *Dr. Jekyll and Mr. Hyde*. Considering the addiction angle, Tracy suddenly felt trapped in a project that threatened to agonize him personally and make a fool of him professionally.

Unfortunately, the shocking realization came on Christmas Eve.

"My Devil Had Been Long-Caged, He Came Out Roaring"

Monday, December 30: *Variety* reported, "Jack Dawn has completed the unusual makeup Spencer Tracy, who plays the dual role, will wear" in *Dr. Jekyll and Mr. Hyde*, and that Joseph Ruttenberg would be the film's cinematographer.[20]

Wednesday, January 8, 1941: "Ingrid Bergman Lent Metro for Lead in *Dr. Jekyll*," headlined *Variety*, three weeks after she tested for Ivy.

Fleming continued makeup tests on Tracy and hoped to start shooting January 15.

Friday, January 10: George E. Phair, in his *Variety* "Retakes" column, joked, "A better idea would be to co-star Spencer Tracy and Mickey Rooney in *Dr. Jekyll and Mr. Hyde* and let them alternate."

January 15 came and went; the film didn't start shooting. The makeup tests continued. There were ideas for MGM's Cartoon department to contribute to the transformations. Tracy and Bergman were virtually the only principals cast.

Wednesday, January 22: *The Hollywood Reporter* wrote that *Jekyll and Hyde* faced "postponement" due to Tracy suffering "a severe attack of the flu." John Lee Mahin, still refining the script, was at his San Fernando Valley home with a cold, and Victor Fleming was also suffering a cold "but still on his feet." He wouldn't be for long: Fleming went home ill and stayed out for a week.

Thursday, January 23: *Dr. Jekyll and Mr. Hyde* was now three weeks past its originally announced January 2 shooting date. The first scene in the film would take place in a church, where Jekyll, Beatrix and Beatrix's father, Sir Charles, attend Sunday services and listen to the bishop's sermon. In the film's first jolt, a disturbed man suddenly jumps up, cackles and lewdly heckles the Bishop.

It was the first scene scheduled to shoot. An MGM Inter-Office Communication on this date addressed the status of Production No. 1178:

Lana Turner as Beatrix, Jekyll's upper-class but hot-blooded fiancée.

> 1. *Tracy, Fleming and Saville wish to make further tests of the characters Jekyll (#1) and Hyde (#1,3, 4-B). Jekyll # 1 works first day according to present layout Jekyll continuity.*
>
> 2. *Beatrix—no one cast. Maureen O'Hara and Ruth Hussey under consideration. Wardrobe sketches, wardrobe, makeup and hairdress all dependent upon casting the character. Character works the first day.*
>
> 3. *Sir Charles—Donald Crisp first in consideration but will not finish with Warner Bros.' picture until Feb. 7th or 8th. Needed first day.*
>
> 4. *Lanyon—Ian Hunter first consideration, contingent upon* Billy the Kid *schedule. Should have more complete information Monday, Jan. 27th. James Stephenson of Warner Bros. is the second choice and will not finish current picture there until Feb. 7th or 8th.*
>
> 5. *Character of Higgins—not set. Needed first day.*
>
> 6. *Character of Mrs. Higgins—not set, contingent upon casting of Mr. Higgins. Needed first day.*
>
> 7. *Bishop—not set. Considering C. Aubrey Smith and Fred Worlock.*

As such, the majority of the players needed to start shooting the film weren't yet confirmed. The memo went on to note:

> *The picture is laid out to shoot all Jekyll script first, then all Hyde, then the transitions from Jekyll to Hyde and vice versa. With all script changes to date it still looks like approximately 45 days. The script is still being re-written.*

Also reported was that "Mr. Sprunk of the Cartoon Dept. would have his first preliminary test ready to show about Jan. 30th," that a Mr. Ceccarini had shot tests with "blue light" but "without sufficiently outstanding results," and that Jack Dawn "will be ready to test the hand transformations on Monday, January 27."

Tuesday, February 4: "Tracy's *Hyde* Lenses," headlined page one of *Variety*, reporting that the film finally started shooting this day. Four other major productions were then in production at MGM: *A Woman's Face,* starring Joan Crawford, *Blossoms in the Dust,* starring Greer Garson, *Love Crazy,* starring William Powell, and *Billy the Kid,* starring Robert Taylor. *Lady Be Good,* a musical starring Eleanor Powell and Ann Sothern, was set to start February 12. On February 10, *Variety* reported that Franz Waxman (whose credits included *Bride of Frankenstein*) would score the picture.

Although coming together tortuously, the new *Jekyll and Hyde* was slowly but surely perversely taking form. Despite Joe Breen, the accent was on sex and sadism, with MGM preparing a uniquely sensual attack that, in its spicy specifics, was original for *Jekyll and Hyde,* and for 1941 Hollywood itself. For Hyde won't be a "tarantula," *à la* Barrymore, or an "ape," like March. He'd be a diabolically handsome man whose "horror" would be primarily in his eyes and his mouth. He would *resemble* Jekyll … purposefully.

He would be the funhouse mirror reflection of the depraved addict Jekyll had self-created.

Part Two: Production

Start of Jekyll & Hyde, *what may well be the worst picture ever made. It will get panned, I will get panned—it will flop!*
> —Spencer Tracy, writing in his journal about *Dr. Jekyll and Mr. Hyde,* February 4, 1941, the first day of shooting[21]

"Good Old Beelzebub," Loose in a Church

The film opens in London on a Sunday in 1887. Its first shot: a church steeple as a choir sings the opening words of the 23rd Psalm, "The Lord Is My Shepherd." C. Aubrey Smith, as the bishop, is in his pulpit, flanked by stained glass windows, sermonizing about the moralistic splendor of Queen Victoria's realm in her Golden Jubilee year. Suddenly, from the congregation, comes a cackle.

"Evil wiped out, eh? So, you want to take all the fun out of life, bishop?"

It emanates from Sam Higgins, referred to in the script pages as a "madman." We learn that he suffered shock in a gas main explosion, and the accident has seemingly unleashed his evil, profane nature. Mrs. Higgins (his wife in the script but referred to as his mother in the film) is seated beside him and tries to calm him. Dr. Harry Jekyll, seated near the front of the church, hears the heckling and turns in his pew, alarmed and curious.

It's a great introduction for Tracy's Jekyll. This Jekyll isn't the Victorian archangel John Barrymore presented, nor the poseur matinee idol that Fredric March offered. He's an idealistic, compassionate rebel, and Tracy sells the character with his eyes … just as he will with Hyde.

MGM had ten actors on its "suggestions" list for the deranged Sam Higgins, including Leo G. Carroll, Harry Cording, George Coulouris and (a surprise) *Greed* star Gibson Gowland. Eventually cast (with sixth billing) was Warner Bros.' toughie Barton MacLane.

Barton MacLane as Higgins, a deranged man who, in the film's opening scene, heckles the bishop profanely and blasphemously in church. The role was highly significant in the scenario; only a few shots and lines ended up in the release print.

John L. Balderston, in a revision to Mahin's script dated December 27, 1940, provided a great soliloquy for Higgins to rant:

> *Evil be thou my good! That's what I say! Evil be thou my good! That's the creed I live by! That's my thirty-nine Articles and my Ten Commandments. Good old Beelzebub! They're always running him down—and he's the winner in the end every time! Blasphemy I call it, to talk like that about*

man's best friend! So, the Bishop thinks he and the Queen are cleaning the evil out of man's heart, does he? Let me go—let me tell him!

The church attendants are trying to drag Higgins out of church as the bishop sermonizes: "The Devil shall be cast into the bottomless pit." "The Madman" continues:

No, no, no, no, no, Bishop. You can't do that to my friend with the goat's horns and the spiked tail! Bottomless pit, my eye! They can't get the Devil into any old pit—he's too smart for 'em, he is. He's here now, every place, in all your minds. And if he weren't, the world would be a mighty dull place. There's plenty of the Old Nick here in this very church, now! Ask these good people what's in their minds, and you'd see—only they won't tell you the truth.
(Maniacal laughter)

It was a startling way to begin *Dr. Jekyll and Mr. Hyde*—unleashed evil, profanely amok in a church! As it was, Fleming compromisingly shot the scene with most of the speech cut, and what remained was largely lost in the background, with only such words as "Beelzebub" and "blasphemy" clearly audible. The scene still works, although one wonders what the impact would have been if Balderston's strikingly chilling speech had been uncut and received a showcase presentation.

Jekyll takes charge of Higgins, sends him to Camden Hospital, comforts Higgins' distraught mother (Sara Allgood), and then resumes his seat next to fiancée Beatrix (Lana Turner) and her father, Sir Charles Emery (Donald Crisp), back in the church pew. All join the congregation in singing a hymn.

Lana Turner's against-type casting as Beatrix works. The baby-talking "Sweater Girl" is an eyeful in her Victorian costumes, so attractive as to explain easily Jekyll's restlessness to marry her. Crisp (who would win the 1941 Best Supporting Actor Academy Award for *How Green Was My Valley*), as Sir Charles, was appropriately stuffy and patrician, yet also sympathetic, as when he gazes at his late wife's portrait and listens to a gramophone playing the waltz to which they used to dance.

Incidentally, among the 30 names on MGM's "Suggestions" list for the role of Sir Charles had been such horror familiars as Lionel Atwill, George Zucco, Claude Rains and Sir Cedric Hardwicke. Also on the list, inexplicably, for a character who represents Victorian repression and dies a horrible death at the hands of Hyde: slapstick comic player Leon Errol!

As for the character of Sam Higgins: John Lee Mahin's November 15, 1940, revised script presents him at Camden Hospital being strapped in bed by two interns as he says to his weeping *wife*:

What are you starin' and mewin' about? I told you I don't want to be wrapped up in an old sack like you. I want me a young woman. Oh, you was young once and fair enough to please. But now you're done in—old, eh? Look at them strings in your neck and them sick cat's eyes. You think those'll keep a man awake nights? No.... I don't think ... but now I'm thinking what will....

In his November 23, 1940, revision, Mahin toned this down. We hear Higgins in the hospital room laughing evilly and ranting: "Don't let that old hen in! Youth! ... Young—slender.... White shoulders!" His wife overhears from the corridor outside the room.

In the release film, we merely hear him raving a few words as his *mother* listens.

At any rate, the character of Higgins is significant: After he dies in the hospital, presumably from his mania, Jekyll, who had hoped to experiment on him, realizes he must be his own guinea pig.

The Dinner Scene—and an Infamous Canard

There's a formal dinner hosted by Mrs. Marley (Doris Lloyd, featured in many horror films of this era). Jekyll joins Beatrix, Sir Charles, the bishop and various upper-class guests, some of them medicos. Among these is Dr. John Lanyon, Jekyll's devoted friend, although opposed to his unorthodox experiments. The studio's list of "suggestions" for Lanyon included 50 names, among them George Sanders, Henry Daniell, David Manners, Vincent Price, Lester Matthews, Basil Rathbone and Laird Cregar. Ian Hunter, the studio's original first choice, however, played the part. (Briefly seen as Lanyon's butler: an unbilled Brandon Hurst. Twenty years earlier, taunting words from Hurst's hedonistic Sir George Carew drove Dr. Jekyll to drink—to drink his potion, that is—in the Barrymore silent.)

Jekyll ventures to deliver his concept of Good vs. Evil:

Good and Evil are so close as to be chained together in the soul. Now, suppose we could break that chain....

Fleming pans the appalled faces of the guests as Jekyll explains his theory. There was another skeptical face, for a different reason, behind the camera. Indeed, while this scene was shot, an "event" occurred that would haunt Tracy, the entire production, and its legacy. Somerset Maugham visited the *Jekyll and Hyde* set, reportedly escorted there by George Cukor. The celebrated author watched Tracy perform, and asked the soon-to-be-notorious question:

"Which one is he playing now?"

The joke spread through Hollywood like wildfire. The odd thing was, Maugham hadn't necessarily meant it as a joke, having learned that Tracy was planning to play Hyde with minimal makeup. Nevertheless, the query became one of the undying zingers of Motion Picture Bitchiness, a harbinger of doom for Tracy's performance and the film itself.

What to do? MGM decided to confront it—sort of. In an issue of *The Lion's Roar*, an in-house magazine devoted to the studio's product, Tracy wrote (or somebody ghost-wrote for him) a feature that head-on addressed the canard tossed off by Maugham (unnamed in the article, and referred to only as "a prominent author"):

That chance remark, after I had recovered from the shock, did a lot to make me understand Jekyll and Hyde. I began to appreciate that the two men had much in common, but their reactions were different. Jekyll would have wanted to commit murder, restraining himself after slight effort. Hyde would have murdered with gleeful relish. This made me see Hyde as a human being, not an overdrawn monster. There is something of Hyde in all of us. The average man, and this is a subject for interesting study, has such impulses, but checks them. For Hyde to have an evil thought was to put it into action.

It made sense; MGM would also include this feature in the film's pressbook. However, Tracy, in fact, was terribly insecure about the performance(s). As the Jekyll scenes were shot first, he had time before playing the Hyde episodes, which he increasingly dreaded.

For Tracy, *Dr. Jekyll and Mr. Hyde* was truly a horror film.

The "Bad Girl"

Ingrid Bergman's first action in *Dr. Jekyll and Mr. Hyde* would be the same as her last: a harrowing scream.

Jekyll and Lanyon are slumming one night when they meet Ivy. A ruffian had attacked her in the street and Jekyll and Lanyon save her. As Ivy, Bergman's less overt than Miriam Hopkins, certainly as sensual and, in her early scenes as she lures Jekyll up to her flat, more sympathetic. Of course, there's no striptease-in-bed that Hopkins performed, rocking her leg with a garter on her thigh. Bergman does remove her blouse, rolls down a black stocking, and gives Jekyll her garter … and a passionate kiss. Lanyon enters and interrupts.

Jekyll makes the diagnosis that Ivy wears her garter too tight. The line will echo later in the film.

Sir Charles has forbidden Jekyll's marriage to Beatrix at this time. Ivy is haunting Jekyll's dreams. His sexual urges are raging.

Here, for *Dr. Jekyll and Mr. Hyde*, Life imitated Art. Jekyll wanted to break free from Victorian society and morality and release his "evil," daring side. MGM wanted to shatter the chains of Joseph Breen's Production Code and produce a sexy, daring film.

The crux was in the depiction of Hyde, including the manner of his transformation.

The Transformation, Freudian Fantasies … and "Bring on the Choppers!"

Any adaptation of *Dr. Jekyll and Mr. Hyde* rises or falls on (a) the effectiveness of the transformations, and (b) the ultimate depiction of Hyde. MGM would experiment throughout the shooting and right into post-wrap retakes with these challenges.

De Sade–esque fantasy: Ingrid Bergman's Ivy and Lana Turner's Beatrix as steeds, whipped by Spencer Tracy's Jekyll as charioteer. The sexual sadism was remarkably daring for 1941 Hollywood.

First, as for the transformation "preludes": John Lee Mahin's original script had Jekyll quaff the potion and experience vague hallucinations of Beatrix and Ivy, just as Jekyll had visions of the two ladies in his life in the 1931 film. Metro decided to top the Mamoulian version.

They went for Freudian sex dreams.

Peter Ballbusch was a 38-year-old Swiss-born special effects expert. He became the man in charge of *Jekyll and Hyde*'s two transformation dream sequences—each showcasing the sadistic carnal temptations in Jekyll's mind. The first offered these spicy vignettes, scored by Franz Waxman's alternately teasing and thunderous music:

- Lily pods floating in water. Beatrix and Ivy float there too, seductively, as the water and lily pads start to spin.
- A hand rising from damp mud. It grasps Ivy and drags her down into the mire.
- Ivy, partly undressed, temptingly rubbing her shoulder.
- A chariot, driven by Jekyll in driving rain, the doctor smiling sadistically as he lashes a dark horse and a white horse. The dark horse transforms into Ivy; the light horse into Beatrix. (This was how Balderston's Plato idea became part of the movie.)
- Jekyll becomes a hungrily prowling lion.

Lana Turner recalled the chariot episode in her memoir:

Creating the scene was hellishly uncomfortable. We had to sit astride mechanical horses, which bucked worse than live ones, while machines drove gale-force winds through our long hair....[22]

For many 2022 audiences, the 81-year-old de Sade–style nightmares in *Jekyll and Hyde* seem laughably overblown. In actuality, they're not only remarkably audacious for the time—they're flamboyantly staged escape acts, designed to elude the scissors of Joseph Breen, who (MGM hoped) would either miss the point, or figure the audience would. Montage #2 offers these visions, also with appropriately surging Franz Waxman scoring:

- A lion menaces Turner, helpless in a field.
- A wine bottle. We see Turner in it. Then we see a corkscrew, extracting a smiling Ingrid Bergman from the bottle. The wine explodes!
- A stallion and lion prowl as Bergman laughs seductively in a bed of flowers. The stallion violently rears on its hind legs, as if about to rape her, hence bringing bestiality into the brew.

When Breen saw these scenes, he demanded two excisions:

- *In the first montage, delete all scenes where Tracy is shown lashing the two girls.*
- *In the second montage, delete all scenes having to do with the swan and the girl, and the stallion and the girl.*

In fact, the only cut MGM made was the swan—the lashing Jekyll and the raping stallion remained in the film, at least in the original release. Other than that small snip, *Jekyll and Hyde*, with its Freudian montage, got away with murder. Even audiences who never heard of Freud or Richard von Krafft-Ebing would get the under-the-skin impression that, in these flash scenes, something wicked this way was truly coming. When the film opened in Baltimore in late August 1941, *The Baltimore Sun* critic Donald Kirkley wrote:

Despite obvious efforts to meet the demands of the morality code, Dr. Jekyll and Mr. Hyde *skirts amazingly close to frontiers which have been closed to picture-makers for some time. Two Freudian dream sequences are full of symbolism which might well startle some of the censors who passed on them.*[23]

Now, as for the first glimpse of Hyde: Mahin's original script had Jekyll rise from the floor:

His back is to the camera…. WE PAN UP WITH HIM, his back like an animal's in a crouch. The top of his head is strangely elongated. His ears are pointed. As yet we do not see his face but FOLLOW HIM as he slowly shuffles, gasping and grunting, to the mirror. There over his shoulder, we get a look at his face for the first time. It is hideous in its transformation into Evil, yet withal containing a strange fascinating Pan-like quality. At first, he starts, as though an animal looking in the mirror for the first time. Then he peers closer. And he starts to laugh, slowly, softly at first, then mounting to loud yelps.

Jekyll (into mirror, like eyeing a work of great art): *Look at you … look at you…. What beautiful, consummate evil!* (shouting exultantly) *There you are! There you are! I made you!* (Laughs louder, triumphantly now) *There it is, Sir Charles! Look at it, Lanyon! Hypocrites! Fools! Blind men! Deny what's in your souls, will you? You can't deny that!*

Then we PAN HIM as he capers about the room, leaping and stretching and jumping up and down like a faun, laughing all the time.

Dr. Jekyll's servant, Poole (Peter Godfrey, who also was the film's technical director on British customs) comes to the lab door, causing Hyde to drink the potion to return to Jekyll.

An elongated head, pointed ears, a Pan-like quality, a yelping laugh, bounding about like a faun: Mahin was asking a lot of the star playing Jekyll and Hyde. Transformation #2, as originally scripted, followed the technique used in the Fredric March version—panning from face to hands and back as makeup is applied—but Mahin's version had its unique flourishes. For one thing, Jekyll gazes at the garter Ivy had given him just before drinking the potion:

In violent convulsions, his face starts to turn. He grips the side of the chair in agony. WE PAN DOWN to his hand. It turns into an animal-like appendage. His four fingers seem to grow together a little bit at the base and then separate in the middle, almost like a cloven hoof.

His neck becomes thick and shorter. WE PAN UP to his face. It is worse than before. WE PAN DOWN to the other hand. The same process is happening here. He is gasping and writhing all the while. WE PAN UP again to his face. The transformation now becomes complete. It is worse in this second stage—more bestial than faun. The head more elongated. His writhing stops. He rises, shakes his head—feel the change in his thoughts…. He hurries over to the mirror to look….

Hyde (into mirror, gleefully): *Yes, Mr. Hyde! Wonderful, Mr. Hyde! It is! You are the modern Narcissus! Your face reflects man's Eternity as it was meant to be….*

The horror is certainly there—the devilish "cloven hoof" an especially grisly touch—and the elongated head seems a nod to Barrymore's cone-headed Hyde. However, Tracy wasn't about to go for that elongated head, those pointed ears, or the Pan-like face. Nor was he likely to leap about like a faun. Indeed, could *any* actor have pulled off this specific makeup and action in a 1941 film without raspberries from the audience?

MGM, aware of the crucial aspect of this scene and speech, remained open to new ideas. On March 24, after the "Hyde" part of the film had started shooting, Keith Winter provided an uncredited rewrite of the second transformation, with all new dialogue:

Jekyll (into mirror): *It isn't true! It isn't true! It can't be! But what is truth? Who said that? Oh yes, Pilate—Pontius Pilate—the man in the Bible. But has this THING read the Bible? Can it read?* (he peers closely into the mirror) *Have you read the Bible, THING?* (the reflection gives back a ghastly grin) *Ah, so we are an actor, are we? Then act something!* (he shakes his fist at the mirror) *Act something, I say!* (the reflection answers:)
   Is this a dagger which I see before me, the handle toward my hand?
   Come let me clutch thee.
   I have thee not.
   And yet I see thee still!
   NO! OH, NO!
(The last "NO" is almost a hysterical scream. With a violent movement, he attempts to wipe his image from the mirror. But there it stays—irrevocable—accusing).

The concepts here—referencing the man who ordered Christ crucified, referring to the image in the mirror as "THING," the quotes from *Macbeth*, were all full of potential. And the idea of Hyde being an "actor" was an inspired one—an excuse for Tracy's overacting as Hyde (which had become evident by the time this scene was written), appearing as if he's overacting *on purpose*. The speech went on, as Hyde became "increasingly diabolical":

Oh Jekyll, what a fool, an ass, and a pompous bore you were! You with your idiotic ideals and ridiculous integrity! And where did they get you? … No, mister, you're the man for me! The world is ours, mister—ours to kick around and spit upon and batter till it squeals for help. Are you ready? Then let's go. Come on, mister! Lead on, MacDuff!
(He bursts into shrieks of horrible laughter)

The new soliloquy actually scored a bullseye on the sexual and religious aspects the film was increasingly tapping. Yet it, too, would be discarded.

Now, finally … as for the first glimpse of Hyde, and the revised soliloquy, in *the finished* film:

After the dream of the chariot and Ivy-Beatrix steeds, Jekyll rises from the floor and makes his way to a mirror. There's a single crashing chord of music, then we see the reflection. At first, it almost appears the potion failed to work, and we're only seeing Jekyll, ill and spent after his wild-ride dream.

Bit by bit, however, *we* see what *he* sees.

Jack Dawn created and applied Tracy's Hyde makeup masterfully; it suggested a degenerated yet supercharged Jekyll after an injection of vile hormones … or, as the MGM creative staff came to call it, "the dope." Tracy's eyes are huge and laughing, his mouth sensual—with specially created Hyde teeth.

"Bring on the choppers!" Tracy would shout on the set.[24]

Tracy as Hyde. The makeup was subtle—too subtle for some audiences—but quite brilliantly revealed Hyde's cruelty, especially in the eyes and mouth.

The soliloquy delivered in the movie was by Paul Osborn, writer of the fantasy play *On Borrowed Time* (which MGM had filmed in 1939). He later received Academy nominations for his screenplays for *East of Eden* (1955) and *Sayonara* (1957). Osborn received no onscreen credit for these *Jekyll and Hyde* rewrites and retakes, actually shot after the film had originally wrapped:

> **Hyde:** *What's … what's this? Whose face is this? That's not my cheek, and yet it is. That's not my mouth, and yet there's something there that's like my mouth. How strange! My eyes! Can this be Evil then—that man has shunned and scorned and hidden deep inside him, that since the start of time, has been the cause of misery and shame? Shame! Misery! I feel no shame! I feel no misery! This Evil has been maligned! This Evil is a pleasant thing! This Evil is a fine thing!*

And he laughs in triumph.

Come the second transformation, Jekyll laughs admiringly, smooths his hair, winks at his reflection … and takes off in the night in search of Ivy.

If you've watched the 1941 *Dr. Jekyll and Mr. Hyde* recently and the speech sounds unfamiliar, there's a reason. MGM long ago cut the Hyde soliloquy, so all that remains in the "official" DVD and TV version is the line, "*Can this be Evil then?*" followed by his laughter.

The intensity and experimentation of the transformation soliloquy, as far as posterity goes, was sadly and ironically all for nothing.

Hyde Seeks "Utopia"

Next, outside the lab, comes the "Baptism" scene, as in the 1931 version: Hyde removes his top hat and lets the rain drench his new face as he laughs wickedly. (This is also an episode that was shot after the film initially wrapped.) He visits Ivy's residence, looking for her, and high-spiritedly delivers a suggestive line to the landlady that somehow eluded Joe Breen: "Don't you realize that Utopia is waiting upstairs, just off that landing?"

The Palace of Frivolities, where Ivy works as a barmaid. A singer in corset, tights and a bonnet sings "You Should See Me Dance the Polka," her chorus girls prancing and kicking behind her. This will cue another Joe Breen decree: "[D]elete the crotch shot of the dancing girls."

Actually, we see what Breen refers to in the film, although it's a long shot; perhaps he'd objected to a close-up. The crowd sings along, and Hyde demands Ivy serve him champagne. "I make my own luck, my dear," says Hyde, "and tonight, I follow the rainbow." He stares at her, one of the greatest cases of undressing-with-the-eyes ever performed by an actor. Hyde causes a brawl, gets Ivy fired, and is waiting for her at his coach when she leaves. He woos her into his cab with money, Tracy high-spiritedly delivering Hyde's over-the-top dialogue:

> *Ivy, my darling, you belong with the immortals. Come with me to Mount Olympus. Drink nectar with the gods. Sing the ancient songs of pleasure. And put Athena and Diana to shame!*

Ivy is bewildered by her leering admirer and, as he goes on, his sly references to things Jekyll would have learned the night he and Ivy met. "I don't know what you're talking about," says Ivy in sad bewilderment.

"Oh, she doesn't know what I'm talking about?" mocks Tracy's Hyde, cruelly parroting her words, his leering face in extreme close-up … one of Tracy's most chilling moments in the film.

He kisses her. Fade out.

A short time later, we see Ivy, wearing a low-cut dressing gown, living in a respectable "love nest"—as Hyde's mistress. (Among the accoutrements, appropriately: a caged bird.) Her friend Marcia (Frances Robinson) pays a call. (MGM considered several actresses for Marcia, including Universal's Evelyn Ankers, who later in 1941 was *The Wolf Man*'s leading lady.) Marcia invites Ivy to go out on the town with her. Ivy goes to change and offscreen, begins taking off her gown.

"*What's that across your* back?" asks Marcia.

We don't see it, but it's clearly the welts from Hyde's whip. Hyde himself appears and suggests a *ménage a trois* for the trio. It doesn't happen.

"Very nice material," he chuckles lecherously after Marcia leaves.

Hyde torments Ivy, who refers to him as "sir." Tracy is terrific as he eats grapes (and spits out the seeds), torments Ivy about possibly going out for the evening, refers to her garter being too tight, suggests she read to him from *Paradise Lost*, and plays "You Should See Me Dance the Polka" at the piano.

"I know what we like!" leers Hyde, rising from the piano.

He forces Ivy to sing the song, until she becomes hysterical. "*Bravo!*" roars Hyde. "A prima donna is born!" He exultantly throws the bouquet of grapes into Ivy's face. (The script had him smearing them across her breasts.)

"The world is yours, my darling!" exults Hyde, climaxing the scene. "The moment is mine!"

Hyde passionately kisses Ivy. His hand goes down her back.

Fade out.

As Donald Kirkley reported in *The Baltimore Sun,* the scene "has something of the impact of a case history from Krafft-Ebing. Sadism in this degree seldom finds expression on the screen."

Life Imitates Art

> *Shall I never be happier in my work? Will I ever get a better part than the little girl Ivy Peterson, a better director than Victor Fleming, a more wonderful leading man than Spencer Tracy, and a better cameraman than Joe Ruttenberg? …For the first time I have broken out from the cage which encloses me…. It is as if I am flying….*
>
> —Ingrid Bergman writing in her journal
> about *Dr. Jekyll and Mr. Hyde*[25]

It was a season for hyper-sensitive stars at MGM. As *Variety* wrote in its "Hollywood Inside" column on March 19:

> *Newspaper writers and gossip columnists are running into difficulties when they ask to visit the sets of* Dr. Jekyll and Mr. Hyde, A Woman's Face *and* Love Crazy *at Metro, all because the principals in each are doing scenes that the studio wishes to avoid advance publicity on. When Spencer Tracy dons his Mr. Hyde makeup, his camera appearance is done behind closed doors. The same thing goes for Joan Crawford, who wears a large scar on her face through much of* A Woman's Face. William Powell *is sensitive about the female impersonation act he is doing at present in* Love Crazy *and has asked for no visitors while scenes are being taken.*

By this time, Tracy, playing the Hyde scenes, was so hung-up about the makeup that a studio limousine drove him to and from the set with the car's curtains closed. The hypersensitivity added to the atmosphere on the set.

Fleming—an emotional director, as noted—had his own Hyde moments. While directing Lana Turner's big scene, where she falls at Jekyll's feet and weeps, he took an extraordinary measure to make her cry: He twisted her arm behind her back until she screamed "Stop it! You're hurting me!" She cried not only during the scene, but for the rest of the day.

Ingrid Bergman recalled, "As soon as [Fleming] came close to me, I could tell by his eyes what he wanted me to do." There was a memorable exception:

> That scene where he wanted a frightened, distraught, hysterical girl, faced by the terrifying Mr. Hyde—I just couldn't do it. So eventually he took me by the shoulder with one hand, spun me around, and struck me backwards and forwards across the face—hard—it hurt. I could feel the tears of what?—surprise, shame—running down my cheeks. I was shattered by his action. I stood there weeping, while he strode back to the camera and shouted, "Action!" Even the camera crew were struck dumb, as I wept my way through the scene. But he'd get the performance he wanted....[26]

The female co-stars would have different overall responses: Turner never worked with Fleming again, but Bergman did (in 1948's *Joan of Arc*, which she blamed for contributing to his fatal heart attack in 1949). As she wrote a bit poutingly about *Dr. Jekyll and Mr. Hyde*:

> By the time the film was over, I was deeply in love with Victor Fleming. But he wasn't in love with me. I was just part of another picture he'd directed.[27]

Apparently, *Dr. Jekyll and Mr. Hyde* was an emotional work-out for Bergman. She was not only in love with Fleming, but—as inferred in James Curtis' biography, *Spencer Tracy*—she was having an affair with Tracy. The spouses of each star were out of town in March of '41 and Tracy and Bergman began to rendezvous at the Beverly Wilshire Hotel. One can only presume Bergman was more comfortable with this situation than Tracy, a lapsed Roman Catholic who, nevertheless, never divorced his wife (despite his later, long-time relationship with Katharine Hepburn). He was buried in 1967 with a Requiem Mass at Immaculate Heart of Mary Church in East Hollywood.

Life imitating art at the Beverly Hills Hotel? Perhaps, in a way. It was a strange arrangement: Tracy in his Hyde makeup and "choppers" masochistically torturing Bergman on the set; then the two players sequestered alone nights away from MGM.

Tracy carried on bravely in the film; however one critically regards his Hyde, he was certainly not dogging it, and had definitely dived into the belly of the beast. Gil Perkins, who doubled Tracy as Hyde in the more physical action, told me in 1991 that he remembered no negativity from Tracy at any time during the shoot:

> All I know is that Tracy did everything very professionally—he always was the ultimate professional. And Victor Fleming was one of the best directors in the business.... Spence had great respect for Vic, and they got along very well.[28]

By now, *Dr. Jekyll and Mr. Hyde* had spun off in a bizarre, surreal way, an intensely emotional experience for its prime movers. Nobody felt the anguish as did Tracy. "Hyde got to the point where he gave me no rest," the star claimed. "I couldn't sleep, I couldn't eat."[29]

Mirror Image

Jekyll, aware of his Hyde behavior, sends £50 to Ivy. Yet she's afraid to run away. She fears Hyde will follow and find her. "If I could do it," she weeps to Marcia, "I'd go down to the river."

Marcia and her friend Freddie suggest that Ivy, on the verge of a complete break-down and a possible suicide, visit the esteemed Dr. Jekyll for help. Ivy did not learn his name the night they met, and recognizes him at once as she visits his home. Berg-man is superb, at times sensing Hyde behind Jekyll's visage, other times seeing him as her savior: "If you can't help me," she pleads, "give me some poison so I can kill myself."

Jekyll promises Ivy that Hyde will never bother her again. As she leaves, Ivy looks back at Jekyll and says cryptically, "For a moment, I thought.... Goodbye."

Jekyll heads in the night to Beatrix's party to announce their wedding. His whistled tune (Robert Bradford dubs Tracy's whistling) changes from "You Should See Me Dance the Polka" to Beatrix's waltz, and back again. Jekyll sits on a park bench and, for the first time in the film, we see the full-before-the-camera transformation. MGM had invested a small fortune in experimentation with the Jekyll-into-Hyde technique. Harold Kress, the film's editor, remembered the disastrous results:

> *They hired 65 animators and were going to do it the way they did the old flip cards. They put this animation stuff on his [Tracy's] face and told me to take it over to Walt Disney to see if they had any ideas.*
> *Disney said, "This is terrible, it's a bunch of crap, you've got to find a better way."*[30]

Ultimately, the studio decided on the traditional lap dissolve technique, later used in 1941 by Universal on *The Wolf Man*. Kress (later the winner of Best Editing Oscars for *How the West Was Won* and *The Towering Inferno*) supervised:

> *Tracy was a dream to work with. There were over 40 makeup changes. To keep the registration perfect, we had to put him back and realign him. An artist sketched him and we lined up his nos-trils. You couldn't touch the camera. I was ten feet away with a remote-control switch. The cam-era was never changed and overnight a guard was on the stage. I would say, "Okay, Spence, get ready, we're rolling, now just a little grimace, a little more, you fight it, fight it, cut." That went on for 46 changes of makeup. There were just a few times when the eyes blurred, but I couldn't help it, I had to make a continuous series of dissolves. The result was that you would stay on his face....*

Back in the "love nest," Ivy is celebrating her freedom from Hyde, which Jekyll had promised her. She gazes at herself in a mirror, drinking champagne, getting tipsy, toast-ing the good doctor: "Here's to my angel…."

The door opens. It's Hyde. He mocks her, taunts her, describes her meeting with Jekyll and quotes her remark "For a moment, I thought…"

> *What did you think? Did you think that Dr. Jekyll was falling in love with you? You, with your cheap little dreams? Or did you think perhaps, that in him, you saw a bit of me—Hyde? Look … look closely, oh so closely. … In me now, Hyde, you can see remnants of our mutual friend, Dr. Jekyll! What about that!*

One imagines the impact that Tracy's taunting and Bergman's rising terror would have created in 1941 if MGM had sold this film not as a horror movie, but as what it

As Jekyll and Beatrix dance, Hyde looms demonically over them.

genuinely is: the saga of a sexual sadist and his victim. As it is, Ivy now knows the truth. She screams, and Hyde strangles her.

Yes ... dance and dream....

A couch blocks the view of the strangled Ivy and, in a hint of necrophilia, Hyde lowers his head and body, as if he's about to embrace—and perhaps rape—the corpse. A crowd, having heard Ivy's scream, gathers outside the room, and Hyde makes his acrobatic escape down the stairs and into the street. Gil Perkins performed most of this action. Australian-born Perkins, who incidentally had appeared in a fight scene in the 1931 *Dr. Jekyll and Mr. Hyde* and would later double Bela Lugosi as the Monster in 1943's *Frankenstein Meets the Wolf Man*, recalled:

> To double Tracy as Hyde, I had to get into the MGM makeup department at 5:30 in the morning, and it would take them a couple of hours to put the rubber mask all over my head. Then they would make up the mask, and put a wig on top of it, and fill in down around the neck…. At lunchtime, I used to have to drink my lunch through a straw, because I couldn't eat anything—I could only get this straw in my rubber mouth. Jack Dawn and Bill Tuttle were the two guys responsible for all that.

Hyde contacts Lanyon, who brings the potion to his home. We—and Lanyon—see the transformation from Hyde to Jekyll. "I warned you, John," says Jekyll. "Even as Hyde, I warned you."

"You've committed the supreme blasphemy," says Lanyon. Ian Hunter plays the scene with both admonition and a sense of sympathy for his friend—even though it's been hinted that Lanyon is also in love with Beatrix. Jekyll promises Lanyon he'll tell Beatrix the truth.

He finds her that night at her home, playing the piano. They go into the greenhouse, where he ends the engagement without telling her about Hyde. Turner is excellent: "Harry, it's all right, if you don't love me any more," she weeps—and as Tracy leaves, she falls to the floor, crying. He hears her, and walks back….

"Oh, you did come back, oh my darling!" rejoices Beatrix, as she sees Jekyll's feet. She hugs his legs, looks up … and sees Hyde.

He attacks her. When Sir Charles runs to rescue her, Hyde beats him to death—so savagely that he breaks his cane. After police arrive, Lanyon recognizes the broken piece and leads them to Jekyll's lab.

There's a magnificently shot chase through the gaslit night fog. Hyde crashes through Jekyll's front window and locks himself in the lab. He takes the potion. Jekyll looks in the mirror, relieved to see his own reflection. Then he hears familiar laughter. It's Hyde, appearing in the mirror, the makeup at its most extreme, suggesting a fetid, rancid Satan:

> HYDE: *Looking for someone, Dr. Jekyll?* (laughing) *Why, you look surprised, Dr. Jekyll—and even a little frightened too! Yes, those nice, kind, gentle features of yours look a little frightened. Poor Dr. Jekyll!*
> JEKYLL: *I..I….*
> HYDE: *I! I!* (laughing) *Why, that doesn't sound like you, Dr. Jekyll. You always know exactly what to say. Yes. You thought you could get away with it, didn't you? Poor*

Hyde, in the laboratory mirror, taunts Jekyll at the climax. This superb scene, Tracy's best in the film, is unfortunately and inexplicably cut from most existing prints of the 1941 *Dr. Jekyll and Mr. Hyde*, including the 2004 DVD.

Jekyll. He didn't have a chance from the start because he had to stick his nose in, didn't he? He had to pry ... he had to peek!

JEKYLL: *No, no.... I never intended ... all these things.* (a knocking at the door) *I never intended....*

HYDE: *That's right, Jekyll. Squirm out of it, if you can. You never intended anything, did you? Go on, squirm out of it, Jekyll! Maybe you can.*

JEKYLL: *Man ... cannot flout the Divinity ... of man....*

HYDE: *Ha, ha! But that doesn't apply to you, Jekyll. You're so good, and so wise.*

(CRIES AND KNOCKING AT THE DOOR)

HYDE: *There's someone at the door. They're trying to get in. They're here, Jekyll! Now here's your chance! Squirm out of it! Squirm out of it, Jekyll, if you can! Maybe we can get out of it together. Together...!* (laughing)

JEKYLL: *No.* (weeping) *NO!*

Jekyll pulls the mirror from the wall, smashing it to the floor. It was a brilliantly played scene, Tracy's best in the film; his heartbreaking anguish as Jekyll, his taunting evil as Hyde, make this episode the movie's dramatic highlight.

As previously noted, it no longer appears in MGM's "official" version on DVD.

Lanyon arrives with the police. Before their eyes, and Poole's, Jekyll transforms into Hyde and puts up a wild last stand in the lab. Hyde, with a knife, vengefully goes after Lanyon, climbing the stairs, Tracy's face in extreme close-up, teeth bared. Lanyon fires three times, and Hyde falls down the stairs.

He's dead. A clock chimes midnight as Hyde transforms back into Jekyll. Poole kneels beside the body and prays: "The Lord is my Shepherd, I shall not want..."

In the 1931 film, the final fadeout showed a boiling cauldron in Jekyll's laboratory fireplace. Mamoulian's metaphor: Jekyll, with Hyde, was going to Hell. In the 1941 film, however, the Franz Waxman music swells beautifully, and a different moral was clear: Hyde had been released into the darkness; Jekyll, having endured his Purgatory here on Earth, faces Salvation. God had recognized his noble endeavor and forgiven him.

"He restoreth my soul," angelically sings the choir.

THE END

*   *   *

The film officially "wrapped" April 8, 1941. It had been in a constant state of rewriting and experimentation all through the production.

Additionally, on April 7, the eve of the close of production, Saville outlined the scenes still remaining to be filmed. Besides the mirror soliloquy, written by Paul Osborn, the revisions included, in Saville's words:

- The first time that Jekyll takes the dope.
- Exterior of the laboratory in the rain where Jekyll sets out for the Palace of Varieties [called the Palace of Frivolities in the completed film].
- Exterior Ivy's rooming house. Scene with the cabby on the way to the Palace of Varieties after leaving Ivy's apartment.

Also, these retakes:

- The corridor of the hospital around the door. Mrs. Higgins approaches the door, listens to a longer conversation from inside, steps back out of picture as Jekyll and Heath come from inside the room. [Dr. Heath in Camden Hospital, played by Frederic Worlock]

- The scene inside the empty room between Heath and Jekyll, and a shot of Lanyon and Jekyll at the door of the children's ward, second floor landing hospital.
- The dinner scene. Two-shot and Close shot of Tracy and Turner throughout the entire scene. Original dialogue.
- Conservatory scene. Close Shot of Tracy and Turner taken in that part of the conservatory in which the present scene finishes. Dialogue—fresh scene from Mr. Paul Osborn.
- Laboratory. A fresh mirror scene played by Tracy the first time he becomes Hyde. Fresh scene written by Paul Osborn.
- Middle of the night scene. In Jekyll's consulting room. Fresh scene. Turner, Tracy and Crisp. New scene as written by Mr. Paul Osborn.
- In Jekyll's consulting room. Between Jekyll and Poole after Ivy has left. Scene to be written by Mr. Paul Osborn.

Franz Waxman recorded most of the score from May 20 to May 23, 1941, having personally composed the great majority of it, including such cues as "The Garter," "The First Transformation," "Hyde's Triumph" and "Prayer and Finale."[31] "Sex Montage" and "Evil Montage" were by Daniele Amfitheatrof, an Italian composer and conductor then under contract to MGM. Ivy's "You Should See Me Dance the Polka" was an 1886 standard written by George Grossmith. In the 1960s, Waxman received a commission from the New York City Opera to write a work of his choice. He decided to compose a work on *Dr. Jekyll and Mr. Hyde,* and had completed the First Act and part of the second at the time he died in 1967.

*   *   *

With uncredited writers, an active "Hyde" stunt double, and even a dubbed whistler for Tracy, *Dr. Jekyll and Mr. Hyde* reached a point of uncredited absurdity when Victor Fleming demanded that Victor Saville receive no onscreen credit as producer. Fleming was likely angry that he had worked for years at MGM, largely perceived as a "producers' studio," and he was certainly still bitterly angry at producer David O. Selznick for the terrors of *Gone with the Wind.*

Thursday, June 26: Saville wrote a "night letter" to Fleming:

My dear Victor:

I have now commenced the final dubbing of Jekyll and Hyde *and am about to give orders for the permanent main title to be made, and therefore I am addressing this last note to you with the hope that you will have changed your mind in regard to my credit.*

Please understand me clearly that everything I do I try to do with enthusiasm and the result means just as much to me as it does to you in the pride of accomplishment. Our business, however, has placed a value on actual credits and no amount of good will or lip service ever assumes the importance of a correct credit. This is something that the industry has established and I am certainly only human enough to wish for a recognized credit on Jekyll and Hyde *on which I so willingly labored as producer.*

Believe me, working with you was both great pleasure and profit. I should not like my memories to be disturbed on such a pleasant association with regrets on the lack of recognition of my work....

Fleming's MGM contract reportedly protected his right to eliminate producer credit. There's no response to this letter in Saville's production file and *Dr. Jekyll and Mr. Hyde* went into release with a title card reading, "Victor Fleming's Production of *Dr. Jekyll and Mr. Hyde,*" as well as a card reading, "Directed by Victor Fleming."

Victor Saville's name is nowhere in the credits.

Part Three: The Previews and Release

Monday, July 21: MGM proudly hosted a trade show of *Dr. Jekyll and Mr. Hyde* at the Ambassador Hotel in Los Angeles. A record crowd of exhibitors attended. *The Hollywood Reporter* was properly impressed:

> *Magnificent are the performances of Spencer Tracy and Ingrid Bergman, the thoughtful direction of Fleming, and the artful screenplay writing of John Lee Mahin....*

The Reporter went on to hail Tracy's Jekyll and Hyde as "the top portrayal of a top actor's career." After the enthusiastic trade reviews, Metro prepared a "pre-release" world premiere of *Dr. Jekyll and Mr. Hyde* at New York's Astor Theatre, opening day set for August 12.

Thursday, August 7: MGM hosted the aforementioned Hyde detector "experiment" at the Astor. International News Service staff writer Inez Robb (who was prematurely gray) managed to infiltrate the crowd of, as she expressed it, "luscious young redheads, blondes and brunettes." She met Dr. Marston ("natty in white flannels and a Phi Beta

Dr. Jekyll and Mr. Hyde was a smash hit at the Astor Theatre in New York City, despite the pans of several Manhattan critics. Note the advertisement's giraffe necks, which allegedly were to be prominent (as phallic symbols) in the de Sade fantasy sequences.

Kappa key") and allowed herself to be hooked up by "a wide, lethal black leather strap" to the emotion-registering "Hyde detector." As Robb wrote:

> … Mr. Hyde leered menacingly from the screen.
> "Look at the register!" Dr. Marston cried excitedly to his assistants….
> Then Mr. Hyde reached a horrible, deadly claw for Ivy's throat. As he did in the poor gal (Ingrid Bergman) Dr. Marston let out a shout.
> "The indicator's jumped the track! What a woman! Get a glass of water for the lady! Get two glasses!"
> …The doc's general observations show that redheads scare least of all, although they are apt to be erratic. Brunettes are hard to intimidate, too. But blondes![32]

Tuesday, August 12: *Jekyll and Hyde* opened at the Astor. The title, stars, promotion and advance word had their effect. As MGM publicist chief Howard Dietz wired the studio in Culver City:

> Jekyll and Hyde *opened sensationally. So far today we have done more business and played to more people than any picture in the history of the Astor Theatre. The reviews will not appear until tomorrow.*

August 13: The New York newspaper reviews were out—and were not what MGM had been anticipating. Destined to be quoted over the decades time and again was this snipe from the *New York Times*:

> …a Grand Guignol chiller with delusions of grandeur…. Mr. Tracy's portrait of Hyde is not so much evil incarnate as it is the ham rampant.[33]

The *Times* had a pretentious Cinema page which panned the overwhelming majority of early 1940s horror films. "The Old Gray Lady" of newspapers lambasted Tracy's Hyde as "an affront to good taste." *Jekyll and Hyde* did have its Manhattan champions, such as *The Wall Street Journal*, whose film reviews of the era were generally more incisive than the *Times*' critiques:

> "Rule of thumb" for a layman who is trying to appraise acting might be, "Do I hate or fear the villain, and do I pity or admire the hero?" By that test, Spencer Tracy has interpreted with horrifying thoroughness his dual role in Dr. Jekyll and Mr. Hyde….
> It will be difficult to eradicate from one's mind the gruesome spectacle of a human being degenerating to a beast, and following his sadistic impulses with fiendish delight. By the same token, when the more pleasant side of his split personality is in evidence, Dr. Jekyll's growing consciousness that he is powerless to control the "devil that is within him" cannot fail to evoke one's pity….
> This picture is, in truth, a demonstration of a madman's dream….[34]

The divided press in New York City had no effect on the box office: The crowds defied the naysayers and packed the Astor. Tracy, in San Francisco with Ingrid Bergman the day of the New York opening, read the reviews and was devastated by the bad ones. He made a journal entry that reads as if the sardonic Hyde himself had written it to torment Jekyll:

> *Worst panning for an actor ever received? The horrible notices of* Mr. Hyde. *He! He![35]*

As indicated by the preceding reviews, *Dr. Jekyll and Mr. Hyde* was itself a dual nature film: perceived as either a sexy, pioneering, all-stops-pulled super-version of a classic story, or an overstuffed, fustian bomb. Nevertheless, the mob loves a train wreck, and word circulated of a new canard, this one tossed off by humorist Harry Hirshfield.

Attending a screening, he wisecracked that Abbott and Costello had suddenly been substituted for Spencer Tracy.

Before the film's Labor Day weekend general release, MGM cut the film ("Studio cutting *Jekyll & Hyde*—but not enough!" Tracy wrote in his journal on August 15).[36] The trims were primarily for pace, eliminating dialogue here and there but basically leaving Tracy's Hyde as is. An example of the more substantial cuts made is the virtual elimination of the scenes of Camden Hospital's Interne Fenwick portrayed by eleventh-billed William Tannen. The release print has him appearing briefly, unnamed and without dialogue.

Thus began a history of ongoing cuts in *Dr. Jekyll and Mr. Hyde*; more on this topic later.

On August 20, *Variety*'s "Picture Grosses" column reported that *Dr. Jekyll and Mr. Hyde* "was doing strictly capacity or better for a sensational $21,700 opening week." The film had reportedly broken the first-two-days record set by *Gone with the Wind*.[37]

Dr. Jekyll and Mr. Hyde opened in late August at the Palace Theatre in Washington, D.C. Nelson B. Bell of *The Washington Post* saluted "the photographic and technical skill developed by the unlimited resources of the Metro-Goldwyn-Mayer studio." He praised the "startlingly real metamorphoses" of Jekyll into Hyde, and wrote, "The gain is wholly on the side of intensified brutality and multiplied repellence":

> Where once Dr. Jekyll and Mr. Hyde *could be contemplated as a mere exercise in melodramatic trickery, it now becomes a stark and disturbingly realistic study in human cruelty and depravity ... [I]t has been executed in the present instance with such frank, such unrestrained and such relentless actuality as to become questionable entertainment—especially for any but adult and nerve-hardened audiences.*

Bell, who clearly "got" what the film was meant to be, praised Tracy, Bergman and Turner, and opined that, considering the emotional impact, the film was "almost too perfectly done."[38]

September 5: *Jekyll and Hyde* opened in Los Angeles at Grauman's Chinese Theatre and Loew's State Theatre, supported by a second feature, MGM's *Down in San Diego*, starring Bonita Granville and Leo Gorcey. "Jekyll, Hyde Field Day for Tracy—Both of Him!" headlined Philip K. Scheuer in the *Los Angeles Times*, writing that the film opened in both houses to "hungry crowds. It goes without saying that they ate it up. ... The theatrical old melodrama, dual personality and all, wowed 'em."

As for the exhibitors, there was Hyde-like gnashing of teeth at the sophisticated horror show. "The prize boner of the year," wrote C.V. Schofield, manager of the Blackhawk Theatre, in Lansing, Iowa ("Small town and rural patronage").[39] Melville Danner, manager of the Kozy Theatre in Granite, Oklahoma ("Small town patronage"), perhaps came close as to why the new *Jekyll and Hyde* put off some audiences:

> *Spencer Tracy turns in his usual grand performance and Ingrid Bergman is very good. Also Lana Turner. This production, from a standpoint of production, directing and acting, is very good, but here is the catch. I depend a lot on kid patronage and 95% of the children under twelve cannot stay and see this feature. After all, our job is to entertain the majority and it just can't be done with this picture. Personally, I think it should not have been produced. Lots of people stayed away because they did not want to see their favorite actor play this part of Dr. Jekyll and Mr. Hyde.*[40]

A box office disaster? Hardly. *Dr. Jekyll and Mr. Hyde*, with a final negative cost of $1,140,000, took in a worldwide rental of $2,351,000.

The profit: $350,000.[41]

A *Dr. Jekyll and Mr. Hyde* promotional drawing by Jacques Kapalik, caricaturing Lana Turner, Spencer Tracy, and Ingrid Bergman.

Dr. Jekyll and Mr. Hyde received three Academy nominations: Joseph Ruttenberg for Black-and-White Cinematography, Franz Waxman for Musical Score, and Harold Kress for Film Editing. There were no wins.

Spencer Tracy never made peace with *Dr. Jekyll and Mr. Hyde*. In a figurative self-flagellation that his Mr. Hyde might have enjoyed, the actor dwelt on the wisecrack that Abbott and Costello had stood in for him during the transformations. He always considered *Dr. Jekyll and Mr. Hyde* his worst performance.

Finally, as for the cuts. MGM apparently trimmed *Dr. Jekyll and Mr. Hyde* for a 1954 theatrical re-release (on a double bill with MGM's *A Woman's Face*), and perhaps yet again for a TV release in 1956. The original print ran 127 minutes; the print released on DVD in 2004 (on a double-bill with the 1931 version) runs 113 minutes. The copy watched for this chapter is a bootleg of a surviving 117-minute version.

Among the missing footage in the DVD version: a shot in which Jekyll carries Ivy upstairs to her room, and Hyde's risqué scene with Ivy's landlady. The most unfortunate excisions: both of Hyde's mirror scene soliloquies, which might have been Tracy's best moments in the movie.

* * *

To sum up with a personal story:

In 1958 when I was seven years old, I saw the 1941 *Dr. Jekyll and Mr. Hyde* on a Saturday night Late Show on Baltimore's Channel 13, competing with Channel 11's *Shock! Theatre*. My dad and mom stayed up to watch with me.

Well … to this child's critical eye, *Dr. Jekyll and Mr. Hyde* played as an awesome classic. The finale, with Tracy's Hyde carcass transforming into an at-peace Jekyll's corpse as his butler recited the 23rd Psalm and an angelic chorus sang "He Restoreth My Soul," moved me to tears. (It was maybe the first time a film made me cry.) The film had the dark feel of a Good Friday High Mass at our nearby Roman Catholic Church … infiltrated by the Devil.

It played, for me, even as a child, as an epic battle of Good vs. Evil. MGM's *Dr. Jekyll and Mr. Hyde* had left its emotional mark—Tracy's Jekyll-Hyde gets to me, movingly and dramatically, every time I watch the film.

It's my favorite *Dr. Jekyll and Mr. Hyde*.

Yes, I love John Barrymore's 1920 *Dr. Jekyll and Mr. Hyde,* and the fact that, to the end of his life, he could go into his Hyde transformation at the snap of a finger (or the promise of a drink).[42] I wrote and narrated the audio commentary for the 2004 DVD release of the "restored" 1931 *Dr. Jekyll and Mr. Hyde*, and I admire the way Fredric March and Miriam Hopkins, clearly at Rouben Mamoulian's inspired direction, dare to play some scenes for black comedy. I'm even a fan of the recent *Jekyll and Hyde* Broadway musical, wherein Jekyll—in a terrific touch the moviemakers all missed over the decades—transforms into Hyde at his wedding.

I've heard and read all the criticisms … among them:

The 1941 film lacks the punch of the pre–Code movie. (That's because the 1941 version *isn't* a pre–Code movie.)

Tracy's Hyde so resembles Tracy's Jekyll that everyone else in the film seems like a dolt for not recognizing him. (Actually, it's no more far-fetched than the 1931 version, where no one in London who passes Hyde seems surprised by the spectacle of a man-size ape adorned in formal wear.)

The film is "Christian." (This is a recent criticism, born of the current times. I can imagine a 2022 critic somehow around in 1941, meeting up with Louis B. Mayer—a Jew—and registering this complaint. Mayer, aghast at such a bigoted remark, would have probably slugged him.)

At any rate, to each his/her own. Surely my exposure as an impressionable child to the film affects my emotion toward it.

The 1941 *Dr. Jekyll and Mr. Hyde* is admittedly one of those "What if...?" films, so populous in the horror genre. One needs to be aware of its sinuous production history to appreciate fully its troubled, tormented genesis, and the film seems to have unseen images and sounds lurking in its shadows....

It's the muffled speech of a madman in a church cackling about Beelzebub.... It's the scripted Hyde that never was, melding with the film Hyde that came to be ... the former's elongated head, pointed ears and cloven hoof, along with the latter's wild eyes and "chopper" teeth ... leaping like a faun, yelping with laughter, invoking Pontius Pilate, smearing Ivy's breasts with grapes. It's the ludicrous cartoon transformations that didn't work ... the Breen-demanded cut scenes of a swan, a stallion, showgirl crotches, and "undue exposure of Ivy's breasts" ... the masterful mirror scene in which Tracy weeps as Hyde taunts, and all the years of other snips and trims that cry for official restoration.

It's a film with shadow images of all the mad science the world's greatest studio attempted to conjure creatively in producing the ultimate *Dr. Jekyll and Mr. Hyde,* with admittedly mixed results ... and with the *angst* of a star who, for all his own hang-ups and addiction, finally dared to look into the mirror literally and figuratively, at the role(s) held up to him.

All the dark, crazy experimentation, passionately trying to make a great film, madly whirling around the surviving film's periphery.

Yet, in one way, the 1941 *Dr. Jekyll and Mr. Hyde* nailed it from the earliest conception. Generally, the movies dogmatically sentence its mad doctors, including other Dr. Jekylls, to Damnation. This one doesn't.

"Jekyll was restored to himself for Eternity," John Lee Mahin wrote in his first draft script, and for all the revisions, this concept never changed.

Forgiveness. Compassion. Salvation. Somehow, they seem strangely novel and subversive in a 1940s horror classic, don't they?

Dr. Jekyll and Mr. Hyde

MGM, 1941. Producers, Victor Fleming, Victor Saville. Director, Victor Fleming. Screenplay, John Lee Mahin, based on the 1886 novella by Robert Louis Stevenson (also based on the 1931 screenplay by Percy Heath and Samuel Hoffenstein); uncredited writers, John L. Balderston, Paul Osborn. Cinematography, Joseph Ruttenberg. Musical Score, Franz Waxman. Dance Director, Ernst Matray. Recording Director, Douglas Shearer. Art Director, Cedric Gibbons. Associate Art Director, Daniel B. Cathcart. Set Decorator, Edwin B. Willis. Special Effects, Warren Newcombe. Montage Effects, Peter Ballbusch. Gowns, Adrian. Men's Wardrobe, Gile Steele. Makeup Artist, Jack Dawn. Editor, Harold F. Kress. Assistant Director, Tom Andre. Orchestrators, Paul Marquardt, Joseph Nussbaum, Leonid Raab. Unit Manager, Keith Weeks. Script Clerk, Carl "Major" Roup. Original running time, 127 minutes. DVD release running time, 113 minutes.

Song "See Me Dance the Polka": music and lyrics, George Grossmith, additional lyrics, John Lee Mahin.

New York opening, Astor Theatre, August 12, 1941. Los Angeles opening, Grauman's Chinese Theatre and Loew's State Theatre, September 5, 1941.

The Cast: Spencer Tracy (Dr. Harry Jekyll/Mr. Edward Hyde), Ingrid Bergman (Ivy Peterson), Lana Turner (Beatrix Emery), Donald Crisp (Sir Charles Emery), Ian Hunter (Dr. John Lanyon), Barton MacLane (Sam Higgins), C. Aubrey Smith (The Bishop), Peter

Godfrey (Poole), Sara Allgood (Mrs. Higgins), Frederic Worlock (Dr. Heath), William Tannen (Interne Fenwick), Frances Robinson (Marcia), Denis Green (Freddie), Billy Bevan (Mr. Weller), Forrester Harvey (Old Prouty), Lumsden Hare (Col. Weymouth), Lawrence Grant (Dr. Courtland), John Barclay (Constable), Aubrey Mather (Inspector), Alec Craig (Tripped Waiter), Doris Lloyd (Mrs. Marley), Lionel Pape (Mr. Marley), Hillary Brooke (Mrs. Arnold), Lydia Bilbrook (Lady Copewell), Winifred Harris (Mrs. Weymouth), Alice Mock (Showgirl Singing "See Me Dance the Polka"), Milton Parsons (Choir Master), Claude King (Uncle Geoffrey), Brandon Hurst (Briggs—Lanyon's Butler), Gwen Gaze (Mrs. French), Martha Wentworth (Landlady), Gil Perkins (Stunt Double for Tracy), Robert Bradford ("Whistler" for Tracy).

9

Monogram's
Nazi Horror Peep Show

Women in Bondage

Its Naked Truth Will Shock You!
—Publicity for *Women in Bondage*, 1943

Thursday night, December 9, 1943. The Palace Theatre, Milwaukee.

There was a gala premiere this night—the world premiere, in fact, of *Women in Bondage*, formerly titled *Hitler's Women*.[1] Monogram, despairing of a major New York or Hollywood opening, had settled on Milwaukee, and the city and Palace management had indulged Monogram in making this premiere a night to remember.

Women in Bondage was a special type of horror film—a Nazi atrocity shocker, following in the tradition of RKO's *Hitler's Children* and MGM's *Hitler's Madman*. It boasted a luridly suggestive title and the novelty of a half-dozen female stars—some of them admittedly slinking down the sad path to cinema oblivion.

A brunette martyr strapped to a whipping post, her lashing overseen by a Nazi blonde. A profane Nazi baptism. A leading lady commanded to bear a child via her Nazi brother-in-law after her husband is paralyzed from the waist down. And all of it daringly shot *without* the blessing of Joseph Breen and his censorship office.

Sex. Sadism. Propaganda … each one begging for risqué, all-stops-pulled sideshow promotion. And this night, in Milwaukee, the exploitation was amok.

Women in Bondage star Gertrude Michael, who played the aforementioned Nazi blonde, made a personal appearance at the Palace, as did Rita Quigley, who played a promiscuous village girl who consorts with the German soldiers. Considering their hateful roles, Michael and Quigley were brave for showing up. Joining them onstage, rather incongruously: H.B. Warner, once Christ in DeMille's *The King of Kings*, now *Women in Bondage*'s aged but valiant holy man.

Floodlights illuminated the Palace front, streamer pennants hooked from the rooftop to the marquee, a 50-foot-wide banner loomed over the main thoroughfare advertising the opening night, and swastikas abounded on the theater doors.

The management had decorated the entire theater lobby as a Nazi Art Museum. All male employees of the palace were costumed as Nazi storm troopers, all female employees as German "Mädchen" in dark skirts, white blouses and ties, and pigtails.

Near the theater, under a giant billboard advertising the attraction, there was a barbed wire enclosure suggesting a concentration camp, with women garbed as prisoners and a man dressed as a Nazi guard, holding a rifle.

Poster for *Women in Bondage* (Monogram, 1943).

Before the film began, a group of uniformed WACs and WAVEs joined the trio of stars onstage, before a large picture of Miss Liberty, and everyone in the theater sang "God Bless America."

All the while, the most sensational attraction of *Women in Bondage*'s premiere night was a local model, dressed in torn, disheveled and revealing Nazi "Mädchen" attire. She lay sprawled and seemingly defiled on a platform in the theater foyer, above which hung a ten-foot-high banner with a swastika.

The banner bore the formidable words, "She Has Served the Reich!"

* * *

It all sounds today like a nightmarishly camp burlesque show, in the style of Mel Brooks' *Springtime for Hitler*, without the intentional laughs. The two luridly suggestive titles, *Hitler's Women* and *Women in Bondage*, failed to do the film any aesthetic favors, nor did the aforementioned accent-on-sex exploitation. The fact that the presenter of the film was Monogram Pictures—Poverty Row's most infamous studio—seemed to be the ultimate kiss of death.

The critical reception was, in many cases, what one would expect. John T. McManus, film critic of New York City's highbrow newspaper *PM*, wrote of *Women in Bondage*:

> When the women (all sprightly lasses, even in Hitler Youth uniforms) are called in for motherhood or marriage examinations, their winding sheets are all fetchingly off-the-shoulder. When Nancy Kelly finally revolts against threatened sterilization and runs away, she hasn't gone a half mile … before her skirt is ripped clear up to here, baring a neat, non-athletic thigh as she flees the pursuing SS men....[2]

In Baltimore, where *Women in Bondage* opened on its strangely timed national release date—Christmas Eve, 1943—Donald Kirkley of the *Sunpaper*s was unsparing in his condemnation: He called it "a peep show."[3]

Yet this wasn't the whole story, and certainly not a fair one. *Women in Bondage* is a curio—produced, directed and written by *émigrés* who had fled Hitler, and played by actresses who seemed to see this woebegone production as a solemn act of patriotism.

The result: a tawdry film by its nature, with a Quixotic desire to transfigure itself and stir an audience.

Amazingly, it did.

Part One: Pre-Production

After Hitler's Children *comes* Hitler's Women. *Just one big unhappy family.*
—George E. Phair, "Retakes," *Variety*, March 8, 1943

In 1943, Monogram, based in its red-brick buildings at 4376 Sunset Drive in East Hollywood, had three major attractions: Belita (one name only), an Olympics ice-skating superstar known as "the Ice Maiden"; the East Side Kids; and Bela Lugosi.

"Better to reign in Hell than serve in Heaven" might have been Monogram's *Paradise Lost* motto.

Yet this wasn't Hell. Hollywood's Stygian Underworld, as least as far as horror films went, belonged to Universal, with its Gothic goblins, and to RKO, with Val Lewton's spooky glamour girls.

Where Monogram resided in the Hollywood firmament was basically *sub*–Hell.

The Lugosi horror films of Monogram might be legendary today but, at the time of their release, they hadn't a chance of playing in a first-run theater such as Hollywood's Hawaii. This was the top "sensation" salon in town, where RKO's 1941 *Citizen Kane* and Universal's 1941 comedy *Hellzapoppin'* held the records.[4] It was the house where RKO's Val Lewton hit *Cat People* had begun its powerhouse 13-week run in early 1943. It was also the favored theater for Universal fare, such as the late 1943 double bill of *Son of Dracula* and *The Mad Ghoul* (see Chapter 13). The mainstream critics basically ignored the Monogram product.

Attempts by the studio over the years to release a major movie had been, overall, hapless.

Take, for example, 1933's *Oliver Twist*, starring Dickie Moore in the title role, and Irving Pichel as Fagin.[5] *The Hollywood Reporter's* February 22, 1933, review headline: "Monogram's *Oliver Twist* Has No Redeeming Feature." The *Reporter* so eviscerated the film that its producer, I.E. Chadwick, took out a full page in the February 26 *Reporter*, protesting the "cavalier-like, unjust and ignorant attack on the director of this picture, Mr. W.J. Cowen, and the finest group of sincere artists it has been my pleasure to present in a picture." On February 28, *Hollywood Reporter* editor Billy Wilkerson responded with a full-page rebuttal, including this broadside:

> [W]e sent not one, but three reviewers to see Oliver Twist. *Each of the three men wrote a review on the picture without knowing that the others were doing likewise, and we ran the* best *of the three reviews....*

Monogram had followed up with 1934's *Jane Eyre*, starring Virginia Bruce as Jane and Colin Clive as Mr. Rochester, and scavenging the *Oliver Twist* sets. It had a handsome, storybook quality, Christy Cabanne directed nicely, and both Bruce and Clive were affecting and picturesque in their roles. Still, how effectively could a film conjure up Charlotte Bronte's novel when it was shot in only eight days?

Monogram temporarily gave up any dreams of prestige and during the period between 1934 and 1941 embraced its standby "B" potboiler program of action, adventure and Westerns. Among familiar faces who appeared in Monogram potboilers during this time were Bela Lugosi and Boris Karloff.

While MGM and Paramount had 1941 profits of $11 million and $9.2 million, and Universal a profit of $2.7 million,[6] Monogram recorded a net profit of $10,897.69.[7]

Come World War II, Monogram was once again restless to break out of its dungeon. The profits of the major studios kept soaring and Monogram's rose too: Its net profit for the year ending June 27, 1942, was $43,306.[8]

Monday, January 11, 1943: Monogram previewed its new Belita-starring musical *Silver Skates* at the Hollywood Paramount Theatre. *Variety,* in its positive review, called it "Monogram's first 'A' production."[9] It was a nice stab at legitimacy.

Monogram was determined to continue its modest ascent. As such, the studio was ready to hit the public, exhibitors and critics right between the eyes.

*   *   *

Thursday, January 14: RKO's *Hitler's Children* premiered at 50 key cities. The story concerned a Hitler Youth (Tim Holt) in love with a village girl (Bonita Granville) who doesn't share his Nazi fervor. The big scenes: A sterilization center for females unfit to bear Nazi children, and a torture episode, with Granville lashed to a post. Edward Dmytryk directed.

Thursday, February 4: "*Hangman* Sold to MGM for Release," headlined page one of *The Hollywood Reporte*r. The film, *The Hangman*, was based on the recent assassination of Reichsprotektor Reinhard Heydrich in Bohemia. Seymour Nebenzal, *avant-garde* German filmmaker who had fled the Nazis, produced the independently made film with the financial backing of wealthy Jews. Playing Heydrich: John Carradine, so satanic a Nazi that he slaps a priest and wipes his boots on sacred cloth. Douglas Sirk, an *émigré* from Hitler, directed. The film was so powerful that MGM bought it, dressed it up and released it under the title *Hitler's Madman.*

Clearly, sensational films based on Nazi horrors were hot. Monogram paid heed.

Wednesday, February 24: On the same date that *Hitler's Children* opened at an additional 75 theaters, including the Pantages and the RKO-Hillstreet in Hollywood, the *Los Angeles Times* headlined, "Russian Will Produce Film About Hitler." The Russian was Herman Millakowsky, "formerly with the UFA and Amelka organizations abroad." The *Time*s wrote:

> After the Fuehrer took over, Millakowsky was identified with the French industry and worked on pictures in which Simone Simon, Erich von Stroheim and Jean-Pierre Aumont appeared. June 11, 1940, he escaped to unoccupied France, Casablanca, and the United States.

The article stated that Monogram had acquired the distribution rights to this new film, and delivered the payoff news: The title of Millakowsky's movie-to-be was *Hitler's Women*.

The title made wildfire news through Hollywood. Would the film be about Eva Braun? Or Hitler's mother? Or Die Fuehrer's old flames?

Wednesday, March 3: Edith Gwynn, in her *Hollywood Reporter* "Rambling Reporter" column, wrote:

> Hear that Monogram is about to make a picture called Hitler's Women—all about his "love life." Which sounds like the worst possible psychology to us….

Perhaps … but *Hitler's Children* had broken "all existing records" at the Pantages Theatre and the RKO-Hillstreet Theatre with a combined first week take that *Variety* estimated at $63,000.[10] The film, with a negative cost of $205,000, would eventually take in an astounding rental: $3,355,000.[11]

Saturday, March 13: MGM, taking its cue, wrapped up added scenes for *Hitler's Madman*. One of the new scenes, shot despite Joseph Breen's objection: Carradine's Heydrich lecherously ogling a gaggle of young village ladies (including MGM starlets Ava Gardner, Frances Rafferty and Vicky Lane) whom he plans to ship as prostitutes to the Russian front. He first sends them to a laboratory for sterilization, prompting one of the ladies to jump to her death from a window.

Monogram, meanwhile, proceeded with plans for *Hitler's Women*.

Thursday, March 18: Still committed to its stand-by favorites, Monogram premiered a double feature: *The Ape Man*, starring Bela Lugosi, and *Kid Dynamite*, starring the East Side Kids, at the 475-seat Colony Theatre on Hollywood Boulevard. Lugosi made a personal appearance at the Colony during the run's second week, and the East Side Kids appeared in person the third week.

Tuesday, May 4: Edwin Schallert, *Los Angeles Times* drama critic, wrote: "Strongest cast that has acted in any Monogram feature in a long time is being sought for the film-ization of *Hitler's Women*, which is expected to have sensational topical values." The article claimed Monogram wanted Francis Lederer as the patriot hero, and Anna Sten "in the most powerful dramatic feminine part." Neither would eventually play in the film.

Wednesday, May 5: George E. Phair wrote in *Variety*: "Monogram may have trouble finding femmes to play *Hitler's Women*. Imagine being typed as one of Odolf's [sic] girlfriends."

The script went into development. Authoring the original story was Frank Bentick Wisbar, a 44-year-old Prussian-born producer-director-writer *émigré* who had worked for UFA and had fled Hitler in 1939. Wisbar, destined to be best-remembered for his Expressionistic direction of PRC's 1946 horror film *Strangler of the Swamp*, had strong motivation for this project: He escaped his homeland with his wife after she had been declared "Non-Aryan."

Incidentally, Wisbar had been production manager on the 1931 German film *Mädchen in Uniform* (1931), an acclaimed lesbian love story taking place in an all-girl boarding school. The Nazi regime later tried unsuccessfully to destroy all copies.[12]

Wednesday, June 2: In a letter to Wisbar at Monogram Studios, Joseph Breen responded to the treatment for *Hitler's Women*. Breen reported that "the basic story" (basic underlined) met Production Code requirements. However:

> On account of the somewhat unusual nature of several angles of your story, you will appreciate the fact that we could not give you any kind of a general clearance until we have had a chance to read carefully your final detailed shooting script.... We are therefore withholding further comment or approval....[13]

Wednesday, June 23: "Leave It to Steve," headlined *Variety*, reporting: "Monogram handed Steve Sekely two director chores with widely divergent themes: *Hitler's Women* and *Dime a Dance* for summer shooting."

As for Sekely, he was a 44-year-old, Budapest-born *émigré* who had directed films in Germany and Hungary. Sekely had directed Monogram's *Revenge of the Zombies* (1943) starring John Carradine as a Nazi doctor hoping to raise a zombie army for the Fuehrer.

Houston Branch, 44-year-old veteran screenwriter from St. Paul, Minnesota, wrote the actual screenplay for *Hitler's Women*. The basic story:

> Margot Bracken returns to Germany and her estate, Brackenfeld, after ten years away. There she meets Gertrude Schneider, a sadistic district leader who heads the Nazi Youth movement. Margot reluctantly agrees to be a section leader of the all-female Nazi Youth trainees. When Margot's husband Ernst returns from the front paralyzed and unable to sire children, the State assigns Otto, Ernst's storm trooper brother, to impregnate Margot and provide another child for the Fuehrer. One of Margot's Youth trainees is Toni Hall, a maid who, forbidden to marry an SS officer because she's myopic, goes about hysterically denouncing the Nazis—with tragic consequences. Another Youth trainee, Herta, a teenage voluptuary, stays out nights with the German troops, defying the protests from her aged grandmother. Grete, the village flower seller and the widow of a German soldier and mother of his infant child, wants to have her baby baptized, thus disobeying the directives of the Nazis. The lives of these women intersect throughout the film and the lines between "good" and "evil" are delineated (with fervent Nazis obviously on the side of "evil").

Clearly, *Hitler's Women* had nothing to do with the Fuehrer's love life. It offered several meaty women's roles, and via Margot's climactic heroics, packed a wallop with an early feminist message. Mainly between the lines were the calculated flourishes of sex, sadism, horror and even blasphemy.

Naturally, these sensations didn't escape the scrutiny of Joseph Breen.

Monday, July 26: Breen wrote to Monogram producer Herman Millakowsky: "[I]n its present form, this material is not acceptable under the provisions of the Production Code, and as written, cannot be approved." Among the objections listed in Breen's three-page letter:

> *Page 1: We suggest that you eliminate the lines, "sterilize every Non-Aryan child"; the word, "breed"; and the line, "For neither party is it important that love enter as a factor."*
>
> *Page 2: We suggest that you eliminate, or rewrite, the lines of Hitler's voice, to get away from the present suggestion that there are "young soldiers standing ready to mate with you in order to produce the first generation of children"....*
>
> *Page 16, et seq: The characterization of Herta, and the details with which this characterization is pointed up, are definitely unacceptable, and will have to be changed. It might be acceptable, simply to indicate that she is a common prostitute; but all dialogue dealing with prostitution is unacceptable....*
>
> *Page 19: We would ask that you eliminate the suggestion, from the radio voice, "go out and look for Nordic warriors and heroes to mate with...." It might be that you can substitute for the first phrase, the word, "marry," making the line read, "Young German girls and young women, marry Nordic warriors and heroes."*
>
> *Page 23: It will be necessary for you to exercise the greatest possible care in order that there will be no offensive sense in and about the clinic, the laboratory, and the examination room. The "pregnant mothers" should not, of course, be visibly pregnant.*
>
> *Page 25, et seq: It occurs to us that there is too much intimate detail in the several scenes inside the clinic....*
>
> *Page 27: Specifically, you should omit the business of the woman doctor feeling Toni's legs, bust and hips.*
>
> *Page 36: Please note that no scenes would be acceptable of the characterization in detail of Herta as a prostitute. There should be no scenes of her having been bruised and beaten with the suggestion that this was done as part of her activities as a prostitute.*
>
> *Page 37: The scenes beginning with #90, between Heinz and Toni, should not be played in a bedroom.*
>
> *Page 88: [W]e suggest that the business of beating Toni should be merely suggested, and not actually shown. It might be that you could show her having been beaten or tortured, but the actual scenes of the beating should be merely suggested.*
>
> *Page 96: You should be careful with the scenes of Litzl riding in the truck with the soldiers, in order that these be not offensively suggestive. The business of their kissing and fondling her promiscuously, is not good.*
>
> *Page 104: It might be well if the sign on the ambulance indicated that Toni was to be taken to an insane asylum, rather than a sterilization center.*

And so it went. As always, Breen was more than willing to work with the studio to develop an acceptable script. Monogram was cooperative too. A meeting followed where Breen and Monogram representatives discussed alterations. Based on the aforementioned letter from Breen and the finished picture, it appears Monogram made every excision and adjustment that Breen demanded.

Friday, July 30: Carl E. Milliken, governor of Maine from 1917 to 1921 and executive secretary of the Motion Picture Producers and Directors Association of America (MPPDA), sent Monogram a letter from the Title Registration Bureau:

> *To assist us in consideration of the approval of your proposed title* Hitler's Women, *it would be appreciated if you would send us a synopsis or outline of the story for which this title is intended.*

The inference was clear: The title, as ever, was controversial, sensational and likely to be rejected. In fact, other studios had already tried to register such a title and had been refused.

Sunday, August 1: In the Real World, U.S. B-24 Liberator bombers were attacking oil refineries at Ploesti, Romania.[14]

Monday, August 2: Also in the Real World, Lieutenant John F. Kennedy's PT-109 was rammed in two and sunk off the Solomon Islands.[15]

Wednesday, August 4: In the Make-Believe World, *Hitler's Women* started shooting. The budget was set at $104,000[16] and the shooting schedule was to be 14 days.[17]

The surprise brazen move: Monogram never sent Breen a revised script for approval—and *Hitler's Women* went into production without his sanction.

Gail Patrick, usually the arch "other woman" in films, was *Women in Bondage*'s gallant heroine.

Part Two: Production

Oh dear, I did Women in Bondage *and it was a huge hit—the censors let us get away with murder! I'm a girl coming back to Germany and getting involved with all the Nazi customs from sterilization to paganism to mercy killings. The trailer had this line: "Blueprint for Shame!" It was a huge hit but Nancy Kelly was in tears over some of the awful dialogue. A lot of actors were in it for the pay—H. B. Warner, Gertrude Michael, Mary Forbes.*
— Gail Patrick, *Classic Images*[18]

"The Greatest Cast In The History Of Monogram"
—Monogram publicity for *Hitler's Women—*
Women in Bondage

The Horror Begins

Women in Bondage opens with an eloquent prologue:

This is the story of the Women of Germany today ... Hitler's Women. You may find it hard to believe that such things are taking place because they could not possibly happen to you. For that, thank a Divine Providence and the Country in which you live. For everything in this picture is true. These things did happen ... are happening to women who are making the voyage called life, now, at the same time you are.

How much of the story is specifically true is open to question, but the prologue captures the overall sincerity of the movie.

Although Breen had objected to the Hitler rantings in the original scenario, the shooting script opened with "stock shots and dissolves" of "women in the German Reich, interspersed with shots of various Nazi leaders, addressing masses of women." The voices "seem to shout back at each other" as they declare such lines as "German women—you are superior to all other women," and "Selective breeding means racial purity." This leads up to a stock shot with Hitler's voice "addressing a mass of emotionally intoxicated women":

> *The conquest of the world begins in the kindergarten. German women—yours is the greatest destiny—to create the Master Race!*

If these scenes were originally included, shot, they were cut. *Women in Bondage* opens with a train, as Margot Bracken returns to Germany and to the family estate at Brackenfeld after a decade away. Top-billed Gail Patrick is a smart, attractive, if rather icy heroine, playing against her usual type of an arch vamp. She joked on the set with columnist Erskine Johnson, who wrote:

> *[S]he is always the gal who slips poison into her husband's coffee, or breaks up somebody's beautiful romance on the screen. This is her first really sympathetic role, and she's happy for the chance to prove to Hollywood that she can be a good girl.*[19]

Incidentally, readers might recall that Ms. Patrick originally came to Hollywood in 1932 as a finalist in Paramount's Panther Woman contest for *Island of Lost Souls* (see Chapter 3).

Margot, whose husband Ernst is fighting at the front, has a reunion with her mother-in-law Gladys (venerable Mary Forbes) and sister-in-law Ruth (fierce Tala Birell). The Romanian-born Birell had once upon a time been a Universal star, notably in 1933's jungle melodrama *Nagana,* in which she was tossed to crocodiles. She now played character roles. As Nazi zealot Ruth, Birell looks appropriately Nordic in her flowing blonde tresses and snug Nazi uniform.

The true she-wolf of *Women in Bondage,* however, is third-billed Gertrude Michael, as Deputy District Director Gertrude Schneider. The Alabama-born blonde enjoyed a special niche in pre–Code Hollywood: She sang "Sweet Marijuana" in Paramount's *Murder at the Vanities* (1934). A horror-related footnote as well: She is supposed to have been the lover of mystery writer Paul Cain (aka Peter Ruric, who received story credit on the Karloff and Lugosi *The Black Cat*). When Cain wrote his sole novel *Fast One,* he allegedly based the story's alcoholic voluptuary on his former flame, Gertrude.

Michael had been having tough times in Hollywood and relished the juicy role of the sinister Schneider. In her tight blonde hairdo and dark Nazi uniform, she suggests a Walkure as she passionately delivers her Nazi ravings to Patrick: "As a good German, as the wife of a German soldier, you must and will want to obey!"

When Margot, as section leader, is introduced to her group of all-female Nazi Youth trainees, we behold a bevy of starlets, all costumed in their Mädchen uniforms. "*Achtung!*" commands Birell's Ruth, and at her command, the Nazi teenage girls parade in step, German march music thundering on the soundtrack.

Among them is Toni Hall, played by second-billed Nancy Kelly, who got the biggest emotional workout in the film. Fans might remember Kelly best in 20th Century–Fox's

Four of the characters you love to hate in *Women in Bondage*, all giving a "*Sieg Heil!*": Alan Baxter, Tala Birell, Gertrude Michael and Anne Nagel.

1939 Western *Jesse James*, as the highly emotional wife of Tyrone Power's Jesse. She has her share of hysterics in *Women in Bondage* as well.

Among the film's other female principals, most of whom have a connection to Hollywood horror:

- Red-haired Anne Nagel, despite fourth billing, played the small role of the assistant deputy director. She'd been on contract to Warner Brothers when her husband, Warners star Ross Alexander, fatally shot himself on January 2, 1937. She later signed with Universal, where she co-starred with Boris Karloff and Bela Lugosi in *Black Friday* (1940) and with Lon Chaney Jr. and Lionel Atwill in *Man Made Monster* (1941). Now remarried and no longer at Universal, she had been leading lady in PRC's 1942 *The Mad Monster*, with George Zucco and Glenn Strange.
- Blonde Maris Wrixon, 26-year-old Washington state-born actress, portrayed Grete Ziegler, the village flower seller, whose husband has died in combat and who wants to have their baby son baptized in her faith. Wrixon was a former Warners starlet, and had played the crippled heroine of Monogram's *The Ape* (1940) starring Boris Karloff.
- Rita Quigley, a 20-year-old Los Angeles native, acted the free-and-easy Herta. She was the older sister of Juanita "Baby Jane" Quigley, who appeared in Universal's *Imitation of Life* (1934). Rita had recently played in PRC's *Isle of Forgotten Sins,*

directed by Edgar G. Ulmer, with John Carradine, Gale Sondergaard and fellow *Women in Bondage* cast member Tala Birell.
- Gray-haired Gisela Werbisek, 68-year-old actress born in Austria-Hungary, played Herta's hapless grandmother, who tries to control Herta's wanton ways. Werbisek, whose film career dated back to 1912, was also an *émigré* who fled Hitler, and had made her Hollywood debut as a grandmother in RKO's *The Hunchback of Notre Dame* (1939).

All these actresses, for whatever celebrity they had enjoyed in the past, found it tough going at Monogram: Wrixon remembered that acting for the studio was "like being in a foxhole."[20] Director Steve Sekely's shooting schedule and budget were mercilessly tight. The first day's shooting, taking place on the Bracken living room set, called for coverage of eight pages and 13 scenes; the second day (Bracken living room and hallway), seven and three-quarter pages and 19 scenes; day three (Bracken Hallway, Railroad Station and Bracken terrace), seven and three-eighths pages and 22 scenes.

It was all a wind-up for Day 4: Sekely shot on the Bracken terrace, church, and Air Defense post sets—11 pages and 35 scenes!

Yet, for all the challenges, Sekely threw himself passionately into the picture, and his cast responded with spirit and gallantry. The director probably had to think only of what was happening in his native country to spark his fervor for shooting *Women in Bondage*.

Nancy Kelly as the doomed Toni, and other village girls, submit to a Nazi-mandated physical— their state of undress one of the "sensations" of *Women in Bondage*.

Additionally, the production got a break: Charlie Chaplin, perhaps admiring Monogram's spunk, provided the *Women in Bondage* company the use of his old studio for exteriors—presumably for a reasonable rental. Sekely and cinematographer Mack Stengler clearly exulted in the open-air freedom of the Tyrolean set and made the most of the pictorial possibilities. Monogram scheduled the Chaplin Studio for two days, where the film would cover 13 and five-eighths pages and 47 scenes.

Among the "big" episodes in the first half of *Women in Bondage*:

The physical examination: Toni and other village ladies, all hoping to wed SS officers, report for a physical to see if they meet the demanding standards. Nancy Kelly (who wears pigtails for most of the film) and her colleagues walk about the medical facility wrapped in white sheets, a titillating sight for 1943 audiences. Toni fails her eye test—myopia. Fraulein Schneider cancels Toni's engagement to SS officer Heinz Radtke (William Henry).

Herta and her grandmother: Rita Quigley as the brazen teenager Herta flounces home after a night of consorting with the German soldiers. Gisela Werbisek, as Herta's grandmother, confronts her, threatening to report her to the authorities for her promiscuous behavior. Herta mocks the old woman, insisting that she's doing precisely what the authorities want her to do. The shooting script provided this bit:

> Herta has taken off her torn shirtwaist, looks down at a bruise on her shoulder, and her brassiere that has been roughly disarranged.

The Baptism scene: Gail Patrick, H.B. Warner and Maris Wrixon.

However, in the film, although Herta starts to strip in front of her grandmother, there's no bruised shoulder and no roughly disarranged brassiere.

The Christian baptism: Maris Wrixon's Grete wants her baby boy baptized. Margot helps her, secretly taking her by night to the church, where Pastor Renz meets them to perform the sacrament. Playing the pastor: 66-year-old H.B. Warner—who appeared as a bishop in *Hitler's Children*.

"In the name of the Father...," prays Pastor Renz at the Baptismal font.

"In the name of the *Fuehrer*!" shouts a Nazi as soldiers intervene, ending the ceremony. The SS officer who spoils the sacrament is Otto Bracken, Margot's brother-in-law. Portraying Otto: Alan Baxter, Yale School of Drama alumnus, noted for playing baby-faced killers—for example, "The Kid" in Karloff's *Night Key* (1937). Right after completing *Women in Bondage*, Baxter joined Moss Hart's *Winged Victory* show and served in the military.

By the way, the shooting script provided an economic suggestion regarding the set for the church, which the production followed:

> *Pastor Renz has lighted a single candle. It pierces the blackness of the church, bringing into relief the font, the altar and the pulpit, but the actual church itself is shrouded in darkness—so it is not needed to be built.*

Toni's hysteria: Toni finds her fiancé Heinz in the village. He's learned she'd failed her physical and rejects her.

"But it's only my eyes," Toni forlornly calls after him. "You always said you liked my eyes—remember?"

Heartbroken, Toni—who, as played by Nancy Kelly and scripted by Houston Branch, presumably isn't totally sound (how else could Hollywood dramatize a woman hopelessly in love with an SS officer?)—goes wild. She runs through the Nazi-occupied village, her hysteria rising as she insists she can see well:

> *I can see you* (to a passerby staring at her)—*you've got a funny little wart on your nose. ...* (heading toward Grete's flower stand) *And I can see you.... I can see your flowers—I can even see the dead ones you hide behind the fresh ones...* (to the deputy director) *And I can see you.... And I can see your eyes and your mouth and you pretending to smile—while all the time beneath you're hard and cruel—and you're very much afraid....*

"What did you say?" demands Anne Nagel's deputy director. Toni responds as the script says, "wildly and recklessly":

> *I said you're afraid ... that's why you are hard, and cruel, and unkind—you're just beasts.... Beasts!—you—and the doctor—and the frau director—and the Fuehrer! You're all beasts!!*

And she runs weeping down the Chaplin Studio street.

The Nazi baptism: On the makeshift altar at the district leader's office is a sword and a copy of *Mein Kampf*. Otto has forced Margot to attend, and she and Grete watch helplessly as a German soldier prepares to bestow on Grete's baby this pagan baptism.

"In the name of the Fuehrer," intones the Nazi.

"In the name of the Father!" shouts Pastor Renz, breaking into the room and christening the baby. The soldiers drag the old man away.

The Horror Climaxes

Just as one thinks the horrific episodes can't get any worse, the movie moves into further atrocities in the second half:

Toni's escape and pursuit: The travails of Nancy Kelly's heartbroken, nearsighted Toni continue. Anne Nagel's deputy director reports on Toni's "mental instability," "hysteria" and "previously established myopia," and Gertrude Michael's Director Schneider replies, "You are right—sterilization recommended." In the DVD version released by Warner Bros., the print has a jump cut where the words "sterilization recommended" appeared.

Nevertheless, sterilization is the plan, and Toni, suspecting such action, flees into the countryside. Monogram visited Sherwood Forest, a popular location site, to film Toni's flight from her pursuers.[21] This episode has all the Teutonic trimmings: Toni fleeing in her slit-up-the-leg black skirt; the Nazi Youth girls pursuing her in their uniforms; a Nazi on a motorcycle with another Nazi riding in the sidecar; and through it all, Edward Kay's poundingly dramatic musical score.

Toni makes her way to Margot's house. "They will sterilize me—then send me to a labor camp for life," laments Toni—these lines also cut from the currently available DVD print. Margot hides her and sneaks her away in the trunk of her car, again to the countryside—where Nazis capture her almost immediately.

Toni's torture scene: We see Toni on the floor, whipped and bound to a post—an imagery very similar to Bonita Granville's whipping in *Hitler's Children*. Fraulein Schneider creeps in for an eyeful of Toni's agony. Toni refuses to admit that Margot helped her escape.

As the Nazis prepare to take Toni (Nancy Kelly) presumably to an asylum, she sees her former fiancé (William Henry) with his new Aryan blonde bride-to-be.

Toni's death: Toni is being led away by the German soldiers to an ambulance. The script had an interesting note:

> *A closed ambulance awaits Toni. The Gestapo men turn her over to a hospital orderly who is dressed in white. (This should indicate clearly enough that her destination is the Sterilization Center—but if desired, there can be a sign on the ambulance indicating it belongs either to a Sterilization Hospital or an Insane Asylum.)*

Meanwhile, a blonde beauty emerges from the physical examination headquarters and approaches Heinz. "The doctor said I am a perfect example of Nordic womanhood!" exults the blonde.

"We can be married this weekend!" says Heinz.

Toni loses it. Heartbroken and (again) hysterical, she breaks away from the soldiers and wildly pursues Heinz (and the blonde) down the village street. The soldiers shoot her in the back. Toni falls, as Grete holds her in her arms.

"They were right about my eyes," says Toni. "I can't see any more" … and she dies.

Margot and motherhood: Margot's husband Ernst (Roland Varno[22]) has returned from the front, wounded and paralyzed below the waist. Director Schneider calls in Margot and delivers a speech that must have been a shocker for 1943 audiences. In fact, it carried such a punch that the Pennsylvania State censor demanded it be trimmed, as noted in the brackets below. The cut version of the speech is what survives in the DVD release:

> *The fact that Captain Ernst Bracken has served his Fatherland well does not mean that the Third Reich should be deprived of his wife's children. The man does not necessarily need to be your husband. [The Nazi Law states concisely that in case of inability of a husband, a deputy husband can be designated. For the sake of the family line, the donor should be the next of kin of the husband. In your case, how fortunate for you, that your husband's brother is such a perfect specimen of German manhood, so exalted in the esteem of his Fuehrer. I have already consulted your brother-in-law, and he...]*

Margot's response to the order that she mate with her brother-in-law? She strikes Director Schneider across the face—which must have received fervent applause from wartime audiences.

The mercy killing: Herta's grandmother is in a prison-like room, inside what the script calls a Mercy Killing Home. On the soundtrack we hear her thoughts: The lines in brackets below were in the script but not in the film:

> *I am a poor old German woman.... In a few minutes, I will be led away to my death—mercy killing, they call it. [That I, an old woman, should die is unimportant—but the reason for my death is. I am dying because I objected to my granddaughter's being turned into a common...]*

A door opens and a Nazi beckons her. As the script details:

> *Up to now she has been a miserable old thing. Now, in the moment of her "Calvary," her face has gained almost majesty—a majesty which her withered, broken body cannot sustain.*

In the film, we see her only from the back. Perhaps Steve Sekely felt the "Calvary" face would add to the melodrama overdose he was trying to avoid.

Ernst's suicide: Tormented by his paralysis, overhearing his mother's disgust at the idea of Otto impregnating Margot, Ernst, pretending he hasn't heard anything, asks Margot to see what music is playing on the radio. As she turns her back, he removes a pistol from his nightstand drawer and shoots himself.

The climax and Margot's revenge: Otto, Margot's proscribed mate, tries to rouse himself to the occasion, sitting in the study, nervously bracing himself with shots of whiskey, a subtle attack by the filmmakers on the SS officer's manhood. Meanwhile, Allied bombers form an air raid over Brackenfeld. Gail Patrick's Margot, looking like a million dollars, seizes the moment, bravely and defiantly opening the curtain covering the skylight and bedroom windows. She has this final speech, which she delivers to Otto:

> *Do you hear the planes, Otto? Do you know what they mean? They mean that the women of all the countries Germany has despoiled and degraded will be free.... Yes—that the women of Germany, too, will be able to lift their heads and hearts again. It means that Toni Hall—all the Toni Halls— had not died in vain.... The dawn of tomorrow is coming, Otto, and with it your doom—and the doom of your kind. The world is tired of you....*

The Allied bombers see the light in the night and take aim. Brackenfeld explodes.

A suicide for Margot? Yes … but one that spares her the indignity of sex with her brother-in-law, cancels out another child for the Fuehrer, and causes the total destruction of the German munitions hidden on the estate.

In a brief coda, we see flashbacks of Toni … the grandmother … the pastor. And for a final fade-out image, we see a Nazi flag in rubble.

The End

Saturday, August 21: After a feverish 16 days of shooting, *Women in Bondage,* only two days over schedule, wrapped up production.

It was all over—and Joseph Breen had never known it had started!

Part Three: Post Production

Pre-Release

Friday, August 27: MGM's *Hitler's Madman,* after playing several cities, opened at the Rialto in New York City. Most critics panned it as overly melodramatic, missing the point that few historical personages were as melodramatic as Reinhard Heydrich.

Monday, August 30: Carl E. Milliken, from his MPPDA office in New York City, sent this telegram to Joseph Breen in Hollywood: "Have you approved script on Monogram's picture presently entitled *Hitler's Women*?"

It was a strange question, considering the film had wrapped nine days previously. Breen's reply telegram of August 31:

> *We have not yet approved shooting script now titled* Hitler's Women. *First script was rejected but at conference we approved verbally certain changes which if properly made will likely result in approved shooting script. No such script has been submitted as yet.*

Breen was a very busy man, and must not have been reading *Variety* or *The Holly-wood Reporter,* which had been covering the shoot of *Hitler's Women.* How he responded when he learned the film was already shot is not evident in the film's censorship file.

September 1: Carl E. Milliken wrote to Monogram with a final decision regarding the title:

You realize, I hope, our desire to be cooperative in every possible way, but the adverse decision seems to be forced upon us, both by the implications in the title itself and by the previous rejections of the same title when offered by members of our Association.

As the weeks passed, Joseph Breen, at some point, rather sportingly gave Monogram's movie, retitled *Women in Bondage*, a pass—and PCA release certificate No. 9617. It was fortunate for Monogram. Had Breen decreed so, he could have refused to release the picture and caused the company to forfeit its entire investment.

Meanwhile, Monogram proceeded with its tried-and-true formulas. In the fall of 1943, the studio filmed two new horror movies: *Return of the Ape Man* and *Voodoo Man*, both boasting the presence of Bela Lugosi, John Carradine and George Zucco.

Release

Monogram proceeded with plans for release and exploitation of *Women in Bondage*. The first move was to try to woo the press.

Tuesday, November 9: Monogram presented a special preview at the Filmarte Theatre in Hollywood for a select audience. The following day, *Variety* ran a positive assessment:

[P]icture carries plenty of drama without recourse to synthetic situations, with excellent results. A strong women's picture, it also holds possibilities for extensive exploitation that can lift grosses to surprising levels.

Thursday, November 11: Edwin Schallert of the *Los Angeles Times* wrote:

A strong brief for the fortitude of women under great stress is promulgated in [this] exceptionally fine study of conditions under the Nazi rule in Germany.... Gail Patrick, Nancy Kelly, Gertrude Michael, Anne Nagel, Tala Birell, Mary Forbes and others supply stunning portrayals ... [T]his picture reaches far beyond such a film as Hitler's Children, *a feature of similar theme, in its earnestness and sincerity. The cast is drawn from some of the most capable people in Hollywood, incidentally, who are too often ignored in the set routines of the major studios. They have risen notably to the occasion.*

Schallert felt so strongly about the merits of the film that, when he realized he'd left director Steve Sekely's name out of his review, he mentioned it the next day in his column. At any rate, these early raves were great news for Monogram. Had the studio actually managed to mix a frankly sensational topic with an impressively somber treatment?

Sunday, November 14: Jimmie Fidler, popular Hollywood columnist and reporter, let loose at the censors on his radio show:

Attention, please, to this editorial. Hitler's Women, *I would say, is one of the best motion picture titles of the year. It is intriguing, timely and provocative. So I was more than surprised when I received news that the title,* Hitler's Women, *had been changed to the dull, meaningless title,* Women in Bondage....

I asked Mr. Trem Carr, head of production at Monogram Studio, why this change had been made. He replied that the Will Hays Office had refused to okay Hitler's Women *on grounds that the title was suggestive. I might add that Mr. Carr was broken-hearted over the loss of his million-dollar title....*[23]

Fidler went on, complaining that the censors allowed films with scenes "I wouldn't want my daughter to see," that the title *Hitler's Women* was "no more suggestive than *Hitler's Children*," and that he'd seen the film and "found it excellent entertainment, not in the least offensive." Fidler concluded, haranguing the Breen Office for picking on "one of the less powerful major studios."

He had a point. In April, Breen had reluctantly approved *Hitler's Madman*, although the film had shot the village-girls-as-prostitutes-heading-for-sterilization-laboratory-causing-one of-them-to-leap-out-a-window-to-her-death episode, in defiance of Breen's order it not be filmed. Breen had surrendered, rationalizing that since it was wartime, certain concessions were allowable. It's possible he also dreaded a nasty battle with all-powerful Metro.

With the rave notices, Monogram was empowered to launch an all-out campaign for *Women in Bondage*, setting a general release date of Christmas Eve, 1943. Meanwhile:

Thursday, November 25: Monogram previewed *Women in Bondage* at New York City's Waldorf-Astoria Hotel for press, radio and invited guests. After the morning viewing, Monogram hosted a luncheon for the attendees.

Wednesday, December 8: Gertrude Michael, Rita Quigley and H.B. Warner arrived in Milwaukee for the premiere of *Women in Bondage* scheduled for the following night.[24] There was a welcoming dinner at Milwaukee's Schroeder Hotel, where Michael and Quigley posed with theater critic Dorothy Lawton as Michael fed Lawton an appetizer of caviar.

Michael said that she had lived in Germany and observed the conditions in the film first-hand. H.B. Warner said he had a son at Pearl Harbor. The Milwaukee *Journal Times* reported that the star trio was "pleasantly friendly." Also present was Monogram vice-president Steve Broidy.

Thursday, December 9: The aforementioned premiere took place at Milwaukee's Palace Theatre. The opening night was one of a set of Wisconsin openings scheduled for "'A' houses" in Racine, Fond du Loc, Green Bay, Appleton, La Crosse, Port Washington, Kenosha, Wausau and Manitowoc. The Hollywood trio was set to appear in some of these cities as well.

Exploitation

Friday, December 24: On the same day that President Franklin D. Roosevelt announced the appointment of General Dwight D. Eisenhower as Allied commander in chief to lead an impending "gigantic attack,"[25] *Women in Bondage* went into general release. It played the country ahead of its New York City and Los Angeles openings. Many exhibitors reveled in the exploitation. On February 26, 1944, *Motion Picture Herald* ran a photo of a woman hitting a mannequin dressed as a German solider on its head with a board. The caption blurb:

> As part of her campaign on Women in Bondage *at Loew's Ohio Theatre, in Cleveland, Gertrude L. Tracy planted a figure of a Nazi soldier in her lobby. Each bond purchaser was permitted to break the sign over the soldier's head. The stunt which was pulled several times a day for three days in advance of the opening helped to sell numerous bonds.*

Thursday, March 2, 1944: At last, the big day arrived: *Women in Bondage* opened at the Hawaii Theatre in Hollywood. Not only did lowly Monogram finally have a headliner at the prestigious 1100-seat Hawaii, *Women in Bondage* also came complete with a Monogram second feature, *Hot Rhythm*.[26]

The Hawaii was appropriately adorned for the opening. A large electric roof

Bond Buyers Crown Nazi

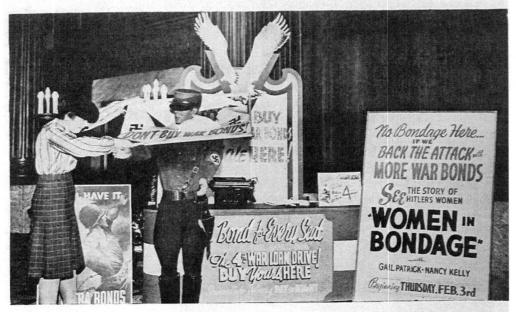

As part of her campaign on "Women in Bondage" at Loew's Ohio theatre, in Cleveland, Gertrude L. Tracy planted a figure of a Nazi soldier in her lobby. Each Bond purchaser was permitted to break the sign over the soldier's head. The stunt which was pulled several times a day for three days in advance of the opening helped to sell numerous bonds.

Theater promotion for *Women in Bondage*.

sign, bearing the original title *Hitler's Women*, was aglow in the night above the marquee. Business was tops. Hawaii manager Al Galston sent a celebratory telegram to Monogram:

> Women in Bondage *opened today to biggest opening day gross in theatre's history. Twenty Five percent higher than opening days of* Citizen Kane *and* Hellzapoppin', *previous record breakers which ran respectively seventeen and fifteen weeks.*[27]

It was a dream come true for Monogram. In less than a day, however, the bubble burst.

Friday, March 3: Joseph Breen wrote to Monogram's Trem Carr:

> *I am presuming to address you to direct your attention to the attached advertisement of the Hawaii Theatre, for your production titled* Women in Bondage.
>   *I direct your particular attention to the lines:*
>   Its Naked Truth Will Shock You!
>   First Terrible Revelations Of Immorality Demanded Of Girls For The Glory Of The Reich!
>   Illicit Romances! Illegitimate Children Encouraged By The Reich!
>   *I think you will agree with me that this is stretching things pretty far. I am sure that this is exactly the kind of advertisement which will give very serious offense to decent people here in Southern California, and thus do a very definite disservice to the industry as a whole.*

A huge electric roof sign and illuminated banner helped to exploit "Women in Bondage" at the Hawaii theatre, Hollywood.

The Hawaii Theatre on Hollywood Boulevard lures the public to see *Women in Bondage.*

Breen had already been in touch with Al Galston at the Hawaii, who had told him all this material came directly from Monogram. Breen wrote to Carr:

> *If this is true, it would seem that in failing to submit this material to the Advertising Advisory Council of this office, your company has thus violated one of the understandings under which the picture was approved by the Production Code Administration....*
> *I think we ought to do something about this kind of advertising? What do you think?*

A series of letters ensued between Monogram and the Production Code Administration, Monogram insisting that the PCA had approved the copy, the PCA investigating and concluding:

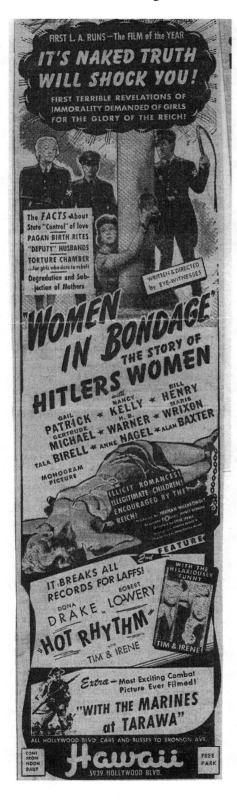

Evidently Monogram provided the Hawaii Theatre with supplementary advertising that was not submitted to this office for approval. These advertising lines are the sort of thing we have been trying to eliminate for the past ten years.

It was foul play by Monogram, especially since Breen had been clement in allowing the picture's release at all. At any rate, the advertising clicked. At the Hawaii, *Women in Bondage* (and *Hot Rhythm*), after setting an opening day record, racked up a first-week take of $9465. This was excellent money; it fell a bit short of the first week take of *Citizen Kane* ($10,000) and *Cat People* ($9600), but exceeded the $8500 of *Hellzapoppin'*. The film did not, however, have a record run: It stayed four weeks at the Hawaii, and took in a total of $22,835.[28] it next played at L.A.'s Orpheum Theatre for one week on a double bill with Monogram's *What a Man!*, and a stage show featuring the Freddie Slack Orchestra and the King Cole Trio. The week's take was $23,800.[29]

Saturday, March 25: Women in Bondage got a Broadway opening. The theater was the Gotham, formerly the Central, and the revamped 900-seat house had reopened especially for the occasion. The reviews were mixed, several of the Big Apple critics admitting respect for the film. In its first several days, the film was "doing well," as *Variety* put it, taking in $13,000. *Women in Bondage* ran at the Gotham for four weeks, taking in $39,300.[30]

Thursday, March 30: The Very Rev. Monsignor J.J. McClafferty, executive secretary of the New York Roman Catholic Diocese, wrote to W. Ray Johnston, Monogram's president:

It is the opinion of this office that advertising on Women in Bondage, *which has appeared in New York City newspapers in connection with the Gotham Theatre showing, is definitely objectionable.*

Whether the advertising material which appeared in the New York City press is part of the general press

This *Women in Bondage* advertisement, prepared for newspapers and a display at the Hawaii Theatre, got the film into major censorship trouble.

book for the exploitation of this picture or whether the material was prepared by an advertising agency for the New York exhibitor, I do not know. But I do know that the material is immodestly suggestive and possibly sadistic.

Wednesday, May 31: "$100,000 Mono Pic Due for $1,000,000 Gross," headlined *Variety*. It referred, of course, to *Women in Bondage*.

Monday, October 16: Steve Broidy, Monogram's vice-president and general sales manager, wrote in the annual anniversary edition of *Variety* that the studio's net "is up 300%." He reported the studio's net for the 39-week period ending March 25, 1944, saw a profit of $149,642, as compared with $43,306 for the comparable period of the previous year. Broidy gave primary credit to *Lady Let's Dance*, a Belita musical; *Where Are My Children* and *Are These Our Parents*, both social issues melodramas; *The Unknown Guest*, starring Victor Jory; and *Women in Bondage*.[31] (Note that neither the Lugosi horror films nor the East Side Kids movies were cited for contributing to Monogram's profit.)

Definitive financial figures on *Women in Bondage* aren't presently available. As noted, Monogram claimed a $1,000,000 gross (the rental would have been considerably less); another source gave the estimated sum as $700,000.[32]

Monogram stayed ambitious, had a big 1945 box office winner with *Dillinger*, but never fully rose in stature in Hollywood. It eventually became Allied Artists. Today, some of the red-brick buildings remain: first as the home of KCET Television, and now the Church of Scientology Media Center.

Lore and Legacy

> *Monogram's upper-bracket dramas provided some of their most impressive films of the period....* Women in Bondage *(1943) dealt with degradation and shame suffered by women in Hitler's Germany, teetering on the lurid side for exploitation purposes and patterned after RKO's successful* Hitler's Children, *but with several meritorious sequences and a well-chosen cast ... all directed firmly by Steve Sekely.*
>
> —Don Miller, *B Movies* (Ballantine Books, 1987)

As for the ladies of *Women in Bondage*:

Gail Patrick was a busy actress throughout the 1940s but eventually left acting and became executive producer of the long-running *Perry Mason* TV series. She served two terms as vice-president of the National Academy of Television Arts & Sciences and died at her estate on La Brea Terrace, Hollywood, in 1980 at age 69.

Nancy Kelly gave full sway to her emotional powers in Broadway's *The Bad Seed* as mother of the demonic child (Patty McCormack); Kelly won a Tony Award and reprised her role in the 1956 film, for which she received an Academy nomination. That same year, she was Emmy-nominated for her portrayal of Sister Mary Aquinas, who turns her students on to science in "The Pilot" (*Studio One in Hollywood*, November 12, 1956). She died at her Bel Air, California, home in 1995 at age 73.

Gertrude Michael continued in films and later TV (including a 1958 episode of *Perry Mason*). Never married, and an alcoholic for many years, she died from heart disease on New Year's Eve of 1964 in Beverly Hills, age 53.[33]

Anne Nagel made strange headlines—considering the nature of *Women in Bondage*. In 1947, she claimed a Hollywood doctor had sterilized her in 1936, that she hadn't realized it until 1947, and sued for $350,000. The surgeon (Dr. Franklyn Thorpe, who'd divorced Mary Astor in the sensational 1936 "diary" case) volleyed that Nagel had been "well aware of the nature of the surgery and its necessity."[34] Nagel and her second husband divorced in 1957. A longtime alcoholic, Nagel died July 6, 1966, following surgery for cancer of the liver. She was 50.

Tala Birell went on to featured roles in such horror films as *The Monster Maker* (PRC, 1944) and *The Frozen Ghost* (Universal, 1945). She eventually returned to Berlin as a Command Entertainment Director and staged shows for U.S. troops. She died of cancer in Germany in 1958 at age 50.

Maris Wrixon appeared in such "B" pictures as *White Pongo* (1945), did some TV work, and died in Santa Monica in 1999 at the age of 82.

Gisela Werbisek won a certain fame as Al-Long, the witch in the cult horror movie *Bride of the Gorilla* (1951). She died in Hollywood in 1956, age 81.

The director of these ladies, Steve Sekely, went on to direct such PRC films as *Lady in the Death House*, with Lionel Atwill and Jean Parker, and *Waterfront*, with John Carradine and J. Carrol Naish (both in 1944). He also directed the notable science fiction film *The Day of the Triffids* (1963). As a countryman of Bela Lugosi, he attended the latter's funeral in 1956, serving as a pallbearer. Sekely died in Palm Springs, California, on March 9, 1980, at the age of 79.

*   *   *

Today, *Women in Bondage*, naturally, has a tough time getting past its title. Yet it's definitely worth the effort. For whatever one ultimately thinks of the movie, it's fascinating to compare it with its rivals, RKO's *Hitler's Children* and MGM's *Hitler's Madman*.

Hitler's Children, the true "sleeper" and best-remembered of the trio, is slick, solid 1943-style studio moviemaking. Tim Holt and Bonita Granville are attractive and moving as the doomed lovers, Edward Dmytryk directs with punch, and the film delivers sensation without ever going overboard. Indeed, it rather underplays the sterilization episode that attracted so much attention. Its success is understandable; it presented the goods without ever becoming offensive.

Hitler's Madman is passionate, to the point of raw melodrama, directed with purple flourish by Douglas Sirk. John Carradine is truly nightmarish as Heydrich and the film's finale, the ghosts of the slaughtered villagers of Lidice reciting Edna St. Vincent Millay's poem "The Murder of Lidice" as the Nazi-destroyed village burns behind them, provides an almost spiritual finale. "Sensational!" proclaimed *Hitler's Madman*'s posters, and it delivered.[35]

Women in Bondage differs profoundly from these predecessors. For all its Poverty Row trappings, and Monogram's obvious craving to cash in on Nazi horror, what prevails is the courage of the title women. It even dares to present its chief Nazi monster as a female; indeed, the male villains are either weak or basically anonymous. Gail Patrick and Nancy Kelly—the latter especially moving, despite her on-the-set weeping about the dialogue—are both excellent, as is Gertrude Michael in her appropriately despicable performance. Director Sekely properly places the accent on the heroics and heartbreak.

One would hardly expect to find a feminist message in a 1943 film from Monogram called *Women in Bondage*, but there it is.

Some years before his death, Steve Sekely had donated his *Women in Bondage* script to the USC Library for Performing Arts. The old script was incomplete, missing pages, but marked throughout with Sekely's annotations. They revealed the passion and intelligence that he, along with his fine and devoted cast, brought to a movie that transfigured its exploitative purpose and become a moving, ahead-of-its-time study of women bravely facing horrific odds.

A "peep show," perhaps ... but a very valiant one.

Women in Bondage

Monogram, 1943. Producer, Herman Millakowsky. Associate Producer, Jeffrey Bernerd. Director, Steve Sekely. Screenplay, Houston Branch. Original Story, Frank Wisbar. Cinematographer, Mack Stengler. Musical Director, Edward Kay. Production Manager, William Strobach. Dialogue Director, Harold Erickson. Technical Director, Dave Milton. Sound Recording, Tom Lambert. Editor, Richard Currier. Makeup Artist, Fred Walker. Wardrobe, Harry Bourne. Set Dresser, Al Greenwood. Assistant Director, Eddie Davis. Technical Adviser, Frank Wisbar. Original title: *Hitler's Women*. Running time, 71 minutes.

World premiere, Palace Theatre, Milwaukee, December 9, 1943. Hollywood opening, Hawaii Theatre, March 2, 1944. New York opening, Gotham Theatre, March 25, 1944.

The Cast: Gail Patrick (Margot Bracken), Nancy Kelly (Toni Hall), Gertrude Michael (Deputy Director Gertrude Schneider), Anne Nagel (Deputy District Director), Tala Birell (Ruth Bracken), Mary Forbes (Gladys Bracken), Maris Wrixon (Grete Ziegler), Gisela Werbisek (Grandmother), Rita Quigley (Herta Rumann), Francine Bordeaux (Litzl Neumann), Una Franks (Blonde), William Henry (Heinz Radtke), H.B. Warner (Pastor Renz), Alan Baxter (Otto Bracken), Felix Basch (Dr. Mensch), Roland Varno (Ernst Bracken), Ralph Lynn (Corp. Mueller), Frederic Brunn (District Leader), John Merton (SS Officer), Wally Patch (German Soldier), Hermine Sterler (German Mother).

The Odyssey of Mildred Davenport— to Acquanetta—to Paula the Ape Woman

Every day was Halloween!
—Acquanetta in 1992, remembering playing
Paula the Ape Woman in *Captive Wild
Woman* and *Jungle Woman*[1]

FLESH of Beauty! SOUL of Satan!
—poster copy for *Jungle Woman*, 1944

Vicious Hitlerian slander ... both Captive Wild Woman *and* Jungle Woman
*imply a natural affinity between Negroes and apes. Nazis in Germany have
been taught such things by Goebbels.*
—David Platt, *The Daily Worker*, July 30, 1944[2]

It just might be the most jaw-dropping moment, sociologically, of any horror film ever released by Universal.

Captive Wild Woman, 1943. A leering mad doctor, played by John Carradine, has brought forth into 1940s melodrama a strange new being, mixing the raging sex hormones of a female patient, the brain of a murdered nurse, and the host body of a female gorilla he stole from a circus. The racy result: a dusky, sexy, pouty young beauty whom the crazed doctor christens Paula Dupree.

Alas, sexual jealousy torments her—and as the animal in Paula cries to be unleashed, she reverts ... not into a gorilla, but into something more tantalizingly horrid ... an Ape Woman.

In between the two stages, Paula turns Black.

Thus, World War II–era Universal, via *Captive Wild Woman*, was virtually proliferating the vile Nazi credo that a Black person is "a half-born ape."[3] The studio was shooting the movie in December 1942, when many families of soldiers fighting the forces of the rabidly racist Nazis were receiving Yuletide season telegrams reporting their sons had been killed in battle.

The most shocking irony of all: The starlet playing Paula the Ape Woman was African-American.

Of course, Universal, at the time, didn't know it. Acquanetta, who had created the role of Paula, was then claiming to be a Native American. And the brief scene of a black Paula the Ape Woman was almost certainly just a horribly bad makeup choice, and not the insidious work of a Hollywood underground Nazi coven poisoning the content of American entertainment.

A Universal *Captive Wild Woman* publicity shot of Acquanetta as Paula Dupree, "the Ape Woman." The chains in the picture are a shocker, especially if one knows the true story of the actress' ancestry (from the John Antosiewicz Collection).

Captive Wild Woman spawned two sequels, *Jungle Woman* (1944) and *The Jungle Captive* (1945). Interestingly, take a poll of Universal horror disciples for "Worst Studio Horror Film of 1931 to 1948," and a major contender certainly would be *Jungle Woman,* the second installment of Paula the Ape Woman's tragic trilogy.

This chapter will try to answer two questions:

Was Acquanetta actually an anguished, freakishly victimized African American starlet?

And does her alter ego, Paula the Ape Woman, lurk in Universal's horror canon as a genuine World War II cinema nightmare?

Part One: Burnu Acquanetta

Tales of a Would-Be Scheherazade

Universal City, California, June 1942.

There was a new starlet, who called herself Burnu Acquanetta. She was a tall, dark-skinned brunette who had been a popular fashion model for both Harry Conover and John Powers in New York City.

Her soubriquet: "The Venezuelan Volcano."

Burnu Acquanetta was en route to Rio when she stopped in at Hollywood's Mocambo night club and attracted the eye of producer Walter Wanger. A Universal screen test resulted.

Monday, June 29, 1942: Walter Wanger's *Arabian Nights*, starring Maria Montez, started shooting at Universal. "Acquanetta" played Ishyia, one of a trio of "Bewitching Harem Queens."

If it all sounds like a Cinderella fable, you should have seen and heard Acquanetta herself tell it.

Fast-forward 50 years to August 1992. Acquanetta—still known simply as Acquanetta—was a guest at the FANEX convention in Baltimore, Maryland. The fans beheld a fireball who proudly admitted to 70, was still tall and shapely, flashed a dazzling smile, and wore a crown of jet-black hair that appeared to be a wig. (Her middle-aged female traveling companion wearily admitted one evening, when Acquanetta was out of earshot, that mornings started very early, due to the ex-star's glamorization rituals.)

Before the convention, on a telephone from her home in Arizona, Acquanetta had regaled me regarding her Hollywood legend and lore, including her discovery:

> *Maria Montez had already been signed for* Arabian Nights. *They tried to get her to give it up and let* me *star in it. Walter Wanger, Dan Kelley* [the casting director], *all the Universal brass—they said of me,* "She is our Scheherazade." *See, Maria Montez—they made her up beautifully, but she didn't have good features.*
>
> *I have* great *features!*

Back to 1942 … *Arabian Nights* continued shooting. All went well until Acquanetta, joining the Screen Actors Guild, had to prove that she was a native of Venezuela and present her passport.

She didn't have one.

First, the starlet accused her hotel of having lost her suitcase in which she had packed the document. Then came a proud confession—from the "Volcano" herself: "I chose the Latin American background because it was exotic and fitted my type," she told reporters. "But … as a matter of fact, boys, I'm proud of being a full-blooded Indian."

"LATINS 'GIFT TO FILMS' JUST U.S. INDIAN GIRL" headlined the July 20, 1942, edition of *The Miami News*. Hollywood gossip columnist Paul Harrison, noting that Acquanetta's accent wavered into Spanish and French, skeptically went after the truth, and published his account on July 28:

> *She said she was born July 17, 1921, at Ozone, Wyoming, but didn't know what part of the state it's in—nor do U.S. postal authorities. Her father, she said, was an Arapaho named Laughing Water, and her mother was an Arapaho named Blue Skies. Her own name was Burning Fire. She claimed to have thought up "Burnu Acquanetta" as a contraction of all three Indian names.*
>
> *She was orphaned at 3, she continued, and went to live with an Indian woman…. For seven years they traveled around Oklahoma and Colorado, Acquanetta said. I asked where, specifically, and she answered vaguely, "Always we leeved on the outskirts of towns, and for a while we leeved in a Gypsy camp, and they sang sad songs."*

Harrison, exasperated, wrote in his column, "I decided that if Burnu Acquanetta's story is accurate in detail, I am the grandmother of General De Gaulle."

Universal starlet "Burnu Acquanetta." She claimed she was Arapaho-born.

Monday, August 24: Acquanetta, as a result of the publicity, received a three-page story and layout in *Life* magazine. Meanwhile, Universal announced that she would join the all-star lineup in its new feature *Flesh and Fantasy*. Maria Montez reluctantly accepted her as a Universal colleague.

At least she's not one of those "hatchet-faced Indians," said La Montez.[4]

Acquanetta appeared destined for kitschy Universal celebrity. Her publicity photos, be they of her in a black negligee or her *Arabian Nights* "Harem Queen" costume, were an eyeful. Her large smile was toothy, almost predatory. Her figure was voluptuous, she had long, shapely legs, and her proud, shoulders-back, fashion-model-on-a-runway walk was a stunner. She had all the ingredients that appealed to the more exotic-minded audiences and the more "extreme" element of fans. In 1944, she made the news after a fan-fetishist stole all 28 pairs of her shoes.[5]

Shadows, however, lurked under the hype.

The Davenport Family

In 1992, Acquanetta explained to me her ancestry and early life. Note the inconsistencies with what she'd told Paul Harrison:

> *My mother was Arapaho, and my father was part Cherokee. Actually, my father had an interesting background: my father's father was the illegitimate son of the king of England and a French Jewess....*
>
> *I was given away to a family in Norristown, Pennsylvania, when I was only a few years old. They had the name of Davenport, and the foster parents gave me the name of Mildred, which I used all through school—and which doesn't suit me at all, at all, at all! But before he left me there, my father sat me down and told me my background, and how my mother had died, and my real name—which, years later, I would take.*

Had Universal truly cared to investigate—and based on later developments, they eventually did—they would have learned the truth, just as Scott Gallinghouse[6] did when he recently explored the true ancestry of Acquanetta:

The 1920 Federal Census listed William Daniel Davenport (1894–1974) and Julia Mae Green Davenport (1892–1980) as married and living in Newberry, South Carolina. The Census noted the family's race as mulatto. By 1920, the Davenports had four children: Edward (1914–2001), Caroline (later referred to as Carolyn, 1916–1998), Winifred (1917–2006) and Horace (1919–2017). When Horace died in 2017, having outlived all his siblings, *The Philadelphia Daily News* headlined his obituary, "HORACE DAVENPORT, 98, FIRST AFRICAN-AMERICAN JUDGE IN MONTCO [Montgomery County]."

Mildred Davenport was born in South Carolina on July 17, 1921 (some sources say 1920). She was followed by a sister, Kathryn (1923–2012), and a brother, William (1924–1995). The Davenports and their seven children, dreaming of a better life, eventually crossed the Mason-Dixon Line and settled in Norristown, about 20 miles northwest of Philadelphia.

In 1938, Mildred Davenport's senior portrait appeared in the yearbook for Norristown Area High School. The smiling teenage girl in the photograph was clearly African-American. Several of the students pictured on the same page were also obviously Black; the others were clearly Caucasian, as many Pennsylvania public schools of that time were integrated.

The Yearbook listed Mildred as having taken the General Course and having been Home Room secretary. She was president of the Social Service Club and a member of the debating team, the correspondence club and the hiking club. Two years later, the 1940 Census reported that William and Julia Davenport were residing on Green Street in Norristown in a house built in 1880. Six of the seven children were still living at home, including Mildred. The house still stands.

At some point in the early 1940s, Mildred decided to pursue her dream. She headed

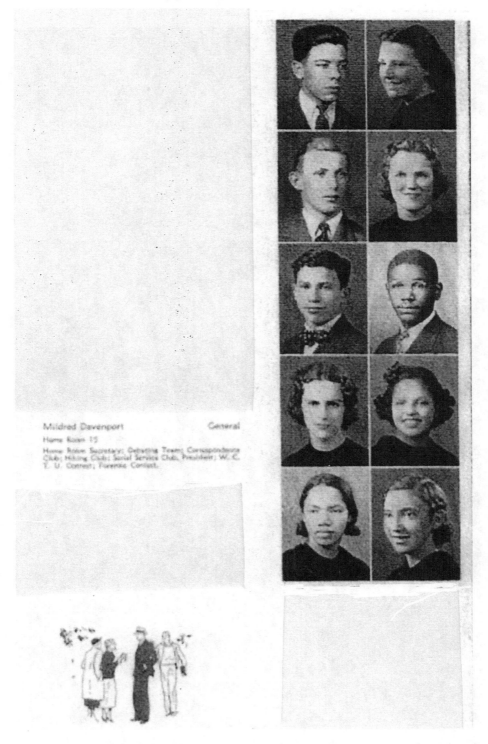

Mildred Davenport's photograph as it appears in the 1938 Norristown Area Senior High School Yearbook (courtesy of Scott Gallinghouse).

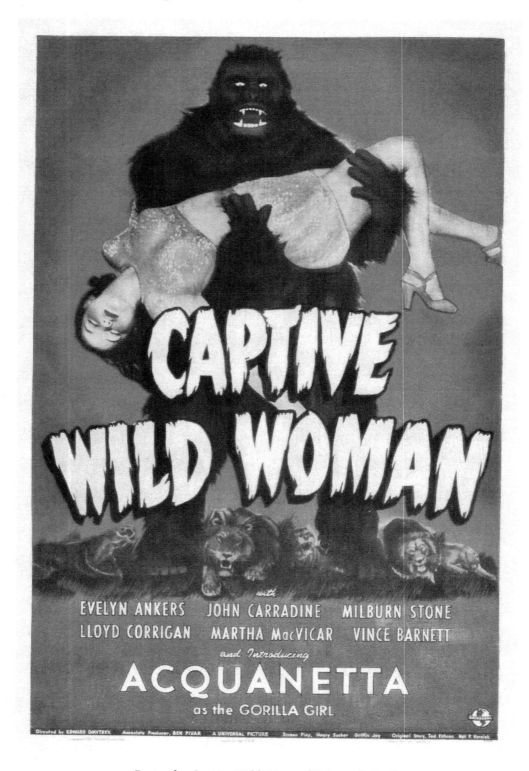

Poster for *Captive Wild Woman* (Universal, 1943).

to New York City, attracted attention, claimed she was from Valencia, Venezuela, and became a high-profile model. The trip to Hollywood followed, and the Universal contract.

Yet Acquanetta's projected takeoff to stardom stalled. The *Flesh and Fantasy* role fell through. The studio tossed her into *Rhythm of the Islands*, a 60-minute musical starring Allan Jones and Jane Frazee. "And Introducing Acquanetta," read the poster for *Rhythm of the Islands*, in which she played a native girl named Luani. Directing the film: Roy William Neill, who had just wrapped *Frankenstein Meets the Wolf Man*.

Meanwhile, a very strange stardom awaited Acquanetta in the wings ... vicious and ready to pounce.

Part Two: Introducing Paula the Ape Woman

Captive Wild Woman

In early December 1942, Universal began shooting *Captive Wild Woman*, a circus horror melodrama whipped up by four male writers.[7]

The film top-billed John Carradine in his first bona fide starring horror role, and it was a wild and worthy one. Dr. Sigmund Walters is a 1942 Dr. Frankenstein, in a black slouch hat and mustache who, the exposition tells us, has managed to "change the breed and sex of animals." He creates his alluring monstrosity Paula Dupree via intriguing sources:

Source One: Pretty patient Dorothy (Martha MacVicar, later known as Martha Vickers), who suffers from a cyst that, as Dr. Walters expresses it, "secretes an abnormal amount of sex hormones"—quite a lurid malady for an early 1940s movie. For film *noir* fans, Dorothy's dire diagnosis was prophetic: Vickers later played Carmen, the thumb-sucking nympho in Warners' *The Big Sleep* (1946) with Bogart and Bacall. (Vickers had been Lon Chaney's full-moon victim in *Frankenstein Meets the Wolf Man*; from 1949 to 1952, she was the third Mrs. Mickey Rooney.)

Source Two: There's Nurse Strand (Fay Helm, victim of Bela Lugosi's werewolf in *The Wolf Man*, and Margaret Ingston, who burns herself alive in *Night Monster*). Nurse Strand warns Dr. Walters of his gorilla-into-girl experiment, "What will you have? A human form with animal instincts!" He responds by killing the nurse and popping her brain into his creation.

Source Three: There's Cheela (Ray "Crash" Corrigan), a female gorilla captured in the jungle and brought to the States for the circus. Carradine's Dr. Walters steals Cheela, strapping her on an operating table in his Crestview Sanitorium laboratory, transforming her into a human female.

By the way, Crestview Sanitorium is "played" by the Universal back lot's Shelby House, originally built—ironically considering *Captive Wild Woman*'s "racist" content—for 1927's *Uncle Tom's Cabin*.[8]

Surgery, accompanied by Hans J. Salter's reprise of *Son of Frankenstein* music, and we behold Walters' unholy Paula. The swarthy young lady (who never speaks) soon

Mad doctor John Carradine unveils his part-animal, part-human creation, Paula Dupree. Acquanetta's features here are rather revealing (from the John Antosiewicz Collection).

reveals a strange power over the Big Top beasts, who sense her unnatural being and fear her. She joins the circus, standing outside the Big Cat cage in her sexy, skimpy, Vera West–designed circus costume as lion tamer Fred Mason (Milburn Stone) handles the roaring cats.

The plot thickens as Paula falls in love (lust?) with Fred … and sees he already has a fiancée, the blonde and rather bountiful Beth (Universal's "Scream Queen" Evelyn Ankers). Sexually jealous, Paula—those transplanted, abnormally vibrant sex hormones raging—vents violently, throws a topsy-turvy tantrum and trashes her dressing room. And, as mentioned earlier, she changes into an Ape Woman, with a Black person transition stage.

Didn't this appall anyone working on the film? What about the 34-year-old director Edward Dmytryk, whose liberal proclivities eventually landed him on the Hollywood Blacklist?[9] (Dmytryk told interviewer Tom Weaver that the dark makeup simply seemed to him to be a natural transition from ape to ape-woman.) What about Jack Pierce, who designed and applied all stages of the Ape Woman makeup, including the heinous middle one?

And, most of all, considering her real-life background … what about Acquanetta herself?

It was the holiday season, and apparently everyone at Universal was merry … and

Left to right: *Captive Wild Woman* **cast members Lloyd Corrigan, Milburn Stone, Evelyn Ankers, Vince Barnett, Acquanetta, and John Carradine (from the John Antosiewicz Collection).**

oblivious. There was John Carradine, visions of stage stardom dancing in his head (he founded John Carradine and His Shakespeare Players the following year), leering away like a Wild West tragedian playing Iago in a Gold Rush saloon. There was Evelyn Ankers, nestled snug in her bed as Paula the Ape Woman crept through her window. There was "Crash" Corrigan, prancing and pawing in his gorilla suit. And there was Milburn Stone, grateful for the gift of a romantic lead, even if he got it only because he was as diminutive as wild animal tamer Clyde Beatty. Shots from Universal's *The Big Cage* (1933), starring Beatty, provided most of the animal action in *Captive Wild Woman.*

A half-century later, Acquanetta bubbled like a wide-eyed starlet as she recalled the prime movers of the *Captive Wild Woman* company:

> *John was beautiful ... always acting—on stage and off! ... He was Carradine—and he wanted people to know it! ... I've always felt he was an actor from his first incarnation! Evelyn ... always very friendly and warm and just a lovely, delightful lady.... Edward Dmytryk? What a nice man. I think he was single at the time, and he tried to date me.... Eddie was just a big brother, with a lot of talent.... Jack Pierce ... very nice, very straight, no kidding around.... The makeup ... sometimes it would take two hours ... the hair on the face and the fangs and all that....*

Of course, Acquanetta had her tall tales too. For example, she vowed that there was a *real* gorilla on the set, and when she showed up in her Ape Woman makeup, the gorilla came bounding after her.

"I mean, it wanted to *embrace* me," she attested, making sure I understood.

She claimed the trainer hit the gorilla with a club, and the ape went away with a chain around him. (Edward Dmytryk told Tom Weaver there was never an actual gorilla on the set.)

Captive Wild Woman climaxed with Cheela, in full gorilla form, released from her cage by Ankers and mauling Carradine to death. Cheela lopes off to the circus this wild night, where a storm has upset the caged beasts, and a lion is chewing Stone. The smitten gorilla enters the cage, saving her man, carrying him over her shoulder to safety. A policeman fires a fatal bullet into Cheela's furry back, and she tumbles into the sawdust.

The Wolf Man, when killed, reverts to Lawrence Talbot. Paula the Ape Woman, when killed, remains Cheela.

George Robinson's camerawork was, as always, aces; so was Hans J. Salter's score. Universal set *Captive Wild Woman* for late spring release.

Paula the Ape Woman, up close and personal (from the John Antosiewicz Collection).

Meanwhile, on New Year's Eve, 1942, as the Allied Forces fought to conquer "the Master Race" in Europe and *Captive Wild Woman* was wrapping up in Hollywood, the Tuskegee Institute of Alabama made a grim announcement. The *New York Times* reported it the next day on page 17, under the headline "Five Negroes Lynched In 1942":

> *Mobs lynched five persons in the United States during 1942, one more than in the preceding year.... The lynchings all took place in the South, and the victims were all Negroes, according to the report.*

"This Film Must Be Stopped"

Wednesday, March 24, 1943. The *Daily Worker*, America's Communist newspaper, picked up the feral scent of *Captive Wild Woman*, although Universal hadn't yet previewed it. On this day, David Platt, who wrote *The Daily Worker*'s "Film Front" column, reported:

> Universal's *Captive Wild Woman is an open and shut case of Hitler propaganda against Negroes but the Hays Office and the OWI [Office of War Information] passed it without comment. Are they blind? ... Do they really expect to get away with it?* The Daily Worker *tried to get the company to show the film before an audience of Negroes and whites but they refused on the grounds that the picture is "not controversial" as far as they are concerned.*
>
> *Universal is guilty and readers of* The Daily Worker *are demanding action....*

Platt's column went on to cite a letter from one Lawrence Pepper ("typical of many received here"). Pepper's letter called *Captive Wild Woman*

> *...a movie which is utterly shocking and a much clearer-cut insult to the Negro people than* Gone with the Wind*.... It shows a doctor trying to make a human being out of an ape; after various glands transplanted, etc., the ape has turned into a Negro girl. The conclusion to be drawn is clear: that the Negro is one step above the ape and one or more steps below the white human being. This film must be stopped. I've already written strong letters to Universal Pictures, [in] New York City, and to the Bureau of Films, OWI, in Washington. Every democratic-minded person should do the same.*

An interesting facet to the above letter was that the writer, who hadn't seen the movie, mistakenly believed the movie presents Acquanetta as "a Negro girl" even in her first scene as Paula, and before the transition-to-ape girl. (In truth, she does appear African-American in her first appearance after Carradine removes the facial bandages.)

Universal's response to the protest?

Tuesday, April 13: "UNIVERSAL SILENT ON *CAPTIVE*," headlined *The Daily Worker*. David Platt went on, hotly waging war against the film and the studio:

> *Why is Universal so reluctant to discuss* Captive Wild Woman, *the horror quickie which* The Daily Worker *recently charged was anti–Negro?*
>
> *If the movie company is innocent as it claims it is, why are Universal's officials so secretive about the picture; why their persistent refusal to test this picture before a select audience of Negroes and whites?*
>
> *Is Universal so impervious to public criticism that they can ignore the protests of the National Negro Congress.... What's behind this public-be-damned attitude?*

The article reported that Joe Bostic, editor of Harlem's *People's Voice* newspaper, was also fighting Universal and receiving a "similar rebuff." The conclusion of Bostic: "[T]he company is not averse to peddling anti–Negro propaganda." A "Mr. Lines" of Universal told Bostic that any comment on the film was "premature and out of order until the picture had been released."

Platt, however, found this argument unacceptable, and wrote:

> *... Universal's officers in New York know all about* Captive Wild Woman, *and they don't seem to care what people think. Bostic said Universal admitted receiving many protests but they are all being ignored "on the ground that they have come from progressive elements."*
>
> *... Universal's secrecy with regard to* Captive Wild Woman *amounts to a confession of guilt.* The Daily Worker *agrees with* People's Voice *that the people should prepare to let this one have all the guns if it does attempt to tell any* Mein Kampf *racial theories.*

The reference to "guns" was probably figurative, although if the rumors were accurate, violence was certainly possible.

Universal decided to take its chances.

Saturday, June 5: Captive Wild Woman opened at the Rialto Theatre, New York City's horror salon. The credits read, "And Introducing Acquanetta"—despite her two previous films. The posters proclaimed,

and introducing a Sensation in Savagery!
ACQUANETTA
As the Gorilla Girl!

Also retrospectively disturbing is a *Captive Wild Woman* production still of Acquanetta: It shows her in a skimpy circus costume, with chains.

The New York Times' Thomas Pryor, reviewing *Captive Wild Woman*, cited no *Mein Kampf* flavoring, yet the film clearly got under his skin:

> In some respects, Universal has outdone itself with its latest monstrous wonder-child, an orang-utan which takes on the appearance of Burnu Acquanetta, and vice versa...Either you decide to meet this bit of scientific hocus-pocus at its own inane level or else you are likely to get hopping mad.... The picture as a whole is in decidedly bad taste.[10]

There were no disturbances reported at the Rialto, and the first week take was $10,800—"stout," as *Variety* described it. The hold-over second week dropped to $6500, with $5000 in its third.[11] *Variety* reported that the film had earned a "substantial profit" for the Rialto.

Tuesday, July 13: Attorney General Francis Biddle announced this night in Washington, D.C. the indictment of 13 persons, including a sheriff and three deputy sheriffs, "in the lynching of a Negro near Paris, Illinois." The victim was James E. Person, who had served in World War II before being honorably discharged. He was lynched October 12, 1942, but his body wasn't discovered until November 26. *The New York Times* reported:

> Person, the indictment set forth, had committed no offense, and no warrant was outstanding for his arrest. It further said that no one had probable or reasonable cause to believe, or reliable information to indicate, that Person had committed, or would commit, any crime.[12]

In a nation where this could happen, was it madness to release and promote *Captive Wild Woman*?

Thursday, July 22: Universal's double bill of *Frankenstein Meets the Wolf Man* and *Captive Wild Woman* ("2nd THRILL HIT! Can You Take It?") opened at Los Angeles' Paramount Theatre as well as Hollywood's Paramount Theatre. The combined first week take was a giant $40,000; the second week, $16,500.[13]

How was Acquanetta faring in the reviews? When *Captive Wild Woman* visited Baltimore's Keith's Theatre, Donald Kirkley of the *Sun* called the movie "[o]ne of the goofiest thriller-dillers ever filmed" and wrote:

> ...the gorilla emerges in the guise of a Latin American–type beauty with a somewhat blank countenance and shapely figure, answering to the name of Acquanetta.... This is Acquanetta's screen debut [sic], and it is a remarkable one, in that she utters not a single word, not even a Tarzanian grunt....
> She shows very little animation, and doesn't even react strongly when her mirror tells her that she is turning back into a gorilla, or when she is prowling by night and digging her fingernails into various necks. In other words, Acquanetta is the tamest wild woman you ever saw.[14]

Acquanetta had her champions: *Photoplay* called her "stunning" in *Captive Wild Woman*. The film was a moderate hit, and truly—despite the conventional wisdom on 80-year-old horror movies—Acquanetta wasn't bad. She wasn't good, either, but she was strikingly attractive as the human Paula, walking like a proud Copacabana showgirl, and wearing her Ape Woman makeup with a quiet dignity (except for the inexcusable flash of her in transitional blackface).

She had *presence* ... and certainly sex appeal.

Thus, with this 61-minute potboiler, Acquanetta sashayed into the pantheon of Universal female monsters—joining the trio of vampire brides and the Woman in White of *Dracula*, Elsa Lanchester's magnificent Bride of Frankenstein, and Gloria Holden's moody Dracula's Daughter. (Louise Allbritton's vampire bride of *Son of Dracula* followed later in 1943.) Surely there was a kinship with Kathleen Burke's tragic Lota, the Panther Woman of Paramount's *Island of Lost Souls,* and her own "stubborn beast flesh creeping back." And Acquanetta was now in a select cinema sorority that claimed Simone Simon and Elizabeth Russell, the two feline beauties of *Cat People*.

Of course, *Captive Wild Woman* fell woefully short of that Big League. There's a stale mixed scent of perfume and circus cages in this erotic yarn, concocted by the male writers who spiked female hormones into mad Dr. Walters' brew. The outrage of *The Daily Worker* and *People's Voice* was painfully valid: *Captive Wild Woman,* for all its fun horror flourishes, was inexcusable entertainment for a 1943 America. It would have fit better in 1943 Germany as the supporting feature in a revival of 1935's Nazi propaganda epic, *Triumph of the Will*.

For 2022 audiences, the film amazes and appalls, although perhaps fortunately, many horror fans take it as simply a rambunctious 79-year-old "B" horror flick. Show *Captive Wild Woman* to the wrong crowd, and you'd likely have a problem. Among its inflammatory ingredients is the death scene of Paula, now fully reverted to Cheela: a policeman shoots her in the back.

The question: What did Acquanetta think of *Captive Wild Woman*?

She was clearly a bright young lady. Did the transformation from white woman to black woman to ape give her pause? Did she feel, considering the facts of her ancestry, that this was an agonizingly ironic "vehicle" to advance her dream of stardom?

Did she privately ponder the abhorrent racism of the film? Did she suppress her feelings because her career was at stake? Did it frighten her? Shame her? Did she imagine the possibility that her parents or siblings would see her in this film? Did she wonder how it might hurt them? Did she specifically think of her sister Carolyn, who in 1942, the year Acquanetta went to Hollywood, began her own very notable career with the NAACP?[15]

Finally, how did it affect *her*? Was the 71-year-old diva at FANEX a performance by a survivor who had compartmentalized all these aspects—and was haunted by how she'd attained her celebrity?

When I interviewed Acquanetta in 1992, I hadn't learned of the protests of the "progressives" in 1943. I knew no specific details of her ancestry. And, admittedly, I treaded lightly about the racist aspects of *Captive Wild Woman*, wrapping them in my remarks about Paula Dupree being the "outsider" that most Universal Monsters were.

She became oddly quiet, suddenly subdued. All the flamboyance and braggadocio disappeared … vanished.

"I *became* her," Acquanetta said softly.

Was Paula Dupree fated to haunt Acquanetta, so that the horror fiction and racial fact would meld?

Or, as an outsider professing to be someone she wasn't, was Acquanetta before 1943, *already* Paula Dupree?

M.I.A. in 1943

In 1943, Universal kept its contractees busy. Evelyn Ankers, for example, appeared in nine releases.

Acquanetta appeared in only two: *Rhythm of the Islands* and *Captive Wild Woman*. And both had been shot in 1942.

In August 1943—after *Captive Wild Woman*'s early engagements and eight months after its production—Universal finally cast Acquanetta in a new film, *The Mummy's Ghost*, starring Lon Chaney as Kharis the Mummy and John Carradine as the Mummy's high priest. Acquanetta's role: Amina, a college coed who is the reincarnation of Kharis' love, the Princess Ananka.

Shooting began Monday, August 23, 1943. Acquanetta lasted until August 25. Walking in a scene in a trance and her nightgown, she fainted, struck her head on a rock, and reportedly suffered a concussion.

On August 27, the *Los Angeles Times* headlined "'HORROR QUEEN' OF SCREEN HURT." As with so many things in Acquanetta's life, this story has multiple versions. Reginald LeBorg, director of *The Mummy's Ghost*, remembered that the actress was so nervous—this was, after all, her first star role with dialogue—that she actually fainted and knocked herself out.[16] Acquanetta claimed she was simply playing her role: Amina was supposed to faint (which is true). She reported that there were "scabs" working that day, replacing striking crew members, and they had used *real* rocks instead of *papier-mâché* rocks. Since she was (in her words) "very realistic" in her acting, she'd fallen, hitting her head on a real rock.

"I could have been killed!" Acquanetta exclaimed.

The inevitable question: Why did there need to be rocks in this scene, and if there had to be rocks, why weren't they cleared from where Acquanetta was supposed to faint? At any rate, the *Los Angeles Examiner* reported that she was unconscious "for more than 16 hours." Keeping watch at her bedside at Cedars of Lebanon Hospital: actor Barry Nelson.[17]

Ramsay Ames replaced Acquanetta as Amina in *The Mummy's Ghost*.

No roles immediately followed, but inane publicity did. For example, on September 19, 1943, the *New York Daily News* announced that a Siberian regiment had selected Acquanetta as "The Girl They'd Like to Sit on the Steppes With."

Then came the concept of making a sequel to *Captive Wild Woman*. This time, Universal might have taken a cue from MGM and Garbo and advertised it with the come-on slogan ACQUANETTA TALKS.

The title originally was *Jungle Queen*. It would soon change to *Jungle Woman*, and posterity would crown it a prime contender for the worst horror film of the era.

Reasons for *Jungle Woman*'s infamy? Shall we count the ways?

- It's a rip-off sequel to 1943's *Captive Wild Woman*, with much of the first 15 minutes of the 60-minute film padded with footage from the previous movie.
- Even super character actor J. Carrol Naish looks blah.
- It tries to emulate the rival Val Lewton horror films in its evocative use of shadows and suggestion, but generally falls flat on its Ape Woman face.
- It showcases Acquanetta, widely regarded as an atrocious actress.
- Although it's largely free of the goose-stepping effrontery of the original film, the mere fact that it was produced at all was enough to doom it.

Part Three: *Jungle Woman*

Pre-Production

Nineteen forty-four was a big year for Horror at Universal City.

Boris Karloff was back on the lot, after his three-year romp in *Arsenic and Old Lace*

Poster for *Jungle Woman* (Universal, 1944).

on Broadway and on tour. Also, 1944 would be the only year in the studio's history in which virtually all the goblins in the Universal canon cavorted in movies filmed within the same 12-month period.

- *The Invisible Man's Revenge* shot in January, with Jon Hall in the title role.
- *House of Frankenstein* shot in April and May, with mad doctor Boris Karloff and

hunchback J. Carrol Naish unleashing Lon Chaney's Wolf Man, John Carradine's
Dracula and Glenn Strange's Frankenstein Monster.
- *The Mummy's Curse* shot in August, Lon Chaney again galumphing as Kharis the
Mummy.

And, as if to celebrate diversity—sexual and (unpublicized) racial—Universal
decided to set Paula Dupree loose on another fling, starring who else but…. Acquanetta?

Thursday, January 27, 1944: Joseph Breen, having read the January 19 first script
for *Jungle Woman*, wrote to Universal: "[We] regret to report that this script appears to
us to be unacceptable under the provisions of the Production by reason of a flavor of
bestiality."[18]

It was a juicy charge, to be sure. Breen wrote that members of his office had met the
previous day with the film's executive producer Ben Pivar[19] and producer Will Cowan,[20]
talking about that "unacceptable flavor" and deciding on a revised script. Breen warned:

- *The District Attorney should be played with dignity and not unsympathetically as
  now indicated.*
- *There should be no suggestion that Paula is naked at any time where she is changing
  from animal to human form.*
- *Unacceptable gruesomeness should be avoided at all times.*

Friday, January 31: As the script underwent revision, Pivar authorized a payment of
$750 to Clyde Beatty for the use of footage of him and his animals from Universal's 1933
The Big Cage to be used here as flashbacks. Beatty, of course, had already collected a payment for the use of this same footage in *Captive Wild Woman*.

The basic revised scenario, as whipped up by Bernard L. Schubert, Henry Sucher
and Edward Dein[21]:

Dr. Carl Fletcher, a brilliant (if not very prepossessing) scientist, is in the circus
audience the fateful stormy night that Cheela, having saved Fred Mason from a lion, is
shot by a policeman. Fascinated, Fletcher attends to the wounded Cheela, detecting a
faint respiration, and he nurses her back to health. Obsessed by her history, he purchases
the late Dr. Sigmund Walters' Crestview Sanitarium and his medical records. Then comes
the moment when Willie, Fletcher's mentally challenged handyman (and patient?),
brings him dire news: Cheela has trashed the lab and disappeared. (Aside from the flashbacks, virtually all of the preceding action is not seen, only described.)

Shortly thereafter, wide-eyed Willie finds a brunette beauty wandering the area, as
if in a trance. At first, she's silent. However, she soon catches a glimpse of young Bob Whitney, fiancé of Fletcher's perky daughter Joan. Lo! Paula speaks to Bob, and at very close range:

Hello. My name is Paula…

Alas, those aberrant hormones that the late Dr. Walters had provided Paula Dupree
are clearly still ping-ponging in her John Powers fashion model body—and she falls into
lust again, forsaking Fred Mason for Bob. That old mad jealousy surfaces. As Bob and
Joan canoodle in a canoe one moonlit night, Paula swims underwater toward them, over-
turning the canoe with her ape-like strength, unsuccessfully trying to drown Joan.

A watchdog and animals in the countryside are found torn asunder. The body of
poor Willie, who's been ogling Paula, is discovered mutilated in the woods. (All these
atrocities are talked about, not seen.) Paula connives to make it appear that Dr. Fletcher
is a sadist who's abusing her. Climactically, Paula, wild with jealousy, stalks Joan through

the woods. Fletcher tracks her in the night. Paula attacks him like … well, a Captive Wild Woman, and he injects her with a hypodermic needle. Meaning to render her unconscious, he accidentally kills her. (The preceding action is seen in shadows.)

The story unfolds in flashback form, with Dr. Fletcher accused of Paula's murder. Fred and Beth, from *Captive Wild Woman*, now married, testify in the coroner's office. The payoff comes in the morgue. As the principals watch, along with the coroner's jury, an attendant rolls out Paula's corpse … and the cadaver is that of the Ape Woman.

The script, frankly, was a hack job, with ten-and-one-quarter pages of the 94-page script calling for *Captive Wild Woman* flashbacks and stock shots. Yet the script was as interesting for what was *not* in it as what *was*:

- There was no reference to Paula's rampant hormones, or the brain transplant.
- There were no transformation scenes of Paula changing from an ape or into an ape.
- Paula was only glimpsed in action as human; the only Ape Woman shot was of her corpse (and only from the neck-up).
- Although Universal would use footage from *Captive Wild Woman* in *Jungle Woman*, it would *not* use the transformation scene where Paula turns from white human to black human to gorilla.

The script, bad as it was, inferred that Universal was semi-sorry for its sins on *Captive Wild Woman* and, while eager to perpetuate Paula, was careful this time not to offend the "progressive elements."

Tuesday, February 8: Breen approved *Jungle Woman*. He noted that his office had conferred with Will Cowan and fired off what was now Breen's big gun concern: "that great restraint be exercised in the direction of the picture to get away from any suggestion that Paula is in love with Bob." This, of course, would have truly been a major problem: It would imply that an animal desires to mate with a human … shades of *Murders in the Rue Morgue* and *Island of Lost Souls*. (See Chapters 1 and 3 of this book.)

It's interesting that, while Joe Breen must have heard about the controversy regarding *Captive Wild Woman* and its accusations of Nazi propaganda, he made no reference to that film, or those problems, in giving a pass to *Jungle Woman*.

Universal's Production Estimate blueprinted *Jungle Woman*, production # 1573:

- *Shooting schedule and budget*: 12 days and $103,000. Universal films in 1944 rarely if ever came any faster or cheaper. For comparison, *House of Frankenstein*—granted an "all-star" horror extravaganza—would have a 30-day schedule and a $354,000 budget.
- *Director*: Reginald LeBorg. The resourceful LeBorg had already done fine work for Universal on *Calling Dr. Death*, *The Mummy's Ghost* and *Weird Woman*. His fee: $2500.
- *Star*: Evelyn Ankers, reprising her role of Beth from *Captive Wild Woman*. Top-billed in *Jungle Woman*, her role was actually so negligible—delivering a few lines of testimony in the coroner's office—that she was set to complete her part in only two days. As she was contract talent, Universal computed her star salary for *Jungle Woman* as a "flat" $400.

Actually, the "legit" name in *Jungle Woman* was second-billed J. Carrol Naish, as Dr. Fletcher. One of Hollywood's great character actors, Naish was very much in-demand; he'd just wrapped up PRC's *The Monster Maker*, which had started shooting February 7

A *Jungle Woman* shot of Acquanetta as Paula and J. Carrol Naish as Dr. Fletcher. "If he hadn't been married, I think I could have fallen in love with him!" Acquanetta said of her co-star (from the John Antosiewicz Collection).

(only eight days before he reported for work on *Jungle Woman*). More impressively, on the night of February 6, the Academy of Motion Pictures Arts and Sciences had announced the Oscar nominees for 1943, and Naish received his first Best Supporting Actor nomination—for his portrayal of the pitiful Italian solder in Columbia's *Sahara*. Naish's deal for *Jungle Woman:* Two weeks and a total of $3000.

Among the other principals: Milburn Stone was back as Fred, for the same two days as Evelyn Ankers. Although he had considerably more dialogue than Ankers, he got third billing and a "flat" $300. Lois Collier as Joan was set for two weeks and a flat $1400; Richard Davis as Bob, for two weeks and a flat $1000; and Samuel S. Hinds, as the coroner, for two days and a flat $700. As shooting loomed, the studio hadn't cast the pivotal roles of the district attorney or Willie.

So, *Jungle Woman* went into production with an Oscar nominee—but there was no denying who Universal regarded as the true attraction. Acquanetta got special billing on screen and on the posters.

She also got the biggest payday: $4000 for the picture.

The Shoot

As the preceding plot summary suggested, *Jungle Woman*, as scripted, was Universal's rip-off of RKO's *Cat People*. It offered its thinly disguised variations on the Lewton movie's two big shock sequences: The stalk in Central Park, and the swimming pool episode.

Monday, February 14: On this Valentine's Day of 1944, *Jungle Woman* started shooting. The Assistant Director's Daily Report marked the day as "Pre-Production," the only player on call was Acquanetta, and the exterior location was Universal's back lot Pollard Lake.

Director LeBorg was presumably experimenting, with cameraman Jack MacKenzie (who later in 1944 was the cinematographer on Val Lewton's *Isle of the Dead*), on the "shock" episode where Paula attacks Joan and Bob in the canoe. This was a "homage" to *Cat People's* pool scene, where Simone Simon (in shadowy leopard form) terrorized Jane Randolph (screaming in the pool), which Jacques Tourneur and company had shot at the basement pool of the Royal Palms Hotel in downtown Los Angeles.

There was one stand-in for Acquanetta and three stunt people to represent Paula, Joan and Bob. (The Assistant Director Daily Reports do not list their names.) The major goal this day: To create the illusion of an underwater creature (i.e., Paula) who pursues the lovers in the canoe.

The ultimate effect: A swimming monster that resembles a shark in a long black wig.

The Assistant Director's Daily Report credited LeBorg with completing a page and a half of script. The Paula-underwater shots had worked, at least well enough, and *Jungle Woman* was ahead of schedule—although the film officially hadn't started filming yet.

"Everyone treated me like a queen at Universal," Acquanetta said; LeBorg—"a gentleman, with the accent on 'gentle'"—was no exception. Vienna-born, 41 years old, with prematurely gray hair and a mustache, he studied art at the Sorbonne and acting at Max Reinhardt's drama school. When he first arrived in Hollywood, LeBorg staged opera episodes in such films as Grace Moore's *One Night of Love* (1934) and was quite social; he became a frequent guest at soirees given by such luminaries as Basil Rathbone. In fact, he once found himself present at one of Lionel Atwill's notorious orgies.

"When I realized what was going on there," LeBorg told me, "I fled!"

Now grinding 'em out for Universal, LeBorg found the *Jungle Woman* script "atrocious." Taking his cue from the script, he hoped to stylize *Jungle Woman* into an ersatz *Cat People*.

It would be an uphill battle, but LeBorg was eager and willing.

Tuesday, February 15: The company gathered for the first actual day of shooting. The back lot exterior: Universal's Shelby House, representing Crestview Sanitarium, just as it had in *Captive Wild Woman*.

Joining Acquanetta this morning were Lois Collier as Joan and Richard Davis as Bob. Collier was a Universal starlet, recently publicized as "Pin-Up of the Pup Tents." Davis had previously appeared in Universal's *Hat Check Honey* (1944); *Jungle Woman* was his second (and last) film. According to syndicated newspaper columnist Walter Winchell, Davis had been wounded in the War and had "half his face shot away at Casablanca" before being refashioned by plastic surgery.[22]

At 1:00 p.m., J. Carrol Naish officially began work as Dr. Fletcher. Acquanetta told me:

> *I have never known anyone that I have ever liked more without being in love with him. I liked Carrol, I liked his wife and daughter—what a wonderful friend and man he was! No one has ever been kinder or gentler, more caring, more sharing, more instructive—he was just a great pal, a great buddy. If he hadn't been married, I think I could have fallen in love with him! A great actor—he would always give me little pointers, like a big brother ... a beautiful man.*

Naish and Acquanetta had something in common. In 20th Century–Fox's *Dr. Renault's Secret* (1942), Naish had played Noel, the ape man creation of mad George Zucco, who had developed Noel from a gorilla. As such, *Jungle Woman* presented, if one wished to see it this way, a union of Paula the Ape Woman and Noel the Ape Man ... starting the day after Valentine's Day.

As for his performance here... Naish was obviously trying to put over the compassion of Dr. Fletcher; after all, he'd just played an oily, smirking mad scientist in *The Monster Maker* and likely wanted variety. He made Fletcher a soft-spoken, sad soul, clearly wracked by his traumas with Paula. At any rate, with old pro Naish on hand, director LeBorg had a productive day, shooting seven and a half pages.

Wednesday, February 16: The locations were the sanitarium grounds and the woods. Acquanetta, Naish, Collier and Davis started work at 9:00 a.m., as did Edward M. Hyans Jr. as "Willie." Hyans reportedly had come to Hollywood after being medically discharged from the Army—a tank had run over him at Fort Knox, Kentucky![23] Hyans played Willie as if he had a signed portrait of Lon Chaney Jr. from *Of Mice and Men* on his wall at home. In fact, the way Hyans ogled Acquanetta reminds one of the way Chaney's Lennie eyeballed Betty Field's doomed Mae.

Willie's mentally enfeebled nature threatened to add a new level of tastelessness to the Paula the Ape Woman saga, but the character didn't last long.

The work this day covered over six script pages, the latter part concentrated on the climactic stalking scene: Paula pursuing Lois Collier in the woods at night. The episode parroted the classic vignette of Simone Simon pursuing Jane Randolph in Central Park in *Cat People*. The reality of the way these two different scenes were shot was stark. On *Cat People*, ace director Jacques Tourneur and superb *noir* cinematographer Nicholas Musuraca shot the stalk on RKO Soundstage 4, with controlled lighting and effects. LeBorg and Jack MacKenzie filmed *Jungle Woman's* stalk on a back lot exterior, using tricks to try to make it appear it was really night, despite the California sunshine.

Additionally, *Cat People* had fastidious producer Val Lewton passionately overseeing the work; *Jungle Woman* had Ben Pivar, whom LeBorg would later describe (probably with a dash of hyperbole) as basically illiterate.

LeBorg, despite the huge odds, hoped for a miracle. His actresses tired. As twilight approached, Acquanetta and Collier struggled through seven bad takes. Nightfall descended, and at 6:20 p.m., LeBorg called it quits and sent both ladies home. Tomorrow was another day.

Thursday, February 17: It was back into the woods. Acquanetta, Collier, Naish, Davis, and Hyans were all on call. LeBorg covered four and a half pages and put finishing touches on the stalk.

Friday, February 18: After four days' work outside, the company moved indoors: Paula's room on Soundstage 8 and the Sanitarium Office on Soundstage 7. It was a good day, as Acquanetta, Naish, Collier, Davis and Hyans played eight and three-quarters script pages. Hyans wrapped up his role, and Nana Bryant began work as Miss Gray, Fletcher's nurse. Once again, fatigue set in at the end of the day—a scene with Acquanetta, Collier and Davis required ten takes.

Saturday, February 19: It was back to the Sanitarium Office set. Acquanetta, Naish, Collier, Davis and Nana Bryant (who completed her role this day) were on call. So was Christian Rub as George, a groundskeeper who tells about the slaughtered animals.[24]

Paula (Acquanetta) drags the body of her victim Willie (Edward M. Hyans Jr.) into the woods. Although the murder occurs in *Jungle Woman's* release version, this view of it does not (from the John Antosiewicz Collection).

Acquanetta finished up at 1:00 p.m. and got an early start on the weekend. Naish, the last to go, worked until 7:25 p.m.

Jungle Woman was almost halfway through its shooting schedule. LeBorg had about 47 pages left to shoot in only seven days.

The schedule and economy made things seem nearly impossible. Yet, based on this week's work, *Jungle Woman* wasn't the debacle that legend will insist. Actually, in some modest ways, the movie was paying off.

The stalk scene, for example: It doesn't hold a proverbial candle to *Cat People's* Central Park "walk," but Acquanetta does appear a semi-force of nature as she storms through the branches, and LeBorg delivers the atmospherics. The temptation for the writers and director to have her revert to gorilla in this sequence must have been strong, but they go for something different. When the sound effects add screeching birds, freaked out by Paula's unnatural presence and the rising tempo of danger, the eerie episode works rather nicely ... especially with Paul Sawtell's music.

Then there was Naish, giving, granted, a strange, off-the-wall performance. Yet the actor's gentle, animal-loving Dr. Fletcher is a total departure from John Carradine's bravura *Captive Wild Woman* portrayal of the breed- and sex-changing, murdering, sadistic and probably perverted Dr. Walters. Naish's Fletcher isn't a creep, but a humanitarian; if Carradine's Dr. Walters is a wanna-be Dr. Moreau, then Naish's Dr. Fletcher is a wanna-be Albert Schweitzer.

Finally, there was Acquanetta herself.

First off, there's her *look*. In certain shots and angles, the lady evokes a mulatto Vampira, playing it deadly straight and, at times, viciously scary. Her fierce eyes, her brisk, strangely deadly walk—she evokes a possessed Earl Carroll showgirl, about to throw herself off the HOLLYWOOD sign (and maybe take a few victims with her). The high-pitched purr of a voice works too. As with other horror films discussed in this book, cut out the horror element—in this case, the gorilla angle—and you get a racy, quirky melodrama. *Jungle Woman* becomes the story of a sexually out-of-control *femme fatale* patient amok in a countryside sanitarium, vamping "Hello, my name is Paula" into the male ingénue's face, insanely jealous, slaughtering helpless animals in her sexual frustration, accusing her caring doctor of physical abuse … a whirlwind of mad, dangerous vanity.

It was only there in flashes, but it was there. Could LeBorg make it all come together in the seven days to come?

Monday, February 21: Acquanetta, Naish, Collier and Davis were ready at 9:00 a.m. for work on the Sanitarium Office on Stage 7 and Paula's Room on Stage 8. Milburn Stone (starting work that day) and Naish reported to Stage 9 and the Fletcher Office set. LeBorg and his actors finished seven and a quarter pages.

Stone, as Fred Mason, delivered fresh, significant information: He claimed that, while capturing Cheela in the Belgian Congo, he learned that she was originally a human being, transformed into a gorilla by, if you'll excuse the expression, black magic. It was almost a throwaway line, but it established that—maybe—Paula Dupree was a human being to begin with, thereby softening (barely) the gorilla-into-woman story.

Tuesday, February 22: Acquanetta, Naish, Davis and Stone reported at 9 a.m., Collier at 1:00 p.m. LeBorg completed five pages, working on the Fletcher's Office set, the Sanitarium Office set, the Entrance Hall (Stage 7) and Bob's Room (Stage 19). It was a long day for Acquanetta: 9:00 a.m. to 7:05 p.m.

Wednesday, February 23: A big day—LeBorg shot ten and a half pages! Acquanetta, Naish, Davis and Collier worked, as did Pierre Watkin, as Dr. Meredith. The sets: Bob's Room, Joan's Room (both on Stage 19) and Dr. Meredith's Office (Stage 11).

Thursday, February 24: The company moved to Stage 9, and the Coroner's Office. Evelyn Ankers joined the show as Beth. Perhaps because she had so little to do, she's dressed to the nines, with a picture hat and a fur wrap, and keeps her favored right profile toward the camera.

Also starting work: Samuel S. Hinds (well-remembered as Judge Thatcher in the Karloff-Lugosi *The Raven*) as the coroner; Douglass Dumbrille (whose villainous filmic atrocities include placing bamboo shoots under Gary Cooper's fingernails in *The Lives of a Bengal Lancer*) as the district attorney; and the actors playing the jurors, including Beatrice Roberts (Queen Azura of Universal's 1938 serial *Flash Gordon's Trip to Mars*). "Bee" Roberts (as the Assistant Director's Daily Report listed her) was a strange presence at Universal: She was allegedly a mistress of Louis B. Mayer, who had an under-the-table deal with Universal to keep her working. Among her recent gigs at the studio: *Frankenstein Meets the Wolf Man* (1943), as the villager Varja.

Naish, Stone, Collier and Davis were there too. LeBorg covered six pages.

Friday, February 25: Work resumed on the Coroner's Office set, with the same players as the previous day. Later they moved to Stage 18 with its set for the Interior Morgue and Corridor sets. This set the stage for the appearance of the corpse of Paula the Ape Woman.

The Assistant Director report listed Acquanetta reporting to the set at 1:30 p.m., which indicates that she likely was made up as the Ape Woman for that very brief shot. LeBorg finished the sequence at 5:00 p.m. and, except for Acquanetta, Naish and Collier, all the players were dismissed.

7:00 p.m. After dinner, shooting took place at the back lot Exterior Cottage set. There LeBorg added a bit to the stalk in the woods sequence, and shot some footage that was seen both at the start of the movie and in the final reel: Paula attacking Fletcher, their shadows cast on the cottage wall. The "Extras and Miscellaneous" section of the Daily Report noted two people hired at $35; this indicates stunt doubles who, based on this information, probably performed the frenetic Paula vs. Fletcher battle. As it is, Lois Collier finished at 9:30 p.m., Acquanetta and Naish at 10:10 p.m., and the company at 10:30 p.m.

Saturday, February 26: Acquanetta, Naish, Collier and Davis worked on the Process Stage, which provided backgrounds for the lake and car scenes. The company also worked on the Fingerprint Office set on Stage 18. Richard Powers played the fingerprint expert. Naish and Powers finished at 6:30 p.m. (Powers was actually cowboy actor Tom Keene, who later played Col. Edwards in 1958's *Plan 9 from Outer Space*.)

Monday, February 28: It was the last day of shooting. On an Interior Circus set on Soundstage 18, Naish played the flashback where he saw Cheela save Fred Mason. He sat in bleachers, surrounded by 20 extras (earning $10.50 a head), watching action that

From *Jungle Woman*: **Acquanetta as Paula and Richard Davis as Bob—whom she desires (from the John Antosiewicz Collection).**

Acquanetta had a striking, fiercely attractive presence on film—as glimpsed in this still with J. Carrol Naish (from the John Antosiewicz Collection).

supposedly took place in *Captive Wild Woman* but actually happened, for the most part, in *The Big Cage*.

Also today, Lois Collier, Richard Davis and Acquanetta worked at Pollard Lake, fleshing out the "scare sequence" where Paula attacks the canoe. Once again, Jack MacKenzie attempted to shoot a "night" sequence in broad daylight (with fair results). They shot different script shots of the sequence than the ones filmed the "pre-production" day on February 14. Acquanetta finished at 11:00 a.m. while Collier and Davis worked until 4:15 p.m.

And thusly was *Jungle Woman* finished, right on schedule. After everything was tabulated, the film would come in at $105,612.72—$2612.72 over budget.

The Bombshell

Tuesday, March 14: Acquanetta started a new Universal film, *Dead Man's Eyes*, an Inner Sanctum entry starring Lon Chaney ("another wonderful man," recalled Acquanetta) and Jean Parker. Acquanetta played a bitchy fashion model named Tanya Czoraki and ended up dead in the movie. Acquanetta begged director Reginald LeBorg to allow her to give way to explosive dramatics. He cautiously and wisely refused.

Meanwhile, about this time, serious trouble loomed behind the scenes.

In *Filmfax* #42, Robert Nott interviewed Edmund L. Hartmann, who was a writer at

Universal in 1944, working on Abbott and Costello films and the Sherlock Holmes series. (Hartmann later scripted several of Bob Hope's hit features and produced TV's *My Three Sons*.) In the Nott interview, he remembered his days at Universal:

> There was an actress on the lot named Acquanetta, who was going to be the next Maria Montez.... Word was sent to all the producers that she had another four months to go on her contract. But while she was there, she was not to be in any scene where she is romantically involved with a white man.... As soon as her contract was up, they dropped her. I told this story to an actress I knew who also knew Acquanetta, and she told me that [Acquanetta's] mother was black. She was at Acquanetta's house and Acquanetta introduced her mother as the cook to try to hide the fact.

A ring of truth? More than that, actually. Acquanetta's contract did expire four months and two days after she started *Dead Man's Eyes*. During that time, she not only didn't appear in a scene "romantically involved with a white man"—she didn't appear in any films at all.

If Hartmann's account is accurate, it must have been a horrible time for Acquanetta: the revelation of the secret she'd so passionately guarded, and would continue to guard for the rest of her life. She, of course, offered her own version of events: that she'd wanted out of her Universal contract due to her dissatisfaction with being mired in "B" films. As we'll see, her version had little credibility.

It was all hitting at a racially sensitive time. That summer, Republican presidential nominee Wendell Wilkie was fighting for "Negro Rights," asking Republicans to come out for anti-lynching laws. (Wilkie was more liberal regarding "Negro Rights" than Franklin D. Roosevelt.) Meanwhile, Universal had *Jungle Woman* on its hands. The studio prepared to release it on a double bill with *The Mummy's Ghost*, the film Acquanetta started just before her unfortunate fainting spell.

Tuesday, June 20: "Mae Tinee," the *Chicago Daily Tribune*'s cleverly named film critic, reviewed both horror movies in verse, writing of *Jungle Woman*:

> *Of jungle woman, too, bewarium!*
> *She's loose in Crestview Sanitarium.*
> *Part human and part anthropoid*
> *And of the milk of kindness void.*
> *She howls and kills and goes a'raidin*
> *An ape—that looks just like a maiden.*
> *She's jealous of the good doc's daughter*
> *And sets out little Joan to slaughter.*
> *[Being a beast she thinks she orter.]*

Monday, July 3: *The Los Angeles Examiner* reported that Acquanetta's Universal contract would expire July 16. (There was no reference in the article to the race issue.) The *Examiner* also revealed that she was moving to Poverty Row's Monogram Studios, supposedly at three times her Universal salary, to act for producer "Jungle Sam" Katzman: "Katzman hopes to make Acquanetta the biggest femme property at Monogram, and is setting out to get a tailor-made script to launch her. Of course, she will still cater to the sarong clientele."

Acquanetta told me that Universal sold her to Monogram without her consent.

Friday, July 14: Two days before Acquanetta's Universal contract expired, *Jungle Woman* opened (as a solo attraction) at New York City's Rialto. "Same Old Ape," headlined the review in the next day's *New York Times*. The Manhattan critics basically saw it as just another lousy horror movie—the *New York Herald Tribune* calling it "pseudosci-entific stuff and nonsense." But on July 16, one critic focused on the beast below the surface. John T. McManus, reviewer for New York's highbrow, liberal-slanted *PM* newspaper, wrote:

> In *Mein Kampf*, *Hitler calls the Negro a "half-born ape." Jungle Woman illustrates the point, changing a Hollywood glamour girl into an ape and vice versa with the Negro stage inserted right where Hitler says.*

This wasn't accurate: *Jungle Woman* has no such scene. McManus continued:

> *Beyond its affinity with Hitler ideas, the film is an out-and-out steal on unsuspecting moviegoers, being mainly old footage [from] Captive Wild Woman. The 1943 version was challenged at the time of its production for its Nazi ideas, but Universal made it anyway. Apparently, it is to be an annual outrage unless somebody passes a law against propounding Nazi race theories in America.*

Meanwhile, *New York Post* critic Archer Winsten, apparently missing the inference that McManus detected, wrote about "a couple flashes of Burnu in an intermediate phase in which she resembles the Wolf Man in burnt cork." The only such "flash" in the film was in the *Captive Wild Woman* flashback and in the morgue.

Jungle Woman took in $9000 at the Rialto its first week ("a puller," noted *Variety*) and $6500 its second week.[25]

Thursday, July 27: *Jungle Woman* and *The Mummy's Ghost* opened at the Hawaii Theatre in Hollywood. The duo ran there for four weeks and tallied $20,480.[26]

Sunday, July 30: Two weeks after Acquanetta departed Universal, and just after *Jungle Woman* wrapped up its run at New York's Rialto, David Platt of *The Daily Worker* again jumped into the fray. He titled his column "A Horror Film That Went Too Far" and recapped the "vicious anti–Negro B horror movie called *Captive Wild Woman*."

"*Jungle Woman* continues this vicious Hitlerian slander," wrote Platt. He went on, attacking *Jungle Woman* for scenes that weren't actually in it, and again took aim at Universal:

> *… It is not even important whether it was malice aforethought or just plain stupidity on their part. The fact remains that both Captive Wild Woman and Jungle Woman imply a natural affinity between Negros and apes. Nazis in Germany have been taught such things by Goebbels. There's no room for such anti-racial theories in America.*

Then Platt delivered his bombshell:

> *Universal claims that Acquanetta is an American Indian, not West Indian. I happen to know that she is a West Indian Negro….*

Platt's revelation of Acquanetta as a "West Indian Negro" was (a) inaccurate, and (b) shockingly cruel. Surely he realized his announcement would circulate; *The Daily Worker* wasn't *Photoplay*, but news like this would likely spread through film circles. Platt had every right to be critical of Universal's Ape Woman series, but he had no right to toll a death bell for Acquanetta's Hollywood career in this pre–civil rights era.

He went on:

> *Universal's business is escapist films … they are becoming known far and wide as the hall of horrors. The danger there is that they might be engulfed by their own horrible creations.*
> *I will say this: Movie studios that refuse to see the handwriting on the wall and continue to turn out such films as Captive Wild Woman and Jungle Woman will go down as surely as a new day is dawning for colored peoples of the globe.*

Platt cared so much about his agenda that he made Acquanetta his sacrificial lamb. Advocating a new dawn for "colored peoples," he had potentially destroyed Acquanetta's career.

Part Four: Aftermath

The Jungle Captive

Thursday, August 31: A month and a day after the *Daily Worker* diatribe, Universal started shooting the third and final Ape Woman entry, *The Jungle Captive*. Brunette (and Caucasian) starlet Vicky Lane, formerly of MGM and then wed to Hollywood "bad boy" Tom Neal, inherited the role of Paula. Otto Kruger was the mad doctor and real-life acromegalic Rondo Hatton was a featured bogey man. Incidentally, *The Jungle Captive* detailed the fate of Dr. Carl Fletcher (who doesn't appear in the movie): Rondo Hatton's Moloch killed him when stealing records from Crestview Sanitarium.

Friday, October 6: *Dead Man's Eyes*, Acquanetta's Universal swan song, opened at the Rialto. Maybe the critics had heard the racial revelation, maybe not, but Acquanetta was the panned movie's prime target. *The New York Post* wrote:

> [J]ungle gal Acquanetta—now done up in dressy finery—goes highly emotional. Her lines are ostensibly dramatic; her delivery of them is something on the order of a six-year-old reading his first-grade primer.[27]

Late 1944 saw reports in the trades about Acquanetta making personal appearances for Monogram on the West Coast. An announced star vehicle for the studio, *Voodoo Queen*, never came to pass. She claimed a half-century later that she'd rejected all the scripts Monogram offered her. At least as credible is the probability that Monogram regretted signing her.

Friday, July 6, 1945: *The Jungle Captive* opened at the Rialto. The *New York Herald Tribune* review claimed that Vicky Lane's Ape Woman "looks like an over-sized woodchuck with a hangover."[28] Otto Kruger was excellent as the mad scientist. *The Jungle Captive* took in $8900 its first week and $6500 its second,[29] trailing *Jungle Woman's* Rialto fortnight total by only $100.

In the eyes of the Rialto audiences, all Ape Women were apparently created equal.

The Best Revenge

When *Shock! Theatre* came to TV in late 1957, *Jungle Woman* was not included in the 52-film package of Universal melodramas. Neither were *Captive Wild Woman* and *The Jungle Captive*, but those two did turn up in the *Son of Shock!* package the following year.

One might suspect Universal had taken *Jungle Woman* and, considering its reputation, dropped it somewhere in the Pacific Ocean, but it showed up on TV in the 1960s. The Ape Woman trilogy failed to get any respect from new audiences; as Denis Gifford

A poster for *The Jungle Captive* (Universal, 1945), third and final entry of the Paula the Ape Woman trilogy. Acquanetta left Universal shortly before its production and Vicky Lane, a Caucasian actress, inherited the role of Paula.

expressed it in his excellent 1973 book *A Pictorial History of Horror Movies*, "Poor Paula, she never even met Abbott and Costello. But she left behind her, if not an interesting body of work, an interesting body.[30]

Eventually, all three films came to home video. In 2020, they were released (along with Paramount's 1941 *The Monster and the Girl*) in the Blu-ray set *Universal Horror Collection Volume 5.*

As for Acquanetta: She had a "comeback" in *Tarzan and the Leopard Woman* (1946) with Johnny Weissmuller ("just like a big kid!" she remembered). In 1946, she married the very wealthy Ludwig (Luciano) Baschuk in Mexico. They had a son, Sergio, and soon divorced. The year 1950 was a bad year for her as she battled Baschuk for a share of his $5 million fortune; he responded that, while he admitted to being Sergio's father, he and Acquanetta had never actually married. *The Pittsburgh Courier* newspaper, which had many Black readers, extensively reported on the trial in Los Angeles and referred to Acquanetta as "a pretty Negro girl who took Hollywood by storm." The *Courier* also reported that, when the question of her race came up in court, Acquanetta's lawyer S.S. Hahn, noted Hollywood attorney, responded, "What difference does it make? Maybe it might not be for her best interests to explain anything about race. She doesn't have to. We're all Americans. There's no difference."[31]

In 1951, Acquanetta admitted having married artist Henry Clive, 69 years old, the previous year. "It was a marriage in name only—never consummated," she told me. A prominent illustrator and painter, Clive had painted Acquanetta years before for covers of Hearst's *The American Weekly.*

She also tried to jump-start her defunct film career. She appeared in *Lost Continent* (1951), starring Cesar Romero, Hillary Brooke and stop-motion dinosaurs. She also was in MGM's *Callaway Went Thataway* and *Take the High Ground* and the indie *The Sword of Monte Cristo.* Her roles were so small that *Film Daily* didn't include her name in any of these three films' cast lists.

In the fall of 1952, Acquanetta's son Sergio died of cancer. The funeral took place at the Little Church of the Flowers at Forest Lawn Memorial Park in Glendale. Acquanetta was reportedly "despondent" for many months.

By the mid–1950s, Acquanetta had divorced Clive (who would die in 1960) and wed again—to Jack Ross, a wealthy Lincoln-Mercury car dealer in Arizona. She advertised Ross' dealership and became a local TV and radio personality. She also became the proud mother of four sons. As Mrs. Jack Ross, she now enjoyed a movie star lifestyle, flying with her husband in their private plane to spend weekends in San Diego, sailing on their yacht that slept 27.[32]

In 1974, she published a book

Post-Universal, Acquanetta created her own personal identity and lived it passionately for the rest of her long life.

of poetry titled *The Audible Silence*. Divorced, she again resumed her career, appearing in the direct-to-video *Grizzly Adams—The Legend Never Dies* (1989). As always, she generously devoted herself to various charities and philanthropic causes.

The years passed. Alzheimer's disease took its toll. One wonders who and where she believed she was during her final years, lost in the shadows of that dreadful illness.

Monday, August 16, 2004: Acquanetta died at Ahwatukee Foothills Alzheimer's Care Center in Arizona. *The Arizona Republic* eulogized her as Paradise Valley's "first television diva" and gave her age as 83.

Saturday, August 21: Acquanetta's funeral took place through Messenger's Indian School mortuary and at Ascension Lutheran Church in Scottsdale. Her sons Lance, 50, Tom, 47, Jack, 45, and Rex, 43, produced a funerary tribute to their mother, whom they "adored," showing on twin screens above the altar shots and posters of their mom in cheesecake poses for such films as *Captive Wild Woman* (including the transformation scene), *Jungle Woman* and *Tarzan and the Leopard Woman*. (Paradise Valley broadcaster Pat McMahon afterwards congratulated Ascension Lutheran Church for its forbearance: "I don't know many parishes that would have allowed some of those posters up there," he joked.)

There were personal photos on display as well, Louis Armstrong's "It's a Wonderful World" played on the soundtrack, and the sons read from their mom's book of poetry. There were more songs and a Native American blessing. The casket was rolled past a six-foot floral display that spelled out Happiness, Acquanetta's favorite word.[33] She was buried in Paradise Memorial Gardens.

A curiosity about the funeral: *The Arizona Republic*, covering the event, called Acquanetta "an Arapaho beauty" and reported she'd been born in Wyoming. It also noted that her brother, 85-year-old Horace Davenport, a retired Pennsylvania judge, attended the funeral. The article didn't include the fact that the deceased's brother was clearly of African-American heritage. It did note that he admitted that he'd never seen any of his sister's movies.

"Now, I'm going to rent the videos," said Judge Davenport.[34]

"Beautiful Monster" and FANEX 6

A year after Acquanetta's death, a tribute (of sorts) came via a grand opera—a very harrowing one—simply titled *Acquanetta*. Michael Gordon and Deborah Altman wrote the piece, and it premiered in 2005 in Aachen, Germany. A "chamber opera" version came in 2018. Daniel Fish (whose *Oklahoma!* won the 2019 Tony for Best Revival of Musical) produced and directed it at Bard College's Richard B. Fisher Center for the Performing Arts at Annandale-on-Hudson, New York, in July 2019. Ben Brantley wrote in his *New York Times* review of the "spine-tingling chamber opera":

> [T]he source of the very genuine terror at the center of Acquanetta *isn't your usual cinematic psychopath, zombie or vampire. The boogeyman is instead golden age Hollywood itself, where a young woman can be so radically and disfiguringly transformed that she'll no longer know who she is.*[35]

Surely Acquanetta, were she alive to see the show (and managed to sit through it), would have protested the depiction of herself as a victim. Nevertheless, the title role was a showcase for African-American soprano Rebecca L. Hargrove, whose performance climaxed with her anguished aria "Beautiful Monster," in which she cries out like an animal.[36] Critic Brantley rhapsodized of Hargrove's performance, and her eyes: "The eyes of the 1940s cult star ... fathomless whirlpools, edged in spiky vegetation, from some alien landscape...."

Author Greg Mank with Acquanetta at the Fanex 6 Convention in Baltimore, Maryland, in August 1992.

I have a story about Acquanetta's eyes as well ... the *real* Acquanetta's. It goes back almost 30 years, to her guest appearance at FANEX 6 in Baltimore.

As previously noted, she was a fireball. Tall, dramatic, maybe a bit vainglorious, adorned in Indian jewelry, giving the most flamboyantly signed autographs I've ever seen ("Happiness" written on all of them), she was smoothly delivering the same superstar public persona performance she'd been playing and perfecting for half a century.

I interviewed her on a Saturday afternoon before an audience of wide-eyed fans. The lady was in great form, regaling the crowd how she'd once turned down Clark Gable, and how she'd once walked out of a party high in Coldwater Canyon after the guests started stripping. She also read her self-composed "My Creed":

> *I believe in the great Spirit.... It gives me hope and faith....*
> *I believe in Prayer ... it is the umbilical cord that ties man to his creator and gives him strength....*
> *I believe imagination is man's greatest gift ... with imagination man can conceive of anything and all things ... without limitation....*

I sat across from her, watching her, fascinated, wondering where the reality and fantasy of Acquanetta met and where, if ever, it shattered. Two weeks prior, I'd spoken at length with her on the phone, amazed at how fervently she told tales that I knew must be false. Why did a very wealthy, beautifully preserved septuagenarian feel a need to create her own reality regarding events that were now so far behind her ... and one would think, no longer able to hurt her?

As such, her words about "imagination" and how it allowed to "conceive of anything and all things," struck me powerfully. And I remembered vividly what she'd said to me on the phone, sadly, softly about her role of Paula the Ape Woman.

I became her....

That night was the 1992 FANEX award ceremony. Actor Russ Tamblyn, actress Veronica Carlson, and special effects artist Jim Danforth were honorees, along with Acquanetta. I was privileged to present her award to her on stage.

She knew from the program when her time came, and as I started my brief speech, I looked at her, seated in all her finery in the front row. My guess was that, with an award about to be bestowed, the lady would be Acquanetta in Excelsis.

What (or who) I saw instead was startling.

As Acquanetta sat in the near-darkness, her diva act had vanished. She looked shy, almost guilty of something ... sadly contrite. In an apparent complete reversal of persona, she didn't appear proud of her fame that we were celebrating this night, but embarrassed, perhaps ashamed, maybe even frightened by it.

"For being a very unique presence in the movies," I said, keeping my eyes on her, actually concerned she might get up and bolt from the auditorium, "and for giving a heart and soul to Paula the Ape Woman ... FANEX honors Acquanetta."

The crowd warmly applauded, she came up on the stage, and our eyes met. Her eyes were grateful, yet strangely, mysteriously sad. She reached out and hugged me, emotionally, almost the way a mourner hugs a fellow mourner at a wake. She accepted the award, and spoke briefly to the audience ... as I remember it, a brief poem of her own about hoping she'd be kindly remembered.

I didn't see her afterward that night. Years later, knowing what I've learned, I wonder if that night she remembered, or perhaps dreamed about, who she'd been over 50 years ago, the trick she tried to play on Hollywood and the terribly cruel trick Hollywood had played back on her. The revelation, the humiliation. Yes … she'd given a heart and soul to Paula the Ape Woman, and Universal Studios, presiding, had consecrated it—knowingly or unknowingly—as an unholy sacrament.

I became her.…

She also became the new post–Hollywood woman she'd desperately and protectively created, built on the ruins of the young, fresh starlet who had perhaps pursued her dream recklessly and foolishly … and crashed and burned … but had survived to continue her masquerade.

The next morning at FANEX, when I saw her, she was her usual Norma Desmond self.

Yet I'd seen behind the mask, and as I write this chapter, the memory's a haunting one. Looking all those years ago into Acquanetta's sad, frightened eyes, had I caught a brief, telling and heartbreaking glimpse of Mildred Davenport?

Was the song "Beautiful Monster" mournfully playing in her head, although it hadn't been written yet?

Captive Wild Woman

Universal 1943. Associate Producer, Ben Pivar. Director, Edward Dmytryk. Screenplay by Griffin Jay and Henry Sucher. Original story by Ted Fithian and Neil P. Varnick. Cinematographer, George Robinson. Art Directors, John B. Goodman and Ralph DeLacy. Editor, Milton Carruth. Sound Director, Bernard B. Brown. Sound Technicians, William Hedgcock and William Fitz. Music, Hans J. Salter. Gowns, Vera West. Set Decorators, Russell A. Gausman and Ira S. Webb. Makeup Artist, Jack P. Pierce. Assistant Director, Melville Shyer. Stock footage, *The Big Cage* (Universal, 1933). Running time, 61 minutes.

New York opening, Rialto Theatre, June 5, 1943. Los Angeles opening, Paramount Downtown and Hollywood Theatres, July 22, 1943 (on a double bill with *Frankenstein Meets the Wolf Man*).

The Cast: John Carradine (Dr. Sigmund Walters), Evelyn Ankers (Beth Colman), Milburn Stone (Fred Mason), Lloyd Corrigan (John Whipple), Fay Helm (Miss Strand), Martha MacVicar aka Martha Vickers (Dorothy Colman), Vince Barnett (Curley), Paul Fix (Gruen), Ray "Crash" Corrigan (Cheela), Fern Emmett (Beth's Murdered Neighbor), Gus Glassmire (Coroner), William Gould (Sheriff), Edward Peil Sr. (Jake—Handler), Frank Mitchell (Handler), Grant Withers (Veterinarian), Anthony Warde (Tony), Harry Holman (Clerk), Ray Walker (Ringmaster), Virginia Engels (Trapeze Artist), Joey Ray (Attendant), Charles McAvoy (Policeman), Alexander Gill (Waiter), Turhan Bey (Narrator of Closing Lines), Clyde Beatty (in footage from *The Big Cage*), and Introducing Acquanetta as Paula Dupree.

Jungle Woman

Universal, 1944. Executive Producer, Ben Pivar. Associate Producer, Will Cowan. Director, Reginald LeBorg. Screenplay, Bernard L. Schubert, Henry Sucher and Edward Dein. Cinematographer, Jack MacKenzie. Music, Paul Sawtell. Editor, Ray Snyder. Art

Directors, John B. Goodman, Abraham Grossman. Set Decorators, Russell A. Gausman, Edward R. Robinson. Gowns, Vera West. Sound, Bernard B. Brown, Jess Moulin. Makeup Artists, Jack P. Pierce and Ed Zimmer. Dialogue Director, Emory Horger. Assistant Directors, Melville Shyer and Ralph Slosser. Script Girl, Mary Chaffee. Camera Operator, Dick Towers. Assistant Cameraman, Phil Lathrop. Special Effects, Red Guthrie. Running time: 60 minutes.

New York opening, Rialto Theatre, July 14, 1944. Los Angeles opening, Hawaii Theatre, July 27, 1944.

The Cast: Acquanetta (Paula Dupree), Evelyn Ankers (Beth Mason), J. Carrol Naish (Dr. Carl Fletcher), Samuel S. Hinds (Coroner), Lois Collier (Joan Fletcher), Milburn Stone (Fred Mason), Douglass Dumbrille (District Attorney), Richard Davis (Bob Whitney), Nana Bryant (Miss Gray), Pierre Watkin (Dr. Meredith), Christian Rub (George—Groundsman), Alec Craig (Morgue Attendant), Edward M. Hyans Jr. (Willie), Tom Keene aka Richard Powers (Joe—Fingerprint Man), Wilson Benge (Court Stenographer), Diane Carroll, Edward Clark, Heinie Conklin, Nolan Leary, Charles Marsh, Beatrice Roberts (Inquest Jurors). Also: In footage from *Captive Wild Woman*: John Carradine (Dr. Sigmund Walters), Ray Walker (Ringmaster).

How to Make a Monster Rally

The Production of *House of Frankenstein*

HORDES OF HORROR ... Spawned by THE DEVIL...!
—Quote from the trailer of *House of Frankenstein*

Tuesday, April 25, 1944: It was the night they feared Boris Karloff had drowned—below the mountains of Universal City, against a background of blazing torches, and in the shadow of Frankenstein's Monster.

The film was *House of Frankenstein*. The company was shooting the climax on Universal's back lot. It was after 2:30 a.m., cold, with frost on the ground.[1]

Karloff was the Mad Doctor of this "monster rally"—a vengeful lunatic who, aided by J. Carrol Naish's hunchback, rabidly lets loose Lon Chaney's Wolf Man, John Carradine's Count Dracula and Glenn Strange's Monster. This night, 50 torch-bearing bit players and extras chased the Monster, who was lugging the Mad Doctor into the Visaria marshes—actually the old jungle from *Nagana* (1933).

"Quicksands!" the Mad Doctor warned the Monster, who just kept galumphing along.

Gaunt, gray, suffering from severe back trouble, Karloff had been at work for 14 hours (with two hours off for meals). He watched from the sidelines as the marsh exploded into flame and the towering Strange lugged Karloff's double, Carey Loftin, into the "quicksands."

For the final shot, however, Karloff had to join Strange in the eight-foot-deep pit of goo ... and sink for the close-up fade-out.

Living legend Karloff didn't need this. His three years as star and investor in *Arsenic and Old Lace* on Broadway and on tour had made him a very wealthy man. And he resented how *House* wasted his "dear old Monster." Still, it was work—and he'd have been a lost soul without work.

At 2:55 a.m., Erle C. Kenton, the director, called for Karloff, who waded into the pond. Strange grasped him. The "villagers" stood by with their torches. The brush blazed like bonfires.

"Action!" cried Kenton.

Strange sunk, lowered on a hydraulic lift under the muck. Then Karloff went down too. "Cut!" called Kenton. The lift rose. Strange emerged.

Karloff didn't.

The company stood by tensely, fearing it might be witnessing the on-the-job middle-of-the-night death of the King of Hollywood Horror. At last, the star arose,

Poster for *House of Frankenstein* (Universal, 1944).

trembling with cold, covered with gunk—and explaining he hadn't wanted to risk ruining the take by surfacing too early.[2]

Everyone went home at 3:00 a.m. *House of Frankenstein* was right on schedule.

* * *

In 1931, when Karloff's Monster pitifully raised his scarred arms and hands to the skylight, it was a profound moment: "Looking at God!" as Mae Clarke, *Frankenstein*'s leading lady, recalled.[3]

Nobody was looking at God in *House of Frankenstein*—or, as it was titled during shooting, *The Devil's Brood*. The studio was looking at box office, the players at a paycheck. Even Elena Verdugo—then 18 years old and in a showcase role as the Gypsy girl who dances, flirts, screams, kills, and dies—was hardy euphoric to be in the film.

"Actors made that kind of movie," Verdugo laughed, "so they could buy their lunch!"[4]

The actors, a quirky pack, were at strange places in their lives. The Mad Doctor was suffering a late midlife personal and professional crisis. The Wolf Man was violent when drunk. Dracula, also an epic imbiber, announced one night that he was Jesus and tried to walk across the pool at the Garden of Allah. The pitiful Hunchback was, in fact, whispered to be a "brawling roisterer." Hollywood at large regarded "the Inspector" as a "sex maniac." And "the Monster," listed at the tail end of the final credits, was a cowboy heavy most horror fans had never heard of.

House of Frankenstein was Universal's declaration of horror supremacy vs. all usurpers, especially RKO, where Val Lewton had created revolutionary shockers such as *Cat People*. When *House of Frankenstein* played New York's Rialto Theatre and Hollywood's Hawaii Theatre on the

On the night of April 24-25, 1944. Glenn Strange's Monster carried Karloff's double, Carey Loftin, into the back lot quicksand. Karloff let himself sink into the goo for the fade-out close-up—with frightening results!

nights before Christmas 1944, it was a record-breaking powerhouse. Panned by the *New York World-Telegram* as "a carnival of monstrosity,"[5] it was, in fact, a three-ring horror super circus, hellbent on showcasing Universal's terror genre dominance, zestfully delivered by an all-star cast of villains rarely (if ever) surpassed in Hollywood history.

As with the new Frankenstein's Monster, what was missing, primarily, was a soul.

Or *was* it?

Part One: Pre-Production

The Prodigal Returns

> *I hope there's a fatted calf awaiting the return of the prodigal....*
> —Boris Karloff as Jonathan, Act I, *Arsenic and Old Lace*

Wednesday, December 29, 1943: "Bogie Man Boris Karloff is coming back to movies to scaaaare you!" reported Louella Parsons in the *Los Angeles Examiner*.

Karloff would arrange to leave the national company of *Arsenic and Old Lace* in late January; he had played over 1000 performances as mad Jonathan Brewster, transformed by a drunken plastic surgeon to resemble Hollywood's #1 Horror star.

"He said I looked like Boris Karloff!" said Jonathan, explaining why he killed a man in cold blood. The line always had brought down the house.

His Universal contract called for 12 weeks, $60,000 and *two* films. The first eight weeks and $40,000 would go to *The Climax*; in this, Karloff's first feature in Technicolor, he played Dr. Hohner, an opera house physician who keeps an embalmed diva in his quarters. Susanna Foster and Turhan Bey co-starred. The other four weeks and $20,000 were left over for what Universal mysteriously listed as "picture to come."

The "picture to come" had actually been in the planning stage for some time. On June 9, 1943, *Variety* had reported:

> *Chiller-diller to end all chiller-dillers is being whipped up by Universal with an appropriate title,* Chamber of Horrors. *Idea, evolved by George Waggner, when he has finished* Cobra Woman, *is to round up Boris Karloff, Bela Lugosi, Peter Lorre, Lon Chaney Jr., George Zucco and other goosepimplers in a ghostly rodeo with Frankenstein, Dracula, the Wolf Man, the Mad Ghoul, the Invisible Man and kindred spirits prowling in one cinematic nightmare.*[6]

The "picture to come" phrasing inferred: (a) Universal hadn't told Karloff about *Chamber of Horrors*, waiting to spring it on him after it was too late for the star to bail, or (b) the studio *had* told him about the horror spectacular, but he was arguing to do a different film.

Meanwhile, on June 13, 1943, Bosley Crowther, lead-off film critic for the *New York Times*, applauded the announcement of *Chamber of Horrors*, writing:

> *[T]he painful fact is that horror pictures have been woefully dull these several years.... Frankenstein's horrible monster, which was a nightmare when he left the assembly line, has become a sort of whimsical jalopy ever since he had that misadventure in the sulfur pit....*[7]

The "sulfur pit" reference was to 1939's *Son of Frankenstein*, the last time Karloff had played the Monster. Crowther hadn't mentioned by name Lon Chaney's Monster in *The Ghost of Frankenstein* (1942) or Bela Lugosi's Monster in *Frankenstein Meets the Wolf Man* (1943), but the inference was clear: For a Frankenstein picture to be truly effective, it needed Boris Karloff.

The actors who would be the *dramatis personae* of this all-stops-pulled shocker carried on, busy personally and professionally.

Friday, December 31: John Carradine walked out on his wife Ardanelle and their two sons, saying he was "madly in love" with Sonia Sorel. She was his Ophelia-Portia-Desdemona from his "John Carradine and His Shakespeare Players" repertory company, which had just folded after a West Coast tour. "All I want are the clothes on my back," Carradine told Ardanelle.[8]

Monday, January 10, 1944: Universal began *The Invisible Man's Revenge,* with Carradine as mad Dr. Drury.

Tuesday, January 18: *Variety* reported that Lon Chaney and actress Ann Savage (soon to play the femme fatale Vera in director Edgar G. Ulmer's *Detour*) were in Memphis, part of the Hollywood Victory Committee's Bond Battalion for the Fourth War Loan Campaign.

Saturday, January 29: Bela Lugosi replaced Boris Karloff in the national company of *Arsenic and Old Lace,* then playing in Oklahoma City. Karloff returned to Hollywood.

Tuesday, February 1: Universal launched *The Climax* with a $742,250 budget, a 47-day schedule, and a call for 1500 extras.[9] George Waggner directed as well as produced.

Wednesday, February 2: Columbia started production on *The Black Parachute*, starring Carradine as a Nazi. Fraught with divorce and money troubles, the actor had moved into Hollywood's Garden of Allah, "living in sin" with Sonia, drinking, and roaring Shakespeare.[10]

Saturday, February 5: Republic released its new 15-chapter "super-serial" *Captain America.* Playing the villain, "the Scarab": Lionel Atwill. This was Atwill's first film since his April 1943 exoneration for perjury (for which he received a five-year sentence on probation) related to "orgies" he allegedly hosted at his Pacific Palisades house during Yuletide of 1940.[11]

Monday, February 7: PRC began *The Monster Maker*, starring the very busy J. Carrol Naish in the title role. Playing Naish's giant henchman Steve: Glenn Strange.

Thursday, February 11: "Boris Karloff has been given an important role in *Destiny*, forthcoming Universal thriller," wrote the *Hollywood Citizen-News. Destiny*, of course, was Universal's generic title for films in development; in this case, it related to the *Chamber of Horrors* project, the script still in the works. If Karloff hadn't clearly seen the nature of his "picture to come," he did now.

As George Waggner was busy producing and directing *The Climax*, he had passed on Karloff Film #2 to Paul Malvern, who had produced the just-released Maria Montez–Jon Hall hit *Ali Baba and the Forty Thieves.*

Monday, February 14: Universal started shooting *Jungle Woman*, sequel to *Captive Wild Woman* (1943). The sequel's star: J. Carrol Naish. (See Chapter 10.)

Tuesday, February 15: Karloff's new radio show, *Creeps by Night*, premiered.

Over the next week, Karloff apparently had discussions with Universal about *Destiny*. Then came an eruption.

The Bombshell

Monday, February 21: The bomb detonated. Hitherto, Karloff had always spoken affectionately of his "dear old Monster" and the horror genre.

Not today.

Frederick Othman published an interview with a hotheaded Karloff in the *Hollywood Citizen-News*, providing a between-the-lines exposé of the star's battle with Universal:

[Karloff] *takes this occasion to announce for all to read, customers and employers alike....
He's through with Frankenstein, and if Universal henceforth finds itself in need of a half-man
half-something else, it'll have to hire another monster.*

*"I will never play Frankenstein's Monster again," he said. "Other people have taken similar
roles and the edge is off of it. I am through with it.... I made these horror films. They were of little
importance in anybody's scheme of things, including my own, and though I did make a disgrace-
ful amount of money, I was getting nowhere. Then out of the blue, three years and one month ago,
came this incredible play."*

The play, of course, was *Arsenic and Old Lace*, which Karloff clearly deeply missed.
At any rate, if Karloff played the Monster, who would essay the star role of the Mad Doctor? And if Karloff was the Mad Doctor, who would play the Monster? It all adds up to a
wild guess, but one that makes sense:

Universal wanted Karloff to play *both* Mad Doctor *and* Monster!

Consider the ideas that likely ping-ponged at Universal as *Destiny*—developed by
Curt Siodmak, who wrote the scripts for *The Wolf Man* and *Frankenstein Meets the Wolf
Man*—evolved over production and script conferences:

- Chaney, who had succeeded Karloff as the Monster in *The Ghost of Frankenstein*,
  would surely play the Wolf Man in *Destiny*.
- Lugosi, who succeeded Chaney as the Monster in *Frankenstein Meets the Wolf
  Man*, if cast here, would surely play Dracula.
- This left no major horror star to play the Monster, except…?
- Universal had planned to cast Chaney as Wolf Man and Monster in *Frankenstein
  Meets the Wolf Man*, right up to the eleventh hour. The studio had already
  mapped out the technicalities with doubles and camerawork for the one actor-
  two Monsters idea.
- Karloff could play the pivotal role of the Mad Doctor *and* the Monster, provided
  the Monster was basically a guest star, running amok only in the film's final
  climactic minutes. (This is what ultimately happened in the release.)
- For the sequence in the ice cavern, where the Mad Doctor and the Hunchback
  discover the Monster, a dummy could play the Monster (and ultimately did in the
  release). A dummy or double could play the thawed-out, comatose Monster. (For
  at least one scene in the release, a dummy did.)
- With the Monster's activity so limited, Karloff could shoot the Monster's climactic
  "action" scenes in only a few days and, with proper scripting and planning, within
  the time period Universal had with him. (Production records reveal that the
  Monster acted "on his feet" for precisely three days.)
- Meanwhile, a double could stand in for the Mad Doctor while Karloff played the
  Monster. (In the release, a double did extensively stand in for the Mad Doctor in
  the finale—and for three days.)
- The showmanship has supercharged potential: Karloff, as Mad Doctor *and* Monster!
- Universal would get *three* performances out of Karloff in only 12 weeks.

As noted, it's a supposition—but Karloff's anti–Monster rant to Othman must have
had some basis; and the mechanics necessary for the double performance, as noted, all
ended up in the finished film.

A possible alternate approach: Star Karloff as the Mad Doctor, and co-star Chaney
as Wolf Man, Dracula and the Monster. After all, Chaney had previously played all three.
The mystery lingers, and Curt Siodmak (who died in 2000) was no help.

"I only wrote the story and I never saw the picture," he told me.[12]

Monday, February 21: Monogram released *Voodoo Man*, starring Bela Lugosi in the title role, John Carradine as his mentally enfeebled minion Toby, and George Zucco as a voodoo high priest. Lugosi kept his dignity while Carradine played a bongo and Zucco chanted and wore war paint.

Tuesday, February 22: Universal started the Olsen and Johnson comedy *Ghost Catchers*. Lon Chaney, in support, appeared in a bear suit.

Wednesday, March 1: John Carradine appeared at the Wilshire-Ebell Theatre, narrating Aaron Copland's symphony *Lincoln's Portrait*, with the Hollywood Canteen Orchestra. The performance was a benefit for Jewish war victims and refugees.

Thursday, March 2: It was Academy Awards night. Susanna Foster opened the ceremony, singing "The Star-Spangled Banner." J. Carrol Naish, a Best Supporting Actor nominee for Columbia's *Sahara*, lost to Charles Coburn for Columbia's *The More the Merrier*. Universal won two Oscars for *Phantom of the Opera*: Color Cinematography and Art Direction.

Friday, March 10: The script was finally completed for *Destiny*, featuring the Mad Doctor, Hunchback, Dracula, Wolf Man and, in a virtual "cameo," Frankenstein's Monster. (The Mad Ghoul and the Invisible Man, originally announced, failed to make the cut.) Curt Siodmak's story earned him $7041.67; Edward T. Lowe's shooting script earned him $5000. Lowe had experience in the realm of hunchbacks and mad doctors, having scripted Universal's *The Hunchback of Notre Dame* (1923), starring Lon Chaney (the Elder) as Quasimodo, and Majestic's *The Vampire Bat* (1933), starring Lionel Atwill as Dr. Otto von Niemann. Maybe in homage to his 1933 film, Lowe named the mad doctor in *The Devil's Brood* Dr. Gustav Niemann.

Meanwhile, Karloff and Universal agreed: He'd play mad Dr. Niemann ... not the Monster.

Friday, March 17: *Waterfront* started filming at PRC, starring J. Carrol Naish and John Carradine.

Tuesday, March 21: "Kenton Directs Karloff" headlined *Variety*: "Erle C. Kenton will direct Boris Karloff's second film for Universal, *The Devil's Brood*. Production gets under way April 3, after Karloff finishes his present assignment at the valley lot, *The Climax*." Note that the film now had a new title. Note too that Kenton had two prize horror credits: Paramount's *Island of Lost Souls* (1932), arguably the wildest of pre–Code horror films, and Universal's own *The Ghost of Frankenstein* (1942).

Monday, March 27: Edward T. Lowe had done a rewrite, and this day, Joseph Breen, head of the Production Code, sent his censorship cautions. Among them:

- *We urge you strongly to avoid all unnecessary gruesomeness, brutality or horror....*
- *All scenes of strangling should be handled with care....*
- *Please exercise your usual good taste, in the scenes of Ilonka to avoid any unacceptable movements in her dance....*

The Nuts, Bolts and Budget

Universal finalized its cast for *The Devil's Brood* and their respective salaries.[13]

Karloff, of course, won—or was now trapped into playing—the top-billed role of Dr. Gustav Niemann. The only other way he could have completed his Universal contract within the next four weeks would have been to join the cast of *The Singing Sheriff*, starring Bob Crosby and set to start shooting April 3.

Chaney took the second star spot as Larry Talbot, the Wolf Man. His fee, as indicated on the budget sheet, was one-half of Karloff's: $10,000.

J. Carrol Naish got special "And" billing as Daniel, the Hunchback. His salary: $1750 per week for four weeks.

John Carradine, after his Universal horror build-up (*Captive Wild Woman*, *The Mummy's Ghost* and *The Invisible Man's Revenge*), was a natural to play the undead Count Dracula. (If Universal wanted Bela Lugosi for Dracula, he was unavailable, committed to wrapping up the *Arsenic and Old Lace* tour.) Carradine's fee: $3500 per week on a two-week guarantee. The casting had its irony: In both *Return of the Ape Man* (yet to be released) and *Voodoo Man* at Monogram, Carradine's role had been definitely subordinate to Lugosi's.

Lionel Atwill, as Inspector Arnz, had a role so small it makes one suspect that Universal was embarrassed by "Pinky's" presence. His fee: $1750 for one week.

George Zucco got a juicy cameo role (and a super death scene) as Prof. Bruno Lampini, whose Chamber of Horrors wagon Karloff's Niemann pirates. His fee: $1500 for one week.

Anne Gwynne, veteran of such Universal horrors as the Karloff-Lugosi *Black Friday* (1940), played Rita, Dracula's intended conquest. Her fee: $3000. Peter Coe, as her newlywed spouse, was set for $3500. Finally, Elena Verdugo, who made a splash as the alluring Native girl in *The Moon and Sixpence* (UA, 1942), landed the role of Ilonka the Gypsy girl—a seeming tribute to Esmeralda of *The Hunchback of Notre Dame* and Maria Montez in the yet-to-be-released *Gypsy Wildcat*. Her fee: $250 per week with a three-week guarantee.

"I was thinking, 'What am I doing in one of *these* things?'" said Verdugo. "That was the kind of film where everybody went, 'Wooooo!'"

As for the Monster: Universal hired 44-year-old Western heavy, fiddle player, singer, songwriter, rodeo rider, Pocahontas descendant Glenn Strange. The 6'5" actor's nickname: "Pee-Wee." He was impressive as Petro, George Zucco's towering werewolf in *The Mad Monster* (PRC, 1942), and as noted, had just skulked about in PRC's *The Monster Maker*. Strange was durable; after Lugosi collapsed on *Frankenstein Meets the Wolf Man*, Universal wanted durability. Frankly, the Monster role was so small that acting ability was hardly a factor—they just needed a big romper-stomper to run amok in the last five minutes. Strange fit the bill, and Jack Pierce thought that Glenn's head was ideal for the Monster makeup. His fee: $250 a week for two weeks.

The budget for *The Devil's Brood*, Universal Production No. 1382, was $354,000—the biggest budget for a Universal Frankenstein film to that time. (Average cost of a 1944 feature: $462,150.[14]) While *Bride of Frankenstein* and *Son of Frankenstein* had exceeded this amount by running considerably over-budget, *The Devil's Brood* budget far surpassed the final cost of 1943's *Frankenstein Meets the Wolf Man*—which had been only $238,071.79.

A few costs listed on the April 3, 1944, budget sheet:

- *Director*: $15,000
- *Set Construction*: $34,000
- *Makeup and Hairdressing*: $3,000
- *Trick, Miniature, Process and Special Effects*: $12,500

The most expensive item: "Cast and Bits." Total: $63,300.

As the first day of shooting neared, perhaps the big mystery was Karloff. On *The Climax,* he gave a frigid performance. He had charmed many leading ladies over the years, but Susanna Foster later likened working with him to "acting with a slab of ice."[15]

Karloff had some reason for his reserve. Although he was back on Universal's hallowed ground, where he'd become a worldwide star in *Frankenstein*, he was also near the back lot hill where, in 1931, James Whale had forced him to carry Colin Clive on his back and up to the windmill, the torch-bearing villagers in pursuit, Whale sadistically demanding take after take.[16] Karloff's back had never been the same. Now his back trouble was so agonizing that the actor feared—accurately, as it turned out—that he'd soon be in a wheelchair.

In *The Devil's Brood*, Karloff basically would be the ringmaster of a Midnight Freak Show. And look how it presented the poor Monster—as a zapped-up dolt!

Is *this* what Karloff could expect from Hollywood … after making theater history in *Arsenic and Old Lace*?

Part Two: The Shoot

Week One: April 4 to April 8, 1944

Tuesday, April 4: "Now will you give me my chalk?"

It was a terrific introductory close-up for Dr. Gustav Niemann. We see him staring wildly through his cell door window, eyes bright but dead, sporting a long gray beard, lightning flashing on his face as he chokes the prison guard—thus instantly giving the monster rally an unholy showmanship only Karloff could deliver.

The interior of Neustadt Prison for the Criminally Insane was Universal's old set from *Green Hell*, an Inca headhunter saga that James Whale had directed in late 1939. Karloff was there at 9:00 a.m., as was Charles Wagenheim as the guard.[17] On the set at 10, also sporting a beard courtesy of Jack P. Pierce—and a hump—was J. Carrol Naish.

"All I have to do is stick on a beard, get an evil glint in my eye, and I'm ready to cut you all up!" laughed Karloff.[18] Well-known for his love of animals, especially canines, Karloff this day delivered one of the more bizarre lines of his career as Niemann, this "would-be Frankenstein," indicated the charts and formulas chalked on his prison wall: "[T]his brain, taken from the man and transplanted into the skull of the dog, would give him the mind of a human being…"

"Then you could give *me* a new body!" sighed J. Carrol Naish's Daniel. Naish was one of Hollywood's greatest character actors and—according to Lee Server in his 2002 biography of Robert Mitchum, *"Baby, I Don't Care"*—not only a "brawling roisterer," but "a rabid and surprisingly successful womanizer."[19] Maybe … but he was wed to his only wife for 44 years (until his death in 1973) and was a proud and doting father. At any rate, Naish instantly made poor deformed Daniel the poster boy for the sexually frustrated. Indeed, his performance, daubed with sadness and loneliness, will take the film into deeper, darker realms.

George Robinson, veteran cameraman of many Universal horrors, masterfully captured the shadows and flashes of special effects lightning. Wagenheim finished at 3:30 p.m., Karloff at 5:05, Naish at 5:45.

After his first day's work on *The Devil's Brood*, workaholic Karloff hosted his evening radio show, *Creeps by Night*.

Wednesday, April 5: Spectacle—a blast from the heavens as lightning struck Neustadt Prison. The special effects crew dumped debris on Karloff and Naish on the *Green Hell* set. After the actors and crew took a break for lunch, they filmed Karloff and Naish's escape, scuttling through the prison sewer—actually the "Pittsburgh Tunnels," originally built by Universal for *Pittsburgh* (1942), starring Marlene Dietrich, John Wayne and Randolph Scott.

The company finished at 6:00 p.m. Karloff drove home to Coldwater Canyon, Naish to Los Feliz. Meanwhile, the assistant director report noted that Elena Verdugo was "rehearsing." She continued rehearsing the next day.

Thursday, April 6: *The Devil's Brood* company was scheduled to work late this night, so the call was 1:00 p.m. George Zucco came in from his Mandeville Canyon ranch to play Prof. Bruno Lampini, pipe-chomping proprietor of a traveling Chamber of Horrors. The interior of his wagon, appropriately, was on Universal's Stage 12, that once housed the castle of *Dracula* and the laboratory of *Frankenstein*. Zucco seemed to delight in recounting the legend of Dracula, whose skeleton Lampini starred in his show, delivering his dialogue with lip-smacking relish:

"I have a collection of the world's most astounding horrors!" boasted Zucco's Lampini.

After dinner, Karloff, Naish and Zucco reported to the back lot's *Gung Ho!* set, where the escaped Niemann and Daniel helped Lampini extricate his wagon from a muddy road. The rain machines did their worst, soaking all three actors plus George Plues, who played the wagon's driver. Zucco finished at 10:20, Karloff and Naish at 10:45. Kenton, Plues and the crew then ventured to the *Tower of London* set, for the opening shot of Lampini's coaches riding past Neustadt Prison. The *faux* rain poured, the fake lightning flashed, and Kenton dismissed the company at 12:35 a.m.

Friday, April 7: The call was 10:30 a.m.—a violation of the 12-hour break that the unions dictated after last night's session. The set was the Gypsy Camp in the village of Frankenstein, based on another venerable Universal back lot site: the grounds of the Shelby House, a Southern Colonial mansion from the studio's 1927 *Uncle Tom's Cabin*. Audiences never see the Civil War–style domicile, of course, in *House of Frankenstein*.

No more beards for Karloff and Naish: Karloff displayed a mustache and wore a cap and dark suit as he masqueraded as Lampini. Naish, clean-shaven, sported the organ grinder's costume that he'd wear for much of the film, somehow avoiding looking silly (for the most part). They rode the Lampini wagon into the village.

Meanwhile, it was the first day of filming for Elena Verdugo. Blonde and pleasingly plump, Elena squeezed into her tights, donned a black wig and instantly lit up in a wildfire performance that was sexy, kitschy and ultimately tragic. As the vivacious lady told me over 50 years later:

> When I first worked at Universal, you drove on this little lot, and all you saw were the hills behind the stages, all full of flowers, and it was very pretty. There was a shoeshine stand at the walkway to the entrance, and the commissary had a screen door to it—a screen door!

William Edmunds played Fejos, Ilonka's Gypsy "pimp" ("smelly pig!" Ilonka calls him); Belle Mitchell was Urla, the Gypsy woman; George Lynn was Gerlach, the gendarme. There were 23 extras. Karloff and Naish reported at 10:45 a.m. Work lasted until 5:45 p.m.

Saturday, April 8: Clouds and wind challenged director Kenton to keep *The Devil's Brood* on schedule. Forty extras and five musicians reported to the Shelby site at 9:00 a.m. for the filming of Ilonka's dance. By 10:00 a.m., due to the weather, they were dismissed.

Kenton scrambled to shoot other scenes. He called for Lon Chaney, who hurried to the studio, but there was little they could rig up for Chaney, so he was dismissed at 12:55 p.m. George Zucco showed up at 1:00 p.m., reported to Stage 12, and he, Karloff and Naish wrapped up the scene in the wagon. Zucco had finished his role in *The Devil's Brood* in two days.

It was Easter eve, and after a studio supper, Karloff, Naish and Elena went to the Nagana Rocks site on the back lot, under a full moon. Karloff finished at 9:45 p.m. Elena nestled under the coach's driver seat, and she and Naish played the scene in which Daniel brought Ilonka tea. She flirted and invited him to come closer:

"You're afraid of me, aren't you, Daniel?" she teased. "If you weren't, you'd come up here, where I could see you better."

The girl can't hide her revulsion when she sees he's a hunchback. Both players acted the episode with delicacy and pathos.

"But you will talk to me ... sometimes ... won't you?" pleads Naish's Daniel.

Easter Eve, April 8: J. Carrol Naish, Elena Verdugo and Boris Karloff work this cloudy, windy night on Universal's back lot "Nagana Rocks" set.

Kenton ("adorable, so sweet," recalled Elena Verdugo) was himself "gung ho" to keep working this night. But the assistant director report notes that, come midnight, it was "too windy to continue." The company dismissed and went home for Easter.

Kenton's first-week performance had been impressive. Despite weather trouble, he had shot 21 pages of the 125-page script in only five days. This was just shy of the four and a half pages he had to average daily to keep the film on schedule.

The director liked horror movies, and told reporter Erskine Johnson:

> *They give us a chance to let our imagination run wild. The art department can go to town on creep sets. Prop men have fun with cobwebs. The cameraman has fun with trick lighting and shadows. The director has fun. We have more fun making a horror picture than a comedy.*[20]

Elena Verdugo, meanwhile, had formed impressions of her co-stars:

> *Working with Boris Karloff, I had the keen awareness that I was working with a "great." He was a serious actor, but never unkind. I was aware that this was a wonderful man who was in his part—really in his part!*
>
> *Lon Chaney was a lovely, friendly man. I remember often sitting and chatting with him.*
>
> *I had met J. Carrol Naish on the set of my first picture,* Down Argentine Way *[1940], when I was 15. He loved working. I simply loved him. Oh, God! What a gentle, sweet soul. He helped, he supported, he gave so much.... He was an Irishman, you know—but he didn't look Irish, did he?*

Karloff could be cold, Chaney raucous, and Naish (allegedly) roistering—but all three men responded sweetly to the young Elena. The teenager saw them all on their best behavior, personally and professionally, and *The Devil's Brood* was a happy set.

Week Two: April 10 to April 15, 1944

Monday, April 10: The week began with gossip queen Hedda Hopper, in her "Looking at Hollywood" column, writing this quip:

> *Someone has a sense of humor. Lionel Atwill of the hot headlines has been added to the horror picture,* Devil's Brood, *at Universal....*[21]

The word "brood" still had a sexual flavor in 1944 Hollywood, and those "hot headlines" had reported Atwill to be a "devil"—hence Hedda's humor. At any rate, Atwill wouldn't start work on the film until late in the month.

Meanwhile, *The Devil's Brood* call was at 1:00 p.m. Karloff, Chaney, Naish and Elena did exterior shooting at Niemann's castle (the *Tower of London* set) and amidst the Frankenstein ruins (once again the sprawling *Green Hell* set). Last to go that night: Karloff and Chaney, at 10:35. Of note: Glenn Strange officially began work this day, reporting for a wardrobe and makeup run-through.

Tuesday, April 11: On this beautiful morning, Kenton shot Ilonka's dance "Gypsy Tantrums" on the Shelby House grounds. Also in the scene were five musicians and 41 extras. The lady remembered:

> *I had to choreograph the Gypsy dance carefully myself. It was difficult, because at the last moment I learned that it was to be done on a slope that had not even been cleared of rocks! All kinds of rocks, and on a slope—everything a dancer hates, you know. When I see the film, I recognize the steps—they're all mine.*

Her Ilonka was a dynamo, and during the dance we get several peeks at her black panties. However, the peacock performance masqueraded a shy teenager:

April 11: Elena Verdugo performs her Gypsy dance on the back lot's Shelby House set.

In dancing, and in Spanish dancing particularly, there's a lot of flirting that goes on; they flirt, and it used to embarrass me so much. I think back on playing Ilonka in House of Frankenstein—*and I could have died! It was my first picture without my mother on the set all the time, and I was so shy—I wouldn't even go into the commissary by myself. I'd grab a couple of candy bars. But my dancing experience gave me the freedom to play a part like Ilonka; I just pretended I was dancing, I suppose.*

Karloff worked this day from 11:00 a.m. to 4:40 p.m. (he had a *Creeps by Night* broadcast that evening), Naish from 10:00 to 4:50, Elena from 9:00 to 5:25.

Wednesday, April 12: Chaney, Naish and Elena started on the exterior "Brook and Trees" set, again on the Shelby estate grounds, where we see Ilonka's infatuation for Larry growing. Karloff joined them at 1:00 p.m. Mid-afternoon, they moved to Stage 17, where they beheld the interior of Niemann's laboratory, packed with impressive electrical gadgetry. Glenn Strange was there in full Monster regalia. Elena Verdugo said:

I'd see Glenn Strange in the makeup department every a.m. Glenn was dear, and Jack Pierce, his makeup man, was a genius. Jack had said to me, "'Lenny,' you want to see how I do all this makeup?" And I thought, "Sure!" So one time, in makeup, he showed me this array of masks, so I understood how he created all the fantasy.

The Frankenstein Monster would come on the set, and everybody'd say, "How you doin', Glenn? How you doin'?" Everyone loved Glenn—just loved him!

Also on this day: Monogram started filming *Alaska*, a Western spectacular (for that studio, anyway). Carradine played a drunken Wild West Shakespearean actor. He'd join *The Devil's Brood* in two weeks.

Thursday, April 13 through Saturday, April 15: The Devil's Brood focused Thursday on the exterior and interior of Lampini's wagon (now on Stage 7), then the company moved to the lab set (Stage 17) for the rest of the week. Some film historians have doubted that the Monster makeup required the three and a half hours that Universal publicized, but the assistant director report states the fact: Strange started "in Make-up" at 6:30 a.m. and reported to the set at 10:00 a.m.

Once there, the actor had nothing to do but lie on a table, comatose and prune-faced. Yet even this was hazardous. In one scene, Niemann thawed out the frozen Monster by lowering a large coffin-like glass case over the figure on his operating table. Prop men pumped steam into the case to create vapor; this made it impossible for Strange to breathe, so they placed small rubber air hoses up his nose. They also installed a panic button for him to push, that would light up a red flash.

Nobody watched for the flash.

As Strange told *Mad Monsters* magazine 20 years later:

> *Sure enough, something went wrong. The hoses were so long, I couldn't breathe out the bad air and I was starting to suffocate. I laid on the panic button they gave me to push if anything happened, and that red cue light was flashing like Fourth of July. Believe me, I almost died before somebody saw the light and got me out of there.*[22]

Karloff, between scenes, coached Strange on playing the Monster in the climax, where he finally rises from his coma. "He showed me how to make the Monster's moves properly," said Strange, "and how to do the walk that makes the Monster so frightening…."

Work for the week ended Saturday at 6:30 p.m. Kenton had shot 49¾ pages of a 125-page script in 11 days. This was almost exactly the four and a half pages a day the film needed to finish on schedule.

Week Three: April 17 to April 22, 1944

Monday, April 17: It was a 9:00 a.m. call on *The Devil's Brood* for Karloff, Naish and Verdugo; Strange joined them at 9:30. Chaney had the day off.

This day saw plenty of climax-centered action: Daniel, after the death of Talbot and Ilonka, attacked Niemann and broke his back. Then the Monster burst his operating table bonds, grabbed Daniel, virtually dribbled the hunchback across the room and hurled him through the skylight. The Daniel death scene was actually a two-parter—inside, the audience will see him crashing through the skylight; outside he'll tumble down the roof, and fall to his death.

This day was the inside shot. Thirty-year-old Carey Loftin, eventually known as the best stunt driver in Hollywood history, wore a gray fright wig as he doubled Karloff. Thirty-one-year-old Billy Jones, born in Ireland and later a John Ford favorite in films such as *Wagon Master* (1950), doubled Naish. Strange had no stunt man.

The shot of Niemann, strangled in shadow, went fine; Karloff left at 5:30 p.m., Loftin at 5:40. For the last shot of the day, Strange's unbound Monster grabbed Billy Jones (as Naish hung around to watch), lifted him in the air and threw him crashing through the skylight. As Strange told *Mad Monsters*, he had a hard time seeing through his Monster eyelids. He also didn't know his own strength. Jones smashed through the breakaway window, missed the mat placed for his landing, and landed smack on the soundstage floor. He suffered no serious injury.

The next day was Billy Jones' 32nd birthday.

Tuesday, April 18: *The Devil's Brood* company reported at 9:00 a.m. to a venerable Universal site: the European Street. Here was where Ludwig had carried the corpse of his daughter Maria in *Frankenstein*.

This morning, Ludwig himself was there: Michael Mark. The bald, mustached, Russian-born actor also played a victim of Karloff's Monster in *Son of Frankenstein,* and appeared in a bit in *The Ghost of Frankenstein,* as well as small parts in such horrors as *The Black Cat*. His role in *The Devil's Brood* was Herr Strauss, who testified against Niemann years before; Karloff and Naish vengefully kidnapped Mark in the village, the sun shining on the Tyrolean archways and cobbled street.

The actors moved to Stage 16 and Lampini's wagon. At 11 a.m., another experienced horror player arrived on the set: Frank Reicher, whose most famous credit was Captain Englehorn in RKO's *King Kong* (1933). Reicher played Herr Ullman, another target of Niemann's revenge. We see Strauss and Ullman bound in the wagon; Niemann announces that Ullman will get the Monster's brain, Strauss, the Wolf Man's brain.

April 18: Niemann (Boris Karloff) has a score to settle with Strauss (Michael Mark), whose testimony sent him to prison. Mark was a veteran of three past Frankenstein films: the 1931 original (as Little Maria's father), *Son* **and** *Ghost***. Pictured left to right, Mark, Karloff and J. Carrol Naish (from the Jim Clatterbaugh Collection).**

"[S]o that all your waking hours," said Karloff, *"will be spent in untold agony, await-ing the full of the moon, which will change you into a werewolf!"*

Lunch … then a wrap-up of the wagon scene. The two players completed their gigs in less than a day: Reicher at 3:45 p.m., Mark at 4:10 p.m.

Then cast and crew went to the interior tavern set, also on Stage 16. Olaf Hytten, Lit-tle Cloestine's father in *The Ghost of Frankenstein*, was Hoffman, the proprietor. Among the villagers: Charles Miller (Toberman, the burgomaster), Philip Van Zandt (Muller, the inspector) and Joe Kirk (Schwartz). The latter was Lou Costello's brother-in-law, a hanger-on in the Abbott and Costello films and Mr. Bacciagalupe in the team's 1952-53 TV series. The company wrapped up at 6:25 p.m.

Wednesday, April 19: The 9:00 a.m. call was for the villagers, who gathered on the "exterior woods" of the Process Stage. Joining them as Dr. Geissler, who examines a Wolf Man victim, was Brandon Hurst, a grand old man of supporting horror players, having appeared in such fare as *Dr. Jekyll and Mr. Hyde* (1920), *The Hunchback of Notre Dame* (1923), *The Man Who Laughs* (1928) and *White Zombie* (1932).

"The jugular vein is severed," said Hurst, "not cut, but torn apart, as though by pow-erful teeth."

Karloff and Strange reported at 3:30 p.m., but Kenton was still busy with the villag-ers, and both actors were dismissed at 4:00 p.m. (Strange had been in makeup for three

April 20: Happy birthday, Elena! Left to right with the birthday girl: Boris Karloff, director Erle C. Kenton and producer Paul Malvern. Lon Chaney looms behind them.

hours for apparently nothing.) The day ended at 6:40—Elena Verdugo at the gun rack, fashioning the Wolf Man–killing silver bullet "fired by one who loves him enough to understand."

Thursday, April 20: It was Elena Verdugo's 19th birthday. The call was at 1:00 p.m. and Elena arrived for a birthday party, complete with cake. Flanking her by the cake were Karloff in his Mad Doctor gown, Strange in Monster makeup, and J. Carrol Naish and Lon Chaney in their "civvies." (Chaney didn't work that day, but nevertheless was there for the party.) Karloff presented Elena with a "Fairy Tales" book, which she kept for many years.

Elena was on call this day primarily for the party; she went home at 4:00 p.m. The villagers had also reported at 1:00, and Kenton spent the afternoon shooting their storming of the castle interior as the Monster carried Niemann. Carey Loftin doubled Karloff in some of this footage and stayed on for the night shooting. Karloff went home at 5:30.

After dinner and come nightfall, Strange's Monster, Carey Loftin, Billy Jones, the "featured" villagers and 45 extras reported to the exterior *Tower of London* set. The scenes filmed included the terrific shot of the Monster coming down the tower steps, the villagers in pursuit with their torches—an iconic image in Universal Frankenstein lore.

The big spectacle this night, however, was the death of Daniel, Part II: The hunchback, having been thrown through the window by the Monster, falls to his death. Jones gave the company a Big Top–style thrill—sliding on his belly down the rooftop, and then falling far below into an off-screen net.

Carey Loftin told film historian Tom Weaver that Jones was cut up doing the stunt because the sloping roof had protruding nails and, instead of tumbling down it as he intended, he found himself sliding.[23] Also: The scream heard in the film, as Daniel falls, was actually Karloff's scream from the *Son of Frankenstein* scene where the Monster discovers that Lugosi's Ygor is dead.

Jones was dismissed at 12:10 a.m., as were Loftin and Strange. Universal served the company a midnight dinner, then work continued, Kenton shooting the villagers until 1:40 a.m. Still the night wasn't over. After the villagers and extras departed, Kenton took another shot of the Neustadt Prison Sign, with rain special effects. The eventful day and night finally ended at 2:30 a.m.

Friday, April 21: Lon Chaney and Elena Verdugo reported at 1:00 p.m. to the Process Stage representing the exterior of Niemann's garden, where they performed the Romeo and Juliet–style death scene—Larry at peace, the self-sacrificing Ilonka (who had shot him with a silver bullet, and been fatally mauled in the process) dragging her dying self through the mist to expire with her head on his chest.

Naish joined them at 7:00 p.m. *House of Frankenstein* has its glitches, and one appears in this episode: As Naish lifted Elena to carry her into the castle, she instinctively grabbed her dress so not to expose her lingerie.

Kenton had planned to complete shooting the climax this night; Karloff, Strange, the featured villagers and 45 extras were there at 7:30 p.m. For reasons not explained in the production report, the studio canceled the back lot shooting and dismissed those players. Chaney, Verdugo and Naish continued working on the Process Stage until 9:15 p.m.

Also on this date, reporter Virginia McPherson filed a newspaper story, "Film Has '5' Horrors." McPherson (who presumably had visited the set earlier in the week) called Karloff's Niemann "a slightly screwier version of Dr. Frankenstein," and opined, "The Monster looks worse in person than he does on the screen—only he smiles once in a while." She also attributed an interesting quote to Chaney:

I've played both Frankenstein's Monster and the Wolf Man before. And for my money, I'd rather be a Monster.[24]

Saturday, April 22: Karloff had the day off—his first since shooting began. Verdugo was on the set at 9:15 a.m. Chaney arrived at 10:45 a.m. in Wolf Man makeup. The scene: Wolf Man and Ilonka killing each other. Elena had never seen Chaney in Wolf Man makeup, and he and Kenton were careful not to let her see him now until they shot the scene. As Elena remembered:

For the horror films at Universal, they used to have professional screamers on the sets. For the scene in which the Wolf Man attacked me—that was spooky! They called one of those screamers to our stage … and I hadn't seen Lon in his makeup. Well, when the Wolf Man jumped out at me, I was so scared and screamed so wildly that they cancelled the professional screamer! They didn't need her! That was my *scream—and I screamed bloody murder!*

Elena managed to have a little fun with Lon this day:

I wasn't aware he had any problem with alcohol, although once, when we were sitting in a little wagon together, outside the soundstage—where the Wolf Man was smoking!—he might have had a beer hidden behind him. Maybe—I mean, I'd hate to be stuck as a Wolf Man! That's a heavy makeup! And the San Fernando Valley gets hot!

For the scene in which the Wolf Man crashed through the doors, the always rambunctious "Lonster" used no double.

Shooting ended at 6:45 p.m.—day 17 of the 30-day schedule. Kenton had shot 72¼ pages of the 125-page script. The film remained right on schedule.

Week Four: April 24 to April 29, 1944

Monday, April 24: The push was on to finish up with Karloff, whose contract called for him to complete all his work that coming Saturday. As blueprinted, the production would focus on the majority of the Dracula scenes after Karloff wrapped up.

This afternoon, Karloff and Naish reported at 1:00 p.m. to the Process Stage, representing the exterior of Lampini's wagon. Come 4:00 p.m., Chaney and Verdugo were on Stage 17, the interior hall set. Elena completed her work on *The Devil's Brood* at 5:15 p.m. She told me:

All in all, I enjoyed making the picture very much. I was a still-growing teenage girl, and all of those fine actors were kind, considerate, and made me feel a part of everything.

That night, they shot the climax in the swamp. Karloff, Strange, the villagers, 45 extras and Karloff's double Carey Loftin were there for the 7:30 night call on the Nagana Rocks set. Karloff greeted each of the extras personally and said how pleased he was to be working with them.[25] They proceeded until 12:10 a.m., when there was a break for a one-hour dinner. There was almost a disaster when the tumbleweed, set afire by the villagers, surprisingly exploded into an inferno of towering flames, almost burning both Strange and Loftin. Strange, in a panic, lunged into the quicksand (sawdust, bran and ground-up cork).

Then, at 2:55 a.m., Karloff performed the aforementioned sinking-into-the-goo. Producer Paul Malvern recalled:

Erle and I were getting ready to dive in when Karloff's head bobbed up. Boris is the best sport I have ever met. When he emerged from the water, he was trembling with cold. But he never uttered a single word of complaint.[26]

Strange wrapped up his Monster role this night. Destined to play the Monster again in *House of Dracula* (1945) and *Abbott and Costello Meet Frankenstein* (1948), he credited his success in the role to the man he called "the greatest man in show business," Boris Karloff. Of course, great actors aren't always great teachers. Strange's Monster came off as a stalking hybrid of zombie and T-Rex—complete with the latter's pea-sized brain.

Tuesday, April 25: After the marathon the previous night, the call was 3:00 p.m. for Karloff, Chaney, Naish and Burgomaster Charles Miller (the latter needed for some extra shots). The three horror stars worked a couple hours on the Ice Caves set on the Process Stage. Karloff had a *Creeps by Night* broadcast this night.

It was in the cavern that Niemann and Daniel discovered the frozen-in-ice Monster and Wolf Man (both dummies), providing Karloff the memorable line, "The undying Monster! The triumphant climax of Frankenstein's genius!"

Chaney had dinner and moved to Stage 17 for scenes shot in Larry's room. He finished at 8:55 p.m. The production report listed Glenn Strange as "carried"—meaning he was still on the payroll. He remained "carried" the rest of the week.

John Carradine arrived at 8:00 p.m. for a Dracula makeup and wardrobe run-through. He nailed it: The test, starting at 9:10, was over by 9:35. Carradine always claimed he wanted to wear a drooping white mustache, which Dracula had worn in the Bram Stoker novel, but Universal nixed it. Perhaps he wore that drooping mustache in the test.

Meanwhile, Carradine's dream of premiering his Shakespeare company on Broadway on the Bard's April 23 birthday had crashed and burned.[27] Now, due to personal travails, he'd sold his soul to Hollywood—as the new Count Dracula.

As the Ghost of Hamlet's father said, "O, horrible! O, horrible! Most horrible!"

Wednesday, April 26: It was back on the Ice Caverns set: Karloff, Chaney and Naish.[28]

Thursday, April 27: *The Devil's Brood* ventured into new Gothic territory this day: Carradine officially started work as Count Dracula.

Karloff and Naish were the first on the "Exterior Cross Roads & Nearby Roads" Process Stage set at 9:00 a.m. Carradine started at 9:30. Lionel Atwill (as Inspector Arnz) and Peter Coe and Anne Gwynne (as Carl and Rita, newlyweds) began work this day too.

The film this day seemed more Western genre than horror. Kenton took shots of the chase scene—Karloff pulled reins and Carradine cracked a whip, pretending to be driving their respective coaches. Atwill sat on a horse. George Plues, who played the driver of Lampini's wagon, returned to double Karloff on the wagon and Atwill on horseback.

It's rather a shock to see Atwill, a horror superstar in such films as 1933's *Mystery of the Wax Museum*, in this virtual bit. And the fact that he was in uniform as an "inspector" reminds one of his terrific portrayal of one-armed Inspector Krogh in *Son of Frankenstein* (1939). The mighty had indeed fallen.

Atwill's best line of the 12 he had in *House of Frankenstein*: "Don't get lost in the fog!"

Yet these were personally happy days for Atwill. "Pinky" was wooing a beautiful, blonde 27-year-old contralto named Paula Pruter.[29] Another possible reason for Atwill's high spirits: The previous Sunday, April 23, the *New York Times* had announced that Mae West ("the lady herself abursting for action") was bringing her new play, *Catherine Was Great*, to New York. The *Times* wrote, "Lionel Atwill, of Hollywood 'heavy' luster, may have one of the leading roles."[30]

One wonders if West considered Atwill partly due to those "hot headlines." At any rate, Atwill was *not* in the cast when *Catherine Was Great* opened on Broadway on August 2, 1944.

April 28: Karloff's Niemann threatens John Carradine's Dracula with a stake. The two stars worked only three days together on *House of Frankenstein*, and were on the set at the same time for only about nine hours (from the Jim Clatterbaugh Collection).

Friday, April 28: The sets were the interior of Dracula's "Booth" (Stage 17) and, on the Process Stage, the interior carriage, exterior of Lampini's wagon, and the coffin on the road. Karloff and Carradine played the memorable scene in which Niemann withdrew the stake from Dracula's skeleton and the vampire appeared, to serve as the Mad Doctor's demon of vengeance. Carradine later claimed the gasp he gave as he came to life was his own concept. (John P. Fulton's unit added the special effect transformation later.) Naish, Gwynne, Coe and Atwill were also on hand.

Saturday, April 29: It was the "Midnight Spook Show," and the last day's shooting for Karloff and Naish. Others on call: Gwynne, Coe, Atwill, Sig Ruman (who started work this day as Hussman, burgomaster of Reigelberg), and 20 extras. The call: 9:00 a.m. for everyone but Karloff (10:00 a.m.) and Carradine (2:30 p.m.), The sets: exterior and interior of Lampini's tent, and exterior carriage and horses on road (Process Stage).

Chaney wasn't on call. Although *House of Frankenstein* was an all-star monster film, there hadn't been a single day when all the star villains had been on the set simultaneously.[31]

Karloff's Niemann did his spook show spiel. Carradine did more carriage-riding process work. Naish finished at 3:00, Karloff at 4:30 and Carradine at 6:00. Kenton completed the week's work at 6:30.

The director had delivered Karloff right on the date of his contract, and was still on schedule, having shot 95¼ pages of the 125-page script. He had seven days to complete the picture.

As for Karloff: His Niemann might remind his fans of the dark, dead-eyed portrayal he later gave in the title role of *Thriller*'s very frightening episode "The Incredible Doktor Markesan" (February 26, 1962). Yet Karloff privately lamented the Monster's degeneration, the movie's cruelty and violence, and probably what had happened to his own film career.

Having revived Dracula, the Wolf Man and the Monster ... where in the hell would Boris Karloff go from here?

Week Five: May 1 to May 8, 1944

Monday, May 1: It was 9:00 a.m. and John Carradine's lanky presence filled Stage 6. The actor, in his stylishly cocked top hat and flowing cape, turned Dracula into Lucifer himself—with dashes of carnival magician and sexual predator. There was also, naturally, a flourish of Shakespeare. As Carradine explained:

> *My attitude would be definitely Shakespearean, with a nod to Richard III. Dracula is a tragic figure—a monarch of the undead, in some respects like Lear, his kingdom gone, forced to live among inferiors, an outcast. I added many of my own ideas to personalize the role—I wore the top hat at an angle because this man could afford to be debonair. I used my eyes like weapons since Dracula could, of course, bend one's will to his own....*[32]

Carradine, Gwynne, Atwill and Ruman worked on the Interior Hussman house set this day. Among the scenes filmed: Dracula's creeping through the doors, wild-eyed, to kill the burgomaster.

Tuesday, May 2: Carradine, Gwynne, Coe, Atwill and Ruman acted on the exterior country road set, the interior carriage, and the interior of Arnz's bedroom. Carradine was so dramatically overpowering that the hopelessly upstaged Peter Coe had a tantrum.

"Don't try to fuck with me!" Coe remembered shouting at Carradine.[33]

Last to finish that day, at 5:15 p.m.: Atwill, filmed in bed, answering Carl's call that the burgomaster is dead. Kenton and crew stayed on until six, getting a process shot of the exterior sky and moon.

Wednesday, May 3, and Thursday, May 4: Carradine, Gwynne, Coe and Ruman worked on the interior and exterior of Hussman's estate set. Atwill wrapped up his role Wednesday at 4:15 p.m. He went home to Pacific Palisades, having worked on *The Devil's Brood* for a total of six days.

Also on Wednesday, John Fulton's special effects unit shot Lon Chaney's Wolf Man transformation. It was impressive, 1944 state-of-the-art movie magic—but as many fans have noticed, Chaney's hands don't change and get hairy. This day's shoot completed Chaney's work on the film.

On Thursday, Ruman finished his role at 10:15 a.m. and work proceeded on the interior and exterior of Hussman's estate on Stage 6 and the interior of Rita's room on Stage 7. Carradine and Gwynne shot sparks as Dracula seduced Rita, and gave her his ring. "I will come for you before the dawn," he soulfully promised.

Gwynne talked about her role of Rita with Michael Fitzgerald in a *Fangoria* interview:

> *The part was nice, but not great. I had fun with it, but I'm only in the first 25 minutes ... and then zap, I'm out for the rest of the film! That's not good showmanship.... John Carradine was a good*

choice for Dracula.... I felt that my scenes with Carradine were some of the best acting I ever did....[34]

Late in Carradine's life, Jack Gourlay asked the actor for his memories of playing this scene with Gwynne, and the aged actor replied, "I don't think I ever worked with her." Gourlay couldn't resist passing this on to Gwynne, who laughed long and loudly.[35]

Also, the May 4 production report noted that the Fulton unit filmed the "Bat and Dracula" scenes in the afternoon from 4:45 to 5:50 p.m.

Friday, May 5: Carradine, Gwynne and Coe, the last three actors on the production, worked 9:00 a.m. to 4:30 p.m. Kenton shot scenes inside Carl and Rita's room on Stage 7. Carradine arrived at 10:00 a.m. and worked with the Fulton unit, which filmed both his skeleton-into-Dracula and Dracula-into-skeleton transformations on the Process Stage. Fulton had this down to a science, and Carradine was done at 2:30 p.m. However, there was a continuity error. As Carradine went into his Dracula death throes, he wore a glove on his left hand; then in a later shot, the glove was gone; and then, as he became a skeleton, the glove was back!

The unit also filmed on this day shots of the dead Wolf Man's feet transforming to human feet (the participation of Chaney wasn't needed).

Saturday, May 6: The three players had the day off as Kenton, crew and eight stunt men left at 8:00 a.m. for Sherwood Forest. They filmed long shots of the chase scene, as the police cavalry pursued the coach of Dracula, who was chasing the coach of Niemann, to get to his coffin before the dawn. George Robinson and his two-camera crew did a nice job of day-for-night shooting, managing an impressive 22 camera set-ups. The picturesque scenes of the wagons riding over a bridge, through a stream and past a mill wheel, gave *The Devil's Brood* another splash of Wild West–style action. The company worked until 4:40 p.m.

Monday, May 8: It was the 30th and final day of shooting of *The Devil's Brood*, focused on the "exterior countryside & roadways." John Carradine, Anne Gwynne and Peter Coe left Universal at 8:00 a.m., along with Kenton, crew, and the eight stunt men, for Sherwood Forest. Once again, George Robinson and the members of his crew completed an amazing 30 set-ups.

Again, there was a gaffe. After the coach tumbled down the hillside, a disheveled Dracula was sprawled in the grass ... and half of Carradine's mustache was gone.

Still, it was a solid day's work and a slam-bang production finale, wrapping up at exactly 5:00 p.m. Erle C. Kenton had completed *The Devil's Brood* precisely on schedule.

Part Three: Post-Production

Interim—and Karloff Defects from the Fold

The actors found new jobs:

- May 15: Universal began shooting *Raiders of Ghost City*, a Western serial, with Lionel Atwill as the star heavy.
- May 31: PRC started *Bluebeard*, with John Carradine in the title role.

- June 9: Universal rolled the new Maria Montez-Jon Hall Technicolor romp *Sudan*, with George Zucco as the villain.
- June 12: Paramount started *A Medal for Benny*, for which J. Carrol Naish received his second Best Supporting Actor Oscar nomination.
- June 19: Universal began *The Frozen Ghost*, a new *Inner Sanctum* with Lon Chaney, Evelyn Ankers, and Elena Verdugo.

The most significant news, however, came Thursday, May 18: Boris Karloff signed an RKO contract to star in two films for Val Lewton. Universal's King of Horror had defected to the competition, whose most recent release had been *The Curse of the Cat People*.

The RKO terms were the same as he signed for at Universal: two films for a total of $60,000. Karloff and Lewton quickly struck a rapport and the producer prepared two vehicles for him: *Isle of the Dead*, inspired by the Bocklin painting, and *The Body Snatcher*, based on the Robert Louis Stevenson story.[36]

Undaunted, Universal launched a "Worldwide Sales Drive." On June 8, William A. Scully, studio vice-president and general sales manager, promised that *The Devil's Brood*, Universal's "all-star horror feature," would be "the largest grosser [that the] company has ever had in this bracket."

Other developments:

Friday, July 7: Lionel Atwill wed Paula Pruter in Las Vegas. She gave birth to their son Lionel in October 1945 (Atwill was 60, Paula 28) and carried a torch for her husband after his 1946 death (despite her remarrying) until her own death in 2002.

Friday, July 14: *Isle of the Dead* started shooting on RKO's Stage 10. Mark Robson was the director. The budget was $180,450 and the shooting schedule was 18 days—about half the budget and shooting days of *The Devil's Brood*. Karloff, as Greek General Pherides on a plague-haunted isle, was ill with severe back trouble, but worked this day from 9:00 a.m. to 5:40 p.m.

Wednesday, July 19: After four days on the *Isle of the Dead* set, part of it spent in a wheelchair, Karloff could no longer make it to work. The company shot around him until Saturday evening, July 22, when RKO's daily shooting report noted, "Show Closed Until Further Notice." Karloff entered the hospital for spinal surgery.

Approximately the same time: John Carradine, suffering a meltdown over his divorce and financial woes, went berserk at the Garden of Allah: After downing 12 double Scotch and sodas, he tried to drown himself in the pool. Three male nurses, answering the Garden's emergency call, restrained him.[37]

Wednesday, July 26: *Variety* reported that Karloff had signed with *Arsenic and Old Lace* producers Howard Lindsay and Russel Crouse to return to Broadway in the play *He Who Sups with the Devil*. (It was never produced.)

Monday, August 21: Universal completed *The Mummy's Curse*. Lon Chaney, drinking heavily during his third Mummy-go-round, had wreaked havoc.

Friday, September 1: The Warner Bros. film version of *Arsenic and Old Lace*, produced and directed by Frank Capra, opened at Broadway's Strand Theatre. Raymond Massey, in Karloff's stage role of Jonathan Brewster, wore a Karloffian makeup (complete with Frankenstein Monster–style scars) and said the line, "He said I look like Boris Karloff." The wildly popular film (earning a rental of $4,784,000 and a profit of $2,074,000[38]) lacked the real-deal Karloff, but certainly added to his iconic stature.

Monday, October 16: Universal ran a two-page trade advertisement for *The Devil's Brood*—now retitled *House of Frankenstein.* The copy read:

> "Man, Oh, Man!
> This show's gonna scare the yell out of
> Satan himself!"

Along with its new title, the film had received a terrific musical score. In 1995, Marco Polo released a CD of the complete *House of Frankenstein* film score by Hans J. Salter and Paul Dessau. John Morgan masterfully recreated the long-lost orchestral scores, William T. Stromberg conducted the Moscow Symphony Orchestra, and Bill Whitaker wrote in his excellent liner notes:

> *A virtual Hollywood camp* Symphonie Fantastique *when heard in its entirety … the* House of Frankenstein *score offers numerous delights to accompany its cast of accursed characters….*

Salter revived monster cues from Universal's past and created new ones, while Dessau (like Salter, a European who fled Hitler) added his own flourishes—notably what Whitaker called the "haunting, transparent night music" of the Dracula episode, and the wild "romp" for the mounted chase after Dracula. As Whitaker wrote, "the real showstoppers" come in the finale, "exploding into a musical maelstrom":

> House of Frankenstein *concludes with an unforgettable musical climax … the utter chaos of the film's bizarre, one-of-a-kind resolution in which, very oddly for a Hollywood programmer of the early 1940s, everybody dies….*

Wednesday, October 18: "Lon Chaney Jr. to Do Dramatic Vaude Act," headlined *Variety*, noting that Chaney

> *will do a quick-change dramatic routine using masks, somewhat reminiscent of the performance of his late father in films years ago. Theatres in Washington, Boston, Columbus, Fall River and Worcester will be played, as well as Loews State, N.Y. Dates are being worked out currently.*

The "routine" was to begin around December 1 and last six weeks. If realized, it would be great publicity for *House of Frankenstein.*

Meanwhile: Since it would take time to re-assemble the *Isle of the Dead* company after its shutdown in July, Val Lewton proceeded with Karloff vehicle #2.

Wednesday, October 25: Karloff, upbeat after his back surgery, began playing the title role in *The Body Snatcher* on RKO's Stage 4. He was "Dear Boris" again—and director Robert Wise found him "an absolute joy … very quick and very keen."[39] The budget was $194,608 and the shooting schedule was 18 days.

In his top hat and scraggly sideburns, Karloff, as cabman John Gray, rode his coach at night through the spectral streets of Edinburgh (actually the old sets from RKO's 1939 *The Hunchback of Notre Dame* on the studio's ranch in Encino). The actor gave a wonderfully nightmarish performance, arguably his best.

Lewton added Bela Lugosi as janitor Joseph, whom Karloff's Gray kills and deposits into a brine vat. Henry Daniell, superb as Dr. MacFarlane, had the true co-starring role, but Lewton hoped the Karloff-Lugosi billing, along with the film's Burke and Hare lore, would make the film a "special" … and RKO's volley to Universal's *House of Frankenstein.*

This put events into place for a true battle of horror supremacy between Universal and RKO.

Saturday, October 28: John Carradine guest starred on the Halloween episode of *Stars Over Hollywood*: "Frankenstein and the Monster."

Friday, November 17: *The Body Snatcher* wrapped at 10:00 p.m. The scene: Karloff killing the little dog guarding the grave of his master. The film took 21 days to shoot (three days over schedule) and had a final cost of $221,000.

House of Frankenstein, meanwhile, had a final cost of $389,636.64—$35,000 over budget. *The Body Snatcher* cost over $168,000 less and took nine days fewer to shoot.

Friday, December 1: Karloff resumed work at RKO on Lewton's *Isle of the Dead.* Katherine Emery had replaced Rose Hobart (who had gone overseas) and sets needed to be rebuilt. Mark Robson continued as director.

Monday, December 11: *Variety* mentioned that Lon Chaney was taking a vacation on his ranch in Cool, California. The "mask" vaudeville tour had apparently fallen through.

The New York premiere of *House of Frankenstein* was four days away.

The Release

There were big shows on Broadway during 1944's Yuletide season: MGM's *National Velvet* at Radio City Music Hall; Warner Bros.' all-star *Hollywood Canteen* at the Strand; RKO's John Wayne Western *Tall in the Saddle* at the Palace. For competition, Universal launched two Boris Karloff films.

Tuesday, December 12: *The Climax* opened at New York City's 1700-seat Criterion Theatre.

Friday, December 15: As Karloff worked this day on Stage 15 of RKO's Pathé lot on *Isle of the Dead, House of Frankenstein* premiered at Broadway's 594-seat Rialto Theatre (see Chapter 13). Arthur Mayer, the theater's manager (and known as "the Merchant of Menace"), gave the film a deluxe showcase presentation, erecting a castle-like entranceway to the Rialto and exhibiting huge pictures of the horror stars.

House of Frankenstein was a sensation. The film was so instantly popular that the Rialto ran the film all night Saturday, its second night. On Wednesday, December 20, *Variety* wrote:

> Perhaps for the first time in Broadway history—and probably the U.S.—a theatre establishes a new high the week ahead of Christmas. It's the bandbox Rialto, which looks to hit $17,000 with House of Frankenstein, *best ever for house by close $1000. It ground through Saturday....*[40]

It would stay there for three more weeks, becoming the Rialto's King of the Horror Hits of the World War II years.

Friday, December 22: The double bill of *House of Frankenstein* and *The Mummy's Curse* opened at the 1100-seat Hawaii Theatre in Hollywood. Elena Verdugo remembered:

> I drove by the theater, at the end of Hollywood Boulevard, and they had pictures all over the outside—pictures of the monsters, pictures of me in that Gypsy costume, pictures all over the front, like a decoupage. The theatre was so adorned with all these huge photos ... a lot of hype and a splurge of publicity. It was elaborate showcasing!

The double feature stayed at the Hawaii for six weeks and made terrific money.[41]

Meanwhile, *Isle of the Dead* finished up on the RKO Pathé lot on December 21 with a final cost—due to Karloff's illness and the suspension in shooting—of $230,287. This was $50,000 over its original budget.

Thursday, January 4, 1945: *Film Daily* reviewed *House of Frankenstein*, and its critique was typical:

Universal spreads a lavish feast for horror lovers. The picture, produced without too much care by Paul Malvern and directed by Erle C. Kenton in slipshod manner ... is a scarer with a vengeance. The story [is] a silly thing that will draw laughs from those who don't take readily to horror entertainment.... The actors make the most of their exaggerated and thankless roles.[42]

House of Frankenstein was a natural for theater ballyhoo. When the film opened at Brooklyn's RKO-Albee Theatre, Dave Ballard, a man over seven feet tall, dressed in a top hat and cape, wandered the downtown Brooklyn streets, passing out heralds reading, "I am the LANDLORD of the *House of Frankenstein*.... Come and Meet the Mad Monsters...!" *Boxoffice* magazine reported that Ballard was "a sensation," and Charles McDonald, the zone manager, dispatched Ballard to go stalking through other neighborhoods.[43]

Wednesday, February 14: *The Body Snatcher* had a sensational opening this Valentine's Day night at the Missouri Theatre in St. Louis. All variety of ballyhoo accompanied the show.

Tuesday, February 20: *House of Frankenstein* and *The Mummy's Curse*, after the dual run at the Hawaii, began a week's run at Los Angeles' 2200-seat Orpheum Theatre, where *Frankenstein* had broken the house record in 1932. The attraction, losing steam, took in $19,700, which *Variety* called "below average." If one counts the double bill's run at the Orpheum, however, its L.A. receipts surpassed *I Walked with a Zombie–The Leopard Man*, but still fell about $12,000 short of the *Cat People–The Gorilla Man* bonanza.

Wednesday, March 14: *Variety* reported that *House of Frankenstein,* after "heavy box office returns," was expected "to pile up a gross of between $1,500,000 and $2,000,000 before another Christmas rolls around."[44]

The article also announced a sequel.

The Sequel and the Rival

House of Dracula, the *Variety* story claimed, was to have a $750,000 budget and star Karloff, who reportedly had been signed by Universal "to a three-picture deal." Paul Malvern was to produce, Erle Kenton direct, Edward T. Lowe write the script, and as *Variety* reported, "Lon Chaney, John Carradine, Lionel Atwill, J. Carrol Naish and others who worked with Karloff in *House* probably will be rounded up for *Dracula*."

The announcement was premature, at least in regard to Karloff and Naish. Karloff had signed a new three-picture, $100,000 RKO contract in January, and then took off to the South Pacific to appear in a G.I. production of *Arsenic and Old Lace*. Upon his return, Universal offered him a three-picture pact, negotiating with him at the time of the *Variety* report, and matching RKO's figure.

However, when Karloff learned *House of Dracula* was to be one of the three films, he rejected Universal's $100,000 deal.

Thursday, May 10: Two days after Germany's surrender, RKO's *The Body Snatcher* opened at Hollywood's Hawaii Theatre. The supporting feature: RKO's *The Brighton Strangler*. *The Body Snatcher* provided Karloff's magnificent title role portrayal, Robert Wise's atmospheric direction, Henry Daniell's bull's-eye performance as the tragic Dr. MacFarlane, Bela Lugosi's excellent cameo, a stirring Roy Webb musical score, and a shock finale. In his incisive book *Alternate Oscars*, Danny Peary awarded Karloff the Best Actor Oscar for 1945 for his Cabman Gray.

Friday, May 25: *The Body Snatcher* opened at the Rialto. In a review that seemed like a potshot at *House of Frankenstein*, *The New York Times* maintained that Lewton's film:

> manages to hold its own with nary a werewolf or vampire! But then, with Karloff on the prowl, what chance would a bloodthirsty hobgoblin stand?

The Body Snatcher reaped the highest worldwide rental of any of the Val Lewton horror films, $547,000.[45] However, in *The Body Snatcher*'s box office battles with *House of Frankenstein* at the Rialto and the Hawaii, the result wasn't even close. (For specifics, see Chapter 13.)

Incidentally, a grisly tale regarding *The Body Snatcher*: On Friday, June 1, 1945, the *Detroit Free Press* headlined on page one, "Skull Taken from Grave by Ghouls":

> Investigation into evidence that a grave in Redford Cemetery had been tampered with, disclosed Thursday that the skull of Mrs. Helen Jackson, who died in 1883, had been removed.
> It was Memorial Day that Mrs. Oliver Herrick, of 15935 Bradner, Plymouth, went to the cemetery to place flowers on her mother's grave.
> She noticed the sod had been removed and replaced carelessly. Nearby were found two old-fashioned coffin handles.
> Permission was obtained to reopen the grave. Police found that the skull had been removed recently from the body.

Saturday, June 23: *Showmen's Trade Review* headlined, "Real Body Snatcher":

> The Capitol Theatre, Detroit, was quick to capitalize on some ready-made publicity recently. While the theatre's press agents were searching for a skeleton or a reasonable facsimile to attract customers to see RKO Radio's *The Body Snatcher*, a real ghoul visited a Detroit cemetery and snatched a body [sic—actually, a skull]. All local newspapers gave it their biggest type. Those headlines adorned the lobby of the Capitol with the caption, "It Happens Here."

Wednesday, July 18: Val Lewton's *Bedlam* started shooting at RKO's Pathé lot, with Karloff as the wicked apothecary general of the infamous asylum.

Thursday, October 25: Universal completed shooting *House of Dracula*. The cast included Lon Chaney (the Wolf Man), John Carradine (Dracula), the Monster (Glenn Strange), Jane Adams (a hunchbacked nurse in false eyelashes) and Onslow Stevens as the Mad Doctor. Universal had continued mentioning Karloff for *House of Dracula* into August, hoping he would change his mind, but the star had held fast. The final cost was about half of what Universal originally publicized: $363,802.29.[46]

Meanwhile, in his own potshot at *House of Frankenstein*, Karloff, in 1946, called the movie "the monster clambake"—and referred to Lewton as "the man who rescued me from the living dead and restored my soul."[47]

Retrospect

The Body Snatcher is arguably the greatest horror film of the 1940s. The movie deals with bodies, but it's actually about souls, and the film, brilliant on so many levels, plays as if it has a soul of its own.

So … does *House of Frankenstein* have a soul?

It definitely has its kinks and quirks. Carradine as Dracula and Anne Gwynne as his kidnapped American bride, passionately sighing dialogue like the stars of a 1944 smoker; Elena Verdugo, brazenly revealing her thighs in her Gypsy dance; J. Carrol Naish's hunchback, in a fit of sexual frustration over Ilonka, lashing the unconscious Monster with a strap. "She hates me because I'm an ugly hunchback," cries Naish, his voice breaking. "If it wasn't for you, I'd have Talbot's body!" And meanwhile the musical track provides a seemingly mocking, "Strap One, Strap Two!" accompaniment.

There are other twists … for example, the eight onscreen deaths of stars and featured players (and various other offscreen demises referred to) almost qualify *House of Frankenstein* as a "snuff" film.

Most of all, however, *House of Frankenstein* is precisely and almost endearingly what fans have always called it: "a monster rally." Here's where the "soul" really manifests itself: the giant professionalism of the monsters themselves as they tackle those "exaggerated and thankless roles."

- See John Carradine, wishing he were playing Hamlet on Broadway for the Bard's 380th birthday, nevertheless serving up a new, sexy Count Dracula, with a wry twist of Shakespeare.
- Watch J. Carrol Naish, recent Academy Award loser, acting as if Daniel could win him an Oscar—but surely knowing a nomination for playing a hunchback in an organ grinder costume in a monster rally was totally out of the question for Academy consideration.
- Enjoy Lon Chaney, futilely dreaming on about being a movie heartthrob— meanwhile investing his "Baby," the Wolf Man, with conviction and tragedy.
- Admire Glenn Strange, hero-worshipping Karloff, trying to do the Monster as Karloff had done it, under the Great Man's tutelage—falling light years short, but not for lack of trying.
- Observe Lionel Atwill, acting with gusto, apparently just pleased to be working again … and
- Salute George Zucco, who once called himself "Hollywood's unhappiest actor" due to horror films, showing no shame at playing the doomed proprietor of a Chamber of Horrors.

Finally, there's Boris Karloff, who—for whatever personal and professional hang-ups that haunted him that spring of 1944, and for however he felt about the film—provided *House of Frankenstein* a gothic authority only he could bestow. There isn't the passion he gave the Monster, the Mummy, high priest Poelzig, Cabman Gray, or other roles he indelibly created. Nevertheless, there's plenty of star presence and heroic professionalism—from a venerable actor who even held his breath in a quicksand pit at 3:00 a.m. on a chilly April night.

After years of fan mail and convention appearances, Elena Verdugo came to regard *House of Frankenstein* with genuine affection—realizing what the film and her performance mean to so many.

"*House of Frankenstein*," she told me, "has enriched my life beyond all expectations."

The irreplaceable actors made the magic happen, and made it last. After 78 years, *House of Frankenstein* still wins the prize … as Hollywood's Greatest Midnight Spook Show of Them All.

House of Frankenstein

Universal, 1944. Producer, Paul Malvern. Executive Producer, Joseph Gershenson. Director, Erle C. Kenton. Screenplay, Edward T. Lowe (based on a story by Curt

Siodmak). Cinematographer, George Robinson. Musical Score and Direction, Hans J. Salter (and Paul Dessau, uncredited). Art Directors, John B. Goodman and Martin Obzina. Sound Director, Bernard B. Brown; Sound Technician, William Hedgcock. Set Decorators, Russell A. Gausman and A.J. Gilmore. Editor, Philip Cahn. Gowns, Vera West. Assistant Directors, William Tummel (and Phil Bowles, uncredited). Special Photography, John P. Fulton (and Carl Elmendorf, uncredited). Makeup, Jack P. Pierce and Otto Lederer. Prop Man, Eddie Keys. Still Photographer, Sherman Clark. Script Clerk, Connie Earle. Shooting title: *The Devil's Brood.* Running time, 70 minutes.

New York Opening, Rialto Theatre, December 15, 1944. Los Angeles Opening, Hawaii Theatre, December 22, 1944.

Boris Karloff (Dr. Gustav Niemann), Lon Chaney (Larry Talbot—the Wolf Man), J. Carrol Naish (Daniel), John Carradine (Count Dracula), Anne Gwynne (Rita Hussman), Peter Coe (Carl Hussman), Lionel Atwill (Inspector Arnz), George Zucco (Prof. Bruno Lampini), Elena Verdugo (Ilonka), Sig Ruman (Hussman), William Edmunds (Fejos), Charles Miller (Toberman), Philip Van Zandt (Inspector Muller), Julius Tannen (Hertz), Hans Herbert (Meier), Dick Dickinson (Born), George Lynn (Gerlach—Gendarme), Michael Mark (Strauss), Olaf Hytten (Hoffman), Frank Reicher (Ullman), Brandon Hurst (Dr. Geissler), Glenn Strange (The Frankenstein Monster), Belle Mitchell (Urla), Joe Kirk (Schwartz), Edmund Cobb (Driver), Charles Wagenheim (Prison Guard), George Plues (Lampini's Wagon Driver/Double for Karloff and Atwill), Carey Loftin (Double for Karloff), Billy Jones (Double for Naish).

12

His 20-Year-Long Last Bow

The Final Act of Basil Rathbone

Halloween night, 1953, was the closing night of the play *Sherlock Holmes*. It had opened only the previous evening at Broadway's New Century Theatre.

The star: Basil Rathbone.

The play had appeared a sure bet. Rathbone was reprising the role he had indelibly played in 14 motion pictures and 275 radio broadcasts. His interpretation of Sir Arthur Conan Doyle's master detective was iconic. The play was set to head to London after New York, and then embark on a world tour. How could it lose?

Well….

Rathbone's wife Ouida, long considered seriously batty by many of the actor's acquaintances, had written the script—her first such work in 30 years. Her script had called for clumsy, heavy sets—including "a chalet at the Reichenbach Falls"—which proved nearly impossible for the stage crew to move. Rathbone, likely sensing disaster, had blown his lines on the first night of the Boston tryout.[1] The star had been playing

Holmes not as the cool analytic genius but as a babbling near-hysteric, possibly due to trying to enliven (and remember) the cumbersome dialogue. The Boston run had closed early.

Opening night in New York, there was an ominous sense of disaster in the air. Critical response was dismal: one favorable review, one "yes-and-no," and five pans.[2] The play was closing after the Friday night opening and the Saturday matinee and evening performances. Ticket sales had been so poor that many in the audience for the final performance received free passes. On this All Hallows' Eve, Rathbone, shattered by this train wreck of a play, felt the professional shadows closing.

A post-mortem of *Sherlock Holmes* revealed a then-gigantic loss of "around $125,000 on a $100,000 investment."[3]

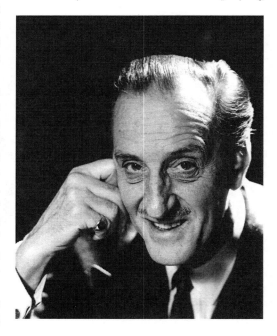

A late portrait of Basil Rathbone.

360

It was a startling and significant low in the last act of Basil Rathbone—a frequently sad final bow that provided an often-cruel variety of failures and humiliations. How he faced them—and, for 20 years, gallantly survived them—reveals a great deal about the man and the actor.

Part One: Pre-1946

Now comes Basil Rathbone, the dark and devious, the long and languorous, the naughty and handsome, philandering his way through The Command to Love, *with Mary Nash and Violet Kemble Cooper, at the Belasco. Is it his fault if every normal girl and woman in the audience feels his breath upon her ear ... thrills to his pleasant villainies, trades places by a feat of imagination with the philandered females of the cast?*

No. Not his fault; but his duty. The matinee idol of the moment, he carries his grave responsibilities well. Let the hearts throb where they may.
—"Now It's Rathbone for Whom Feminine Hearts Beat Wildly,"
Los Angeles Examiner, June 10, 1928

Professional Success

As the aforementioned stage review shows, Basil Rathbone in his heyday had been a theatrical sex symbol and spellbinder. And in 1928, his greatest successes were all ahead of him.

Born in South Africa, a decorated soldier in World War I, he made his stage bow in 1911 and his film debut in 1921. It was from 1935 to 1946 that Rathbone enjoyed his apogee in the Golden Age in the Movies. Hollywood's top villain, he was unforgettable in MGM's *David Copperfield* (1935) as the cruel Mr. Murdstone, mercilessly beating little Freddie Bartholomew with a cane. His most famous weapon, however, was a sword, and he was magnificent, dueling with such heroic foes as Errol Flynn in Warner Bros.' *Captain Blood* (1935) and *The Adventures of Robin Hood* (1938), and Tyrone Power in 20th Century–Fox's *The Mark of Zorro* (1940).

He received two Academy Best Supporting Actor nominations—for his quicksilver Tybalt of *Romeo and Juliet* (MGM, 1936, in which he dueled with Leslie Howard and John Barrymore) and his cackling, hunchbacked King Louis in *If I Were King* (Paramount, 1938). He easily should have won, especially for the latter, but in those days, the extras always voted for Walter Brennan (a former extra, who defeated Rathbone both times).[4]

He had a special flair, as if he had bounded out of the pages of classical literature, with a wolfhound handsomeness ("two profiles glued to one another," sniped Dorothy Parker), a golden voice, and an acting style of contained majesty that he delicately keyed for the camera.

Rathbone even made his mark in horror films. As Dr. Wolf von Frankenstein in Universal's *Son of Frankenstein* (1939), he played his Gothic role as one big, gradual, flamboyant nervous breakdown, and had star billing over Boris Karloff as the Monster, Bela Lugosi as broken-necked Ygor, and Lionel Atwill as one-armed Inspector Krogh.

Then, in his next film, 20th Century–Fox's *The Hound of the Baskervilles,* he played Sherlock Holmes. He reprised the role in Fox's *The Adventures of Sherlock Holmes* (1939), with Nigel Bruce his Dr. Watson in both films. Rathbone and Bruce began the radio series, and in 1942, they commenced the modernized Holmes series for Universal. During the World War II years, he was under contract to MGM, who farmed him out for the Holmes movies and films at other studios, and paid him a salary of $5000 a week.

Of course, Rathbone gave many great performances (see Chapter 9 on *Tower of London*): There are a number of films from the early 1940s where he's the only good thing *in* them. An example: Paramount's Technicolor (but dreadful) *Frenchman's Creek* (1944), in which Rathbone's villain hopes to rape Joan Fontaine's heroine and stalks her up a staircase ... until she kills him by pushing a suit of armor atop him. But eclipsing his respect as an actor, steadily, was his doppelganger, Sherlock Holmes.

The identification, understandably, finally paled. So, in 1946, Rathbone, 54 years old, moved out of his mansion at 10728 Bellagio Road in Bel Air, gave up his Sherlock Holmes franchise (much to the unhappiness of Nigel Bruce), and went back to New York.

In understanding Rathbone's motives and inspirations, however, it's essential to profile his wife, Ouida.

Ouida

Ouida Bergère was a fascinating self-creation. Rathbone often extolled her as the true love of his life. Others saw her as the great curse of his existence.

Although reputedly born on a train as it arrived in Madrid on December 14 in (probably) 1886, Eunie Branch (her real name) was more likely born in Arkansas. When Rathbone met her, she was a petite, red-haired dynamo, well-known as a "motion picture and scenario writer" and (so she claimed) an actor manager whose clients included such theatrical superstars as Nazimova and Lionel Atwill. She was married at the time to George Fitzmaurice, a film director. In fact, a large number of Ouida's "scenarios" had been for her husband, and starred such silent screen divas as Fannie Ward (*A Japanese Nightingale*, 1918), Mae Murray (*Idols of Clay*, 1920) and Pola Negri (*Bella Donna*, 1923).

As such, many of Ouida's influences were of the World War I, silent-films era. She was also five and a half years older than her husband-to-be, Rathbone.

Sunday, April 18, 1926: "Ouida Bergere to Wed," headlined the *New York Times*.[5] Ouida and Basil (his name conspicuously missing from the headline) married this day at the Beekman Mansion, 439 East 51st Street. Rathbone had recently closed in the Broadway play *Port O'London* and Ouida was giving up her career to be Mrs. Rathbone. In order to marry, they had both secured divorces: Ouida from Fitzmaurice, Basil from his first wife Ethel Marion Foreman. (Basil and Ethel had a son, Rodion, born in 1915.)

Then, only 54 days after the Rathbone-Bergère marriage, there came another *New York Times* headline:

Friday, June 11, 1926: "Ouida Bergere Bankrupt."[6]

The article reported that her liabilities tallied $9399, with creditors in New York, London, Paris and San Francisco. Her only assets: her "wearing apparel," valued at $150.

Thus began 40-plus years of Basil Rathbone heroically and desperately bailing Ouida out of debt.

Still, he claimed to adore her.

Hollywood in the late 1930s: Rodion Rathbone, Basil's son by his first marriage, poses with Basil's second wife Ouida and his father.

Of interest: On September 29, 1926, shortly after Ouida's bankruptcy claim, Rathbone opened in *The Captive* at New York's Empire Theatre, playing a man who marries a lesbian (Helen Menken), with Act III presenting tragedy for all. The play was a hit, but on February 9, police arrested company members of *The Captive* (including Rathbone and

Menken), *Sex* (starring Mae West) and *The Virgin Man;* the charge was violation of section 1140 A of the criminal code, which forbid "indecent performances." There were 41 arrests in all, and they were taken to night court.[7]

Rathbone cast Ouida as his personal heroine of this real-life melodrama. They had come into town together that night, from the Long Island home at which they were staying, and Ouida had gone to see another play. As Rathbone wrote of the police arrest in his 1962 memoir, *In and Out of Character*:

> *Ouida arrived from the play she had seen and, as she has always done under duress, faced the situation impassively, except to announce to the police that wherever I was going she was coming with me. Ouida can be very determined upon occasion and the police soon gave up and submitted to her request....*
>
> *It was a miserable ride back to Long Island, but as usual Ouida faced facts with much more courage than was at my command. She calmly wrapped up the past and with her incurable optimism looked boldly forward into the future.*[8]

Was Ouida that captivating an enchantress? Not likely. Most people I've spoken to about Rathbone refer to Ouida as actor Alan Napier did: "that crazy wife of Basil's."[9] The truth was that Rathbone's personality—in certain situations, at least—was that of a bounding St. Bernard dog who pretended to be oblivious to any panic or impending disaster. Frances Drake, the lovely leading lady of such melodramas as 1935's *Mad Love* (see Chapter 6), socialized with the Rathbones in the late 1930s. She told me:

Ouida and Basil at their Bel Air estate, circa 1939. The couple reigned over Hollywood's aristocracy.

Oh, Basil was marvelous! He and his wife Ouida were dear friends of mine. I remember once, dancing with Basil at a party; I had been a dancer—and Basil couldn't dance at all! "You're shoving me across the floor!" I said. "No, no, everything's fine," he said—so enthusiastic, you know! Basil, really, was darling....[10]

Thus was his nature. He would be far less incurably upbeat about such topics as Sherlock Holmes, or his *Anna Karenina* co-star Greta Garbo (she refused to give him an autographed picture), or *Son of Frankenstein* (which he apparently never mentioned at all). As far as Ouida, however, he refused to say any words less than rapturous.

Then there were the Rathbone parties. If Basil was to be the most marketable legitimately trained British actor in Hollywood, Ouida was going to be the film colony's premiere hostess. It wasn't for nothing that their home in the late 1930s at

Cynthia, the child whom Basil and Ouida adopted in 1939, with her famous father.

5424 Los Feliz Boulevard had its own ballroom. On March 30, 1937, Reine Davies of the *Los Angeles Examiner* gushed:

> *What is so dear to a Thespian's heart as a spectacular entrance? Well, Ouida and Basil Rathbone's "Bride and Groom" party at the Victor Hugo Restaurant provided the picture colony with endless opportunities to make entrances that were ENTRANCES. On they came in breath-taking loveliness, ingenious originality or in amusing comedy get-ups, while an orchestra played the "Wedding March," and the flickering glow of many candelabra lighted an aisle of effulgent Easter lilies.*

Rathbone and Ouida wore costumes as Emperor Joseph and Empress Elizabeth of Austria. Among the guests: Edward G. Robinson and his wife as Napoleon and Josephine, Fredric March and spouse Florence Eldridge as a Stone Age couple in leopard skins, Jeanette MacDonald and Gene Raymond as an all-in-white Romeo and Juliet, Theda Bara in an all-black gown and veil with her husband Charles Brabin as Dracula, and Marlene Dietrich—who came solo in her famous tuxedo and top hat. There were many more. Footing the bill for the orchestra, the Easter lilies, and all the bountiful food and drink consumed by these celebrated guests: Basil.

Late in 1939, the year the Rathbones moved to Bellagio Road in Bel Air, they adopted a daughter, Barbara Cynthia (called Cynthia), who had been born the previous April. She was seven years old when the family moved east. Her life would be complex and eventually tragic.

Part Two: Late 1946–1954

Ups and Downs

Tuesday, October 1, 1946: Rathbone's first Broadway appearance after his return to New York was *Obsession*, a two-character play that opened this night at the Plymouth Theatre. The story: Maurice (Rathbone) and Nadya (Eugenie Leontovich) marry; she's still under the control of a lover; Maurice kills the lover. Will he be caught? *Obsession* lasted only 31 performances.

Monday, September 29, 1947: Major success for Rathbone came this night when *The Heiress*, based on Henry James' *Washington Square*, opened at Broadway's Biltmore Theatre. He starred as the bearded Dr. Austin Sloper, whose love (lust?) for his spinster daughter (Wendy Hiller) makes her life a living hell.

Ouida had objected to *The Heiress*: She hadn't wanted her husband to play an unsympathetic role, especially one in which he wore a beard. She'd also insisted on rewriting the play by Ruth and Augustus Goetz, although her own writing career had ended with overblown silent-film sex melodramas nearly 25 years previously. Director Jed Harris navigated smoothly through the troubles. As the *New York Times*' Brooks Atkinson wrote, "As Dr. Sloper, Catherine's keenly inhuman parent, Mr. Rathbone has one of his most actable parts. He plays it perfectly with irony and arrogance."[11]

The Heiress ran for 410 performances in New York. On the night of March 28, 1948, Rathbone won a Tony Award for *The Heiress*. Also receiving Best Actor Tonys that night: Henry Fonda for *Mister Roberts* and Paul Kelly for *Command Decision*.[12]

Rathbone became third vice-president of Actors Equity. He starred in his own radio series, *Tales of Fatima*. He toured in *The Heiress*. If there was a disappointment, it came in Sir Ralph Richardson playing Dr. Sloper in Paramount's 1949 film version of *The Heiress* for which Olivia de Havilland, Rathbone's Maid Marian of *The Adventures of Robin Hood*, won an Oscar.

The only film work Rathbone did at this time was Walt Disney's 1949 *The Adventures of Ichabod and Mr. Toad*, for which he narrated "The Wind in the Willows." The lack of Hollywood money was impacting the patrician lifestyle that he and Ouida had enjoyed in California.

Friday, October 21, 1949: Rathbone starred on TV's *The Ford Theatre Hour* in "On Borrowed Time," playing Mr. Brink (aka Death) to Walter Hampden's Gramps. He guest-starred on over three dozen TV shows during the 1950s, including playing Dr. Jekyll and Mr. Hyde on *Suspense* (March 6, 1951). He also frequently appeared on TV as himself, including at least seven visits to *The Milton Berle Show*.

Friday, March 31, 1950: The music-loving Rathbone was narrator of *The Nightingale and the Rose*, a symphonic poem composed by Alexander Steinert based on Oscar Wilde's fairy tale. The world premiere took place this afternoon in Philadelphia, with Eugene Ormandy conducting the Philadelphia Orchestra.

Tuesday, June 20, 1950: Rathbone played Cassius in *Julius Caesar*, presented at the Arena Theatre in New York's Hotel Edison. His reviews were excellent and the limited run played for 31 performances.

Saturday, October 7, 1950: Rathbone starred in Aldous Huxley's *The Giocanda Smile,* which opened this night at Broadway's Lyceum Theatre. "Chills and Karma" headlined *The Wall Street Journal*'s rave review. The melodrama was about a venomous woman (Valerie Taylor) who poisons her best friend, an invalid, to snare her husband (Rathbone). When he marries someone else, the poisoner frames him for the murder and the play becomes, as the critic described it, a saga of "horrid vengeance." *The Giocanda Smile* was a big hit in London, but on Broadway it lasted only 41 performances. Rathbone revived it in 1951 in summer stock.

Also in 1950, he toured summer stock in *The Winslow Boy* as Sir Robert Morton. During its Washington, D.C., run, Rathbone spoke with *The Washington Post* regarding television. Although he had by now appeared on TV a good number of times, he vented—his hot words indicative of the wrath the usually gentlemanly actor could dispense on occasion:

> I loathe it. It is the most inadequate medium ever offered to the public. It is puerile, infantile, moronic. It is an atrocity.
>
> Television borrows from everything and contributes nothing. It is wonderful for the advertiser and for people who want to see how to cook a chicken. But it is totally unrelated to art.
>
> There you are, six inches high, while your six-foot voice comes booming out. It's absurd....
>
> And to have one's children subjected to it is simply monstrous. How can they grow up with an appreciation of art if all they see is the same cowboy story over and over again with nothing new except the leading man?[13]

He freely admitted that he himself appeared on TV because, as the article expressed it, "the call of a substantial check."

As early as 1951, the actor was touring in a one-man show, *An Evening with Basil Rathbone*, giving dramatic readings.

Friday, February 1, 1952: Rathbone returned to Broadway in *Jane*, written by S.N. Behrman, based on a Somerset Maugham story. Edna Best was his co-star, Cyril Ritchard directed, and Rathbone played William Tower. Brooks Atkinson wrote, "Mr. Rathbone is ideal in the part. He is crisp, immaculate and good-humored, and he speaks some elaborately written lines with wry punctilio."[14] *Jane* ran 100 performances.

The work never stopped.

Among the output of the time:

Sunday, July 13, 1952: Rathbone began hosting a summer replacement TV game show, *Your Lucky Clue.*

Tuesday, May 26, 1953: He played Sherlock Holmes again on TV's *Suspense* in the episode, "The Adventure of the Black Baronet" with British actor Martyn Green as Watson. It was Rathbone's last performance of Holmes on film.

Wednesday, July 8, 1953: Paramount's *Casanova's Big Night*, Rathbone's first film appearance in over seven years, started shooting. The film starred Bob Hope posing as Casanova, Joan Fontaine as leading lady, and Rathbone as Lucio, valet to the fake Casanova. Other Hollywood heavies in the cast: John Carradine (as a nobleman), Lon Chaney Jr. (as a bearded dungeon prisoner), and—unbilled as the real Casanova—Vincent Price. The film was released in 1954.

All of this led to the *Sherlock Holmes* play.

Sherlock Holmes—An Unfortunate Reprise

As noted, it was written by Ouida, and based on several of Sir Arthur Conan Doyle's stories: "The Adventure of the Bruce-Partington Plan," "The Adventure of the Second

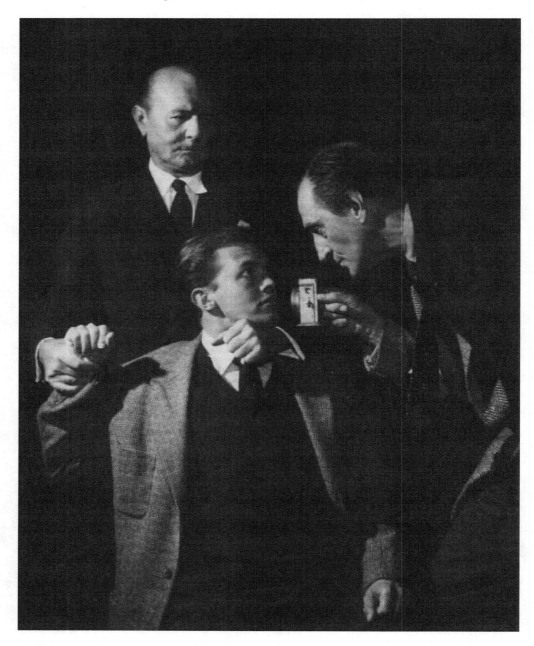

The 1953 Broadway disaster *Sherlock Holmes*. Left to right: Jack Raine as Watson, Terence Kilburn-Walker (formerly child actor Terry Kilburn) and Rathbone as Holmes.

Stain" and "A Scandal in Bohemia." Rathbone had hoped Nigel Bruce would come east to play Watson, but he was ill, and Australian actor Jack Raine took the role (and was reportedly excellent). Mme. Jarmila Novotna, a Metropolitan opera star, played Irene Adler ("*the* woman") and Thomas Gomez assayed the part of the sinister Professor Moriarty. The play's poster noted that it was directed by Reginald "*Dial M for Murder*" Denham.

Rathbone and Ouida clearly saw the play as their financial salvation; Rathbone admitted as much in his 1962 memoir. Perhaps fate revealed a "curse" on the production when, on October 8, 1953—two days before *Sherlock Holmes* premiered at Boston's Majestic Theatre—Nigel Bruce died in California.

Variety reviewed the opening performance in Boston:

> *[It is] in too rough a shape to allow a definite prediction…. Basil Rathbone, in the title role, reads his lines much too fast and presents a nervous and tensely emotional Sherlock rather than the more cerebral and deliberate character that seems appropriate…. The next three weeks will tell.*[15]

Friday, October 30, 1953: Sherlock Holmes opened at Broadway's New Century Theatre and lasted the three previously mentioned hapless performances. Basil and Ouida were devastated, both emotionally and financially.

Cynthia Rathbone was 14 years old when *Sherlock Holmes* fell in flames. In his memoir, Rathbone wrote that Cynthia, learning of the play's colossal failure, "cried bitterly" and sent him a letter from her convent school:

> *Despair is dangerous for men. Despair means that a man has given up hope. A man without hope has nothing to live for, nothing to seek, nothing to gain. He can neither respect himself, or not others, nor love God. Since he no longer trusts the divine power, he has no means by which to advance to God and the mercy God will give him to draw him from despair.*[16]

In some of the most revealing words of his discreet memoir, Rathbone wrote, "I have carried this little piece of paper with me everywhere, all over the world. I am never without it."[17]

More and more as the years went on, he would need the comfort the words offered.

Part Three: Finale 1954–1967

The Bills Never Stop

Thursday, June 17, 1954: Paramount's *We're No Angels* started shooting. It starred Humphrey Bogart, Aldo Ray and Peter Ustinov as Devil's Island escapees, running afoul of Rathbone's comically wicked Andre Trochard—who meets his end via Ray's pet snake. (Henry Daniell played Trochard in the Broadway play.) The movie was released in 1955.

During the filming of *We're No Angels*, Rathbone showed a surprising side of his sense of humor when he and daughter Cynthia, who had accompanied her father to California for the shoot, decided to play a trick on the company. Gloria Talbott, a *We're No Angels* co-star, told historian Tom Weaver:

> *There was a bunch of Russian teenagers or young adults who were going to be visiting the set … and so Basil, who was always doing strange and funny things anyway, bought a nice,* beautiful *piece of wet* shit *from a novelty store … it was sort of like Silly Putty, and it was horrible and wet-looking! And as you opened the stage door you'd step in one and then take the* second *step and you'd step right into the shit (he had it fixed so that it wouldn't slide)….*
>
> *Well, the first person he caught was Bogie! And of course, the expletives flew…. Bogie kicked his leg and the shit dropped off. He looked down … and he looked around … and of course everybody was watching. Basil said to Bogie, "Good morning, old boy!"—and Bogie just looked up at him*

with that look *of his, his head down and his eyes up. Then he turned, and went* straight *into his dressing room! After that, everybody came in, including the Russians, and we caught at* least *the first seven people … everybody was screaming and yelling…. I wet my pants, it was so funny!*[18]

It was about this time that Rathbone and Cynthia came home to New York from California to find that Ouida had moved the family residence to the Langham, a luxury apartment building at 135 Central Park West. It had opened for rental in 1907, and was entered into the National Register of Historic Places on November 9, 1982. The Rathbone quarters on the eleventh (top) floor, overlooking Central Park, provided panoramic views north, east and south.

Rathbone's name for his dwelling: "our ivory tower."[19]

It was very expensive to live in an ivory tower and Rathbone, who resided at the Langham for the rest of his life, felt the pinch. He was working harder than ever.

Among his many, *many* credits at this time:

Monday, November 22, 1954: Paramount's *The Court Jester*, starring Danny Kaye, began shooting. It happily returned Rathbone to the swashbuckling genre: He was the wicked Sir Ravenhurst, amok in a splendid cast that boasted Glynis Johns, Angela Lansbury, John Carradine and Alan Napier. Losing a rapier duel with Kaye, Rathbone's Sir Ravenhurst makes his final exit launched out of the film by catapult into the sea. Now 62 years old, Rathbone finally had to surrender to a sword double for some of his duel with the frenetic Kaye, but it doesn't detract from his wonderfully high-spirited portrayal, featuring this memorable exchange of dialogue:

Basil and his co-star in *The Court Jester*, Angela Lansbury, in the Paramount commissary. The film began shooting in late 1954 and was released in 1956 (from the Frank J. Dello Stritto Collection).

KAYE: *I'd like to get in, get on with it, get it over with, and get out. Get it?*
RATHBONE: *Got it.*
KAYE: *Good!*

But there was also a tense moment, during the Danny Kaye–Rathbone swordfight, when the comedian did a couple of unexpected forward leaps and the point of his epee bounced off Rathbone's forehead and then slid across the top of his head—cutting his

Rathbone as Marley's Ghost in 1954 (from the John Antosiewicz Collection).

wig up the middle! Michael Pate, who played Rathbone's equally evil sidekick, told interviewer Tom Weaver, "I don't remember whether there were stitches but there was quite a lot of blood."

The Court Jester was released in 1956. Surely Rathbone was amused by its opening: Behind the cast and crew credits, a singing and dancing Danny Kaye twice wards away the name Basil Rathbone which keeps reappearing and zooming toward him. It was a nice tribute to Rathbone's high station in the swashbuckler genre.

Thursday, December 23, 1954: Rathbone appeared on TV's *Shower of Stars* as Marley's Ghost in a musical version of *A Christmas Carol*. Fredric March portrayed Scrooge, the libretto was by Maxwell Anderson, and the score by Bernard Herrmann. The show was re-run on *Shower of Stars* for the next two Christmases.

Saturday, July 30, 1955: He starred in the 90-minute NBC musical special *Svengali and the Blonde*. He, of course, was Svengali, and Carol Channing was Trilby (i.e., the Blonde). Ethel Barrymore narrated.

Rathbone as Svengali in the TV special *Svengali and the Blonde* (1955) (from the John Antosiewicz Collection).

Thursday, February 9, 1956: The *Black Sleep*, which began shooting this day, was a film that would prove significant in Rathbone's career and legacy. The horror film top-billed Rathbone as Sir Joel Cadman, a distinguished but ruthless brain surgeon, experimenting in his gloomy castle to bring his beloved young wife from a coma. Akim Tamiroff played his Gypsy henchman, and three horror legends played the wretched results of Rathbone's pioneering brain surgery: Lon Chaney was Mungo, a lumbering mute monster; John Carradine was Borg, who wears a long gray beard, believes himself a medieval crusader, and roars "Kill the infidels"; and Bela Lugosi was a mute butler. Producer Howard W. Koch told historian Tom Weaver:

> *Basil Rathbone was the dignified Englishman, just wonderful. I loved to talk to him just to hear him speak. He'd talk to me about his days on Errol Flynn pictures, and how much he loved doing them ... a lovely gentleman.*[20]

The Black Sleep was shot at the old PRC Studios, 7324 Santa Monica Boulevard. Director Reginald LeBorg had known Rathbone in Hollywood in the Golden days and nights and the two had a fine rapport. Unfortunately, Rathbone had never had a rapport with Lugosi who, about six months before *The Black Sleep* began shooting, had been through a widely reported three-month treatment for drug addiction. Both Lugosi's fourth wife Lillian (married to the actor from 1933 until their divorce in 1953) and his fifth wife Hope (whom he married in August of 1955) were outspoken in their interviews with

The Black Sleep, 1956. Rathbone and Lon Chaney Jr. pose with Bela Lugosi, who was trying for a "comeback" after his recovery from drug addiction (from the John Antosiewicz Collection).

me that Lugosi strongly disliked Rathbone,[21] with whom he'd worked in Universal's *Son of Frankenstein* (1939) and *The Black Cat* (1941). Neither was specific about why Lugosi had this aversion.

All those years later, Lugosi, a recovering drug addict but an alcoholic who was drinking on the set, still bristled at the very sight of Rathbone. Aware of it, Rathbone wrote him a note:

> *Dear Bela,*
> *I found this in a reading last night. "That which is past is irrevocable; and wise men have enough to do with things present and to come. Therefore, they do not trifle with themselves that labour in the past matters."*[22]

Lugosi, who'd die on August 16 that same year, saved the note.

The Black Sleep, on a double bill with *The Creeping Unknown*, was a huge box office hit. Rathbone's excellent, dominating and sympathetic performance did much to persuade his new audiences that he was a horror star.

Also notable in 1956: *The Alcoa Hour's* Christmas special "The Stingiest Man in Town," telecast Sunday, December 23. Rathbone starred as Scrooge, acting with wonderful high spirits, and singing "Listen to the Sound of the Christmas Spirit" and "Mankind Should Be My Business."

Sunday, February 10, 1957: NBC's *Hallmark Hall of Fame* brought to TV Jean Anouilh's 1955-56 Broadway play *The Lark*. Julie Harris (who starred as Joan of Arc) and Boris Karloff (who played the bishop) reprised their stage roles. For TV, Rathbone was the inquisitor; Joseph Wiseman had played the role on stage.

Tuesday, April 2, 1957: *Hide and Seek* opened at the Ethel Barrymore Theatre. The story: a scientist's son (Peter Lazar)

Rathbone as the Inquisitor confronts Julie Harris' Joan of Arc in "The Lark," a 1957 presentation of TV's *Hallmark Hall of Fame* (from the John Antosiewicz Collection).

is believed to be contaminated by radioactive material. Geraldine Fitzgerald played the boy's mother, Barry Morse his scientist father (replacing Franchot Tone shortly before opening night), and Rathbone played Sir Roger Johnson, a cool-headed leader of scientists who address the potentially tragic situation. *Variety* was direct in its assessment: "This, to put it bluntly, is a fiasco."[23] The play closed after only seven performances.

Rathbone also did plenty of stock stage work. Several examples of his prodigious output include *A Midsummer Night's Dream* (as Oberon, with Leopold Stokowski conducting, Ellenville, New York, 1956) and *Witness for the Prosecution* (as Sir Wilfrid Robarts, Q.C.—the part played by Charles Laughton in the film version—Rhode Island, 1957).

Wednesday, November 20, 1957: Rathbone played the Duke in *Huck Finn*, Mark Twain's classic set to music, on *The United States Steel Hour*. Jack Carson played the King, his partner in crime, and they duetted singing "The Boasting Song."

Friday, February 21, 1958: Rathbone played the emperor in "Aladdin" on CBS's *Dupont Show of the Month*. S.J. Perelman wrote the script, Cole Porter composed the songs; Rathbone's song "Wouldn't It Be Fun" was the last song Porter ever wrote.

In 1958, Columbia released *The Last Hurrah*, Rathbone's first and only time working with director John Ford and star Spencer Tracy. The film, based on the Edwin O'Connor novel, cast Rathbone as Norman Cass Sr., a conservative enemy of Tracy's liberal Boston mayor. John Carradine, who played Rathbone's political ally, told Rathbone biographer Michael Druxman:

> *John Ford didn't usually like actors trained in the theater and would often ridicule them. He* didn't *ridicule Basil Rathbone.*[24]

Meanwhile, Rathbone took work as a "pitchman." On May 28, 1958, *Variety* reported that the actor would be a spokesman for Prudential and Nytol. On March 18, 1959, the trade paper announced that Fuller Fabrics had recruited him to appear in its ads as the chauffeur. Much more work of this sort followed.

Wednesday, March 11, 1959: Rathbone arrived in Southampton, back in England for the first time in over 20 years, to make two TV appearances: *Tales from Dickens*, in which he played Scrooge, and the documentary series *Time to Remember*. He was back in the United States—Chicago, specifically—by Monday, March 30, for what, at the time, was his professional nadir.

On this night, Chicago's long-closed Studebaker Theatre re-opened for *Fun Time*, a revue with various "acts." The producer was Jules Pfeiffer, a garish showman whose dubious distinction had been as producer of the infamously racy play *Maid of the Ozarks*. Topping the bill: Jack E. Leonard, famed insult comic, and Basil Rathbone. Also, on the bill: Nip Nelson, impressionist; Nick and Noel, an adagio team; and the Ivy V, "songsters."

Variety caught the first night, when the re-opened theater still had dust on the seats. The audience witnessed a cheap production that the trade paper likened to "makeshift bailing wire":

> *As a designation,* Fun Time *is antique....*
> *It is altogether unfunny, in the Pfeiffer concept, when Basil Rathbone finales the show with 30 minutes of Shakespeare soliloquies. Actor's turn, it's to be emphasized, is a generally fine and moving thing apart, but is so far out of the evening's context as to border on bathos....*
> *Rathbone, because of the light-hearted stuff that forewent, had difficulty the first five minutes or so, achieving a sympathetic mood, though from its reaction audience never did quite warm to him. ... Actor prologued that Shakespeare wrote for "the people," a truth that didn't seem to sway first-nighters.*[25]

Pfeiffer's response was immediate, as reported by *Variety*:

> *One of the least happy in the cast was Rathbone, who* [after playing] *the windup spot the first night, then switched to lead-off at considerably reduced time when it was decided his Shakespearean readings were anticlimactic in a "fun" show.*[26]

Rathbone dons a deerstalker hat *à la* Sherlock Holmes as he arrives in Southampton, England, in March 1959 (from the John Antosiewicz Collection).

Incredibly, things grew worse. On Monday, April 6, Pfeiffer fired Jack E. Leonard for making insulting remarks about him.[27]

Pfeiffer took over Leonard's spot himself, delivering a deadly 55-minute monologue before an audience of less than 100 people. Pfeiffer made anti–Semitic jokes before a Jewish audience, screamed "Drop dead!" at hecklers, and created, in *Variety*'s words, "a shocking public exhibition." Pfeiffer refused refunds to outraged patrons, many of whom called the Chicago Better Business Bureau.

As for Rathbone: *Variety*, following the ongoing debacle, reported on April 15 that Pfeiffer

> *had begun harassing "special guest star" Basil Rathbone, switching the actor from closing to opening spot, drastically cutting his time for Shakespeare readings, and ordering the band to play a hard "Cow-Cow Boogie" accompaniment. Asked why he stood it, Rathbone, plainly shaken, said he'd been through two world wars and could endure this.*

Pfeiffer claimed he had the right to humiliate Rathbone because the actor had allegedly reneged on an arranged publicity tie-up with a Chicago department store. Rathbone claimed he'd never agreed to such a promotion, but to avoid further atrocities, he humbly consented to the P.R. stint. Pfeiffer responded by restoring 25 minutes of Rathbone's stage time and canning the "Cow-Cow Boogie" music.

Nevertheless, the stint remained a shocker. Forrest Tucker, in Chicago as star of the national company of *The Music Man*, went on a late-night radio talk show to lambast Pfeiffer for his treatment of Rathbone. Pfeiffer naturally responded by attacking Tucker. At any rate, by April 21, *Fun Time* was a one-man show, starring Jules Pfeiffer. Devastated by this nightmarish engagement, Rathbone went home to New York, bloody but as always unbowed, surely due for a break.[28]

Fortunately, he got one.

Monday, June 8, 1959: Rathbone succeeded Raymond Massey in Archibald MacLeish's Pulitzer Prize–winning *J.B.* at Broadway's ANTA Theatre. The play, a modern retelling of the Biblical story of Job, was now in its 26th week and playing to about 50 percent capacity. Rathbone had succeeded Massey as Mr. Zuss with the option that he would eventually replace Christopher Plummer as Nickles. He also played Nickles on tour.

Wednesday, March 30, 1960: *Variety* ran the squib "'Legit's Loaded with Amateurs,' Sez Rathbone." In Philadelphia, where he was starring in *J.B.*, the actor lamented:

> *I've been in America almost forty years and except for a spell in the movies have been identified with Broadway. I can count the number of worthwhile shows I've been in on one hand—The Czarina (not a financial success), The Swan, Command to Love, The Heiress and the current J.B., at the Locust. There was another good show, The Captive, an investigation of lesbianism, but the police in 1926 clamped down after a brief run. It would seem pretty tame stuff in these days of Williams and Faulkner.*
>
> *Our business is loaded with amateurs. There are no standards such as you have in music. In music, you either know your business and can play, or you don't. And you're always performing some work by a great composer.*

On April 20, *Variety* published a rebuttal from Bob Downing (described by *Variety* in 1953 as "a theatrical jack-of-all-trades" as he was a noted stage manager as well as an actor and writer):

> *Basil Rathbone is entitled to his opinion that the theatre "is loaded with amateurs," but he is mistaken when he complains that legit "has no standards as in music." The odious comparison to one*

Ouida and Rathbone, circa 1960.

side, show biz happens to be loaded with people of all ages who know their business and love it. My 20 years on Broadway has given me the greatest respect and admiration for the dedication of most stage youngsters … [T]hey are concerned for the future of the profession, and very few have time to bellyache about the shortcomings of others.

Rathbone should have known better than to vent in an arena where he wouldn't get the last word.

In and Out of Character, the White House, AIP and Other Output

In 1960, Basil Rathbone toured Australia in the four-character comic play *The Marriage Go-Round* as Professor Delville.

In January 1961, the fantasy film *The Magic Sword* began shooting at the Goldwyn Studio. Based on the legend of St. George and the Dragon, the Bert I. Gordon–directed indie gave Rathbone star billing as Lodac, a wicked wizard … who keeps a dragon. Gary Lockwood was Sir George, and among the featured players were Estelle Winwood (as Sybil the sorceress) and Maila Nurmi (aka Vampira, as "The Hag"). Talking to Tom Weaver in 2009, Lockwood remembered,

Rathbone didn't particularly like me and I didn't particularly like him. …He was traditional, more of a theater type, and I just don't think he approved of me. I was a young rogue asshole to him, I think. Because he was an uptight guy, I didn't even deal with it. …There was just no relationship, there was no connection between us. I mean, when the job was over, I said, "Take care," and he said, "Goodbye." There weren't any encomiums!

Released in 1962, *The Magic Sword* provided a juicy star role for Rathbone.

In 1962, AIP added to its Vincent Price–Edgar Allan Poe series with *Tales of Terror*, a horror anthology comprised of "Morella," in which Price keeps his 26-years-dead wife as a mummified corpse; "The Black Cat" (actually a blend of that Poe tale and "The Cask

AIP's *Tales of Terror* (1962): Rathbone, Vincent Price, David Frankham and Debra Paget.

of Amontillado"), in which Peter Lorre walls up his voluptuous wife (Joyce Jameson) and her wine-tasting lover (Price) in his cellar; and "The Facts in the Case of M. Valdemar," in which Rathbone played Mr. Carmichael, a hypnotist who threatens to keep Valdemar (Price) in an unholy trance that is neither life nor death until Valdemar's young wife (Debra Paget) agrees to marry him. When he attacks her, Price's Valdemar rises from his bed, turns into "detestable putridity" (as Poe wrote in the final words of his story) and fatally oozes all over Rathbone's Carmichael.

David Frankham, the excellent British actor, played the young doctor who wishes to marry Paget. He idolized the three stars and wrote in his engaging memoir *Which One Was David?*:

> When we filmed Tales of Terror, I was thirty-five and Basil was seventy, and yet he was challenging me for Debra Paget's hand in marriage! That irony wasn't lost on me during the production. I admired Basil's vitality, his enthusiasm, his discipline, his enduring talent, you name it. He was a marvel—as energetic at seven p.m. as he was on set at seven a.m.
>
> … I marveled at sharing the screen with one of my idols, Errol Flynn's and Tyrone Power's nemesis! I had seen Basil and his sword fights with Flynn and Power. I just thought he was the best villain ever.
>
> Much to my surprise, Basil rated Power's swordsmanship as vastly superior to Flynn's; he said Flynn didn't take it seriously enough and much preferred to have his stunt double do as many long shots as he could get away with in a scene…. When Basil did a job, though, he wanted to tackle it thoroughly. He had been taught well to fence properly, thus, his judgment of Flynn's talent—or lack thereof. "No," he told me, "old Flynn used to have a double more often than not."
>
> The energy level of Basil and Vincent was something to behold…. By four p.m. I needed a break or a nap but not Basil. I saw that he gave so much in a scene. Just being around him was one of the great satisfactions of my life.[29]

The *New York Times'* judgment of *Tales of Terror*: "A dull, absurd and trashy adaptation…broadly draped around the shoulders of such people as Vincent Price, Peter Lorre and Basil Rathbone (who at least bothers to act)."[30]

It was also in 1962 that Rathbone appeared in the mysterious *Two Before Zero*, a bizarre film in which the actor, dressed in vestments before a podium, lectures a woman (Mary Murphy, co-star of Marlon Brando's *The Wild One*) on the horrors of Communism and atheism. He makes his points with Communist horrific-atrocity footage. The film must be taken in historical context—1962 was the year of the Cuban Missile Crisis.

In late 1962, Doubleday published Rathbone's memoir, *In and Out of Character*. The book was certainly indicative of Rathbone's personality, from the dedication ("To my Ouida with Love") to the large amount of exclamation points the author used to tell his stories. Although it was clear that his true professional affection was for the Theater, he related a number of memorable Hollywood anecdotes: how it agonized him to have to lash Freddie Bartholomew over and over in *David Copperfield* ("When it was over I rushed over to Freddie and took him in my arms and kissed him"), how Garbo had refused to give him a signed picture on the set of *Anna Karenina* ("[L]ike a wax figure in Madame Tussaud's, she said, 'I never give picture'"), how John Barrymore profanely ad-libbed Shakespeare in *Romeo and Juliet* ("He heareth not, he stirreth not, he *pisseth* not!"). He naturally addressed his screen matches with Errol Flynn:

> I believe him to have been quite fearless, and subconsciously possessed of his own self-destruction. I would say that he was fond of me, for what reasons I shall never know. It was always "dear old Bazzz," and he would flash that smile that was both defiant and cruel, but which for me always

had a tinge of affection in it. We only crossed swords, never words, and he was generous and appreciative of my work. I liked him and he liked me.

He also explained his exasperation with Sherlock Holmes:

One was jealous of Holmes, of course. Yes, of course, that was it. One was jealous. Jealous of his mastery of all things, both material and mystical … he was sort of a god in his way, seated on some Anglo-Saxon Olympus of his own design and making! Yes, there was no question about it, he had given me an acute inferiority complex!

The book didn't sell well, partially because it lacked salacious anecdotes; Rathbone knew plenty of them, but refused to betray confidences. Rathbone fans tend to be underwhelmed by the book, which they consider overly discreet; his horror fans are put off by the omission of *Son of Frankenstein, Tower of London* and all similar melodramas. (It did include a picture of himself from *Tower of London* as Richard III.) Rathbone does mention his favorite Moriarty from the Holmes series: It's not George Zucco from *The Adventures of Sherlock Holmes,* nor Lionel Atwill from *Sherlock Holmes and the Secret Weapon,* but Henry Daniell in *The Woman in Green.* "There were other Moriartys," wrote Rathbone, "but none so delectably dangerous as was that of Henry Daniell."

Sunday night, April 30, 1963: Rathbone enjoyed a special honor: He appeared at John F. Kennedy's White House. "Elizabethan Music and Verse Scheduled at the White House," headlined the *New York Times*, reporting:

The Elizabethan era will be recreated in music and poetry at a White House dinner tomorrow night for Grand Duchess Charlotte of Luxembourg (her first visit since the WWII years).

Performers at the after-dinner program in the East Room will be Basil Rathbone and the Consort Players, directed by Sydney Beck of New York. Mr. Rathbone will present excerpts from the works of Shakespeare, Christopher Marlowe and Ben Jonson.

The Consort Players will perform on such Elizabethan instruments as the virginal (a small English harpsichord), cittern, treble viol, bass viol, flute, lute and pandora.

Also on the program will be Helen Boatwright, soprano, and Robert White, tenor.

Rathbone was there at the special invitation of First Lady Jacqueline Kennedy, and the two corresponded about the choice of material. Among her requests: Shakespeare's "Shall I Compare Thee to a Summer's Day," John Donne's "Go and Catch a Falling Star" and Christopher Marlowe's "Come Live with Me and Be My Love." As an encore, and at President Kennedy's request, Rathbone recited "The Battle for Agincourt" from Shakespeare's *Henry V.*[31]

Rathbone saved Mrs. Kennedy's letters. More about them later.

Sunday, June 30, 1963: Rathbone once again performed with a mixture of Shakespeare and music, this time at Lewisohn Stadium in New York. Alan Rich, critic for the *New York Times,* judged that the evening "didn't quite work out," partly because some of the music didn't fit the verses, but also…

The second reason for the partial failure of the program was the pompous and self-indulgent manner in which Basil Rathbone delivered the speeches. Mr. Rathbone is a fine actor, but at this concert he seemed anxious to revive the ghost of an orotund Shakespearean manner long and justly dead.[32]

A new offer came from AIP in Hollywood, for what was Rathbone's last great screen performance: John F. Black, the Shakespeare-obsessed, mad-as-a-hatter landlord who absolutely refuses to die in *The Comedy of Terrors* (1963).

The zesty spoof starred Vincent Price, Peter Lorre and Boris Karloff, as well as

High spirits between scenes on *The Comedy of Terrors* (1964). Rathbone, Boris Karloff, Peter Lorre and Vincent Price.

blonde, buxom Joyce Jameson (who, as the *New York Times* reported, "looks as though she could flatten all three of them"). Rathbone gave the film's most memorable portrayal, running about his mansion at night in nightcap and robe, waving a sword, spouting *Macbeth*, and finally "murdered" by undertaker Price because business was slow. However, Rathbone's Black rises from his mausoleum (causing Joe E. Brown, as the cemetery caretaker, to emit his fabled howl), attacks Price's household with an axe, is killed again (and again)—but keeps rising to ask, "What place is this?" and to go on and on in Shakespearean pentameter.

Originally, Rathbone was set for Karloff's role—Price's ancient, senile father-in-law—while Karloff was to play John F. Black. As Karloff was in bad physical shape due to his arthritis, he and Rathbone swapped parts. It was a happy switch. Karloff had his moments as the doddering old fool (giving a eulogy for Rathbone's character, he can't remember the name of the deceased!), while Rathbone had a field day.

Richard Matheson, who wrote *The Comedy of Terrors*, remembered the film as his "happiest experience" on a movie set. He told Mick Martin in *Cinefantastique*:

> All the principals loved the script ... the shooting was great fun. Basil Rathbone ... was forever full of energy and delightful anecdotes. He told me all about the shooting of Robin Hood *with Errol Flynn, which remains one of my favorite films....*[33]

Director Jacques Tourneur, whose credits included Val Lewton's original *Cat People* (1942) and *Curse of the Demon* (1957), helmed the satire. Matheson remembered:

> He had only a two-week shooting schedule, and he wasn't too happy with the heaviness of the actors' approach to comedy, which may or may not be true. He visualized it more as a very crisp British comedy, and felt that only Basil Rathbone handled it deftly and lightly enough, and he was sensational in it....[34]

As Rathbone told the *Los Angeles Times* during the shooting:

> We like each other. We respect each other. As an example, Vinnie said, "I've asked them to favor you with the camera in this scene because it's your entrance." This is not usual. You won't find this with many stars. Boris Karloff and I have been friends in pictures for a long time. Vinnie and I have done several pictures together.... We all know each other—three old pals.[35]

Yet Rathbone insisted, as always, that he wasn't enamored of Hollywood horror: "It doesn't amuse me to chase someone down a corridor with an axe."[36]

Rathbone had one problem in *The Comedy of Terrors*: He hated having to lie in the coffin. According to Price, Rathbone was "almost violent" about getting out of the casket after a scene and that "he fought like hell to avoid retakes!"[37]

Nevertheless, Rathbone's John F. Black is riotous and remarkable—almost a *Monty Python's Flying Circus*–style performance, nearly a decade before *Monty Python*. One of the best moments: in the middle of the night, Rathbone's Black, in robe and nightcap, comes out of his trance in the cellar of Price and Lorre's undertaking parlor. He sees Price and Lorre staring at him. His query, delivered with classic understated British dismay:

> *"What jiggery-pokery is this?"*[38]

In 1964 U.S. Films released *Pontius Pilate*, an Italian-French co-production. Jean Marais played the title role (which Rathbone had played in RKO's 1935 *The Last Days of Pompeii*), Jeanne Crain was leading lady, and Rathbone played Caiaphas the high priest. It was shot in Rome in the summer of 1961, at the same time that 20th Century–Fox was there filming Elizabeth Taylor's *Cleopatra*. The film came and went with barely any notice. A curiosity: John Drew Barrymore played in the movie as both Jesus *and* Judas.

Wednesday, April 7, 1965: Rathbone guest-starred on TV's *Burke's Law*, in the episode, "Who Killed Hamlet?" Among the other guest stars: Agnes Moorehead, Edward Everett Horton and John Cassavetes,

Thursday, April 8, 1965: Production began on *Queen of Blood*, at the Harlequin

International Studios in Hollywood. Basil Rathbone starred, with future *Easy Rider* star Dennis Hopper, John Saxon, Judi Meredith and Florence Marly as the "space vampire." Directing the film was Curtis Harrington, who in addition to being a fine and resource-ful director, was a great fan of Old Hollywood and thrilled to be working with Rathbone.

Forrest J Ackerman, editor of *Famous Monsters of Filmland* magazine, visited the set.[39] As Ackerman remembered, an awkward introduction was made:

> **HARRINGTON:** "*Mr. Rathbone, this is the editor of* Famous Monsters, *the original filmonster magazine.*"
> **RATHBONE:** "*Yes, well, of course, I'm not in* that *category.*"

As Ackerman wrote, Rathbone "made it so painfully plain that he was not keen about being identified as a horror actor that my hopes for a Karloff- or Price-type inter-view were immediately dashed." Ackerman had a bit role in *Queen of Blood* as an assistant to Rathbone's Dr. Farraday, and in his usual fanboy style, wrote exultantly of the experi-ence in *Monster World*, a spin-off of *Famous Monsters*:

> *I had never dreamed when I was only 22 years old and thrilled to* Son of Frankenstein *when it was new that one day, I would be standing face to face, in makeup, before a motion picture cam-era, being photographed in a scene with Basil Rathbone!*

Be that as it may, Ackerman was a bit snippy in his interview, later published under the title, "Smile If You … Call Him MONSTER! Basil Rathbone Will Eat You Alive if You Don't!" Opposite the title page: an unflattering full-page close-up of Rathbone from *The Magic Sword*. The story made the star sound arrogant and at times condescending—pos-sibly because he *was* arrogant and condescending that day; for example, when asked if he believed the aged, arthritis-suffering Karloff would ever retire, Rathbone said:

> *Retire? Oh no, not Boris! Not if he can help it. Of course, he's almost doubled up now, the poor dear man, but he'll never say die!*

Not published at the time was Ackerman's eyewitness account of a Rathbone melt-down on the *Queen of Blood* set at the end of shooting.[40] The film, of course, had a paltry budget and schedule, and Harrington was forced to work his cast hard to finish up the last day. After the final shot, Rathbone frigidly asked the cameraman if the take was okay and the sound recorder if it all came through properly.

Then, assured there was no need for a retake, he exploded.

"*You*, sir," Rathbone thundered at Harrington, "are surely one of those people who do not respect we thespians properly. A *dog* would not be treated the way I have been this day!"

He vented, Ackerman likening Rathbone to a Roman emperor swirling his toga, and made a tempestuously dramatic exit from the set. Harrington, shaken by the tantrum, didn't speak publicly of it.

For all his dismay, Rathbone—who worked on *Queen of Blood* for $3000 per day—agreed to do a two-page scene for AIP's made-for-TV *Voyage to a Prehistoric Planet*. His co-star was Faith Domergue.

Wednesday, July 14, 1965: *Variety* reported that a new version of *Dr. Jekyll and Mr. Hyde* was about to go into the works, for Allied Artists release. The title: *Dr. Rock and Mr. Roll*. The article stated that the title roles weren't yet cast, but that there would be ten rock'n'roll groups—and that Basil Rathbone and former Bowery Boy Huntz Hall had been signed as "a couple of cops." Production was to take place in New York, and report-edly started August 10.[41] The horrid project was presumably never completed.

Wednesday, August 18, 1965: *Variety* reported that Basil Rathbone was in Chicago, "currently in town to tape the opening and close of *Sherlock Holmes Theatre*, WGN-TV's new feature mystery film series."[42]

Crushing Humiliations

Then came a new debacle: Rathbone decided to sell the letters that Jacqueline Kennedy wrote to him in 1963. Charles Hamilton, famed auctioneer, wrote in his 1981 book *Auction Madness*:

> When I first met Basil Rathbone he was 71, but he looked as if he had just stepped out of one of Conan Doyle's Holmes stories. He was tall and handsome, impeccably dressed, with a sharp twinkling eye that flashed like a Toledo rapier. He had a rich voice of pure gold. There was an awesome severity in his appearance that momentarily, but only momentarily, hid the warmth of his personality.... He had spent his life in stintless giving, and now in the twilight of his great career he was broke.[43]

It was a group of seven letters in all, and Hamilton was set to auction them at the Gotham Hotel in New York City on September 30, 1965. Starting bid price: $1500. Of course, John F. Kennedy had been assassinated less than two years before this auction, and Rathbone's decision to part with the letters struck many as a tasteless insult to an American martyr and his widow.[44]

Once again, Rathbone was devastated.

He claimed the letters revealed Mrs. Kennedy "in the most charming light," and as "a woman of intelligence, taste and culture." He appealed to Hamilton ("What have I done, Charles? Have I really done something wicked?"). The situation worsened: The media reported that Mrs. Kennedy herself was offended by the sale.

Hamilton recalled Rathbone telephoning him—"I could tell that he'd been and perhaps still was crying"—and asking to take the letters out of the sale. Fearful for Rathbone's health, Hamilton made a "special appeal." He sent a letter marked "Very Personal" to Mrs. Kennedy's secretary Pamela Turnure, at 400 Park Avenue, where the former First Lady was living. He wrote in his book that he hadn't kept a copy of the letter, but summarized it thusly:

> *Dear Mrs. Kennedy:*
>
> *Mr. Rathbone is extremely distressed and depressed because he has read in the newspapers and heard over the radio that you disapprove of the sale of your letters to him.*
>
> *Were he not strapped for money, I'm certain that Mr. Rathbone would never part with your letters, for he counts them among his greatest treasures. But he has very little income and earns only a meager living by recitals at schools and colleges for which he receives a fee of $100 per appearance, plus travel expenses.*
>
> *Mr. Rathbone's daughter, Cynthia, has long been ill with hepatitis. With the money he receives from the sale of your letters, he hopes to take his daughter on a much-needed vacation.*
>
> *If you could find some way to deny the newspaper reports of your displeasure at the sale of the letters, I know that it would buoy Mr. Rathbone's spirits and make him a very happy man.*
>
> *Only you and I must know that I wrote this letter.*
>
> *Sincerely,*
> *Charles Hamilton*

The response from Ms. Turnure was immediate.

Mrs. Kennedy isn't aware of the sale, as far as I know. I have not discussed this with Mrs. Kennedy. We (Mrs. Kennedy's New York office) only learned of it through reporters calling us.[45]

Rathbone was still fired up about the matter, saying that reports of Mrs. Kennedy's ire was "so much bosh" and telling the press:

All she has to do is get in touch with me. I'd be the first to agree not to let them go. But I'll bet a million dollars to a nickel that she doesn't ask me…. I wanted them to fall into the hands of someone who could perpetuate them. I can't. It's a shame for me to have them lying here in a closet.[46]

Although it all could have been worse, it was a crushing humiliation for Rathbone. The situation made it painfully obvious he was in financial straits and the fact that he'd sell personal letters from Jacqueline Kennedy, the most revered woman in the country, showcased his desperation.

It didn't help that he was lined up for a new AIP movie tentatively titled *Pajama Party in a Haunted House.*

It became *The Ghost in the Invisible Bikini* and started shooting Wednesday, September 29, 1965. The stars were Tommy Kirk, former Mouseketeer, and Deborah Walley, who played the title role in *Gidget Goes Hawaiian* (1961). The featured cast included Nancy Sinatra (who sings "Geronimo") and Francis X. Bushman (his last film). The

Oldtimers on the set of *The Ghost in the Invisible Bikini* (1966): **Boris Karloff, Francis X. Bushman and Rathbone. The combined age of the three actors at the time of this shot: 233 (from the John Antosiewicz Collection).**

villains: Rathbone as Reginald Ripper and Quinn O'Hara as his redheaded daughter Sinistra.

The film was a curio, produced at a time that the hippie culture was working its way into Hollywood's identity, spawning a totally different world than the one Rathbone had enjoyed in his prime. Yet he entered the job with his usual professionalism and high spirits. Tommy Kirk went on record about Rathbone's charm and that, as always, he was "a wonderful raconteur" on the set.

Partly due to a director (Don Weis) who was reportedly pie-eyed through the entire shoot, the finished film was nearly incomprehensible. This necessitated the addition of new characters (the title Ghost, played by Susan Hart, and the Corpse, played by Boris Karloff) who appeared in scenes written and shot in post-production, observing and commenting on the action (and making things less confusing). Their uncredited director: former kid actor Ronald Sinclair, who played the boy king murdered by Karloff and Rathbone in 1939's *Tower of London*!

The indignities seemed endless. Booth Colman, veteran actor and friend of Rathbone, told Tom Weaver about seeing Rathbone in a late stage production in Los Angeles:

> [H]e was old and tired and working in some Grand Guignol [stage] show that they did here, in the Santa Monica High School, I believe. It was *awful*, a terrible comedown for him … a Grand Guignol play with the side of someone's face being fried in a pan and all that. It was *unfitting* to see him doing that stuff. I was so sorry that he felt he had to.

Afterwards, Colman and some friends drove Rathbone to his hotel. Colman never saw him again.

Monday, December 27 and Tuesday, December 28, 1965: Rathbone guest-starred on a *Dr. Kildare* two-parter titled (Part 1) "Perfect Is Hard to Be" and (Part 2) "Duet for One Hand." He played a celebrated pianist who required life-saving surgery that might have ended his musical career. Playing his son was David Frankham, who'd acted with him in *Tales of Terror* and was delighted to meet up with him again:

> Basil was still the same, straining at the leash to get going on the day's shooting. He was staying at the Chateau Marmont Hotel in West Hollywood. Because most of our scenes were together, we had the same call each morning. On our first day of work, we discovered that each of us had taken a separate cab to get to work. Basil decided that we could share a cab since we were both in West Hollywood. He was picked up first, and then he directed the cab to my place on the way to work! We had to report to the set at 7:30, but he liked to get there thirty minutes early at seven, so each morning for two weeks there was one of the silver screen's all-time great actors sticking his head over my fence and calling that our cab was ready!

Dr. Kildare was filmed at MGM, where Rathbone had played in such 1930s classics as *David Copperfield*, *A Tale of Two Cities* and *Romeo and Juliet*, and where he'd been under contract during the World War II years. Frankham wrote:

> Because we got to work early, he gave me a personal tour of the studio each morning! He could still remember and point out the soundstages where he had worked with Norma Shearer or with Greta Garbo in Anna Karenina. It was like a wonderful, first-hand guided Hollywood tour, every morning for ten days![47]

The glory days were behind Rathbone, and his 1966 credits wouldn't help.

Thursday, June 16, 1966: Rathbone narrated ABC's special *The Baffling World of ESP*.

Friday, August 26, 1966: He guested in the unsold pilot, *The Pirates of Flounder Bay*.

Wednesday, September 7, 1966: "Rathbone, Carradine, Mitchell in Mex *Ghost*," head-lined *Variety*. The film's full title was *Autopsia de un Fantasma* (*Autopsy of a Ghost*) and it would be produced and directed by Ismael Rodriguez from his own script. The reported budget: $280,000. Shooting was to start October 3 in Mexico City.

"Rathbone plays the 'ghost,'" wrote *Variety*.

The result was the cold rock bottom of Rathbone's career, an atrocity shot by a shamelessly self-indulgent Rodriguez, who apparently reveled in his reputation as Mexico's "mad genius" writer-director. The story: The ghost of Perez (Rathbone), a great lover and a 1567 suicide, sleeps in a coffin (which could hardly have pleased the actor), lives with a talking skeleton, and wears medieval finery … along with the heavy makeup and a flowing black wig that basically disfigures the star. The Devil (Carradine, with horns and a long, pointed tail) challenges the ghost to find a woman who will kill herself for his sake. Humiliations follow. In one episode, Rathbone wears a Cyrano de Bergerac nose as he woos a bikini-clad blonde who stands imperiously on a bed and orders him out of the boudoir. In another, he wears a Beatle wig and holds an electric guitar, seductively bending a different woman onto a bed—and she knocks him across the room. In a third "wooing" scene, he dresses as a seedy Apache dancer, and dances with a third woman who, in keeping with the sado-maso humor of the piece, also mops up the floor with him.

Meanwhile, a mad inventor (Cameron Mitchell) creates robots, including a female one with a red wig and false eyelashes. An explosion near the end of the 105-minute(!) film destroys the female robot, and we see a forlorn Rathbone carrying her various parts. Apparently, the "ghost" has fallen in love with the robot, and maybe vice versa. It's hard to tell; Spanish actors dubbed the dialogue for Rathbone and Carradine, and the version I watched had no subtitles. (At one point, Rathbone recites, in English, "To be, or not to be" to a skull. It sounds like the actor's own voice, and to suddenly hear it in this farrago gives one a chill.)

In his positive-energy-in-the-face-of-disaster way, Rathbone entered the project with high spirits, making the 2500-mile trip from New York to Mexico City. "He thought it was a brilliant script," remembered Cameron Mitchell (who performed his own lines in Spanish). "Basil was still very young at heart."[48]

Carradine, whose hamming as the Devil bordered on the maniacal, remembered:

> [Rathbone] was hopping and jumping and leaping around like a man of 30. But at the end of the day he was tired—because of the altitude, a mile high there. At dinner one night, he said, "John, I'll never do this again." And I said, "What do you mean?" And he said, "Work at this altitude." That's what killed him….[49]

Rathbone's psyched-up enthusiasm eventually dwindled as the altitude, the heat, and the spastic nature of the abominable film ganged up on him. In another interview, Carradine claimed that Rathbone suffered a heart attack on location.[50]

Rathbone probably saw that he had two choices: Do this wretched film, and earn the $15,000 it reportedly paid him, or face his increasingly dire financial woes and the eventual loss of his "ivory tower" in New York. If he did, the humiliation might have killed Ouida.

He had to go on.

Monday, November 14, 1966: Rathbone got a boost when the *New York Times* reviewed three new recordings he made for the Caedmon label: *Edgar Allan Poe, Volume*

3; The Scarlet Letter and The Great Stone Face; and *The Poems of Rudyard Kipling*. Critic Thomas Lask favorably wrote of the actor's work on all three records, notably the Poe album (for which Rathbone read "The Tell-Tale Heart" and "The Fall of the House of Usher," as well as the poems "The Haunted Palace" and "The Bells").

"If Poe can still horrify you," wrote Lask, "Mr. Rathbone will do it."[51]

Wednesday, November 30, 1966: A new film began: *Hillbillys in a Haunted House.* The hillbillys were Ferlin Husky, Joi Lansing and Don Bowman and the villains were John Carradine, Lon Chaney and Basil Rathbone. The horror stars played foreign spies who, hoping to steal rocket propellant from a nearby base, set up a supposedly haunted house. Among the spooky accoutrements: Anatole the gorilla (played by George Barrows). At one point, Carradine steals the ape's banana.

The budget was $240,000 and Rathbone, whose character was named Gregor (although at one point, Carradine calls him George), earned $10,000 of it. It was good money for two weeks' work, but the film offered yet another indignity—the credits read:

> *John Carradine*
> *Lon Chaney*
> *Linda Ho*
> *Basil Rathbone*

Linda Ho, 26 years old, played the villainous Madame Wong.

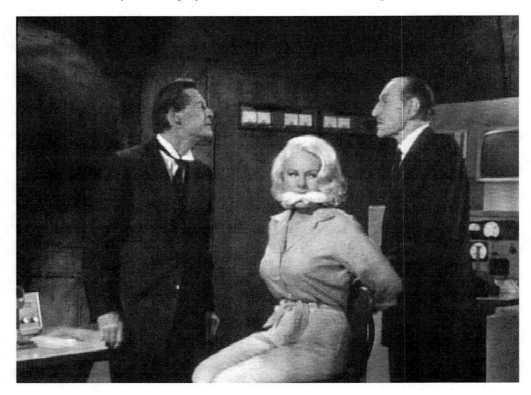

Hillbillys in a Haunted House (1967): **Rathbone in his final film, with John Carradine and Joi Lansing.**

Rathbone looks gaunt but still handsome, sporting a dark double-breasted suit and lending his presence gracefully to the film which, while silly, isn't horrible *à la Autopsy de un Fantasma*. Late in the movie, scared by what he thinks is a *real* ghost, Rathbone rolls around on the floor in a white sheet, somehow avoiding looking ridiculous.

Hillbillys producer Bernard Woolner recalled that Rathbone "was a real gentleman, and we all enjoyed working with him."[52]

At this point, it may have been an alternative for the Rathbones to have thrown in the towel and entered the Motion Picture Country House and Lodge in Woodland Hills, California, where Ouida might have re-established an old-style Hollywood aristocracy among the residents. The very idea, however, would surely have shocked her.

Therefore, Basil would keep taking whatever he could get.

* * *

Wednesday, April 26, 1967: NBC's *Hallmark Hall of Fame* presented "Soldier in Love," starring Jean Simmons, Claire Bloom and Keith Michell. Rathbone had the small role of the Duke of York. The job was rather a consolation prize: Rathbone had been writing to the series' producer-director, George Schaefer, requesting starring roles in the announced productions of *Anastasia* and *The Admirable Crichton*.

Wednesday, May 24, 1967: Rathbone was a guest of Duncan MacDonald on his 2:30 p.m. radio show on New York's WQXR-AM.

The Final Act

At last, during 1967's Summer of Love, a new film offer came ... and from Rathbone's native England.

Tigon British Films had produced *The Sorcerers* starring Boris Karloff—a millionaire, whose various homes included his top-floor apartment in the Dakota at 1 West 72nd Street, a block from the Rathbones' home. Tigon was now preparing to film *Death's Head Vampire* (later released as *The Blood Beast Terror*). Its plot: Inspector Quennell investigates horrific murders committed by a human-sized, flying, blood-sucking Moth Woman—created by mad Dr. Mallinger.

In his excellent feature "The Making of the *Blood Beast Terror*" in *Little Shoppe of Horrors* magazine, film historian John Hamilton reported that Peter Cushing wanted the Quennell part, and Tigon offered the Mallinger role to Rathbone.[53] There was a certain showmanship, at least for film fans: two "Sherlock Holmes" in the same movie (Cushing had played Holmes in Hammer's 1959 *The Hound of the Baskervilles*). Executive producer Tony Tenser told Hamilton:

> I spoke to Basil Rathbone's agent. He said [Rathbone] *would love to do it. So, I said: "Okay, let's do a deal and send him over." That was all there was to it. It was a bit of a coup for us. I doubt he had ever heard of Tigon.*

Hamilton wrote that Rathbone

> *seemed to be looking forward to the challenges offered by Professor Mallinger, and he wrote an enthusiastic letter to Tenser confirming his travel arrangements to London. Insisting that once the script "is under my belt, I find it difficult to unlearn," the actor expressed hopes that there would not be too many last-minute changes—a point that suggests he was indeed unfamiliar with Tigon!*

It would be a homecoming, in a way, and his first feature film in England since 1937's *Love from a Stranger*. Surely he'd get along famously with the gentle and charming Peter Cushing. And after *Autopsia de un Fantasma* and *Hillbillys in a Haunted House*, it would certainly seem *Death's Head Vampire* could only be an improvement.

The role of Clare, aka the "Death's Head Vampire," went to Wanda Ventham who, in 1976, became the mother of Benedict Cumberbatch. Hamilton wrote:

> With script in place, cast and crew hired and production arrangements confirmed, [director] Vernon Sewell probably felt he was on the home strait, but nothing in Tigon's world was ever that straightforward. Basil Rathbone was due to arrive in London on 4th of August for costume fittings at Bermans, the renowned London costumers, and then on to dinner with Sewell and the producers. A hotel and driver had been booked for the duration of his stay, and Professor Mallinger was expected to make his first appearance on the set the following week....

According to biographer Michael Druxman, Rathbone didn't have the financial luxury to rest up before his trip abroad. Rather, he embarked on a midsummer round of readings. He came home, as Ouida told Druxman, "looking very tired."

Friday, July 21, 1967: As Ouida told Druxman:

> Basil was very sad, because an old friend of his had died. We were in the living room of our apartment discussing it, when he suddenly said, "You know, I'm not afraid to die, but I just wish it didn't have to be."[54]

As Ouida talked with him, he seemed "to cheer up a bit," and went into his study to play a record he'd just purchased.

A few moments later, Basil Rathbone died of a heart attack. He was 75 years old.

The New York Times reported that his daughter Cynthia found him dead on the floor of his study. (Ouida told Druxman that she herself found the body.) The *Times* eulogized Rathbone as "the suave Shakespearean actor who won motion-picture fame in the early nineteen-forties as Sherlock Holmes—and regretted the identification the rest of his life."[55]

Tuesday, July 25, 1967: The funeral for Basil Rathbone took place this morning at St. James Episcopal Church, 865 Madison Avenue. Ouida and Cynthia were there, as was his son Rodion. The approximately 350 mourners included actor Cyril Ritchard and Ouida's niece, Mrs. David Huxley. The Reverend Dr. Arthur Lee Kinsolving, St. James' rector, eulogized Rathbone, speaking of his

> singular gifts of person and personality; verve and enthusiasm in his dedication to good theater; imagination and vision in the roles he played; warmth and kindness in personal relationships; devotion to his church, his home and his ideals.

Author-actress Cornelia Otis Skinner paid tribute, saying, "Basil Rathbone was a warm and witty gentleman in the true sense of the word." She read Elizabeth Barrett Browning's "How Do I Love Thee?" which Basil had often read to Ouida. She also read what Rathbone had stipulated in his will be read: Rupert Brooke's "The Soldier":

> If I should die, think only this of me:
> That there's some corner of a foreign field
> That is for ever England....[56]

Rathbone was interred at Ferncliff Cemetery's Shrine of Memories Mausoleum in Hartsdale, New York. His crypt is number 117, Unit One, left side, top tier. The actor's will specified:

I wish to be buried beside my wife—so close that, if it were possible, we might hold each other's hand....

I wish to be buried above ground, as I look upon death as a gateway to an ascension and elevation—not a descent.[57]

* * *

Robert Flemyng replaced Rathbone as Dr. Mallinger in *Death's Head Vampire*, which was released as *The Blood Beast Terror* (1968). Peter Cushing, usually gentlemanly and discreet, called it his all-time worst film.

Talk show host Dick Cavett, a Rathbone fan, shared a funny story about Rathbone with interviewer Jack Gourlay in 2007:

I had a friend who saw him in an airport bathroom and said to him as he was rinsing his hands, "Oh my God, Mr. Rathbone—you're my favorite actor! Would you give me your autograph?" But he didn't have a pen handy, and Rathbone exploded, "What's the matter with you people? You don't even have the proper tools!"

* * *

Friday, August 18, 1967: Rathbone's will was filed in Manhattan's Surrogates Court. His assets were estimated at $10,000 to $20,000, and left to widow Ouida and son Rodion. (Rodion, a Brooklyn resident, was reportedly never close to his father, partly because of Ouida's presence. There are stories that Rodion did assist his father in his finances late in life.) There was, apparently, no provision made for Cynthia, who lived with her parents. The *New York Times*, publishing the information, noted that Rathbone at his death had been "a British subject."[58]

The modest estate, reflective of Rathbone's financial perils, soon caused Ouida to depart the "ivory tower" at 135 Central Park West. She and Cynthia moved to an apartment a block away, at 15 West 72nd Street. Cynthia worked as an assistant art director for the Hockaday Advertising Agency.

Cynthia's life, plagued by illness, living in the shadow of her increasingly out-of-touch parents, was a difficult one. She was, by various accounts, a sad young woman. Residing with her aging and not-always-sound mother must have been an often-frightening challenge.

Wednesday, June 4, 1969: Barbara Cynthia Rathbone died at New York's Roosevelt Hospital. The published cause of death was acute anemia. She was only 30.[59]

There were other accounts of her death. Dick Cavett candidly told Jack Gourlay:

At the end, [Rathbone] deserved better than those shit movies he was making. He died the same year I started my show. The son was estranged and his daughter, Cynthia, committed suicide. She was not gifted in the looks department and was depressed, and the face probably didn't help.

There have also been claims that Cynthia was addicted to alcohol and/or drugs and died of an overdose. If this was true, it might have been another reason for Rathbone's financial perils.

The true cause of Cynthia's death remains a mystery. One hopes she knew her father carried her 1953 note with him at all times.

* * *

Ouida Rathbone survived, as Michael Druxman wrote, "with little more than her memories." She stayed on at 15 West 72nd Street, with failing eyesight and a desperate ongoing battle with finances. Her name bylined the feature "Happy Birthday, W.R," ("W.R." being William Randolph Hearst) in the Christmas 1972 issue of *Esquire*. It featured her floridly written reminiscences and pictures from Hearst's extravagant parties, which she and Basil had attended. Yet Ouida Rathbone was now basically a ghost, living on into her late eighties without her famous and devoted husband and her sad, sickly daughter. News of her straits reached Hollywood, and the old filmland aristocracy took up a collection on her behalf.

Reginald LeBorg visited her shortly before her death, finding her nearly blind but desperately clinging to memories:

> *I think she had a little bit of regret, but I had attended many of her parties in the 1930s, when she had been hostess to the crème de la crème of Hollywood, so we reminisced about those times.*[60]

Many of her "friends" in Hollywood, who had long mocked her airs and extravagance, morbidly kept a long-distance death watch. Yet Ouida went on, and one imagines some of the well-to-do old guard in Southern California feared she would outlive them all.

Friday, November 29, 1974: Ouida Rathbone died in New York's Roosevelt Hospital, due to complications from a broken hip she suffered a month previously. She was about two weeks away from her 88th birthday. Ouida would have been pleased that the UPI story regarding her death eulogized her as "one of the first women to attain prominence in the early days of film" and stated that she had been a writer "for Paramount, Pathé, and movie mogul Sam Goldwyn."[61]

She was entombed beside her husband at Ferncliff Cemetery. There are no reports as to where Cynthia was buried.

Thursday, August 22, 1996: Rodion Rathbone died in Brooklyn. He was 81.[62]

*   *   *

Basil Rathbone's death was the end of an era ... although the era that he favored had ended long ago. He and his Ouida, whom he devotedly adored despite all the hardships she created, had seen him play a horridly humiliating final act, pocked by his reciting Shakespeare to "Cow-Cow Boogie" and playing a guitar in a Beatle wig.

For Captain Levasseur, Sir Guy of Gisbourne, Sherlock Holmes and (although he probably didn't count it) Dr. Wolf von Frankenstein, it was too cruel a fate.

Yet, he'd kept going. He knew he had conquered the theater world in his youth, even gone to jail one night for the sake of Art, and there had been later stage triumphs as well. In Hollywood he lived luxuriantly, part of the most memorable magic of the Movies ... including Sherwood Forest and 221-B Baker Street. He wrote a memoir that did not become a best-seller, but neither had it betrayed any confidences which, for him, was more important. The business had turned on him, sentencing him to a long Limbo, but he had marched on "into the breach."

And on the nights that age and finances gnawed at him, and he wished that death "didn't have to be," he still was with his Ouida, in the "ivory tower" above Central Park and the lights of New York City, facing it all with her.

At the close of his *An Evening with Basil Rathbone*, he recited from Shakespeare's *The Tempest*:

We are such stuff
As dreams are made on; and our little life
Is rounded with a sleep.

Basil Rathbone's dreams had come true, whatever cruel restitution the final act had demanded. For all the whips and scorns of time, he had realized it, savored it ... and lived it.

He had been gallantly bloody and unbowed.

13

Horror Box Office

I now find myself working for an abysmally ignorant and stupid gentleman called Jack Gross.... Gross is the man who has been making those Universal horror films and so had a particular grudge against me, as our pictures had shown up his films not only from an artistic viewpoint, but also from the standpoint of profits.
— Val Lewton, letter to his mother and sister, August 20, 1944[1]

House of Frankenstein, *Universal's horror classic, starring all its Titans of Terror, has broken all existing records at the Rialto Theatre on Broadway, New York. This again proves that Universal knows when and how to make this type of boxoffice bonanza....*
— *Showmen's Trade Review,* January 6, 1945[2]

In researching the Great Hollywood studios of Yesteryear, it's generally easier to learn which stars wore toupees, falsies and dentures than it is to find out how much money a movie made or lost.

The Internet includes budgets and grosses for recent films, and there have always been the trade paper lists of all-time blockbusters. Yet for films of the Golden Age, the studios vigilantly safeguarded their cost/profit/loss ledgers.

For the most part, all these years later, they still do.

Hence, in this final chapter, we boldly go where few (if any) horror historians have gone before: the dark realm of Film Revenue. The "money angle" of Classic Horror has rarely rated discussion, partly because of the aforementioned secrecy. What would be the value of such arcane knowledge? A great deal, actually. Full disclosure on profits/losses would reveal, in cold, factual numbers, which films *truly* attracted the crowds, which stars *really* packed 'em in, and which studio *actually* was tops in horror.

This would be especially fascinating in the Hollywood of World War II, when Universal and RKO waged war for horror genre supremacy.

Frankenstein's Monster, Dracula, the Wolf Man and other goblins capered about the Universal back lot's Grimm Brothers sets, while a hyper-sexual beauty parade, featuring a cat woman, a blonde zombie and a female Satanist sashayed through RKO's oddly erotic Val Lewton films. Both studios proudly professed victory, so a dollar-to-dollar comparison as to who actually won would be a fun discovery.

It is also, alas, a staggering challenge!

Muddying the waters even further is the fact that many movies of that era involved intricate profit and revenue sharing deals among movie studios, moviemakers and investors. Lou Costello, who owned a piece of his Universal films, once complained that every time he made a film, the studio painted its buildings and charged it to his picture.

Some viable dollar figures have eventually emerged. RKO closed in 1956, and its cost/profit/loss records have long been available, revealing to the penny, for example, how much *King Kong* and the Lewton horrors cost, and how much they earned or lost. Universal, still booming today, is a different story—although, cool grab bags of significant financial figures now and then escape the fortress of Universal's corporate Black Tower. Unfortunately, since many of Universal's figures are still under lock and key, a full comparison is currently impossible.

What *is* possible, on a *far* more limited scope, is to compare the box office tallies at the Rialto Theatre in New York City and the Hawaii Theatre in Hollywood. These were the country's most notorious horror salons of the early 1940s, playing (in most cases) both the Universal *and* the RKO product. The two theaters had slick showmanship, a loyal fan base, a history with each studio ... and both reported their precise weekly takes to *Variety*.

Of course, the Hawaii vs. Rialto records do *not* reflect the individual films' overall success/failure (and in at least one startling case, stray far from the final mark). Nor does such a sharply focused overview fully take into account such issues as varying ticket costs, national preoccupations, weather, the War, and other situations that would make for a more detailed (and lengthy) examination. A definitive, comprehensive history of horror movie revenue is still in the future.

Acclaimed film historian Frank Dello Stritto has contributed valuable insights and information in developing this chapter as I attempt to "show you the money," partially but significantly, during the Golden Age of Horror and the World War II years.

Part One: Horror Film Financials of the 1930s

Did Horror Films Really Save Universal and RKO?

Some horror fans have become cynical about the oft-repeated mantra that certain horror classics "saved" their respective studios. Were *Dracula* and *Frankenstein* truly the salvation of Universal? Did *King Kong* actually rescue RKO from corporate oblivion?

In a word ... yes.

In the summer of 1932, 16 months after the release of *Dracula* and seven months after the release of *Frankenstein*, *Variety* reported the rentals on each film. (Note: Rental is *not* gross; it's the amount of money the studio receives after the theaters take their cut. Throughout this chapter, I will be using rental figures, *not* gross figures.)

Dracula's rental: $1,200,000. *Frankenstein*'s rental: $1,400,000.[3]

Profit figures vary. However, given that *Dracula* cost $341,191.20 and *Frankenstein* cost $291,129.13, both films, based on the rentals, made giant profits.[4] The lush receipts came at a time when Universal was in dire financial peril despite the international success of its Academy Award–winning *All Quiet on the Western Front*.

As for *King Kong*, the film cost $672,254.75, took in worldwide rentals of $1,856,000, and earned RKO a profit of $626,945.[5] This was in an era where RKO had suffered a 1932 loss of $10,000,000[6] and was in such hot water that it was about to go into receivership.

The company's *Flying Down to Rio* and *Little Women*, both released in 1933, joined *King Kong* as huge profit makers.

By the way, other factors affect box office. *King Kong*, which enjoyed excellent business in its opening week, might have done even better had not its premiere coincided with Franklin Roosevelt's Bank Holiday, implemented two days after his inauguration. From March 6 until March 13 (approximately—it's complicated), moviegoers could only spend what money they had in their pockets (approximately—that's complicated, too).

Fair and succinct conclusion: Universal would likely have gone under by 1933 had it not been for *Dracula* and *Frankenstein*. RKO probably would have given up the ghost the same year without *King Kong*.

Was Horror Always Big Box Office in the Pre–Code Early 1930s?

The answer: Sometimes.

During Hollywood's pre–Code era, 1930 to 1934, the Depression forced filmmakers to be more daring so as to attract moviegoers. Sound gave the studios a new dimension to make their films more effective. Censorship remained a bit behind the times, a sleeping giant before awakening in 1934. Until Joseph Breen, as head of the Production Code Administration, cracked the whip, moviemakers could (and did) put a lot on the screen that would later be forbidden.

Inspired by the gothic megahits of 1931, Hollywood studios turned out about one horror every two months from 1932 through 1934. Every major studio contributed: four from Universal, three each from RKO and Paramount, two each from Warner Brothers, MGM and Columbia, and one from Fox. The independent studios—none of whom survived the Depression years—added another half dozen.

Let's look at ten films of this era, in order of release. The key here is worldwide *rentals*, not the final profit/loss, as to determining how big an audience the film attracted. In some cases that follow, worldwide rentals are available but not profit/loss, or vice versa.[7]

Svengali (Warners–First National, New York, opening, May 1, 1931). John Barrymore in his greatest screen performance, Marian Marsh as a sexy, doomed Trilby, and a from-the-rear nude scene (performed by Marsh's double in a body stocking).

Cost: $499,000. Worldwide rental: $498,000. Loss: $225,000.

The Mad Genius (Warners–First National, New York opening, October 23, 1931). Barrymore and Marsh again, he as a dance instructor with a club foot, she as a ballerina.

Cost: $441,000. Worldwide rental: $400,000. Loss: $241,000.

Murders in the Rue Morgue (Universal, New York opening, February 10, 1932). Poe and bestiality, as Bela Lugosi's Dr. Mirakle hopes to mate Erik the Ape with a French ingénue.

Cost: $190,099.45. Worldwide rental: unavailable. Profit: $63,000. (See Chapter 1 for much more information about this audacious film.)

Freaks (MGM, New York opening, July 8, 1932). Metro's notorious shocker with genuine sideshow attractions, directed by Tod Browning.

Cost: $310,607.37. Worldwide rental: $331,000—barely more than its cost. Loss: $305,000.[8]

White Zombie (United Artists, New York opening, July 28, 1932). Bela Lugosi in one

Posters for various early 1930s pre–Code Horror Classics.

of his milestone performances as Murder the zombie master. The film was reportedly shot in 11 days.

Cost: $62,000. Worldwide rental: $370,000. Profit: unavailable (however, considering the very low cost, the profit must have been considerable).[9]

Doctor X (Warners—First National, New York opening, August 3, 1932). Lionel Atwill in his horror debut, Fay Wray screaming away, and Preston Foster as a sex-crazed, one-armed cannibal … all in early Technicolor.

Cost: $224,000. Worldwide rental: $594,000. Profit: $72,000.

The Mask of Fu Manchu (MGM, New York opening, December 2, 1932). MGM's wild comic-book horror hoot, with Karloff's Fu ranting, "Conquer and breed! Kill the white man and take his women!" and Myrna Loy as his nymphomaniacal daughter.

Cost: $338,000. Worldwide rental: $625,000. Profit: $62,000.

The Mummy (Universal, Chicago opening, December 24, 1932). "Karloff the Uncanny," as the posters proclaimed him, in two magnificent Jack P. Pierce makeups: the head-to-toe rotting bandaged Mummy, and the shriveled Ardath Bey. Nubile Zita Johann, as his reincarnated love, helps make this fantasy a strangely sexy love saga.

Cost: $196,000. Worldwide rental: unavailable. Profit: $148,000.

Mystery of the Wax Museum (Warners–First National, Los Angeles opening, February 9, 1933). Fay Wray cracks Lionel Atwill's wax mask, as he hopes to exhibit her cadaver as a wax-coated Marie Antoinette in this Technicolor production.

Cost: $279,000. Worldwide rental: A giant $1,106,000. Profit: A walloping $400,000.

The Black Cat (Universal, Hollywood opening, May 3, 1934). The first "KARLOFF and BELA LUGOSI" teaming, with Karloff's Lucifer Incarnate, skinned on a rack by Lugosi's avenging angel. A perversely blasphemous climax to pre–Code Horror with powerhouse performances by the two stars.

Cost: $92,323.76. Worldwide rental: $438,000. Profit: $155,000.

Unfortunately, no specific rental/profit/loss figures are available on Paramount's 1931 *Dr. Jekyll and Mr. Hyde*, for which Fredric March won a Best Actor Academy Award (box office business was described in the trade papers as very good); Universal's 1932 *The Old Dark House*, starring Karloff and directed by James Whale (national box office announced as moderate); Paramount's 1932 *Island of Lost Souls*, starring Charles Laughton and Bela Lugosi (box office reported nationally as below expectations; banned in various other countries); and Universal's 1933 *The Invisible Man*, starring Claude Rains and directed by James Whale (a near record-breaker in New York, but a flop in Los Angeles).

A few points on the films covered:

1. *Mystery of the Wax Museum* is the only movie of the ten on the list to have earned a rental of over $1,000,000.

2. Four of the ten had profits of over $100,000; three had losses of over $100,000.

3. A hasty review of these tabulations can create misleading assumptions. While *The Black Cat* was proclaimed Universal's "hit of the season" and made a rosy profit, it almost *had* to make money, due to its low cost. At the same time, Warners' *Svengali* appears a flop due to its considerable loss, but as the worldwide rental shows, more audiences saw *Svengali* than saw *The Black Cat*.

Also demanding attention: Until the late 1940s, when the courts decreed the breakup of the major studio-theater conglomerates, movies from the majors played mainly at their own theaters. The "Big Five"—Warner Brothers, MGM, Paramount, RKO and Fox—operated massive chains of cinemas. Major cities had motion picture palaces bearing the names of those companies (except MGM, whose theaters were named for its parent corporation, Loews). Films from the Big Five had an easier time turning profits thanks to the number of screens on which they played. And many a manager of those theaters chafed at having to end the profitable run of a hit film from Universal or Columbia (the "Little Two") to make way for a routine offering from their corporate cousin.

Doctor X and *Mystery of the Wax Museum* came from Warners, which had a far bigger theater chain than Universal. Just so, the worldwide rental on MGM's *The Mask of Fu Manchu* far exceeding that of *The Black Cat* is hardly a surprise, as Metro had the largest fleet of theaters of any 1930s studio.

What one can distill from all these figures and qualifiers is that horror films were risky ventures in the early 1930s. Based on the precise profit/loss figures for nine of these ten films (excluding *White Zombie* for which there is no profit/loss figure), the final numbers are close:

Profits: $800,000. Losses: $771,000.

Horror in Full Bloom: 1935–1936

Come 1934, Joseph Breen spearheaded rigid enforcement of the newly strengthened Production Code. Nevertheless, the studios' often slyly creative defiance made for fascinating films and Hollywood history in 1935 and 1936.[10]

Bride of Frankenstein (Universal, San Francisco opening, April 19, 1935). Karloff's Monster and Colin Clive's monster-maker return in the apogee of 1930s Horror. (See Chapter 4 for an examination of this landmark film's censorship difficulties.)

Cost: $397,023.97. Worldwide rental: unavailable. Profit: $166,000 (as of late 1937).[11]

Mark of the Vampire (MGM, New York opening, May 1, 1935). This film asks the question: Have vampires truly committed a murder? Fourteen turgid minutes were cut between preview and release—none of them dealing with the legendary "incest" scenes featuring Bela Lugosi and Carroll Borland as father-and-daughter vampires (and which were never shot at all). The 61-minute film had Tod Browning's atmospherics and MGM gloss.

Cost: $305,177.90. Worldwide rental: $563,000. Profit: $54,000.

The Raven (Universal, New York opening, July 4, 1935). The second Karloff-Lugosi vehicle: Poe-obsessed Lugosi transforms gangster Karloff into a hideous pumpkin-head.

Cost: $115,209.01. Worldwide rental: $335,000. Profit: $72,000.[12]

Mad Love (MGM, Hollywood opening, July 24, 1935). Mad Peter Lorre, tormented Colin Clive, foxy Frances Drake, and director Karl Freund mixing Grand Guignol theater with surgical amputations. (See Chapter 6 for additional *Mad Love* information.)

Cost: $257,562.14. Worldwide rental: $364,000. Loss: $39,000.[13]

The Invisible Ray (Universal, New York opening, January 10, 1936). Karloff as a Radium X–poisoned scientist; Lugosi, a sympathetic fellow scientist and his final victim. Universal poured much more money and production value into this Karloff–Lugosi horror–science fiction melodrama than it had the stars' two previous teamings. Frances Drake, dazzling John P. Fulton special effects and an original Franz Waxman score contributed to its final cost. The film attracted bigger business than *The Black Cat* (barely) and *The Raven* (by a good margin).

Posters for several mid–1930s horror films, made after Joseph Breen strengthened the Production Code Administration.

Cost: $234,875.74. Worldwide rental: $448,000. Loss: $11,000.

The Walking Dead (Warners–First National, New York opening, February 29, 1936). Warners' street-wise answer to *Frankenstein*. Karloff goes to the electric chair, comes back to life via Edmund Gwenn's laboratory, then scares the gangsters to death. The studio gave this melodrama its top dog director Michael Curtiz and ace cameraman Hal Mohr, and the film emerged as a slickly packaged blend of horror show, gangster saga and religious message.

Cost: $217,000. Worldwide rental: $589,000. Profit: $94,750.

The Devil-Doll (MGM, New York opening, August 7, 1936). Lionel Barrymore, in drag as an old lady, shrinking people and animals. Tod Browning directs and special effects run rampant.

Cost: $391,000. Worldwide rental: $729,000. Profit: $68,000.[14]

Several points:

1. *Bride of Frankenstein* was the only one of these seven films to register a profit over $100,000—although *The Walking Dead* came close.
2. Two of the seven films lost money.
3. To a greater or lesser extent, all seven ran afoul of Joseph Breen.
4. The ultimate figures on the seven films:
Profits: $454,750. Losses: $50,000.

There are no rental figures available for Universal's *WereWolf of London* (1935) or *Dracula's Daughter* (1936), neither of which were reported to be major moneymakers. Come mid–1936, the censorship fracas and the sale of Universal to new management— combined with Great Britain eventually keeping its threat to ban children from seeing horror films—nailed the lid on the horror genre's coffin.

A miracle was needed to bring horror back. It came two and a half years later.

Sometimes, They Come Back

Movie horror's comeback began as a gimmick at a Beverly Hills theater to coax moviegoers into the hot, humid summer nights (no air conditioning in 1938). The neighborhood curiosity became a West Coast sensation and then a national and international phenomenon. The full-page *Variety* ad of October 12, 1938, said it all:

> Throw Away the Books! Forget All You Ever Knew About Showmanship
> Because HORROR Is Paying Off Again!
> DRACULA and FRANKENSTEIN
> You Play Them Together! You Dare Them to See It.
> AND THEN THE CROWDS BREAK DOWN YOUR DOORS

The ad hardly exaggerated. The Regina Theatre in Beverly Hills booked a triple bill of *Dracula*, *Frankenstein* and 1933's *The Son of Kong* for a half-week (i.e., August 4–7, Thursday–Sunday). The theater immediately filled, and stayed full all day. Lines stretched along Wilshire Boulevard with sweating patrons waiting for seats to become available. (In 1938 and well after, a moviegoer—once seated—could stay in the theater all day.) The half-week passed, but the triple bill played on. Seats tended to empty when *The Son of Kong* played. The excitement centered on seeing Count Dracula and Frankenstein's Monster playing for the first time together.

A trade advertisement for the sensationally popular double bill release of Dracula and Frankenstein in late 1938.

To keep the momentum going, Bela Lugosi, who had hardly worked since horror film production ceased in 1936, made personal appearances starting on August 11 each night at 9 p.m.

Universal acknowledged the news in an offbeat way. Edward Ludwig, then directing

That Certain Age starring Deanna Durbin, Universal's 16-year-old singing sensation, tossed a "horror party" for Deanna and the rest of the movie's cast at Eaton's Restaurant in Los Angeles. The party showed *Frankenstein,* but instead of *Dracula,* played *The Invisible Man.* Deanna and the other "youngsters" put on their own show accompanied by an orchestra and followed by a buffet. (Deanna in horror makeup? The mind boggles!)[15]

The half-week at the Regina Theatre eventually became a three-and-a-half–week run. By then, double bills of *Dracula* and *Frankenstein* played through the western states, including at the Gordon Theatre only two miles from the Regina. Box office reports defied belief. House records were set in theaters throughout the west. The double bill routinely drew bigger audiences than new movies. The monsters had the temerity to outdraw Universal's Durbin starrer *Mad About Music.*

An oft-repeated story started at the Warner's Theatre in Fresno: The double-bill did outstanding business, but had to be pulled to play a Warner Brothers movie. As soon as that obligation was filled, *Dracula* and *Frankenstein* returned.

Perhaps the oddest story came from Salt Lake City:

> At the Victory Theatre, the house was sold out by 10 o'clock in the morning. Four thousand frenzied Mormons milled around outside, finally broke through the police lines, smashed the plate glass box office, bent the front doors and tore off one of the door checks in their eagerness to get in and be frightened. The manager rented an empty theater across the street, bicycled reels to it and in 20 minutes had it packed to the gunwales, with the street still full of frustrated phobiaphiles clamoring for admission.[16]

Universal, caught unawares by the SRO business, did not have enough prints of the two films to satisfy demand. Five hundred fresh prints were struck, while the studio pondered what to do next. The phenomenal double bill headed east, reaching New York's Rialto on October 18, 1938, and running there 24 hours a day. In its first week at the Rialto, *Dracula* and *Frankenstein* grossed $12,000; the average weekly take at the theater was $5500.[17]

It also traveled across the Atlantic despite the ban in Britain, which did not outlaw horror films, but put them off limits to anyone under 16 years old. Adults came, and the kids sneaked in behind them.

The day after Universal ran its full-page *Variety* ad came another announcement in the same trade journal:

New Universal Horror Picture Ready;
Lorre, Karloff, Lugosi Star

The new picture wasn't quite ready. Peter Lorre would be replaced by Basil Rathbone, with Lionel Atwill added. But horror was back.

Son of Frankenstein

The accepted legend is that *Son of Frankenstein,* premiering in January 1939, was a box office smash, resurrecting Hollywood horror. Actually, the story is considerably more shaded and complex … with a variety of resounding repercussions.

Rowland V. Lee, who produced and directed *Son of Frankenstein*, had a theory: Build an impressive melodrama, cast box office draws Basil Rathbone (as Dr. Wolf von Frankenstein), Boris Karloff (as the Monster), Bela Lugosi (as Ygor) and Lionel Atwill (as Inspector Krogh), dress up the film with sets and spectacle, and the people would come—*because* it was a horror film, and *despite* it being a horror film. Universal had originally hoped for a modest production, but Lee, basically winging the script with Wyllis Cooper, went perilously over the estimated schedule and budget. The final cost: $420,000,[18] making it Universal's most expensive horror film of 1930–1938.

Meanwhile, the *Son* company had fun. On Christmas Eve, 1938, *Variety* reported:

> *Weirdest pre–Christmas party came as surprise last night to principals and director on Universal's* Son of Frankenstein *set when crew and assistants tossed a parody on the chiller, with Wyllis Cooper, author of original, writing the satire…. Gil Valle, assistant director, played the Monster in a sissy version; script girl parodied Bela Lugosi's role; 200-pound prop man impersonated little Donnie Dunagan; and Otto Lederer burlesqued Basil Rathbone.*[19]

The stakes for Universal (which hadn't had a profitable fiscal year since 1934) and for *Son of Frankenstein* were frighteningly high. The new studio regime was prodigally gambling on a genre considered dead and buried.

On January, Friday the 13th, 1939, Universal opened *Son of Frankenstein* in Los Angeles at the Hollywood Pantages and the RKO-Hillstreet Theatre, double-billed at both with the RKO comedy *Next Time I Marry*. The film also had key openings that weekend across the country.

There came a curse worthy of the Frankensteins: A Friday the 13th snowstorm affected the East Coast, reducing theater business by 10 to 20 percent. At any rate, by January 18, *Variety* was reporting *Son of Frankenstein*'s openings: At Chicago's Palace Theatre, the film was a "smash"; at Keith's Memorial in Boston, it was one of the city's "standouts"; at Keith's in Baltimore, it was "hitting strong pace for biggest take in weeks." However, the film was merely "Oke" at Keith's in Washington, D.C., while at Cleveland's Hippodrome, it was dismissed as "a bit too corny for this stand and just a fill-in."

As for the L.A. openings: *Variety* reported *Son of Frankenstein*'s first week at the Hollywood Pantages to be $7600—"just fair." At the RKO Hillstreet, the first week was listed at $9200—"good."[20]

Overall, box office was solid, and impressive in some cities, especially for a genre that had been extinct for over two years. However, Universal felt compelled to exaggerate the film's first week, with *Variety* running this notice:

> *Universal has ordered twice as many prints as originally contemplated on* Son of Frankenstein *to meet demand for rush bookings. Openings of chiller in Los Angeles, Boston and Richmond last week brought in grosses which company declares are greater than any other Universal picture ever played in these keys.*[21]

It wasn't true. In Boston, for example, *Frankenstein*'s first week tally in December 1931 had been $41,200.[22] *Son of Frankenstein*'s first-week receipts: $18,500.[23]

Son received a large number of hold-over dates. For the second week in Los Angeles, the Pantages take was $3900, and the Hillstreet tally $4350. The total for the two weeks at both theaters: $24,550. In comparison, Warner Bros.' *Devil's Island*, starring Karloff, had opened in Los Angeles on New Year's Eve, 1938, playing at the Warners Downtown Theatre and Warners Hollywood Theatre, double-billed with Warner Bros.' *Going Places*. Its two-week total: $34,700.[24]

As for Broadway: *Son of Frankenstein* reached the Rivoli Theatre in late January 1939 and did $31,000 in two weeks, which *Variety* called "under hopes."[25]

Nevertheless, the February 1, 1939, issue of *Box Office Digest* headlined on page one, "Universal Tops for Week with *Son of Frankenstein* Scoring." The trade journal called *Son* "the top box office attraction this week" and reported that the film was performing "116%"

NATIONAL BOX OFFICE DIGEST
★   ★   *"Honor Box"*   ★   ★
THE BIGGEST GROSSING PICTURE OF THE PAST WEEK

This Week UNIVERSAL Wins With
"SON OF FRANKENSTEIN" - 116%

★

Producer-Director
ROWLAND V. LEE

Original Screenplay
WILLIS COOPER

Featured
LIONEL ATWILL
DONNIE DUNCAN

BORIS KARLOFF

Film Editor
TED KENT

Photography
GEORGE ROBINSON

★

BELA LUGOSI   JOSEPHINE HUTCHINSON   BASIL RATHBONE

National Box Office Digest **salutes the success of Universal's** *Son of Frankenstein* **(1939).**

business ("very good under current conditions"). Still, the reporter, Norman Webb, refer-ring to the recent double-bill release of *Dracula* and *Frankenstein*, wrote,

> [S]trange as it may seem, this double-header even did more business than Universal's new Son of Frankenstein *has done in certain spots. The fact that the reissue beat the new picture in many instances may be due to the exhibitor showmen who sold Lugosi and Karloff, while the standard*

advertising on the new production is trying to sell Rathbone—a fine actor, but not a ticket seller. Hollywood forgets that Rathbone is still a character actor as far as marquees are concerned....

All in all, *Son of Frankenstein* earned a worldwide rental of $921,000.[26] This was a very impressive figure, and over *double* the rental on *The Invisible Ray*, which had previously held the highest rental figure for the films co-starring Karloff and Lugosi. However, as noted, *The Invisible Ray* ended up slightly in the red because of its higher-than-usual production cost. There's no definitive profit/loss number currently available for *Son*, but based on its production tab, it's likely that the film barely broke even.

Indeed, in May 1939, *Variety* burst Universal's bubble by reporting, "*Son of Frankenstein* missed the honorable mention class" among the studio's recent releases and had performed at 91 percent of the figure Universal had set for profitability.[27]

In summary: As a horror film, *Son of Frankenstein* had performed "socko" at the box office; as a slightly-above-moderate-cost mainstream "A" feature, it had fallen just short of its target.

Fast-forward to a different Rowland V. Lee production for 1939: *Tower of London*. As noted in Chapter 7, the medieval melodrama starring Rathbone, Karloff and Vincent Price was a smash at Broadway's Rialto, a theater that catered to the horror and thriller crowd. The film performed far less impressively at other big city venues.

By late 1939, the New Universal had learned several show business facts of life:

1. There was definitely an audience for horror films.
2. If these chillers were to be profitable, the studio had to slash production costs.
3. Horror films would perform best in specialty houses that offered splashy promotion and attracted faithful genre audiences, such as the Rialto.
4. Although top-priced actors might demand star billing, the exploitation had to center on the monsters and the actors who portrayed them.

Once again, as Milton put it, "Better to reign in Hell than serve in Heaven"— and a theater perfectly suited to provide a cozy "Hell" for the horror trade opened in Hollywood.

Its name: The Hawaii.

Part Two: Horror Film Financials of the 1940s

The Hawaii Theatre and The Rialto Theatre

Located at 5939 Hollywood Boulevard, the Hawaii opened on May 5, 1940, with an RKO double feature: *Abe Lincoln in Illinois* and *Courageous Dr. Christian*. The theater had 1100 seats, a tropical motif with a mural of a volcano and a dancing girl, and a trademark gimmick of decorating its facade to promote its films. The Hawaii truly came into its own when it presented RKO's *Citizen Kane* for 17 weeks in 1941, followed by a 15-week run of Universal's Olsen and Johnson comedy *Hellzapoppin'*.[28] The managers were Albert Galston and Jay Sutton.

Meanwhile, the Rialto was at full blast in New York City. Located at 1481 Broadway,

The opening night of the Hawaii Theatre on Hollywood Boulevard, May 1940. Many of the Universal and RKO horror hits of the World War II years played at this movie house.

the northwest corner of 42nd Street and Seventh Avenue, the theater had risen from the ashes of a previous Rialto, once known as "The Temple of the Motion Picture," demolished in 1935. (As noted in Chapter 5, the wrecking ball swung after the first week's engagement of *WereWolf of London*.) Opening on Christmas Day 1935, the new Rialto was an art deco house with an 80-foot-tall glass tower and only 750 seats (mysteriously down to 594 seats in 1941). Its first feature: Frank Buck's *Fang and Claw*.

The Rialto's manager, Harvard-educated Arthur Mayer, was formerly the mastermind of Paramount's Panther Woman Contest for *Island of Lost Souls* in 1932. As Mayer wrote in his 1953 book, *Merely Colossal*:

> *Across the street, the New Amsterdam Theatre, under Flo Ziegfeld, had once declared that its ideal was to glorify the American girl. Ours was to glorify the American ghoul…. I became known up and down Broadway as the Merchant of Menace, and I achieved the Broadway equivalent of immortality when it was printed in a newspaper gossip column one day that Sam Goldwyn had said, "When I see the pictures they play in that theater it makes the hair stand on the edge of my seat." It was a delicate compliment and I saw to it that it was reprinted and reprinted. (Its true author was, I am told, the Hollywood director Michael Curtiz.) We were not officially launched, however, until* The New York Times *summed up one year's record with, "No hits, no runs, just terrors."*[29]

Mayer claimed the Rialto appealed (in his words) to the "ancient and unquenchable male thirst for mystery, menace and manslaughter." His "tarting up" of the theater with lurid displays at the entranceway and marquee became legendary.

The Rialto and the Hawaii usually played the same product, often with similar box

Boris Karloff, then starring in the mega-hit Broadway play *Arsenic and Old Lace*, visits Arthur Mayer, manager of New York City's Rialto Theatre, where the attraction is Karloff's *The Devil Commands* (Columbia, 1941). The Rialto was New York's showcase horror movie salon (from the John Antosiewicz Collection).

office impact, but sometimes not. Also, the Rialto showed the films one at a time, while the Hawaii was a double feature house. Nevertheless, ticket prices were comparable in 1943: The Rialto tickets cost 28¢–65¢, while the Hawaii cost 40¢–75¢. Also, during the period in question, the Hawaii (1100 seats) had almost double the capacity of the Rialto (594 seats) yet the box office figures for both theaters were usually comparable.

The "war" was on, and here's how some of the films fared at the Rialto and the Hawaii.

1. *Cat People* (RKO, Rialto opening, December 5, 1942/Hawaii opening, January 14, 1943). Val Lewton's dark, sexy maiden production starred Simone Simon as the tragic Irena, convinced that her sexual arousal and jealousy will transform her into a leopard. While the film did nicely at the Rialto, it was a sensation at the Hawaii, supported by Warner Bros.' *The Gorilla Man* (a wartime melodrama, despite its title).

	Co-Feature	1st Week BO	Run	Total
Rialto		$10,000	2 weeks	$17,000[30]
Hawaii	*The Gorilla Man*	$9,600	13 weeks	$68,731[31]

Cat People played the Rialto Theatre, with "tarted-up" exploitation.

The lobby of the Rialto Theatre, during *Cat People*'s run.

Cat People was a 13-week attraction at Hollywood's Hawaii, supported by Warners' *The Gorilla Man*—which was not a horror film, but a yarn about Nazi spies.

  2. *I Walked with a Zombie* (RKO, Rialto opening, April 21, 1943/Hawaii opening, September 2, 1943). In Lewton's second film, set in the Caribbean, a nurse (Frances Dee) tends the catatonic wife of a plantation owner. Is the illness a tropical disease or a curse for infidelity (with her brother-in-law)? Once again, the film did well at the Rialto but was a smash at the Hawaii, where it was double-billed with Lewton's third film, *The Leopard Man*. The double-bill's first week's take at the Hawaii topped *Cat People*'s (and *Citizen Kane*'s!).

	Co-Feature	1st Week BO	Run	Total
Rialto		$12,000	2 weeks	$19,500[32]
Hawaii	*The Leopard Man*	$10,950	7 weeks	$37,986[33]

  3. *Son of Dracula* (Universal, Rialto opening, November 4, 1943/Hawaii opening, November 10, 1943). Horror fans have squawked long and loud about Lon Chaney's beef-trust bloodsucker, but he packed 'em in at both the Rialto and the Hawaii, although one suspects Louise Allbritton's sexpot female vampire and Robert Siodmak's velvety direction helped. *Variety* reported that its first week take at the Rialto was "one of the highest figures ever registered"[34] for one week at that theater. At the Hawaii, *Son of Dracula* was supported by Universal's *The Mad Ghoul* (ace screamer Evelyn Ankers graced both films). The double feature, *Variety* reported, was "breaking the house record"; on the first Sunday showing, the Hawaii had "lines continually from 1 til 11 P.M."[35]

	Co-Feature	1st Week BO	Run	Total
Rialto		$16,300	4 weeks	$40,300[36]
Hawaii	*The Mad Ghoul*	$10,600	5 weeks	$33,555[37]

The ticket booth of the Hawaii Theatre, felinely re-designed for *Cat People*.

4. *The Ghost Ship* (RKO, Hawaii opening, December 23, 1943/Rialto opening, December 24, 1943). The Yuletide 1943 show at the Hawaii was a new Val Lewton double feature: *The Ghost Ship* and *The Seventh Victim*. The stars practically screamed "Merry Christmas": Richard Dix's Captain Stone of *The Ghost Ship*, a psychopathic murderer on a ship that's a motif for Hell, and Jean Brooks' Jacqueline of *The Seventh Victim*, a moon-eyed Satanist in a Cleopatra wig who hangs herself. One wonders just what compelled anyone in the City of Angels to spend Christmas Eve or Day at the

Hawaii that year, but as *Variety* reported of the Hawaii, "House got sold-out lines all Saturday [December 25] and Sunday [December 26] and also went big for Christmas Eve trade...."[38] At the Rialto, *The Ghost Ship* was also the 1943 Christmas attraction, and did excellent business.

	Co-Feature	1st Week BO	Run	Total
Rialto		$12,000	3 weeks	$27,900[39]
Hawaii	*The Seventh Victim*	$7,800	5 weeks	$25,011[40]

5. *House of Frankenstein* (Universal, Rialto opening, December 15, 1944/Hawaii opening, December 22, 1944—for more information about this movie, see Chapter 11). Universal's monster rally, a spectacular 1944 Christmas present to horror disciples, *perhaps* made Broadway history, as noted, by setting a new high at a theater the week before Christmas. At the Hawaii, *House of Frankenstein* was paired with Universal's *The Mummy's Curse,* which featured *two* mummies: Lon Chaney's Kharis and, emerging from the swamp, Virginia Christine's Princess Ananka. The double feature did blockbuster business there as well.

	Co-Feature	1st Week BO	Run	Total
Rialto		$17,000	4 weeks	$57,800[41]
Hawaii	*The Mummy's Curse*	$11,700	6 weeks	$36,850[42]

The Rialto offers *House of Frankenstein* as a record-breaking 1944 Christmas attraction.

6. *The Body Snatcher* (RKO, Hawaii opening, May 10, 1945/Rialto opening, May 25, 1945). As noted in Chapter 11, Val Lewton and RKO saw *The Body Snatcher* as its "throw-down-the-gauntlet" challenge to Universal's *House of Frankenstein*. Karloff's wicked Cabman Gray, Henry Daniell's tragic Dr. MacFarlane, Bela Lugosi's doomed Joseph, Robert Wise's atmospheric direction…RKO had every reason to anticipate giant box office success, having made what's retrospectively regarded as perhaps the greatest horror film of the 1940s.

The Body Snatcher opened at the Hawaii on a double bill with RKO's *The Brighton Strangler*. Note that the contest between *House of Frankenstein* and *The Body Snatcher*—at least at the Hawaii and the Rialto—wasn't even close.[43]

	Co-Feature	1st Week BO	Run	Total
Rialto		$11,400	4 weeks	$26,400[44]
Hawaii	*The Brighton Strangler*	$7,800	3 weeks	$21,200[45]

The Body Snatcher earned the highest worldwide rental of any of the Lewton horrors: $547,000.[46] Perhaps its Hollywood release, two days after VE Day and the ensuing euphoria, limited its appeal at both the Hawaii and the Rialto.[47]

As noted, with complete profits/losses figures unavailable, the Hawaii vs. the Rialto give only a small piece of the story.

Away from the Hawaii in L.A.

Of course, not all of the horror films of the era played the Hawaii and the Rialto. For example:

Universal's *Frankenstein Meets the Wolf Man* played the Rialto in New York starting on March 5, 1943. It did a terrific first week of $15,500[48] and a four-week total of $42,000.[49] However, in Los Angeles, it played the Paramount Downtown Theatre and the Paramount Hollywood Theatre (supported by *Captive Wild Woman*—see Chapter 10) for two weeks starting July 22, 1943. In its two-week run at those two theaters, it reaped a huge $56,500 combined.[50]

Universal's 1945 *House of Dracula* opened on December 21, 1945, at the Rialto, did a big $14,000 its first week[51] and, in a three-week run, earned $35,000.[52] In Los Angeles, *House of Dracula,* double-billed with Universal's *The Daltons Ride Again* (co-starring Lon Chaney), opened on February 6, 1946, at four theaters: the Guild, the United Artists, the Wilshire and the Vogue. The double-feature earned what *Variety* called a record combined first-week gross of $45,500.[53]

Perhaps most dramatically, RKO's 1946 *Bedlam,* Karloff's third and final Lewton film, opened Good Friday, April 19, 1946, the Easter attraction at the Rialto. The first week business was a huge $13,900[54] and the four-week run took in $37,000,[55] making it one of the Rialto's biggest horror hits. In Los Angeles, however, *Bedlam* forlornly opened on New Year's Eve 1946 at Hollywood's Marcal Theatre. The film headed what *Variety* called an unspecified "horror bill." Lewton had left RKO, the studio's new management failed to promote *Bedlam,* and the movie's worldwide loss was $40,000.[56]

Other Studios and Conclusions

As for worldwide rentals, it's important to note that except perhaps for Universal's 1943 *Phantom of the Opera* (figures unavailable, but reportedly high), none of the RKO and Universal horror films matched the numbers on these three movies from other studios[57]:

Dr. Jekyll and Mr. Hyde (MGM, 1941). Spencer Tracy, Ingrid Bergman and Lana Turner in this censor-defying romantic triangle (quadrangle?). Worldwide rental: $2,351,000. (See Chapter 8 for an in-depth analysis of this controversial film version of the classic tale.)

The Lodger (20th Century–Fox, 1944). Laird Cregar in his bravura portrayal of Jack the Ripper. Worldwide rental: $2,295,500.

The Picture of Dorian Gray (MGM, 1945). Hurd Hatfield in the title role, George Sanders as Lord Henry Wotton, 18-year-old Angela Lansbury in an Academy Award–nominated performance as lovely, ill-used Sibyl Vane, and Oscar-winning cinematography by Harry Stradling. Worldwide rental: $2,975,000.

*   *   *

A major take-away from all these numbers: Hollywood Horror was still hot throughout World War II and might have gone on indefinitely. It was the change in front

The Hawaii Theatre, at the time it presented *Citizen Kane* for 17 weeks in 1941.

A 2016 photograph of what used to be the Hawaii Theatre, now a Salvation Army headquarters (photograph by the author).

office policy in postwar Universal and RKO—not fickle public taste—that killed off the genre.

The end of World War II brought abrupt changes to the output of Hollywood studios. Film franchises that had flourished through the war years evaporated. Recurring characters, from Mickey Rooney's Andy Hardy to Basil Rathbone's Sherlock Holmes, made their last appearances in 1946.

Lest we forget: Universal (now Universal-International) made a mint with 1948's *Abbott and Costello Meet Frankenstein*, with worldwide rentals of $2,250,000.[58]

* * *

As for the fate of the movie houses:

The Rialto fell in 2002 to make way for a high-rise New York City office building.

The Hawaii, which gave up as a theater in the summer of 1963, still stands on the not-so-nice-anymore northeast end of Hollywood Boulevard. Its interior was gutted decades ago and the building has served as a Salvation Army Tabernacle. When I last saw the Hawaii in 2016, it looked forlorn, a depressing chunk of archaic L.A. real estate.

Part and parcel of "Haunted Hollywood"?

No doubt!

Chapter Notes

Chapter 1

1. Bonhams and Butterfields offered this painting for auction in 2013. It sold for $30,000.

2. Lugosi kept several scrapbooks. The one containing clippings from *Murders in the Rue Morgue* belonged at one time to John Antosiewicz, who'd made copies of these pages and generously shared them with me. Many thanks, John!

3. Universal publicity in the Motion Picture Producers and Directors Association of America (the MPPDA) File, on *Murders in the Rue Morgue*, Margaret Herrick Library, Academy of Motion Picture Arts & Sciences, Los Angeles, CA. This file also contains all the censorship material cited in this chapter. Thanks to Kristine Krueger.

4. Suit Uncovered in Girl Killing," *Los Angeles Times*, 27 September 1931, p. 15.

5. "Women Quizzed in Girl Murder," *Los Angeles Times*, 1 October 1931, p. A8.

6. "Women Sought in Girl Killing," *Los Angeles Times*, 2 October 1931, p. A5.

7. "Crime Record Undiminished," *Los Angeles Times*, 6 October 1931, p. A3.

8. Poe earned $56 for *Murders in the Rue Morgue*, as opposed to the $9 he'd earned for 1845's *The Raven*.

9. Robert Florey was still perfecting his English when he directed this film. Groucho Marx allegedly said of the film's directors, Florey and Joseph Santley (a former dance director), "One of them didn't understand English, and the other one didn't understand comedy."

10. Brian Taves, *Robert Florey: The French Expressionist* (Scarecrow Press, Metuchen, NJ, 1987).

11. "Great Horror Figure Dies," *Famous Monsters of Filmland*, December 1964, No. 31, p. 50.

12. Rick Atkins, *Let's Scare 'Em!: Grand Interviews and a Filmography of Horrific Proportions, 1930–1961* (McFarland, Jefferson, North Carolina, 1997).

13. The mystery remains unsolved. A picture of Lugosi in his *Frankenstein* test make-up has yet to emerge. As for the test itself, Universal destroyed all its test footage and outtakes after World War II. Karloff, repeating what make-up artist Jack Pierce had probably told him, claimed Lugosi made himself up as an "awful, hairy creature, not at all like our Monster." This author's personal belief is that Florey was not honest in his recollections and that Lugosi made himself up rather like T.P Cooke had looked as the Monster in 1823, evoking a frightening, flowing-haired angel.

14. "*Frankenstein* Finished," *New York Times*, 11 October 1931, p. X5.

15. Taves.

16. James Curtis, ed., *Featured Player: An Oral Autobiography of Mae Clarke* (Scarecrow Press, Lanham, MD, 1996), p. 89.

17. Among the earlier stabs at a script was one dated September 17, 1931, by Francis Edward Faragoh, one of the writers on *Frankenstein*. In his book *Screams of Reason*, David J. Skal discusses this script: "Faragoh named his caped madman Dr. Ramey and had him operate a traveling wax museum and freak show as a front for his evolutionary experiment. "My fame is great," he tells a visitor to his tent. "I am the creator of the bird-boy, of the two-headed dog, of a thousand and one amazing, stupendous monsters...But my new handiwork will be greater than any of them! That's why I needed these women...that's why they've had to die...for science...for my secret...to produce a new freak...the crowning glory of my career!" The precise nature of this freak is not revealed until the end. It is a new female being, carrying within its human and simian blood: "A freak greater than any ever created! Ape-woman! Ape-girl!" (*Screams of Reason: Mad Science and Modern Culture* [W.W. Norton & Company, New York, 1998], p. 133).

18. Author's telephone interviews with Evelyn Moriarty, Los Angeles, CA, 26 and 27 April 1993. Ms. Moriarty was Junior's lady friend for nearly 40 years, up to his death in 1979. Ms. Moriarty died in 2008.

19. See G. D. Hamann, *Carl Laemmle, Jr. In the 30's* (Filming Today Press, Hollywood, CA, 2012), which contains newspaper articles which mention Junior's incapacitation. Hamann's books (which collect newspaper articles and reviews re: actors, directors, etc.) are highly recommended!

20. Thanks to John Antosiewicz, who owns this letter and provided me a copy.

21. Robert E. Sherwood, "A Big-Game Hunting Picture That Includes Sex Interest," *The Baltimore Sun*, 25 May 1930, p. MR1.

22. "Hays Bars *Ingagi* Film: Movie of Jungle Life Called Nature Faking by Business Bureau," *New York Times*, 12 June 1930, p. 37.

23. Andrew Erish, "Illegitimate Dad of Kong," *Los Angeles Times*, 8 January 2006, p. E6. Erish's article provides a good summary of the *Ingagi* furor.

24. *Ibid.*

25. J. Brooks Atkinson, "The Play," *New York Times*, 6 May 1930, p. 37.

26. Naturally, there was no newspaper/fan magazine coverage in 1931 that reported Laemmle Jr., and Sidney Fox to be "lovers." It was, however, well-known within the industry at that time. DeWitt Bodeen (1904–1988), the screenwriter of such films as *Cat People* (1942) and a prominent film historian, confirmed the rumors regarding the Laemmle-Fox relationship in conversations with me.

27. Elisabeth Goldbeck, "Five Feet of Stardom," unsourced magazine article. Thanks to Gary Don Rhodes.

28. *Los Angeles Times* unsourced clipping.

29. Jerry Hoffman, "Sidney Fox Explodes That High-Hat Rumor," *Los Angeles Examiner*, 8 November 1931.

30. *Murders in the Rue Morgue* file, Universal Collection, USC Cinematic Arts Library, Los Angeles, CA. Thanks to Ned Comstock. All cost/budget and shooting dates information in this chapter comes from that file.

31. Press release dated 11 May 1932. The release was in the *Los Angeles Examiner* files on Ms. Fox at the USC Cinematic Arts Library. Thanks to Ned Comstock.

32. Leon Ames later toured with Lugosi in a *Dracula* stage revival in 1932. In 1933, he'd been an early member of the Screen Actors Guild, along with Boris Karloff and Bela Lugosi, and was President of SAG 1957/1958. He enjoyed a quite amazing career: films such as *The Postman Always Rings Twice* (1946); the TV series *Life with Father* (1953–1955), *Father of the Bride* (1961–1962), and 40 episodes of *Mr. Ed*, as Ed's and Wilbur's neighbor, Gordon. His last film was *Peggy Sue Got Married*, released in 1986, the year Ames turned 84 years old. In addition to continuing to act into his 80s, Ames owned four Ford dealerships in Southern California in the early 1960s. Leon Ames died in Laguna Beach in 1993 at the age of 91.

33. Tom Weaver, Michael Brunas, and John Brunas, *Universal Horrors: The Studio's Classic Films, 1931–1946 Second Edition* (McFarland, Jefferson, North Carolina, 2007), p. 53.

34. "'Ape-Man' Hunt Traps Suspect," *Los Angeles Times*, 24 October 1931, p. A2.

35. The pre-shooting censorship letter to Universal regarding this film refers to the Mirakle-and-Prostitute episode as the "opening episode." An early studio-prepared synopsis does as well. The introduction of Lugosi in this episode, emerging from the coach in the night mist, sets up his character far more effectively than does the rearranged opening in the carnival, where Camille refers to Mirakle, "What a funny-looking man!"

36. David J. Skal, *The Monster Show: A Cultural History of Horror* (W. W. Norton & Company, New York, 1993), pgs. 163, 164.

37. D'Arcy Corrigan's death certificate. Thanks to Scott Wilson.

38. See the author's book *Women in Horror Films, 1930s* (McFarland, Jefferson, North Carolina, 1999) for full chapters on these two actresses (and more).

39. Robert Florey letter to Richard Bojarski. Thanks to John Antosiewicz.

40. This was apparently from the pressbook for *Murders in the Rue Morgue* and Lugosi cut the page out and saved it in his scrapbook. Thanks to John Antosiewicz.

41. Jimmy Starr, *Los Angeles Evening Express*, 7 November 1931.

42. As for the "funsters" in this episode: Herman Bing provided comedy relief in 1934's *The Black Cat*, but was cut from the picture before release; Agostino Borgato had played Captain Jacobi in the 1931 *The Maltese Falcon*; and Torben Meyer played the gentle servant in Karloff's 1935 *The Black Room* and an ominous Gypsy in 1943's *Frankenstein Meets the Wolf Man*.

43. Among his horror credits: John Barrymore's 1920 *Dr. Jekyll and Mr. Hyde*, Conrad Veidt's 1928 *The Man Who Laughs*, and 1944's *House of Frankenstein* (see Chapter 10).

44. Hays had been the U.S. Postmaster in 1921/1922 and had become the first head of the MPPDA, enforcing film censorship.

45. According to a story synopsis prepared by Universal the film opened with the Woman of the Streets episode; then came Pierre's visit to the morgue; then came the Morgue Keeper's visit to the apartment with the specimen; and then came the Carnival episode. Following this was the scene in which Pierre visits Mirakle at the Carnival; Pierre then goes to Camille's flat for their love scene (split into two separate scenes in the release version). The story synopsis for the original cut follows through from that point to the end the same as it does in the release version. Several film historians have re-edited the film to conform to what's widely believed to have been its original form. Universal Studios has not.

46. Film Reviews" *Variety*, 16 February 1932, p. 24.

47. Skal, *The Monster Show: A Cultural History of Horror*, p. 167.

48. Thanks to Dr. Karl Thiede.

49. Danny Peary, *Guide for the Film Fanatic* (Simon & Schuster, New York, 1986), p. 286.

50. Tom Weaver, Michael Brunas, and John Brunas, p. 49.

51. Jack Spears, "Robert Florey," *Films in Review*, April 1960, p. 225.

52. "Sidney Fox Asks Divorce Over Row at Reconciliation," *Los Angeles Examiner*, 21 February 1934.

53. Divorce Won by Sidney Fox," *Los Angeles Examiner*, 20 April 1934.

54. "Maybe Sidney Will Oblige," *Los Angeles Examiner*, 9 June 1934.

55. "Sidney Fox Will Sue for Divorce," *Los Angeles Examiner*, 11 October 1940.

56. Sidney Fox's death certificate.

57. Thanks to Scott Wilson, who sent me a photo of Ms. Fox's marker.

58. Obituaries," *Variety*, 20 August 1968, p. 14.

Chapter 2

1. Sir David Napley, *Rasputin in Hollywood* (Weidenfeld & Nicolson, London, 1989), p. 35.

2. Joseph T. Fuhrmann, *Rasputin: The Untold Story* (John Wiley & Sons, New Jersey, 2013), p. 210.

3. Greg King, *The Man Who Killed Rasputin* (Carol Publishing Group, New York, 1995).

4. Maria Rasputin, with Patte Barham, *Rasputin: The Man Behind the Myth* (Prentice Hall, New Jersey, 1977).

5. Napley, p. 41.

6. Charles Higham, *Louis B. Mayer, M.G.M and the Secret Hollywood* (Donald I. Fine, New York, 1993), p. 182.

7. Cobbett Feinberg, *Reel Facts* (Vintage Books, New York, 1978), p. 394.

8. "Studios Busy Grinding Out Films," *New York Times*, 20 March 1932, p. X6. The *Times* was quoting the report in *The London Daily Telegraph*.

9. John Barrymore, "Those Incredible Barrymores," *The American Magazine*, February 1933. This article, as well as the follow-up "How I Escaped a Great Lover's Doom," in *The American Magazine*, April 1933, were actually ghost written by Jerome Beatty, a long-time friend of John's who'd heard him tell these stories and captured John's personality and humor in the articles.

10. James Kotsilibas-Davis, *The Barrymores: The Royal Family of Hollywood* (Crown Publishers, New York, 1981), p. 129.

11. *Ibid.*, p. 140.

12. *Ibid.*, p. 128.

13. The play *Laugh, Clown, Laugh!* opened November 28, 1923, at the Belasco Theatre and ran 133 performances. Lionel Barrymore played "Tio Beppi,"and his wife, Irene Fenwick, appeared in the play as "Simonetta." When MGM produced the 1928 film version, the studio awarded Lon Chaney the star role and offered Lionel a supporting part. Lionel said, "No." As John wrote, "The way he said 'No!' is still a historical event in Hollywood. It took him ten minutes, and he decorated that little two-letter word with the choicest garlands and festoons of ancient, medieval, modern and futuristic oaths that had ever been heard, even in a motion picture studio."

14. The most comprehensive and in-depth Barrymore book is *The House of Barrymore*, by Margot Peters (Alfred A. Knopf, New York, 1990). Ms. Peters' book details and documents the addictions of John, Ethel, and Lionel.

15. Donald Kirkley, "School for Scandal," *The Baltimore Su*n, 22 May 1932, p. 14.

16. "Three Barrymores to Appear in Talkie," *New York Times*, 28 May 1932, p. 18.

17. Kotsilibas-Davis, p. 124.

18. Bob Thomas, *Thalberg: Life and Legend* (Doubleday, New York, 1969), p. 210.

19. Peters, p. 229.

20. The play was by Benn W. Levy, who also directed. Basil Rathbone starred as the Devil in the disguise of a preacher. Each of the other characters joined him in the game "Truth," in which they confessed what they most wanted from Life. Ernest Thesiger played an unsuccessful novelist who craved fame. *The New York Times* wrote that Diana Wynyard acted "with limpid charm and dexterity." The play ran in New York for 96 performances.

21. The totem pole later belonged to Vincent Price, who displayed it on his Benedict Canyon estate. When Price and his second wife divorced, they donated the totem pole to the Honolulu Museum of Art. It was found there in recent years stored in three sections, and in 2015 was returned to the tribal people of Tuxecan.

22. Thanks to Ned Comstock of the USC Cinematic Arts Library, who made available, from the library's MGM Collection, a full-length draft of the final *Rasputin and the Empress* script. The pages are dated and indicate the order in which the scenes were written and shot.

23. John Barrymore, "Those Incredible Barrymores," p. 70.

24. *Ibid.*

25. Bob Thomas, *Thalberg: Life and Legend* (Doubleday, New York, 1969), p. 212.

26. Peters, p. 344.

27. Kotsilibas-Davis, p. 139.

28. John Barrymore, "Those Incredible Barrymores," p. 72.

29. Mark Vieira, *Forbidden Hollywood: The Pre-Code Era (1930–1934) When Sin Ruled the Movies* (Running Press, Philadelphia, 2019), p. 125.

30. John Barrymore, "Those Incredible Barrymores."

31. *Ibid.*

32. Peters, p. 341.

33. John Barrymore, "How I Escaped a Great Lover's Doom."

34. John Kobler, *Damned in Paradise: The Life of John Barrymore* (Atheneum, New York, 1977), p. 278.

35. Jean Parker related this account to James Kotsilibas-Davis in his book *The Barrymores: The Royal Family of Hollywood*, pgs. 134–135.

36. John Barrymore, "How I Escaped a Great Lover's Doom," p. 77.

37. Peters, p. 344.

38. *Ibid.*, p. 343.

39. Barondess (1907–2000) and Hyman almost became involved in MGM's major scandal regarding Paul Bern's death in 1932. The night before his suicide (or was it murder?), Bern provided a rendezvous for Hyman and Barondess at the Ambassador Hotel in Los Angeles. Nevertheless, they avoided any publicity. Barondess later became a noted interior decorator.

40. All of these lines appear in the original shooting script.

41. Marx, *Mayer and Thalberg: The Make-Believe Saints* (Random House, New York, 1975), p. 213.

42. In his previously-cited book *Rasputin in Hollywood*, Sir David Napley described a different ending. The assassination of the Tsar and his family isn't shown; instead, "The film ends in Soho Square, London. There we see Lieutenant Paul Chegodieff of the British army. He has acquired an artificial leg, having presumably, lost his own in the British army." Natasha is there too. "With them is Dr. Remezov, who imparts the knowledge that the Imperial family has been horribly massacred…. They are inconsolable, but Natasha reminds Paul of the Empress's parting words to her before she left Russia: 'Find happiness, Natasha.' 'Natasha … beloved,' says Paul, and the film ends." This scene doesn't exist in the surviving shooting script. It was perhaps filmed and shot later as an alternate finale for the British release.

43. Theatre Receipts," *Motion Picture Herald*, 14 January 1933, p. 36.

44. "The Theatre," *Wall Street Journal*, 25 December 1932, p. 3.

45. Donald Kirkley, "Three Barrymores Appear in *Rasputin* at The Maryland," *The Baltimore Sun*, 31 January 1933, p. 9.

46. "The Shadow Stage," *Photoplay*, March 1933, p. 58.

47. The majority of information included here regarding the trial that centered on *Rasputin and the Empress* comes from Napley's *Rasputin in Hollywood*.

48. Mark A. Vieira, *Sin in Soft Focus: Pre-Code Hollywood* (Harry N. Abrams, New York, 1999), p. 221.

49. Feinberg, p. 394.

50. "Chatter," *Variety*, 20 October 1937, p. 61; "M-G's 2D 'Rasputin' Libel Settlement," *Variety*, 17 November 1937, p. 12.

51. Kotsilibas-Davis, p. 140.

52. "C.B.S. Again Stalled on Youssoupoff Case on Script Sources," *New York Times*, 2 November 1965, p. 21; "News Summary and Index," *New York Times*, 16 October 1965, p. 29.

53. "*Izvestia* Criticizes Rasputin Verdict," *New York Times*, 11 November 1965, p. 49.

54. Ironically, Fanny Holtzmann became a close confidante of Louis B. Mayer who referred to her as "a female Solomon." In fact, based on Scott Eyman's book *Lion of Hollywood: The Life and Legend of Louis B. Mayer* (Simon & Schuster, New York, 2005, pgs. 185–186), Holtzmann was already a trusted friend of Mayer before the *Rasputin and the Empress* trial. Eyman reports that Holtzmann, at some time prior to midsummer of 1932, counseled Mayer not to fire John Gilbert, whom Mayer detested, and who was a major casualty of Sound pictures. "So leave him alone and maybe he'll drink himself to death," advised Holtzmann. Gilbert did, dying in 1936.

55. Bob Fairbanks, "Rasputin's Daughter Maintains Father Was Wise and Generous," *Los Angeles Times*, 25 September 1967, p. A1.

56. David Bramwell and Jo Tinsley, *The Odysseium: Strange Journeys That Obliterated Convention* (Chambers Publishing Limited, United States and Great Britain, 2018).

Chapter 3

1. Elsa Lanchester, *Charles Laughton and I* (Harcourt Brace and Company, New York, 1938).

2. Richard Watts, Jr., "On the Screen," *New York Herald Tribune*, 13 January 1933.

3. Patrick Parrinder and Robert M. Philmus, *H.G. Wells's Literary Criticism* (Barnes and Noble, 1980), p. 243.

4. "Organize to Fight Vivisection of Dogs," *New York Times*, 17 January 1932, p. 22.

5. "Doctors Urge War on Anti-Vivisection," *New York Times*, 24 May 1932, p. 21.

6. Mark Vieira, *Forbidden Hollywood: The Pre-Code Era (1930–1934), When Sin Ruled the Movies* (Running Press, Philadelphia, 2019), p. 147.

7. All of the studio production history cited in this chapter, including budgets, salaries, quotes from the shooting script, and location shooting data, comes from the *Island of Lost Souls* file, the Paramount Collection, Margaret Herrick Library, Academy of Motion Picture Arts & Sciences, Los Angeles. Thanks to Kristine Krueger for making it possible for me to examine this material.

8. All the censorship information quoted in this chapter *for Island of Lost Souls'* release and re-release comes from the *Island of Lost Souls* file, the MPPDA Collection, Margaret Herrick Library. Thanks to Kristine Krueger.

9. David J. Skal, *Screams of Reason* (W.W. Norton & Company, New York, 1998), p. 143.

10. "More Than Two-Score Girls in "Panther Woman' Contest," *Atlanta Constitution*, 20 July 1932, p. 18.

11. Arthur Mayer, *Merely Colossal* (Simon & Schuster, New York, 1953), pgs. 129, 130.

12. Author's telephone interview with Verna Hillie, New York City, 5 February 1994. All quotes from Ms. Hillie in this chapter come from that interview.

13. For a full account of the Wells and West relationship see J. R. Hammond, *H. G. Wells and Rebecca West* (Palgrave MacMillan, 1991).

14. Vieira, *Forbidden Hollywood*, p. 170.

15. James Curtis, *James Whale: A New World of Gods and Monsters* (Faber and Faber, Boston, 1998), p. 48.

16. Author's telephone interview with Gloria Stuart, Brentwood, CA, 19 May 1986.

17. Charles Higham, *Hollywood Cameramen* (Indiana University Press, 1970), p. 129.

18. Actually, the line in the shooting script reads: "Mr. Parker—do you know what it means to feel like God," which is precisely how Laughton says it in the movie.

19. Dan Thomas, "Panther Girl's Diary Lists

Fears and Joys of Debut," *The Pittsburgh Press*, 22 November 1932, p. 15.

20. Mayer, p. 130.

21. *Standard Sentinel* (Hazelton, PA), 11 November 1932, p. 13.

22. Higham, p. 129.

23. On page 39 of his book *Charles Laughton: An Intimate Biography* (Doubleday and Company, Garden City, NY, 1976), the late Charles Higham wrote that during the trip to Catalina Island for the shooting of *Island of Lost Souls*, "a tiger lashed out and tore one man's arm almost from its socket." I have been unable to find any documentation regarding this incident.

24. Some reports claim Joe Bonomo played the gorilla in *The Sign of the Cross*, wearing Charles Gemora's ape suit.

25. Elsa Lanchester, *Elsa Lanchester Herself* (St. Martin's Press, New York, 1983), p. 142.

26. Samuel A. Peeples, "Films on 8 & 16," *Films in Review*, June-July 1976, p. 366.

27. Thomas, p. 15.

28. Thanks to John Antosiewicz, who formerly owned this scrapbook and made a copy of its *Island of Lost Souls*-related contents for me.

29. Thanks to Frank Dello Stritto, who has copies of Lugosi's bankruptcy papers and shared them with me.

30. Dello Stritto.

31. The Blondie song "Island of Lost Souls" has no relation to the 1932 film except the title.

32. Such treadmills were used in prisons at the beginning of the 20th century. Some of the *Island of Lost Souls'* first audiences might even have worked on them themselves.

33. My thanks to David Knight, Stonyhurst archivist and editor of *The Stonyhurst Record,* for this information. Mr. Knight included this data on Laughton while providing material for my book *"One Man Crazy!" The Life and Death of Colin Clive* (Midnight Marquee Press, Baltimore, 2019).

34. Philip K. Scheuer, "Panther Woman Laps Up Blood? No. Malted Milks," *Los Angeles Times*, 20 November 1932, p. B13.

35. Kurt Singer, *The Laughton Story* (The John C. Winston Company, Philadelphia and Toronto, 1954), p. 103.

36. Higham, *Charles Laughton: An Intimate Biography*, p. 39.

37. Dello Stritto.

38. Scheuer, p. B13.

39. Grace Kingsley, "'Hurricane' to Save Marlene," *Los Angeles Times*, 13 October 1932, p. 11.

40. George Shaffer, "'Panther Girl' Wins Her First Studio Battle," *Chicago Daily Tribune*, 29 October 1932, p. 16.

41. "Long Pig" means human flesh.

42. Higham, *Hollywood Cameramen*, p. 129.

43. *Motion Picture Herald*, May 13, 1933, p. 55.

44. William L. Laurence, "Undying Universe Visioned by Tolman In Relativity Idea," *New York Times*, 30 December 1932, p. 1.

45. "Theatre Receipts," *Motion Picture Herald*, 21 January 1933, p. 36.

46. "Theatre Receipts," *Motion Picture Herald*, 28 January 1933; "Theatre Receipts," 11 February 1933. Note that this was the original 1,960-seat Rialto Theatre which would be demolished two years later and replaced with the smaller 594-seat Rialto.

47. *Island of Lost Souls* review, *Variety*, 17 January 1933, p. 15.

48. Pearl Katzman, "H.G. Wells Talks About the Movies!" *Screenland,* July 1935, pgs. 20–21.

49. Lanchester, *Charles Laughton and I.*

50. *The Island of Dr. Moreau* (1977) starred Burt Lancaster as a subdued Moreau. Michael York was the shipwrecked hero, Richard Basehart was the Sayer of the Law, and Barbara Carrera was the Panther Woman, complete with a layout publicizing the film in *Playboy*. Don Taylor directed, and John Chambers created the makeup. One of the several scripted endings had the Panther Woman give birth to a tiger kitten, but the producers opted for a Happy Ending...she remained human. *The Island of Dr. Moreau* (1996), released on the 100th anniversary of the novel's publication, starred Marlon Brando as Moreau. Brando weighed nearly 400 pounds at the time, and his Moreau seemed a cross between a Renaissance Pope and Jabba the Hutt. Val Kilmer was a very twisted Montgomery, Ron Perlman was the Sayer of the Law, and Fairuza Balk was the regressing-to-beast female lead. John Frankenheimer directed, Stan Winston did the makeup, and the production was a disaster.

51. These quotes come from correspondence Karl Struss and Richard Bojarski shared in February and March of 1978. Thanks to John Antosiewicz.

52. Thanks to Scott Wilson.

53. James Bawden, "Gail Patrick," *Films in Review*, May 1981, p. 287.

Chapter 4

1. For details on the various screenplay versions of *The Return of Frankenstein,* I'm grateful to the book *The Return of Frankenstein* (BearManor Media, OK, 2012), edited by the late Philip J. Riley. The details on those early versions come from this book, unless otherwise noted.

2. Stephen Pendo, "Universal's Golden Age of Horror: 1931–1941," *Films in Review*, March 1975, p. 157.

3. For the Censorship information in this chapter, thanks to Ms. Kristine Krueger of the National Film Information Service, Margaret Herrick Library, Academy of Motion Picture Arts & Sciences, Los Angeles, CA, for making the MPPDA File available for my examination. The package Ms. Krueger sent contained 62 pages of material related to *Bride of Frankenstein* and was postmarked 30 July 2014. All quoted material in this chapter regarding censorship of *Bride of Frankenstein* comes from that file.

4. George Turner (editor), *The Cinema of Adventure, Romance & Terror* (The ASC Press, Hollywood, CA, 1989), p. 171.

5. He also wrote the screenplay for Karloff's *The*

Body Snatcher (RKO, 1945), which Val Lewton, the film's producer, extensively rewrote before shooting.

6. Information on *The Black Cat* comes from the Universal Collection, USC Cinematic Arts Library, Los Angeles, CA. Thanks to Ned Comstock.

7. MPPDA file on *The Black Cat*. Thanks to Kristine Krueger.

8. These expressions were used by Joseph Breen in a 1932 letter to a Catholic priest regarding the populace of Hollywood. Scott Eyman, *Lion of Hollywood: The Life and Times of Louis B. Mayer* (Simon & Schuster, New York), pgs. 342, 343.

9. Universal Collection, USC.

10. Universal Collection, USC.

11. *Gift of Gab* file, Universal Collection, USC.

12. Karloff's *Gift of Gab* costume was similar to what he wore as "the Mesmerist" in the 1926 silent film *The Bells*. Lugosi's attire looked much like those he wore in his first New York English language stage role, "Fernando the Apache" in 1922's *The Red Poppy*.

13. *One More River,* MPPDA file, Margaret Herrick Library.

14. *Imitation of Life,* MPPDA File, Margaret Herrick Library.

15. "Film Trend Told Pope," *Los Angeles Times*, 27 September 1934, p. 1.

16. Chip Cleary, "Universal, The Industry's Phoenix," unsourced clipping, Universal Studios File, Margaret Herrick Library, Los Angeles, CA.

17. Jane Jackson, "Society in Filmland," *Hollywood Citizen News*, 24 October 1934. This article and the other Los Angeles newspaper reports about Junior Laemmle's going-away party and the ensuing fights with his father come from G. D. Hamann, editor, *Carl Laemmle, Jr., in the 30's* (Filming Today Press, Hollywood, CA, 2012).

18. "Laemmle Seeking New Stars," *New York Times*, 7 November 1934, p. 32.

19. Jimmy Starr, *Evening Herald Express*, 20 December 1934.

20. All dialogue and stage directions for *Bride of the Lamb* comes from the published script by William J. Hurlburt (Boni and Liveright, 1926).

21. *Bride of Frankenstein* file, Universal Collection, USC. All dates and financial figures regarding budget and salaries in this chapter comes from this file.

22. This wasn't mere publicity. A candid shot from *Frankenstein* shows Karloff with Jack Pierce, outside at Universal, wearing a veil over his head. Elsa Lanchester also remembered Karloff wearing the scrim head sack during *Bride of Frankenstein*.

23. *WereWolf of London* file, Universal Collection, USC. All dates and financial figures regarding budget and salaries in this chapter comes from this file.

24. The information comes from an undated interview that the late Richard Bojarski conducted with Ms. Darling (who died in 1991). Mr. Bojarski sent me a transcript of the brief interview.

25. Author's telephone interview with Valerie Hobson, Basinstoke, England, 19 April 1989.

26. David Del Valle, "Curtis Harrington on James Whale," *Films in Review*, January/February 1996, p. 5.

27. David J. Skal, *The Monster Show: A Cultural History of Horror* (W.W. Norton & Company, New York, 1993), p. 189.

28. James Curtis, *James Whale: A New World of Gods and Monsters* (Faber and Faber, London, 1998), p. 186.

29. Cleary.

30. "Film Studio Observes 20th Birthday—High Papal Honors Bestowed Here," *Los Angeles Times*, 18 March 1935, p. 16.

31. "They Give Hollywood the Horrors," *Picturegoer*, 11 May 1935, p. 9.

32. "Unit Plan for U with Bergerman Leaving," *Variety*, 24 April 1935, pgs. 1, 4.

33. See John McElwee's excellent "Ballyhoo and the *Bride of Frankenstein*," *Monsters from the Vault* No. 31.

34. "Picture Grosses," *Variety*, 22 May 1935, p. 9.

35. "Picture Grosses," *Variety*, 3 December 1934, p. 9.

36. "Picture Grosses," *Variety*, 22 May 1935, p. 9.

37. Thanks to Dr. Karl Thiede.

38. Patrick McCray, "Bride of Frankenstein." In Wallace McBride, ed., *Monster Serial: Morbid Love Letters to Horror Cinema* (Penny Dreadful Books, Columbia, SC, 2014) p. 166.

Chapter 5

1. This memorandum dated 15 January 1935 and written by John Stuart of the Production Code Administration is in the MPPDA file on *WereWolf of London,* Margaret Herrick Library, Academy of Motion Picture Arts and Sciences, Los Angeles, CA. All quoted material from the MPPDA /Production Code Administration used in this chapter comes from that file. Thanks to Kristine Krueger.

2. Lyle Rooks, "Genius in a Rouge Box," *Daily Boston Globe*, 20 October 1935, p. 8.

3. Author's interview with Cortlandt Hull, Mars, PA, 23 June 2019. Mr. Hull is the creator/designer/manager of the remarkable *Witches' Dungeon* in Plainville Ct. He's also the great nephew of Henry Hull. Thanks to Mr. Hull for sharing his memories and for generously providing several rare illustrations from Henry Hull's personal archive that appear in this chapter.

4. Lugosi's salary for Universal's *The Raven* which followed *WereWolf of London* was $5,000 whereas Oland's salary for *WereWolf...* was $12,000.

5. E.J. Fleming, *Hollywood Death and Scandal Sites* (McFarland, Jefferson, North Carolina, 2000), p. 182.

6. "Mr. Colton of *Rain*," *New York Times*, 7 February 1926, p. X2. This same article provided information on Colton's early life.

7. Mark A. Vieira, *Sin in Soft-Focus: Pre-Code Hollywood* (Harry N. Abrams, New York, 1999), p. 221.

8. "Inside Stuff—Legit," *Variety*, 17 January 1933, p. 48.

9. Tom Weaver, Michael Brunas and John Brunas, *Universal Horrors: The Studio's Classic Films, 1931–1946*, Second Edition (McFarland, Jefferson, North Carolina, 2007), p. 138.

10. "Plays on Broadway," *Variety*, 12 December 1933, p. 55.

11. All production information in this chapter—budgets, salaries, shooting dates, final cost—come from the *WereWolf of London* file, Universal collection, USC. Many thanks to Ned Comstock, who also provided access to the shooting script.

12. The name of the flower proved problematic. When Colton first mentions it in his script, he calls it "Mariphasa Lumino Lupino." When Henry Hull first says it, he says, "Mariphasa Lupino Lumino." Later the script standardizes the name of the flower as the "Mariphasa Lumina Lupina"—which is what it will be called throughout this chapter.

13. "Fantastic 'Trick' Shots Now Taboo," *The Boston Globe*, 26 May 1935, p. 46.

14. Author's telephone interview with Elsa Lanchester, Hollywood, CA, 10 June 1979.

15. "Ogre of the Make-Up Box: Mr. Pierce, Who Turns Men into Beasts, Plots the Return of a Monster," *New York Times*, 31 March 1935, p. X3. Note that the article ran more than a month after the completion of the film.

16. E.C.S., "Monitor Movie Guide," *The Christian Science Monitor*, 13 April 1935

17. Author's telephone interview with Valerie Hobson, Basinstoke, England, 19 April 1989. All quotes from Ms. Hobson in this chapter come from that interview. Valerie Hobson died 13 November 1998. For a profile of her life and career, see the author's *Women in Horror Films, 1930s*.

18. "Hollywood Finds a Live Flower Eats Frogs, Mice," *The Chicago Defender*, 4 May 1935, p. 12.

19. Oland, after a divorce in 1937 and suffering from alcoholism and a nervous breakdown, walked off a Charlie Chan film at 20th Century-Fox, sailed to Sweden, reportedly to recuperate, and died there 6 August 1938.

20. Some film analysts, learning John Colton was homosexual, assume he fashioned his scripts to center on homosexuality. A study of his works, notably *Rain* and *The Shanghai Gesture*, reveal a totally different focus—i.e., extolling dominant sensual females. As such, the character of Lisa Glendon in *WereWolf of London* probably interested Colton more than either Wilfred Glendon or Dr. Yogami.

21. When Bela Lugosi played the Frankenstein Monster in Universal's *Frankenstein Meets the Wolf Man* (1943), Jack Pierce apparently posed for no photos applying Lugosi's makeup. He posed with Karloff, Lon Chaney, Jr., and Glenn Strange when they appeared as the Monster during his time at the studio.

22. The bar that Mrs. Whack and Mrs. Moncaster frequent is apparently a popular watering hole for hags. At the bar, we see an old harridan (Tempe Pigott), who, at the sight of the grim-faced Glendon, cackles, "He seems to have a secret sorrow!"

23. Apparently the only screen role played by Jeanne Bartlett (1905–1997) was Daisy in *WereWolf of London*. She later was a screenwriter whose credits included *Son of Lassie* (MGM, 1945), *Gallant Bess* (MGM, 1946), and *Man-Eater of Kumaon* (Republic, 1948). Presumably, Ms. Bartlett lived wealthily in Malibu. She was the mother of Johnny Fain, a famed surfer who appeared in a number of AIP's "Beach" movies.

24. Weaver, Brunas and Brunas, p. 135.

25. Research for *WereWolf of London* indicates that in this scene the stunt man for Hull was George DeNormand (who doubled Reginald Barlow as "Hans" in the windmill fall in the opening of *Bride of Frankenstein*); the stunt man for Matthews was Eddie Parker (who later doubled, at least briefly, Bela Lugosi as the Monster in *Frankenstein Meets the Wolf Man*). However, watching this fight in the film, it appears that neither Hull nor Matthews is being doubled. Possibly DeNormand and Parker doubled Hull and Matthews later in the climax.

26. "The Preview Parade of Universal Pictures," *Universal Weekly*, 4 May 1935, p. 8.

27. The information on the title contest, and its entries, are in the *WereWolf of London* file, Universal Collection, USC.

28. "Belasco Slates Matinee; Two Productions Due Soon," *Los Angeles Times*, 23 March, 1935, p. 11.

29. "Unit Plan for U with Bergerman Leaving," *Variety*, 24 April 1935, pgs. 1 and 4.

30. Despite his boost to "Associate Producer" status at Universal, Stuart Walker continued to direct films. Come late summer of 1935, he fought with Universal's front office about needing more preparation time for the Karloff and Bela Lugosi vehicle *The Invisible Ray*. The fracas resulted in him leaving the studio. (Lambert Hillyer would direct *The Invisible Ray*.) Walker departed for Paramount, serving as an associate producer there for 15 "B" films, including seven of the *Bulldogg Drummond* pictures. Stuart Walker died of a heart attack March 13, 1941, in Beverly Hills. He was 61 years old and is buried in his native Cincinnati at Spring Grove Cemetery.

31. Stanley Bergerman thereafter never produced another movie and became a very successful talent agent. He died 13 July 1998, at the age of 94, having outlived Junior Laemmle by almost 29 years.

32. Frank S. Nugent, "At the Rialto," *New York Times*, 10 May 1935, p. 25.

33. "Picture Grosses," *Variety*, 22 May 1935, p. 9.

34. "'Dad's Swell' as Werewolf, Son Thinks," *The Hartford Courant*, 2 June 1935, p. C6.

35. Thanks to Tom Johnson for sending me this page from *To-Day's Cinema*, which featured this quote from *The Observer*.

36. In the Gypsy carnival episode in *The Wolf Man*, a bright light can be seen in the background, which might be the moon, but probably is a carnival light. If it *is* the moon, it gets no lovingly moody coverage.

37. "John Colton, Author, Dies," *The Baltimore Sun,* 29 December 1946, p. 7.

38. Scott Wilson, *Resting Places: The Burial Sites of More Than 14,000 Famous Persons, Third Edition* (McFarland and Company, Jefferson, North Carolina, 2016), p. 149.

39. Weaver, Brunas and Brunas, p. 138.

40. Wilson, p. 360.

Chapter 6

1. Lorre's curtain speech is included in the file with *Mad Love's* "Advertising Approach, Box Office Analysis" packet, from the *Mad Love* file in the MGM Collection at the Margaret Herrick Library, Academy of Motion Picture Arts and Sciences, Los Angeles, CA. Thanks to Kristine Krueger.

2. Ronald Haver, *David O. Selznick's Hollywood* (Bonanza Books, New York, 1980), p. 146.

3. David Stenn, *Bombshell: The Life and Death of Jean Harlow* (Doubleday, New York, 1993), p. 182.

4. Cobbett Feinberg, *Reel Facts* (Vintage Books, New York, 1978), p. 394.

5. Stephen D. Youngkin, *The Lost One: A Life of Peter Lorre* (University Press of Kentucky, 2005).

6. See the author's book *"One Man Crazy!" The Life and Death of Colin Clive* (Midnight Marque Press, Baltimore, 2018).

7. Production File on *Mad Love*, MGM Collection, USC Cinematic Arts Library, Los Angeles. Thanks to Ned Comstock. All of the production information on this film in this chapter, as well as the various script drafts and studio communications, come (unless otherwise noted) from that file.

8. William K. Everson, *Classics of the Horror Film* (Citadel Press, Secaucus, New Jersey, 1974), p. 93.

9. Author's telephone interview with Carroll Borland, Los Angeles, CA, 7 June 1988.

10. All censorship material quoted in this chapter comes from the *Mad Love* MPPDA file, Margaret Herrick Library, Los Angeles, CA. Thanks to Kristine Krueger.

11. The house over the years has been the residence of actors Hurd Hatfield and later Dean Jagger.

12. Author's interview with Frances Drake, Beverly Hills, CA, 13 July 1987.

13. *Mad Love* has quite a number of other horror movie homages as well, some which remained in the finished film and some of which were cut before the movie's original release. Among them:

i. Frances Drake stood in for her own wax dummy as had Fay Wray for the wax Marie Antoinette in Warners' 1933 *Mystery of the Wax Museum.*

ii. May Beatty's Francoise character seems to have been fashioned as an homage to Universal's 1935 *Bride of Frankenstein's* Minnie character (played to perfection by Una O'Connor).

iii. Michael Mark's presence as one of the execution officials in *Mad Love* is certainly an homage to his numerous character roles in classic horror movies—most notably as Little Maria's father in *Frankenstein.*

iv. Peter Lorre's Dr. Gogol's triumphant organ playing is an homage to a number of other horror characters (Karloff's Poelzig in *The Black Cat,* Fredric March's Dr. Jekyll in Paramount's 1931's *Dr. Jekyll and Mr. Hyde,* Bela Lugosi's Dr. Vollin in Universal's 1935 *The Raven,* et. al.)

v. Francoise again—her going to answer the door during a scene in which Reagan arrives at Gogol's house, shows her mumbling her way down the stairs just as Dwight Frye's Fritz mumbled and scuttled his way down the tower staircase in *Frankenstein.*

vi. Shortly after Francoise delivers her homage to *Frankenstein's* "It's alive!" she delivers the line "It went out for a little walk"—quite similar to the famous Bramwell Fletcher line "He went for a little walk" in Universal's 1932 *The Mummy.*

14. "Times Square Chatter," *Variety,* 8 May 1935, p. 77.

15. Thanks to Dr. Karl Thiede for this cost and schedule information.

16. Whitney Williams, "Peter Lorre Acclaimed the World's Greatest Actor," *Silver Screen,* August 1935, p. 22.

17. Andre Sennwald, "Noted for the Record: Fragments of Recollection Culled from a Recent Visit to the Film City," *The New York Times,* 4 August 1935, p. X3.

18. Author's interview with Zita Johann, West Nyack, New York, 27 December 1979.

19. Stephen D. Youngkin, pgs. 131–132.

20. Gogol's poem to Yvonne is a paraphrase of several lines in Robert Browning's poem "Porphyria's Lover."

21. An early script treatment for *Mad Love* originally offered a happy ending: "Yvonne and Stephen recover from weeks of horror and Stephen becomes master of his own hands once more. He gets a position as a conductor of a great orchestra and he and Yvonne live in happiness."

22. Thanks to Dr. Karl Thiede.

23. "The Screen," *New York Times,* 5 August 1935, p. 20.

24. "Picture Grosses," *Variety,* 14 August 1935, p. 9.

25. "What the Picture Did for Me," *Motion Picture Herald,* 28 September 1935, p. 354.

26. "What the Picture Did for Me," *Motion Picture Herald,* 16 November 1935, p. 68.

27. "Sally Rand Fans Big $30,000 Into Boston; Melody 35 G in Two Houses," *Variety,* 2 October 1935, p. 11 (10/9 says $25,000 and "Sally Rand on stage, latter rating all the draw")

28. Thanks to Dr. Karl Thiede.

29. Thanks to Dr. Karl Thiede.

30. Ted Healy's death certificate. Thanks to Scott Wilson.

31. Danny Peary, *Guide for the Film Fanatic* (Simon & Schuster, New York, 1986), p. 255.

32. See "Andre Sennwald, Times Film Critic, Killed as Explosion Wrecks West End Av. Home,"

New York Times, 12 January 1936, p. 1; "Sennwald's Death Laid to Gas Fumes; Medical Examiner, Pending an Inquiry, Finds the Film Critic Was Probably Suicide. Blast Caused by Spark. Detectives Learn his Sight Was Threatened— Funeral to be Held Tomorrow," *New York Times*, 13 January 1936, p. 18.

Chapter 7

1. Henry Chu, "The World: Bones Found May Be English King; The Skeletal Remains Unearthed in Leicester Match the Profile of Richard III," *Los Angeles Times*, 13 September 2012, p. A3; John F. Burris, "Discovery of Skeleton Puts Richard III In Battle Once Again," *New York Times*, 24 September 2012, p. A9.

2. Sylvia Hut, "King Richard III Gets Proper Burial Ceremony," *Chicago Tribune*, 23 March 2015, p. 13.

3. *The Tower of London Souvenir Guidebook*. In 2019, my wife Barbara and I visited the Tower of London, a tremendously colorful and fascinating experience. The 80-page souvenir guidebook contains a wealth of information about the site and its remarkable history.

4. Thanks to Ned Comstock and the USC Cinematic Library for providing, from The Universal Collection, the Weekly Production Records on *Tower of London*, as well as those on *Service De Luxe*, *Son of Frankenstein*, *The Sun Never Sets*, and *Rio*. These records contain shooting dates, budget figures, and an enormous amount of information on life at Universal during the production of these respective films.

5. Rathbone had hoped to pursue romantic roles and had tested in August of 1938 for the doctor role in Bette Davis's *Dark Victory* at Warner Bros. The actor believed David Lewis, the film's producer, didn't want him in the role (ultimately played by George Brent) and had sabotaged Rathbone's test. See Rudy Behlmer, *Inside Warner Bros. (1935–1951)* (Viking, New York, 1985), pgs. 76 to 78.

6. The incomplete script problem was also contagious. A good number of Universal's 1938/1939 productions started shooting without a completed script, including the W.C. Fields and Edgar Bergen and Charlie McCarthy *You Can't Cheat an Honest Man*, the Deanna Durbin vehicles *Three Smart Girls Grow Up* and *First Love*, and the Marlene Dietrich and James Stewart western *Destry Rides Again*. Thanks to Ned Comstock for providing the Weekly Production Reports on these films.

7. Francis Edward Faragoh, aka Francis Edwards Faragoh (1895–1966), was one of the screenwriters on *Frankenstein*.

8. For the Censorship information from the MPPDA archive, thanks to Kristine Krueger, Margaret Herrick Library, Academy of Motion Picture Arts & Sciences.

9. This Louella Parsons item from the *Los Angeles Examiner* comes from G.D. Hamann's book *Basil Rathbone in the 1930's* (Filming Today Press,

Hollywood, CA, 2013), p. 114. The book contains many newspaper articles on Rathbone from the era.

10. Donlevy received a Best Supporting Actor Academy Award nomination for *Beau Geste*. He lost to Thomas Mitchell of *Stagecoach*. Mitchell was excellent but Donlevy should have won.

11. The film was a reunion of Claire Trevor and John Wayne, after they'd starred in John Ford's *Stagecoach* (UA, 1939).

12. Harry Mines, "Raves and Raps," *Los Angeles Daily News*, 22 August 1939.

13. Frank S. Nugent, "The Screen," *New York Times*, 12 December 1939, p. 37.

14. Scott Allen Nollen, *Boris Karloff: A Gentleman's Life* (Midnight Marquee Press, Baltimore, 1999), p. 124.

15. Robinson (1890–1958) would have been a potentially wonderful interview subject: *The Invisible Ray*, *Son of Frankenstein*, *The Mummy's Tomb*, *Frankenstein Meets the Wolf Man*, *Captive Wild Woman*, *House of Frankenstein* and *House of Dracula* were all filmed by him.

16. Author's telephone interviews with Donnie Dunagan, San Angelo, TX, 13 August and 23 October 2004. All quotes from Dunagan in this chapter come from those interviews.

17. Steve Biodrowski, David Del Valle, and Lawrence French, "Vincent Price: Looking Back on Forty Years as Horror's Crown Prince," *Cinefantastique*, Vol. 19, No. 2, January 1989, p. 46.

18. Carl Laemmle, Jr., who never produced another picture after new management took over Universal in 1936, died September 24, 1979, the 40th anniversary of his father's death.

19. Hedda Hopper, "In Hollywood," *The Washington Post*, 30 September 1939, p. 16.

20. Beebe died on his 90th birthday, 26 November 1978.

21. Dr. Bruno David Ussher, *Music in the Films, 1937–1941*. This book was edited by G.D. Hamann from newspaper articles Dr. Ussher had written about film music (Filming Today Press, Hollywood, CA, 2003), pgs. 116, 117.

22. Preston Neal Jones, "The Ghost of Hans J. Salter," *Cinefantastique*, Vol. 7, No, 2, Summer 1978, p. 14.

23. Among other showcases for the Tower: Universal-International's *The Black Castle* (1952), which starred Richard Greene, Stephen McNally, Boris Karloff, and Lon Chaney. It also appears prominently in the opening of the *Thriller* TV episode "A Wig for Miss Devore" (January 29, 1962) as the medieval witch of the opening (Pamela Searle) is hanged in the castle courtyard.

24. Gene Brown, *Movie Time* (Macmillan, New York, 1995), p. 153.

25. Erskine Johnson, *Los Angeles Daily News*, 8 December 1939.

26. "Picture Grosses," *Variety*, 13 December 1939, p. 9.

27. *Ibid.*, p. 7.

28. "Picture Grosses," *Variety*, 20 December 1939, p. 7.

29. *Ibid.*, p. 9.

30. Cynthia Lindsay, *Dear Boris* (Alfred A. Knopf, New York, 1975), p. 101.

31. Karl Wray, "Rowland V. Lee," *Films in Review*, January 1986, p. 8.

32. The death and cemetery information on the Lee brothers comes from Scott Wilson, *Resting Places Vol. 1* (McFarland, Jefferson, North Carolina, 2016), p. 434.

Chapter 8

1. Jill Lepore, *The Secret History of Wonder Woman* (Alfred A. Knopf, New York, 2014), pgs 183–209.

2. James P. Cunningham, "Asides and Interludes," *Motion Picture Herald,* 23 August 1941, p. 39.

3. George E. Phair, "Retakes," *Variety*, 1 July 1941.

4. Donald Rumbelow, *The Complete Jack the Ripper* (Penguin Books, London, 2004), p. 112. Rumbelow notes that the writer who accused Richard Mansfield of being the Ripper "had not been able to rest for a day and a night after seeing the performance, claiming that no man could disguise himself so well and that, since Mansfield worked himself up into such a frenzy on stage, he probably did the real-life murders too."

5. Margot Peters, *The House of Barrymore* (Alfred A. Knopf, New York, 1990), p. 197. Peters writes that at the Bronx Zoo, Barrymore had seen "a particularly evil-looking red tarantula, its back rubbed bald from struggling to squeeze out of its cage." Barrymore joked, "He looks just like Richard the Third." Barrymore clearly took inspiration from the tarantula for his Hyde and his *Richard III* (which opened on Broadway on March 6, 1920).

6. John Barrymore, "Those Incredible Barrymores," *The American Magazine*, February 1933.

7. Charles Higham, *Hollywood Cameramen* (Indiana University Press, Bloomington, 1970), p. 123.

8. Mason Wiley and Damien Bona, *Inside Oscar: The Unofficial History of the Academy Awards* (Ballantine Books, New York, 1987), p. 41.

9. The production facts, figures, letters, memos, etc., on the shooting of the 1941 *Dr. Jekyll and Mr. Hyde* come from the personal MGM production file of Victor Saville, who produced the film. Saville's file is in the MGM Collection at the USC Cinematic Arts Library, Los Angeles, CA. Many thanks to Ned Comstock for making it available to me.

10. Mahin (1902–1984) received two Oscar nominations: *Captains Courageous* (1937, shared with Marc Connelly and Dale Van Every) and *Heaven Knows, Mr. Allison* (1957, shared with John Huston).

11. Mark A. Vieira, *Hollywood Horror: From Gothic to Cosmic* (Harry N. Abrams, New York, 2003), p. 106.

12. The censorship file for *Dr. Jekyll and Mr. Hyde* is accessible digitally from the MPPDA files at the Margaret Herrick Library.

13. The strip was later largely deleted. When the 1931 *Dr. Jekyll and Mr. Hyde* was restored for DVD release in 2004, most of Miriam Hopkins' removal of clothing was put back into the film, although there are rumors that a racy snippet or two are still out there somewhere.

14. John Gallagher, "Victor Fleming," *Films in Review*, March 1983, p. 146. Gallagher writes that, in addition to Fleming's 45 percent, Sam Wood directed 15 percent, production designer William Cameron Menzies directed 15 percent, George Cukor directed 5 percent, B. Reeves Eason directed 2 percent, and 18 percent of the film "was second unit or process shots."

15. Scott Eyman, *Lion of Hollywood: The Life and Legend of Louis B. Mayer* (Simon & Schuster, New York, 2005), p. 225.

16. Gallagher, p. 135.

17. James Curtis, *Spencer Tracy: A Biography* (Alfred A. Knopf, New York, 2011), p. 410.

18. For this clipping from *The Hollywood Reporter*, thanks to Tom Weaver.

19. Curtis, p. 410.

20. Ruttenberg (1889–1983) won four Oscars for his cinematography—*The Great Waltz* (1938), *Mrs. Miniver* (1942), *Somebody Up There Likes Me* (1956), and *Gigi* (1958).

21. Curtis, p. 412.

22. Lana Turner, *Lana: The Lady, the Legend, the Truth* (Dutton, 1982).

23. Donald Kirkley, "*Dr. Jekyll and Mr. Hyde*: Spencer Tracy Plays Dual Role in Robert Louis Stevenson Classic," *The Baltimore Sun*, 30 August 1941, p. 6.

24. Victor Saville and Roy Moseley, *Evergreen: Victor Saville in his Own Words* (Southern Illinois University Press, 2000).

25. Ingrid Bergman and Alan Burgess, *Ingrid Bergman: My Story* (Delacorte Press, 1980).

26. *Ibid.*

27. Gallagher, p. 148.

28. Author's telephone interview with Gil Perkins, Los Angeles, CA, 25 August 1991.

29. Spencer Tracy, *The Lion's Roar* (publicity publication put out by MGM).

30. Vincent LoBrutto, *Selected Takes: Film Editors on Editing* (Praeger, Santa Barbara, CA, 1991), pgs. 6, 7.

31. MGM Music Department Collection, USC Cinematic Arts Library, Los Angeles. Thanks to Ned Comstock.

32. Inez Robb, "Inez Gives Her All (To Science) to Show Why Men Like Blondes: Gray-Haired Writer Finds She Doesn't Scare as Easily," *The Washington Post*, 8 August 1941, p. 15.

33. "Spencer Tracy Essays Dual Role of *Dr. Jekyll and Mr. Hyde*, Which Opened Yesterday at the Astor," *New York Times*, 13 August 1941, p. 13.

34. "The Theatre: New Actors—Old Play," *Wall Street Journal*, 15 August 1941, p. 11.

35. Curtis, p. 422.

36. *Ibid.*, p. 423.

37. "'Kiss the Boys Good-bye' Opens Socko for 9Gs," *Variety*, 14 August 1941, p. 1.

38. Nelson B. Bell, "Dr. Jekyll and Mr. Hyde Takes on a New Realism," *The Washington Post*, 29 August 1941, p. 18.

39. "What the Picture Did for Me," *Motion Picture Herald*, 25 April 1942, p. 49.

40. "What the Picture Did for Me," *Motion Picture Herald*, 27 December 1941, p. 63.

41. For the rental and profit figures, thanks to Dr. Karl Thiede.

42. Elaine Barrie and Sandford Dody, *All My Sins Remembered* (Appleton-Century, New York, 1964), pgs. 190–193. Barrie, Barrymore's fourth and final wife, gives a marvelously hair-raising account of her offering to get Barrymore a beer one night at home if he'd perform his Hyde transformation for her. He did it so horrifically that he terrified both her and their dog!

Chapter 9

1. "Big Campaign Sells Milwaukee *Women in Bondage*," *Showmen's Trade Review*, 1 January 1944, p. 20.

2. John T. McManus, "'Bondage' Plays with Nazi Fire," *New York Newspaper PM*, 26 March 1944.

3. Donald Kirkley, "Women in Bondage," *The Baltimore Sun*, 27 December 1943, p. 10.

4. Due to its notoriety and troubles with William Randolph Hearst, *Citizen Kane* was considered a "sensational" film.

5. The film had a colorful back story. When Herbert Brenon, originally set to direct *Oliver Twist*, learned that I.E. Chadwick, an independent producer, planned to release the film though Monogram, he jumped ship and announced he'd produce and direct it independently at Universal, hoping for Boris Karloff as Fagan or Bill Sikes. Chadwick proceeded with his production anyway, engaging William Cowen to direct, and maintaining the releasing arrangement with Monogram. Brenon's *Oliver Twist* for Universal fell through when Universal demanded Brenon agree to cover any damages Monogram would pursue. See "Brenon Quits Chadwick: Will Make 'Twist' at 'U,'" *The Hollywood Reporter*, 12 January 1933, p. 1. "Brenon-'U' Deal for 'Twist' Cold," *The Hollywood Reporter*, 17 January 1933, p. 4.

6. Cobbett Feinberg, *Reel Facts* (Vintage Books, New York, 1978), p. 394.

7. "Financial," *The 1942 Film Daily Yearbook*, p. 911.

8. "Monogram 39-Week Net Profit $43,306," *Motion Picture Herald*, 26 June 1943, p. 48.

9. "Preview," *Variety*, 12 January 1943, p. 3.

10. "Week-End Pic Biz in Boom: 'Children' Is Setting Records," *Variety*, 1 March 1943, p. 8.

11. Thanks to Dr. Karl Thiede.

12. He directed such films as *Devil Bat's Daughter* (PRC, 1946), and later did TV work, including directing 214 episodes of *Fireside Theatre* (1950–1955). He returned to Germany and won the German Film Award for Best Direction for *Hunde, wollt ihr ewig eben* (aka *Stalingrad: Dogs, Do You Want to Live Forever?* 1959). Wisbar died in Germany in 1967.

13. MPPDA File, *Women in Bondage*, Margaret Herrick Library, Academy of Motion Picture Arts & Sciences, Los Angeles, CA. All censorship quotes cited in this chapter come from that file. Thanks to Kristine Krueger.

14. James Dugan and Carroll Stewart, *Ploesti* (Bantam Books, New York, 1963), p. 82.

15. "John F. Kennedy and PT-109," The John F. Kennedy Presidential Library and Museum Website.

16. "$100,000 MONO PIC DUE FOR $1,000,000 GROSS," *Variety*, 31 May 1944, page one.

17. Thanks to Ned Comstock, USC Cinematic Arts Library, Los Angeles, CA, who provided me a copy of Steve Sekely's shooting script which contained the shooting schedule in the back.

18. James Bawden, "Dream Factory Time: Gail Patrick," *Classic Images*, posted 29 April 2014.

19. Erskine Johnson, "In Hollywood with Johnson," *Tallahassee Democrat*, 3 September 1943.

20. Tom Weaver, *Poverty Row Horrors!* (McFarland, Jefferson, North Carolina, 1993), p. 11.

21. The area, in the San Fernando Valley, has been a location site for many films, including Warner Bros.' *The Adventures of Robin Hood* (1938) and the early MGM Tarzan films.

22. Varno co-starred with Bela Lugosi in Columbia's *Return of the Vampire*, which began shooting August 21—the same day that *Women in Bondage* finished shooting.

23. A copy of Jimmie Fidler's letter is in the MPPDA file on *Women in Bondage*.

24. "Film Stars Are Guests at Reception," *The Journal Times* (Racine, Wisconsin), 9 December 1943.

25. "Roosevelt's Talk in Brief," *The Baltimore Sun*, 26 December 1943, p. 3.

26. A comedy with songs, *Hot Rhythm* was directed by William Beaudine and starred Robert Lowery, Dona Drake, and Irene Ryan (later "Granny" on TV's *The Beverly Hillbillies*). Ryan's real-life husband, Tim Ryan, played a featured role and co-wrote the screenplay.

27. A reproduction of Al Galston's letter appeared in a full-page advertisement that Monogram ran in *Variety*, 6 March 1944, p. 27.

28. Weekly B.O. Clicks of First Runs," *Variety*, 16 October 1944, p. 385. *Women in Bondage* took in $9,465 in its first week at the Hawaii, $6,241 in its second week, $4,312 in its third week, and $2,817 in its fourth and final week.

29. "Weekly B.O. Clicks of First Runs," *Variety*, 16 October 1944, p. 380.

30. "Picture Grosses," *Variety*, 29 March, 5 April, 12 April, and 19 April 1944.

31. Steve Broidy, "Mono Moves Mightily," *Variety*, 16 October 1944, p. 517.

32. "Picturedom's 'Little Three' Have Come Of Age," *Variety*, 16 October 1944, p. 18.

33. An oddity, Hollywood Gothic style: The ashes of both Gertrude Michael, who played Deputy

Director Schneider, and H. B. Warner, who played the Pastor who defied the Nazis (and who had died 21 December 1958), are in "Vaultage" at the Chapel of the Pines Crematory, Los Angeles.

34. "Anne Nagel Answered in Suit Over Operation," *Los Angeles Examiner*, 23 January 1948.

35. For a detailed examination of *Hitler's Madman*, see Chapter 10 in my book *The Very Witching Time of Night: Dark Alleys of Classic Horror Cinema* (McFarland, Jefferson, North Carolina, 2014).

Chapter 10

1. "Every day was Halloween!" This quote, and all others from Acquanetta (unless otherwise cited), come from the author's telephone interview with her (Phoenix, AZ, 29 July 1992) and Baltimore, MD (14–16 August 1992).

2. David Platt, *The Daily Worker*, 30 July1944. Thanks to Ned Comstock for providing all the material from *The Daily Worker* regarding *Captive Wild Woman* and *Jungle Woman* cited in this chapter.

3. John T. McManus used this expression from *Mein Kampf* in his *New York Newspaper PM* review ("*Jungle Woman*," 16 July 1944).

4. Louella O. Parsons, *Los Angeles Examiner*, 28 October 1942.

5. "All Actress' Shoes Stolen," *Los Angeles Times*, 14 April 1944.

6. Mr. Gallinghouse discovered much material on Acquanetta's early life, including census reports and her high school yearbook. Scott wrote and recorded the audio commentary for the Blu-Ray of the third "Paula the Ape Woman" film, *The Jungle Captive*.

7. Ted Fithian collaborated on the original story; according to my research, this was his only film credit. Neil P. Varnick, who collaborated with Fithian, also wrote the original stories for Universal's *The Mummy's Tomb* and *Danger in the Pacific* (both 1942). Griffin Jay worked on screenplays for such Universal films as *The Mummy's Hand* (1940), *The Mummy's Tomb*, *The Mummy's Ghost* (1944), as well as Columbia's *The Return of the Vampire* and *Cry of the Werewolf* (both 1944), and PRC's *Devil Bat's Daughter* (1946). Henry Sucher worked on screenplays for Universal's *The Mummy's Tomb*, *The Mummy's Ghost*, *The Frozen Ghost* (1945), and would contribute to *Captive Wild Woman*'s sequel *Jungle Woman*. Finally, a mystery: some sources also list Maurice Pivar as a contributing writer. Pivar was a long-time editor at Universal Studios.

8. It would appear in many films and survive at Universal until 2005, when it was destroyed to provide expanded room for the *Desperate Housewives* TV show.

9. Tom Weaver includes this quote from Dmytryk in his audio commentary for *Captive Wild Woman* on the 2020 Blu-ray release *Universal Horror Collection Vol. 5*.

10. Thomas M. Pryor, "The Screen," *New York Times*, 7 June 1943, p. 9.

11. "Picture Grosses," *Variety*, 16 June 1943, p. 9, 23 June 1943, p. 27.

12. "13 Are Indicted in Lynching Case: Federal Grand Jury Acts on Killing in Paris, Ill," *New York Times*, 14 July 1943, p. 40.

13. "Record First Run LA BO Totals," *Variety*, 29 October 1943, p. 45.

14. Donald Kirkley, "*Captive Wild Woman*: Female Gorilla Used as Subject of Experiment in Melodrama Shown on the Screen at Keith's," *The Baltimore Sun*, 6 August 1943, p. 14.

15. "Obituary: Carolyn Moore, 82, a civil-rights leader," *The Philadelphia Inquirer*, 3 December 1998, p. 36.

16. The author interviewed Reginald Le Borg several times by telephone, during which time the director discussed his memories of *Jungle Woman*, as well as Acquanetta's collapse on *The Mummy's Ghost* (West Hollywood, CA, 20 and 27 September 1988). All quotes from Le Borg in this chapter come from those interviews.

17. "Snapshots of Hollywood: Collected at Random," *Los Angeles Examiner*, 2 September, 1943.

18. The censorship and production material regarding budgets, salaries, shooting dates, sets, etc., on *Jungle Woman* come from the Universal Collection, USC. Many thanks to Ned Comstock!

19. Ben Pivar (1901–1963), born in Manchester, England, was a very busy producer at Universal whose credits included *The Mummy's Hand* (1940), *Horror Island* (1941), *The Mummy's Tomb* (1942), *The Mad Ghoul* (1943), *Calling Dr. Death* (1943), *The Mummy's Ghost* (1944), *The Mummy's Curse* (1944), *House of Horrors* (1946), and many more. He was later a producer for TV's *Confidential File* (1953–1958).

20. Will Cowan (1911–1994), born in Scotland, produced almost 200 movies, directed over 120, and was a credited writer on a dozen more. Among his production credits were the Inner Sanctum movies *Dead Man's Eyes* (1944) and *The Frozen Ghost* (1945).

21. Schubert (1895–1988) was one of the writers on *Mark of the Vampire* (MGM, 1935), co-wrote screenplays for such films as Universal's *The Mummy's Curse* (1944) and *The Frozen Ghost* (1945), and was later a TV producer on such 1950s series as *Mr. and Mrs. North* and *Topper*. Sucher (1894–1986) had been one of the co-writers on *Captive Wild Woman* and was a co-writer on *The Mummy's Tomb* (1942), *The Mummy's Curse*, and *The Frozen Ghost*. Dein (1907–1984) worked on Val Lewton's *The Leopard Woman* (1943) , wrote the original screenplay for *Calling Dr. Death* (Universal's first "Inner Sanctum" film, 1943), directed and co-wrote the "horror/western" *Curse of the Undead* (U-I, 1959), and directed *The Leech Woman* (U-I, 1960), for which Ben Pivar provided the story.

22. Walter Winchell's column, the *Wilkes Barre Times Leader*, 4 April 1945. Thanks to Laura Wagner, who provided this item.

23. "It's Hollywood," *The Record*, Hackensack, NJ, 25 February 1944.

24. Rub had been the model for and voice of Geppetto in Disney's *Pinocchio* (1940).

25. "Picture Grosses," *Variety*, 26 July 1944, p. 17; 2 August 1944, p. 16.

26. "Weekly B.O. Clicks of First Runs," *Variety*, 16 October 1944, p. 385.

27. Irene Thirer, "'Dead Man's Eyes' Whodunit Shocker on Screen at Rialto," *The New York Post,* 7 October 1944.

28. Bert McCord, "'Jungle Captive' Rialto," *The New York Herald Tribune,* 7 July 1945.

29. "Picture Grosses," *Variety*, 18 July 1945, p. 31.

30. Denis Gifford, *A Pictorial History of Horror Movies* (The Hamlyn Publishing Company Limited, London, 1973), p. 166.

31. "Acquanetta Loses Fight to Obtain Part of Fortune," *The Pittsburgh Courier*, 21 January 1950.

32. Richard Lamparski, *2nd Annual Lamparski's Whatever Became of...* (Bantam Books, New York, 1977), p. 115.

33. Kaye Nolan, "Acquanetta leaves in Hollywood style," *Arizona Republic* (Phoenix, AZ), 22 August 2004.

34. Horace Davenport died at his home in Norristown, PA, on March 21, 2017. See "Horace Davenport, 98, first African American judge in Montco," *Philadelphia Daily News*, 6 April 2017.

35. Ben Brantley, "In This Chilling Opera, The Eyes Have It," *New York Times,* 15 July 2019, p. C6.

36. On the CD recording of *Acquanetta*, Mikaela Bennett sings the title role, beautifully.

Chapter 11

1. The dates and descriptions of the shooting of the various scenes in *House of Frankenstein* come from the Asst. Director Daily Production Reports, part of the *House of Frankenstein* file, Universal Collection, USC Cinematic Arts Library, Los Angeles, CA. So do the production financial figures and the censorship papers. Thanks to Ned Comstock.

2. The specific details about Karloff in the quagmire come from Tom Weaver, "Universal's World of Frankenstein," *Frankenstein* (*Gorezone* magazine special issue, no. 27), 1994, p. 19.

3. Author's interview with Mae Clarke, Woodland Hills, CA, 11 May 1983.

4. All quotes from Elena Verdugo in this chapter come from a personal letter she sent to the author (15 October 1979), as well as a telephone interview with Ms. Verdugo (Chula Vista, CA, 22 October 1994) and conversations with her at the "Fanex 9" Convention in Baltimore in July 1995.

5. Alton Cook, "Carnival of Monstrosity Holds Forth at Rialto," *New York World-Telegram,* 15 December 1944.

6. "This Will Do It," *Variety,* 9 June 1943, p. 4.

7. Bosley Crowther, "Old Black Magic: A Note on the General Deficiency in Screen Gorgons, Hydras, and Such," *New York Times*, 13 June 1943, p. X3.

8. John Carradine clipping file, Margaret Herrick Library, Academy of Motion Picture Arts & Sciences, Los Angeles, CA.

9. *The Climax* file, Universal Collection, USC Cinematic Arts Library.

10. Sheilah Graham, *The Garden of Allah* (Crown Publishers New York, 1970), pgs. 205–206.

11. For the full story on Atwill's parties and legal travails, see the author's *Hollywood's Maddest Doctors* (Midnight Marquee Press, Baltimore, 1999).

12. Author's telephone interviews with Curt Siodmak, Three Rivers, CA, 8 April and 1 July 1980.

13. This area requires clarification. Various interpretations of how much the actors actually received for *House of Frankenstein* have come forward, some wildly off the mark. To try to explain: Boris Karloff, on a two-picture contract, received a combined $60,000 for *The Climax* and *House of Frankenstein*. I've examined his Universal contract for those films, and he did *not* receive a percentage of this, as some historians have conjectured, but the entire amount. As to the fees received by the contract players, Universal would charge a part of his/her yearly salary against a film, based in part on the production's schedule. Lon Chaney, for example, was probably earning about $1,250 a week for 40-weeks-per-year at this point at Universal, or $50,000 a year. $10,000 of this was set for *House of Frankenstein;* other amounts were added for other films during that year until the figure reached $50,000. Anne Gwynne, told of *House of Frankenstein's* salary sheet setting her fee at $3,000, laughed, "I was never paid that much for a movie in my entire career!" In fact, the $3,000 represents a part of her 1944 Universal salary the studio charged to this film.

14. Gene Brown, *Movie Time* (Macmillan, New York, 1995), p. 173, p. 8.

15. Author's interview with Susanna Foster, Glendale, CA, 10 December 1981.

16. Cynthia Lindsay, *Dear Boris* (Alfred A. Knopf, New York, 1975), pgs. 55–57.

17. Tragically, in real life, Wagenheim was fated for death by bludgeoning in his Hollywood apartment in 1979, at age 83.

18. Virginia McPherson, "Film Links '5' Horrors," *The Youngstown Daily Vindicator*, Ohio, 21 April 1944. Thanks to Dr. Robert Kiss for providing this item.

19. Lee Server, *Robert Mitchum "Baby, I Don't Care"* (St. Martin's Press, New York, 2002).

20. Erskine Johnson, "In Hollywood," *Miami Daily News-Record*, Miami, Oklahoma, 11 May 1944, p. 6. Thanks to Dr. Robert Kiss.

21. Hedda Hopper, "Looking at Hollywood," *Chicago Daily Tribune*, 18 April 1944, p. 18. Thanks to Dr. Robert Kiss.

22. "My Life as a Monster!" *Mad Monsters* magazine. All quotes from Strange in this chapter come from that source.

23. The information of Jones' wounds suffered in action on *House of Frankenstein* comes from Tom Weaver, Michael Brunas and John Brunas, *Universal Horrors: The Studio's Classic Horror Films,*

1931–1946 (McFarland, Jefferson, North Carolina, 2007), p. 455.

24. McPherson.

25. Thanks to John Eccles, Jr., for providing this information.

26. Weaver, p. 19.

27. For detailed coverage of John Carradine's 1943 Shakespeare company, see the chapter "John Carradine and His 'Traveling Circus'" in the author's *The Very Witching Time of Night* (McFarland, Jefferson, North Carolina, 2014), pgs. 330–364.

28. Incidentally: On this day, Basil Rathbone, Nigel Bruce, Evelyn Ankers, and Rondo Hatton were all at work at Universal's new Sherlock Holmes saga, *The Pearl of Death*, on Stages 7 and 16. Thanks to Ned Comstock, Universal Collection, USC.

29. For information on Atwill's last marriage and his final years, see the author's interview with Atwill's son, Lionel Anthony Atwill, in the chapter "The Mystery of Lionel Atwill" in *The Very Witching Time of Night*, pgs. 91–115.

30. "Rialto Gossip: Rehearsals for 'Catherine Was Great' to Start With Mae West—Other Items," *New York Times,* 23 April 1944, p. X1.

31. On December 10, 1944, the *New York Times* ran a feature, "A Witches' Sabbath," by Edward J. Eustace. He claimed he'd interviewed Karloff, Chaney, Carradine, Naish, and Strange after they'd been "shooting some night scenes for *House of Frankenstein*." Anne Gwynne and Elena Verdugo appear in the article too. Apparently, Eustace had been on the set at some point, but his account of the stars all together and hobnobbing after night shooting was whimsical "fake news."

32. David Del Valle, "Shakespeare's Dracula!" *Famous Monsters of Filmland*, #227, August/September 1999, p. 51.

33. Weaver, Brunas and Brunas, p. 455.

34. Michael Fitzgerald, "Universal Appeal," *Fangoria*, #115, August 1992, p. 17.

35. Thanks to Jack Gourlay for providing this information.

36. All the production information, including dates, salaries, budgets and costs cited on *Isle of the Dead*, *The Body Snatcher*, and *Bedlam* come from the RKO Archives UCLA Cinema Library, Los Angeles, CA. Thanks to Julie Graham.

37. This action was covered in mid-1940s newspaper accounts of Carradine's divorce from his wife Ardanelle and marriage to second wife Sonia. These reports cite the drowning attempt as happening in "the summer of 1944."

38. Thanks to Dr. Karl Thiede.

39. Letter to author from Robert Wise, Los Angeles, CA, 24 June 1976.

40. "Picture Grosses," *Variety*, 20 December 1944, p. 13.

41. For financial specifics on the Rialto and Hawaii theatres showing *House of Frankenstein* and *The Body Snatcher* see Chapter 13.

42. "Reviews of the New Films," *The Film Daily*, 4 January 1945, p. 6.

43. "Showmandizer," *Boxoffice* magazine, 27 January 1945, p. 3.

44. "U Will Shoot $750,000 on New Super-Chiller," *Variety,* 14 March 1945, p. 3.

45. Thanks to Dr. Karl Thiede.

46. Thanks to Dr. Karl Thiede.

47. Louis Berg, "Farewell to Monsters," *Los Angeles Times*, 12 May 1946.

Chapter 12

1. Basil Rathbone, *In and Out of Character* (Doubleday, New York, 1962; Limelight Editions, New York, 1991), p. 211.

2. "Legitimate," *Variety*, 4 November 1953, p. 59.

3. *Ibid.*

4. After Brennan won three Oscars in five years, the Academy changed its rules to exclude extras from voting.

5. *New York Times*, 18 April 1926, p. 30.

6. "Ouida Bergère Bankrupt," *New York Times*, 11 June 1926, p. 7.

7. "Police Raid Three Shows, *Sex, Captive* and *Virgin Man*, Hold Actors and Managers, All go to Night Court," *New York Times*, 10 February 1927, p. 1.

8. Rathbone, pgs. 103, 104.

9. Author's interview with Alan Napier, Pacific Palisades, CA, 15 May 1983.

10. Author's interview with Frances Drake, Beverly Hills, CA, 13 July, 1987.

11. Brooks Atkinson, "The New Play," *New York Times*, 30 September 1947, p. 22.

12. "*Mister Roberts* Wins Perry Award," *New York Times*, 29 March 1948, p. 23.

13. Sonia Stein, "Video? Its Moronic, Sneers Rathbone," *The Washington Post*, 12 August 1950, p. B11.

14. Brooks Atkinson, "S.N. Behrman's *Jane*," *New York Times*, 10 February 1952, p. 97.

15. "Legit Tryout: *Sherlock Holmes*," *Variety*, 12 October 1953, p. 2.

16. Rathbone, p. 212.

17. *Ibid.*

18. Tom Weaver, "The Black Sleep," *Bela Lugosi, Midnight Marquee Actors Series,* Gary J. and Susan Svehla, eds. (Midnight Marquee Press, Baltimore, 1995), p. 262.

19. Rathbone, p. 266.

20. Tom Weaver, telephone interview with Howard W. Koch, Los Angeles, CA, 31 March and 1 April 1985.

21. Author's telephone interview with Lillian Lugosi Donlevy, Culver City, CA, 13 December 1974; author's telephone interview with Hope Lugosi, Honolulu, HI, 15 July 1993.

22. Robert Cremer, *Lugosi: The Man Behind the Cape* (Regnery, Chicago, IL, 1976) p. 235.

23. "Broadway Opening," *Variety*, 3 April, 1957, p. 10.

24. Michael B. Druxman, *Basil Rathbone: His Life and His Films* (A.S. Barnes, Cranbury, NJ, 1975), p. 331.

25. "Unit Review," *Variety*, 8 April 1959, p. 64.

26. "Charity Party Sans Money Just a Lot of Sad Sacks to No- Show 'Fun Time,'" *Variety*, 8 April 1959, p. 64.

27. "Jack E. Leonard Axed," *Variety*, 8 April 1959, p. 64.

28. Jack Pitman, "Some 'Fun Time,' Eh, Kids! Pfeiffer's Not-So-Pvt.-War with Jack E. Leonard," *Variety*, 15 April 1959, p. 2 and p. 159. This article gives a comprehensive narrative of the entire fiasco.

29. David Frankham (with Jim Hollifield), *Which One Was David?* (BearManor Media, OK, 2012), pgs. 346–351.

30. Howard Thompson, "Supernatural Thriller is on Double Bill," *New York Times*, 5 July 1962, p. 20. The other film on the double bill was *Burn, Witch, Burn.*

31. "Elizabethan Music and Verse Scheduled at White House," *New York Times*, 30 April 1963, p. 27, and "Grand Duchess Has Elizabethan Evening," *New York Times*, 1 May 1963, p. 3.

32. Alan Rich, "Stadium Centers on Shakespeare," *New York Times*, 1 July 1963, p. 18.

33. Mick Martin, "Matheson: A Name to Conjure With!" *Cinefantastique*, Vol. 3, #2, Spring 1974, p. 10.

34. *Ibid.*, p. 13.

35. Don Alpert, "What Ever Happened to Basil? He's Much Alive, Not Kicking," *Los Angeles Times*, 22 September 1963.

36. *Ibid.*

37. Druxman, p. 342.

38. Richard Matheson had an idea for another Price/Lorre/Karloff/Rathbone AIP movie—co-starring Tallulah Bankhead!

> so I wrote, I think, a very funny script called Sweethearts and Horrors about the Sweetheart family where Peter Lorre was a magician who had a fire sequence in his magic act and burned down every theatre he ever worked in—and Boris Karloff had a children's show, he was "Uncle Dudley," the kindly old television host who hated children. Vincent Price was a ventriloquist and Basil Rathbone as an ageing music-hall comedy star, and Tallulah Bankhead was a movie actress, an ex-big star. And they were all completely vicious to each other, except for Peter Lorre, of course. You couldn't make Peter Lorre vicious. He had to be the victim, really. It was filled with sight gags. It would have made a wonderful picture. I don't know why they never made it…well, I do know…about three or four of them died before they could make it, so that kind of took the wind out of the sails.

Stephen Jacobs, *Boris Karloff: More Than a Monster* (Tomahawk Press, England, 2011), pgs. 461–462.

39. Forrest J Ackerman, "Smile If You Call Him MONSTER! Basil Rathbone Will Eat You Alive if You Don't!" *Monster World* #7, 1965, pgs. 10–15. All the following quotes and information about Forrest J Ackerman's exchange with Basil Rathbone at the time of the shooting of *Queen of Blood* comes from this source unless otherwise noted.

40. Ackerman related this *Queen of Blood* story at the FANEX 3 Convention, Baltimore, September 1989.

41. "'Dr. Rock and Mr. Roll' For Mammoth Monster Market; 'Not Art But Well-Done,'" *Variety*, 14 July 1965, pgs. 5 and 21.

42. "TV Radio Production Centres," *Variety*, 18 August 1965, p. 34.

43. Charles Hamilton, "Basil Rathbone's Last Adventure," *Auction Madness: An Uncensored Look Behind the Velvet Drapes of the Great Auction Houses* (Everest House Publishers, New York, 1981), pgs. 104–110. All the following quotes and information about Hamilton's dealings with Basil Rathbone regarding the Kennedy letters comes from this source unless otherwise noted.

44. Elizabeth Shelton, "Letters to, From Mrs. JFK to Be Sold," *The Washington Post, Times Herald*, 21 September 1965, p. A1.

45. "Basil Wants to Share Letters," *The Washington Post, Times Herald*, 25 September 1965, p. C3.

46. "Actor Bets 20 Million to One," *The Baltimore Sun*, 25 September 1965, p. 5.

47. Frankham, pgs. 383–384.

48. Druxman, p. 354.

49. Tom Weaver, *John Carradine: The Films* (McFarland, Jefferson, North Carolina, 1999), p. 274.

50. Jack Gourlay, "John Carradine Interview—'Unhappy with Horror,'" *Filmfax* #14, March–April, 1989, p. 89.

51. Thomas Lask, "Greater Than the Sum of Its Parts," *The New York Times*, 14 November 1965, p. X21.

52. Druxman, p. 356.

53. John Hamilton, "'They'll Never Believe This at the Yard. They'll Never Believe It …Anywhere!' The Making of *The Blood Beast Terror*," *Little Shoppe of Horrors*, #43, 2019, pgs. 73, 77. All the following quotes and information regarding this film come from this source.

54. Druxman, pp. 103–104.

55. "Basil Rathbone, 75, Dies at Home Here," *New York Times*, 22 July 1967, p. 1.

56. "Rathbone Rites Attended By 350," *New York Times*, 26 July 1967, p. 39.

57. Druxman, p. 105.

58. "Rathbone Will Filed," *New York Times*, 19 August 1967, p. 22.

59. "Barbara Rathbone," *New York Times*, 5 June 1969, p. 47.

60. Author's telephone interviews with Reginald LeBorg, West Hollywood, CA, 20 and 27 September 1988.

61. "Ouida Rathbone: Writer, Wife of Late Actor," UPI, *The Washington Post*, 2 December 1974, p. C8.

62. Rodion Rathbone, aka John Rodion, was married to Caroline Fischer with whom he had three children, apparently none of whom were close to their grandfather.

Chapter 13

1. Joel E. Siegel, *Val Lewton: The Reality of Terror* (The Viking Press, New York, 1973), p. 66.

2. *Showmen's Trade Review,* 6 January 1945, p. 5.

3. "Big Sound Grosses," *Variety,* 21 June 1932, p. 62.

4. The Cost figures of these films come from the Universal Collection, USC. Thanks to Ned Comstock.

5. Mark A. Vieira, *Sin in Soft Focus: Pre-Code Hollywood* (Harry N. Abrams, New York, 1999), p. 221.

6. John McElwee's excellent book *Showmen, Sell It Hot! Movies as Merchandise in Golden Era Hollywood* (GoodKnight Books, Pittsburgh, 2013), p. 29.

7. For cost/profit/loss figures listed for the pre–Code films of the 1930s, thanks to Dr. Karl Thiede. Figures vary according to alternate sources, but for the purpose of this chapter, I have used only Dr. Thiede's figures for consistency.

8. Probably no film of the era from an American major studio suffered more censorship and condemnation, including a 30-year ban in the United Kingdom. Within the uncertainty of the data, *Freaks* saw the largest loss of the films listed here.

9. *White Zombie* is the only film in the list not from a major studio. United Artists released and distributed the film, but *White Zombie* was produced by Halperin Productions (brothers Edward and Victor). The rental total seems low, and may not be the total, but what either party received.

10. For cost/profit/loss figures listed for the films of 1935–1936, again thanks to Dr. Karl Thiede. Figures vary according to alternate sources, but for the purpose of this chapter, I have used only Dr. Thiede's figures for consistency.

11. Although no world-wide rental figure is available, considering *Bride of Frankenstein*'s cost, and late 1937 profit, this would suggest a worldwide rental of about $1,000,000.

12. The rental figure for *The Raven* was about $100,000 less than the rental on *The Black Cat,* and its profit was less than half of *The Black Cat's.* Possible reasons: the growing Censorship controversy over horror films, and a hostile press.

13. As the rental figure shows, however, more people saw *Mad Love* than did *The Raven.*

14. World-wide rental for *The Devil-Doll* is high—more than *Mad Love* and *The Raven* combined.

15. Alta Durant, "Gab," *Variety,* 12 August 1938, p. 3.

16. "Revival of the Undead: The Monster and the Vampire Go Barnstorming and Scare Up Business," *New York Times,* 16 October 1938, p. 160.

17. "'Space Ships,' 'Death Rays,' 'Terror' Trend Brings New Theatre Business," *Motion Picture Herald,* 17 December 1938, p. 17.

18. *Son of Frankenstein* file, Universal collection, USC.

19. Alta Durant, "Gab," *Variety,* 24 December 1938, p. 3.

20. "Picture Grosses," *Variety,* 25 January 1939, p. 8.

21. "U Doubles Prints For *Son of Frankenstein* After Big Draw," *Variety,* 18 January 1939, p. 7.

22. "*Frankenstein* $67,000 on Two Boston Weeks," *Variety,* 8 December 1931, p. 11.

23. "Picture Grosses," *Variety,* 25 January 1939, p. 9.

24. "Here's Record of First Run Grosses Here," *Variety,* 30 October 1939, p. 158.

25. "Picture Grosses," *Variety,* 8 February 1939, p. 9.

26. Thanks to Dr. Karl Thiede.

27. "Top Money Pix This Year," *Variety,* 10 May 1939, p. 1.

28. "Detailed Record of LA First Run Grosses in '42," *Variety,* 19 October 1942, p. 266.

29. Arthur Mayer, *Merely Colossal* (Simon & Schuster, New York, 1953), p. 170.

30. "Picture Grosses," *Variety,* 9 December, 1942, p. 9; 16 December 1942, p. 9.

31. "Record First Run LA BO Totals," *Daily Variety,* 29 October 1943, p. 48.

32. "Picture Grosses," *Variety,* 5 May 1943, p. 9.

33. "Weekly B.O. Clicks of First Runs," *Daily Variety,* 16 October 1944, p. 384.

34. "Picture Grosses," *Variety,* 17 November 1943, p. 13.

35. "*Lassie* and Horror Duo Give Tilt to B.O.," *Variety,* 23 November 1943, p. 12.

36. "Picture Grosses," *Variety,* 10 November 1943, p. 27; 17 November 1943, p. 13; 1 December 1943, p. 11.

37. "Weekly B.O. Clicks of First Runs," *Variety,* 16 October 1944, p. 384.

38. "Christmas Crowds Send Box Office Figures Zooming," *Variety,* 27 December 1943, p. 4.

39. "Picture Grosses," *Variety,* 5 January 1944, p. 27; 12 January, 1944, p. 19.

40. "Weekly B.O. Clicks of First Runs," *Variety,* 16 October 1944, p. 384.

41. "Picture Grosses," *Variety,* 20 December 1944, p. 13; 27 December 1944, p. 13; 3 January 1945, p. 47; 10 January, 1945, p. 13; 17 January, 1945, p. 16.

42. "How Pix Drew in First Runs," *Variety,* 29 October 1945, p. 457.

43. It should be noted that, in Los Angeles, *The Body Snatcher* had a simultaneous run at the Elite Theatre (financial figures not available). However, *House of Frankenstein* also had an additional L.A. run at the Orpheum February 20 to February 26, 1945 (taking in $19,700).

44. "Picture Grosses," *Variety,* 6 June 1945, p. 18; "Picture Grosses," *Variety,* 13 June 1945, p. 21.

45. "How Pix Drew in First Runs," *Variety,* 29 October 1945, p. 457.

46. Thanks to Dr. Karl Thiede.

47. On page 77 of his excellent book, *Val Lewton: The Reality of Terror* (Viking Press, New York, 1973), the late Joel E. Siegel wrote, "*The Body Snatcher* broke all first-week attendance records at the Hawaii Theatre in Hollywood and was almost as popular at the Rialto in New York." This claim was probably made by RKO publicists. As the primary sources for this chapter show, the film did not do nearly as well.

48. "Picture Grosses," *Variety,* 17 March 1943, p. 9.

49. "Picture Grosses," *Variety,* 24 March, 31 March, and 7 April 1943.

50. *Variety,* 29 October 1943, p. 45.

51. "Picture Grosses," *Variety,* 2 January 1946, p. 12.

52. "Picture Grosses," *Variety,* 2 January 1946, p. 12; 9 January 1946, p. 81; 16 January 1946, p. 13.

53. "'Daltons' and 'Dracula' In Record 45G Week," *Variety,* 14 February 1946, p. 3.

54. "Picture Grosses," *Variety,* 1 May 1946, p. 13.

55. "Picture Grosses," *Variety,* 1 May 1946, p. 13; 8 May 1946, p. 13; 15 May 1946, p. 13; 22 May 1946, p. 15.

56. Thanks to Dr. Karl Thiede.

57. For all figures cited for *Dr. Jekyll and Mr. Hyde, The Lodger,* and *The Picture of Dorian Gray,* thanks to Dr. Karl Thiede.

58. "Top Grossers of 1948," *Variety,* 5 January 1949, p. 46.

Bibliography

Interviews

Acquanetta, Phoenix, AZ, 29 July 1992 and Baltimore, MD 14–16 August 1992

Lionel Anthony Atwill, Dorset, VT, 9 October 2003 and 16 July 2004.

DeWitt Bodeen, Woodland Hills, CA, 8 December 1981.

Carroll Borland, Los Angeles, CA, 7 June 1988.

Mae Clarke, Woodland Hills, CA, 11 May 1983.

Lillian Lugosi Donlevy, Culver City, CA, 13 December 1974.

Frances Drake, Beverly Hills, CA, 7 June 1986 and 13 July 1987.

Donnie Dunagan, San Angelo, TX, 13 August and 23 October 2004.

Susanna Foster, Glendale, CA 10 December 1981.

Verna Hillie, New York City, NY, 5 February 1994.

Valerie Hobson, Basinstoke, England, 19 April 1989.

Cortlandt Hull, Mars, PA, 23 June 2019.

Zita Johann, West Nyack, NY, 3 November and 27 December 1979.

Elsa Lanchester, Hollywood CA, 10 June 1979 and 11 December 1981.

Reginald Le Borg, West Hollywood, CA, 20 and 27 September 1988.

Hope Lugosi, Honolulu, HI, 15 July and 12 August 1993.

Evelyn Moriarty, Los Angeles, CA, 26 and 27 April 1993.

Alan Napier, Pacific Palisades, CA 15 May 1983.

Gil Perkins, Los Angeles, CA, 25 August 1991.

Curt Siodmak, Three Rivers, CA, 8 April and 1 July 1980.

Gloria Stuart, Brentwood, CA, 19 May 1986,

Elena Verdugo, Chula Vista, CA, 22 October 1994 and Fanex 9, July 1995.

Robert Wise, Los Angeles, CA, 13 May 1994 and Baltimore, MD, 27 July 1996.

Archives

Billy Rose Library for the Performing Arts, Lincoln Center, New York City, New York

Margaret Herrick Library, The Academy of Motion Picture Arts and Sciences, Los Angeles, CA

University of Southern California Film and Television Library, Los Angeles, CA

University of Southern California, Los Angeles, Performing Arts Archive, Los Angeles, CA

Books

Rick Atkins, *Let's Scare 'Em! Grand Interviews and a Filmography of Horrific Proportions, 1930–1961* (McFarland, Jefferson, North Carolina, 1997).

Elaine Barrie and Sandford Dody, *All My Sins Remembered* (Appleton-Century, New York, 1964).

Rudy Behlmer, *Inside Warner Bros. (1935–1951)* (Viking, New York, 1985).

Ingrid Bergman and Alan Burgess, *Ingrid Bergman: My Story* (Delacorte Press, 1980).

David Bramwell and Jo Tinsley, *The Odyssetum: Strange Journeys That Obliterated Convention* (Chambers Publishing Limited, United States and Great Britain, 2018).

James Curtis, *James Whale: A New World of Gods and Monsters* (Faber & Faber, Boston, 1998).

James Curtis, *Spencer Tracy: A Biography* (Alfred A. Knopf, New York, 2011).

James Curtis, ed., *Featured Player: An Oral Autobiography of Mae Clarke* (Scarecrow Press, Lanham, MD, 1996).

Frank J. Dello Stritto, *A Quaint & Curious Volume of Forgotten Lore: The Mythology & History of Classic Horror Films* (Cult Movies Press, Los Angeles, 2003).

Michael B. Druxman, *Basil Rathbone: His Life and His Films* (A.S. Barnes and Co., Cranbury, NJ, 1975).

James Dugan and Carroll Stewart, *Ploesti* (Bantam Books, New York, 1963).

Scott Eyman, *Lion of Hollywood: The Life and Legend of Louis B. Mayer* (Simon & Schuster, New York, 2005).

Cobbett Feinberg, *Reel Facts* (Vintage Books, New York, 1978).

E.J. Fleming, *Hollywood Death and Scandal Sites* (McFarland, Jefferson, North Carolina, 2000).

David Frankham (with Jim Hollifield), *Which One Was David?* (BearManor Media, OK, 2012).

Joseph T. Fuhrmann, *Rasputin: The Untold Story* (John Wiley & Sons, New Jersey, 2013).

Bob Furmanek and Ron Palumbo, *Abbott & Costello in Hollywood* (Perigee Books, New York, 1991).

Denis Gifford, *A Pictorial History of Horror Movies* (The Hamlyn Publishing Company Limited, London, 1973).

G.D. Hamann, *Basil Rathbone In the 1930's* (Filming Today Press, Hollywood, CA, 2013).

G.D. Hamann, *Carl Laemmle, Jr. In the 30's* (Filming Today Press, Hollywood, CA, 2012).

Charles Hamilton, *Auction Madness: An Uncensored Look Behind the Velvet Drapes of the Great Auction Houses* (Everest House Publishers, New York, 1981).

J.R. Hammond, *H. G. Wells and Rebecca West* (Palgrave MacMillan, 1991).

Ronald Haver, *David O. Selznick's Hollywood* (Bonanza Books, New York, 1980).

Charles Higham, *Charles Laughton: An Intimate Biography* (Doubleday & Company, Garden City, New York, 1976).

Charles Higham, *Hollywood Cameramen* (Indiana University Press, Bloomington, 1970).

Charles Higham, *Louis B. Mayer, M.G.M and the Secret Hollywood* (Donald I. Fine, New York, 1993).

Stephen Jacobs, *Boris Karloff: More Than a Monster* (Tomahawk Press, England, 2011).

Greg King, *The Man Who Killed Rasputin* (Carol Publishing Group, New York, 1995).

John Kobler, *Damned in Paradise: The Life of John Barrymore* (Atheneum, New York, 1977).

James Kotsilibas-Davis, *The Barrymores: The Royal Family of Hollywood* (Crown Publishers, New York, 1981).

Richard Lamparski, *2nd Annual Lamparski's Whatever Became of...* (Bantam Books, New York, 1977).

Elsa Lanchester, *Charles Laughton and I* (Harcourt Brace, New York, 1938).

Elsa Lanchester, *Elsa Lanchester Herself* (St. Martin's Press, New York, 1983).

Cynthia Lindsay, *Dear Boris: The Life of William Henry Pratt a.k.a. Boris Karloff* (Alfred A. Knopf, New York, 1975).

Vincent LoBrutto, *Selected Takes: Film Editors on Editing* (Praeger, Santa Barbara, CA, 1991).

Samuel Marx, *Mayer and Thalberg: The Make-Believe Saints* (Random House, New York, 1975).

Arthur Mayer, *Merely Colossal* (Simon & Schuster, New York, 1953).

Wallace McBride ed., *Monster Serial: Morbid Love Letters to Horror Cinema* (Penny Dreadful Books, Columbia, SC, 2014).

John McElwee, *Showmen, Sell It Hot! Movies as Merchandise in Golden Era Hollywood* (GoodKnight Books, Pittsburgh, PA, 2013).

Sir David Napley, *Rasputin in Hollywood* (Weidenfeld & Nicolson, London, 1989).

Scott Allen Nollen, *Boris Karloff: A Gentleman's Life* (Midnight Marquee Press, Baltimore, 1999).

Patrick Parrinder and Robert M. Philmus, *H.G. Wells's Literary Criticism* (Barnes and Noble, 1980).

Danny Peary, *Guide for the Film Fanatic* (Simon & Schuster, New York, 1986).

Margot Peters, *The House of Barrymore* (Alfred A. Knopf, New York, 1990).

Maria Rasputin, with Patte Barham, *Rasputin: The Man Behind the Myth* (Prentice Hall, New Jersey, 1977).

Basil Rathbone, *In and Out of Character* (Doubleday, New York, 1962; Limelight Editions, New York, 1991).

Gary Don Rhodes, *Lugosi: His Life in Films, on Stage, and in the Hearts of Horror Lovers* (McFarland, Jefferson, North Carolina, 1997).

Philip J. Riley, Editor, *The Return of Frankenstein* (BearManor Media, OK, 2012).

Donald Rumbelow, *The Complete Jack the Ripper* (Penguin Books, London, 2004).

Victor Saville and Roy Moseley, *Evergreen: Victor Saville in his Own Words* (Southern Illinois University Press, 2000).

Lee Server, *Robert Mitchum "Baby, I Don't Care"* (St. Martin's Press, New York, 2002).

Kurt Singer, *The Laughton Story* (The John C. Winston Company, Philadelphia, 1954).

David J. Skal, *Screams of Reason: Mad Science and Modern Culture* (W.W. Norton & Company, New York, 1998).

David J. Skal, *The Monster Show: A Cultural History of Horror* (W.W. Norton & Company, New York, 1993).

David Stenn, *Bombshell: The Life and Death of Jean Harlow* (Doubleday, New York, 1993).

Brian Taves, *Robert Florey: The French Expressionist* (Scarecrow Press, Metuchen, NJ, 1987).

Bob Thomas, *Thalberg: Life and Legend* (Doubleday, New York, 1969).

Lana Turner, *Lana: The Lady, the Legend, the Truth* (E.P. Dutton, New York, 1982).

Dr. Bruno David Ussher, *Music in the Films, 1937–1941* (Filming Today Press, Hollywood CA, 2003). This book was edited by G.D. Hamann.

Mark Vieira, *Forbidden Hollywood: The Pre-Code Era (1930–1934), When Sin Ruled the Movies* (Running Press, Philadelphia, 2019).

Mark A. Vieira, *Hollywood Dreams Made Real: Irving Thalberg and the Rise of M-G-M* (Harry N. Abrams, New York, 2008).

Mark A. Vieira, *Hollywood Horror: From Gothic to Cosmic* (Harry N. Abrams, New York, 2003).

Mark A. Vieira, *Sin in Soft Focus: Pre-Code Hollywood* (Harry N. Abrams, New York, 1999).

Tom Weaver, *Poverty Row Horrors!* (McFarland, Jefferson, North Carolina, 1993).

Tom Weaver, Michael Brunas, and John Brunas, *Universal Horrors: The Studio's Classic Films, 1931–1946*, Second Edition (McFarland, Jefferson, North Carolina, 2007).

Mason Wiley and Damien Bona, *Inside Oscar: The Unofficial History of the Academy Awards* (Ballantine Books, New York, 1987).

Scott Wilson, *Resting Places (Third Edition), The*

Burial Sites of More Than 14,000 Famous Persons, Vol. 1 and Vol. 2 (McFarland, Jefferson, North Carolina, 2016).

Stephen D. Youngkin, *The Lost One: A Life of Peter Lorre* (University Press of Kentucky, 2005).

Felix Yousoupoff, *Lost Splendor: The Amazing Memoirs of the Man Who Killed Rasputin* (Turtle Point Press, Brooklyn, 2003).

Magazines, Newspapers, and Trade Journals

The American Magazine
Arizona Republic (Phoenix, Arizona)
The Baltimore Sun
Boxoffice Magazine
Chicago Daily Tribune
Chicago Tribune
The Christian Science Monitor
Cinefantastique
Classic Images
Daily Boston Globe
The Daily Worker
The Evening News (Wilkes-Barre, PA)
Famous Monsters of Filmland
Films in Review
Hollywood Citizen News
The Hollywood Herald
The Hollywood Reporter
The Journal Times (Racine, Wisconsin)
The Lion's Roar
Little Shoppe of Horrors
Los Angeles Daily News
Los Angeles Evening Herald Express
Los Angeles Examiner
Los Angeles Record
Los Angeles Times
Mad Monsters
Miami Daily News-Record (Miami, Oklahoma).
Monsters from the Vault
Motion Picture Herald
New York Newspaper PM
New York Times
Philadelphia Daily News
Photoplay
Picturegoer
San Francisco Examiner
San Francisco News
Showmen's Trade Review
Silver Screen Magazine
Tallahassee Democrat
Variety
Wall Street Journal
The Washington Post
Wilkes Barre Times Leader
The Youngstown Daily Vindicator (Ohio)

Index

Abbott and Costello 267, 269, 321, 324, 346, 394
Abbott and Costello Meet Frankenstein (film) 349, 415
Abe Lincoln in Illinois (film) 406
Ackerman, Forrest J 383
Acquanetta (opera) 326
Acquanetta, Burnu (aka *Davenport, Mildred*) 296–330
Adams, Jane 357
Adventures of Ichabod and Mr. Toad (film) 366
The Adventures of King Paulsole (film) 35
The Adventures of Robin Hood (1938 film) 210, 361, 366, 382
The Adventures of Sherlock Holmes (1939 film) 213, 362, 380
"The Adventures of the Black Baronet" (episode of TV's *Suspense*) 367
"Aladdin" (episode of TV's *Dupont Show of the Month*) 374
Alaska (1944 film) 343
Alexander, Ross 281
Alexander, Tad 42, 50, 52, 54
Alfred Hitchcock Presents (TV series) 35
Ali Baba and the Forty Thieves (1944 film) 335
All Quiet on the Western Front (1930 film) 7, 13, 182, 395
Allbritton, Louise 308, 410
Allegheny Uprising (film) 215, 216
Allgood, Sara 251
Altman, Deborah 326
Ames, Leon (aka Waycoff, Leon) 15, 16, 24, 27, 93
Ames, Ramsay 310
Amfitheatrof, Daniele 264
Anderson, Maxwell 372
Andre, Lona 80, 84, 85, 86
Ankers, Evelyn 173, 258, 304, 305, 306, 309, 313, 314, 318, 353, 410
Anna Karenina (1935 film) 177, 365, 379, 386
Anouilh, Jean 374
Antosiewicz, John 227
The Ape (film) 281

The Ape Man (film) 37, 276
Arabian Nights (1942 film) 298, 299
Are These Our Parents (film) 293
Arlen, Richard 73, 83, 86, 87, 88, 91, 92, 96, 98, 99
Armstrong, Everhardt 32
Armstrong, Louis 326
Arnold, Edward 54
Arnsbiter, Bernice 6
Arsene Lupin (film) 45
Arsenic and Old Lace (1944 film) 144, 353
Arsenic and Old Lace (play) 144, 310, 331, 334, 335, 336, 338, 339, 353, 356, 408
Ashley, Arthur 44
Ashly, Edward 246
Asther, Nils 143
Astor, Mary 294
Atkinson, Brooks 366, 367
Atwill, Lionel 97, 105, 107, 181, 211, 251, 281, 294, 315, 332, 335, 337, 338, 342, 349, 350, 351, 352, 353, 356, 358, 361, 362, 380, 398, 403
Atwill, Lionel Anthony 353
Auer, Mischa 63, 232, 233
Aumont, Jean-Pierre 276
Auster, Iselin 122, 127, 129
Autopsy of a Ghost (aka *Autopsia de un Fantasma*) 387, 389, 390
Avory, Judge Horace Edmund 68
Ayres, Lew 35

Babes in Toyland (1934 film) 90
Baby Sandy 223, 224
Bacall, Lauren 303
The Bad Seed (play and film) 293
Bad Sister (film) 13
The Baffling World of ESP (TV special) 386
Baily, Tom 96
Balderston, John L. 109, 115, 116, 117, 120, 187, 188, 189, 193, 197, 201, 206, 246, 247, 250, 251, 254
Ballard, Dave 356
Ballbusch, Peter 254
Bankhead, Tallulah 50
Bara, Theda 48, 365
Barbary Coast (1935 film) 207
Barbier, George 92, 95

Barlow, Reginald 167
Barnett, Vince 305
Barnum, P.T. 103
Barondess, Barbara 60, 61
Barrett, Edith 219
Barrows, George 388
Barrymore Ethel 2, 40, 42, 45, 47, 49, 50, 51, 54, 55, 58, 59, 60, 65, 69, 70, 71, 72, 372
Barrymore, John 2, 13, 26, 39, 40, 44, 45, 46, 47, 49, 50, 51, 52, 54, 55, 56, 57, 58, 62, 63, 64, 65, 67, 68, 70, 71, 72, 146, 212, 241, 242, 243, 246, 249, 255, 269, 361, 379, 396
Barrymore, John Drew 48, 59, 70, 382
Barrymore, Lionel 2, 39, 40, 44, 45, 47, 49, 52, 53, 54, 55, 56, 57, 58, 60, 61, 62, 63, 64, 65, 66, 67, 70, 71, 72, 143, 178, 181, 401
Barrymore, Maurice 70
Bartholomew, Freddie 361, 379
Bartlett, Jeanne, 165
Baschuk, Ludwig Luciano 325
Baschuk, Sergio 325
Basshe, Emjou 87
The Bat (play) 146
Baum, Vicki 146
Baxter, Alan 281, 284
Beahan, Charles 35, 36, 37
The Beast of the City (film) 48
The Beast with Five Fingers (film) 34
Beatty, Clyde 305, 312
Beau Geste (1939 film) 214
Beaudine, William 37
Beavers, Louise 116
Beck, Sydney 380
Bedlam (film) 357, 413
Beebe, Ford 227, 228, 229
Beery, Noah, Sr. 78
Beery, Wallace 44, 205, 242
Beetson, Fred W. 10
Behrman, S.N. 367
Belais, Diana 76
Belasco, David 144, 145, 146
Belita 274, 275, 293
Bell, Nelson B. 267
Bella Donna (1923 film) 362
Belmore, Lionel 234
Beloved Bachelor (film) 193

Ben-Hur (1926 film) 48
Ben-Hur (1959 film) 235
Bennett, Constance 210
Bennett, Joan 235
Bergen, Edgar 234
Bergerman, Rosabelle Laemmle 118, 140
Bergerman, Stanley 118, 119, 120, 123, 124, 125, 127, 131, 140, 141, 142, 147, 148, 149, 150, 160, 171
Bergman, Ingrid 173, 238, 240, 245, 246, 247, 252, 253, 254, 258, 259, 260, 265, 266, 267, 268, 414
Bergman, Teddy "Blubber" (aka Reed, Alan) 133
Bern, Paul 55, 59
Best, Edna 367
Bey, Turhan 334
Biddle, Atty. Gen. Francis 308
The Big Cage (film) 305, 312, 320
The Big Fisherman (film) 235
The Big Sleep (film) 303
A Bill of Divorcement (1932 film) 48, 59
Billiet, Phil 203
Billy the Kid (1941 film) 248, 249
Bing, Herman 26
Birell, Tala 32, 280, 281, 282, 288, 294
Bizet, Georges 9
The Black Cat (1934 film) 21, 33, 87, 114, 115, 116, 118, 124, 134, 151, 171, 234, 280, 345, 397, 398, 399
The Black Cat (1941 film) 373
"The Black Cat" (segment of *Tales of Terror*) 378
Black Friday (1940 film) 281, 338
The Black Parachute (film) 335
"The Black Prophet" (episode of TV's *Suspense!*) 70
The Black Room (1935 film) 189
The Black Sleep (film) 372, 373, 374
Blochman, Lawrence G. 113, 114
The Blood Beast Terror (1968 film) 389, 391; see also *Death's Head Vampire*
Blonde Venus (film) 76
Bloom, Claire 389
Blossoms in the Dust (film) 249
Bluebeard (1944 film) 352
Boatwright, Helen 380
Bocklin, Arnold 353
The Body Snatcher (film) 353, 354, 355, 356, 357, 413
Boehm, David 170
Bogart, Humphrey 303, 369
Bogeaus, Benedict 235
La Bohème (1926 film) 9, 14
Bojarski, Richard 11, 107, 227
Boles, John 14, 113
Boleslavsky, Richard 58, 60
Bonomo, Joe 28, 86
Booth, Junius Brutus 45, 46
Borden, Lizzie 144

Borgato, Agostino 26
Borland, Carroll 185, 399
Borzage, Frank 235
Bostic, Joe 307
Bow, Clara 3
Bowman, Don 388
Boyack, James Edmund 238
Boyer, Charles 234
Boys Town (film) 243
Brabin, Charles 48, 50, 58, 365
Bradford, Robert 260
Brady, Alice 119
Brahm, John 214
Branch, Eunie *see* Rathbone, Ouida Bergere
Branch, Houston 277, 284
Brando, Marlon 379
Brantley, Ben 326
Braun, Eva 276
Brecher, Egon 151
Breen, Joseph 2, 33, 105, 109, 114, 115, 116, 117, 118, 120, 121, 122, 123, 124, 127, 128, 129, 133, 134, 141, 147, 148, 150, 151, 152, 161, 163, 164, 166, 171, 180, 185, 186, 188, 189, 201, 214, 215, 217, 224, 229, 238, 244, 245, 249, 253, 254, 257, 272, 276, 277, 278, 279, 280, 287, 288, 289, 290, 291, 312, 313, 337, 396, 399, 400
Brennan, Walter 361
Brent, Evelyn 13
Bride of Frankenstein (aka *The Return of Frankenstein*, 1935 film) 1, 2, 21, 26, 87, 105, 109–137, 138, 142, 148, 150, 152, 162, 169, 170, 171, 172, 180, 183, 186, 187, 201, 202, 205, 206, 207, 246, 249, 308, 338, 399, 401
Bride of the Gorilla (film) 294
Bride of the Lamb (play) 119, 120
The Bridge of San Luis Rey (film) 235
The Brighton Strangler (film) 356, 413
A Briny Boob (film) 161
Broadway Melody of 1936 (film) 178, 183, 192
Broccoli, Albert "Cubby," 205
Brodie, Buster 87, 90
Broidy, Steve 289, 293
Bronte, Charlotte 275
Brooke, Hillary 325
Brooke, Rupert 390
Brooks, Jean 411
Brooks, Mel 137, 274
Brooks, Phyllis 159
Brophy, Edward 189, 195
Brown, David 205
Brown, Joe E. 118, 381
Browne, Frederick, 246
Browning, Elizabeth Barrett 390
Browning, Tod 9, 150, 175, 181, 206, 396, 399, 401
Bruce, Nigel 362, 368, 369
Bruce, Virginia 183, 187, 275
Brunas, John 33

Brunas, Michael 33
Bryant, Nana 316
Buck, Frank 407
Burditte, Jack 87
Burke, Billee 118
Burke, Eulalia 81
Burke, Kathleen 35, 73, 75, 80, 84, 85, 86, 88, 91, 92, 95, 97, 98, 99, 100, 102, 104, 105, 107, 108, 149, 308
Burke's Law (TV series) 382
Burnette, W.R. 213
Burns, Bob 17, 18
Bushman, Francis X 385
Butler, David 234
Buzzell, Edward 147
Byington, Spring 150, 153

Cabanne, Christy 275
The Cabinet of Dr. Caligari (film) 9, 182
Cain, Paul (aka *Ruric, Peter*) 280
Caldwell, Erskine 146
Calhern, Louis 235
Callaway Went Thataway (film) 325
Calling Dr. Death (film) 313
Cantwell, Bishop John J. 118
Capra, Frank 118, 233, 353
Captain America (serial) 335
Captain Blood (film) 361
Captain Kidd (1945 film) 235
Captains Courageous (1937 film) 242, 243, 245
The Captive (play) 363, 376
Captive Wild Woman (1943 film) 2, 296, 297, 302, 303, 304, 305, 306, 307, 308, 309, 310, 312, 313, 315, 320, 322, 323, 326, 335, 338, 413
Carlson, Veronica 328
Carson, Jack 374
Carr, Trem 288, 290
Carradine, Ardanelle 334
Carradine, John 276, 277, 282, 288, 294, 296, 303, 304, 305, 306, 309, 312, 317, 331, 332, 334, 335, 337, 338, 344, 349, 350, 351, 352, 353, 354, 356, 357, 358, 367, 370, 372, 375, 387, 388
Carroll, Earl 318
Carroll, Harrison 112, 123, 219, 222
Carroll, Joan 221, 229
Carroll, Leo G. 234, 249
Carroll, Nancy 78, 83
Casanova's Big Night (film) 367
Cassavetes John 382
The Cat and the Canary (play) 146
Cat People (1942 film) 275, 292, 309, 314, 316, 317, 356, 382, 408, 409, 410, 411
Catherine Was Great (play) 349
Cavalcade (film) 59, 65, 67
Cavett, Dick 391

Ceccarini, Mr. (MGM lightning expert) 248
Chadwick, I.E. 275
Chaliapin, Feodor 35
The Chamber of Horrors (shooting title) 334, 335; see also *Destiny Devil's Brood*; *House of Frankenstein*)
The Champ (1931 film) 242
Chandler, Helen 10, 12, 23
Chandu the Magician (film) 93
Chaney, Lon, Jr. 127, 140, 160, 161, 172, 173, 175, 281, 303, 309, 312, 316, 320, 331, 332, 334, 335, 336, 337, 338, 341, 342, 343, 344, 346, 347, 348, 349, 350, 351, 353, 354, 355, 356, 357, 358, 367, 372, 373, 388, 410, 412, 413
Chaney, Lon, Sr. 12, 26, 47, 77, 87, 127, 190, 337
Channing, Carol 372
Chaplin, Charlie 201, 203
Charlotte of Luxembourg, Grand Duchess 380
Chegodieff, Prince Alexis Pavlovich 69
Chegodieff, Princess Elena 69
The Chimp (three-reeler) 35, 90
China Seas (film) 183
Christine, Virginia 412
A Christmas Carol (1938 film) 23
"A Christmas Carol" (episode of TV's *Shower of Stars*) 372
Churchill, Douglas W. 245
Citizen Kane (film) 81. 275, 290, 292, 406, 410
Clarke, Betsy Ross 23, 26, 27
Clarke, Mae 6, 9, 23, 332
Clemente, Steve 191, 192
Cleopatra (1962 film) 382
The Climax (1944 film) 334, 335, 337, 339
Clive, Colin 1, 6, 19, 61, 84, 96, 112, 115, 123, 124, 126, 127, 130, 136, 150, 177, 180, 187, 189, 192, 193, 194, 199, 201, 202, 204, 205, 206, 275, 339, 399
Clive, E.E. 129
Clive, Henry 325
Cobra Woman (film) 334
Coburn, Charles 337
The Cocoanuts (1929 film) 7
Coe, Peter 338, 349, 350, 351, 352
Coffee, Lenore 48
The Cohens and Kellys in Hollywood (film) 35
Colbert, Claudette 76, 81, 92, 116, 118
Collier, Lois, 314, 315, 316, 318, 319, 320
Colman, Booth 386
Colman, Ronald 207
Colt, Ethel 47, 48
Colt, John Drew 47, 48
Colt, Samuel 47, 48
Colton, John 47, 48, 138, 142, 143,

144, 147, 150, 155, 157, 159, 161, 164, 166, 173, 174
Colton, Marcus 174
The Comedy of Terrors (film) 234, 380
Command Decision (play) 366
The Command to Love (play) 361, 376
Conan Doyle, Sir Arthur 7, 360, 367, 384
Conover, Harry 298
Considine, John Jr. 183, 185, 192, 202
The Constant Wife (1926 play) 47
Cooper, Gary 76, 207, 318
Cooper, Jackie 83
Cooper, Violet Kemble 361
Cooper, Wyllis 211, 404
Coote, Robert 235
Copland, Aaron 337
Cording, Harry 234
The Corn Is Green (play) 70
Corrigan, D'Arcy 23, 27
Corrigan, Lloyd 305
Corrigan, Ray "Crash," 303, 305
Costello, Dolores 48, 59
Coulouris, George 249
The Count of Monte Cristo (1934 film) 235
Courageous Dr. Christian (film) 406
The Court Jester (film) 370, 371, 372
Cowan, Will 312, 313
Cowen, W.J. 275
Cowles, Jules 87
Crabbe, Buster 95
Crain, Jeanne 382
Crawford, Joan 44, 121, 143, 178, 187, 249, 258
The Creeping Unknown (film) 374
Creeps by Night (Radio series) 335, 340, 343, 349
Cregar, Laird 1, 252, 414
Crime and Punishment (1935 film) 187
Crisp, Donald 248, 251, 264
Crosby, Bing 147, 234
Crosby, Bob 338
Crouse, Russel 353
Crowther, Bosley 334
Cukor, George 252
Cumberbatch, Benedict 390
Cummings, Irving 44
Currie, Louise 37
The Curse of the Cat People (film) 353
Curse of the Demon (film) 382
Curtis, James 9, 247, 259
Curtiz, Michael 401, 407
Cushing, Peter 389, 390, 391
The Czarina (play) 376

Dade, Frances 13
The Daltons Ride Again (film) 413
Dancing Lady (film) 177, 183, 185
Danforth, Jim 328

Daniell, Henry 252, 354, 356, 369, 380, 413
Daniels, William (cinematographer) 50, 54
Danner, Melville 267
Darling, Anne 118, 125
Darwin, Charles 18, 98
Datig, Fred 85
Daughter of the Dragon (film) 142
Davenport, Caroline 300, 309
Davenport, Edward 300
Davenport, Horace 300, 326
Davenport, Julia Mae Green 300
Davenport, Kathryn 300
Davenport, Mildred see Acquanetta, Burnu
Davenport, William 300
Davenport, William Daniel 300
Davenport, Winifred 300
David Copperfield (1935 film) 361, 379, 386
Davies, Marion 81
Davis, Bette 13
Davis, Richard 314, 315, 316, 318, 319, 320
Dawn, Jack 247, 248, 256, 262
The Dawn Patrol (1938 film) 219
The Day of the Triffids (film) 294
Dayne, Eleta 133
De Acosta, Mercedes 49, 142
Dead Man's Eyes (film) 320, 321, 323
Death's Head Vampire (film) 389, 390; see also *The Blood Beast Terror*
De Gaulle, General Charles 298
De Havilland, Olivia 366
Dein, Edward 312
Dello Stritto, Frank 395
Del Rio, Dolores 114
DeMille, Cecil B. 81, 83, 85, 272
Denham, Reginald 368
Dessau, Paul 354
The Destiny (shooting title) 335, 336, 337; see also *Chamber of Horrors Devil's Brood*; *House of Frankenstein*
Destry Rides Again (1939 film) 216, 226, 227, 234
Detour (1945 film) 335
Devil and the Deep (film) 82
The Devil Commands (film) 408
The Devil-Doll (film) 400, 401
The Devil Passes (play) 49
The Devil's Brood (shooting title) 332, 337, 338, 339, 340, 341, 342, 344, 345, 348, 349, 351, 352, 353, 354; see also *Chamber of Horrors*; *Destiny*; *House of Frankenstein*
The Devil's Disciple (play) 243
Devil's Island (film) 404
Devo (New Wave band) 95
Dial M for Murder (play) 368
Diehl, Karl Ludwig 45

Dietrich, Marlene 34, 76, 96, 114, 216, 226, 227, 234, 340, 365
Dietz, Howard 200, 266
Dillinger (1945 film) 293
Dime a Dance (film) 277
Dinner at Eight (film) 40, 69
Disney, Walt 50, 260, 366
The Divine Woman 143
The Divorcee (1919 film) 47
Dix, Richard 411
Dmytryk, Edward 276, 294, 304, 305, 306
Le docteur Miracle (operetta) 9
Dr. Jekyll and Mr. Hyde (1920 film) 26, 47, 241, 242, 246, 269, 346
Dr. Jekyll and Mr. Hyde (1931 film) 30, 32, 76, 83, 89, 92, 102, 234, 241, 242, 245, 262, 269, 398
Dr. Jekyll and Mr. Hyde (1941 film) 1, 2, 238–271, 414
"Dr. Jekyll and Mr. Hyde" (episode of TV's *Suspense*) 366
Dr. Jekyll and Mr. Hyde (opera) 264
Dr. Kildare (TV series), 386
Dr. Renault's Secret (film) 316
Dr. Rock and Mr. Roll (uncompleted film) 383
Doctor X (film) 398, 399
Domergue, Faith 383
Don Quixote (film) 35
Donat, Robert 242, 243
Donlevy, Brian 207, 214, 215, 216
Donne, John 380
Douglas, Lloyd C. 235
Down Argentine Way (film) 342
Down in San Diego (film) 267
Downing, Bob 376, 378
Dracula (1931 film) 3, 4, 7 , 9, 13 , 14, 17, 25, 30, 32, 33, 34, 76, 77, 93, 105, 115, 150, 151, 160, 170, 182, 246, 308, 340, 395, 396, 401, 402, 403, 405
Dracula (1931 Spanish film), 9
Dracula (play) 25, 187
Dracula's Daughter (film) 215, 308, 401
Drake, Frances 122, 147, 173, 179, 180, 181, 187, 188, 190, 191, 192, 193, 194, 199, 200, 201, 202, 205, 206, 364, 365, 399
Dreier, Hans 90
Druxman, Michael 375, 390
Dudgeon, Elspeth 129
"Duet for One Hand" (episode of TV's *Dr. Kildare*) 386
Dumbrille, Douglass 318
Dunagan, Donnie 221, 222, 229, 404
Dunlap, John 136
Dunne, Irene 118, 234
Dupont, E.A. 23
Durant, Alta 213, 219, 224
Durante, Jimmy 13
Durbin, Deanna 234, 403

Eagels, Jeanne 142
The Eagle and the Hawk (film) 149
Earthquake (film) 210
East of Eden (film) 257
The East Side Kids 274, 276 , 293
East Side of Heaven (film) 234
Easy Rider (film) 383
Edeson, Arthur 182
Edgar Allan Poe, Volume 3 (record album) 387
Edmunds, William 340
Edward V 209
Eisenhower, General Dwight D. 289
Eldridge, Florence 365
Emery, Katherine 355
Encore (play) 49, 60
End of the Trail (film) 83
Endore, Guy 182, 183, 185
Errol, Leon 251
Estabrook, Howard 235
An Evening with Basil Rathbone (one-man play) 367
Everson, William K. 182
Eyman, Scott 245
Ezekian, Harry 86, 88

"Facts in the Case of M. Valdemar" (segment of *Tales of Terror*) 379
Fair Warning (film) 204
Fairbanks, Douglas, Jr. *211*
Fang and Claw (film) 407
Faragoh, Francis 213
Fast One (novel) 280
Faulkner, William 376
Fenwick, Irene 49
Fidler, Jimmie 288, 289
Field, Betty 316
Fields, Stanley 88
Fields, W.C. 76, 234
Fish, Daniel 326
Fish, George F. 242
Fitzgerald, Geraldine 374
Fitzgerald, Michael 351
Fitzmaurice, George 362
Flash Gordon (serial) 86
Flash Gordon's Trip to Mars (serial) 318
Fleming, Victor 240, 245, 246, 247, 248, 251, 258, 259, 264, 265
Flemyng, Robert 391
Flesh and Fantasy (film) 299, 303
The Florentine Dagger (film) 34
Florey, Robert 5, 7, 8, 9, 10, 11, 12, 15, 17, 20, 21, 24, 25, 28, 29, 32, 33, 34, 37, 112
The Fly (1958 film) 107
Flying Down to Rio (film) 396
Flynn, Errol 219, 361, 372, 379, 380, 382
Fonda, Henry 366
Fontaine, Joan 362, 367
Forbes, Mary 279, 280, 288
Forbes, Ralph 228, 230
Forbidden Planet (film) 77

Ford, John 113, 114, 344, 374, 375
Foreman, Ethel Marion 362
Forepaugh, Luella 242
Forsaking All Others (film) 121, 187
Fort, Garrett 29, 77
Foster, Preston 398
Foster, Susanna 334, 337, 339
Fox, Sidney 4, 5, 8, 13, 14, 16, 23, 24, 25, 26, 28, 29, 30, 32, 33, 35, 36, 37
F.P.I. Antwortet Nicht (film) 187
Francis, Arlene 20, 22, 28, 31, 32
Frankenstein (1931 film) 3, 5, 6, 7, 8, 9, 11, 14, 17, 19, 20, 22, 25, 28, 29, 30, 32, 33, 34, 75, 76, 77, 81, 84, 90, 93, 96, 101, 103, 111, 112, 115, 122, 136, 160, 180, 184, 187, 188, 189, 201, 234, 246, 332, 339, 340, 345, 356, 395, 396, 401, 402, 403, 405
"Frankenstein and the Monster" (episode of radio's *Stars Over Hollywood*) 354
Frankenstein Meets the Wolf Man (film) 138, 262, 303, 308, 318, 334, 336, 338, 413
Frankham, David 378, 379, 386
Frazee, Joan 303
Freaks (1932 film) 3, 32, 44, 75, 76, 83, 100, 113, 189, 396, 397
A Free Soul (film) 47
Freeman, Helen 52
Fremont, John C. 144, 175
Frenchman's Creek (film) 90, 362
Freud, Sigmund 254
Freund, Karl 8, 9, 17, 20, 21, 23, 24, 29, 33, 34, 116, 118, 182, 183, 185, 189, 192, 193, 199, 202, 205, 206, 247, 399
Friderici, Blanche 35
Frobe, Gert 71
The Front Page (play) 50
The Frozen Ghost (film) 294, 353
Fulton, John P. 158, 350, 351, 352, 399
Fun Time (stage show) 375
Furhmann, Joseph T. 41, 43
Frye, Dwight 17, 126, 129, 136

Gable, Clark 47, 90, 121, 147, 177, 178, 183, 187, 192, 242, 246, 328
The Gae Foster Girls 133, 202
Gallagher, John 246
Gallinghouse, Scott 300
Galston, Al 290, 291, 406
Galsworthy, John 115
Garbo, Greta 44, 49, 50, 57, 142, 143, 177, 365, 379, 386
Gardner, Ava 276
Garland, Judy 246
Garson, Greer 241, 249
Gates, Harvey 150
The Gay Diplomat (film) 58
Gemora, Charles 12, 14, 17, 18, 26, 28, 35, 76, 90

General Electric Theatre (TV series) 34
George, John 87
Ghost Catchers (film) 337
The Ghost in the Invisible Bikini (aka *Pajama Party in a Haunted House*) 385
The Ghost of Frankenstein (film) 107, 214, 334, 336, 337, 345, 346
The Ghost Ship (film) 411, 412
Ghosts (play, adapted for radio's *NBC Shell Show*) 120
Gidget Goes Hawaiian (film) 385
Gifford, Denis 323
Gift of Gab (film) 116
Gilbert, John 9
The Giocanda Smile (play) 367
Gish, Lillian 9, 144
Godfrey, Peter 255
Goebbels, Joseph 322
Goetz, Augustus 366
Goetz, Ruth 366
Going Places (film) 404
Goldfinger (film) 71
Goldwyn, Samuel 189, 214, 392, 407
Der Golem (1920 film) 7, 9, 182
Gomez, Thomas 368
Gone with the Wind (film) 100, 173, 215, 240, 242, 245, 246, 264, 267, 307
The Good Earth (film) 35, 205
The Good Fairy (film) 127
Goodbye, Mr. Chips (1939 film) 242
Gorcey, Leo 267
Gordon, Bert I. 378
Gordon, Mary 128
Gordon, Michael 326
The Gorilla (1930 film) 12
The Gorilla Man (film) 356, 408
Gould, Charlie 228
Gourlay, Jack 352, 391
Gowland, Gibson 249
Grand Hotel (1930 play) 146
Grand Hotel (1932 film) 44, 45, 57, 146
Grant, Cary 92, 149
Grant, Helena 155
Grant, Lawrence 161
Granville, Bonita 267, 276, 285, 294
Graubart, Julius 87
Gray, Glen 232
Great Expectations (1934 film) 119, 147, 150, 159
The Great Train Robbery (1903 film) 87
Greed (film) 249
Green, Martyn 367
Green Hell (film) 215, 216, 339, 340, 342
Greene, Graham 177, 202
Gregory, Dr. William K. 103
The Gretonas 133
Grey, Nan 212, 215, 227, 232, 233
Griffies, Ethel 141, 162, 163

Griffith, D.W. 146
Grizzly Adams—The Legend Never Dies (film) 326
Gross, Jack 394
Grossmith, George 264
Gung Ho! (film) 340
Gurie, Sigrid 214
Gwenn, Edmund 401
Gwynn, Edith 276
Gwynne, Anne 338, 349, 350, 351, 352, 357
Gypsy Wildcat (film) 338

Hahn, S.S. 325
Hajos, Karl 170
Hall, Huntz 383
Hall, Jon 335, 353
Halliday, Richard 242
Hamilton, Charles 384
Hamilton, John 389
Hamlet (1922 Broadway stage production) 47
Hampden, Walter 366
Hands of Orlac (British title) 202; see also *The Hands of Orlac; Mad Love*
The Hands of Orlac (alternate title) 200; see also *Hands of Orlac; Mad Love*
The Hands of Orlac (1924 film) 182
The Hands of Orlac (novel) 182
The Hangman see *Hitler's Madman*
Hardwicke, Sir Cedric 214, 215, 251
Hargrove, Rebecca L. 326
Harlow, Jean 6, 13, 44, 48, 55, 59, 118, 162, 177, 178, 183, 185
Harrington, Curtis 125, 383
Harris, Jed 366
Harris, Julie 374
Harris, Marilyn 20, 90
Harris, Robert 142, 148, 150, 152, 161, 170
Harrison, Paul 298
Hart, Moss 284
Hart, Susan 386
Hartmann, Edmund L. 320, 321
Harvey (1950 film) 144
Harvey (play) 144
Hassel, Jeffrey 165
Hastings, Sir Patrick 68
Hat Check Honey (film) 315
Hatfield, Hurd 414
Hatton, Rondo 323
Hayes, Gabby 118
Hayes, Helen 50
Hays, Richard E. 32
Hays, Will H. 29, 32, 117, 133, 288
Hayward, Louis 235
Hayward, Susan 246, 247
He Who Sups With the Devil (unproduced play) 353
Healy, Ted 189, 193, 202, 205
Hearst, William Randolph 81, 392

Heart of Africa (documentary) 11
Heath, Percy 242
Hecht, Ben 48, 50
Heggie, O.P. 127, 169
The Heiress (film) 366
The Heiress (play) 366, 376
Hell Divers (film) 67
Hell's Angels (1930 film) 77, 105
Hellzapoppin' (film) 275, 290, 292, 406
Helm, Brigitte 182
Helm, Fay 303
Henry, William 283, 285
Hepburn, Katharine 48, 59, 243, 244, 259
Herrick, Mrs. Oliver 357
Herrmann, Bernard 372
Heydrich, Reinhard 276
Hide and Seek (play) 374
Hillbillys in a Haunted House (film) 388, 389, 390
Hiller, Wendy 366
Hillie, Verna 79, 80, 84, 85, 86, 99
Hinds, Samuel S. 314, 318
Hirshfield, Harry 266
His Creatures (play) 77
Hitchcock, Alfred 173, 187, 235
Hitler, Adolf 190, 277, 280, 322, 354
Hitler's Children (film) 272, 276, 284, 285, 288, 293, 294
Hitler's Madman (film) 272, 276, 287, 289, 294 (aka *The Hangman*)
Hitler's Women (shooting title) 274, 276, 277, 287, 290; see also *Women in Bondage*
Ho, Linda 388
Hobart, Rose 234, 242, 355
Hobson, Valerie 125, 126, 127, 130, 132, 136, 139, 141, 150, 152, 153, 155, 156, 158, 160, 167, 169, 170, 173, 205
Hoffenstein, Samuel 242
Hoffman, J.J. 102
Hohl, Arthur 86, 87, 88
Holden, Gloria 215, 308
Hollywood Canteen (film) 355
Holt, Tim 276, 294
Holtzmann, Fanny 68, 70, 71
Hope, Bob 321, 367
Hopkins, Arthur 49, 59
Hopkins, Miriam 76, 242, 245, 253, 269
Hopper, Dennis 383
Hopper, Hedda 227, 342
Horton, Edward Everett 382
Hossein, Robert 71
Hot Rhythm (film) 289, 292
The Hound of the Baskervilles (1939 film) 211, 362
The Hound of the Baskervilles (1959 film) 389
A House Divided (film) 10
House of Dracula (film) 107, 349, 356, 357, 413

House of Frankenstein (film) 107, 230, 311, 313, 331–359, 394, 412; see also *Chamber of Horrors*; *Destiny*; *The Devil's Brood*
House of Pain (song) 95
The House of Rothschild (film) 114
How Green Was My Valley (film) 251
How the West Was Won (film) 260
Howard, the Hon. Cecil John Arthur 205
Howard, Leslie 361
Huber, Harold 199
"Huck Finn" (musical episode of TV's *The United States Steel Hour*) 374
Hughes, Howard 118
Hugo, Victor 92
Hull, Cortlandt 160, 169, 170, 174
Hull, Henry 44, 118, 138, 144, 145, 146, 147, 148, 150, 151, 152, 153, 154, 156, 158, 159, 160, 161, 164, 165, 167, 168, 169, 171, 172, 173, 174, 175
Hull, Josephine 144
Hull, Shelley 172
Hume, Cyril 77
The Hunchback of Notre Dame (1923 film) 26, 86, 337, 346
The Hunchback of Notre Dame (1939 film) 213, 214, 215, 217, 227, 282, 354
Hunter, Ian 215, 216, 248, 252, 262
Hurlbut, William J. 119, 120
Hurst, Brandon 26, 27, 252, 346
Hurst, Fannie 116, 119
Hurst, Paul 100
Huskey, Ferlin 388
Hussey, Ruth 248
Huston, John 9, 10
Huston, Walter 10, 143
Hutchinson, Josephine 118
Huxley, Aldous 367
Huxley, Mrs. David 390
Huxley, Julian 98
Huxley, T.H. 98
Hyams, Leila 83, 86, 88, 89, 92, 100, 103
Hyans, Edward M., Jr. 316, 317
Hyman, Bernie 48, 49, 60, 65
Hytten Olaf 346

I Love Lucy (TV series) 205
I Walked with a Zombie (film) 356, 410
Ibsen, Henrik 120
Idols of Clay (film), 362
If I Had a Million (film) 82
If I Should Die (1963 TV drama) 70
If I Were King (1938 film) 361
Imitation of Life (1934 film) 116 , 118, 119, 133, 281
In Old Chicago (film) 119

"The Incredible Dr. Markesan" (episode of TV's *Thriller*) 35, 351
Ingagi (film), 11, 12, 19, 34, 77
The Invisible Man (1933 film) 114, 162, 398, 403
The Invisible Man (proposed film) 29, 33
The Invisible Man's Revenge (film) 311 335, 338
The Invisible Ray (film) 147, 173, 187, 399, 400, 406
The Island of Dr. Moreau (novel) 73, 75, 77
Island of Lost Souls (1932 film) 2, 34, 35, 66, 73- 108, 149, 280, 308, 313, 337, 398, 407
Isle of Forgotten Sins (film) 281
Isle of the Dead (film) 315, 353, 354, 355, 355
It Happened One Night (film) 170
Ivano, Paul 7
The Ivy V 375

Jackson, Helen 357
J'ai tu'e Raspoutine (film) 71
James, Henry 366
Jameson, Joyce 379, 381
Jane (play) 367
Jane Eyre (1934 film) 275
Jannings, Emil 34, 35
A Japanese Nightingale (film) 362
J.B. (play) 376
Jekyll and Hyde (musical) 269
Jesse James (1939 film) 151, 281
Jewell, Isabel 189, 197, 199
Joan of Arc (1948 film) 259
Jocko Homo (song) 95
Johann, Zita 97, 192, 398
Johann the Coffin Maker (three-reel film) 7
John Carradine and his Shakespeare Players (stage company) 335
Johns, Glynis 370
Johnson, Erskine 232, 280, 342
Johnson, Noble 8, 17
Johnston, W. Ray 292
Jo-Jo the Dog-Faced Boy 103
Jones, Allan 303
Jones, Billy 230, 344, 345, 347
Jonson, Ben 380
Jory, Victor 293
Jowett, Sir William 68
Joy, Col. Jason 10, 29, 30, 77, 83, 96
Julius Caesar (play) 366
The Jungle Captive (film) 297, 323
Jungle Queen see *Jungle Woman*
Jungle Woman (1944 film) 2, 296, 297, 310, 311, 312, 313, 314, 315, 316, 317, 318, 319, 320, 321, 322, 323, 326, 335

Kapalik, Jacques 268
Karloff, Boris 5, 6, 7, 13, 20, 21,

28, 29, 32, 34, 35, 50, 55, 58, 70, 73, 78, 81, 82, 85, 90, 93, 97, 109, 111, 112, 113, 114, 115, 116, 118, 119, 120, 121, 124, 125, 126, 127, 128, 130, 136, 138, 147, 150, 151, 152, 170, 173, 180, 182, 183, 189, 190, 205, 209, 210, 211, 213, 215, 217, 218, 219, 221, 223, 224, 225, 227, 228, 229, 230, 231, 232, 233, 234, 235, 275, 280, 281, 284, 310, 311, 318, 331, 332, 334, 335, 336, 337, 338, 340, 341, 342, 343, 344, 345, 346, 347, 348, 349, 350, 353, 354, 355, 356, 357, 361, 374, 380, 381, 382, 383, 385, 389, 398, 399, 401, 403, 406, 408, 413
Karloff, Dorothy 218
Karloff, Sara Jane 218
Katzman, Sam 321
Kay, Edward 285
Kaye, Danny 370, 371, 372
Kazanjian, Aram 31, 32
Keel, Howard 235
Keene, Tom *see* Powers, Richard
Kelley, Dan 298
Kelly, Nancy 274, 279, 280, 282, 283, 284, 285, 288, 293, 294
Kelly, Paul 366
Kende, Geza 3
Kennedy, Jacqueline 380, 384, 385
Kennedy, John F. 279, 380, 384
Kennedy, Noel 155
Kenton, Erle C. 83, 85, 87, 88, 89, 92, 95, 98, 99, 103, 107, 331, 337, 340, 341, 342, 344, 346, 347, 348, 349, 350, 351, 352, 356
Kerrigan, J.M. 155
Kid Dynamite (film) 276
Kilburn-Walker, Terence 368
King, Greg 42, 43
King Cole Trio 292
King Kong (1933 film) 12, 17, 345, 395, 396
The King of Kings (1927 film) 272
Kinsolving, Dr. Arthur Lee 390
Kirk, Joe 346
Kirk, Tommy 385, 386
Kirkland, Jack 146
Kirkley, Donald 3, 32, 47, 67, 115, 131, 254, 258, 274, 308
Knowling, Meriel 68
Koch, Howard W. 372
Kolker, Henry 193
Komai, Tetsu 86, 88, 89
Koster, Henry 234
Kress, Harold 260, 268
Krieger, Paul 131, 132
Kruger, Otto 323

Ladd, Alan 95
Lady Be Good (film) 249
Lady in the Death House (film) 294
Lady Let's Dance (film) 293
Lady Tubbs (film) 171
Laemmle, Carla 170

Laemmle, Carl, Jr. 3, 5, 7, 9, 10, 12, 13, 14, 20, 28, 29, 30, 32, 35, 109, 112, 113, 115, 118, 119, 120, 123, 124, 125, 126, 127, 129, 131, 133, 135, 140, 141, 142, 148, 150, 160, 171

Laemmle, Carl, Sr. 7, 10, 109, 112, 115, 118, 119, 120, 123, 124, 125, 127, 131, 135, 140, 141, 142, 170, 171, 227

Lahr, Bert 246

Lanchester, Elsa 73, 82, 90, 106, 107, 125, 126, 127, 136, 137, 152, 180, 205, 308

Lane, Vicky 276, 323, 324

Lang, Fritz 186

Lansbury, Angela 370, 414

Lansing, Joi 388

"The Lark" (episode of NBC's *Hallmark Hall of Fame*) 374

Lask, Thomas 388

The Last Days of Pompeii (1935 film) 382

The Last Hurrah (1958 film) 374

Laugh, Clown, Laugh (film) 47

Laugh, Clown, Laugh (play) 47

Laughton, Charles 73, 75, 81, 82, 83, 86, 87, 88, 90, 91, 92, 93, 95, 96, 97, 98, 99, 100, 101, 102, 103, 104, 105, 106, 107, 108, 178, 183, 192, 213, 227, 235, 374, 398

Laurel and Hardy 16, 35

Lawton, Dorothy 289

Lazar, Peter 374

Lazovert, Dr. Stanislaw 41

LeBorg, Reginald 310, 313, 315, 316, 317, 318, 319, 320, 372, 392

Lederer, Francis 277

Lederer, Otto 87, 404

Lee, Christopher 71

Lee, Robert N. 213, 217, 228, 235

Lee, Rowland V. 210, 211, 212, 214, 217, 220, 227, 228, 229, 230, 231, 232, 234, 235, 403, 404, 406

Leonard, Jack E. 375, 376

Leontovich, Eugenie 366

The Leopard Man (film) 356, 410

Leslie, Maude 155

Levee, William A. 203

Lewis, David 124, 126

Lewton, Val 310, 315, 316, 332, 353, 354, 357, 394, 395, 411, 413

Light of the World (radio series) 107

Lincoln's Portrait (symphony) 337

Lindsay, Cynthia 234

Lindsay, Howard 353

Little Caesar (1931 film) 213

Little Shoppe of Horrors (film and play) 155

Little Women (1933 film) 396

The Lives of a Bengal Lancer (film) 107, 207, 318

Lloyd, Doris 252

Lockwood, Gary 378

The Lodger (1944 film) 214, 414

Lodijensky, Theodore 59

Loftin, Carey 331, 333, 344, 347, 348

Lombard, Carole 149

London After Midnight (film) 77

Lorre, Peter 34, 177, 179, 180, 186, 189, 190, 193, 194, 195, 197, 199, 200, 201, 202, 203, 204, 205, 206, 207, 234, 334, 379, 380, 381, 399, 403

Losch, Tilly 36

Lost Continent (film) 325

The Lost Patrol (film) 113, 114, 124

Lost Sheep (play) 12, 13

Love, Montagu 44, 146

Love and the Devil (film) 162

Love Crazy (film) 249, 258

Love from a Stranger (film) 210, 390

Lovsky, Celia 187, 194

Lowe, Edward T. 337, 356

Loy, Myrna 55, 78, 398

Lubitsch, Ernst 85

Ludwig, Edward 234, 402

Lugosi, Bela 1, 3, 4, 5, 6, 8, 9, 11, 12, 13, 14, 17, 18, 22 , 23, 24, 25, 26, 29, 30, 31, 32, 33, 34, 35, 37, 50, 73, 76, 78, 79, 92, 93, 94, 95, 98, 101, 102, 103, 107, 108, 114, 115, 116, 118, 127, 141, 148, 150, 151, 156, 160, 173, 181, 182, 183, 187, 211, 227, 232, 233, 262, 274, 275, 276, 280, 281, 288, 293, 294, 318, 334, 335, 336, 337, 338, 347, 354, 356, 361, 372, 373, 396, 398, 399, 402, 403, 404, 406, 413

Lugosi, Hope 372

Lugosi, Lillian 372

Lukas, Paul 13, 118

Luke, Keye 194, 195

Lulu Belle (play) 145, 146

Lynn, George 340

Lyons, Chester 189, 192, 204

M (1931 film) 179, 186

M Squad (TV series) 34

MacArthur, Charles 50, 53, 54, 60, 62, 67

Macbeth (play) 256

MacDonald, Duncan 389

MacDonald, Jeanette 147, 178, 365

MacDonald, Philip 113

Mack, Freddy 202

MacKenzie, Jack 315, 316, 320

MacKenzie, Lady Grace 11

MacLane, Barton 249, 250

MacLeish, Archibald 376

MacVicar, Martha (aka Martha Vickers) 303

Mad About Music (film) 403

The Mad Genius (1931 film) 56, 57, 396

The Mad Ghoul (film) 275, 410

Mad Love (1935 film) 2, 105, 134, 147, 177–208, 246, 247, 364, 399; see also *Hands of Orlac*; *The Hands of Orlac*

The Mad Monster (film) 281, 338

Madame Butterfly (film) 89

Madame Du Barry (film) 114, 118

Madame X (1929 film) 47

Mädchen in Uniform (film) 277

The Magic Sword (film) 378, 383

Mahin, John Lee 48, 242, 246, 247, 250, 251, 254, 255, 265, 270

Maid of the Ozarks (play) 375

Malden, Karl 35

Malvern, Paul 335, 346, 348, 356

Mamoulian, Rouben 76, 83, 85, 118, 241, 254, 269

The Man Called Back (film) 33

Man Made Monster (film) 281

The Man Who Came Back (play), 146

The Man Who Knew Too Much (1934 film) 187

The Man Who Laughs (film) 346

A Man with Red Hair (play) 81, 82, 83

Mander, Miles 217

Manhattan Moon (film) 202

Manners, David 252

Mansfield, Martha 241

Mansfield, Richard 241, 246

Marais, Jean 382

March, Fredric 50, 76, 89, 92, 102, 149, 183, 241, 242, 243, 245, 246, 249, 255, 269, 365, 372, 398

March, Joseph Moncure 77

Marie Antoinette 44

Marion, Edna 16

Mark, Michael 234, 345, 346

Mark of the Vampire (1935 film) 150, 181, 183, 185, 187, 189, 203, 206, 207, 399, 400

The Mark of Zorro (1940 film) 361

Marlowe, Christopher 380

Marly, Florence 383

The Marriage-Go-Round (play) 378

Marsh, Marian 13, 55, 396

Marshall, George 234

Marston, Dr. William Moulton 238, 240, 265, 266

Martin, Mick 382

Marx, Samuel 64

The Marx Brothers, 7, 76, 95, 178

The Mask of Fu Machu (1932 film) 2, 13, 55, 58, 97, 161, 210, 398, 399

Massey, Raymond 353, 376

Matheson, Richard 382

Matthews, Lester 150, 158, 160, 252

Maugham, W. Somerset 142, 252, 367

Mayer, Arthur 78, 85, 105, 355, 407, 408

Mayer, Louis B. 45, 47, 52, 58, 177, 180, 186, 244, 269, 318

McClafferty, the Very Rev. Monsignor J.J. 292

McCray, Patrick 136

McDonald, Charles 356

McEnery, Peter 71
McFarland, Wilma 5, 6, 19
McKim, Josephine 125
McCormick, Patty 293
McLaglen, Victor 235
McLean, Evelyn Walsh 50
McMahon, Pat 326
McManus, John T. 274, 322
McPherson, Virginia 347
A Medal for Benny (film) 353
Medford, J.J. 67
Medina, Patricia 35
Meehan, John 48
Meet Me in St. Louis (film) 15
Melford, George 9
Men in White (film) 58
Men of Boys Town (film) 245
Menken, Helen 143, 363, 364
Meredith, Judi 383
Mescall, John J. 111, 125, 205
Metropolis (1927 film) 9, 182
Meyer, Torben 26
Michael, Gertrude 272 279, 280,
    281, 285, 288, 289, 293, 294
Michell, Keith 389
Mickey's Gala Premiere (cartoon)
    50
A Midsummer Night's Dream
    (play) 374
Milasch, Robert 87
Milestone, Lewis, 118
Millakowsky, Herman 276, 278
Miller, Charles 346, 349
Miller, Don 293
Miller, Elizabeth 170
Miller, Llewellyn 12
Milliken, Carl E. 278, 287
Milton (poet) 406
The Milton Berle Show (TV series)
    366
Mines, Harry 219
Miracles for Sale (film) 175
Les Miserables (1935 film) 58, 192
Mister Roberts (play) 366
Mr. Smith Goes to Washington
    (film) 242
Mitchell, Belle 340
Mitchell, Cameron 387
Mitchum, Robert 339
Mix, Tom 35
Mohr, Hal 401
The Monster and the Girl (film)
    35, 325
The Monster Maker (film) 294,
    313, 316, 335, 338
Montez, Maria 298, 299, 321, 335,
    338, 353
Montgomery, Robert 121, 187
"Moonstone" (episode of TV's
    The Outer Limits) 35
Moore, Dickie 275
Moore, Grace 315
Moorehead, Agnes 382
The More the Merrier (film) 337
"Morella" (segment of *Tales of
    Terror*) 378
Morgan, John 354

Morgan, Ralph 42, 50, 54
Morison, Patricia 246, 247
Morley, Karen 13, 48
Morse, Barry 374
The Mummy (1932 film) 17, 33,
    34, 97, 111, 112, 115, 118, 151, 182,
    187, 192, 246, 397, 398
The Mummy's Curse (film) 312,
    353, 355, 356, 412
The Mummy's Ghost (film) 309,
    313, 321, 338
Muni, Paul 36
Munson, Ona 173
Murder at the Vanities (film)
    280
Murder by the Clock (play and
    film) 35
The Murder of Lidice (poem) 294
Murdered Alive (play) 93
Murders in the Rue Morgue (1932
    film) 3–38 40, 76, 77, 86, 90,
    93, 114, 182, 313, 396
Murders in the Rue Morgue (short
    story) 5, 7
Murders in the Zoo (film) 105,
    107
Murnau, F.W. 83
Murphy, Mary 379
Murphy, M.F. 210, 211, 214, 219,
    221, 225, 227, 228
Murray, Mae 362
The Music Man (musical play)
    376
Musuraca, Nicholas 316
Mutiny on the Bounty (1935 film)
    90, 178, 192, 207
My Friend Flicka (TV series) 107
My Three Sons (TV series) 321
Mystery of Edwin Drood (1935
    film) 149
Mystery of the Wax Museum (1933
    film) 97, 349, 397, 398, 399

Nagana (film) 280, 331
Nagel, Anne 281, 284, 285, 288,
    293, 294
Naish, J. Carrol 230, 294, 310,
    312, 313, 314, 315, 316, 317, 318,
    319, 320, 331, 332, 335, 337, 338,
    339, 340, 341, 342, 343, 344,
    345, 347, 348, 349, 350, 353,
    356, 357, 358
Naldi, Nita 241
Napier, Alan 364, 370
Napley, Sir David 40
Nash, Mary 361
National Velvet (film) 355
Nazimova, Alla 235, 362
NBC Shell Show (radio series)
    120
Neal, Tom 323
Nebenzal, Seymour 276
Negri, Pola 362
Neill, Roy William 303
Nelson, Barry 310
Nelson, Nip 375
Neumann, Kurt 113, 147, 149

*The New Adventures of
    Frankenstein–The Monster
    Lives!* (proposed film) 112
Next Time I Marry (film) 404
Niblo, Fred 48
Nice Women (film) 14
Nick and Noel 375
The Nigger (play) 145
A Night at the Opera (film) 178
Night Fight (film) 69
Night Key (film) 284
Night Monster (film), 303
The Night They Killed Rasputin
    (film) 70
Night World (film) 33
The Nightingale and the Rose
    (symphony) 366
Nine Pine Street (play) 144
1984 (record album) 95
None But the Lonely Heart (film)
    70
Norman, Amber 161, 162
North, Wilfred 127
Nosferatu (film) 9
Notre Dame (play) 92
Nott, Robert 320
Novotna, Mme. Jarmila 368
Nugent, Frank S. 218
Nurmi, Maila *see* Vampira

O'Brien, Edmond 235
Obsession (play) 366
O'Connor, Edwin 374
O'Connor, Una 123, 136, 162
Odom, Walter Sr., 67
Of Mice and Men (1939 film) 316
O'Hara, Maureen 213, 248
O'Hara, Quinn 386
Oklahoma! (2019 Broadway
    revival) 326
Oland, Warner 141, 142, 149, 150,
    153, 156, 168, 173
The Old Dark House (1932 film)
    33, 34, 82, 111, 398
Oliver Twist (1933 film) 275
Olivier, Sir Laurence 210, 234
Olsen and Johnson 337, 406
"On Borrowed Time" (June
    30, 1950 episode of *The Ford
    Theatre Hour*) 175
On Borrowed Time (1939 film)
    214, 257
"On Borrowed Time" (October
    21, 1949 episode of *The Ford
    Theatre Hour*) 366
Once in a Lifetime (film) 35
One Exciting Night (film) 146
One More River (film) 61, 115, 116,
    117, 118, 119, 124
One Night of Love (film) 315
O'Neil, Barbara 215, 219, 232
Orlova, Madam Barry 173
Ormandy, Eugene 366
Osborn, Paul 257, 263, 264
O'Sullivan, Maureen 44, 82, 125
Othman, Frederick 335, 336
Otterson, Jack 117

Ouspenskaya, Maria 58
The Outer Limits (TV series) 35

Pabst, G.W. 35
Paget, Debra 378, 379
Pajama Party in a Haunted House
see *The Ghost in the Invisible
Bikini*
Parker, Dorothy 361
Parker, Jean 42, 51, 54, 58, 294,
320
Parsons, Louella 214, 334
Pate, Michael 372
Patrick, Gail 80, 84, 85, 86, 107,
279, 280, 283, 287, 288, 293, 294
Payment Deferred (film) 82
Payment Deferred (play) 82
Pearson, Edmund 120, 150
Peary, Danny, 33, 75, 206, 356
Pepper, Lawrence 307
Perelman, S.J. 374
"Perfect Is Hard to Be" (episode
of TV's *Dr. Kildare*) 386
Perkins, Gil 259, 261, 262
Perry Mason (TV series) 293
Person, James E. 308
Peters, Margot 69
Peterson, Fred 19
Pfeiffer, Jules 375, 376
Phair, George E. 209, 215, 241,
247, 274, 277
The Phantom Creeps (serial) 227
Phantom of the Opera (1943 film)
337, 414
The Phantom of the Rue Morgue
(film) 35
Pichel, Irving 275
The Picture of Dorian Gray (1945
film) 414
Pierce, Jack P. 7, 17, 87, 125, 138,
147, 152, 153, 154, 158, 159, 160,
167, 169, 170, 172, 175, 217, 219,
304, 305, 338, 343, 398
Pigott, Tempe 28
"The Pilot" (episode of TV's
Studio One in Hollywood) 293
The Pirates of Flounder Bay
(unsold TV pilot) 386
Pittsburgh (film) 340
Pivar, Ben 312, 316
Plan 9 from Outer Space (film)
319
Plato 247, 254
Platt, David 296, 306, 307, 322,
323
Plues, George 340, 349
Plumes in the Dust (play) 174
Plummer, Christopher 376
Poe, Edgar Allan 3, 4, 5, 9, 27, 30,
32, 378, 396
The Poems of Rudyard Kipling
(record album) 388
Pontius Pilate (film) 382
Pope Pius XI 118
Port O'London (play) 362
Porter, Cole 374
Powder Town (film) 235

Powell, Eleanor 192, 249
Powell, William 118, 249, 258
Power, Tyrone 281, 361, 379
Powers, John 298
Powers, Richard (aka Tom Keene)
319
Previn, Charles 228, 232
Price, Vincent 210, 216, 219, 224,
225, 229, 230, 232, 234, 235,
252, 367, 378, 379, 380, 381, 382,
383, 406
The Private Life of Henry VIII
(film) 102
Pruter, Paula 349, 353
Pryor, Thomas 308
The Public Defender (TV series)
197
Purdom, Edmund 70

Queen of Blood (film) 382, 383
*Question: Are We Not Men?
Answer: We Are Devo!* (record
album) 95
Quigley, Rita 272, 281, 283, 289

Racket Squad (TV series) 107
Rafferty, Frances 276
Rage in Heaven (film), 246
Raiders of Ghost City (serial) 352
Rain (1932 film) 143
Rain (play) 47, 142
Raine, Jack 368
Rains, Claude 114, 149, 186, 251,
398
Rand, Sally 203
Randolph, Clemence 142
Randolph, Jane 315, 316
Rardin, Glen 98, 99, 102, 107
Rasputin, Grigori Yefimovich 40,
41, 42 , 45, 68, 71
Rasputin, Maria 43, 44, 59, 71, 72
Rasputin and the Empress (1932
film) 1, 2, 39,-72, 143
The Rasputin Black Monk (film)
44, 146
Rasputin, Demon with Women
(film) 45, 68
Rasputin the Mad Monk (film) 71
Rathbone, Barbara Cynthia 365,
369, 370, 384, 390, 391, 392
Rathbone, Basil 49, 210, 211, 213,
214, 215, 216, 217, 218, 219, 221,
222, 224, 226, 227, 228, 229,
230, 231, 232, 234, 235, 252, 315,
360–393, 403, 404, 406, 415
Rathbone, Ouida Bergere (aka
Eunie Branch) 360, 362, 363,
364, 365, 366, 367, 368, 369,
370, 377, 387, 389, 390, 391, 392
Rathbone, Rodion (aka Rodion,
John) 219, 229, 362, 363, 390,
391, 392
The Raven (1935 film) 34, 105,
127, 134, 170, 171, 183, 203, 207,
318, 399, 400
Ray, Aldo 369
Raymond, Gene 365

Reckless (film) 185
Red Dust (film) 245
Red-Headed Woman (film) 44
Reed, Alan see Bergman, Teddy
"Blubber"
Reed, Florence 142, 147
Reed, Tom 10, 112, 113, 116
Reicher, Frank 345, 346
Reinhardt, Max 315
Rembrandt 44
Renard, Maurice 182
The Return of Frankenstein see
Bride of Frankenstein
Return of the Ape Man (film)
288, 338
Revenge of the Zombies (film)
277
Rhythm of the Islands (film) 303,
309
Rich, Alan 380
Richard III, King 209, 235
Richard III (1920 Broadway stage
production) 47
Richard III (1955 film) 210, 234
Richard of Shrewsbury 209
Richardson, Sir Ralph 366
Rio (1939 film) 213, 214, 216, 217,
221
Ritchard, Cyril 367, 390
Roach, Bert, 15, 16
Roach, Hal 90
The Road to Mandalay (film) 87
Robb, Inez 265, 266
Roberts, Beatrice 318
Roberts, Stephen 192
Robertson, John Stuart 241
Robinson, Edward G. 118, 365
Robinson, Frances 258
Robinson, George 219, 230, 306,
340, 352
Robson, Mark 353, 355
Rockne, Knute 13
Rockne, Mrs. Knute 13
Roderick, Olga 100
Rodion, John see Rathbone,
Rodion
Rodriguez, Ismael 387
Romance in the Rain (film) 150
Romanov, Grand Duchess
Anastasia 42
Romanov, Grand Duchess Maria
42
Romanov, Grand Duchess Olga
42
Romanov, Grand Duchess
Tatiana 42
Romanov, Tsar Nicholas II 40,
42, 58
Romanov, Tsarevich Alexei 40,
42
Romanov, Tsarina Alexandra 40,
41, 42
Romeo and Juliet (1936 film) 361,
379, 386
Romero, Cesar 325
Rooney, Mickey 241, 247, 303,
415

Roosevelt, President Franklin D. 289, 321
Rosenthal, Harry 13
Rosher, Charles 83
Ross, Jack 325
Ross, Jack, Jr. 326
Ross, Lance 326
Ross, Rex 326
Ross, Tom 326
Rub, Christian 316
Ruman, Sig 350, 351
Ruric, Peter *see* Cain, Paul
Russell, Elizabeth 309
Russell, Lillian 120, 126, 127, 148, 150
Ruttenberg, Joseph 247, 258, 268

Sadie Thompson (1928 film) 143
Sahara (film) 314, 337
St. Johns, Adela Rogers 3, 32
St. Vincent Millay, Edna 294
Saint Wench (play) 143
Salter, Hans J. 228, 229, 303, 306, 354
Samson and Delilah (film) 90
Sanders, George 215, 235, 252, 414
Santley, Joseph 7
Savage, Ann 335
Saville, Victor 1, 243, 246, 247, 248, 263, 264
Sawtell, Paul 317
Saxon, John 383
Sayonara (film) 257
The Scarlet Empress (film) 114, 118
The Scarlet Letter (1926 and 1934 film versions) 87
The Scarlet Letter and the Great Stone Face (record album) 388
Scarlet Sister Mary (play) 47
Schaefer, George 389
Schallert, Edwin 115, 277, 288
Scheuer, Philip K. 267
Schlitz Playhouse (TV series) 34
Schofield, C. V. 267
School for Girls (film) 35
The School for Scandal (play) 47
Schubert, Bernard L. 312
Schubert, Lulu 3, 5, 98
Schulberg, B.P. 77
Scott, Randolph 83, 95, 340
Scully, William A. 353
The Sea Beast (1926 film) 46
Secret of the Blue Room (film) 147
Sekely, Steve 277, 282, 283, 286, 288, 293, 294, 295
Selznick, David O. 77, 107, 246, 264
Sennett, Mack 83
Sennwald, Andre 190, 202, 207
Sequoia (film) 189
Server, Lee 339
Service De Luxe (film) 210, 211
The Seventh Victim (film) 411, 412
Sewell, Vernon 390
Sex (play) 364

Shakespeare, William 209, 212, 380, 392
Shanghai Express (film) 105
The Shanghai Gesture (1941 film) 173
The Shanghai Gesture (1932 play) 47, 142, 143, 147
Shaw, George Bernard 243
Shearer, Norma 47, 386
Shelley, Mary Wollstonecraft 120, 130
Sherlock Holmes (1953 play) 360, 367, 368
Sherlock Holmes and the Secret Weapon (film) 380
Sherlock Holmes Theatre (TV series) 384
Sherriff, R.C. 114, 119, 120
Sherwood, Robert E. 48
Shirley, Anne 42, 51, 52
Short, Antrim 220
Shortt, Edward 202, 203
The Show of Shows (film) 212
Shower of Stars (TV series) 372
Shurlock, Geoffrey 96, 122, 123, 126, 127
Sidney, Sylvia 76, 89, 92
The Sign of the Cross (film) 81, 82, 83, 90
Silver Skates (film) 275
Simmons, Jean 389
Simon, Simone 276, 309, 315, 316, 408
Sinatra, Nancy 385
Sinclair, Ronald 386
Sing Me a Love Song (film) 171
Singerman, Sydney 131
The Singing Sheriff (film) 338
Siodmak, Curt 172, 336, 337
Siodmak, Robert 410
Sirk, Douglas 276, 294
Skal, David J. 126
Skinner, Cornelia Otis 390
Skinner, Dr. (Ohio State Censor) 131, 132
Skinner, Frank 228, 232
Skippy (film) 83
Slack, Freddie 292
Small, Edward 235
Smith, B.J. 232, 233
Smith, C. Aubrey 248, 249
"Soldier in Love" (episode of TV's *Hallmark Hall of Fame*) 389
Son of Dracula (film) 275, 308, 410
Son of Frankenstein (film) 161, 210, 211, 213, 214, 221, 229, 234, 303, 334, 338, 345, 347, 349, 361, 365, 373, 380, 383, 403, 404, 405, 406
The Son of Kong (1933 film) 17, 401
The Son of Monte Cristo (film) 235
Sondergaard, Gale 82
The Sorcerers (film) 389
Sorel, Sonia 335

Sothern, Ann 249
The Spirit of Notre Dame (film) 13
Sprunk, Mr. (MGM cartoon dept.) 248
Stahl, John 116, 149, 234
Stallings, Laurence 48
Starr, Jimmy 25, 124, 125
Stars Over Hollywood (Radio series) 354
Steinert, Alexander 366
Steinke, Hans 86, 88, 103
Sten, Anna 277
Stengler, Mack 283
Stephenson, James 248
Stevens, Onslow 357
Stevenson, Robert Louis 240, 242, 353
Stewart, James 216, 234, 242
"The Stingiest Man in Town" (episode of TV's *Alcoa Hour*) 374
Stoker, Bram 349
Stokowski, Leopold 374
Stone, Lewis 44
Stone, Milburn 304, 305, 314, 318
Stradling, Harry 414
Strange, Glenn 230, 281, 312, 331, 332, 333, 335, 338, 342, 343, 344, 345, 347, 348, 349, 357, 358
Strange Case of Dr. Jekyll and Mr. Hyde (1886 novella) 241
The Strange Case of Dr. Jekyll and Mr. Hyde (1887 play) 241
Strangers on a Train (film) 235
Strangler of the Swamp (film) 277
Strickling, Howard 49
Strictly Dishonorable (1931 film) 13, 14
Stromberg, William T. 354
Struss, Karl 83, 87, 88, 89, 92, 102, 107, 242
Stuart, Gloria 35, 82, 147
Stuart, John 148
Studio One in Hollywood (TV series) 293
Stumar, Charles 151, 170
Sturges, Preston 13
Sucher, Henry 312
Sudan (film) 353
Sullavan, Margaret 118, 127
Sullivan, C. Gardner 48
Sullivan, Ed 141, 142
Sullivan, Lucile 182
Sullivan, Thomas Russell 241
The Sun Never Sets (film) 211, 215
Sunrise (film) 83
Sunset Blvd. (film) 90
Sutton, Jay 406
Sutton, John 215, 218, 227, 230, 232, 233
Svengali (1931 film) 13, 47, 55, 57, 396, 397, 398
Svengali and the Blonde (NBC TV musical special) 372
The Swan (play) 376
Swanson, Gloria 143

The Sword of Monte Cristo (film) 325

Take the High Ground (film) 325
Talbott, Gloria 369
A Tale of Two Cities (1935 film) 200, 207, 386
Tales from Dickens (British TV series) 375
Tales of Fatima (Radio series) 366
Tales of Terror (film) 378, 379, 386
Tall in the Saddle (film) 355
Tamblyn, Russ 328
Tamiroff, Akim 235, 372
Tannen, William 267
Tarantula (film) 234
Tarzan and His Mate (film) 125
Tarzan and the Leopard Woman (film) 325, 326
Tarzan the Ape Man (1932 film) 44, 77
Taurog, Norman 83, 85
Taves, Brian 7
Taylor, Elizabeth 382
Taylor, Robert 249
Taylor, Valerie 367
Tenser, Tony 389
Terry and the Pirates (serial) 86
Test Pilot (film) 245
The Texan (TV series) 107
Thalberg, Irving G. 45, 48, 52, 59, 65, 118
That Certain Age (film) 234, 403
Theatre of Blood (film) 235
Thesiger, Ernest 49, 120, 123, 126, 136, 205
Thorpe, Dr. Franklyn 294
The Three Musketeers (1935 film) 210
Three Smart Girls Grow Up (film) 234
The Three Stooges 86, 189
Three Wise Girls (1932 film) 6
Thriller (TV series) 35, 351
Tilbury, Zeffie 141, 162, 163
Time to Remember (British TV documentary series) 375
Tinee, Mae 103
Tiomkin, Dimitri 200, 206
Tobacco Road (play) 144, 146, 147, 159, 170, 171
Tobin, Genevieve 35
Toland, Gregg 189, 192
Tomorrow and Tomorrow (film) 103
Tone, Franchot 374
Tourneur, Jacques 315, 316, 382
Tower of London (1939 film) 2, 209–237, 340, 342, 347, 362, 380, 386, 406
Tower of London (1962 film) 225
The Towering Inferno (film) 260
Tracy, Gertrude L. 289, 290
Tracy, Spencer 238, 240, 241, 242, 243, 244, 245, 246, 247, 248,

249, 252, 253, 254, 255, 256, 257, 258, 259, 260, 261, 262, 263, 264, 265, 266, 267, 268, 269, 374, 414
Transient Lady (film) 147
Triumph of the Will (film) 309
The Trumpet Blows (film) 191
Tucker, Forrest 376
Turner, Lana 238, 240, 248, 251, 253, 254, 259, 261, 262, 264, 267, 268, 414
Turnure, Pamela 384, 385
Tuttle, William 262
20th Century (1934 film) 69
The Twilight Zone (TV series) 35
Two Before Zero (film) 379

Ulmer, Edgar G. 114, 115, 282, 335
Ulric, Lenore 145, 146
Uncle Tom's Cabin (1927 film) 303, 340
Under Capricorn (film and play) 173
The Unholy Three (1930 film) 12
The Unknown (film) 87
The Unknown Guest (film) 283
Ussher, Bruno David 228, 232
Ustinov, Peter 369

Valle, Gil 404
Vampira (aka Maila Nurmi), 318, 378
The Vampire Bat (film) 337
Van Every, Dale 9, 10
Van Halen (Hard Rock band) 95
Van Horn, Emil 37
Van Sloan, Edward 7, 201
Van Wyck, Juliet 144, 146, 170, 175
Van Zandt, Philip 346
Variety (film) 9, 23
Varno, Roland 286
Veidt, Conrad 34, 45, 182
Ventham, Wanda 390
Verdugo, Elena 332, 338, 340, 341, 342, 343, 344, 346, 347, 348, 353, 355, 357, 358
Vickers, Martha *see* MacVicar, Martha
Vidor, Charles 58
Vidor, King 9
Vieira, Mark A. 52
The Virgin Man (play) 364
Visaroff, Michael 17
Vogel, Paul 247
Von Fursternburg, Ira 71
Von Krafft-Ebing, Richard 254
Von Seyffertitz, Gustav 4
Von Sternberg, Josef 173, 187
Von Stroheim, Erich 276
Voodoo Man (film) 288, 337, 338
Voodoo Queen (proposed film) 323
Voyage to a Prehistoric Planet 383
Vreeland, Frank 77
Vyroubova, Madame 68

Wagenheim, Charles 339, 340
Waggner, George 334, 335
Wagner, Carolyn 170
Wagon Master (film) 344
Wagon Train (TV series) 34
Walker, Stuart 85, 86, 118, 141, 147, 149, 150, 152, 153, 161, 165, 166, 169, 171, 173
The Walking Dead (1936 film) 400, 401
Walley, Deborah 385
Walpole, Hugh 81
Wanger, Walter 298
Ward, Fannie 362
Warner, H.B. 272, 279, 283, 284, 289
Warner, Jack L. 34
The Washington Masquerade (film) 48
Waterfront (film), 294
Waterloo Bridge (1931 film) 112
Watkin, Pierre 318
Waxman, Franz 129, 137, 206, 240, 249, 254, 263, 264, 268, 399
Waycoff, Leon *see* Ames, Leon
Wayne, John 118, 340, 355
Weaver, Tom, 33, 304, 306, 347, 369, 372, 378, 386
Webb, Norman 405
Webb, Roy 356
Wegener, Paul 182
Weird Woman (film) 313
Weis, Don 386
Weissmuller, Johnny 44, 178, 325
Welles, Orson 81
Wells, H.G. 29, 73, 75, 81, 93, 105, 107
Werbisek, Gisela 282, 283
We're No Angels (film) 369
We're No Angels (play) 369
WereWolf of London (1935 film) 2, 44, 47, 86, 125, 138–176, 199, 203, 207, 401, 407
Werewolf of Paris (novel) 182
West, Anthony 81
West, Mae 76, 349, 364
West, Rebecca 81
West, Vera 304
West of the Divide (film) 118
Westmore, Frank 244
Westmore, Wally 73, 88, 89, 92, 242
Whale, James 5, 6, 7, 9, 13, 19, 29, 32, 34, 61, 81, 82, 109, 111, 112, 113, 114, 115, 116, 117, 118, 120, 121, 122, 123, 124, 125, 126, 127, 128, 129, 130, 133, 136, 149, 150, 152, 169, 205, 206, 215, 339, 398
What a Man! (film) 292
When Tomorrow Comes (film) 234
When Worlds Collide (film) 77
Where Are Our Children (film) 223
Whitaker, Bill 354

White, Robert 380
White Pongo (film) 294
White Zombie (film) 26, 34, 93, 346, 396, 397, 398, 399
"Who Killed Hamlet?" (episode of TV's *Burke's Law*) 382
Widow Brown (radio show) 79
Wiene, Robert 182
The Wild One (film) 379
Wild Orchids (film) 143
The Wild Party (poem) 77
Wilde, Oscar 366
Wilder, Billy 194
Wilder, Thornton 235
Wilkerson, Billy 275
Wilkie, Wendell 321
Williams, Clark 151, 153
Williams, Tennessee 376
Wilson, Carey 48
Winchell, Walter 315
Wingate, James 102, 111, 112, 113
Winged Victory (play) 284
Wings (1927 film) 83
The Winslow Boy (play) 367
Winsten, Archer 322
Winter, Keith 255
Winwood, Estelle 378
Wisbar, Frank Bentick 277
Wise, Robert 354, 356, 413
Wiseman, Joseph 374

Witness for the Prosecution (1957 film) 374
Witness for the Prosecution (play) 374
The Wizard of Oz (1939 film) 90, 245, 246
Wodehouse, P.G. 48
The Wolf Man (1941 film) 140, 172, 172, 175, 258, 303, 336
Wolfe, Ian 189, 197
Wolfson, P.J. 185
The Woman in Green (1945 film) 380
A Woman's Face (1941 film) 249, 258, 269
Women in Bondage (1943 film) 2, 272–295; see also *Hitler's Women*
Wood, Natalie 89
Woolf, Edgar Allan 202
Woolner, Bernard 389
Work, Cliff 214
Worlock, Frederic 248, 263
Wray, Fay 97, 167, 398
Wrixon, Maris 281, 282, 283, 284, 294
Wyler, William 118, 149
Wylie, Philip 77, 87
Wynyard, Diana 49, 50, 51, 52, 59, 60, 61, 65, 115

Yeaman, Elizabeth 12, 48, 92
York, Duke 86
You Can't Cheat an Honest Man (film) 234
You Can't Take It with You (1938 film) 233
Young, Brigham 77
Young, Waldemar 77, 87
Young Frankenstein (film) 137
Youngkin, Stephen D. 194
Your Lucky Clue (summer replacement TV show) 367
Youssoupoff, Prince Felix Felixovich 40, 41, 42, 43, 44, 45, 65, 68, 69, 71
Youssoupoff, Princess Irina 40, 41, 44, 61, 68, 69, 71

Zane Grey Theatre (TV series) 34
Zanuck, Darryl F. 177
Zehner, Harry, 33, 112, 127, 129, 133, 148, 152
Zenaide, Princess 40
Ziegfeld, Florenz 407
Zoo in Budapest (film) 210
Zucco, George 251, 281, 288, 316, 334, 337, 338, 340, 341, 353, 358, 380